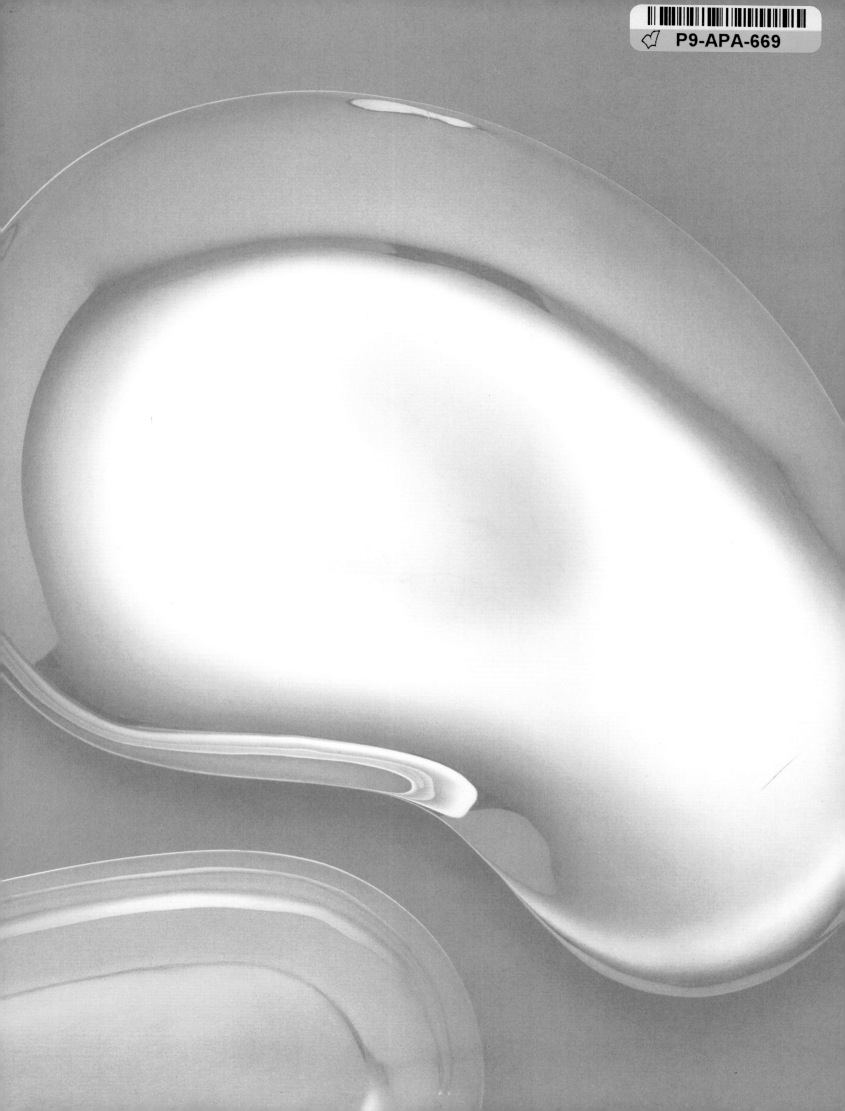

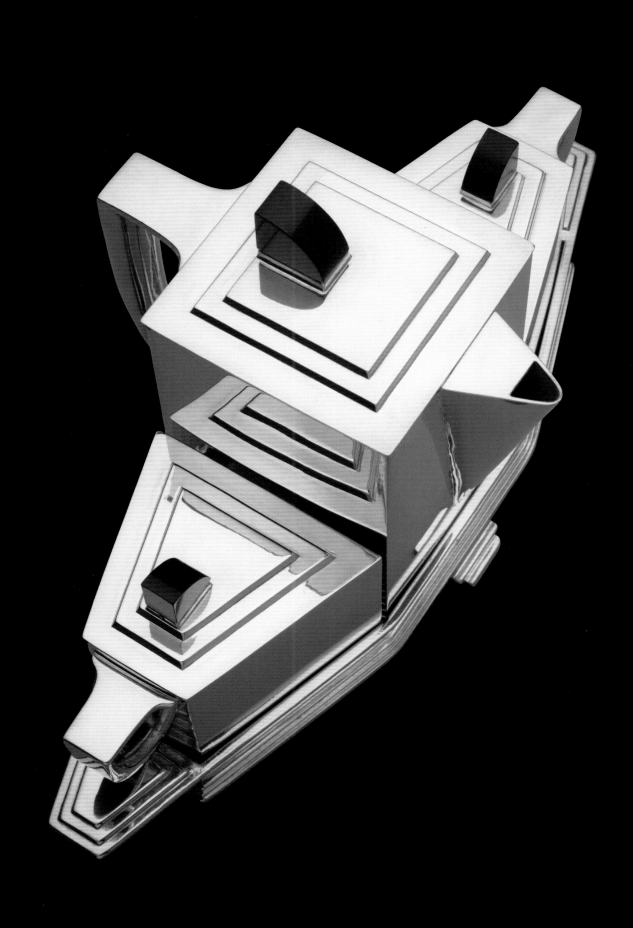

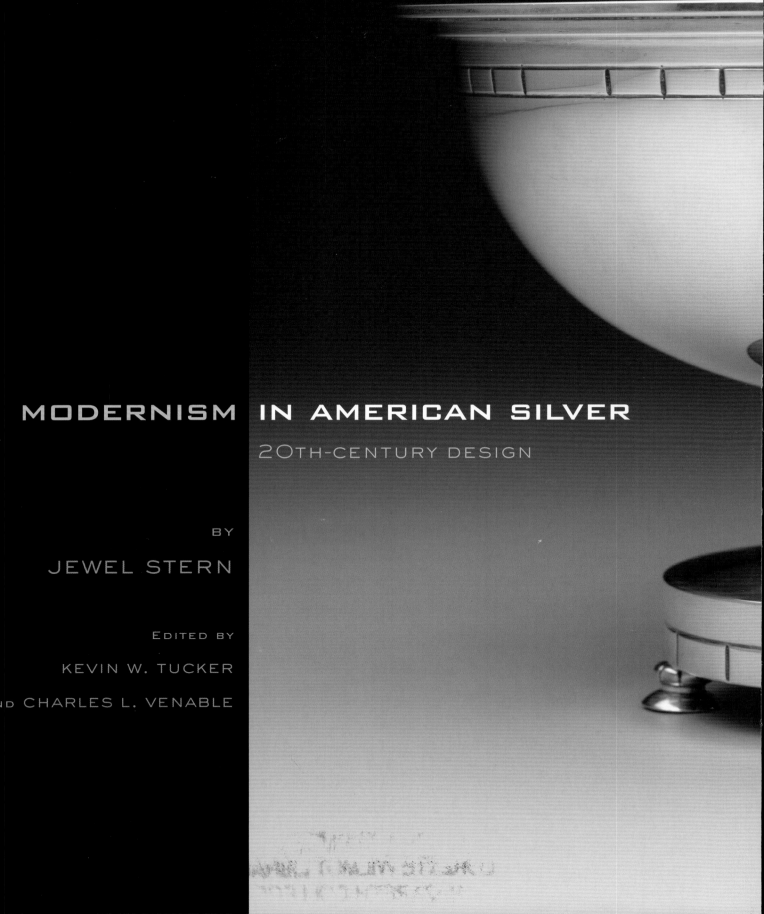

MODERNISM IN AMERICAN SILVER

20TH-CENTURY DESIGN

BY

JEWEL STERN

EDITED BY

KEVIN W. TUCKER

AND CHARLES L. VENABLE

DALLAS MUSEUM OF ART

YALE UNIVERSITY PRESS
NEW HAVEN AND LONDON

The exhibition *Modernism in American Silver: 20th-Century Design* was organized by the Dallas Museum of Art.

The exhibition was supported by a generous grant from the National Endowment for the Arts.

NATIONAL
ENDOWMENT
FOR THE ARTS

Additional support was provided by Judith and Richard Bressler / The Bressler Foundation, the Ajax Foundation, and the General Mills Foundation.

Publication of the exhibition catalogue was underwritten by the Tiffany & Co. Foundation.

Exhibition itinerary:

Renwick Gallery of the Smithsonian American Art Museum
Washington, D.C.
September 16, 2005–January 22, 2006

Nevada Museum of Art
Reno, Nevada
February 11–May 14, 2006

Dallas Museum of Art
Dallas, Texas
June 18–September 24, 2006

The Wolfsonian–Florida International University
Miami Beach, Florida
November 17, 2006–March 25, 2007

The Dixon Gallery and Gardens
Memphis, Tennessee
April 22–July 15, 2007

Published by Yale University Press in association with the Dallas Museum of Art

Note to the reader: In the captions the dates are those for the design, rather than for the production, of the objects illustrated.

Library of Congress Control Number: 2005927187

ISBN: 0-300-10927-X

Jacket front: *Diament* dinette set (detail), 1928 (cat. 126)
Jacket spine: *King Richard* candlestick, 1983 (cat. 225)
Jacket back: *Celestial Centerpiece*, 1964 (cat. 80)
Page 1: *Diament* dinette set, 1928 (cat. 126)
Frontispiece: *Modern American* bowl, 1928 (cat. 23)
Pages 20–21: *Modernist* gravy boat and tray, 1928 (cat. 159)
Pages 190–91: Clockwise from extreme left—sandwich plate, 1955 (cat. 184); *Flair* roll tray, 1954 (cat. 99); salad dish, 1959 (cat. 195); *Modern "Avocado"* centerpiece, c. 1955–1960 (cat. 41)

Dallas Museum of Art
Kevin W. Tucker, The Margot B. Perot Curator of Decorative Arts and Design
Tamara Wootton-Bonner, Director of Exhibitions and Publications
Brad Flowers, Principal Photographer
Eric Zeidler, Publications Assistant
Rebecca Cooper, McDermott Curatorial Intern
Sarah Rector, McDermott Curatorial Intern

Edited by Gerald W. R. Ward and Frances Bowles
Proofread by Jessica Eber
Index by Frances Bowles
Designed by Jeff Wincapaw and Zach Hooker
Typeset in Whitman by Marissa Meyer
Color separations by iocolor, Seattle
Produced by Marquand Books, Inc., Seattle
    www.marquand.com
Printed and bound in China by C&C Offset Printing Co., Ltd.

CONTENTS

The preparation and publication of this volume was underwritten
by a generous gift from The Tiffany & Co. Foundation

LENDERS TO THE EXHIBITION

John P. Axelrod

The Cleveland Museum of Art

Stephen Dweck

Peter Forss

John Loring

Museum of Art, Rhode Island School of Design,
   Providence

Mr. and Mrs. Roger D. Redden

Susan Saarinen

The Jewel Stern American Silver Collection

The United States Navy

Charles L. Venable and Martin K. Webb

John C. Waddell

Mitchell Wolfson Jr.

The Wolfsonian–Florida International University,
   Miami Beach, Florida, The Mitchell Wolfson Jr.
   Collection

and several lenders who wish to remain anonymous

American silver has played a vital role in shaping the identity of the Dallas Museum of Art. Within a decade of the inception of the decorative arts department in 1985, the DMA's commitment to the presentation and interpretation of silverware, particularly the achievements of American manufacturers after 1840, resulted in the landmark exhibition and accompanying catalogue *Silver in America, 1840–1940: A Century of Splendor*. That comprehensive project chronicled the importance and artistic richness of late nineteenth-century American silver and proclaimed the Museum's successful efforts to establish a world-renowned collection of such works. Until then, few museums had accorded much significance to American silver of the mid- to late nineteenth century—the period during which the modern industry evolved, with the growth of large silver manufacturing and retailing concerns, new production techniques, and the resultant ability to produce richly ornamental, fashionable designs with ever-greater efficiency.

Since the publication of *Silver in America* in 1994, a number of writers have furthered our understanding of later American silver. What has been missing is an intensive study of American industrial silver made between 1925 and the end of the twentieth century. *Modernism in American Silver: 20th-Century Design* reveals the aesthetic legacy of this largely unexplored and underappreciated aspect of the silver industry and reaffirms the DMA's commitment to scholarship in the field.

When considered at all, the history of manufactured silver in the twentieth century has traditionally been perceived as that of an industry in decline, largely dependent upon stolid, conservative designs and beset by the difficulties of social change, the introduction of newer, cheaper materials, and corresponding challenges to the market for luxury tableware. Presented in this context, *Modernism in American Silver* is the first major exhibition and publication to address the important role that modernist design played in the revitalization of American silverware as a medium for creative expression. Indeed, the story of modern silver in America is best reflected by those designers, manufacturers, and consumers who stood at the forefront of progressive design in a medium emblematic of great opulence, tradition, and history. As such, it is our hope that this project will provide revealing perspectives upon the design, production, marketing, and consumption of American silver of this era and, importantly, will acknowledge the pioneering achievements of a host of heretofore little-known designers and industry leaders.

For the ability of the Dallas Museum of Art to address this worthy subject, we are greatly indebted to the efforts of the collector and scholar Jewel Stern. During nearly two decades of acquiring works that would ultimately constitute the most comprehensive collection of its kind, Stern dedicated countless hours to identifying related archival material, securing interviews with designers and their circle of associates, and amassing an extra-ordinary personal knowledge of the subject. With the DMA's subsequent acquisition of the Jewel Stern American Silver Collection in 2002 and Stern's participation as the author of the catalogue and guest co-curator of the exhibition, *Modernism in American Silver: 20th-Century Design* marks the realization of her scholarly pursuits. For her dedication, expertise, and many contributions to the enrichment of the DMA's decorative arts and design program, we offer our most sincere gratitude.

We gratefully recognize Charles L. Venable, Deputy Director for Collections and Programs at the Cleveland Museum of Art, who formerly held several senior management positions at the DMA and, from 1985 to 2002, served the Museum as founding Curator of Decorative Arts, for his participation as project director and guest co-curator and for his introduction chronicling his development of the DMA's holdings of American silver, culminating with the acquisition of the Jewel Stern American Silver Collection. We extend expressions of sincere appreciation to Kevin W. Tucker, The Margot B. Perot Curator of Decorative Arts and Design, who joined the DMA's staff in June of 2003. In addition to his recent efforts to develop the Museum's acclaimed silver collections, he marked the beginning of his tenure as DMA project director, curator of the exhibition at the DMA, and essayist for *Modernism in American Silver*, guiding this catalogue and exhibition to fruition.

We offer thanks to Gerald W. R. Ward, The Katharine Lane Weems Senior Curator of Decorative Arts and Sculpture at the Museum of Fine Arts, Boston, for his thoughtful and expert contributions as editor. And, for their efforts in regard to the creation of this publication, we also extend our appreciation to Frances Bowles, the copyeditor; to Ed Marquand, Marie Weiler, Jeff Wincapaw, Zach Hooker, Marissa Meyer, and the entire staff of Marquand Books; and, representing Yale University Press, Patricia Fidler. The exhibition and this publication were produced through the efforts of Dallas Museum of Art staff members Jacqueline Allen, Jennifer Bueter, Kevin Button, Giselle Castro-Brightenberg, Rebecca Cooper, John Dennis, Diana Duke Duncan, Sarah Evans, Evan Forfar, Brad Flowers, Carol Griffin, Heidi Lamb, Mary Leonard, Michael Mazurek, Ron Moody, John Moore, Debra Phares, Bonnie Pitman, Sarah Rector, Chad Redmon, Wood Roberdeau, Elayne Rush, Barbara Scott, Gabriela Truly, Tamara Wootton-Bonner, and Eric Zeidler; each played an important role in this complex and splendid project.

We thank the Tiffany & Co. Foundation for its most generous support for the publication, the National Endowment for the Arts for its grant in support of the exhibition, and extend our gratitude to Judith and Richard Bressler and the Bressler Foundation, the Ajax Foundation, and the General Mills Foundation for their early gifts for the research and planning of both the exhibition and the catalogue.

For their supportive engagement with the presentation of this exhibition at their respective institutions, we thank our colleagues, Elizabeth Broun, Director, Rachel Allen, Deputy Director, Jane Milosch, Curator, Robyn Kennedy, Chief, and Marie Elena Amatangelo, Exhibitions Coordinator, of the Smithsonian American Art Museum, Washington, D.C.; Steven High, Director and CEO, and Diane Deming, Curator, of the Nevada Museum of Art; Cathy Leff, Director, Melissa Smith Levine, Director of Financial Administration, and Marianne Lamonaca, Assistant Director for Exhibitions and Curatorial Affairs, of the Wolfsonian–Florida International University, Miami Beach, Florida; and Jay Kamm, Director of the Dixon Gallery and Gardens, Memphis, Tennessee.

Our particular appreciation also goes to the supporters of the 1995 Silver Supper, the Alconda-Owsley Foundation, an anonymous contributor, Beverly Hart Bremer, Marie Chiles, the Decorative Arts Guild of North Texas, Everts Jewelry Company, DMA Friends of the Decorative Arts, the Estate of Patsy Lacy Griffith (by exchange), Gerald Gulotta, Sherry Hayslip and Cole Smith, Daniel Morris and Denis Gallion, Reed & Barton Silversmiths, Jolie and Robert Shelton, Jewel Stern, Tiffany & Co., Kevin W. Tucker, and Charles L. Venable and Martin K. Webb for their prescient gifts of modernist silver that prominently represent the Museum's permanent collection in this exhibition and catalogue.

We are deeply obliged to the museums, corporations, and private collectors who have so kindly lent or contributed objects to the exhibition. Their cooperation has been exemplary and has allowed us to reveal a richer, more meaningful understanding of the influence of modernism within the realm of twentieth-century American silver design.

John R. Lane
The Eugene McDermott Director

AUTHOR'S ACKNOWLEDGMENTS

Although it is not possible to recognize everyone who has contributed to many years of research, I want to express my gratitude to all the generous individuals—including many unnamed here—who have expanded my knowledge of modern American silver.

I am indebted to Charles L. Venable, my esteemed colleague, whose passion for American silver led to the acquisition of my collection by the Dallas Museum of Art. For Jack Lane, Bonnie Pitman, and the board of trustees of the Dallas Museum of Art, my appreciation is unbounded; I salute you for your extraordinary vision. I am most grateful to Kevin W. Tucker, the Margot B. Perot Curator of Decorative Arts and Design at the DMA, who has superbly overseen the realization of both the catalogue and the exhibition. I thank Gerald W. R. Ward and Frances Bowles for their perceptive and meticulous editing, which has enhanced this catalogue. I join Jack Lane in recognizing all the members of the DMA staff who have contributed to this magnificent result. I have worked most closely with Brad Flowers, whom I thank for his stunning photography, and with Rebecca Cooper, Sarah Rector, Tamara Wootton-Bonner, and Eric Zeidler. To them I offer a deeply felt appreciation. I also wish to recognize Zach Hooker and Jeff Wincapaw of Marquand Books for their elegant design of the catalogue.

During the course of my research, I was graciously assisted by Kevin L. Stayton and Deborah Wythe at the Brooklyn Museum of Art; Gail S. Davidson at Cooper-Hewitt, National Design Museum; Gregory M. Wittkopp at Cranbrook Art Museum and Mark Coir at Cranbrook Archives; Ashley Brown Callahan at the Henry D. Green Center for the Decorative Arts, Georgia Museum of Art; Stephen G. Harrison (a participant at the inception of the project, when he was the assistant curator of decorative arts in Dallas) at the High Museum of Art; Jeannie James and Barbara File at the Metropolitan Museum of Art Archives; Ulysses G. Dietz at the Newark Museum; Kurt G. F. Helfrich at the University Art Museum, University of California, Santa Barbara; and Karen Davies (Lucic) at Yale University Art Gallery.

I owe special thanks to Bernice Morehouse and Allen L. Weathers of the Meriden Historical Society for their help with my research on the International Silver Company, and, for their invaluable support, to representatives of the silver industry: David Rogers at Gorham; Paul Gebhardt at Oneida Limited; Ray Haberstrow, Susan Kindberg MacKenzie, Clark L. Lofgren, and Sinclair Weeks Jr. at Reed & Barton; Herman Schulte of Syratech; and John Loring and Annamarie V. Sandecki at Tiffany & Co.

For sharing their archival materials and experiences with me on many occasions, I thank the designers (all now retired) Robert J. King and Stuart A. Young of the International Silver Company, Robert H. Ramp of Reed & Barton, and Richard L. Huggins of Gorham. Marc Hacker, the former vice president of design and development there, has been enormously helpful on the subject of Swid Powell, as has Debbie Son at Dweck Industries on the work of Stephen Dweck. For many years Donald Cameron has been the finest resource for the work of Tommi Parzinger. Helen Rice, who has shared her pioneering work on Belle Kogan, and Bernard A. Banet, who has compiled material on Kogan, have both enriched my work. Renate Reiss has enlightened me on the Winold Reiss Art School and the circle of artists around Mr. Reiss. Lisa Christoffersen has been a generous source of information on the life and work of her father. I have also benefited from the research of other experts in the field, especially W. Scott Braznell, Jeannine Falino, Dr. William P. Hood Jr., Samuel J. Hough, and Janet Zapata.

The support of John C. Waddell, a friend and fellow aficionado of American modernism, has been exceptional. Others who have enthusiastically followed the unfolding of this project include Constance R. Caplan, Sal J. Fusaro, Leila Marcus, Dahlia Morgan, John A. Stuart, Susan Tunick, Laurie Wilson, and Lori Zabar.

In addition, I wish to recognize my family. I began my silver collection with the encouragement of my late husband, Edward A. Stern, and his support was a source of strength over the years of research. I thank my children, Lori Schainuck and James Schainuck, for their interest and patience, and for being there to cheerlead.

Jewel Stern

DALLAS'S PASSION FOR SILVER: AN INTRODUCTION

Charles L. Venable
Deputy Director for Collections and Programs
Cleveland Museum of Art

The Dallas Museum of Art has a profound interest in the aesthetic and cultural history of silver. As is revealed in the story of its collecting activities that follows, the museum has done an exceptional job in building a collection of artistically significant silver objects made in American factories after 1850. Furthermore, the institution has shown a strong commitment to scholarship in the field, developing two major exhibitions accompanied by book-length studies of the complicated American silverware industry since its industrialization in the early nineteenth century.

The second of these projects, *Modernism in American Silver: 20th-Century Design,* grew directly out of the first, *Silver in America, 1840–1940: A Century of Splendor,* which appeared as an exhibition and as a book by the same title in 1994.[1] The earlier project traced the development of the silverware industry in the United States from the antebellum period in which machinery, steam power, and piecework initially became widespread, through the last years of the nineteenth century, when American firms were the largest in the world, to World War II, when factories were forced to cease producing silverware due to material shortages. This new effort retraces and expands on the brief, general survey of the interwar years done in *Silver in America* and documents the last flowering of the American silverware industry in the postwar period and its rapid decline in the last quarter of the century.

As reflected in its title, this book and the accompanying exhibition are organized around the aesthetics of silver design. As the aesthetic story unfolds, issues of production, marketing, and consumption are woven in to give the history of design depth and the silver context. And, like its predecessor volume, this one includes informative catalogue entries and biographies of designers. The illustration of more than three hundred examples of American modernist silverware, in and of itself, should prove a great resource.

The ability of the Dallas Museum of Art to execute this project is due to the efforts of the collector and scholar Jewel Stern. For almost two decades, Stern worked to build an exceptionally comprehensive collection of modern American industrial silver produced after 1925. Simultaneously, she spent countless hours researching the subject in archives and interviewing industry leaders and designers. *Modernism in American Silver* brings her collecting and scholarly efforts together in the form of this groundbreaking exhibition and book. This accomplishment is especially meaningful to the Dallas Museum of Art since, as we shall see, it acquired the Stern Collection in 2002 and continues to develop it.

More than celebrating an acquisition of great magnitude, however, this project reestablishes Dallas's commitment to further silver scholarship. Since the completion of the manuscript for *Silver in America* in the early 1990s, some significant advances have been made in our understanding of later American silver. For example, thanks to Jeannine Falino's essay "Women Silversmiths" (2000), we now know more about the role of female silversmiths and silver designers. W. Scott Braznell's essay "Metalsmithing and Jewelrymaking, 1900–1920" (1993) shed new light on handmade silver from the first quarter of the twentieth century. Similarly, the work of several other authors has enhanced our knowledge of a variety of silversmiths, including Arthur J. Stone, Janet Payne Bowles, and Margret Craver.[2] No one has, however, written extensively on American industrial silver made between 1925 and 2000. In fact, some studies that logically should have included significant contributions to our knowledge of twentieth-century industrially produced American silver, such as *Silver of a New Era: International Highlights of Precious Metalware from 1880 to 1940* (1992), *Cutlery* (1997), and *Vital Forms: American Art and Design in the Atomic Age, 1940–1960* (2001), simply neglected the subject.[3] Others have sketched in the history of manufactured silver from this period in highly circumscribed ways. Among these writers are Annette Tapert, with her book *Swid Powell: Objects by Architects* (1990), and Jeannine Falino, with a brief essay "American Metalwork between the Wars" (2003). Of all such writings, Jewel Stern's essay "Striking the Modern Note in Metal" in *Craft in the Machine Age, 1920–1945* (1995) is the most notable for its breadth and its illustration of new examples.[4]

Given that there was still work to be done on both craft and industrial silverware, some readers may wonder why this project did not attempt to address both sides of silver making and thus cover the entire twentieth century. First, we felt that, although the history of handmade silver in America does need additional scholarly research, especially in the post–World War II period, that story only periodically intersects with that of factory-made silver. Although it is true that a few craftsmen, most notably John Prip, worked in industry designing objects for mass production, the vast majority of traditional craftpersons eschewed such work. Rather, they typically lived to create entire pieces of silverware by hand and avoided factory life, with its rapid rhythm of production and need to make concessions to the marketplace. Thus the history of American industrial silver is a story unto itself, shaped only occasionally by the parallel world of craft. As for covering the entire twentieth century, Dallas's first show, *Silver in America*, treated American silver from the period 1840 to 1925 more thoroughly than it did later work. More importantly, the stylistic shift from Arts and Crafts and Art

Nouveau aesthetics of the first two decades of the past century to those of European modernism, *art moderne*, and American streamlining in the late 1920s and 1930s provided a natural starting point to the story of modernism in American silver.

Thus it is no accident that this volume opens in Paris rather than in an American city. International design was a great influence on American, factory-made silverware. Against the backdrop of an industry trying to regain the momentum it had lost during the recession of the early 1920s, embracing aspects of modern design as seen at the 1925 international design fair in Paris was believed to be a means of capturing consumers' attention and thereby increasing sales. The same was true of Germanic functionalist designs in the 1930s, Scandinavian aesthetics in the 1950s, and Space Age imagery in the 1960s. But such influences and other innovations must be seen within the context of America as an aesthetically conservative country in which the vast majority of consumers have traditional tastes. Thus, in exploring the development of progressive American silver, readers of this volume should keep in mind that, for every piece of modern silver that left a factory, hundreds more in the rococo and colonial-revival styles were produced. In many ways silver was both too expensive and too symbolically powerful to gamble on modernism. Silver is often given as a gift to mark seminal moments in life, such as marriage or a major anniversary; for most people tradition proved far more comfortable and pleasing than did austere modernism. In the end, it typically was that small group of people who looked toward the future, rather than to the past, who embraced a progressive aesthetic in this, the most traditional of metals. *Modernism in American Silver* celebrates those consumers, as well as the designers and manufacturers who created silverware for them, as they ventured beyond the safe confines of traditional good taste. It is our fervent hope that this study will enhance the appreciation and understanding of the progressive, modern objects they admired and owned.

The story of how the Dallas Museum of Art became a center for post-1850 silver research is worthy of recounting briefly here. In less than two decades, the DMA has built an exceptional collection of American silver, and its holdings of industrially produced silverware made in America between 1850 and 2000 are arguably the finest in the world. The rapid development of a collection of such quality, size, and importance in such a brief period is truly extraordinary.

When I arrived in late 1986 as its first curator of decorative arts, no one could have predicted that the DMA would someday hold a great collection of American silver. There were few examples in the museum: some pieces of mid-twentieth-century studio craft silver made by local silversmiths and a single, wonderful Japanese-style punch bowl produced by Tiffany & Co. in 1881 and given to the museum by its maker 101 years later in advance of the opening of the museum's new downtown building. In fact, it was only in 1983 that the museum decided, with the acceptance of the gift of the Wendy and Emery Reves Collection of impressionist paintings and European decorative arts, "officially" to collect decorative art. Highly personal, the Reves Collection contained diverse works of applied art including significant examples of Spanish carpets and glass, English silver, French furniture, fans, and picture frames, and Chinese export porcelain. In 1985, as the collection was being installed in galleries that were re-creations of rooms from the donors' villa on the French Riviera, the DMA purchased the Faith P. and Charles L. Bybee Collection of American furniture dating from the eighteenth and early nineteenth centuries. Although both the Reves and Bybee collections contained many exceptional objects, the disparate nature of the holdings made for an odd miscellany of things. It was difficult to see how the museum could knit the material together into a coherent institutional collection that reflected the cultural and stylistic evolution of European and American design over the past four hundred years. This was especially true given the presence of a single curator, the absence of dedicated institutional funds for decorative arts, the relative lack of major, local collectors of early material, and the soaring prices for exceptional American and European furniture from the seventeenth to the early nineteenth centuries.

Although collecting decorative art was in its infancy at the DMA, there was great enthusiasm for the undertaking in the vibrant city of Dallas itself. The Dallas Glass Club and the Dallas Antiques and Fine Arts Society allied themselves to the museum and in 1987 the DMA founded a support group called the Friends of Decorative Arts. In that same year, a major gift of silver was donated to the museum by the Hoblitzelle Foundation. Combined with the fine examples in the Reves Collection, the Karl and Esther Hoblitzelle Collection gave the museum a strong start in the area of eighteenth-century English and Irish silver. The Hoblitzelles, society leaders between the 1920s and 1960s, had been important in Dallas's business community and had acquired a collection that contained some extraordinary objects, including great examples by one of England's foremost silversmiths, Paul de Lamerie. However, the collection also contained scores of extra pieces ranging from

duplicates of exceptional objects to numerous items that had been wonderfully useful for entertaining, but were not of museum quality. To enhance the original collection, the Hoblitzelle Foundation allowed the museum to sell some minor pieces and use the proceeds to acquire additional stellar examples of British silver.

Some items, however, were not sold. Karl and Esther Hoblitzelle had built their collection in order to entertain in grand style, and their holdings included large sets of sterling plates, soup bowls, and salt cellars. Following their custom, the museum decided to use the table silver as the focus of an annual fundraiser to benefit the young decorative art department, and in 1988 the first Silver Supper was held. Initially the funds raised through the Silver Supper underwrote the purchase of a piece of silver. During this period several important American objects were acquired, including Gorham's Nautilus Yachting Trophy designed for the 1893 Chicago World's Fair and a monumental Tiffany centerpiece with candelabra from 1949, which is in this exhibition and illustrated in this volume (see fig. 8.22). Although the works acquired through the Silver Suppers were all of great quality, we needed to plan for the future, and in 1996 proceeds from the event were directed to the newly established Decorative Arts Discretionary Endowment Fund. Chaired by exceptional hosts and hostesses, the Silver Suppers have generated substantial, essential support for the museum's mission.

With nascent support growing for the decorative arts department through an annual fundraiser, a support group, and the enthusiasm of numerous individuals, the museum developed a two-part strategy for building the DMA's collection of decorative arts. Using the recently acquired collections as a foundation, the museum decided to build a representative survey collection of Western decorative arts by acquiring fine examples of European and American furniture, silver, glass, ceramics, and textiles dating from 1600 onward. Simultaneously, it would build collections of quality and depth in one or two underappreciated areas ahead of other institutions. American silver was the first area of specialization identified. Later, ceramic and glass tableware became another and resulted in the major book and touring exhibition *China and Glass in America, 1880–1980: From Tabletop to TV Tray*.[5]

The late 1980s were a heady time of soaring prices in the American decorative art market, especially for furniture. Exceptional examples of seventeenth- and eighteenth-century colonial silver became increasingly scarce, and it was difficult to envision how the DMA could ever rival older East Coast institutions that had formed core collections decades earlier. Furthermore, few Dallasites held family heirlooms of major colonial silver nor were there other local collectors of this material. The odds seemed better for building holdings in nineteenth- and twentieth-century American silver, especially industrially produced silver made after 1850. Other museums did hold important works of this kind, but none had treated the material thoroughly in terms of quality, form, and material. Large private collections acquired by museums were often of uneven quality, holloware being typically valued more highly than flatware and sterling more than silverplate. Among private collectors the major styles such as rococo, classical, Renaissance, and colonial revival were generally unappreciated, as was virtually all the silver of the post–World War II era.

With the support of the director Richard Brettell, the trustees on the acquisition committee, and contributions from a host of individuals and groups, several fine pieces of silver in these underappreciated styles were purchased in the late 1980s, as was silver in the Arts and Crafts mode and the Japanese taste. As our interaction with collectors, dealers, auction houses, and curators increased, it became evident that interest in nineteenth-century American silver would escalate rapidly because of the quality of the best examples and their availability in the marketplace. This conviction was bolstered upon viewing the Sam Wagstaff Collection at the New-York Historical Society in 1987. Observations of the intense discussions generated by that collection indicated that the Dallas Museum of Art would have to move rapidly if it wished to build a collection of note in this area before broader interest among collectors forced prices upward. Ironically, our first big opportunity arrived with the announcement that the Wagstaff Collection would be sold in January 1989.

At this time the decorative art department had no dedicated funds and was still in the process of purchasing the Bybee Collection of early American furniture. Purchases of single silver objects had generally been made with funds solicited from individual donors. To bid successfully on a group of pieces in the Wagstaff sale, adequate funds had to be raised rapidly. Margaret McDermott, one of Dallas's most generous philanthropists and a longtime supporter of the DMA, generously pledged significant funds for acquisitions from the sale, and we identified about a dozen desirable objects. Although prices for nineteenth-century American silver had been relatively reasonable, at the Wagstaff sale lots were hammered down for unprecedented sums. The prices realized were well beyond expectations and numerous records were set for different types of nineteenth-century American silver. The sale was a watershed in the American silver market. In the end, the museum successfully acquired five lots. Two were made by Tiffany: an iron and silver Japanese-style vase and a water pitcher lavishly decorated with chrysanthemums

FIGURE 1 Ice bowl with spoon, c. 1871. Gorham Manufacturing Company, Silver. Dallas Museum of Art, The Eugene and Margaret McDermott Art Fund, Inc.

and exhibited at the 1893 Chicago World's Fair. The other three works, all by Gorham, were a pair of shell-form salad servers, a Japanese-style fruit plate, and an ice bowl and spoon in the Arctic taste replete with icicles and polar bears (fig. 1).[6] Because the DMA was one of the most successful institutional bidders and paid a record price for the Arctic ice bowl, the museum garnered much media attention after the sale. Within days the museum was offered exceptional examples of silver from dealers and private owners across the country.

In the evolution of the DMA's collecting of American silver, it is significant that a pair of splendid salad servers and an ice spoon were among the lots acquired at the Wagstaff sale. Although American firms had arguably created the widest array and highest quality flatware in the world during the second half of the nineteenth century, most museums had ignored flat silver in favor of holloware. As a result, great flatware in virtually every style was available well into the 1990s at prices much lower than those for comparable holloware. The museum moved to take advantage of this opportunity and built up its holdings of outstanding flatware. Aiding this process was the DMA's close connection to several major flatware collectors. In 1991, the best pieces from the Houston-based Charles R. Masling and John E. Furen Collection were acquired, followed in 1992–1993 by highlights from the V. Stephen Vaughan Collection in Boston. Meanwhile, through the anonymous gift

FIGURE 2   Cover of *Silver in America:* a selection of flatware representing the wide variety of forms and designs made in the United States between 1860 and 1890

of the Oberod Collection of *Martelé* that consisted of fifteen pieces, the DMA avoided the rise in prices that occurred later in the decade for Gorham's Art Nouveau *Martelé* line.

As exceptional examples of holloware and flatware entered the DMA's collection in greater numbers, it soon became apparent, as noted, that the history of silver in the nineteenth and twentieth centuries was an extremely complicated story about which all too little had been written. Consequently, I decided to tackle the subject as my dissertation for Boston University with the hope of turning that research into a book and exhibition on the subject. Completed in 1993, the dissertation formed the basis for the book *Silver in America, 1840–1940: A Century of Splendor* that accompanied the DMA's touring exhibition by the same name in 1994 (fig. 2). With stops at the Carnegie Museum of Art in Pittsburgh, the Milwaukee Art Museum, and the Henry Francis du Pont Winterthur Museum in Winterthur, Delaware, in addition to the DMA, the show touched a responsive chord in the silver world, and a second edition of the book was issued. Most of the objects included in this extensive exhibition were in the DMA's permanent collection, illustrating how the museum's holdings had grown in numbers and quality. Noting this, several important private collectors, previously unconnected to the DMA, felt that the institution had put their collecting interest on the map and thus gave or promised

significant pieces of silver from their own collections. Similarly, the museum's efforts inspired several Dallasites to collect in the area. A few major foundations and arts patrons periodically funded important silver purchases, such as the Belmont-Rothschild humidor (1889) by Tiffany & Co.[7]

Although most of our collecting and scholarly research had focused on nineteenth- and early twentieth-century American silver, the seeds of an industrial design collection that included modernist silver were also sown during the early 1990s. For example, the museum's first piece of the silver created by Gorham's designer Erik Magnussen in the 1920s was purchased in 1990 (see fig. 1.7). Meanwhile, the Dallas-born, New York collector David T. Owsley encouraged the museum to move into the industrial design field through the gift of several pieces of furniture and metalwork in 1990. However, the greatest inspiration for collecting in this area was provided by the philanthropist-collector Liliane Stewart in Montreal, who in association with the consulting curator David Hanks, rapidly built an important collection of international midcentury modernist industrial design of all media that is now housed in the Montreal Museum of Fine Arts.[8] Following suit, a group of Dallas donors established the Twentieth-Century Design Fund, the goal of which was to provide fifty thousand dollars annually to purchase significant examples of industrial design. Importantly, the museum's curator had discretionary power to commit to select acquisitions so that the DMA could move expeditiously in the marketplace.

The Twentieth-Century Design Fund supported numerous acquisitions. Due to it, as well as to gifts of funds and objects from other sources, especially the bequest in 2000 of the Patsy Lacy Griffith Collection of European and American material dating from the 1920s and 1930s, the DMA mounted the major exhibition *China and Glass in America, 1880–1980: From Tabletop to TV Tray* in 2000, drawn almost exclusively from its own holdings. In addition, a series of three design exhibitions were held to mark the turn of the millennium: *Circa 1900: Design at the Turn of the Century* in 2001, *Art Deco and Streamlined Modern: Design 1920–1950,* and *Boomerangs and Baby Boomers: Design 1945–2000* in 2002, each of them containing twentieth-century American silver. Capping this stage of the DMA's development in the silver field was the long-pursued acquisition of the amazing *Martelé* silver dressing table and stool by Gorham (fig. 3) that had been the centerpiece of its display at the 1900 Paris World's Fair. As with the purchases from the Wagstaff sale over a decade earlier, this seminal acquisition was made possible through the generosity of Margaret McDermott. The dressing table made its debut as part of the permanent collection in

FIGURE 3 *Martelé* dressing table and stool, 1899. Gorham Manu-
facturing Company. Silver, glass, fabric, ivory. Dallas Museum of Art,
The Eugene and Margaret McDermott Art Fund, Inc. in honor of
Dr. Charles L. Venable

the exhibition *Out of the Vault: Silver and Golden Treasures* (2000), organized by Stephen G. Harrison, then
associate curator of decorative art. Although progress
had been made by 2000 in acquiring twentieth-century
American silver, the collection was heavily weighted
toward the pre–World War I period as exemplified by
Gorham's dressing table. The acquisition through partial purchase and partial gift of the Jewel Stern American Silver Collection in 2002 dramatically corrected
this imbalance.

I first learned of Jewel Stern in 1991 during a visit to the Wolfsonian Foundation in Miami Beach to examine its silver collection for possible loans to the *Silver in America* exhibition. Wendy Kaplan, the curator of the Wolfsonian at the time, showed me the silver and mentioned that it had been catalogued by a local scholar named Jewel Stern. During the next few years, we became acquainted, and in each of our exchanges I was impressed by her knowledge and willingness to share her research. In January 1999, Stephen G. Harrison and I traveled to Miami to see the Stern Collection. Amidst an energetic discussion of American silver and popular culture, Jewel showed us her entire collection of more than 150 objects, spanning the years from *art moderne* to postmodernism. Through the Stern Collection, we could see the ebb and flow of modern American design and the final flowering of functional American silver.

During the following months, the possibility of organizing an exhibition as a sequel to *Silver in America* on the subject of twentieth-century modern American silver made by leading manufacturers and featuring the Stern collection began to develop. It became evident that Jewel's knowledge of the subject, her research in archival materials, and her willingness to share were probably unsurpassed, and that she was the ideal person to write an exhibition catalogue should the DMA undertake such a project. Furthermore, the Stern Collection would provide the foundation for such an exhibition. It contained some unique works, as well as many that were produced in such limited quantities that we would be unlikely to find other examples elsewhere. Therefore, it seemed important that, if possible, the DMA should try to both mount an exhibition and acquire the Stern Collection. Following further discussions and a formal presentation of the concept to the director Jack Lane and other colleagues at the museum, it was agreed that the DMA would begin developing an exhibition on modern American silver.

To start the process, Stephen Harrison and I photographed the Stern Collection in Miami in August 2000. While documenting the collection, we defined the parameters of the show, the main topics for the catalogue, and drafted a preliminary checklist. Subsequent meetings and conversations during the rest of 2000 and early 2001 enabled us to shape and refine these aspects of the exhibition. Then in June 2001 Jewel Stern called and said that she had come to the conclusion that the Dallas Museum of Art was the best place for her collection. I was elated and quickly informed Jack Lane. With his support and following many conversations with trustees, appraisers, lawyers, and accountants, an arrangement was arrived at by which Jewel Stern would donate some of her most important and iconic pieces and the museum would purchase the remainder of the collection. Luckily for the DMA, the timing was fortuitous in terms of funding because of the recent bequest from the modernist collector Patsy Lacy Griffith, who loved silver, and the maturity of the museum's Decorative Arts Discretionary Endowment Fund. With Jewel donating key objects, Griffith funds acquiring works from the 1920s and 1930s, and the endowment interest securing the post–World War II pieces, the Jewel Stern American Silver Collection, which by then contained more than three hundred objects, was officially acquired by the Dallas Museum of Art in May 2002 by a unanimous vote of the Trustee Committee on Collections. As part of the arrangement, Jewel's collection records came to the museum, as will her extensive archives in the future. Since that time Jewel Stern has continued to collect, and this book and exhibition contain many of her most recent gifts and promised gifts to the Dallas Museum of Art. By obtaining such a strong and deep collection of American industrial silver dating from 1925 to 2000, and pairing it with its exceptional holdings produced after 1850, the DMA had assembled in just fifteen years the most comprehensive survey of silver of its kind in the world.

The acquisition of the Stern Collection was the culmination of my collecting for the DMA. After sixteen years of service, I decided to leave my duties as deputy director, chief curator, and curator of decorative arts to accept the position of deputy director for collections and programs at the Cleveland Museum of Art in mid-2002. I have been pleased to continue to work with the DMA's new curator of decorative arts and design, Kevin W. Tucker, and with Jewel Stern, to complete this project that Jewel and I dreamed up together five years ago. Through the years my friendship with Jewel has steadily grown stronger, and I have learned much during the countless hours in mutual discussion about designers, manufacturers, consumers, and the marketplace. But perhaps most of all, it has been inspiring to watch Jewel as she organized and articulated the story of modernist, industrial silver design that she has spent nearly twenty years researching. As someone who has tackled another aspect of the history of the enormously complicated American silver industry, I have nothing but the highest respect for her.

NOTES

1. Charles L. Venable, *Silver in America, 1840–1940: A Century of Splendor,* exh. cat. (Dallas, Tex.: Dallas Museum of Art, 1994).

2. Jeannine Falino, "Women Silversmiths," in Pat Kirkham, ed., *Women Designers in the USA, 1900–2000* (New Haven, Conn.: Yale University Press, 2000), 223–45; W. Scott Braznell, "Metalsmithing and Jewelrymaking, 1900–1920," in Janet Kardon, ed., *The Ideal Home, 1900–1920: The History of Twentieth-Century American Craft* (New York: Abrams, 1993), 55–63; Elenita C. Chickering and Sarah Morgan Ross, *Arthur J. Stone, 1847–1938: Designer and Silversmith* (Boston: Boston Athenaeum, 1994); Barry Shifman, W. Scott Braznell, and Sharon S. Darling, *The Arts & Crafts Metalwork of Janet Payne Bowles* (Indianapolis: Indianapolis Museum of Art, 1993); and Jane L. Port, *Margret Craver and Her Contemporaries* (Boston: Museum of Fine Arts, Boston, 1992), an exhibition brochure.

3. A. Krekel-Aalberse, J. R. ter Molen, and R. J. Willink, eds., *Silver of a New Era: International Highlights of Precious Metalware from 1880 to 1940,* exh. cat. Museum Boymans van-Beuningen, Rotterdam, and Museum voor Sierkunst, Ghent (Seattle: University of Washington Press, 1992); Marco Ferreri, ed., *Cutlery* (Mantua, Italy: Corraini Editore, 1997); and Brooke Kamin Rapaport and Kevin L. Stayton, *Vital Forms: American Art and Design in the Atomic Age, 1940–1960,* exh. cat. Brooklyn Museum of Art (New York: Abrams, 2001).

4. Annette Tapert, *Swid Powell: Objects by Architects* (New York: Rizzoli, 1990); Jeannine Falino, "American Metalwork between the Wars," in Charlotte Benton, Tim Benton, and Ghislaine Wood, eds., *Art Deco, 1910–1939* (New York: Bulfinch Press, 2003): 344–47; and Jewel Stern, "Striking the Modern Note in Metal," in Janet Kardon, ed., *Craft in the Machine Age, 1920–1945: The History of Twentieth-Century American Craft* (New York: Abrams, in association with the American Craft Museum, 1995), 122–34.

5. Charles L. Venable, *China and Glass in America 1880–1980: From Tabletop to TV Tray,* exh. cat. (Dallas: Dallas Museum of Art, 2000).

6. Christie, Manson, and Woods International, Inc., *The Sam Wagstaff Collection of American Silver,* sale catalogue, New York, Jan. 20, 1989, lots 86, 158, 188, 218, and 227.

7. See Venable, *Silver in America,* 193.

8. Martin Eidelberg, ed., *Design 1935–1965: What Modern Was: Selections from the Liliane and David M. Stewart Collection,* exh. cat. Montreal Museum of Fine Art (New York: Abrams, 1991).

PART ONE MODERNISM IN AMERICA, 1925–1950

CHAPTER ONE

ART MODERNE COMES TO AMERICA

American decorative arts underwent profound and swift stylistic transformations during the period between the world wars, the decades of the 1920s and 1930s. The acceleration of change from Arts and Crafts ideals and historicism to one in harmony with the new, modern age had an impact on virtually all manufacturers, especially those of silverware, objects deeply associated in the American consciousness with tradition and continuity. The turning point and catalyst was a French international exposition originally scheduled for 1915 but postponed because of World War I and reconstruction. The *Exposition Internationale des Arts Décoratifs et Industriels Modernes* held in Paris in 1925 was the first international exposition limited to decorative and industrial arts as distinct from the fine arts, and the first confined to works of "new inspiration and real originality."[1] Reproductions or derivations of historic styles were officially excluded. The United States was invited to participate in the exposition, and a choice site was reserved for a pavilion on the Right Bank of the Seine. The invitation was declined by the government on the grounds that "American manufacturers and craftsmen had almost nothing to exhibit conceived in the modern spirit, and in harmony with the spirit of the official specifications."[2] Exceptions did exist, but the government's response was a reflection of general conditions and attitudes during the early 1920s, a period in which colonial and other revival styles proliferated, innovation was at a low ebb, and there was limited exposure to or interest in progressive design. As early as 1904 at the *Louisiana Purchase International Exposition* in St. Louis, the Austrian architects Josef Hoffmann and Joseph Maria Olbrich of the Darmstadt Artists' Colony had exhibited their wares.[3] Spurred by John Cotton Dana in 1912, the Newark Museum had sponsored *Deutsches Kunst-Gewerbe,* an exhibition of modern German and Austrian applied art that traveled to six other venues, and, in 1922, the museum hosted another exhibition assembled by the Deutscher Werkbund exclusively for Newark. But none of these three events had much effect on domestic design.[4] For the most part early European modernism had little appeal for the American public. For example, a branch of the Wiener Werkstätte (Vienna workshops) directed by the Austrian émigré architect Joseph Urban opened in New York City in 1922. Although the store received critical acclaim and exhibited its "artistic products," including works in silver, at the Art Institute of Chicago, the branch closed in less than two years.[5] To enhance the appreciation of progressive design, Herbert Hoover, as secretary of commerce, appointed a commission, its members drawn from art and industry and headed by Professor Charles R. Richards, the director of the American Association of Museums, to visit, study, and report on the exhibits at the Paris exposition for their potential effect on the design and production of American goods.[6]

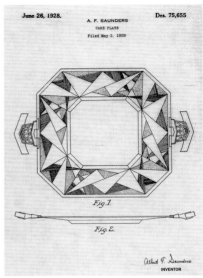

FIGURE 1.1   Pavillon Pomone, *Exposition Internationale des Arts Décoratifs et Industriels Modernes*, Paris, 1925; L. H. Boileau, architect

FIGURE 1.2   Patent application for a cake plate, 1928. T. N. Benedict Manufacturing Company, Albert F. Saunders, designer. See cat. 3

Although the exposition—with twenty-six nations exhibiting—was deemed international, only France was represented comprehensively. In the years immediately before World War I, France had lagged behind Germany and Austria in the decorative and applied arts. The exposition was a national effort to showcase the renaissance in French design and to reassert French leadership in the field. Ironically, the creators of French *art moderne* had assimilated much from earlier German and Austrian progressives, especially Josef Hoffmann and the Wiener Werkstätte.

Notwithstanding the absence of official representation, Americans visited the exposition, and detailed accounts were widely published in journals and newspapers. The first impression of the French pavilions and exhibits (fig. 1.1) was generally one of shock, although the aesthetic would soon influence American design (fig. 1.2). Opinions varied. The architectural decorator W. Francklyn Paris was disparaging: "The dreary iteration of angles, triangles, cubes, octagons, squares, and rectangles does not so much create a spirit of revolt as one of amusement. . . . It cannot be that this art is meant to endure."[7] More importantly, Helen Appleton Read, the influential art critic for the *Brooklyn Daily Eagle* and a delegate to the commission, wrote a series of four articles for the Sunday edition on the importance of the exposition to American artists and designers.[8] Read applauded the controversial event for a "deep-seated urge to create forms in harmony with the Zeitgeist," and observed that "those who look for the influences which have determined the new movement lay it either to the door of cubism or the age of the machine." Read commented on the formal simplicity of the silverware that was exhibited, on the predominance of "octagonal shapes rather than curves," and on the lavish use of color in accents of jade,[9] onyx, and coral, which in her view, were "so important a note of the movement."[10] To Read, the significance of the exposition was its potential to arouse American receptivity to a modern idiom, and she predicted correctly the influence of the event.[11]

At home the American public was introduced to the *art moderne* style in an exhibition of decorative arts derived from the Paris exposition and organized by the American Association of Museums. Selected by the director, Charles R. Richards, the traveling exhibition, consisting of about four hundred objects in a variety of mediums, opened at the Metropolitan Museum of Art in New York in February 1926.[12] Read reviewed the show, noting the consequences of the Paris event to American design:

The American public was strangely inert to the fact that a modern movement, a distinct period of style, was taking its place beside the historic periods . . . Many who visited the Paris Exposition came away entirely unaware of what it was all about—saw only the bizarre and the ultra. But such is the germinating quality of ideas that all unbeknown the idea took root. Among our manufactures first, and through the medium of dress materials and accessories the idea has been first disseminated. Our aesthetic senses are becoming gradually accustomed to geometric shapes and plain flat colors and unornamented surfaces. The new decor has crept into our consciousness unawares, and there is no designer who can create in quite the same spirit from now on than if the Exposition had not existed.[13]

Read also commented on the severe geometric shapes of the silverware exhibited, and she reiterated her admiration for colorful jade and lapis lazuli accents, a treatment she found to be in harmony with the "new spirit."[14] The introduction of semiprecious stones for color contrast and highlights was a feature of French silverware that was adopted by American makers for

FIGURE 1.3   Sandwich tray, 1928. Gorham Manufacturing Company. Silver, jade. Dallas Museum of Art, The Jewel Stern American Silver Collection (hereafter DMA, JSASC), cat. 67

the luxury market (fig. 1.3). Less expensive Bakelite and Catalin in bright colors were employed in pieces made for a wider public (see fig. 3.52). Another way of expressing modernity was the application of new designs in sterling silver overlay onto the surface of ceramic and glass objects that had traditional shapes. One example is the abstract leafy branching that was derived from cubism in the silver overlay decoration of a Lenox porcelain coffeepot and demitasse cup and saucer whose shapes predate 1920.[15] Executed by the Rockwell Silver Company of Meriden, Connecticut, the pattern was aptly named *Moderne*. Another, also done by Rockwell, is the leaping gazelle in a sylvan setting (a popular *art moderne* motif) that embellished a black glass plate by the Pairpoint Manufacturing Company of New Bedford, Massachusetts (fig. 1.4, top left).

Although the onset of World War I in 1914 and American conservatism had prevented Austrian and German progressive design from taking root, modern design as showcased in Paris succeeded because Americans admired French taste in art and fashion. Although reviews were mixed at first, *art moderne* gained immediate acceptance in chic New York circles. Ironically, a colony of progressive émigré designers, few of them French, played a major role. On the eve of World War I, a small, but remarkably influential influx of Austrian and German architects and designers, among them Winold Reiss, Paul T. Frankl, and Joseph Urban, moved

FIGURE 1.4 Left: Plate, c. 1925–1935. Attributed to Pairpoint Manufacturing Company. Glass, silver overlay, cat. 211. Right: *Moderne* coffeepot, demitasse cup and saucer, c. 1930. Lenox China, Rockwell Silver Company. Porcelain, silver overlay, cat. 210. Dallas Museum of Art

Modern Movement in Decoration" to be directed by the omnipresent and influential émigré designer Paul T. Frankl: "When one has gone through these six lessons, he will know from the hands of a master all one should know about this the greatest epoch making revolution in the art of design that has come across the horizon for ages. A movement, which for years, has kept Europe afire with admiration and which, today, has penetrated into almost every hamlet in America."[17] The same year a writer for *Good Furniture Magazine*, commenting on the growing interest in *art moderne*, declared: "Decoration— the way of furnishing a home—has become almost as lively an issue as the political situation!"[18] Significantly, from 1925 until the end of the decade the periodical employed Howell S. Cresswell as a special editorial representative in Paris to keep its readers abreast of the latest in French design.[19]

ERIK MAGNUSSEN AND GORHAM

The report of the commission to the Paris exposition called on progressive industrial leaders to renounce "slavish copying" and "the fixed paths of our present practices" and to venture into "new fields" so that America could "reap real advantage both economically and aesthetically from the modern movement."[20] Ahead of the wave, even before the report was published, Gorham had become the first American silver manufacturer to respond to the modern impulse from Europe.

Shortly after the 1925 exposition closed, Gorham brought Erik Magnussen, an accomplished Danish silversmith with an international reputation, to Providence to design modern handwrought silver with an eye to developing a contemporary machine-made line.[21] Magnussen proved a good choice because his Scandinavian modernism was more compatible with American taste than were the avant-garde designs of the French master Jean Puiforcat and other Europeans. Gorham executives would have been aware, too, of the success of Georg Jensen, another Danish silversmith, in the American market. The ambitious Georg Jensen Sølvsmedie (silversmithy), formed in 1904 in Copenhagen, had expanded rapidly before World War I with a branch in Berlin and, during the war, developed a market in Sweden. Eager to expand internationally and with continental Europe and England off limits due to the war, Jensen sent a collection to the 1915 *Panama-Pacific Exposition* in San Francisco. William Randolph Hearst saw the Jensen exhibit and reputedly purchased most of the collection, thus enhancing the firm's cachet in the United States.[22] By 1920 Danish silverware was recognized as a contemporary alternative to stale period-revival styles. Lauded in an American trade journal as a "breeze of fresh air," examples were illustrated to "enlighten" those who were "as yet unacquainted" with its "style and forms."[23] Late in

to New York. Among them, too, were the Hungarian designer Ilonka Karasz and the German painter Elsa Tennhardt, women who would create modern designs for the silver industry in the late 1920s. Together with a handful of Americans, such as Eugene Schoen, who had studied in Europe, they formed the nucleus of New York's avant-garde design community. The devastating economic situation in Europe after World War I propelled a second wave of emigrants that included the silversmith Peter Mueller-Munk and Alfons Bach, Germans who would design industrial silver in the 1930s. It was these designers who facilitated the rapid transition to a modern idiom that had been sparked by the 1925 Paris exposition. Mueller-Munk,[16] who worked in handwrought silver, and the Danish-born Erik Magnussen at the Gorham Company in Providence, Rhode Island, became modern giants in the field in the late 1920s. With the assistance of these talented émigrés, pioneering American department stores that emulated the promotional role of the Galeries Lafayette, Printemps, and Bon Marché—their counterparts in France, exhibitions organized by museums, and proselytizing journalists, variants of *art moderne* were popularized and spread throughout the United States. Symptomatic in 1928 was the missionary zeal with which the periodical *Arts and Decoration* announced a "Home Study Course on the

FIGURE 1.5 Erik Magnussen in his studio at the Gorham Manufacturing Company, 1926

1922 Jensen silverware was exhibited at the Art Center in New York, and the firm's first American retail store, located at 159 West Fifty-seventh Street, was advertised the following year.[24] From New York, the Jensen firm effectively promoted its naturalistic blend of tradition and modernity.[25] By the 1925 Paris exposition, in which

Jensen's silverware was exhibited in the Danish section, the firm had established a foothold in America and its influence on American silver manufacturers is a thread that wove through silver design for the balance of the twentieth century. There is no doubt that it was to take a share of Jensen's market that Gorham hired Magnussen.

Erik Magnussen introduced modern design to silver manufactured in America, and he was recognized early on in publications and exhibitions. In June 1926, only nine months after he arrived in the United States, two profiles appeared in journals, replete with photographs of Magnussen at work in his studio at Gorham (fig. 1.5) and illustrating several items of holloware.[26] Among these was a pair of candlesticks and a vase (fig. 1.6) in which the primary decorative treatment was the incising of elements with a variety of radiating lines, some evoking abstract floral motifs. The segmenting of rounded surfaces with radiating incised lines to emphasize the form was one of Magnussen's favorite decorative

FIGURE 1.6 Candlesticks and vase, 1927. Gorham Manufacturing Company, Erik Magnussen, designer. Silver. Dallas Museum of Art, cat. 20

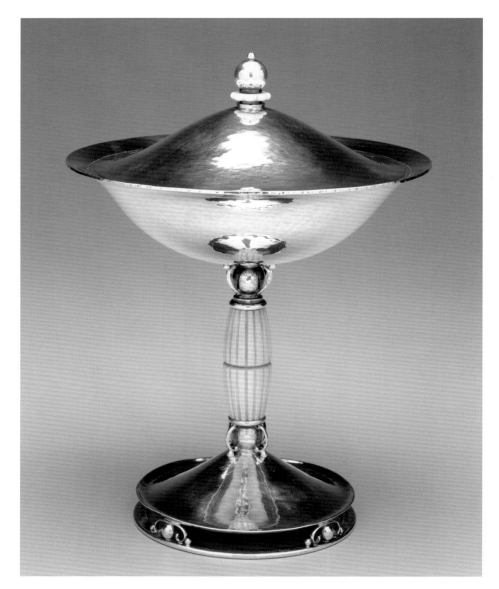

FIGURE 1.7   Candy jar, 1926. Gorham Manufacturing Company, Erik Magnussen, designer. Silver, ivory. Dallas Museum of Art, cat. 18

FIGURE 1.8   Erik Magnussen's EM mark, c. 1928

devices and was widely copied by American silver manufacturers in the late 1920s.[27] A candy jar of 1926 (fig. 1.7) demonstrates other motifs used by Magnussen and characterizing early twentieth-century Danish silver: gently swelling forms derived from nature, restrained scrolling and beadwork, and the addition of semiprecious stones and ivory. In his less formal work for Gorham, playful animal and marine subjects figured strongly, often as silhouetted supports for containers and as finials (see fig. 3.48). To emphasize the fact that these pieces were the work of a famous designer, Gorham marked all of the silver that Magnussen designed, except for very early pieces, with his distinctive EM mark (fig. 1.8).

Much more avant-garde was Magnussen's gilded and oxidized *Cubic* holloware of 1927, a design linked to cubism in sculpture and painting and to contemporary European silverwork influenced by cubist innovations,

particularly the breaking up of surfaces into angular planes. The coffee service (fig. 1.9), first exhibited in Gorham's Fifth Avenue showroom late in 1927, was dubbed "Lights and Shadows of Manhattan," and instantly became an object of controversy. A reporter for the *New Republic* wrote that the display was "both painful and funny," and observed that "our skyscraper worship has produced some pretty sad results; but I think this cubistic claptrap in silver is about the worst I have seen."[28] Two other writers were more complimentary. One approved of the associations with the skyscraper city and of the pattern's "strong response to the spirit of modern America."[29] The other played it safe by completely ignoring the *Cubic* design and depicting Magnussen as a "traditional modernist."[30] A *Cubic* salad bowl and servers (fig. 1.10) were made at Gorham and a photograph of the set appeared in *Arts and Decoration* in 1928.[31] In addition to the coffee service and salad set, Magnussen's drawings survive for a *Cubic* candlestick, sandwich tray, and bonbon dish (fig. 1.11).[32] The sharp faceting and triangular planes of color created by gilding and oxidation that defined *Cubic* holloware apparently

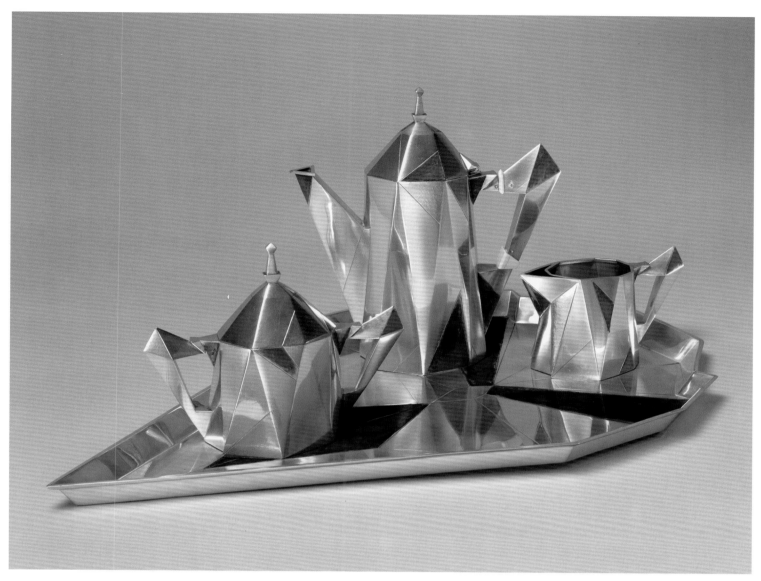

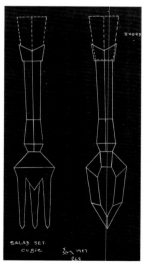

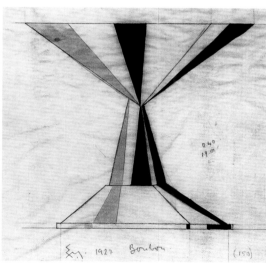

FIGURE 1.9   *Cubic* coffee service, 1927. Gorham Manufacturing Company, Erik Magnussen, designer. Silver with patinated and gilt decoration. Museum of Art, Rhode Island School of Design, cat. 21

FIGURE 1.10   Drawing, *Cubic* salad servers, Erik Magnussen, 1927

FIGURE 1.11   Drawing, *Cubic* bonbon dish, Erik Magnussen, 1927

FIGURE 1.12   "Mulholland Modern-Mode Hollow-ware," Mulholland Silver Company advertisement, 1928

proved too extreme for consumers. The design nonetheless provoked a profusion of manufactured imitations (fig. 1.12), much to the consternation of both Magnussen and Gorham. Smarting from the failed *Cubic* experiment, the manufacturer, in promotional literature for another design by Magnussen, felt compelled to deny that it had intended to produce a commercial line based on *Cubic*:

[The] impressionistic tea set . . . based on tall buildings seen from various perspectives and from sun shadows on set-back skyscrapers . . . was intended merely for exhibition . . . a piece of Fine Art . . . technically sound and admirably wrought. . . . The fact that it was intended for exhibition not for daily use . . . was harder to grasp . . . and soon the market saw a dozen undigested modifications of the set . . . offered as the last word in true American Applied Art.[33]

Gorham's stance is surprising in light of an earlier article in *Arts and Decoration* that referred to the *Cubic*

FIGURE 1.13 *Modern American* bowl, 1928. Gorham Manufacturing Company, Erik Magnussen, designer. Silver. DMA, JSASC, cat. 23

FIGURE 1.14 "The Modern American," Gorham Manufacturing Company advertisement, 1928

of the wood handles (fig. 1.17). A window display of Gorham products included a *Modern American* coffee service and candlesticks shown with earlier pieces by Magnussen, including a tall vase from 1926, and small items enhanced with animal figures and semiprecious stones or accented with ivory (fig. 1.18; see also fig. 1.6). The fullest selection of *Modern American* was shown at the *First Annual Exhibition of Modern American Decorative Arts* of the Art Center of New York, where the silverware was integrated with room interiors.[36] A pitcher and goblets and the coffee set graced living area groupings and a dining table was set with flatware (fig. 1.19), service plates, candlesticks, bowls, and salt and pepper shakers, all in the *Modern American* pattern. A critic found the silver "almost too severe," yet "quite in tune with the modern note" and observed that the table setting "attracted as much attention as anything in

coffee set as part of a complete sterling holloware and flatware service, implying that it was being produced and expanded.[34]

Magnussen's determination to create "something of America, and for America" led to the introduction, in 1928, of *Modern American,* a line of holloware and flatware that evolved more naturally from his formal work than had *Cubic* (figs. 1.13, 1.14).[35] Comparison of a drawing for a *Modern American* candlestick (fig. 1.15) with a drawing of a Danish-style candlestick from the year before (fig. 1.16) shows how Magnussen, responding to modernism, transformed the earlier candlestick into a stepped, geometrical object by abstracting its elements. Scoring was retained but altered into a strict horizontal and vertical pattern that alluded to classical triglyphs. On most, but not all of the pieces in the service, Magnussen kept the multiple feet, still curved, but simplified. In the coffee set Magnussen departed somewhat from this scheme by eliminating the stepped elements and adding carved ivory finials, a flourish that bespoke his Danish roots, as did the shape

FIGURE 1.15 Drawing, *Modern American* candlestick, Erik Magnussen, 1928

FIGURE 1.16 Drawing, candlestick, Erik Magnussen, 1927

the show." That the "ultra-modern lines" of the pattern struck the "popular fancy" was attributed to its "forthright honesty."[37] Gorham sought to position *Modern American* in a niche that appealed to buyers interested in high society, fashion, and the arts. In an elaborate brochure for the pattern, directed to jewelers who carried silverware, a drawing (fig. 1.20) depicted an elegantly dressed flapper and her escort admiring a *Modern American* covered compote on a tall pedestal. Through a window in the background a stepped skyscraper towers over them, while in the foreground a debonair gentleman in formal attire holds a walking stick and ponders a rendition of the *Cubic* coffee service.[38] Notwithstanding the sophisticated campaign, the pattern was not commercially successful and was discontinued during the Depression. Magnussen left Gorham in 1929 and, after brief sojourns in New York City and Chicago,

FIGURE 1.17 *Modern American* coffee service, 1928. Gorham Manufacturing Company, Erik Magnussen, designer. Silver, ivory, wood. Dallas Museum of Art, cat. 22

FIGURE 1.18 Demonstration window display, Gorham Manufacturing Company, c. 1928

FIGURE 1.19 *Modern American* teaspoon, 1928. Gorham Manufacturing Company, Erik Magnussen, designer. Silver. DMA, JSASC, cat. 25

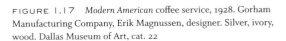

FIGURE 1.20 "The Modern American," brochure, Gorham
Manufacturing Company, 1928

established his own design studio for handcrafted silver
in Los Angeles.[39] Although his silver continued to be
exhibited, he did not regain his prominence in America. In 1939 he returned to Denmark, where he died
in 1961.[40]

ADVERTISING CAMPAIGNS OF 1928

The American silver industry responded vigorously to
the excitement generated by modern design from abroad
and by Gorham's early efforts. By 1928 firms such as the
International Silver Company of Meriden, Connecticut,
Reed & Barton of Taunton, Massachusetts, Bernard
Rice's Sons of New York City, Sheets-Rockford Silver
Company of Rockford, Illinois, Benedict Manufacturing Company of East Syracuse, New York, Mulholland
Silver Company of Aurora, Illinois, and Marshall Field
& Company of Chicago, were advertising snappy new
silverware. International and Reed & Barton were the
largest manufacturers to be galvanized by the challenge
from Gorham, and both jumped on the bandwagon with
aggressive advertising campaigns to attract consumers

and gain market share. With a fanfare International
introduced its new sterling holloware series the *Spirit of
Today* by Alfred G. Kintz, a staff designer.[41] There were
three patterns in the series (see fig. 1.21), and a bowl
in each of the patterns was illustrated in the advertisement and accompanied by sensuous copy and sketches
(fig. 1.22). *Ebb Tide* was described as "the reluctant waves
sliding back—back—leaving ruffled fingermarks on the
wet sand." *Northern Lights* was touted as "all the flashing
life, the cold and colorful mystery of the Aurora—caught
in solid silver." *Tropical Sunrise* was dramatized for its
"palmetto leaves outlined against the glorious rays of
the rising sun." Although perhaps a bit bombastic, International's assessment of the series proved prescient:
"These pieces are as inspiringly conceived and finely
wrought as museum treasures; and it is not predicting
too much to say that in a few years they will have as great
historic value as the work of Early American silversmiths
has now."[42] Despite the bravado, International was care-
ful not to offend its conservative clientele and risk losing these customers. Giving them the nod, the company
declared: "NOW comes a series of holloware designs
that are as distinctive as *Pine Tree*," a traditional pattern
that had been introduced in 1927.

FIGURE 1.21   Left: *Ebb Tide* candlesticks, 1928, cat. 104; center: *Tropical Sunrise* compote, 1928, cat. 101; right: *Northern Lights* whipped cream bowl with ladle, 1928, cat. 105. International Silver Company, Alfred G. Kintz, designer. Silver. DMA, JSASC

FIGURE 1.22   "The Spirit of Today," International Silver Company advertisement, 1928

FIGURE 1.23   "tea service in the modern spirit," International Silver Company advertisement, 1928

In the most striking graphic advertisement for modern silverware in the 1920s, International's Wilcox Silver Plate division presented a revolutionary compact fitted tea service named *Diament* (fig. 1.23; see also fig. 3.13). *Diament* was one of three "dinette sets" produced in 1928 and designed by Jean G. Theobald, a staff designer, in consultation with the pioneering American product stylist Virginia Hamill.[43] Geared to the "modern minded woman," these dinette sets were promoted by International as space savers for the smaller rooms common in modern urban apartments (figs. 1.24, 1.26).[44] Clearly, as the advertisement suggests, *Diament*'s angular "sculpturesque" shape and stepped, layered details were intended to embody the "modern spirit." For the other dinette sets the severe angularity of *Diament* was eschewed in favor of rounded forms. Their riveted wood handles and flat lids were inspired by contemporary European designs by Marianne Brandt at the Bauhaus in Germany, Jean Puiforcat in Paris (fig. 1.25), and Christian Fjerdingstad, a Danish silversmith who worked for Christofle in Paris. The level of sophistication demonstrated by the fitted services is not surprising given Hamill's extensive exposure to European modernism and her active role in the modern industrial expositions held in the

FIGURE 1.24   Dinette set, 1928, Wilcox Silver Plate Company. Jean G. Theobald, designer. Silverplate, wood. The Wolfsonian–Florida International University, Miami Beach, Florida, The Mitchell Wolfson Jr. Collection, cat. 125

FIGURE 1.25   Photograph: Teapot, c. 1928. Jean Puiforcat, designer

FIGURE 1.26   Dinette set, 1928. Wilcox Silver Plate Company.
Jean G. Theobald, designer. Silverplate, wood. DMA, JSASC, cat. 124

FIGURE 1.27 "Sensibly Interpreting the Spirit of Modernism,"
Reed & Barton advertisement, 1928

R. H. Macy & Company department store in New York in 1927 and 1928 (see chapter 2).

Reed & Barton's approach was more subdued. In its pitch for business the company tried to ensure that its sterling holloware would not be perceived as bizarre, but rather as discreetly modern and functional. The headline in its 1928 advertising campaign was "Sensibly Interpreting the Spirit of Modernism" (fig. 1.27). The text read: "Faithfully interpreting the spirit of the day, silver in modern design by Reed & Barton takes note of utility, as well as beauty. Here are pieces one likes to live with, to enjoy, to *use.* Here the influences of modern decoration are applied, *sensibly,* to necessary silver [emphasis in the original]."[45] Although the forms are not as aggressively modern as those of other makers, two vases and a tray with cocktail cups had stylish geometric, angular, and faceted shapes. A series of telescoping bulges formed the vessels of an idiosyncratic after-dinner coffee set. The shape of a pair of candlesticks and matching vase flared out above a recessed and rounded portion of the objects, a design reminiscent of Austrian pieces made during the first two decades of the twentieth century.

Notes

1. Charles R. Richards, Henry Creange, and Frank Graham Homes, *Report of Commission Appointed by the Secretary of Commerce to Visit and Report upon the International Exposition of Modern Decorative and Industrial Art in Paris 1925* (Washington, D.C.: U.S. Government Printing Office, 1926), 17.

2. Ibid., 16.

3. Irving K. Pond, "German Arts and Crafts at St. Louis," *Architectural Record* 17 (Feb. 1905): 119–25.

4. The 1912 exhibition was organized with Karl Ernst Osthaus, director of the Deutsche Museum für Kunst im Handel und Gewerbe in Hagen, Germany. Other venues were St. Louis, Chicago, Indianapolis, Cincinnati, Pittsburgh, and (not listed in the catalogue) New York. The massive catalogue of the exhibition lists 1,337 items in eleven categories: graphics, advertising, bookbinding, wall and floor coverings, textiles, ceramics, glass, metalwork, wood and ivory carving, photography, and architecture, and includes silverwork by Josef Hoffmann, Kolomon (Kolo) Moser, and Carl Otto Czeschka. See *Deutsches Kunst-Gewerbe*, exh. cat., 1912–1913; courtesy of Newark Museum. For the 1922 exhibition in which Waldemar Raemisch and Josef Wilm of Berlin exhibited silver, see Newark Museum, *The Applied Arts*, exh. cat. (Newark, N.J., 1922).

5. "Exhibition Brings Viennese Art Here; Wiener Werkstaetter [*sic*] of America Makes Unique Display at 581 Fifth Avenue," *New York Times*, June 25, 1922, 6; and "Two Exhibitions of Modern Art," *Bulletin of the Art Institute of Chicago* 16 (Oct. 1922): 67–68.

6. Richards, Creange, and Homes, *Report of Commission*, 6–10.

7. W. Francklyn Paris, "The International Exposition of Modern Industrial and Decorative Art in Paris: Part II: General Features," *Architectural Record* 58 (Oct. 1925): 379, 384.

8. The first of the four articles by Read was "New Architecture at the International Exposition of Decorative Arts in Paris Illustrating the Use of Reinforced Concrete; Strange Geometric Shapes," *Brooklyn Daily Eagle*, Aug. 16, 1925 (Archives of American Art, Helen Appleton Read papers [hereafter as AAA, Read papers], reel N736, frame 112).

9. Carved antique pieces of jade were sometimes incorporated into new objects.

10. Helen Appleton Read, "International Exposition of Decorative Arts in Paris Has Practical Background for Display of the Bizarre and Exotic Atmosphere of Luxury," *Brooklyn Daily Eagle*, Aug. 23, 1925 (AAA, Read papers, reel N736, frame 113).

11. Helen Appleton Read, "International Art Exposition in Paris Opens New Era in Field of Decorative Work: Philosophy of Beauty Goes Hand in Hand with Present Economic Changes," *Brooklyn Daily Eagle*, Sept. 6, 1925 (AAA, Read papers, reel N736, frame 115).

12. The exhibition, *A Selected Collection of Objects from the International Exposition of Modern Decorative and Industrial Art*, traveled to Boston, Cleveland, Chicago, Detroit, St. Louis, Minneapolis, Pittsburgh, and Philadelphia; Nellie C. Sanford, "The Loan Exhibition from the Paris Exposition shown in the Metropolitan Museum of Art," *Good Furniture Magazine* 26 (Apr. 1926): 185.

13. Helen Appleton Read, "Selections from French Exposition come to Metropolitan Museum," *Brooklyn Daily Eagle*, Feb. 21, 1926 (AAA, Read papers, reel N736, frame 138).

14. Ibid.

15. See Charles L. Venable, *China and Glass in America 1880–1980: From Tabletop to TV Tray* (Dallas, Tex.: Dallas Museum of Art, 2000), 160.

16. Although the German spelling (Müller-Munk) appears in a few period references, he adopted the English spelling for signed articles as well as for the advertisement of his signature holloware designed for Poole in the mid-1930s.

17. "The Modern Movement in Decoration," *Arts and Decoration* 29 (July 1928): 91.

18. Ella Burns Myers, "Trends in Decoration," *Good Furniture Magazine* 31 (Dec. 1928): 291. Myers also noted the "lively debates" on *art moderne* in "magazines as diverse as *The New Yorker* and the *International Studio*."

19. Determined by author from *Good Furniture Magazine*, 1925–1931.

20. Richards, Creange, and Homes, *Report of Commission*, 20–23.

21. Charles H. Carpenter, *Gorham Silver 1831–1981* (New York: Dodd, Mead, 1982), 256–58.

22. Renwick Gallery, *Georg Jensen Silversmithy: 77 Artists, 75 Years*, exh. cat. (Washington, D.C.: Smithsonian Institution Press, 1980), 16.

23. "A Word About Danish Silverware," *Jewelers Weekly* 80 (May 19, 1920): 1.

24. Karen Davies, *At Home in Manhattan: Modern Decorative Arts, 1925 to the Depression*, exh. cat. (New Haven, Conn.: Yale University Art Gallery, 1983), 94.

25. See, for example, "New Designs in Jensen Silver" in Art: Exhibitions of the Week, *New York Times*, Nov. 9, 1924, 8. Illustrations of pieces by Georg Jensen proliferated in articles on silverware in periodicals during the 1920s.

26. "Modern Silver Design: Erik Magnussen Leads a Trend Toward Plainer Patterns," *Good Furniture Magazine* 26 (June 1926): 291; and "A New Master Silver Craftsman in America," in Art Objects & Antiques, *Harper's Magazine* 153 (June 1926), n.p.

27. The International Silver Company's *Art Moderne* sterling holloware pattern, c. 1928–1929, is an example. In the line were a five-piece tea service and waiter, a console set, a mayonnaise bowl, and several compotiers; the low version compote is number T91; see *Catalogue of International Sterling Hollow Ware, 1929* (International Silver Company Archives, Meriden Historical Society, Meriden, Conn.). For a three-piece coffee set, see Lee Mecca, "Sterling Silver 1929," *Country Life* 56 (May–June 1929): 94.

28. A New York Diary, *New Republic* 53 (Jan. 4, 1928): 192.

29. Elizabeth Lounsbery, "Modernistic Influence on Sterling Silver: The Lights and Shadows of a Skyscraper Are Reflected in this New Table Silver," *Arts and Decoration* 28 (Apr. 1928): 52.

30. Augusta Owen Patterson, "The Decorative Arts," *Town and Country* 83 (Apr. 15, 1928): 71.

31. Lounsbery, "Modernistic Influence," 52. The whereabouts of the salad bowl is not known. The salad servers are in the collection of the Museum of Art, Rhode Island School of Design.

32. On Magnussen's drawings the objects are named "Cubic." Drawings reviewed by author, May 29, 1991, Gorham Company Archives, Smithfield, R.I.

33. Gorham Manufacturing Company, *The Modern American* (New York, 1928).

34. Lounsbery, "Modernistic Influence," 52.

35. "Modern Silver Design," 291. See also "The Modern American," Gorham Company advertisement, *Jewelers' Circular* 96 (July 5, 1928): 2–3.

36. "Gallery Notes: American Decorative Arts Show," *Art Center Bulletin* (Art Center, New York) 7 (October 1928): 1–3; and "American Decorative Art at the Art Center," *Good Furniture Magazine* 32 (Jan. 1929): 46–48. The exhibition opened October 8, 1928.

37. "American Decorative Art," 47.

38. Gorham, *Modern American*.

39. "Sculptor Revives Lost Art of Working Precious Metals," *Popular Science Monthly* 125 (Oct. 1934): 40; and Dorothy Rainwater, *Encyclopedia of American Silver Manufacturers*, 3rd ed. rev. (West Chester, Penn.: Schiffer, 1986), 115.

40. Rainwater, *Encyclopedia*, 115.

41. Patricia F. Singer, "Alfred G. Kintz, an American Designer," *Silver* 19 (Sept.–Oct. 1986): 14–19.

42. "Second great sterling achievement of 1928! International's new holloware series The SPIRIT of TODAY," International Silver Company advertisement, *Jewelers' Circular* 96 (May 10, 1928): 34, 35.

43. For Theobald as designer of the third unpatented set, see "Editorial Footnote," *Creative Art* 4 (Jan. 1929): xxii, where Theobald's first name was mistakenly spelled "Gene" instead of "Jean."

44. "Tea service in the modern spirit," International Silverplate advertisement, *House and Garden* 54 (Dec. 1928): 145.

45. "Sensibly Interpreting the Spirit of Modernism," Reed & Barton advertisement, *House and Garden* 53 (June 1928): 123.

CHAPTER TWO

DEPARTMENT STORES ADVANCE

MODERN DESIGN IN THE 1920s

For manufacturers in general, and for those of silverware in particular, relationships with retailers who promoted stylistic change were uneasy. Mass production demanded efficiency and volume to be profitable. Because retooling to keep apace of fashion was expensive, upheavals in consumer taste were financially threatening to the industry. Yet it was critical to be competitive, indeed, to foresee trends. The advent of the stylist, an innovation made by department stores to determine the public pulse, to monitor trends, and to align a store's merchandise with new currents, had repercussions for silver manufacturers.[1] As large manufacturers maintained their own design departments, in which revival styles prevailed, such consultants had been rare in the industry. Staff designers were, however, not trained to produce the fashionable novelties demanded by consumers in the late 1920s. Manufacturers therefore looked to stylists and designers in other media to update their lines. Sheldon and Martha Cheney underscored this phenomenon in their book *Art and the Machine* (1936). In their analysis of the emergence of industrial design as a profession, they cited the year 1927 as the turning point when, as a result of consumer demand for "higher standards of appearance," talented outsiders were "summoned to the factory for service in unfamiliar design fields."[2]

The International Silver Company, for instance, engaged Virginia Hamill, a pioneering woman stylist who worked for R. H. Macy & Co. in New York City, to advise its staff designers on trends for goods to be introduced in 1928. Hamill (fig. 2.1), a socialite from a prominent Illinois family (her paternal uncle Alfred E. Hamill was a trustee of the Art Institute of Chicago), had lived with her art-minded, widowed mother in Europe and had been educated there between the ages of ten and sixteen.[3] Dynamic, determined, and sophisticated, Hamill graduated from the New York School of Fine Arts and found her métier in the 1920s as a stylist for department stores and manufacturers.[4] She established her own business in New York City as a Decorative Art Consultant, becoming one of the most successful in the field during the 1920s and 1930s.[5] Hamill was publicly credited as the stylist for *Diament* and one other dinette set produced by International and as an influence on the *Spirit of Today* holloware series.[6] The designation of stylist and its prestige gradually diminished in the 1930s, when industrial design became a recognized profession. Hamill was American, but many consultants for the silver industry in the late 1920s were foreign born. The most notable for their modern silver designs were Ilonka Karasz, who worked for Paye & Baker of North Attleboro, Massachusetts, Elsa Tennhardt, who worked for E. & J. Bass of New York City, Kem Weber, who worked for Friedman Silver Company in Brooklyn, New York, and Eliel Saarinen, who worked for International, Dominick & Haff in New York, and Reed & Barton.

Department stores played a pivotal role in disseminating *art moderne* after the 1925 Paris exposition. Percy S. Straus, vice president of Macy's, noted the example set by French department stores: "Inspired by the lead of their Parisian fellow merchants, the department stores of New York are beginning to interest themselves in the development of industrial art." In Straus's view this reflected a "change in the outlook of their clientele," and he urged merchants, "as purveyors to the desires of the people" to respond to this "new consciousness."[7] The role of department stores in introducing the new style, in elevating taste, and as a liaison between the consumer and manufacturer was rapidly recognized. In 1926, Charles R. Richards claimed that "our department stores were our best museums of contemporary industrial art."[8] In the next few years others who were prominent in the field concurred. Robert W. de Forest, president of the Metropolitan Museum of Art, who was involved in the expositions that Macy's mounted in 1927 and 1928, declared that department stores had "a potential leadership of the utmost importance in guiding and moulding public taste and in improving standards of design."[9] J. H. Fairclough Jr. of the Jordan Marsh store in Boston regarded department stores as "the museums of today" and a "great educating force."[10]

Questions arose, however, about the appropriateness of a department store's assuming the role of a museum. Helen Appleton Read addressed the issue in her review of *Exposition of Art in Trade at Macy's* in 1927. Arguing that, because there were no American museums of industrial art and that a department store was a "living museum of the industrial and decorative arts," Read said that it was both "fitting and logical" an assumption. In an indirect attack on the Metropolitan Museum of Art, she criticized previous museum exhibitions of industrial arts as "dull and lifeless" in comparison to the "modern note" that was stressed by Macy's. Read also criticized the lack of sponsorship of the arts by the American government and the absence of supportive societies such as the Werkbund in Germany and concluded that it was "left to private enterprise to sponsor such an exhibition."[11] Later in 1927 Read wrote an article with the provocative title "Department Stores Rival Museum in the Formation of Taste in Industrial Art," a challenge that may have spurred the Metropolitan Museum of Art to mount its acclaimed *Architect and the Industrial Arts* exhibition in 1929.[12]

Most of the department stores that promoted modern design were in New York: Wanamaker's, Macy's, Lord & Taylor, B. Altman, Saks Fifth Avenue, and Abraham & Straus (in Brooklyn). Macy's in 1927 and 1928 and Lord & Taylor in 1928 organized major exhibitions, the latter exclusively French. Wanamaker's, however, was the first, showing modern European designs in 1925 after the Paris exposition, and in 1927 inaugurating the Venturus Shop, a special department devoted exclusively to modern European and American furniture and decorative arts and the venue for an exhibition, *Modern Art in a Department Store*, of European and American merchandise shown together.[13]

MODERNITY IN 1927: EXPOSITION OF ART IN TRADE AT MACY'S

In reviewing the progress of modernism in the United States in the 1920s, the architect Robert A. M. Stern isolated the year 1927 for the "special spirit of 'modernity' which suddenly" took form and is "difficult to recapture."[14] For evidence Stern turned to the Cheneys, contemporary interpreters of the period: "In 1927, there was, as Sheldon and Martha Cheney put it, 'a spreading machine age consciousness.'"[15] Among the events of 1927 enumerated by Stern were the establishment of the first national radio networks, the advent of sound in movies, Charles Lindbergh's solo flight across the Atlantic Ocean, and the Machine Age Exposition in New York organized by the editors of the *Little Review*.[16] He neglected to mention Macy's presentation in 1927 of modern manufactured products, an event that was emphatically in step with the zeitgeist.

The *Exposition of Art in Trade at Macy's*, held in the spring of 1927, became a prelude to a more evolved and expansive endeavor in 1928, and together they were the most influential of the exhibitions of American products mounted by department stores in New York at the time. For the title of its first exposition, Macy's borrowed the name of the Art-in-Trades Club, an organization dedicated to bringing the consumer and manufacturing sectors closer together, which had held its fifth annual exposition at the Waldorf-Astoria Hotel in New York City in 1926.[17] The store, however, identified its venture with the industrial art exhibitions at the Metropolitan Museum of Art, with whom it had established a collaborative relationship.[18] Macy's expositions had the imprimatur of the Metropolitan,[19] and the title of the 1928 exposition, *An International Exposition of Art in Industry*, was an attempt to associate Macy's with the museum's series of exhibitions of art in industry.

Robert W. de Forest, the president of the museum, was chairman of an advisory committee formed for Macy's first exposition. Among the organizations and publications represented by the thirteen committee members were the National Arts Club, the New York School of Fine and Applied Art, the Arts Council of New York City, the Architectural League of New York, the *New York Times*, the *New York Sun*, *Vogue*, and *House and Garden*.[20] In a departure from precedent, Lee Simonson, a stage designer, was hired as art director and designer.[21] Simonson's creative installation received rave reviews for its modish but subdued emulation of *art moderne*. He was engaged again in 1928 and given the title of exposition architect. The stylist Virginia Hamill was appointed executive director, a position she retained in 1928.[22]

The installation occupied an entire floor in the store's new West Building in what was described in the catalogue as a "dramatic setting, contrived in the modern spirit . . . to illustrate the new alliance between the manufacturer and the fine arts."[23] In her review, Read extolled the exposition as "epoch-making," the first "art-in-trade exhibition" to have excluded "copies of period motives," and the broadest artistically installed representation of American decorative arts to date.[24] A lively program of twenty-two lectures was presented in the store during the opening week and broadcast by the radio station WJZ. Among the topics addressed were "The Skyscraper in Decoration" by the interior decorator and furniture designer Paul T. Frankl, "Modern Industrial and Decorative Art" by Charles R. Richards, and "Moods in Color" by Hamill.[25]

Under the category Metalwork in the exhibition catalogue, objects classified as Hand Wrought Silver were listed separately from those classified as Silver, which in this context indicated industrially produced pieces. International Silver and the Towle Manufacturing Company of Newburyport, Massachusetts, were the contributing silver manufacturers, although neither had yet introduced a full line in the modern spirit.[26] Surprisingly, Gorham, the early leader in the field with its designs by Erik Magnussen, was not represented, possibly because Magnussen's pieces were expensive

and so potentially less marketable. The absence of modern industrial silver would be remedied in the following exposition, where both International and Reed & Barton were well represented with their new modern lines. These two manufacturers were attuned to the message from a critic of the 1927 exposition: "This is indeed a machine age. . . . The spirit of the machine age is quantity production at a low cost per unit with rapid consumption and frequent changes in style and design."[27]

Macy's 1928: An International Exposition of Art in Industry

In 1928 Macy's heralded exposition offered a broader overview of the industrial arts and was a more ambitious undertaking than its effort the previous year.[28] The international scope of the exposition was immediately apparent from the catalogue, which listed an advisory committee headed by Robert W. de Forest and consisting of distinguished members from France, Germany, Sweden, Italy, Austria, and the United States.[29] Hamill described the development of the event:

Last year we staged an exposition which was modernistic and largely American. This year it is international. For the first exposition we had difficulty in finding sufficient material to stage a worth-while exhibit of modern design in industry. This year our problem has been one of elimination and selection from a wealth of offerings. . . . Now we combine with our American modernism French genius for catering to the luxuries of life; German recognition of the artistic possibilities of the machine; Italy's facility in projecting classicism into modern forms; Austria's imaginative treatment of decorative effects; and Sweden's modernistic adaptation of its traditional national art in the media of glassware and metals.[30]

The format in 1928 differed in other ways. In 1927, European and American goods were intermixed. For example, in the Hand Wrought Silver section, Georg Jensen and Puiforcat were grouped together with American silversmiths. In 1928, the works of the three American silver exhibitors, International, Reed & Barton, and the silversmith Peter Mueller-Munk, were listed independently and appear to have been displayed separately. Information about specific works in the 1927 exposition is limited because they were not listed in the catalogue. In 1928 this omission was corrected. The waning influence of the Arts and Crafts movement was obvious from the exclusion of all the American Arts and Crafts silversmiths who had exhibited in 1927 and the introduction in 1928 of the modernist Peter Mueller-Munk, a recent German émigré and the sole exponent of American handcrafted silver.

Writing in the catalogue, de Forest recognized fresh evidence that "the America of huge factories and of mass production is beginning to harness the attractive force of good design in team with the tractive power of her

FIGURE 2.2 Court of Honor, R. H. Macy & Company, *An International Exposition of Art in Industry*, 1928

machinery."[31] The improvement of standards in design and taste and the potential leadership of department stores in accomplishing this goal were themes de Forest underscored. "It is to be expected," he continued, "that the manufacturers will therefore take their cue from the interest of these retail centers and will anticipate the trend towards design which will catch the spirit and rhythm of modern life."[32] International and Reed & Barton were two silver manufacturers that did take their cues, each introducing modern lines that were included

in the exposition. Of all the department store exhibitions in the 1920s, this one by Macy's provided modern American industrial silver with the most exposure.

A visitor entered the exposition through the Court of Honor, a spacious reception area that had show-window–style cases filled with small objects arranged dramatically at angles around a central fountain. The silver displays were in this section (fig. 2.2). Of the fifteen objects by International, several can be identified from the patterns named in the catalogue. All three designs in the *Spirit of Today* holloware series (see fig. 1.21) were exhibited: *Tropical Sunrise* was represented with a sandwich plate and bowl (fig. 2.3), *Ebb Tide* by a single bowl similar to the compote in the pattern (fig. 2.4), and *Northern Lights* by a luncheon plate and a compote.[33] In a photograph of the Court of Honor (fig. 2.5), the candelabra in *Evening Sea*, a little-known and now rare holloware pattern by International in sterling (fig. 2.6), is visible in the foreground of a silver display. International romanticized the inspiration for this pattern as "waves gently lapping the shore in the evening quiet after the

FIGURE 2.3 *Tropical Sunrise* bowl, 1928. International Silver Company, Alfred G. Kintz, designer. Silver. DMA, JSASC, cat. 101

FIGURE 2.4 *Ebb Tide* compote, 1928. International Silver Company, Alfred G. Kintz, designer. Silver. DMA, JSASC, cat. 103

FIGURE 2.5   Court of Honor (detail), R. H. Macy & Company,
An International Exposition of Art in Industry, 1928

wind has died."[34] An *Evening Sea* luncheon tray (fig. 2.7) is very similar to the bowl in that pattern that was exhibited. A coffee set with ebony handles and knobs (fig. 2.8), which was produced in the Barbour Sterling Fine Arts Division of International and identified only as "Coffee set, with ebony" in the catalogue, can be discerned in the same show window.[35] Also listed in the catalogue was a silverplated tea set with triangular bodies named for the French transatlantic liner *Ile de France.* The liner's *art moderne* décor caused a sensation on its maiden voyage in June 1927 and International sought to capitalize on the chic connotations of the name in a line of holloware produced and aggressively advertised in 1928.[36] Because the name *Ile de France* was included in the hallmark, it is often incorrectly assumed that these objects were made for the ocean liner.[37]

Reed & Barton, the other American silver manufacturer represented in the exposition, contributed only six items. Although it is not clear from the catalogue entries, research at Reed & Barton strongly suggests that at least four of the six were *Modernist* pattern holloware objects that are illustrated in Reed & Barton salesmen's catalogues and in the company's 1928 advertising campaign titled "Sensibly Interpreting the Spirit of Modernism"

(see fig. 1.27).[38] These four objects were described in the Macy's catalogue as "Silver coffee pot, sugar bowl, and tray" (fig. 2.9); "Silver cocktail tray and six glasses" (see fig. 7.1); and "Small silver vase," and "Tall silver vase" (figs. 2.10, 2.11). A loving cup and compotier completed Reed & Barton's contribution. Eight of Peter Mueller-Munk's works were exhibited in a display case in the Court of Honor and credited to him.[39] In addition, several pieces of his silver adorned the living room designed by Eugene Schoen for the exposition, as did a triangular bowl by Elsa Tennhardt for E. & J. Bass that was not listed in the catalogue (see fig. 3.17 for a creamer and sugar bowl by Tennhardt in the same pattern).[40]

Visitors flocked to see the modern designs. It was estimated that more than two hundred and fifty thousand people attended, and if this is true, it would be at least four times the number for the exposition in 1927.[41] The popularity may have been the catalyst for the sponsorship by *Arts and Decoration* of the "Home Study Course on the Modern Movement in Decoration" written by Paul T. Frankl and advertised in the magazine just two months after the exposition closed.[42] For the industrial silver exhibitors, International and Reed & Barton, the exposure must have been a marketing coup. Another advantage for manufacturers was the centrally located Sales Information Bureau set up by Macy's so that customers could order the merchandise on exhibit, and in certain cases purchase samples directly.[43]

OTHERS FOLLOW SUIT

Early in 1928, before Macy's second exhibition, the Lord & Taylor department store on Fifth Avenue had mounted *An Exposition of Modern French Decorative Art,* a full-blown selection of furniture and objects designed and produced in France and intended for a sophisticated, affluent clientele. Among the decorators invited were Emile-Jacques Ruhlmann, Pierre Chareau, Jean Dunand, and Francis Jourdain. Organized by Dorothy Shaver, who was Lord & Taylor's director of fashion and decoration and the niece of Samuel W. Reyburn, the head of the store, the luxurious installation occupied an entire floor and was designed by the urbane American architect Ely Jacques Kahn.[44] The silverware showcased in the Salon of French Decorative Accessories was exclusively French and primarily the work of Puiforcat and Christofle.[45] However, periodicals from 1928 and 1929 indicate that Lord & Taylor was also a source

FIGURE 2.6   *Evening Sea* candelabra, 1928. Wilcox & Evertsen Fine Arts. Silver. DMA, JSASC, cat. 117

FIGURE 2.7   *Evening Sea* luncheon tray, 1928. Wilcox & Evertsen Fine Arts. Silver. DMA, JSASC, cat. 118

FIGURE 2.8   Pages 48–49: Coffee service, c. 1928–1929. Barbour Sterling Fine Arts. Silver, ebony. DMA, JSASC, cat. 84

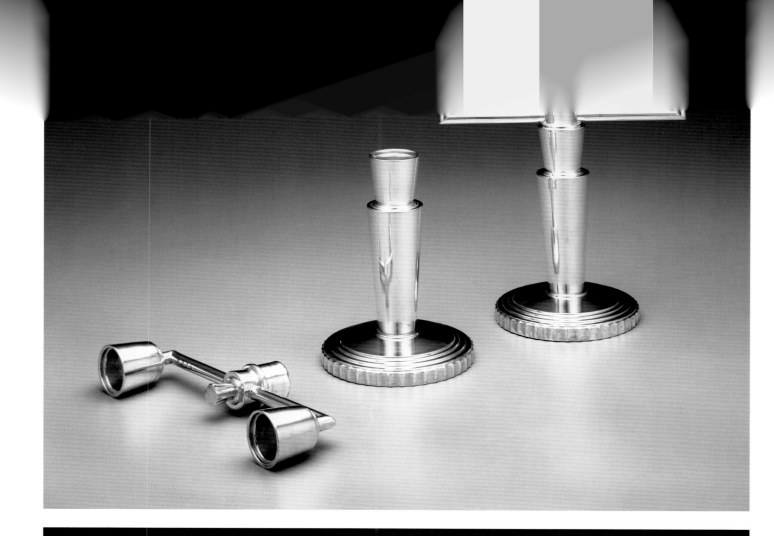

FIGURE 2.9 *Modernist* coffee service, 1928. Reed & Barton. Silver.
DMA, JSASC, cat. 153

FIGURE 2.10 *Modernist* vase, 1928. Reed & Barton. Silver. DMA, JSASC, cat. 155

FIGURE 2.11 *Modernist* vase, 1928. Reed & Barton. Silver. DMA, JSASC, cat. 156

for high-styled modern American silver holloware. A four-piece *Sky-scraper* tea service by Bernard Rice's Sons and an *Ile de France* cocktail shaker set with cups on a matching mirrored tray by International, both in silverplate and illustrated by courtesy of Lord & Taylor, appeared in two different articles by Helen Appleton Read for *Vogue* (see fig. 3.28).[46] Christmas shoppers in 1929 were treated to a dazzling display of silverware at Lord & Taylor in the store's "newly styled gift shops" (fig. 2.12).[47] Standing proudly on one of the stepped bases was an unusually shaped pitcher formed in three bulbous telescoping tiers and resembling Michelin's Bibendum mascot (fig. 2.13). On others were International's horizontally positioned dinette set (see fig. 1.26) and a group of conical pieces by Ilonka Karasz for Paye & Baker (see fig. 3.41).

Marking the peak of commercial promotion of modern design, several other department stores took up the cause in 1928. Abraham & Straus in Brooklyn, for example, intent on modernizing its image, called in Paul T. Frankl to update and transform its *Livable House* exhibit, which in 1926 consisted of American colonial and period revival styles, to a design more compatible with contemporary predilections.[48] In New York City, the B. Altman store presented model room interiors by French and American designers as new expressions of twentieth-century taste.[49] In conservative Boston, the Jordan Marsh Company showed modern furniture as early as 1927.[50] In Chicago, Mandel Brothers staged modern room displays in 1928, as did the Rike-Kumler Department Store in Dayton, Ohio.[51] Early in 1929 on the west coast, Bullock's in Los Angeles presented *An*

Exposition of the Decorative Arts of To-day that included French and American ensembles.[52]

In the early years of the twentieth century when Arts and Crafts ideals had prevailed, Marshall Field & Company, a major Chicago retail department store, established its own Craft Shop to satisfy the demand for handmade metalwork and to profit from it. Although the store also carried industrial silverware from outside manufacturers, it maintained a fully functioning and equipped workroom that produced holloware and flatware and jewelry and accessories in various metals, including silver, through the 1930s.[53] As mass marketing was its goal, Marshall Field did not eschew machine work, and handmade and assembly-line processes coexisted in the workroom. A wide selection of objects that bore the hallmark of the store was available at its counters. In addition to regular stock from the Craft Shop, the store offered its affluent patrons the option of ordering custom-made articles. An elegant Marshall Field *art moderne* sterling silver holloware table suite consisting of compotes, candlesticks, castors, and a cream and sugar dessert set, may well have been a one-of-a-kind design executed to order for a discriminating client in the late 1920s.[54] The dessert set in the suite embodies the main characteristics of the ensemble: rectangular, angled forms that taper downward and rest

FIGURE 2.12   Silver display, Lord & Taylor department store, New York, 1929

on stepped, squared bases, and incised horizontal bands spaced closely together in the upper zones for minimal decoration (fig. 2.14). In keeping with the geometric styling, the cream pitcher has a sharp triangular spout and its wood handle and those of the sugar bowl are squared.[55] From the store's publication *Fashions of the Hour*, we know that in the late 1920s Marshall Field and Company, like enterprising retailers on the East Coast and elsewhere, sold *art moderne* industrial silverware that was influenced by the Paris exposition (see fig. 3.7).[56]

In another manifestation of the modernist impulse at the end of the 1920s, a group of designers—not to be outdone by department stores—banded together as the American Designers' Gallery. Financed by Edgar A. Levy, a banker and aficionado of modernism, the group's opening exhibition took place in November 1928 in New York City on the fifth floor of the Chase Bank Building at 145 West Fifty-seventh Street and was open to the public without charge for six weeks.[57] Herman Rosse, president of the organization, heralded the presentation as "the first complete showing of the united opinion of fifteen of the most experienced designers in America."[58] The roster of exhibitors included the members Donald Deskey, Robert E. Locher, Ralph T. Walker, and Ilonka Karasz, all of whom became consultants to the silver industry in the late 1920s and 1930s.[59] A production-line reeded tea service in silverplate by Karasz for the

silver manufacturer Paye & Baker was exhibited (see fig. 3.38).[60]

Indicative of the intense interest in modern design in 1928 was the formation of two other independent organizations in New York.[61] One was Contempora, which had only three members—Lucian Bernhardt, Bruno Paul, and Rockwell Kent—and was meant solely to advance their own work. More important was the American Union of Decorative Artists and Craftsmen, known by its acronym AUDAC, which attracted outstanding artists, architects, and designers engaged in the industrial, decorative, and applied arts, as well as nonprofessional enthusiasts of modernism. At its height in 1931, AUDAC had more than 150 members in four categories.[62] The group's major contribution was a book, *Annual of American Design 1931*, and an exhibition at the Brooklyn Museum in 1931 that was intended to awaken a "larger section of the public to an appreciation of the value of modern design in its homes, business interiors, in graphic arts, textiles and all the objects of daily use."[63] In the brochure for the exhibition, the group stated its goals of elevating "standards in contemporary design" and developing a cohesive "STYLE rather than styles."[64] Both AUDAC and the Brooklyn Museum expressed the hope that designers and manufacturers would be stimulated to experiment further and to "develop a distinctive form of decoration appropriate to all phases of modern life."[65] Inexplicably, industrially produced silver

FIGURE 2.13   Water pitcher, c. 1928. Meriden Silver Plate Company. Silverplate. DMA, JSASC, cat. 93

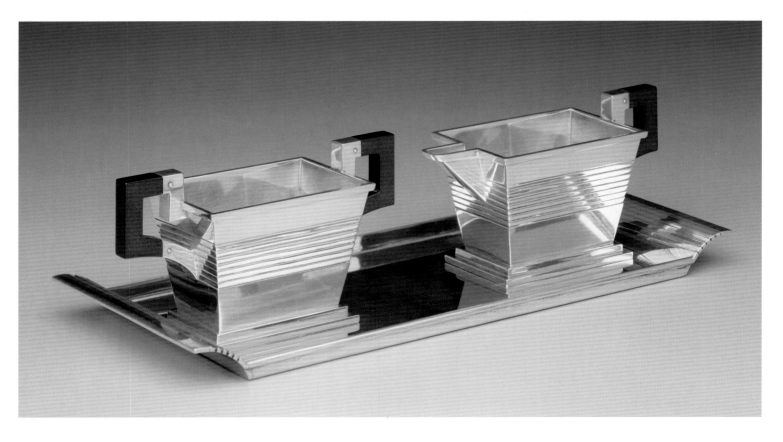

FIGURE 2.14   Cream and sugar set with tray, c. 1929. Marshall Field & Company. Silver, ebony. DMA, JSASC, cat. 136

holloware and flatware were not represented in the exhibition.[66] However, two silverplate vases designed by a member, Kem Weber, for the Friedman Silver Company were illustrated in the group's book.[67] A handwrought silver bowl by Erik Magnussen, also illustrated, was not credited to Gorham although it is identical to Gorham's ashtray with a cockatoo handle that was made about 1927 or 1928 and marked EM 86.[68]

Unfortunately, the creative programs of AUDAC and the American Designers' Gallery were short lived. The deepening Depression closed these organizations in the early 1930s and the members dispersed. Even after the Depression lifted, the esprit de corps and momentum of the late 1920s were never regained. The heyday of department stores as advocates of progressive design was over, too. During the distressed economic decade of the 1930s the modern industrial silver that was produced, especially in holloware, would be showcased primarily in museum exhibitions and international expositions at home and abroad.

NOTES

1. For a discussion of the role of the stylist, see Jeffrey L. Meikle, *Twentieth Century Limited: Industrial Design in America, 1925–1939* (Philadelphia: Temple University Press, 1979), 17.

2. Sheldon Cheney and Martha Candler Cheney, *Art and the Machine* (New York: Whittlesey House, 1936), 7. See also Helen Sprackling, "Modern Art and the Artist; The farseeing Manufacturer is proving that he appreciates the Value of the Artist," *House Beautiful* 65 (Feb. 1929): 151–55.

3. Nick Krezitsky, telephone conversation with author, Sept. 5, 1990; and "Only in the U.S.A.," *House and Garden* 96 (July 1949): 31.

4. "Other Weddings: Johnson-Hamill," *New York Times,* Sept. 19, 1930, 20.

5. Catharine Oglesby, "Big Business Finds That Beauty Pays," *Independent Woman* 16 (Sept. 1937): 282–83; and Felix Payant, "The Editor's Page," *Design* 37 (Feb. 1936): 9. On her letterhead of the later 1930s, Hamill identified herself as a "Merchandising and Design Consultant." See "Magazines File," box 364, series 2, America at Home, 1939 New York World's Fair Collection, Manuscripts and Archives Div., New York Public Library, New York.

6. Douglas Haskell, "A Fine Industrial Design," *Creative Art* 3 (Dec. 1928): 1; Helen Appleton Read, "Twentieth-Century Decoration: The Modern Theme Finds a Distinctive Medium in American Silver," *Vogue* 72 (July 1, 1928): 94.

7. "World Art Exhibit Opened by Macy's," *New York Times,* May 15, 1928, 8.

8. Quoted by Helen Appleton Read, in "Art-in-Trades Club Features American Design in Annual Exhibition," *Brooklyn Daily Eagle,* Oct. 24, 1926 (Archives of American Art, Helen Appleton Read Papers [hereafter AAA, Read papers], reel N736, frame 151).

9. Meikle, *Twentieth Century Limited,* 16n48.

10. Ibid.

11. Helen Appleton Read, "Art-in-Trade Exposition Stresses the Modern Note," *Brooklyn Daily Eagle,* May 8, 1927 (AAA, Read papers, reel N736, frame 151).

12. Helen Appleton Read, "Department Stores Rival Museum in the Formation of Taste in Industrial Art," *Brooklyn Daily Eagle,* Dec. 25, 1927 (AAA, Read papers, reel N736, frame 198).

13. Robert A. M. Stern, Gregory Gilmartin, and Thomas Mellins, *New York 1930: Architecture and Urbanism Between the Two World Wars* (New York: Rizzoli, 1987), 336.

14. Robert A. M. Stern, "Relevance of the Decade," *Journal of the Society of Architectural Historians* 24 (Mar. 1965): 6.

15. Ibid., 9.

16. Ibid., 7–9.

17. Read, "Art-in-Trades Club."

18. For a detailed study of the relationship between the Metropolitan Museum of Art and R. H. Macy & Co., see Marilyn F. Friedman, "An Unlikely Alliance: R. H. Macy & Co. and the Metropolitan Museum of Art Popularize Modern Design in New York City 1914–1928" (master's thesis, Cooper-Hewitt, National Design Museum, New York, 2003).

19. R. H. Macy & Co., "The Exposition Follows the Plan of Exhibitions Held by the Metropolitan Museum of Art," in *The Catalog of the Exposition of Art in Trade at Macy's* (New York: R. H. Macy, 1927), cover.

20. Ibid., 2.

21. "Bringing Art into Trade," *Literary Digest* 93 (May 28, 1927): 26. For photographs of the installation, see "Art Works for a Living," *Independent* 119 (July 9, 1927): 35–37.

22. A reviewer noted that Hamill was "finding the career of stylist a most congenial and successful one" (William H. Baldwin, "Modern Art and the Machine," *Independent* 119 [July 9, 1927]: 39).

23. R. H. Macy, "Exposition Follows the Plan," 3.

24. Read, "Art-in-Trade Exposition."

25. R. H. Macy, "Exposition Follows the Plan," 6–7. Frankl exhibited his skyscraper bookcase. See "Bringing Art into Trade."

26. R. H. Macy, "Exposition Follows the Plan," 8. Individual objects were not listed in the catalogue. Under "Hand Wrought Silver," the metalsmiths Rebecca Gauman [*sic*], John P. Petterson, George C. Gebelein, and Gyllenberg & Swanson were listed, "Courtesy of the Boston Society of Arts & Crafts, New York Branch." The other two contributors in the category were Georg Jensen and Puiforcat, "Courtesy of Tessa Kosta."

27. Baldwin, "Modern Art," 39.

28. R. H. Macy & Co., *An International Exposition of Art in Industry at Macy's* (New York: R. H. Macy, 1928).

29. Ibid., 7. In the American group, eight of the fifteen had been involved in the 1927 exposition. Among those were Richard F. Bach, Charles R. Richards, and representatives of the *New York Times* and *House and Garden*. *Vogue* did not participate again.

30. N. C. Sanford, "An International Exhibit of Modern Art; Macy's of New York Sponsored Forward-Looking Event," *Good Furniture Magazine* 31 (July 1928): 20.

31. Robert W. de Forest, Foreword, in R. H. Macy, *An International Exposition*, 3.

32. Ibid., 6.

33. R. H. Macy, *An International Exposition*, 70.

34. Dudley T. Fagan, "Modernism: Its Possibilities in America," *National Jeweler* 25 (Jan. 1929): 26.

35. R. H. Macy, *An International Exposition*, 70. International made high-quality production-line sterling holloware in smaller quantities in its Barbour Sterling Fine Arts Division in Factory "A" in Meriden, Conn. The Depression forced the closing of the factory about 1931 (Edmund P. Hogan, *An American Heritage: A Book About the International Silver Company* [Dallas, Tex.: Taylor, 1977], 159).

36. Other items in the *Ile de France* line were cigarette boxes in two designs, a mixer set with cups and mirrored and stepped waiter, and a sandwich tray.

37. The other objects by International that were listed in the exposition were a compote with ebony inserts and disk base, a pair of candlesticks with ebony inserts and disk base, a cocktail shaker, a tea set with macassar handles, a trophy cup, and a silverplate beverage mixer with six cups and mirror tray.

38. Determined from research at Reed & Barton, Taunton, Mass., by the author, 1991.

39. Determined from photograph 267N17, Sigurd Fischer Collection, Library of Congress, Washington, D.C. (hereafter as Fischer Coll.).

40. Photograph of a living room designed by Schoen in "Various Countries Exhibit Modern Art," *American Architect* 133 (June 20, 1928): 827; see also photograph 267N4, Fischer Coll.

41. Attendance figure from R. H. Macy & Co., Inc.; see advertisement, *New York Times*, May 28, 1928, 9.

42. "The Modern Movement in Decoration," *Arts and Decoration* 29 (July 1928): 91. Surprisingly, Frankl, who participated in Macy's exposition in 1927, was not included in 1928. Perhaps the course was a way of keeping himself in the public eye.

43. R. H. Macy, *An International Exposition*, following p. 76.

44. Lord & Taylor, *An Exposition of Modern French Decorative Art* (New York: Lord & Taylor, 1928), [iii]; and Isabelle Croce, conversation with author, New York City, July 27, 1983.

45. For list of objects by Puiforcat and Christofle, see Lord & Taylor, *An Exposition*, 24. For Salon of French Decorative Accessories, see "Lord & Taylor Exhibition of Modern Decorative Art," *Kaleidoscope* 1 (Apr. 1928): 8. See also "French Art Moderne Exposition in New York," *Good Furniture Magazine* 30 (Mar. 1928): 119–22.

46. *Sky-scraper* service in Helen Appleton Read, "Twentieth Century Decoration," *Vogue* 71 (June 1, 1928): 16; and *Ile de France* cocktail shaker set in Read, "Shopping for the Modern House," *Vogue* 98 (Mar. 16, 1929): 99.

47. Reynolds G. Rockwell, "Have You a Table of Contents?" *Gift and Art Shop* 21 (Dec. 1929): 23.

48. Stern, Gilmartin, and Mellins, *New York 1930*, 336–37.

49. Ibid., 336.

50. N. C. Stanford, "Decorating in Art Moderne," *Good Furniture Magazine* 31 (Nov. 1928): 2245.

51. For Mandel Brothers, see "Modern Rooms in New York and Chicago," *Good Furniture Magazine* 31 (Dec. 1928): 315. For Rike-Kumler, see "At the Rike-Kumler Exposition of Modern Art," *Women's Wear Daily*, Sept. 15, 1928, 15.

52. For Bullock's, see "Contemporary Art in Current Exhibitions," *Good Furniture Magazine* 32 (May 1929): 241.

53. Sharon S. Darling, *Chicago Metalsmiths* (Chicago: Chicago Historical Society, 1977), 74–75.

54. For the entire suite, see Sotheby's *Important 20th Century Decorative Arts*, auction cat., June 17, 1989 (New York: Sotheby's, 1989), lots 432–35.

55. To emphasize the geometric character of the suite, silver spheres were added as decorative supports to the compotes and candlesticks.

56. See, for example, Wallace *Rhythm* flatware in Marshall Field & Co., *Fashions of the Hour*, exposition number (Chicago: Marshall Field, 1929), 29.

57. "Exhibit of American Designers' Gallery," *Good Furniture Magazine* 32 (Jan. 1929): 40–45. A tour to important department stores in ten cities was reported but there is no record that the exhibition traveled; see David A. Hanks, Jennifer Toher, and Jeffrey L. Meikle, *Donald Deskey Decorative Designs and Interiors* (New York: E. P. Dutton, 1987), 21.

58. Herman Rosse, Foreword, in American Designers' Gallery, *American Designers' Gallery Inc.*, exh. cat. (New York, 1928); and American Designers' Gallery, "Exposition of American Contemporary Art," advertisement, *Metal Arts* 1 (Nov. 1928): vi. The group staged one other exhibition in New York City in 1929.

59. The other charter members of American Designers' Gallery were George Biddle, Wolfgang Hoffmann, Raymond Hood, Ely Jacques Kahn, Henry Varnum Poor, Ruth Reeves, Winold Reiss, Herman Rosse, Martha Ryther, Carolyn Simonson, and Joseph Urban.

60. Karasz's service is illustrated in "Interior Architecture; American Designers' Gallery Exhibits Modern American Art," *American Architect* 134 (Dec. 5, 1928): 751.

61. Helen Appleton Read, "The Moderns Organize; American Designers Form Societies to Push American Made Designs," *Brooklyn Daily Eagle*, Oct. 28, 1928 (AAA, Read papers, reel N736, frame 220).

62. Membership lists, American Union of Decorative Artists and Craftsmen (AUDAC), "AUDAC Exhibition, May–June 1931," exh. brochure, Brooklyn Museum of Art Archives. Among those listed as active members were Donald Deskey, Frederick Kiesler, Kem Weber, Frank Lloyd Wright, and Russel Wright.

63. Josiah P. Marvel and Lee Simonson, Joint Statement, "AUDAC Exhibition."

64. Ibid.

65. Ibid.

66. Ibid., checklist. Works by the metalsmiths Bernard W. Fischer, Gustav B. Jensen, and Erik Magnussen (who was no longer at Gorham) were in the exhibition.

67. R. L. Leonard and C. A. Glassgold, eds., American Union of Decorative Artists and Craftsmen, *Annual of American Design 1931* (New York: Ives Washburn, 1930), 175. For Weber, see David Gebhard and Hariette Von Breton, *Kem Weber: The Moderne in Southern California 1920 through 1941*, exh. cat. (Santa Barbara, Calif.: Art Galleries, University of California, 1969).

68. Leonard and Glassgold, *Annual*, 96. Photograph of Gorham EM 86 ash tray in Gorham Archives, John Hay Library, Brown University, Providence, R.I.

CHAPTER THREE

NEW STYLES FOR A NEW AGE

The French influence on American industrial silver was pervasive in the years immediately following the 1925 Paris exposition. Looking back, C. A. Glassgold, the editor of a landmark survey of modern American design that was published in 1930 by the American Union of Decorative Artists and Craftsmen (AUDAC), recognized the phenomenon:

The Paris Exposition of 1925 is for us, the significant date in the history of [the contemporary movement in design] for it brought clearly to us the realization that Europe had brewed a stimulating potion while we were pottering about in our own unsavory stew. The effect upon American design was stupendous. Little wonder then that our first experiments should have been closely modeled upon French design to be followed later by translations from the German and Austrian.[1]

French silverware exhibited at the 1925 Paris exposition by Gérard Sandoz, for example, and especially that of Puiforcat, on view in three locations, was an initial source. Also exhibiting were the influential French silver firms Orfèvrerie Christofle, Maison Cardeilhac, and Maison Lapparra.

In French modernist silverware two streams, one conservative and the other avant-garde, can be discerned. In the former, traditional forms, especially rounded volumes segmented or lobed with clearly defined curves, were preferred, and decoration, usually imbued with classical allusions, was minimal. In the latter, planarity, angles, sharp edges, and squared shapes, all derivations from radical geometric cubism, were stressed. In both, semiprecious stones and rare exotic woods were introduced for richness and color contrast. Several photographs of holloware by the French maker Tétard Frères that were found in a scrapbook in the Gorham Archive at Brown University attest to the attention paid to French design by a major manufacturer.[2] The pieces selected for reference by Gorham illustrated both French tendencies, smoothly rounded and sharply squared forms. Decoration was limited to contrasting materials for handles and finials, and edges were emphasized.

Between 1925 and 1929 there were ample opportunities for American silver manufacturers to study modern French silverware at home in various exhibitions and through illustrations in periodicals. From the first exhibition in 1926 of selections from the Paris exposition at the Metropolitan Museum of Art, the museum acquired several components of a curved and paneled tea service by Puiforcat with lapis lazuli handles and finials (fig. 3.1). These pieces were illustrated afterward in *The Spur*.[3] In 1927 Wanamaker's Venturus Shop in New York City held an exhibition, *Modern Art in a Department Store*, that featured a dining room by the French firm Primavera set with modernist flatware by Puiforcat, and his work was on display in the *Exposition of Art*

FIGURE 3.1 Photograph: Tea and coffee service, 1925. Jean Puiforcat. Silver, lapis lazuli, ivory. The Metropolitan Museum of Art, Purchase, Edward C. Moore, Jr. Gift, 1923 and 1925 (23.177.1-3; 25.230.1-4)

in Trade at Macy's.[4] The same year *Arts and Decoration* illustrated works by Puiforcat and Gérard Sandoz in an article titled "New Silhouettes in the French Tea Service."[5] Puiforcat and Christofle were prominently featured in the silver category of Lord & Taylor's *Exposition of Modern French Decorative Art*, in which highlights were Christofle's soup tureen and two matching table decorations with lapis lazuli elements.[6]

It was at Saks Fifth Avenue, the luxury department store, which moved to its present location in 1924, that the widest selection of Puiforcat's holloware and flatware was available in the late 1920s. No doubt this was the idea of Adam Gimbel, who became president of the establishment in 1926 at the age of thirty-two after the sudden death of Horace Saks, one of the store's founders. Following his return from the Paris exposition, the youthful Gimbel introduced the "new modernistic décor" in window displays and store interiors by employing vanguard designers such as Frederick Kiesler and Donald Deskey.[7] Gimbel stocked the store with costly imported goods including French silver by Puiforcat, which was represented in New York exclusively at Saks in a new department established in 1928 for "individual gifts." Saks devoted a full-page advertisement in the *New Yorker* to announce the opening of the boutique and to introduce the work of two French modern masters, Puiforcat in silverware and Raymond Templier in fine jewelry. In promoting Puiforcat's work, Saks addressed both modernists and traditionalists: "Modern silverware by Jean Puiforcat is virtually without embellishment; it has a stark beauty of line which is balanced by profoundly considered proportions; it is made for the tables of today *but it will harmonize with those of other periods* [emphasis in original]."[8] Because holloware executed exclusively for the store was stamped "jean e. puiforcat / france / saks fifth avenue," pieces are easily identified.[9] By the late 1920s periodicals such as *Vogue* and *Arts and Decoration* illustrated a rich variety of Puiforcat's designs for sale at the store.[10]

A piece of silver made by Reed & Barton that shows the influence of Puiforcat in 1928 is a sterling compote with a layered, stepped base and ribbed, reeded foot (fig. 3.2). Except for the substitution of a silver foot for semiprecious stone, it was almost a direct copy but larger in size than the original by the French master. Also in 1928 the Wilcox & Evertsen Fine Arts Division of International Silver adapted French elements for a three-piece sterling coffee set with stepped bases.[11] A fluted finial terminates the stepped lid of the coffeepot (fig. 3.3), which has a carved macassar ebony handle. The half-crescent spouts of coffeepot and creamer conform to the contours of the vessels and bring to mind those in a tea service by the French silversmith Gérard Sandoz that was exhibited in the 1925 Paris exposition (fig. 3.4, bottom).[12]

Assimilated by the French from early twentieth-century designs by the Austrian Josef Hoffmann and others, stepped or terraced forms (sometimes referred to as layered and staggered) were abundantly evident at the Paris exposition. Widely embraced afterward by American manufacturers, this formal device, reminiscent of a stepped skyscraper, became ubiquitous in late-1920s holloware. Classical motifs were often paired with stepped elements, as for the fluted finial

FIGURE 3.2 *Modernist* compote, 1928. Reed & Barton. Silver. DMA, JSASC, cat. 157

FIGURE 3.3   Coffeepot, 1928. International Silver Company.
Silver, ebony. DMA, JSASC, cat. 120

FIGURE 3.4   Illustration of *Tête à Tête* services, c. 1925.
Gérard Sandoz, designer

FIGURE 3.5   Salt and pepper shakers with original box, 1929.
Weidlich Brothers Manufacturing Company, Alfred J. Flauder, designer.
Silverplate. Dallas Museum of Art, cat. 306

of International's coffeepot. Another example by International is the *Evening Sea* candelabrum (see fig. 2.6). Alfred J. Flauder, a designer for the Weidlich Brothers Manufacturing Company of Bridgeport, Connecticut, added another element to the classical fluting and stepping of his flamboyant salt and pepper shaker set, imposing a stylized *art moderne* pattern on a fan-shaped motif for each hexagonal shaker (fig. 3.5). Stepping was often combined in an object with its inversion, which gave the impression of "telescoping." This effect is the exclusive decorative element in sterling candlesticks by Tuttle Silversmiths of Boston, Massachusetts (fig. 3.6, right), and in a *Ritz*-pattern compote and almond set designed in 1929 by Harold E. Nock, the head designer for Towle (fig. 3.6, center). Kem Weber employed telescoping in

his *Silver Style* cocktail shaker for the Friedman Silver Company (fig. 3.6, left).[13]

Other makers adopted characteristics of modern French silver. The A. L. Wagner Manufacturing Company of New York endowed a tea and coffee service with an amalgam of these features (fig. 3.7). This service was offered by Marshall Field & Company of Chicago and illustrated in the Christmas 1928 issue of the department store's publication *Fashions of the Hour*.[14] The segmenting of the vessels into narrow fluted ribs, a frequent device in conservative *art moderne* silver, recalls a tea service made in 1925 by Lapparra and an after-dinner coffee service that was illustrated in *House and Garden* in 1927.[15] The triggerlike spouts may have been derived from objects made by Tétard Frères, which employed them. Among the precedents for the quarter-round ebony "ponytail" handles were two services by Puiforcat, one with lapis lazuli handles that was exhibited in the 1925 Paris exposition (see fig. 3.1) and another that was illustrated in *Vogue*.[16] A late-1920s sterling mayonnaise dish (fig. 3.8) by R. Wallace and Sons Manufacturing Company of Wallingford, Connecticut, has a fluted Catalin foot and base and a segmented and notched

FIGURE 3.6 Left: *Silver Style* cocktail shaker, 1928. Friedman Silver Company, Kem Weber, designer. Silverplate, rosewood. Dallas Museum of Art, cat. 17; center: *Ritz* almond set (three of six small compotes), 1929. Towle Silversmiths, Harold E. Nock, designer. Silver. DMA, JSASC, cat. 253; right: Candlesticks, c. 1929–1933. Tuttle Silversmiths. Silver. DMA, JSASC, cat. 278

FIGURE 3.7 Tea and coffee service, 1928. A. L. Wagner Manufacturing Company, Inc. Silver, ebony. DMA, JSASC, cat. 280

bowl that evoked the classicism and color contrasts prevalent in silverware at the 1925 Paris exposition.

One of the most elegant American objects to emulate the curvaceous variant of *art moderne* was made in sterling by Reed & Barton and called a "fruit dish" (fig. 3.9).[17] Introduced in the early 1930s, the piece demonstrated the lingering appeal of French taste after the stock market crash of 1929, when production plummeted and design became more conservative and less lavish. The low-slung, gracefully curved body rests on two delicate rods that serve as feet and are also used as terminals of the handles that unfurl from a central panel in the body of the dish. The fact that, in 1934 Cartier, the sophisticated and renowned French jeweler, retailed an example of this dish, with its own name stamped on it, indicates the affinity of the design with modern French aesthetics.[18]

The cutting edge of design in French silver at the Paris exposition was expressed in a vocabulary of form that was derived mainly from cubism, even though the taut geometric forms were antithetical to the flow and malleability of the material. The square, rectangle, triangle, hexagon, octagon, and prism informed these shapes. Angles, edges, planes, and facets were the primary and, at times, the exclusive decoration. Prismatic effects that heightened light and shadow were relished. Geometry ruled. A crisp, linear octagonal tea and coffee service with angular spouts (see fig. 3.4, top) made by Gérard Sandoz and exhibited at the 1925 Paris exposition is an example of the aspect of *art moderne* that drew inspiration from cubism.[19] Another example that heralded the aesthetic at the exposition is the hexagonal, faceted service with exotic wood handles by Puiforcat (fig. 3.10) that was offered afterward at Saks Fifth Avenue. Initially Americans found such innovative designs "bizarre," but the angularity and severity were soon accepted as quintessential expressions of modernity. Symptomatic was an advertisement, headlined "Angles and Triangles," that appeared in the *New Yorker* in 1928 for jewelry at B. Altman & Co. on Fifth Avenue.[20] This trend, derived from cubism and especially cubistic sculpture, was widespread in modern American silver holloware at the peak of the production of the style in the years 1928 and 1929. An octagonal bowl by Reed & Barton and illustrated in *Country Life* in 1928 (fig. 3.11, top) was almost a direct quotation of one designed in

1925 by the Danish silversmith Christian Fjerdingstad for the French maker Christofle (fig. 3.12).[21] The iconic *Diament* fitted dinette set, a bold geometric composition produced by International Silver, is a study in angles and sharp edges (fig. 3.13). The rectangular pot has a quarter-circle finial and elongated triangular spout. The tray and its handles conform to the sharply angled covered creamer and sugar bowl, and stepping is the prominent element on the lids of the vessels and on the handles, base, and feet of the tray.

Other examples that demonstrate the influence of geometry abound. Although Reed & Barton initially marketed its wares as "sensibly" modern in styling, most of its sterling holloware in the *Modernist* pattern had angular and rectangular shapes and geometric borders. The gravy boat on a tray is rectangular, angled, and has a triangular spout (fig. 3.14). The vertical handle supported by lateral extensions is another borrowing from French modeling.[22] The separate rectangular tray has a border of narrow applied strips that overlap to create a relief effect. The border treatment was repeated on assorted square and rectangular vegetable and meat serving dishes and trays, and was similar to those on earlier geometrical trays by Puiforcat and Sandoz.[23]

CUBISM

The influence of Erik Magnussen's *Cubic* service designed in 1927 (fig. 1.9) was enormous and iterations of it proliferated during 1928 and 1929, the years of efflorescence in Jazz-Age modern silver. Because vogues were generally transitory and silverplate entailed less of an investment in the precious metal, cautious manufacturers aware of financial risks produced their spin-offs primarily in plate. It was hoped that these moderately priced yet stylish wares would appeal to fashion-conscious, middle-class consumers. Economy was also achieved by imitating the three-dimensionality of *Cubic* but without breaking the surface into complex faceted planes. The most exuberant designs were produced by divisions of International, Bernard Rice's Sons, Weidlich Brothers, Benedict, Friedman, and E. & J. Bass.

Elsa Tennhardt (fig. 3.16), a largely unknown émigré artist from Germany, who worked in the mid-1920s at the Winold Reiss Art School on Christopher Street

FIGURE 3.8   Mayonnaise dish, c. 1929. R. Wallace & Sons Manufacturing Company. Silver, plastic. DMA, JSASC, cat. 285

FIGURE 3.9   Fruit dish, c. 1933. Reed & Barton. Silver, DMA, JSASC, cat. 162

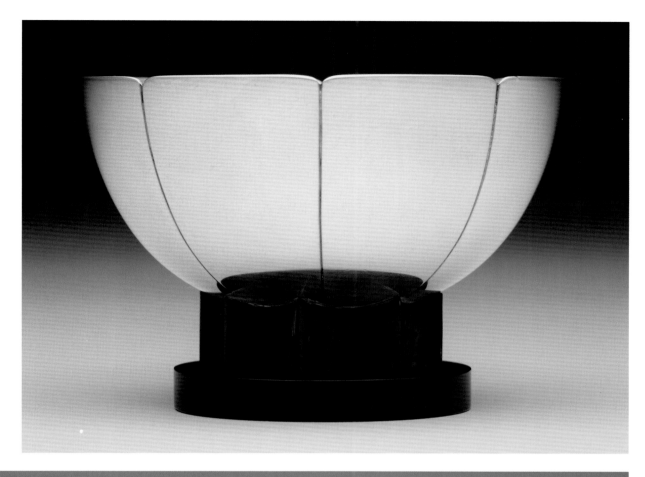

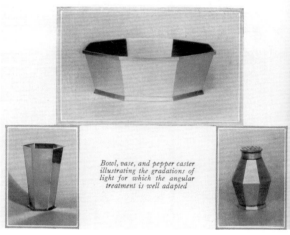

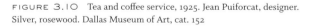

Bowl, vase, and pepper caster illustrating the gradations of light for which the angular treatment is well adapted

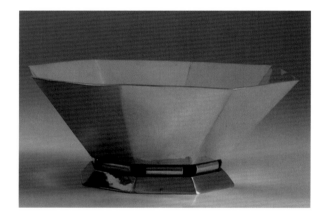

FIGURE 3.10   Tea and coffee service, 1925. Jean Puiforcat, designer. Silver, rosewood. Dallas Museum of Art, cat. 152

FIGURE 3.11   Photograph: Bowl, vase, and pepper castor, Reed & Barton, 1928

FIGURE 3.12   Photograph: Bowl, c. 1925. Orfèvrerie Christofle, Paris, Christian Fjerdingstad, designer

in New York City and was peripherally associated with his circle, designed holloware and vanity articles in a cubist style in 1928. Unless they were famous, designers in the silver trade routinely worked anonymously and were rarely credited by name. Were it not for the patents granted in her name as assignor to the manufacturer E. & J. Bass, Tennhardt would never have been identified.[24] When her cocktail shaker set complete with cocktail cups, tray, and ice bowl was illustrated in *Harper's Bazaar*, she was not named as the designer.[25] In the patent application for "a dish" that was the basis for her holloware series, which included a vigorous, cubist-inspired triangular creamer and sugar bowl set (fig. 3.17) with superimposed angular planes that were originally gilded, Tennhardt wrote: "The dominant feature of the design resides in the employment of long triangular areas . . . of contrasting color placed about the edges of a triangular pyramid and arranged so that the apex of one

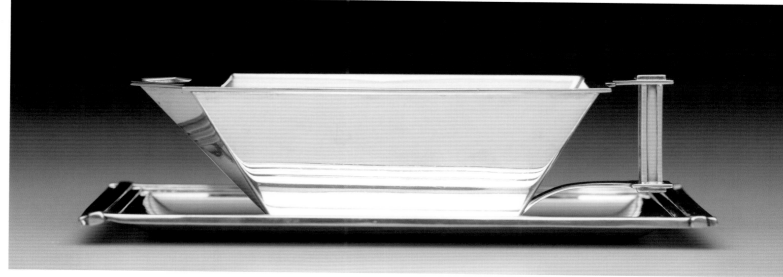

FIGURE 3.13 *Diament* dinette set, 1928. Wilcox Silver Plate Company, Jean G. Theobald, designer. Silverplate, plastic. DMA, JSASC, cat. 126

FIGURE 3.14 *Modernist* gravy boat and tray, 1928. Reed & Barton. Silver. DMA, JSASC, cat. 159

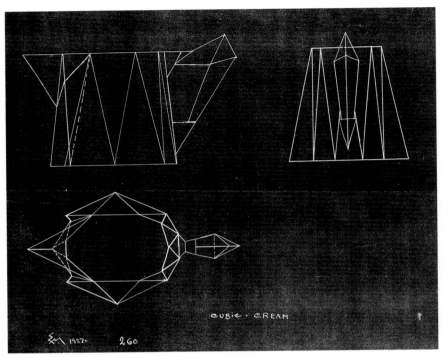

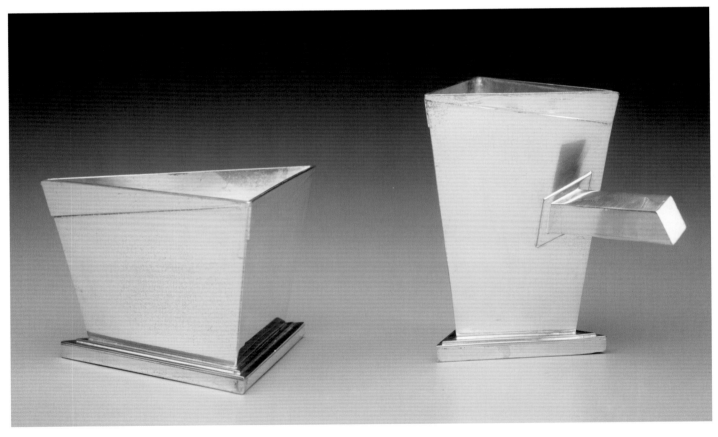

FIGURE 3.15   Drawing, *Cubic* creamer, Erik Magnussen, 1927

FIGURE 3.16   Elsa Tennhardt, c. 1920

FIGURE 3.17   Creamer and sugar bowl, 1928. E. & J. Bass, Elsa Tennhardt, designer. Silverplate with traces of original gilding. DMA, JSASC, cat. 1

FIGURE 3.18 Photograph: Candy box, 1926. Jean Puiforcat, designer. Silver, ebony

triangular area is near the base of the next triangular area."[26] The effect brings to mind Magnussen's *Cubic* coffee service, and the complexity and refinement of design indicates a critical, sophisticated sensibility. When viewing her objects, the eye darts from plane to plane and angle to angle in a constantly shifting dynamic similar to that of cubism in painting and sculpture, where the object cannot be grasped as a static entirety, but only in the oscillation of its fractured planes.[27]

The extent of Tennhardt's training is not known. She returned to Germany on an extended family visit in 1926 with a side trip to France where, given her association with the Reiss Art School, she was probably exposed to contemporary Parisian design.[28] A precedent for the cocktail shaker set may have been Puiforcat's rigorous triangular candy box of 1926 (fig. 3.18) and his striking tea and coffee service with angular components that was illustrated in *Arts and Decoration* in 1927 (fig. 3.19).

Sharply angular holloware by Alois Worle of Munich with bases similar to those employed by Tennhardt had been illustrated in *Dekorative Kunst* even earlier.[29] The ubiquitous triangle motif was the basis of Tennhardt's spirited vanity set (fig. 3.20). It shaped the hairbrush, powder box, and mirror, their openwork handles, and those of the tray as well as the triangular atomizer that rests at an angle on a flat triangular base. The primary decorative device, graduated triangular borders in relief, is a play on the shape and reinforces the geometry of the design.

In 1928, Apollo Gift Lines, a subsidiary of Bernard Rice's Sons, a maker of silverplated holloware and novelties, launched a holloware group with a curiously spelled name, *Shadowardt*. The name may have been an effort to associate the pattern with "The Lights and Shadows of Manhattan," an often-published reference to Magnussen's *Cubic* service. The designer of this pattern responded directly, although crudely, to the *Cubic* service.[30] Unlike the *Cubic* vessels, those in *Shadowardt* were not faceted. Their smooth surfaces were simply inscribed with triangles filled in with either oxidization or gilding to mimic the prismatic effects of *Cubic* (fig. 3.21). A full line of holloware was produced in *Shadowardt*, including a cocktail shaker service with cocktail cups, ice bowl, and tray.

The Friedman Silver Company introduced two silverplated groups of cubist-inspired holloware without applied decoration. In one pattern crenelated rims predominated. The pieces in the other pattern were prismatic in shape (achieved by folding the metal) and had triangular handles. The handles and finials in both

FIGURE 3.19 Photograph: Tea and coffee service, 1927. Jean Puiforcat, designer. Silver, mahogany

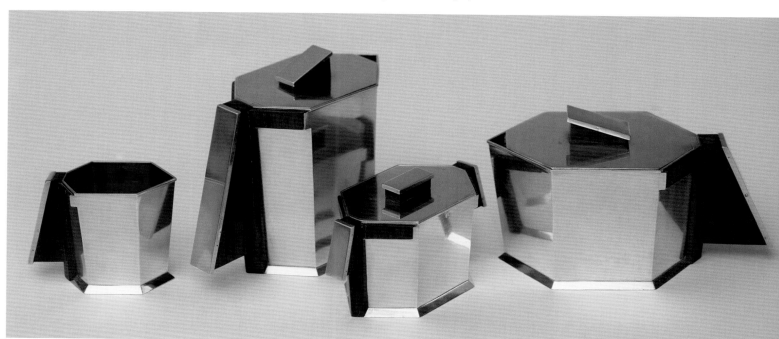

FIGURE 3.20 Vanity set, 1928. E. & J. Bass, Elsa Tennhardt, designer. Silverplate, glass. The Mr. and Mrs. Roger D. Redden Collection, cat. 2

FIGURE 3.21   *Shadowardt* gravy boat, 1928. Apollo Studios, a division of Bernard Rice's Sons. Patinated silverplate. DMA, JSASC, cat. 208

groups were made in either colored plastic, primarily blue and green, or wood. Designed by Howard L. Budd, each pattern was patented and assigned to the manufacturer. A cream and sugar set in the crenelated pattern has angular notched rims and squared dark blue wood handles (fig. 3.22). The tall vase in the prismatic pattern has a zigzag rim, stepped base, and emphatic green triangular handles (fig. 3.23).

Other manufacturers resorted to die stamping angular patterns onto the surface of the metal to give the illusion of three-dimensional fractured planes and to capture the exuberance of the cubist variant of *art moderne*. A prime example is a holloware pattern by Weidlich Brothers that was later dubbed "Sunray" for its quotation of a popular motif in late-1920s goods. The surfaces of the objects were stamped in a complex allover layered pattern of smooth and striped radiating bands against a brushed background of shaded facets (fig. 3.24).[31]

The Benedict Manufacturing Company used a similar procedure in one of its *modernistic plate* lines. In this patented design by Albert F. Saunders, three overlapping triangular patterns form a wide border that surrounds a plain central panel (see fig. 1.2), or the reverse, a plain border that surrounds a patterned center. The pitcher has a handle modeled on Magnussen's *Cubic* handles and, below the angled neck and spout, a different decorative border, also by Saunders, in which a stylized French floral motif was juxtaposed with a rhythmic, overlapping geometric pattern (fig. 3.25). In its introductory advertisement to the trade, the company positioned its *modernistic plate* as "the period silver of tomorrow" and yet "*the silver of Today!*" and proclaimed that the "spirited angularity" was not bizarre; on the contrary, it reflected the "*modern woman in her modern home.*"[32] A subsequent advertisement associated *modernistic plate* with both French and American fine arts and

with authentic *art moderne* and drew attention to the colored plastic accents:

Smart as the day after tomorrow and as charming in its own individuality, as the colorings of a Monet or a Rockwell Kent. . . . Embracing the spirit of true "Art Moderne," benedict [*sic*] modernistic plate is as *colorful* as it is striking in design. Tips, handles, key up its silver sheen with a dash of Carnelian Red. . . . Undeniably smart, yet moderately priced, benedict [*sic*] modernistic plate is now evidencing unusually attractive selling potentials (emphasis in the original) (see fig. 3.26).[33]

SKYSCRAPERS

The setback towers of 1920s skyscrapers became synonymous with American enterprise, especially in New York City, where a building boom was in progress. As early as 1926 it was observed that "an American art based on its modern architecture" had "taken its place besides the modernity of France, Germany, and Italy."[34] In 1916 a pioneering zoning law in New York City forced a new formula of design upon architects, who recast the skyscraper into a dramatic study of mass and silhouette. The dynamic outline of the setback skyscraper was adopted nationwide for consumer products in all mediums. Paul T. Frankl's skyscraper bookcase that was shown at Macy's *Art in Trade* exposition in 1927 is a quintessential example.[35] Later in the year, Erik Magnussen's *Cubic* coffee service was heralded as "The Lights and Shadows of Manhattan" and displayed beneath a painting of a congested cityscape of skyscrapers fractured into cubist planes (fig. 3.27). From a photograph in Gorham's archives, a 1929 trade publication, and an article in *House and Garden*, we know that Magnussen also designed a few serving pieces in a flatware pattern named *Manhattan* that were recognized

as having been "inspired by American skyscraper architecture."[36] Partly oxidized and layered for contrast, the
handles had setback outlines and graphic engraving to
suggest the windowed elevation of a skyscraper. Edwin
Avery Park, a professor of architecture at Yale University and author of *New Backgrounds for a New Age* (1928),
commented in *Arts and Decoration* on the ubiquity of the
imagery: "The skyscraper with its angular setbacks has
today influenced the decoration of every object from
bookcases to handkerchiefs."[37] This was certainly true
of silverware.

The most salient reference to setback imagery was
the *Sky-scraper* silverplate line produced by the Apollo
Gift Lines division of Bernard Rice's Sons. In the advertising promotion the manufacturer connected the shape
of the line with its model, the urban setback skyscraper,
as a symbol of American industrial power.[38] The vessels in the pattern were canted, perhaps to simulate a
viewer's perspective at street level when looking up at
a skyscraper. The shape is reiterated in the graphics of
the advertisement, where the stepped framing is canted
around the featured *Sky-scraper* tea and coffee service
(figs. 3.28, 3.29). The text directed the reader's attention
to the dark handles of the vessels, which were said to
emulate the "black smoke-stacks" of skyscrapers that

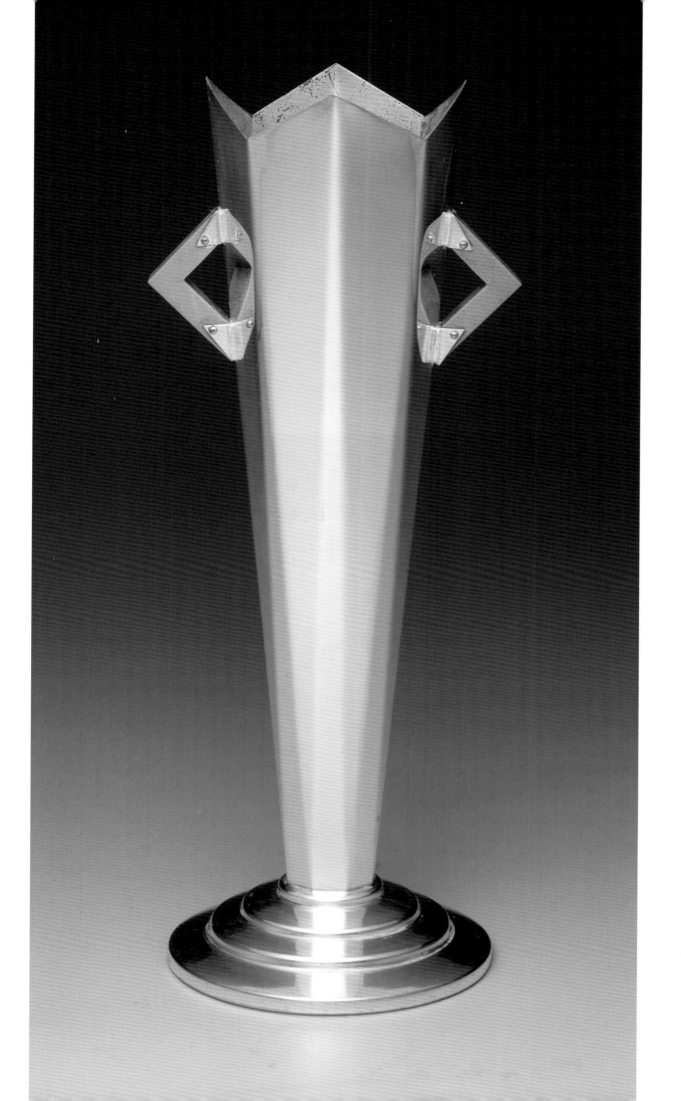

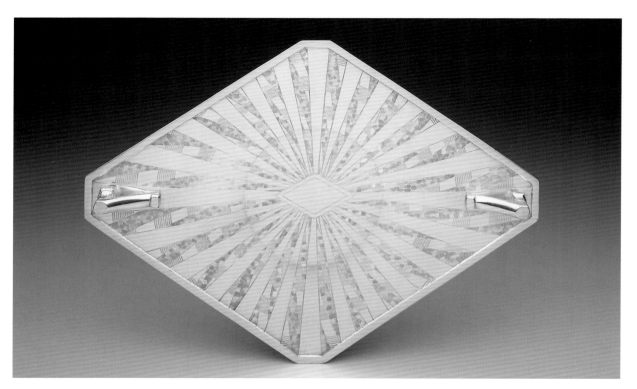

punctuated skylines. A full line was offered and fourteen items were listed, including gravy boat and tray, chop dish, beverage shaker, ice tub, and candlesticks.[39]

In 1928, Reed & Barton introduced sterling silver candlesticks and compotes in what was described in *Harper's Bazaar* as a "radically modern design deriving its inspiration from the structural steel of the skyscraper" (fig. 3.30).[40] The writer was referring to the openwork supports of these pieces, which were composed of four slim, square vertical bars linked closely together at intervals by slightly cantilevered horizontal bands. They suggested, to the reviewer, the steel skeleton frame of modern skyscraper construction. The geometric banded borders on the bases were a distinctive motif in Reed & Barton's 1928 *Modernist* group (see fig. 3.14).

The slogan "The inevitable choice of youth!" headlined the advertising campaign to celebrate and continue the successful marketing of *Rhythm*, a sterling flatware and holloware pattern first produced by Wallace in 1929.[41] The popular stepped motif, a metaphor of American originality in architecture, was combined here with a radiating border that expressed the exuberant beat of the Jazz Age. The same treatment informed the long, narrow rectangular waiter of the *Rhythm* tea and coffee service (fig. 3.31). Vertical incised lines hint of classicism on the subtly swelling octagonal vessels. Repetitive incising on the four unusual curved and stepped feet of all pieces in the service and on the borders of the notched lids unifies the ensemble. Stepped layering is prominent on the handles. Faceted pyramidal finials of white Catalin (which tends to age in color to shades of caramel) and insulators of the same material

contrast with the gleaming metal. Although *Rhythm* holloware was offered in two variants, the 3900 and 3909 series, that were coordinated to mix and match, a tea and coffee service was produced solely in the 3900 series. Holloware in the 3909 series was designed with four equally spaced stepped motifs inserted within wider circular borders, and the squared, stepped edges of the 3900 series were eliminated (fig. 3.32).[42] Wallace used the setback motif in several other items, among them a pierced sandwich plate (see fig. 3.43), a tea strainer and drip with a marbleized green Catalin handle (fig. 3.33), and three dresser sets, produced in 1928 and 1929 and aptly named *Vogue, Fashion,* and *Classic.*

Not to be outdone by its competitors, Gorham introduced a small production-line group of serving dishes in 1929 called *Modernistic* that appropriated skyscraper setbacks for its focal motif.[43] Although skyscraper imagery in American silver peaked in 1929, it occasionally occurred in the 1930s. Reed & Barton's *Maid of Honor* (1935) flatware in silverplate is an example (fig. 3.34). In a late entry by Merle F. Faber Products, a small manufacturer of holloware and novelties in San Francisco, the form was effectively employed in spare silverplated candlesticks that are reminiscent of the reductive slab construction of skyscrapers in New York's Rockefeller Center (fig. 3.35).[44]

ILONKA KARASZ: A PROPONENT OF BAUHAUS GEOMETRY

The multitalented Hungarian-born designer Ilonka Karasz (fig. 3.36), an important member of New York City's émigré colony, was engaged by the silver manufacturer Paye & Baker to design several modern silverplated holloware lines introduced in 1928. Karasz's silver was

FIGURE 3.24   Tray ("Sunray"), c. 1928. Weidlich Brothers Manufacturing Company. Silverplate. DMA, JSASC, cat. 305

FIGURE 3.25   *Modernistic plate* pitcher, 1928. Benedict Manufacturing Corporation, Albert F. Saunders, ornament designer. Silverplate. DMA, JSASC, cat. 4

FIGURE 3.26   *Modernistic plate* tray, 1928. Benedict Manufacturing Corporation, Albert F. Saunders, designer. Silverplate, plastic. DMA, JSASC, cat. 3

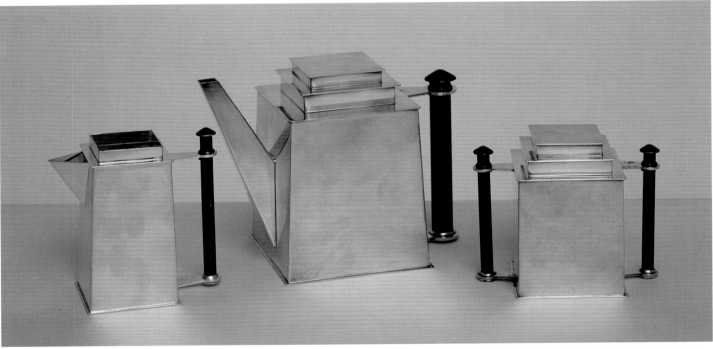

FIGURE 3.27 Gorham *Cubic* "Lights and Shadows of Manhattan" demonstration window display, c. 1928

FIGURE 3.28 *"Sky-scraper,"* advertisement, 1928

FIGURE 3.29 *Sky-scraper* three-piece tea set, 1928. Apollo Studios, division of Bernard Rice's Sons, Louis M. Rice, designer. Patinated silverplate. The John P. Axelrod Collection, Boston, Mass., cat. 209

FIGURE 3.30 *Modernist* candlesticks and compote, 1928. Reed & Barton. Silver. The John P. Axelrod Collection, Boston, Mass., cat. 158

FIGURE 3.31 *Rhythm* tea and coffee service, 1929. R. Wallace &
Sons Manufacturing Company, Percy B. Ball, designer. Silver, plastic.
DMA, JSASC, cat. 283

FIGURE 3.32 *Rhythm* compote, 1929. R. Wallace & Sons Manufacturing Company, Percy B. Ball, designer. Silver. DMA, JSASC, cat. 284

FIGURE 3.33 Tea strainer and drip, c. 1929. R. Wallace & Sons Manufacturing Company. Silver, plastic. DMA, JSASC, cat. 286

FIGURE 3.34 *Maid of Honor* flatware, 1935. Reed & Barton. Silverplate, stainless steel. DMA, JSASC, cat. 164

FIGURE 3.35 Candlesticks, c. 1943–1950. Merle F. Faber Products, Merle Fenelon Faber, designer. Silverplate. DMA, JSASC, cat. 13

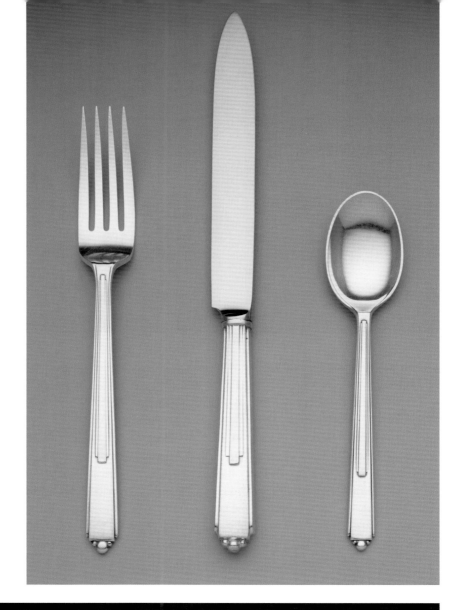

illustrated in periodicals such as *House Beautiful, American Architect,* and *Creative Art* during 1928 and 1929, and in the book *Form and Re-Form* by Paul T. Frankl, which was published in 1930. Her work was also shown at the American Designers' Gallery in 1928 and 1929 and in the Newark Museum's exhibition *Modern American Design in Metal* in 1929. In every instance Karasz, who was one of only a handful of prominent women designers in the 1920s, was recognized by name as the designer.

Her father, Samuel Karasz, had been a silversmith in Budapest,[45] and the influence of the German Bauhaus design school on her work was pronounced. The rigorous reduction of form to cylinder, sphere, cube, or cone was an aspect of Bauhaus theory and practice that was taught by László Moholy-Nagy in the metal workshop, as was serial production after 1923. Karasz's silver designs demonstrate her knowledge of and alignment with these ideals. For the objects she designed for Paye & Baker, which can be identified from period publications and contemporary collections, Karasz drew from Bauhaus ideology and from objects designed by Marianne

FIGURE 3.36   Ilonka Karasz, c. 1920

FIGURE 3.37   Photograph: Coffee and tea service and candlesticks. Ilonka Karasz, designer, 1928

Brandt and fabricated in the Bauhaus metal workshops, especially Brandt's early work in Weimar. Karasz would have known German metalwork from European design periodicals and from published accounts of two exhibitions that had been held in 1927, the *International Art Trade Exhibition* in Monza, Italy, and the *European Applied Arts Exhibition* in Leipzig, Germany, in which a coffee and tea service by Brandt was exhibited and later illustrated in *Dekorative Kunst*.[46] Ashley Callahan, a recent biographer of Karasz, noted that "many of her closest peers, initially, were from Germany," and that she frequently traveled to Europe.[47]

FIGURE 3.38   Photograph: Tea and coffee service, 1928. Paye & Baker Manufacturing Company, Ilonka Karasz, designer. Silverplate, wood

FIGURE 3.39   Drawing, *To-Day* pattern cocktail shaker. Friedman Silver Company, Kem Weber, designer, c. 1928

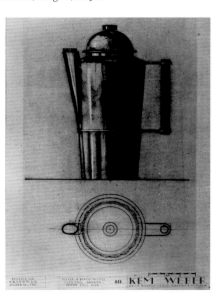

Her exclusion of decoration and reliance on elementary form in the tea and coffee service of one design for Paye & Baker (fig. 3.37) made it the most severely minimal service to have been produced industrially in America in the 1920s. The cylindrical shape of the vessels was reiterated in the circular push-down lids and stubby cylindrical finials of black Bakelite sandwiched between silver disks that were elevated so that they appeared to float above the lid and added a spatial dimension. Although the post-style handles were squared for contrast, the ends of the slim cantilevered silver supports were curved, as were the beaklike triangular spouts. In this well-thought-out design, the cohesiveness of the composition was maintained with care.[48] Although greatly admired now, in 1928 an untested design this extreme that reflected a German

FIGURE 3.40 Tea infuser and strainer, 1924. Marianne Brandt, designer. Silver, ebony. The Metropolitan Museum of Art, the Beatrice G. Warren and Leila W. Redstone Fund, 2000 (2000.63a-c)

FIGURE 3.41 Tea ball and stand, 1928. Paye & Baker Manufacturing Company, Ilonka Karasz, designer. Silverplate. JSASC, cat. 151

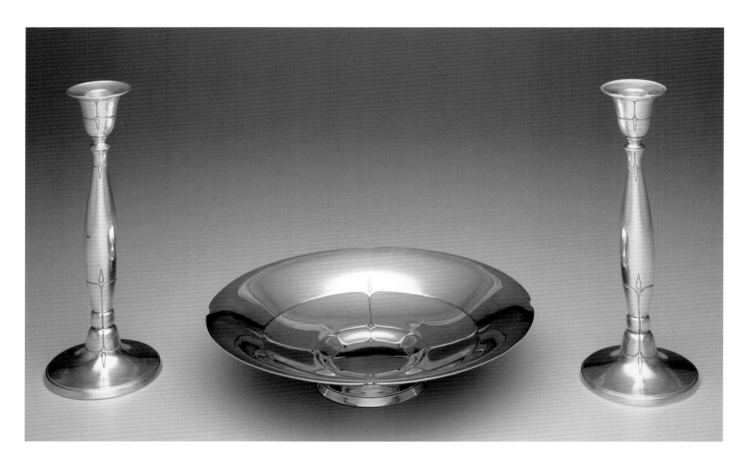

FIGURE 3.42   Console set, 1928. Gorham Manufacturing Company. Silver. DMA, JSASC, cat. 26

rather than a French aesthetic was a substantial risk for the manufacturer. Judging from the dearth of surviving examples, very few were made.[49] In another group by Karasz (fig. 3.38), the same handles, finials, and bodies (in slightly different heights) were modified to soften the design and to make it more marketable as well as to reduce the manufacturer's costs for tooling.[50] Here, classical reeding wrapped around the smooth bodies, and walnut handles and finials were substituted for Bakelite. Interestingly, there is a correspondence between this group by Karasz and Kem Weber's *To-Day* line for Friedman. Both were produced in 1928 and both have reeding around the circumference of vessels and post-style cantilevered handles. The similarity is apparent in Weber's drawing of the *To-Day* cocktail shaker (fig. 3.39).

The pieces in the third group by Karasz were conical, a shape perhaps influenced by a popular cocktail set made by the French firm Maison Desny. The flangelike cruciform supports, a device that Brandt had used for hemispheric vessels as early as 1924 (fig. 3.40), were new in American industrial silver.[51] For the suspended tea ball in the group, two perforated cones, reversed and hinged together, hang harmoniously over its conical receptacle (fig. 3.41). A tea ball and stand was made in the reeded pattern (see fig. 3.38), but no drawing, illustration, or produced example in the severe cylindrical version has yet come to light.[52] Some objects in the conical group were made with an inverted cone-shaped base. Several, including a tea ball and stand, a candlestick,

and shakers for salt and pepper were illustrated in *Creative Art* in 1928.[53] An ashtray in the same form as the conical stand for the tea ball appeared on a shelf in the penthouse designed by William Lescaze for Macy's *International Exposition of Art in Industry* in 1928,[54] and Karasz placed a large conical fruit bowl on the buffet of the dining room that she designed for the second American Designers' Gallery exhibition in 1929.[55] A conical creamer and sugar bowl were made with the cruciform supports, and although one of Karasz's drawing shows a teapot to match, it is not known if one were produced.[56]

GORHAM BROADENS THE MARKET

While some companies were pushing the boundaries of modern design, Gorham sought less controversial ways to broaden its market. Although the Arts and Crafts movement had run its course by the late 1920s and had been supplanted by a desire for conservative colonial-revival styles or progressive modernism, Gorham recognized that there was a lingering niche for craft work and produced a three-piece Arts and Crafts style console set. Consisting of a low compotier and candlesticks, the set was one of four discrete sets offered by Gorham in its sterling silver catalogue for 1929 and the only example of the distinctive, earlier aesthetic in the holloware

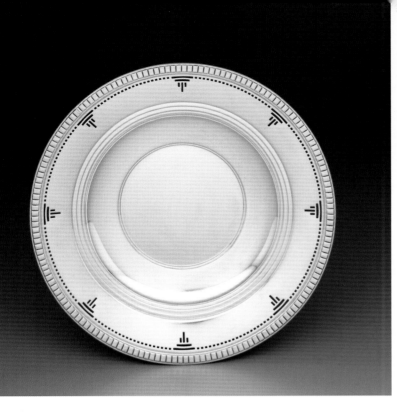
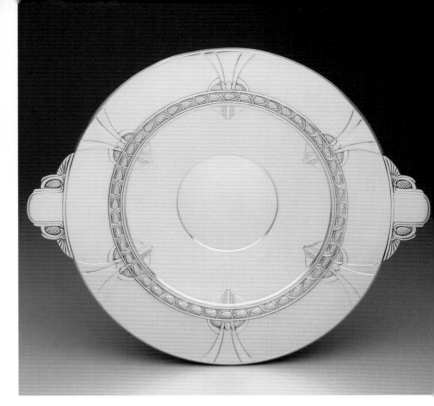

illustrated in the catalogue (fig. 3.42).[57] The other console sets were Erik Magnussen's *Modern American* and two eighteenth-century revivals.

The notched rim of Gorham's low compotier is reminiscent of a similar treatment of bowls by Chicago's Kalo Shop and of circular box covers by the Boston metalsmith Rebecca Cauman, who had relocated to New York City.[58] The hand-chased, quarter-lobed interior of Gorham's compotier, accented at each joint with a stylized bud form, was a simplified version of the decoration favored by the master silversmith

Clockwise from top left:

FIGURE 3.43   Sandwich tray, c. 1928. R. Wallace & Sons Manufacturing Company. Silver. DMA, JSASC, cat. 282

FIGURE 3.44   *Franconia* sandwich plate, 1930. Gorham Manufacturing Company. Silver. DMA, JSASC, cat. 29

FIGURE 3.45   Luncheon plate, 1930. Alvin Corporation. Silver. DMA, JSASC, cat. 66

FIGURE 3.46   *Gift Line* sandwich plate, 1930. Alvin Corporation. Silver. DMA, JSASC, cat. 65

Arthur J. Stone of Gardner, Massachusetts.[59] The lobe-and-bud theme was carried through in the candlesticks to unite the ensemble harmoniously. Like many modern designs of 1928–1929, production of the console set did not survive the Depression. In November 1932, after two price reductions, the compotier was discontinued.[60]

More innovative was Gorham's experiment in mixing styles. These late-1920s holloware designs were idiosyncratic pastiches that defy a crisp, retrospective categorization. Gorham and one of its subsidiaries, the Alvin Corporation of Providence, Rhode Island, introduced several in sterling in 1930. The Gorham *Franconia* line, stamped with the name of the pattern, was by an unknown designer who drew from classical, Egyptian, and skyscraper imagery as well as fantasy.[61] In the sandwich plate (fig. 3.44) and other pieces in the line, a narrow, pinecone-embellished ring overlaps six equally spaced medallions with flaring "wings" and stepped "noses" that are aimed like projectiles toward the center. For the curved handles, the pinecone motif was repeated with stylized palmate surrounds. Although based more closely on Egyptian sources, the unusual medallions on a luncheon plate by Alvin (fig. 3.45) are similar in feeling to those in the *Franconia* pattern and may have been by the same designer. Alvin also produced *Gift Line*, a moderately

priced, extensive holloware line. This series has a rhythmic, arched design combined with a narrow border of traditional motifs that together give a curiously medieval effect (fig. 3.46).

COLOR AND CONTRAST

Objects accented with rare and exotic woods or semiprecious stones appeared frequently in the *art moderne* silverware at the Paris exposition in 1925. American silver manufacturers adopted this treatment to enhance and heighten the appeal of their progressive lines. In addition to wood and semiprecious stones for accents, they applied enamel in decorative modern designs and experimented with new colorful plastics for accents.

EXOTIC WOOD

In the 1920s, macassar ebony and Brazilian rosewood, often hand carved, were the woods favored by Puiforcat and other French makers for elements such as finials and handles. Occasionally mahogany was used, as for a teapot by Sandoz that was illustrated in *Arts and Decoration* in 1927.[62] Although mahogany was seldom used in 1920s American silver, a mahogany finial does adorn a sterling box made by International (fig. 3.47). The shape of the box has an affinity with Chinese designs and may have been influenced by earlier twentieth-century Austrian works for which Chinese prototypes were a source.[63] The incised borders are, however, classical distillations. Other sterling silverware with exotic wood elements by International and its divisions include a coffeepot with carved macassar ebony handle (see fig. 3.3) and a coffee set by the Barbour division that has carved macassar ebony handles and finial (see fig. 2.8).

At International, exotic wood was not reserved exclusively for sterling wares. The *Ile de France* line in silverplate had finials and handles of macassar ebony. The Friedman Silver Company enriched its two silver-plated holloware lines by Kem Weber, *Silver Style* and *To-Day*, with ebony or rosewood handles, bases, and finials (see fig. 3.6).

SEMIPRECIOUS STONES

The use of semiprecious stones to enhance silverware exhibited at the 1925 Paris exposition was widely commented on by reviewers and, not surprisingly, was emulated by American manufacturers for the luxury market. Gorham was the leader in mixing silver and semiprecious stones, first with Erik Magnussen's designs of 1926. Magnussen's holloware was embellished with the widest variety of semiprecious stones, including agate, amber, turquoise, jade, amethyst, lapis lazuli, and carnelian. One example is a bonbon dish with flat, giraffe-shaped supports balanced on spheres of carnelian (fig. 3.48, center). In 1928, Gorham's Durgin division in Concord, New Hampshire, introduced a small number of holloware pieces set with stones, especially lapis lazuli and jade, some with matching flatware servers. The designer of this luxury line may have been Charles F. Sims, of whom little is known except that he lived in Concord and worked for Concord Silversmiths after that company took over the Durgin plant in 1931.[64] In an article published in *Vogue* in 1928, Helen Appleton Read illustrated a covered dish and flatware server decorated with lapis lazuli by "Charles Sims, an American who is a special designer for Gorham."[65] Extremely rare now, the pieces made by Durgin for Gorham are

FIGURE 3.48 Left: Bonbon dish, 1928. International Silver Company. Silver, rose quartz, cat. 106; center: Bonbon dish, 1927. Gorham Manufacturing Company, Erik Magnussen, designer. Silver, carnelian, cat. 19; right: Tea caddy and spoon, 1928. William B. Durgin Company. Silver, rose quartz, cat. 68. DMA, JSASC

known principally from illustrations in period journals and from Gorham's promotional campaigns.[66] In the introductory advertisement in the *New Yorker* in 1928 the company called its "stone trimmed sterling" the "newest thing by Gorham" and the "smartest thing in silver" and was quick to add, however, that "Jade and Lapis lend their beauty and add a color accent to designs charming in themselves."[67] The three pieces pictured, a round bowl with lapis lazuli trim, a mayonnaise bowl and tray, and a tea caddy and spoon, the latter two with jade trim, were available only at Gorham's store on Fifth Avenue at Forty-seventh Street in New York City. One of the few objects of this provenance that have come to light is a sandwich tray with four pieces of carved Asian jade inset into the rim. These intersect the lively border of alternating and reversed half-circle motifs to approximate handles and to define the incised bands that divide the tray into four equal sections (see fig. 1.3).[68] Another exceptionally fine piece is a tea caddy with an elephant finial in rose quartz on its stepped lid and a matching teaspoon ornamented with the same stone (see fig. 3.48, right). Gorham optimistically promoted its inventory of silver holloware with jade decoration even after the stock market crashed in 1929. An advertisement that appeared in *Town and Country* early in 1930 played up the mystique: "Jade, old as the hills and green as the hills, was the lucky stone of the ancients. . . . Today, you find it used in modern ways that will delight you—contrasted with the brilliancy of diamonds, or

used as a new note of color on silver."[69] A drawing of an oval dish with carved rectangular jade handles and a matching flatware server paired with a diamond and jade openwork brooch was used in the advertisement to make the point.

Indicative of Gorham's intent to find new customers was the publication in 1929 of a small book entitled *The Art of Table Setting*, issued to guide prospective hostesses through the so-called rules for every type of home entertaining. Among the nine occasions described were afternoon tea, the bridge party, semiformal and formal dinners, and buffets. A special section was devoted to Serving of Tray, the refined manner of sending a breakfast tray to a guest's room. To illustrate the proper scenario, a drawing showed a smart *art moderne* interior decorated with a zigzag wall border and skyscraper stepped bed. A maid in a black uniform complete with starched apron, collar, and cap is offering the lounging guest her breakfast on a tray laden with silver (fig. 3.49).[70]

The other major manufacturer to combine silver with semiprecious stones, although not to the extent that Gorham did, was International. A sterling covered bonbon dish by International recalls the shape of American sugar urns of the classical period.[71] The graceful shoulders sweep up to a cylindrical finial of rose quartz

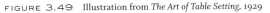

FIGURE 3.49   Illustration from *The Art of Table Setting*, 1929

FIGURE 3.50 *Vogue* centerpiece with flower frog, 1928. Meriden Silver Plate Company. Silverplate, plastic. Dallas Museum of Art, cat. 92

topped with a silver ball (see fig. 3.48, left). International also used cylinders of rose quartz for the pedestals of a bowl and compotes made by its Wilcox & Evertsen Fine Arts Division and for the ring-shaped handles of a huge centerpiece bowl made by its Charter division.[72]

Plastics

In the late 1920s, silver manufacturers also turned to plastics, primarily Bakelite and Catalin, for color accents. Sturdy plastics were especially suitable for finials, bases, posts, and handles. More economical than semiprecious stones and enameling, these advanced modern materials were used to add a new note to sterling silver and to enliven moderately priced, trendy lines in silverplate.

Dr. Leo Baekeland, an émigré Belgian chemist, discovered a method of combining phenol and formaldehyde to form the first synthetic plastic in 1907. The trademark name he gave this pressure-molded and thermosetting plastic was Bakelite. Because the material was molded with fibrous fillers that required black or dark brown pigments to conceal them, its uses were limited. Then, in 1928, the American Catalin Corporation

imported a German process of casting the components, a process that eliminated the need for fillers and thus widened the possibilities of color.[73] Catalin became the trade name of the resulting translucent colored plastic in which colors could also be mixed to create a marbled effect. Catalin was subsequently licensed to DuPont and other firms, including the Bakelite Corporation. It quickly became available from suppliers in standard sizes and colors and in cast forms such as rods, tubes, and blocks that could be cut for decorative elements.[74] The clarity, brightness, uniformity of color, durability, and reasonable cost of Catalin made it an ideal material for silver manufacturers to use in modernizing their products and to exploit the vogue for color. Although Bakelite has since become the umbrella term for the colored plastics used in the 1920s and 1930s, during the period the name Catalin was most often used to distinguish it from the earlier Bakelite. Occasionally, the term *Bakelite* appeared in advertisements when the material was actually Catalin, confusing identification. For example, the Sheets-Rockford Silver Company advertised its *Art Modernë* (the accent on the *n* is curious and unexplained) silverplate line as having Bakelite handles, even though the handles were of translucent green Catalin (see figs. 3.53, 3.54).[75] A possible explanation is that Sheets-Rockford obtained its plastic in 1928 from the Bakelite Corporation.[76] International identified the material used for the handles, tips, and pillars of objects in its *Vogue* pattern for silverplated holloware, which was introduced in 1928, as "Ivory Catalin Stone." The large fluted *Vogue* centerpiece (fig. 3.50), which has a flower frog with a Catalin finial, is the most striking and showy object in this extensive line.[77]

In 1929 Wallace marketed a number of sterling novelties with colored plastic trim (all of which it referred to as Catalin).[78] The items were well thought out, and the red or green Catalin, with black for contrast, was used to highlight the most innovative elements, such as the inverted skyscraper handle of a tea bell that had angular incising to resemble facets, the telescoping handle of a tea strainer, and the gear-shaped bases of salt and pepper shakers (fig. 3.51). The Frank M. Whiting Company of North Attleboro, Massachusetts, used white and black plastic caps to differentiate the salt and pepper shakers in a subtly telescoping set.[79]

White Catalin, now faded to a rich caramel color, originally was used as a substitute for ivory in Towle's sterling coffee service with matching tray in the *Ritz* pattern (fig. 3.52). In this jaunty design Towle expressed the restless, upbeat energy of the Jazz Age by incorporating the most popular characteristics of late-1920s styling. The rim of the tray is stepped. The handles of the coffeepot and creamer are eclipsed octagons. The coffeepot spout is stepped back and layered. The base of each vessel is stepped up and the lids of the coffeepot and sugar bowl are stepped back. The four faceted feet on each vessel were a quotation of, and perhaps a salute to, Erik Magnussen's *Modern American* coffee set of 1928 (see fig. 1.17).

One of the most successful designs in silverplate for which colored plastic details were used (primarily for slim rectangular handles) was the *Art Modernë* holloware from the Sheets-Rockford Silver Company. Introduced by the maker in 1928 as a "splendid pattern" that "is exactly adapted to the demands of the day," the pieces had bright green handles that were said to "lend a modish touch of color."[80] Soft curves were eschewed in this pattern in favor of the hard-edged octagonal shapes observed by Helen Appleton Read at the 1925 Paris exposition. The setback motif was adapted for rims of the canted vessels, a decorative device that evokes crenelated battlements, enlivens the form, and is most effective in the water pitcher (fig. 3.53). The motif, combined with sharp, angular, planar elements, was repeated for the handles of trays, serving dishes, and platters. The double vegetable dish is the best-resolved object in the line (fig. 3.54). Another striking silverplated object with plastic elements is a conical vase by Charter. In this sleek design, a pair of narrow, triangular finlike red plastic extensions that suggest handles spring from a red and black plastic dome that surmounts a stepped base (fig. 3.55).[81]

ENAMEL

In the late 1920s a few expensive silver objects made for the luxury trade were enhanced by the application of colored enamel used to articulate design motifs. Perhaps the most ambitious essay in enamel decoration during this period was a sterling beverage set comprising a cocktail shaker, twelve cocktail cups, and a tray, all decorated with motifs in the then-popular red and black color combination. The stylized enamel decoration on this ensemble was conceived as a linear abstraction of an arched colonnade with stepped capitals. The hybrid design is most prominent on the cocktail shaker that steps back in stages to a domed finial (fig. 3.56). The tall shaker has a monumental presence that is heightened by black enamel lines that represent columns and lead the eye upward to the area

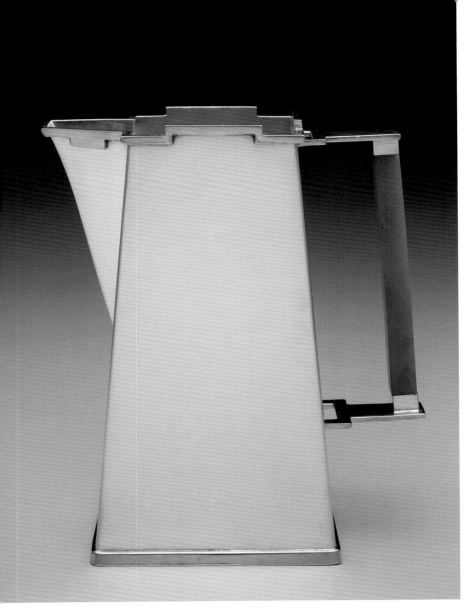

FIGURE 3.53 *Art Moderńe* water pitcher, 1928. Sheets-Rockford Silver Plate Company. Silverplate, plastic. DMA, JSASC, cat. 220

FIGURE 3.54 *Art Moderńe* double vegetable dish, 1928. Sheets-Rockford Silver Plate Company. Silverplate, plastic. DMA, JSASC, cat. 219

FIGURE 3.55 Vase, c. 1929–1935. Barbour Silver Company. Silverplate, plastic. DMA, JSASC, cat. 85

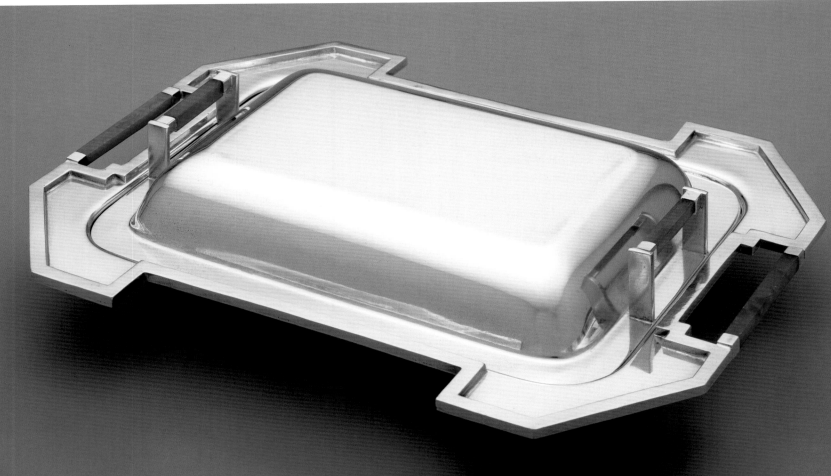

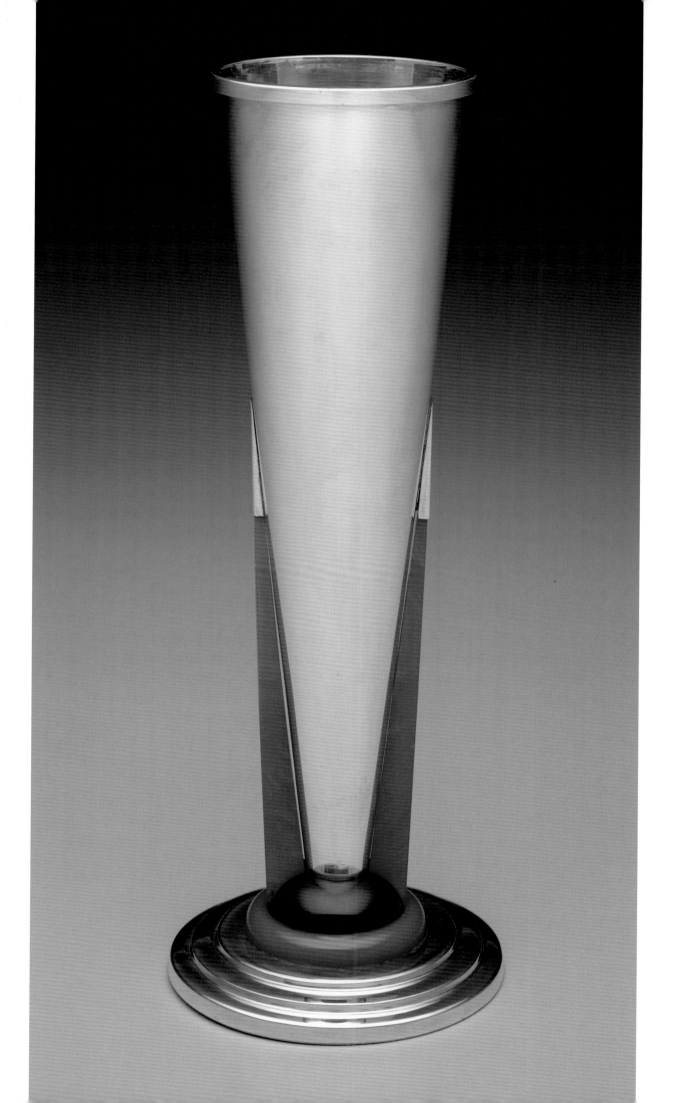

of concentrated decoration. A sales catalogue indicates that the set, made by Barbour, was offered with and without enamel decoration at a considerable difference in price. The complete set enameled cost $725, a fortune at the time.[82] Without enamel, the set was still expensive at $495.[83]

In the Wilcox & Evertsen Fine Arts Division of International a sterling cigarette container with a jade knob was made with four different motifs in red and black enamel. Taking a cue from Erik Magnussen at Gorham, the designer decorated two versions with playful trios of flamingos or giraffes; the others had individual abstract patterns (fig. 3.57, right). In the sales catalogue illustrating the cigarette holders, it was noted that "the magic element of color has been added to sterling silver" and that each cigarette holder was "equipped with [a] silverplated lift to raise cigarettes."[84]

Gorham was best known for using semiprecious stones in combination with sterling, but the company also produced some outstanding enameled pieces. A black enameled cigarette box with red enamel accents is a sophisticated example (fig. 3.57, left). The decoration is focused on the lid, where stepped motifs mirror each other, define the edges, and frame the centered and stepped octagonal panel. Even though the severely distressed economy in the 1930s limited the production of luxury goods with or without semiprecious

stones and enamel, Tiffany & Co. advertised in *Harper's Bazaar* in 1937 and in the *New Yorker* in 1939 an elegant sterling cigarette box with a stylized classical design that was available in combinations of black with emerald green, bright red, or cobalt blue enamel (fig. 3.58).[85]

THE MYTH OF MASS PRODUCTION

The term *mass production* generally connotes numbers in the thousands. During the 1920s and 1930s, however, a production run for modernist silver holloware could result in as few as six objects, and 250 pieces would be an exceptionally large quantity. These small runs would account for the rarity of objects from this period. For example, Gorham's records indicate that, in Erik Magnussen's *Modern American* line, the holloware items were made in multiples of six and twelve, with most of the objects being made in runs of twelve or twenty-four pieces and, for some, no more than six were ever produced.[86] In Gorham's *Franconia* holloware

FIGURE 3.56   Cocktail shaker, 1928. Charter Company. Enameled silver, wood. DMA, JSASC, cat. 86

FIGURE 3.57   Left: Cigarette box, c. 1928. Gorham Manufacturing Company. Enameled silver, cat. 27; right: Cigarette container, c. 1928. International Silver Company. Enameled silver, jade, cat. 119. DMA, JSASC

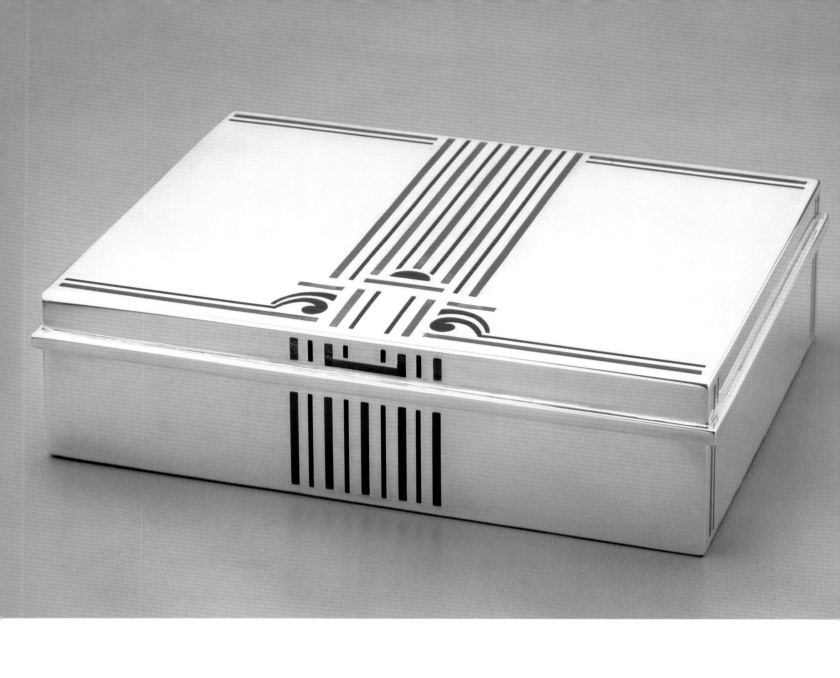

FIGURE 3.58 Cigarette box, c. 1937. Tiffany & Co. Enameled silver.
DMA, JSASC, cat. 243

introduced in 1930, at most only thirty-six sandwich plates were made in each of the four versions, and in *Modernistic,* introduced the same year, one hundred bonbon dishes were produced.[87] For a wider market the Alvin division of Gorham offered the less expensive *Gift Line* series, for which 250 bonbon dishes were made.[88]

Because of the stock market crash in 1929 and the devastating Depression that followed, many lively modernist designs that had been introduced in 1928 and 1929 went out of production in less than two years. Wallace tea strainers and a mayonnaise dish in sterling silver and colored plastic were examples (see figs. 3.51 and 3.8).[89] During most of the 1930s, silver manufacturers, more reluctant to take risks than they had been in the prosperous late 1920s, offered fewer innovative designs, especially in sterling silver. They also faced stiff competition from manufacturers of tableware in less expensive, more easily maintained materials such as aluminum and chromium-plated metal.

The fickle nature of fashion or the lack of commercial success, or both, also limited production runs and shortened production cycles. It was not uncommon for the most progressive designs—those that are sought after now—to remain in production for very short periods. The fate of International's *Gift Ware* signature line in silverplate, which was designed by Lurelle Guild and introduced in the spring of 1934, is a case in point. Notwithstanding a sophisticated advertising campaign, the two cocktail shaker sets and other items in the line were discontinued by December 1935, and by December 1936 the entire *Gift Ware* line was out of production.[90]

NOTES

1. C. A. Glassgold, "Design in America," in R. L. Leonard and C. A. Glassgold, eds., American Union of Decorative Artists and Craftsmen, *Annual of American Design 1931* (New York: Ives Washburn, 1930), 174.

2. Gorham scrapbook, n.p. (Gorham Archive, John Hay Library, Brown University, Providence, R. I.; hereafter Gorham Archive). The objects by Tétard Frères in the photographs were square and rectilinear serving dishes, a squat ovoid tea pot with matching covered sugar bowl, a faceted jug, and a golf trophy.

3. Burton Stillman, "The Modern Spirit in Silver," *Spur* 42 (Sept. 15, 1928): 64. Three pieces had been acquired in 1923; the four additions in 1925 completed the service; see R. Craig Miller, *Modern Design in the Metropolitan Museum of Art 1890–1990* (New York: Metropolitan Museum of Art and Abrams, 1990), 162.

4. "Modern Art in the Department Store," *Good Furniture Magazine* 30 (Jan. 1928): 33–35; and Marilyn F. Friedman, "An Unlikely Alliance: R. H. Macy & Co. and the Metropolitan Museum of Art Popularize Modern Design in New York City 1914–1928" (master's thesis, Cooper-Hewitt, National Design Museum, New York, 2003), 33.

5. "New Silhouettes in the French Tea Service," *Arts and Decoration* 27 (Sept. 1927): 51–52.

6. Lord & Taylor, *An Exposition of Modern French Decorative Art,* exh. cat. (New York: Lord & Taylor, 1928), 24.

7. "Saks is Very . . . ," *Fortune* 18 (Nov. 1938): 126; Donald Deskey, one of the innovative creators of windows for Saks in 1927, was commissioned that year to design a glamorous rendition of the modern idiom for Gimbel's own luxurious apartment; see David A. Hanks, Jennifer Toher, and Jeffrey L. Meikle, *Donald Deskey Decorative Designs and Interiors* (New York: E. P. Dutton, 1987), 10–11, 75–79. Frederick Kiesler also designed display windows for Saks c. 1927–28; see Frederick Kiesler, *Contemporary Art Applied to the Store and Its Display* (New York: Brentano's, c. 1930), 67.

8. "Two Young Men," Saks-Fifth Avenue advertisement, *New Yorker* 4 (June 9, 1928): 8.

9. Thus far only a handful of Puiforcat pieces sold through Saks have been located. In addition to the Puiforcat service in the Dallas collection (see fig. 3.10), see Karen Davies (*At Home in Manhattan; Modern Decorative Arts, 1925 to the Depression,* exh. cat. [New Haven, Conn.: Yale University Art Gallery, 1983], 94), for a vase.

10. See "Modernistic Silver for Many Types of Rooms," *Arts and Decoration* 31 (May 1929): 86; and "Modern Tea-Sets," *Vogue* 74 (July 6, 1929): 55.

11. In the late 1920s, the Wilcox & Evertsen Fine Arts Division of International, located in Meriden, Conn., produced modern sterling holloware similar to that produced by another division of International, the Barbour Sterling Fine Arts Division, which was also in Meriden.

12. *Furniture, Hardware and Accessories,* vol. 5, *Exposition Internationale des Arts Décoratifs et Industriels Modernes 1925* (New York and London: Garland Publishing, 1977), pl. 36.

13. Other pieces for which the "telescoping" effect was employed include a small bowl with a zigzag border, production number WV3, by International, and a boat-shaped bread tray, production number 4339, by Wallace.

14. Marshall Field & Co., *Fashions of the Hour,* Christmas number (Chicago: Marshall Field, 1928), 5.

15. For the service by Lapparra, see Tony Bouilhet, *L'Orfèvrerie française au Xxe* (Paris: Editions Emile-Paul Frères, n.d.), 12. For the after-dinner coffee set, see "Silver in Modern Designs," *House and Garden* 52 (Nov. 1927): 106.

16. "Modern Tea-Sets," 55. A Belgian tea service in the 1925 Paris exposition had similar handles; see *Furniture, Hardware, and Accessories,* pl. 39. For a service with a version of ponytail handles that was designed by Josef Hoffmann in 1928 and made by the Wiener Werkstätte, see A. Krekel-Aalberse, J. R. ter Molen, and R. J. Willink, eds., *Silver of a New Era: International Highlights of Precious Metalware from 1880 to 1940,* exh. cat. Museum Boymans van-Beuningen, Rotterdam, and Museum voor Sierkunst, Ghent (Seattle: University of Washington Press, 1992), 211.

17. "Fruit dish" was the name Reed & Barton gave this object; Reed & Barton file card no. X952A, Reed & Barton Archives, Taunton, Mass.

18. This piece is in a private collection.

19. *Furniture, Hardware, and Accessories,* pl. 36.

20. "Angles and Triangles," B. Altman & Co. advertisement, *New Yorker* 3 (Feb. 11, 1928): 1.

21. Lee McCann, "Sterling Goes Modernist," *Country Life* 54 (May 1928): 93.

22. For the spherical tea service by Puiforcat (1928), see Françoise de Bonneville, *Jean Puiforcat* (Paris: Editions du Regard, 1986), 121.

23. Ibid., 142–43, for square trays with a similar border by Puiforcat.

24. Elsa Tennhardt's design patents assigned to E. & J. Bass, all 1928: 75,937, 75,938, 75,939, 76,360, and 76,361.

25. "Gifts That Solve the Man Problem," *Harper's Bazaar* 63 (Dec. 1928): 92.

26. Design patent 75,939 for a dish or article of analogous nature, Elsa Tennhardt assignor to E. & J. Bass, filed May 23, 1928, granted July 31, 1928.

27. See, especially, Tennhardt's centerpiece with matching candlesticks in Jean Clair, ed., *The 1920s: Age of the Metropolis*, exh. cat. (Montreal: Montreal Museum of Fine Arts, 1991), 206.

28. Mr. and Mrs. Gerhardt Steudte, conversation with author, Southampton, N.Y., June 18, 2002.

29. *Dekorative Kunst* (Munich) 33 (Feb. 1925): 134–35.

30. A four-piece *Shadowardt* tea and coffee service with matching tray was illustrated in a Bernard Rice's Son's advertisement in *Keystone* 56 (Nov. 1928): 31.

31. Another item in the "Sunray" pattern is the water pitcher, production number 3806.

32. "The Period Silver of Tomorrow," Benedict Manufacturing Company advertisement, *Keystone* 56 (Nov. 1928): 25.

33. "Smart as the day after tomorrow," Benedict Manufacturing Company advertisement, *Keystone* 56 (Dec. 1928): 25.

34. "American Modern Art, Its History and Characteristics," *Good Furniture Magazine* 27 (Oct. 1926): 173.

35. Other examples with literal imagery are Ruth Reeves's *Manhattan* textile (1930) and Viktor Schreckengost's *Jazz* bowls (1931).

36. A. Frederic Saunders, "From L'Art Nouveau to L'Art Moderne," *Jewelers' Circular* 98 (Feb. 1929): 106. A *Manhattan* salad fork, a *Cubic* spoon, and a serving spoon with a multistepped handle were illustrated in the article. The last, unidentified, may also have been designed by Magnussen. A *Manhattan* salad fork and spoon set was illustrated but not identified by name or by designer, in "Modern Designs in Silver," *House and Garden* 54 (Sept. 1928): 87. The caption read: "The ubiquitous skyscraper motif is again apparent in the handles of a silver salad spoon and fork. Sections of these are given an oxidized finish to accentuate the architectural effect. From Gorham." For a photograph of a *Manhattan* berry spoon, a serving spoon, and a fork, see Charles H. Carpenter Jr., *Gorham Silver 1831–1981* (New York: Dodd, Mead, 1982), 261.

37. Edwin Avery Park, quoted in Mary Fanton Roberts, "Modernistic Movement in Arts and Crafts," *Arts and Decoration* 28 (Apr. 1928): 101. Setback imagery may also be considered similar to Native American and Mayan motifs, influences that were in the amalgam of sources for *art moderne* and may have indirectly entered the decorative vocabulary of American industrial silver of the late 1920s. However, the setbacks of skyscrapers were the primary, overt reference.

38. "*Sky-scraper*," Bernard Rice's Sons advertisement, *Keystone* 55 (May 1928): 23.

39. The remaining items, in addition to the tea and coffee sets, were a "waiter," a bread tray, a "well and tree platter," a meat platter, a vegetable dish, a centerpiece, beakers, and an ice pail; the pitcher was not listed.

40. "June . . . Weddings . . . And Silver . . . Now and Forever," *Harper's Bazaar* 64 (June 1929): 93.

41. "Rhythm . . . the inevitable choice of youth!" *National Jeweler* 25 (Oct. 1929): 4.

42. Each series had the name "RHYTHM" stamped in capital letters in the hallmark. The 3900 series was more closely aligned with the stepped pattern of *Rhythm* flatware.

43. *Sterling Silver by Gorham,* sales catalogue, 1929 (Gorham Archive); see, for example, the *Modernistic* bonbon dish, production number A13775.

44. See the entry for Merle F. Faber Products in the Catalogue of Selected Works, in this volume, for other objects in the line.

45. Ashley Callahan, *Enchanting Modern: Ilonka Karasz*, exh. cat. (Athens: Georgia Museum of Art, University of Georgia, 2003), 11.

46. Annelies Krekel-Aalberse, *Art Nouveau and Art Deco Silver* (London: Thames and Hudson, 1989), 148–49.

47. Callahan, *Enchanting Modern*, 16.

48. For a photograph of the service and a pair of candlesticks by Karasz, see Paul T. Frankl, *Form and Re-Form: A Practical Handbook of Modern Interiors* (New York: Harper & Brothers, 1930), 152.

49. The complete service with tray was included in the exhibition at the Newark Museum in 1929 and priced at eighty-five dollars (Newark Museum Archives, Newark, N.J.).

50. W. Scott Braznell called attention to the variation in height; see Braznell, "Sterling Character," *Spirit* (Aug. 1990): 46.

51. For Brandt's tea service with cruciform bases, see Krekel-Aalberse, ter Molen, and Willink, eds., *Silver of a New Era*, 139.

52. Ashley Callahan, e-mail communication with author, Oct. 19, 2004.

53. "Mirror Table," *Creative Art* 3 (Dec. 1928): 452; see Helen Sprackling, "Modern Art and the Artist," *House Beautiful* 65 (Feb. 1929): 153.

54. Friedman, "An Unlikely Alliance," 100.

55. Callahan, *Enchanting Modern*, 81.

56. For the creamer and sugar bowl without a lid, see "Modernism at the Armory," *Art and Auction* (November 1994): 159; for Karasz's drawing, see Callahan, *Enchanting Modern*, 78.

57. *Sterling Silver* (Gorham Archive). For a design of the same period in which elements of the Arts and Crafts aesthetic—swelling, segmented, and lobed bodies—were retained, but used in conjunction with an *art moderne* flourish in the stepped finials of the caps, see Reed & Barton salt and pepper shakers, production number 250.

58. For a bowl from the Kalo Shop, see Sharon S. Darling, *Chicago Metalsmiths* (Chicago: Chicago Historical Society, 1977), 50. For Cauman's life and work, see Marilee Boyd Meyer, ed., *Inspiring Reform: Boston's Arts and Crafts Movement*, exh. cat. (Wellesley, Mass.: Davis Museum and Cultural Center, 1997), 72, 75, 82, 85; see also an example of Cauman's work, a box (accession number 1987.266) in the Art Institute of Chicago.

59. For a bowl, by Stone, with similar chasing, see catalogue number 95–1, Ark Antiques, *Fine, Early 20th Century American Craftsman Silver, Jewelry & Metal,* trade cat. (New Haven, Conn.: Ark Antiques, 1995), 14.

60. Samuel J. Hough, "Report on the Gorham sterling compotier A13748," June 2, 1988 (Jewel Stern Archives, Coral Gables, Fla.; hereafter, Stern Archives).

61. Even though the décor of the ship predated *art moderne*, the pattern may have been named retrospectively for the Cunard ocean liner *Franconia*, whose maiden voyage was in 1923.

62. M. Therese Bonney, "New Silhouettes in the French Tea Service," *Arts and Decoration* 27 (Sept. 1927): 50.

63. W. Scott Braznell made this point about a box of the same design except for its semiprecious stone finial; see Braznell, "The Advent of Modern American Silver," *The Magazine Antiques* 125 (Jan. 1984): 238.

64. While he was living in Concord during the 1930s, Sims's designs for flatware and novelties were patented by Concord Silversmiths.

65. Helen Appleton Read, "Twentieth-Century Decoration: The Modern Theme Finds a Distinctive Medium in American Silver," *Vogue* 72 (July 1, 1928): 58. See also a salad set embellished with turquoise in "3 of the Newest Additions to Gorham's offering of individual designs in Sterling Gifts that have no duplicate" (Gorham advertisement, *New Yorker* 4 [July 7, 1928]: 5), where the designer's name is misspelled as Simms.

66. For Gorham's tea caddy and spoon and sandwich tray and server, both with jade trim, see "Modern Designs in Silver," 85. For Gorham's bowl and matching spoon with lapis lazuli trim, see "Simplicity and Elegance in Modern Silverware," *Arts and Decoration* 29 (Aug. 1928): 59. For Gorham's salad dish and pie plate with servers, and cocktail shaker, both with jade trim, see Augusta Owen Patterson, "The Decorative Arts," *Town and Country* 84 (Mar. 1, 1930): 71–72. For Gorham's Durgin sandwich tray with carnelian trim, see Braznell, "Advent of Modern," 238–39. The objects mentioned in these articles were not identified as having been made by Durgin, but other pieces, either identical or very similar, in private and public collections all have the Durgin mark.

67. "Stone Trimmed Sterling; The Newest Thing by Gorham; The Smartest Thing in Silver," Gorham advertisement, *New Yorker* 4 (Apr. 21, 1928): 69.

68. Illustrated in "Modern Designs in Silver," 86.

69. Black Starr & Frost-Gorham, Inc., advertisement, *Town and Country* 85 (Mar. 15, 1930): 81.

70. Lilian M. Gunn, *The Art of Table Setting* (Providence, R.I.: Gorham, 1929), 29.

71. The classical taste, c. 1776–1812, expressed the ideals of the early republic; see Graham Hood, *American Silver: A History of Style, 1650–1900*, rev. ed. (1971; reprint New York: E. P. Dutton, 1989), 178–79.

72. The production numbers of the International Silver bowl and compotes with rose quartz pedestal are WD49, WT24, and WT23, respectively. The Charter Company bowl is in a private collection. Interestingly, a bowl on an oriental teakwood stand, number WD40 in the Wilcox & Evertsen Fine Arts Division sales catalogue, had imitation lapis lazuli handles (International Silver Company

Archives, Meriden Historical Society, Meriden, Conn.; hereafter International Silver Archives).

73. Jeffrey L. Meikle, *American Plastic: A Cultural History* (New Brunswick, N.J.: Rutgers University Press, 1995), 75.

74. Ibid., 76.

75. "Why Not Have the Newest Things," Sheets-Rockford Silver Company advertisement, *Keystone* 56 (Sept. 1928): 198.

76. By 1933, Bakelite had developed its own cast product; see Meikle, *American Plastic*, 76.

77. *International Silver Company Silver Plated Hollowware Catalog No. 34, 1928*, 2, 4 (International Silver Archives).

78. R. Wallace & Sons catalogue (Stern Archives).

79. Production number 870.

80. "Why Not Have the Newest Things," 198. The covered vegetable dish and cream and sugar with tray were illustrated.

81. The date of the vase is not known. The vase was not pictured in a catalogue produced by Barbour in 1930 (International Silver Archives), but the stamped product number is close to those on other objects made in 1929 and 1930. For a mid-1920s French vase by André Rivir with somewhat similar handles in ivory, see Christopher Finch, "Antiques: Modern French Silver," *Art Digest* 50 (May 1993): 158.

82. For prices, see Barbour Silver Company, salesman's catalogue, n.d., pl. 1195S, 93 (International Silver Archives).

83. The shaker in the plain version was illustrated in *Vogue* in 1928 and 1931; see Read, "Twentieth-Century Decoration," 59; and "Rewards for the faithful on wedding anniversaries," *Vogue* 78 (Aug. 1, 1931): 59. Pieces sold by Barbour and the Charter division of International were produced in the same plant in Meriden, Conn.; Dorothy T. Rainwater, *Encyclopedia of American Silver Manufacturers*, 3rd rev. ed. (West Chester, Pa.: Schiffer, 1986), 24. This may account for the Charter leaf trademark on an enameled cocktail shaker in this design (see fig. 3.56). In the Chrysler Museum in Norfolk, Va., a matching cocktail cup is stamped "104," the same number as given in the Barbour catalogue, but has the symbol mark of the Wilcox & Evertsen Fine Arts Division of International Silver. Apparently, the marks of the Barbour, Charter, and Wilcox & Evertsen Fine Arts divisions of International Silver were all used for this design. However, because the Wilcox & Evertsen mark is similar to that of Old Newbury Crafters, the Chrysler Museum attributed its cup, incorrectly, to that company; see David Revere McFadden and Mark A. Clark, *Treasures for the Table: Silver from the Chrysler Museum*, exh. cat. (New York: Hudson Hills Press; Washington, D.C.: American Federation of Arts, 1989), 76.

84. Wilcox & Evertsen Fine Arts Division, salesman's catalogue, n.d., pl. 4724 W, 13 (International Silver Archives).

85. Tiffany advertisements in *Harper's Bazaar* 70 (Sept. 1, 1937): 1; and *New Yorker* 15 (Dec. 16, 1939): 1.

86. Research by author, Gorham Archive.

87. Samuel J. Hough, "Report on two pieces of Gorham sterling hollowware 'Franconia,'" June 2, 1988; and, for the *Modernistic* bonbon dish, see idem, "Report on Gorham sterling Bon Bon Dish A13775," June 2, 1988 (Stern Archives).

88. Idem, "Report on Alvin sterling pieces from 'Gift Line,'" June 3, 1988 (Stern Archives).

89. *Wallace Sterling Silver Hollow Ware*, catalogue S-31 (Wallingford, Conn.: R. Wallace & Sons Mfg. Co., 1931).

90. "All Giftware Disc. Dec. 1936," handwritten on pl. 4431, *Wilcox Silver Plate Co., Meriden, Conn., U.S.A.*, salesman's catalogue, [1934] (International Silver Archives).

CHAPTER FOUR

MUSEUM EXHIBITIONS, 1929–1931

Although department stores were in the vanguard in introducing *art moderne* and its iterations to the American public following the Paris exposition, by 1928 museums were organizing their own formidable responses. From 1929 through 1931, four important exhibitions that included modern American industrial silver were staged, two by the Metropolitan Museum of Art in New York, one by the Newark Museum, and the fourth was a traveling exhibition sponsored by the American Federation of Arts. The imprimatur of these museums enhanced the prestige of American modernist design in general, and the exhibitions showcased some outstanding silverware.

In the fall of 1928 planning began for the Metropolitan Museum's eleventh American industrial art exhibition, *The Architect and the Industrial Arts,* a collaboration of manufacturers, designers, craftsmen, and architects, which opened on February 12, 1929. The concept took shape under the leadership of the English émigré ceramic designer Leon Solon in a Co-operating Committee that consisted of the architects Raymond Hood, Ely Jacques Kahn, Eliel Saarinen, Eugene Schoen, Ralph T. Walker, John Wellborn Root, and Joseph Urban and the landscape architect Armistead Fitzhugh. The cosmopolitan makeup of the committee was significant. Solon was English, Saarinen was Finnish, Urban was Austrian, and the three Americans had trained in Europe—Schoen in Vienna and Kahn and Hood at the Ecole des Beaux-Arts in Paris. Over weekly luncheons at the Architectural League of New York, the members hammered out the theme. Edward Robinson, the director of the museum, noted in the catalogue that this exhibition was unique for the museum in that the architects had planned it from "the general design of the gallery as a whole" to "the minutiae of their individual exhibits."[1] It was also the first unified advancement of a modern idiom by the museum for its industrial art annuals since the inception of the series in 1917. Although a breakthrough had occurred in the tenth annual of 1926–1927, when original designs were introduced, until then, historical revivalism had been the norm.[2] In his catalogue essay Richard F. Bach, the director of industrial relations at the museum, proudly pointed out that "not only are the objects shown all of contemporary design and of American conception and execution throughout, but they have been designed for the specific purpose of this showing."[3] The objects were arranged in thirteen displays that simulated room arrangements. The public response was overwhelmingly positive and validated the concept. Throngs attracted to modern design visited the exhibition. Interest was so great that the viewing was extended from March 24 until September 2, an additional five months. With 185,256 visitors, this exhibition had the highest recorded attendance of any in the museum's series of fifteen American industrial art annuals between 1917 and 1940.[4]

FIGURE 4.1 Dining Room, Eliel Saarinen, designer. Exhibit in *The Architect and the Industrial Arts*, The Metropolitan Museum of Art, 1929

In 1922 Eliel Saarinen had won second prize in the competition to design the Tribune Tower in Chicago. It was this award that had brought him renown in the United States and had led to a major role in the exhibition. He formulated the general spatial treatment of the entire installation and designed a separate Dining Room that showcased his own outstanding modernist silver (fig. 4.1). For the dining-room table Saarinen designed a massive twenty-inch handwrought sterling silver center-piece bowl with chased decoration that was made by the International Silver Company.[5] Of special interest is International's production-line footed bowl (fig. 4.2) for which the Metropolitan centerpiece was the prototype. The bowl was made in sterling silver in several sizes and marketed as a reproduction of the bowl by Eliel Saarinen, "a Finnish master among modern masters," and as "one of the gems which delighted connoisseurs" at the exhibition.[6] Although the foot was simplified, the linear segmenting that subtly fans out at the rim of the bowl was true to the chasing of the original. The production-line bowl was widely copied. One of the most successful versions was made in Gorham's *Hunt Club* pattern to match the flatware introduced in 1930.

Early on Saarinen recognized the commercial potential of industrial design for mass consumption, and he designed four flatware prototypes for the exhibition.[7] These were handmade by International, Reed & Barton, Towle, and Rogers, Lunt & Bowlen of Greenfield, Massachusetts. The only known photograph illustrating all four patterns, but each with only a knife and a fork, appeared in *Country Life* in 1929 (fig. 4.3).[8] For the exhibition each pattern was represented by a seven-piece place setting.[9] The knives had a distinctive feature, long handles and shorter blades, a type that became known in the trade as *Viande,* and was a registered trademark of the International Silver Company.[10] Saarinen first applied for a patent on the knife in November 1929 as assignor to International.[11] His idea was to alleviate the discomfort incurred in pressing the extended index finger against the blade of a conventional knife. Saarinen may have been influenced by early twentieth-century modernist flatware by the Scottish architect Charles Rennie Mackintosh and the Austrian architects Josef Hoffmann and Joseph Maria Olbrich.[12] In his catalogue statement Solon made a special point of mentioning the *Viande* design: "Familiar utensils were regarded from new angles and the need for radical revision—as in the case of Saarinen's table knife. . . ."[13]

Of Saarinen's four flatware prototypes, only Reed & Barton's was mass produced. This design, the handle of which shows the influence of the *art moderne* "frozen fountain" motif, became *Candide* (1929) in silverplate and *Contempora* (1930) in sterling (fig. 4.4). Although Reed & Barton was credited with the prototype in the exhibition catalogue and the flatware design patent was assigned to the company by Saarinen, *Contempora* initially bore the mark of Dominick & Haff, an old and respected name in high-quality sterling flatware and holloware. Reed & Barton had acquired the New York manufacturer in 1928 in order to expand its sterling lines.[14] A full sterling silver holloware service by Saarinen in *Contempora*, which included a "salad dish" with a stepped base (fig. 4.5), was heralded in Dominick & Haff's extensive promotional catalogue.[15] Notwithstanding his designing of *Contempora,* and the availability of the economical silverplate equivalent, *Candide,* Saarinen did *not* select it for Cranbrook. As the architect and founding director of the school, he chose instead International's *Silhouette* pattern of 1930 (fig. 4.6) in silverplate by the staff designer Leslie A. Brown.[16] Saarinen's relationship as a consultant with International, which continued through the 1930s, was probably a factor. Moreover, *Silhouette* was produced with *Viande* styling and, as noted in an advertisement, was closely identified with Saarinen at the time.[17]

Take the regular knife in your hand, pretend you're cutting meat, and notice how your forefinger presses down on the back of the blade itself. Notice how more than half the blade is unused, "excess baggage." Look at the groove it leaves on your fingertip. Then try a Viande knife. Your finger pressed *the handle,* as it should. Note the perfection of balance and "feel." And then sit back and wonder why no one ever thought of it before. The Viande Knife is the creation of Eliel Saarinen, renowned architect and designer, whose work is recognized as embodying the best tendencies of modern *design* [emphasis in original].[18]

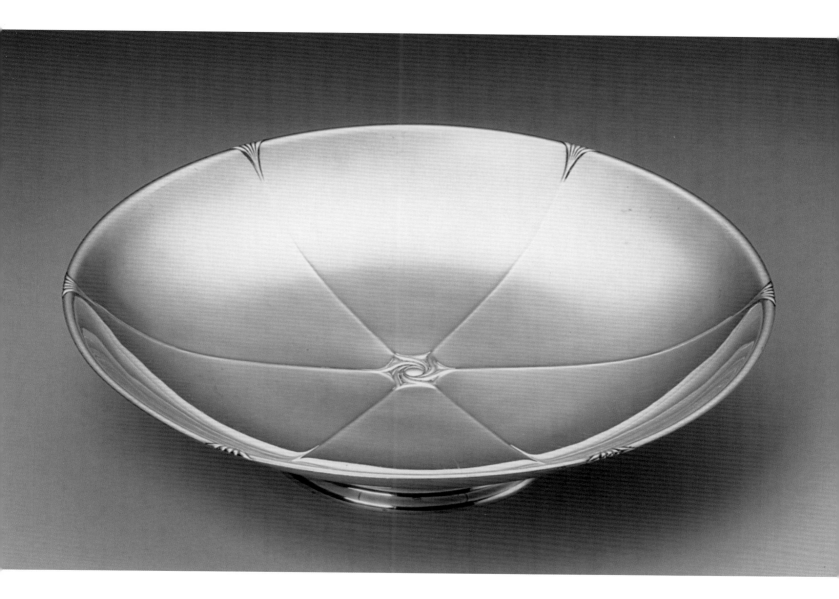

FIGURE 4.2   Centerpiece, c. 1929. Charter Company, Eliel Saarinen,
designer. Silver. The John C. Waddell Collection, cat. 87

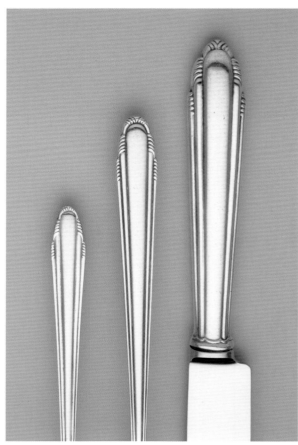

FIGURE 4.3 Photograph of flatware prototypes, c. 1928, Eliel Saarinen, designer. Exhibited in *The Architect and the Industrial Arts*, Metropolitan Museum of Art, 1929

FIGURE 4.4 *Contempora* flatware (detail), 1930. Dominick & Haff, Eliel Saarinen, designer. Silver. Dallas Museum of Art, cat. 206

One other silver object in the Metropolitan's 1929 exhibition received notice, a sterling cocktail shaker with matching cups and tray in the Man's Study for a Country House by Ralph T. Walker. The handmade and hand-chased set was designed by Walker in collaboration with Charles Graff of Graff, Washbourne and Dunn, a silver manufacturer in New York. Innovative features were the pair of handles and the double spouts, which facilitated pouring and prevented the interior strainers from becoming clogged.[19] Like the *Viande* knife, the shaker was recognized for the designer's utilitarian reinterpretation of a familiar form.[20] The shape of the shaker resembled that of a traditional Greek amphora, but its decoration was an amalgam of stylized decorative motifs from Paris with an emphasis on zigzag borders.[21]

The Newark Museum mounted *Modern American Design in Metal,* an exhibition that opened for a month on March 19, 1929,[22] and overlapped with *The Architect and the Industrial Arts* at the Metropolitan. Consisting of more than one hundred objects in a wide variety of metals and types, the exhibition included the work of several designers—Gilbert Rohde, Walter Von Nessen, Donald Deskey, and Winold Reiss, among others—and the architects Ely Jacques Kahn and William Lescaze. The objects, in chromium, aluminum, iron, bronze, brass, copper, steel, gold, and silver, ranged from a novel grand piano, called *Modernique,* designed by Lee Simonson, and made by the Hardman Company, that had setback details and angular metal legs that alluded to skyscrapers, to an austere Bauhaus-inspired tea and

FIGURE 4.5 *Contempora* salad dish, 1930. Dominick & Haff, Eliel Saarinen, designer. Silver. DMA, JSASC, cat. 207

coffee service in silverplate designed by Ilonka Karasz for Paye & Baker (see fig. 3.37).[23] The only other modern industrial silverware in the exhibition were four otherwise unidentified pieces of "table silver" designed by Kem Weber for the Friedman Silver Company.[24] These would have been examples from either or both of the two holloware groups that Weber had designed for Friedman, *Silver Style* and *To-Day* (see figs. 3.6, 3.39). The silversmith Peter Mueller-Munk exhibited handwrought pieces of which several were loans from L. Bamberger & Co., a department store in Newark that sold his work.[25]

Two exhibitions during 1930 and 1931 featured American industrial silver. The first was *Decorative Metalwork and Cotton Textiles: The Third International Exhibition of Contemporary Industrial Art*, an exhibition that was organized by the American Federation of Arts and traveled during 1930 and 1931. On the itinerary were the Museum of Fine Arts, Boston, the Art Institute of Chicago, the Cleveland Museum of Art, and the Metropolitan Museum of Art in New York City. In the catalogue Charles R. Richards, the director of the American Association of Museums, complained of the under-representation of American industrial silver, especially the dearth of holloware: "Outside of flatware, our prominent establishments are very poorly represented. This lack of professional cooperation on the part of many of our foremost producers has marked these international exhibitions of industrial art from the first. It is to be hoped that the generous example of foreign

craftsmen and manufacturers may have its influence in future undertakings."[26]

The sterling flatware patterns that can be identified in a photograph from the catalogue are *Hunt Club* (1930) by Gorham, *Orchid* (1930) by International, and *Miss America* (1932) by Alvin, and in silverplate, *Silhouette* (1930) by International (see fig. 4.6). The flatware prototypes that Eliel Saarinen had designed for International, Towle, and Reed & Barton and exhibited in the 1929 Metropolitan exhibition were also illustrated in the catalogue.[27] Listed but otherwise unidentified were patterns by the staff designers William S. Warren for Wallace and Harold E. Nock for Towle.[28] The only entries of American silver holloware were a bowl and sandwich plate by Gorham. The roster of individual contributors of handmade silver, however, was impressive and two of them, Paul A. Lobel and Peter Mueller-Munk, later designed silverware for industry.[29]

Although Germany, France, Switzerland, and Holland were represented in the exhibition, the silverware from Sweden and Denmark was most important for its influence on American production (fig. 4.7). The appreciation of modern Scandinavian design had become evident in 1927, from the response to the Metropolitan Museum of Art's *Exhibition of Swedish Contemporary Decorative Art*, which had included silverware. Acclaimed

FIGURE 4.6 "New Viande Pieces," in *1847 Rogers Bros. Original and Genuine Rogers Silverplate* catalogue, 1930

FIGURE 4.7 Gallery view of Danish silver, Cleveland Museum of Art, 1931. Exhibit in *Decorative Metalwork and Cotton Textiles, Third International Exhibiton of Contemporary Industrial Art*, The American Federation of Arts, 1930–1931

by Helen Appleton Read for its "vitality and rationalism," this was the first show of Scandinavian work to be held at the museum. Read understood the fundamental appeal of Scandinavian modernism for Americans, and she quoted the curator of decorative arts at the Metropolitan, Joseph Breck, who grasped one characteristic of Scandinavian design that resonated with traditional American values: "These Swedish productions give an impression of permanency—of belonging—which is often missing in the applied arts of other countries, where they are more dependent upon the varying tastes of individuals."[30]

Another attractive aspect of Swedish decorative art in general was its lack of pretension and its relative affordability to the "comfortable middle class," qualities that at the time were perceived as democratic rather than elitist.[31] Initial interest in Scandinavian silver was not limited to the East Coast. At the Minneapolis Institute of Arts, for example, two large cases of Jensen's silver were exhibited in the *Modern Decorative Art* exhibition organized and held at the museum in 1928.[32]

In the fall of 1931, the *Twelfth Exhibition of Contemporary American Industrial Art* was mounted in the Metropolitan's Gallery of Special Exhibitions. Although a small catalogue was published without specific entries, records in the museum's archives indicate that silver manufacturers loaned their latest flatware patterns by staff designers. In sterling, *Symphony* (1931) by Harold E. Nock for Towle, *American Directoire* (1931) by Frederick W. Koonz for Rogers, Lunt & Bowlen, and *Elsinore* (1931) by Alfred G. Kintz for International were shown. Reed & Barton sent *Stylist* (1931), its new silverplate pattern, a design related to Saarinen's *Contempora*. Taking place near the depth of the Depression, this American industrial art exhibition had a relatively low attendance, drawing only 33,972 visitors between October 12 and November 22.[33]

Notes

1. Edward Robinson, Acknowledgments, in *The Architect and the Industrial Arts: An Exhibition of Contemporary American Design*, exh. cat. (New York: Metropolitan Museum of Art, 1929), 12.

2. For a history of the annuals, see R. Craig Miller, *Modern Design in the Metropolitan Museum of Art 1890–1990* (New York: Metropolitan Museum of Art and Abrams, 1990), 8–30.

3. Richard F. Bach, "American Industrial Art," in *Architect and the Industrial Arts*, 24.

4. Exhibition file, Metropolitan Museum of Art Archives, New York.

5. "Modern Art Expressed in Silver," *Jewelers' Circular* 98 (Mar. 7, 1929): 55.

6. Saarinen's hand-chased and embossed bowl was produced by the Charter Company, a subsidiary of International, in three diameters: 11, 13, and 15 inches, and a compote in the design, 7 inches in diameter, was also available; See Charter Company sterling catalogue [c. 1930], plate 2S (International Silver Company Archives, Meriden Historical Society, Meriden, Conn.; hereafter International Silver Archives). The pieces were stamped "By Saarinen" in script.

7. Robert Judson Clark, et al., *Design in America: The Cranbrook Vision, 1925–1950* (New York: Abrams, in association with the Detroit Institute of Arts and the Metropolitan Museum of Art, 1983), 162.

8. Lee McCann, "Sterling Silver, 1929," part 2, *Country Life* 56 (June 1929): 94.

9. The seven pieces were a fish fork, salad fork, dinner fork, fish knife, dinner knife, teaspoon, and tablespoon.

10. The long-handled, short-bladed knife was called both *Grille* and *Vogue*; see William P. Hood Jr., "Modern Flatware Design: The Viande/Grille/Vogue Style," *The Magazine Antiques* 158 (Feb. 2003): 78–85. For the *Viande* trademark, see Earl Chapin May, *A Century of Silver 1847–1947: Connecticut Yankees and a Noble Metal* (New York: Robert M. McBride, 1947), 342.

11. Design patent 84,654 for a knife, Eliel Saarinen assignor to International Silver Company, filed Nov. 7, 1929, granted July 14, 1931.

12. Hood, "Modern Flatware Design," 80–81.

13. Leon Solon, Acknowledgments, in *Architect and the Industrial Arts*, 17.

14. The merger signaled the company's shift from producing plated ware, especially commercial, to producing, predominantly, sterling; see Renee Garrelick, *Sterling Seasons: The Reed & Barton Story* (Taunton, Mass.: Reed & Barton, 1998), 61.

15. *Dominick & Haff Present a New Pattern Contempora: Sterling in the Contemporary Art*, promotional flatware and holloware catalogue (n.d.), courtesy of Reed & Barton.

16. *Silhouette* was acquired for the dining room of Kingswood School for girls at the Cranbrook Educational Community, see Martha Cross Neumann, ed., *Kingswood: Study in Design* (Bloomfield Hills, Mich.: Kingswood School Cranbrook, 1982), 20. An inducement may have been a price discount from International.

17. *Candide* and *Contempora* did not come with *Viande* knives. "Reed & Barton has never made any pattern with viande blades" (Natalie Glavin, Reed & Barton, memorandum to author, May 4, 1988).

18. "Presenting the Viande Knife," International Silver Company advertisement, 1929 (Dallas Museum of Art object file 1995.102.1–3).

19. "Modern Art Expressed in Silver," 46.

20. Solon, Acknowledgments, 17.

21. For an illustration of Walker's cocktail shaker ensemble, see Jean Clair, ed., *The 1920s: Age of the Metropolis*, exh. cat. (Montreal: Montreal Museum of Fine Arts, 1991), 621.

22. *Modern American Design in Metal* was held in the second-floor east gallery of the Newark Museum from March 19 to April 18, 1929.

23. "The Metal Exhibit," *Museum* 2 (April 1929): 51–52. Karasz's tea service identified from a photograph at the museum. Also on the registrar's list for Karasz is a pair of unidentified candlesticks. The tea service in the exhibition is illustrated, with a pair of candlesticks, in Paul T. Frankl, *Form and Re-Form: A Practical Handbook of Modern Interiors* (New York: Harper & Brothers, 1930), 152.

24. "Metal Exhibit," 52, and Newark Museum Archives, Newark, N.J.

25. Newark Museum Archives. Mueller-Munk's bowl from the exhibition was acquired by the museum, accession number 29.472.

26. Charles R. Richards, Introduction, in *Decorative Metalwork and Cotton Textiles: Third International Exhibition of Contemporary Industrial Art*, American Federation of Arts, New York, 1930–1931, n.p. See also Richard F. Bach, "Materials Achieve New Values," *American Magazine of Art* 24 (Apr. 1932): 271, 274.

27. The fourth pattern, the flatware designed by Saarinen and fabricated by Rogers, Lunt & Bowlen, was omitted.

28. *Hunt Club, Silhouette, Miss America,* and *Orchid* were illustrated in *Decorative Metalwork and Cotton*, n.p.; see also, "Cotton and Metal," *Good Furniture Design* 35 (Nov. 1930): 255.

29. Donald Deskey was another exhibitor who later designed silver for industry.

30. Helen Appleton Read, "Swedish Decorative Art Display at the Metropolitan Museum," *Brooklyn Daily Eagle*, Jan. 16, 1927 (Archives of American Art, Helen Appleton Read Papers, reel N736, frame 166).

31. Miller, *Modern Design*, 17–18.

32. "At the Minneapolis Art Institute," *American Magazine of Art* 19 (May 1928): 279.

33. Exhibition file, Metropolitan Museum of Art Archives.

CHAPTER FIVE

THE DEPRESSION: A SOBERING REALITY

Between 1926 and 1929, French *art moderne* had been enthusiastically received, popularized, and adapted. The heady ferment
in design came to an abrupt halt when the stock market crashed
on Black Thursday, October 24, 1929. The euphoria of the Roaring Twenties was over. The Depression brought the economy to
a standstill in the early 1930s and the effect on manufacturers
of deluxe, nonessential goods such as silverware was devastating. A reaction against the dizzying excesses of the prosperity of
the 1920s and a subsequent retreat to period revival styles was
observed in a trade journal early in 1931: "The present-day trend in
silverware design clearly indicates a return to more conservative
lines of artistic expression, and the sobering influences of the past
twelve months have undoubtedly been a contributing factor in
bringing about this reaction to the extremes of so-called modernism . . . the increasing demand for antique reproductions during
the past year or two indicates most clearly the turn of the tide in
silverware styles."[1]

By the end of 1931 the total value of American-made silverware had dropped from nearly eighty-six million dollars in 1929
to about forty-six million dollars.[2] Between 1929 and 1933 the
number of silver manufacturers fell from 179 to 126.[3] By the time
the economy improved somewhat in 1933, the fever of the 1920s
had cooled. The mood was sober and designers turned to a lean
modern classicism and streamlining, symbols of a new aesthetic
and social order, to express the Machine Age. In contrast to the
agitated, irregular planarity of cubism that infused 1920s *art
moderne,* the geometry of 1930s neoclassicism and streamlining
would be derived from machines and would emulate their formal
functional purity and lack of surface ornament. In this respect,
the new modernism was more aligned with the German Bauhaus
ideology of the 1920s.

The exaggeration of the angular in form noted when modern silver was
first brought out some seasons ago has entirely disappeared. It is now freely
admitted that it was not acceptable and such pieces were discontinued one
by one, going into the melting pot, the effort representing a considerable
loss to the concerns which had brought them out. The elimination of all
superfluous ornamentation is retained as a good feature, and some of the
best designers are responsible for modern silver which is entirely guiltless
of extraneous ornament.[4]

The silver industry's struggle for economic survival was ex-
acerbated by the emergence of competition from high-styled
tableware in chromium-plated metal from manufacturers such as
Chase Brass & Copper Company of Waterbury, Connecticut, and
in aluminum from Kensington of New Kensington, Pennsylvania,
a division of Alcoa, the Aluminum Company of America. Tableware in these materials was easy to care for, affordable, and aggressively advertised. Moreover, it was identified with the casual style

of home entertaining that had become fashionable in the 1930s and anticipated the relaxed climate of the post–World War II era with the consequent declining importance of silver in American life. In addition to its own talented employees, Chase engaged prominent industrial designers as consultants, among them Walter Von Nessen, Russel Wright, and Lurelle Guild; the latter also designed Kensington's initial line in 1934.[5] Revere Copper and Brass of Rome, New York, a competitor, initiated a metal giftware line in 1935 designed by Norman Bel Geddes. In 1936, Revere introduced a water pitcher in chromium-plated brass designed by Peter Mueller-Munk and named for the new French ocean liner *Normandie*. Although he was a silversmith and trained to produce unique objects in silver, Mueller-Munk's most celebrated design, paradoxically, is this sleek, mass-produced pitcher, which has become a symbol of 1930s streamlining (fig. 5.1).

Silver manufacturers countered with production-line silverplate in ultramodern patterns as an inexpensive, informal alternative to sterling silver. International's *Gift Ware* signature holloware line in silverplate designed by Guild and introduced in 1934 was the most ambitious undertaking by the trade (see figs. 6.24, 7.3). Later in the decade International promoted a moderately priced thematic group named *Tropical* (see figs. 6.32, 6.33). Cumulatively, extant pieces from the 1930s confirm that, in contrast to the 1920s, investment, dictated by the realities of the economy and demand, was overwhelmingly in silverplate.

The silverware industry did rally, but for the balance of the twentieth century it never regained the financial position and status it had held before the Depression. Nonetheless, in the 1930s a limited amount of silverware in step with contemporary design, both neoclassical and streamlined, was produced and recognized in major exhibitions here and abroad. The most innovative manufacturers were International and Reed & Barton in both silverplate and sterling, and in silverplate, the Napier Company of Meriden, Connecticut, and to some extent Wallace. The Watson Company of Attleboro, Massachusetts, along with Rogers, Lunt & Bowlen, produced a few compelling modernist designs in sterling. Gorham, active in the 1920s, left the field. Tiffany & Co., conservative and slow to embrace *art moderne* in the 1920s, hit a high note in 1937 with the *Century* pattern in flatware and holloware that commemorated its centennial (see fig. 8.3).

In 1937 the Metropolitan Museum of Art in New York and the Brooklyn Museum held exhibitions of silver that marked the apogee of silverware for the 1930s. In the same year, American industrial silver garnered awards in the *Exposition Internationale des Arts et des Techniques dans la Vie Moderne* (International exposition of arts and crafts in modern life) in Paris. With the exception of Tiffany's extravagant display in the House of Jewels at the New York World's Fair in 1939 and 1940 (see fig. 8.12), International's *Tropical* line (see fig. 6.31), and a few individual designs such as the specially commissioned trophy designed by Viktor Schreckengost and made by Gorham (see fig. 6.26), the creative impulse waned in the late 1930s. Symptomatic was the absence of industrial silver in the Metropolitan Museum of Art's fifteenth exhibition of *Contemporary American Industrial Art* in 1940, where handwrought silver took center stage, a portent of the revival of crafts after World War II. America's entry into World War II at the end of 1941 forestalled further innovation and effectively brought this period of modernist design to a close.

CONTEMPORARY AMERICAN INDUSTRIAL ART, 1934

The early years of the Depression created a deep divide between design in the 1920s and design in the 1930s. In 1934, as the economy slowly revived, the Metropolitan Museum of Art's *Contemporary American Industrial Art* exhibition sent a clear message that *art moderne*, the early, exhilarating phase of modernism, had passed. In contrast to the museum's previous exhibition in the series in 1929, the thirteenth, in 1934, was, as Richard F. Bach, the museum's director of industrial relations, observed, "designed and produced in a time

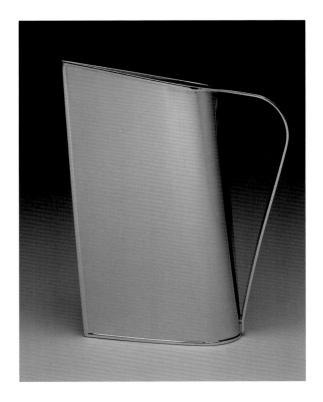

FIGURE 5.1 *Normandie* pitcher, 1935. Revere Copper and Brass Company, Peter Mueller-Munk, designer. Chromium-plated brass. Dallas Museum of Art, 20th-Century Design Fund

FIGURE 5.2   Room for a Lady, Eliel Saarinen, designer. Exhibit in *Contemporary American Industrial Art*, The Metropolitan Museum of Art, 1934

of depression and economic stress when integrity of design is worth more than exuberance and when any purchase implies a need. . . . Now every piece exhibited must carry a promise of marketability."[6] The organizers realized that the demand for unique and expensive articles was limited and that prototypes in the exhibition should be designed for quantity production and at reasonable prices to reach the masses. It was an ideal, yet pragmatic concept for the Machine Age—the democratization of good design. Arthur Loomis Harmon, the chairman of the Central Gallery Unit, underscored these considerations: "The Co-operating Committee agreed that in contradistinction to the exhibition held in the lush period of five years ago, this one was to show what might be achieved at a low cost."[7]

More than two hundred firms and designers worked with Bach on the exhibition. A Co-operating Committee consisting of twenty architects and industrial designers chose more than one thousand objects for the various home furnishings categories. All were American made, newly designed, and shown for the first time. Many were prototypes awaiting public approval before being manufactured. Bach argued against using the term *mass production*. In his opinion *quantity production* or *serial manufacture* were more suitable because his definition

of the term was based on the premise of duplication, rather than of numbers.[8] Quantity production for him could be used for as few as six or as many as six thousand objects. Therefore, the exhibition in 1934 differed strongly from that of 1929 in its "adherence to the quantity viewpoint," and to the "industrial product" as the "chief consideration."[9]

The five-year interval between the exhibitions evidenced a significant alteration in the attitude toward modernism. In this exhibition Bach proclaimed that the "strength and reason" of modernism in design was "fully demonstrated."[10] Ely Jacques Kahn, the chairman of the West Gallery Unit, remarked that in 1929 original designs were stipulated, whereas in 1934 that was considered unnecessary; it was taken for granted that only new forms would be presented.[11] The Depression had dampened the national mood, and austere functionalism as advanced by the newly founded Museum of Modern Art was more in line with the spirit of the time. In this climate designers turned to powerful symbols of progress, transportation machines, and streamlining for inspiration. In dramatic services commissioned for the exhibition, the architect Eliel Saarinen and the metalsmith Paul A. Lobel both used the sphere as the form to create stunning objects that have become Machine Age icons.

The spherical tea urn by Saarinen was a highlight in his Room for a Lady (fig. 5.2), a streamlined interior scheme in shades of eggshell, coral, and black, that, when compared with his Dining Room of 1929 (see

FIGURE 5.3   Photograph: Tea urn and tray, 1934. Wilcox Silver Plate Company, Eliel Saarinen, designer. Silverplate. Cranbrook Art Museum, Bloomfield Hills, Mich. See also cat. 127

FIGURE 5.4   Photograph: Sports trophy (covered cup), 1902. Würbel & Czokally, Vinzenz Mayer's Söhne, Josef Hoffmann, designer. Silver, lapis lazuli

fig. 4.1), demonstrated the gulf between the priorities of the two exhibitions.[12] The urn and its round tray, a production-line version executed by International Silver, the primary fabricator of silverware for the exhibition, were derived from the prototype by Saarinen now in the Cranbrook Art Museum (fig. 5.3).[13] The larger production-line model in the exhibition held twenty-six rather than the sixteen cups of the prototype, had wider slats that partly concealed the heating element, and a base that was flat, without the ball feet of the prototype.[14] The distinctive faucet handle was the abstract crested-crane motif that Saarinen designed for the urn and later incorporated into the Nichols gate at Cranbrook.[15] A likely precedent for the urn was a spherical covered cup designed in 1902 by Josef Hoffmann (fig. 5.4). The unusual foot on Hoffmann's cup may have been adapted by Saarinen to enclose and hide the heating mechanism and to support the urn. Early in the century Hoffmann and other Viennese designers at the Wiener Werkstätte, including Carl Otto Czeschka, had used decorative openwork for the feet of covered cups.[16] Saarinen created a serial openwork pattern that was rhythmic and abstract by piercing the collar around the heating element with very narrow, uniform vertical openings to give the effect of slats. Elegant, elongated finials similar to the one on the urn are to be seen frequently in Austrian silverwork, as are flat, round bases.[17] Although much larger in diameter than the bases of those earlier cups, the under tray for the urn reflects the treatment. Another detail that suggests the Austrian influence were the ball feet (characteristic of many of Hoffmann's silver objects) on the prototype.

Three other silver objects, a vase, a compote, and a bowl, by Saarinen adorned the Room for a Lady. Displayed on the chest of drawers, these were prototypes fabricated in silverplate by International.[18] Their clean lines harmonized with the urn and with the décor of the room, their only decorative element an allusion to classical fluting on the foot. The sphere was repeated for the small vase, and the shallow compote stood on a tall, slender column. The flat disk bases of all three were, in size and proportion, again reminiscent of early twentieth-century Austrian design.

Like Saarinen, Lobel based his design for the four-piece tea service on the sphere. With the components arranged horizontally on a rectilinear tray, the service was displayed in the east case of the central gallery unit at the entrance to the exhibition (fig. 5.5).[19] Contemporaneous photographs and a newsletter published by International Silver indicate that the columnar handles of the exhibited prototype were black Catalin, as were details of the finials.[20] The later production-line version, called a coffee set (fig. 5.6) is, however, entirely silver-plated except for the coffeepot insulator.[21] In a brilliant maneuver Lobel devised a hidden method of anchoring the three vessels to the rimless tray in order to prevent them from sliding off and to maintain the aesthetic spacing of the ensemble. The round bases of the vessels were made with shallow hollow compartments to slip like a sleeve over metal disks permanently attached to the tray.[22] The vessels are thus easily lifted for use and yet

FIGURE 5.5 View of central gallery east case. Exhibit in *Contemporary American Industrial Art*, The Metropolitan Museum of Art, 1934

FIGURE 5.6 Coffee set, 1934. Wilcox Silver Plate Company, Paul A. Lobel, designer. Silverplate, alpaca, Britannia pewter, wood. The John C. Waddell Collection, cat. 128

do not move on the tray when displayed or carried. Cantilevered on extensions parallel to the planes of the tray and at right angles to the spherical bodies, the handles act as a balancing counterpoint to the predominance of curved lines. The relationships of the horizontal planes to one another and of the horizontal to the vertical planes and of both planes to the spherical vessels were compositionally important in this work and in others of the 1930s, such as Saarinen's tea urn, in which pure form dominated and applied decoration was eschewed. The small contoured spouts and sharp fin-shaped finials have aquatic connotations that also suggest aerodynamic movement and activate the static forms. The ponytail handles reinforce the illusion that the vessels are in formation and ready to take flight, an impression heightened when the objects are viewed from certain angles. An imaginative journalist associated the form of the vessels to munitions: "The form is extraordinary, like a hand grenade with handles springing out at right angles."[23] However, a spherical tea service designed by Puiforcat in the late 1920s (fig. 5.7) may have been a source of inspiration. Although they are similar, Puiforcat's design is both rigid and heavy, whereas Lobel's simplified bases and handles and his subtle organic references imbue his masterpiece of Machine Age precision with an enduring liveliness.[24] For the exhibition Lobel also designed a cocktail shaker with a spherical body, a dark Catalin base and cover, and an elongated neck wound with what was described as natural rattan,

which was shown in the General Group in the West Gallery Unit on a tray designed by Alfons Bach.[25] Lobel's shaker later went into production in silverplate and, for economy, the Catalin trim was eliminated.[26]

International also made silver objects designed by Lurelle Guild and Donald Deskey for the exhibition. A cocktail shaker that Guild designed was exhibited in the East Case on the shelf above Lobel's service and was illustrated in *Arts and Decoration*, but whether it went into production is not known.[27] It is doubtful, too, that Deskey's coffee set, and bowl with matching bonbon and almond dishes in his Dining Room exhibit (fig. 5.8; see also fig. 8.25) were marketed.[28]

A little-known holloware group designed by Peter Mueller-Munk (fig. 5.9) was exhibited in Paul Philippe Cret's East Gallery General Group (fig. 5.10), displayed in the only exclusively silver showcase in the exhibition. The showcase was situated across from another filled with metal objects by Russel Wright.[29] This design and one other by Mueller-Munk were manufactured briefly by the Poole Silver Company of Taunton, Massachusetts, as the *Silvermode* signature line in silverplate (fig. 5.11).[30] The only ornamental details on the pitcher and on several other items shown by Mueller-Munk were pointed applied strips that refer to the candelabra commissioned by the Detroit Institute of Arts in 1928.[31]

FIGURE 5.7   Photograph: Teapot, 1928. Jean Puiforcat, designer

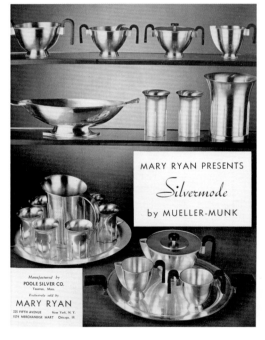

Clockwise from top left:

FIGURE 5.8 Dining Room (detail), Donald Deskey, designer. Exhibited in *Contemporary American Industrial Art,* at the Metropolitan Museum of Art, 1934

FIGURE 5.9 Peter Mueller-Munk, 1935

FIGURE 5.10 View of East Gallery, General Group, Paul Philippe Cret, architect. Exhibited in *Contemporary American Industrial Art,* at the Metropolitan Museum of Art, 1934

FIGURE 5.11 "Mary Ryan presents Silvermode by Mueller-Munk." Mary Ryan advertisement, 1935

The three-piece hemispheric coffee set, tray, and bowls had black plastic ponytail handles similar to those on vessels by Josef Hoffmann and the Wiener Werkstätte.[32] The form of the coffeepot and its spout is similar to that of one made in about 1930 by Puiforcat (see fig. 1.25). Although Puiforcat and Marianne Brandt had employed the hemispheric shape for vessels in the 1920s, it was not until the mid-1930s that it appeared with any frequency in American silver. The decorative components of Mueller-Munk's *Silvermode* line reflected his German roots and were more retrospective than prospective.

Although the exhibition was not held over, the attendance during the run of the show, from November 5, 1934, to January 6, 1935, signaled a considerable rise of public interest in modernism. For the sixty-three days that this show was open, 139,261 visitors were recorded, twice the average daily attendance of the previous exhibition in 1929, which was open for more than six months and visited by a total of 185,256 people.[33]

NOTES

1. A. Frederic Saunders, "The Trend in Silverware Design," *Jewelers' Circular* 101 (Mar. 1931): 94.

2. Charles L. Venable, *Silver in America, 1840–1940: A Century of Splendor*, exh. cat. (Dallas, Tex.: Dallas Museum of Art, 1994), 229.

3. Ibid., 230.

4. Ethel Walton Everett, "Table Silver Feels Change," *New York Sun*, Oct. 30, 1936, n.p.

5. Occasionally, Chase offered articles in silverplate. A little-known novelty early in the decade was a boxed "frozen dessert" set comprising four dishes and matching plates, the dishes designed to fit electric refrigerator freezing trays so that dessert could be made in them and served directly from the refrigerator to the table. The set was mentioned in an article on silver as an attractive and practical "unit" of the Frigidaire refrigerator, but it was discontinued before the first known Chase catalogue appeared in 1933; see "New Designs in Silver," *Good Furniture Magazine* 34 (May 1930): 273. The Chase flyer is illustrated in Donald-Brian Johnson and Leslie Piña, *The Chase Era* (Atglen, Pa.: Schiffer, 2001), 18. For the boxed set, see Jim Linz, *Art Deco Chrome* (Atglen, Pa.: Schiffer, 1999), 47. My thanks to Vicki Matranga and John C. Waddell for their assistance in this research. See also Sarah C. Nichols et al., *Aluminum By Design*, exh. cat. (New York: Abrams, in association with Carnegie Museum of Art, Pittsburgh, 2000).

6. Richard F. Bach, "Contemporary American Industrial Art: 1934," in *Contemporary American Industrial Art*, exh. cat. Metropolitan Museum of Art, New York, 1934, 8.

7. "Contemporary American Industrial Art," *Bulletin of the Metropolitan Museum of Art* 29 (Dec. 1934): 204.

8. Bach, "Contemporary American Industrial Art," 8–9.

9. Ibid., 10.

10. Ibid., 7.

11. Ibid., 205.

12. For the colors in the Room for a Lady, see "Clearly Contemporary," *Country Life* 67 (Jan. 1935): 65.

13. Produced in the Wilcox Silver Plate division of International as "number 5873 urn, $80," and "number 5875 tray, diameter 18 inches, $30" (International Silver Company Archives, Meriden Historical Society, Meriden, Conn.; hereafter International Silver Archives). The prototype urn and tray are in the Cranbrook Art Museum, accession number 1935.8.

14. My thanks to John C. Waddell for sharing his research on Saarinen's urn and tray.

15. Saarinen's gate, with the crested crane motif, is located on Lone Pine Road at the south end and axis of the Triton pools. The gate, executed by Walter Nichols (1864–1951), a blacksmith at Cranbrook, was installed in July 1941, and is commonly referred to as the "Nichols" gate. My thanks to Gary S. Griffin and Leslie Edwards of Cranbrook for their research on and images of the gate.

16. For Czeschka, see A. Krekel-Aalberse, J. R. ter Molen, and R. J. Willink, eds., *Silver of a New Era: International Highlights of Precious Metalware from 1880 to 1940*, exh. cat. Museum Boymans van-Beuningen, Rotterdam, and Museum voor Sierkunst, Ghent (Seattle: University of Washington Press, 1992), 196. See also a group of similar Austrian covered cups originally in *Dekorative Kunst* (Munich) 11 (1903): 40 and illustrated in *Viennese Silver, Modern Design, 1780–1918*, exh. cat., Neue Galerie, New York, 2003, 182.

17. The attenuated finial of the urn is similar to the finial on Czeschka's covered cup; see Krekel-Aalberse, ter Molen, and Willink, *Silver of a New Era*, 196, 198.

18. Prototypes in the Cranbrook Art Museum, accession numbers 1936.1, 1936.2, and 1936.3. No evidence has been found that any of the three went into production.

19. The exhibition was installed in three sections in the Gallery of Special Exhibitions (D6): the Central Gallery Unit, West Gallery Unit, and East Gallery Unit.

20. "At Metropolitan Museum," *International Silver Service* newsletter 3 (Jan.–Feb. 1935): 6. The whereabouts of the exhibited prototype is not known.

21. Lobel's service was produced by the Wilcox Silver Plate division of International as "number 5873 coffee set, four pieces, $65." Each of the four pieces was also offered individually. In the exhibition catalogue the set was called a "tea service," but the production-line version was called a "coffee set" by International in its Wilcox Silver Plate division salesman's catalogue, plate 4449 (International Silver Archives).

22. My thanks to John C. Waddell for alerting me to this feature.

23. Everett, "Table Silver Feels Change."

24. A three-piece coffee set by Lobel, but without the tray and marked "made exclusively for Carole Stupell," an upscale tabletop and accessory shop in New York City at the time, has come to light; see Claude Blair, ed., *History of Silver* (New York: Ballantine, 1987), 211.

25. Both the shaker and the tray were produced by International; see "At Metropolitan Museum." Lobel's cocktail shaker was also illustrated in "A Parade of Contemporary Achievements at the Metropolitan Museum," *Arts and Decoration* 42 (Dec. 1934): 13.

26. Lobel's shaker was produced by the Wilcox Silver Plate division of International as "number 5874 mixer, height 11 inches, wicker wound neck, $12" (salesman's catalogue, plate 4468; International Silver Archives). For Catalin, see "At Metropolitan Museum."

27. A photograph of Guild's shaker was published, but no examples have come to light, nor has research in the International Silver Archives confirmed production. This shaker was not part of the *Gift Ware* or *Contemporary Group* signature holloware designed by Guild for International. From the archival photograph of the East Case of the Central Unit it is not possible to identify conclusively the covered dish by Guild. Other pieces by Guild were displayed in the West Case, directly across from the East Case in the Central Gallery Unit, but these, too, have not been conclusively identified.

28. The whereabouts of Deskey's coffee set and bonbon and almond dishes are not known.

29. Mueller-Munk's holloware was moved from the General Group in the West Gallery Unit, its original location. See "Additions and Changes," *Contemporary American Industrial Art*.

30. See "Original Designs in Silver," *Arts and Decoration* 42 (Apr. 1935): 28.

31. For Mueller-Munk's candelabra, see Janet Kardon, ed., *Craft in the Machine Age 1920–1945: The History of Twentieth-Century American Craft*, exh. cat. (New York: Abrams, in association with the American Craft Museum, 1995), 182.

32. "Tea Services by Famous Viennese Craftsmen," *Arts and Decoration* 32 (Nov. 1929): 55; and C. G. Holme, ed., *Decorative Art Year-Book* (London: The Studio, 1931), 158.

33. Exhibition files, Metropolitan Museum of Art Archives.

CHAPTER SIX

STYLES OF THE 1930S

Stylistically, the design vocabulary of the 1930s differed in major ways from that of the 1920s. Two trends predominated: a modern interpretation of classicism and a freshly minted aesthetic derived from the design of modern machines, particularly those for transportation. Although more abstract, the former retained the classicism of *art moderne,* while the latter, known as streamlining, was a quintessential American response to the Machine Age. "Speed lines" and rounded corners became emblematic of streamlined product design including silver. Naturalistic elements in imported Scandinavian silver, especially that of Georg Jensen, were emulated by manufacturers to satisfy more conservative taste. A fascination with lush, exotic locations opened to tourism by Pan American Airways in the mid-1930s influenced the design of silverware at the end of the decade.

Modern Classicism

Neoclassicism had been an important current in *art moderne,* and in the 1920s modern American silver had incorporated references to it in combination with others in vogue. For example, a compote (fig. 6.1) made in 1928–1929 and described by International as "a very unusual and artistic piece so classic that it reminds one of ancient Greek incense altars" has stepped layering in the base and in other elements.[1] In 1932 International introduced *Empress,* a sterling flatware pattern by the staff designer Alfred G. Kintz, with a classical fan-shaped lotus-palmette at the tip of the handles (fig. 6.2).

The improvement in the economy that began slowly in about 1933 ushered in a classical revival in architecture and design. The classicism that burst upon the scene in 1934 and persisted for the rest of the decade differed from earlier iterations in its extreme simplification and abstraction. It is often referred to in architecture and design as "stripped" or "modern" classicism. Modern classicism and streamlining were the two dominant design idioms of the decade. This phenomenon was clearly articulated by an astute contemporary observer writing on tableware in 1937:

The present day trend of modern design in its reflection in tableware of all kinds is a distinctly simple severe style with little or no ornamentation. Simplicity of form with the emphasis on form itself is an essential characteristic. . . . Streamlining has affected the design not only of airplanes, ships and automobiles, but also silver, china and glassware. . . . There are two schools of thought, one which has ostensibly discarded all previous conceptions of design and attacked the problem at hand from a purely utilitarian point of view and working from that to a realization of beauty through refining or emphasizing the structural basis; *the other starting point is the classic form, adapting and simplifying them* [sic] *to our present-day uses without losing the essential idea* [emphasis added].[2]

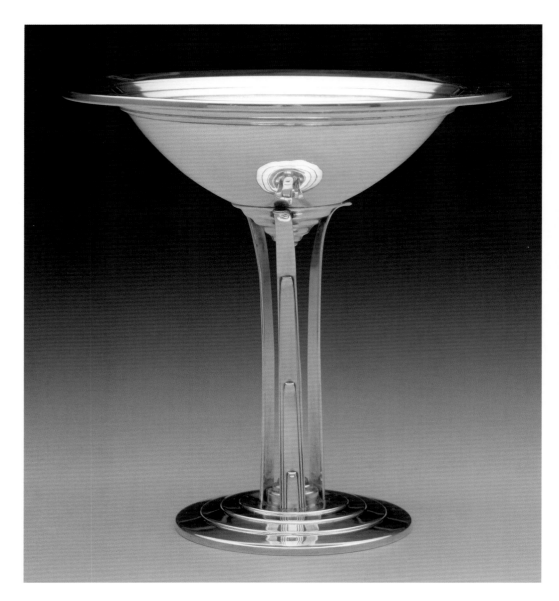

In the forefront of the modern classical revival in silver was the manufacturer Rogers, Lunt & Bowlen, which in 1934 introduced a new sterling flatware and holloware pattern named *Modern Classic* created by the outside consultant Robert E. Locher (1888–1956), an internationally renowned American interior designer. On the heels of *Modern Classic* came *Dorian* from the Watson Company, *Classic Modern* from Wallace, and others styled similarly.

The contrast between the decorative *Empress* of only two years earlier (see fig. 6.2) and Locher's reductive *Modern Classic* demonstrates the difference between earlier interpretations of classicism and post-1933 abstractions. In the spring of 1934 the manufacturer announced the pattern with a two-page advertisement in *House Beautiful* (fig. 6.3). The designer was acknowledged in a photograph (fig. 6.4) and his accomplishments praised in the caption, a rare gesture of recognition in the silver trade, although it had been granted to Erik Magnussen by Gorham in 1928 for *Modern American*. The credit was clearly meant to elevate the status of the pattern by association with Locher's notable

FIGURE 6.1   Compote, 1928–1929. Wilcox & Evertson Fine Arts. Silver. The Jewel Stern American Silver Collection, cat. 121

FIGURE 6.2   *Empress* place fork, 1932. Wilcox & Evertsen Fine Arts, Alfred G. Kintz, designer. Silver. Dallas Museum of Art, cat. 122

reputation and prominent clients. Classicism was hailed as the "essence of the modern spirit" and the pattern as a "modern classic." The proportions of the slim handles and the raised center panel that rolled over the top into a "trim and effective scroll on the back" were extolled as classic.[3] From 1934 on, new applications of classicism became widespread throughout industrial design.[4]

The reception of *Modern Classic* was resounding. A contemporary critic lauded Locher for reaching a new height with his "purity of line,"[5] which is the most prominent attribute of Locher's massive *Modern Classic* floral centerpiece with a mesh cover and circular tray (fig. 6.5). The scale and weight of this rare centerpiece and under tray, which like all the holloware in the line were stamped with the signature of the designer, were extraordinary in light of the still-distressed economy. Exemplary of stripped classicism, the smooth surfaces of the bowl and tray are unadorned. The mesh carries the classical allusions of the composition, openwork in a graphic pattern that evokes the coffered ceiling of the dome of the Pantheon in Rome, and is discreetly accented by a diminutive, scroll-shaped handle in its center that echoes the flatware. *Modern Classic* was popular for the balance of the decade. In 1936, *Arts and Decoration* deemed the pattern "perhaps the most dramatic of the settings for this winter's functions" and its name entered the lexicon of the 1930s as a term that delineated a style.[6] A trade publication in 1936, for example, described an International tea service as "modern-classic" and in "perfect keeping with the modern trend."[7] In tandem with the New York World's Fair in 1939, the McCutcheon's store on Fifth Avenue presented an invitational exhibit entitled *The Masculine Slant on Smart Table Settings,* in which Locher's entry was a Luncheon for a Designer's Board set with *Modern Classic* flatware.[8]

The Watson Company introduced *Dorian,* a sterling pattern in flatware and holloware by the English-born industrial silver designer Percy B. Ball (1879–1957), in the spring of 1935. In the advertisement the association of the name with the Doric column in Greek architecture was accentuated with a drawing of a Doric capital (fig. 6.6). In the text Watson assured readers that classic tradition was "continually reasserting itself" and was "eternally correct for all formal or informal occasions." The copy emphasized the simplicity and modernity of *Dorian* and noted that it met the "demand" of consumers for a "plainer" pattern.[9] Interestingly, in an article he wrote for *Country Life,* Locher heaped praise on the illustrated *Dorian* coffeepot for being "up-to-date yet classic in its flowing lines" (see fig. 8.2, right).[10] *Dorian* holloware was also shown in the Metropolitan Museum

of Art's *Silver: An Exhibition of Contemporary American Design by Manufacturers, Designers and Craftsmen* in 1937, and examples were illustrated in upscale magazines, among them, *Arts and Decoration* and *Creative Design.*[11]

In 1935 Wallace Silversmiths introduced *Vogue* by the company's English-born head designer William S. Warren (1887–1965), a silverplated flatware pattern also derived from Greek architecture. With its scroll tip and fluted stem, the *Vogue* handle (see fig. 8.8) was a more literal appropriation of the Ionic order than *Dorian* was of the Doric order. A distinctive element is the narrow panel that continued the vertical line of the handle into the bowls. The flatware was designed to be sold for informal buffet service, a concept becoming more socially acceptable during stressful economic times, and the layout of the advertisement (fig. 6.7) underscored that by showing a full service for eight together with serving pieces. In the copy the fresh interpretation of classicism in *Vogue* was described as "modern" and "smart" and the flatware all a "young hostess' heart could desire."[12] Wallace produced a moderately priced silverplated holloware group with classical motifs cleverly named *Classic Modern* though unrelated to *Vogue.* For this pattern *art moderne* stepped bases were retained, vessels were fluted, and the rims of dishes and trays were notched, an allusion to classical columns and moldings (fig. 6.8, right).[13]

International (unlike Rogers, Lunt & Bowlen, Watson, or Wallace) did not produce a new flatware pattern to capitalize on the taste for modern classicism, but

FIGURE 6.3 "Announcing MODERN CLASSIC," Rogers, Lunt & Bowlen advertisement, 1934

FIGURE 6.4 Robert E. Locher, c. 1934

FIGURE 6.5 *Modern Classic* centerpiece, 1934. Rogers, Lunt &
Bowlen, Robert E. Locher, designer. Silver. DMA, JSASC, cat. 215

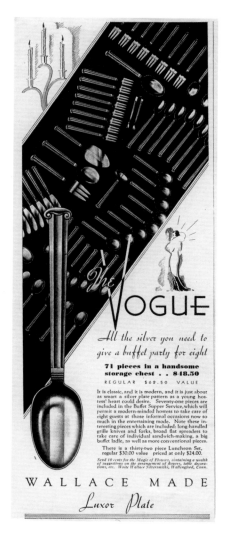

FIGURE 6.6 "Fascinating Dorian," Watson Company advertisement, 1935

FIGURE 6.7 "The Vogue," R. Wallace & Sons advertisement, 1935

did incorporate classical elements, especially fluting and reeding, in its holloware. Like the designs of other manufacturers, many were hybrids that combined classicism with streamlining and residues of *art moderne*. A luxurious six-piece sterling and ivory tea and coffee service with a matching tray was inexplicably named *Continental,* although it was unrelated to the austere *Continental* flatware pattern of 1934. Attempts have been made to attribute this service to Donald Deskey because the bodies, spouts, and lids of the vessels appear identical to the prototype coffee set he designed for the Metropolitan Museum of Art's exhibition *Contemporary American Industrial Art* in 1934 (see fig. 5.8).[14] Deskey, however, reportedly said that his prototype did not go into production and there is no record of it in the International Silver Company's archives.[15] Manufacturers often recycle dies in order to minimize costs, adding new elements to transform earlier designs. Although the whereabouts of Deskey's coffee set is unknown, a comparison of a photograph of it with the *Continental* service coffeepot (fig. 6.9) strongly suggests that International was recycling parts for the latter. Deskey's prototype had overlapping silver and black plastic or wood handles in an abstract configuration; the handles of the *Continental* service are silver and ivory in the ponytail

shape. The *Continental* service has ivory finials and fluted bases, whereas those on Deskey's set were black plastic or wood, respectively, and smooth. The trays for the services are completely unalike. Although the ponytail handles had a precedent in a tea service designed in 1928 by Josef Hoffmann at the Wiener Werkstätte,[16] the inspiration for the *Continental* service was more likely to have been Poole's *Silvermode* coffee set with ponytail handles that had been designed by Peter Mueller-Munk and also shown at the Metropolitan Museum of Art in 1934 (see fig. 5.11). The price of the complete *Continental* service, which was probably produced between 1935 and 1938, was $750, astonishingly expensive for those years and for International. By comparison, the company was offering a modernist five-piece sterling tea service complete with kettle, stand, and tray for $375, about half the price.[17] The high cost of the former indicates that it was developed for the upper end of the market and that production was limited.

Although not in the vanguard, Reed & Barton responded to the cues from competitors and entered

the field in 1936 with *Jubilee*, a sterling flatware pattern designed by the architect Carl Conrad Braun (1905–1998), and holloware lines by the industrial designer Belle Kogan, both of whom were consultants to the company. In the introductory advertisement Reed & Barton claimed that *Jubilee* skillfully interpreted the "decorative mood of the moment," and boasted that it would become the "sterling classic of its era."[18] Clearly meant to compete with earlier modern classic patterns, the flatware has pointed handles that are reeded and taper at the join to a motif based on Greek key frets (fig. 6.10). Braun also designed an elaborate and expensive seven-piece sterling tea service named *Vogue*, for which his patented *Jubilee* handle was the primary motif (fig. 6.11).[19] A highly decorative hybrid design that had in addition to the applied *Jubilee* motif, carved reeded handles and finials, flared and fanned spouts, and stepped lids, the *Vogue* service was a more traditional rendition of classicism than were other objects of the period.[20] In promotional material to the trade Reed & Barton stressed the design's classical references and aura of luxury: "This distinctive service, though modern in the best sense of the word is inspired

FIGURE 6.8   Left: Salad bowl, 1936. Reed & Barton, Belle Kogan, designer. Silver, cat. 169; right: *Classic Modern* pitcher, c. 1935. R. Wallace & Sons Manufacturing Company. Silverplate, cat. 295. DMA, JSASC

FIGURE 6.9   *Continental* coffeepot, c. 1935–1938. International Silver Company. Silver, ivory. The Wolfsonian–Florida International University, Miami Beach, Florida, The Mitchell Wolfson Jr. Collection, cat. 109

FIGURE 6.10 *Jubilee* flatware, 1936. Reed & Barton, Carl Conrad
Braun, designer. Silver, stainless steel. Dallas Museum of Art, cat. 168

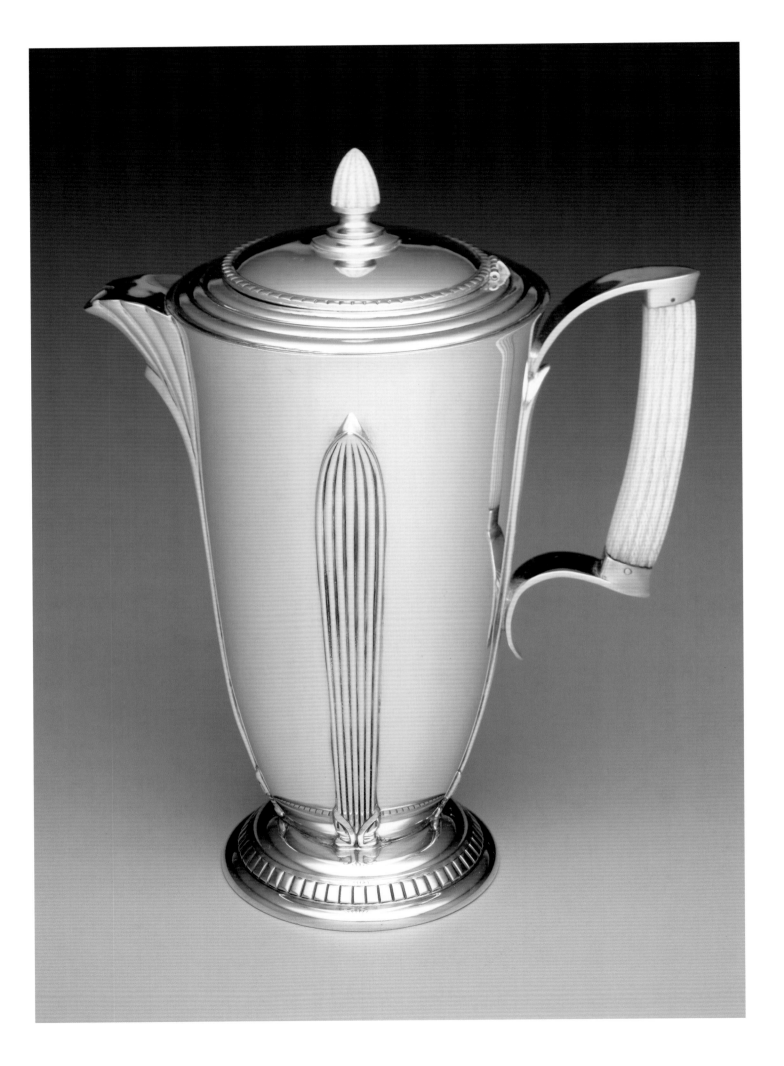

FIGURE 6.11 *Vogue* coffeepot, 1938. Reed & Barton, Carl Conrad Braun, designer. Silver, ivory. DMA, JSASC, cat. 175

FIGURE 6.12 Left: Sandwich tray, 1939. Tiffany & Co. Silver, cat. 244; right: Bowl, 1936. Reed & Barton. Silver, cat. 165. DMA, JSASC

by the noble creations of the early Greeks and Etruscans. The exquisite fluting of the leaf motif is reminiscent of the Parthenon's graceful columns, and the elegant hand-carved ivory handles hark back to the luxurious days of ancient Rome."[21] In contrast to International's *Continental* service, this one would have appealed to a more conservative yet affluent clientele, and undoubtedly Reed & Barton oriented the *Vogue* service to that sector of the market. Another example of the company's essay into classicism is a sterling bowl (fig. 6.12, right), the work of a staff designer, that has motifs that suggest fluting, but also a stepped base encircled with a classical frieze.

Tiffany's contribution to modern classicism appeared later in the 1930s. In 1937 the company produced

a vibrant design for flatware serving pieces that prominently featured the Greek anthemion motif derived from the Egyptian lotus-palmette. The tip of the layered handle, however, relied on more recent precedents in *art moderne* and the high-styled French jewelry of the late 1930s (fig. 6.13). For a small group of holloware objects Tiffany resorted, in 1939, to restrained classical motifs, a border embellished with leaf and flower festoons at equal intervals with linear incising between them to suggest fluting (see fig. 6.12, left).

BELLE KOGAN: "THE SILVER LADY"

One of the earliest women industrial designers, Belle Kogan (1902–2000; fig. 6.14), who had been born in Russia but educated in America, created her first silverware about 1929 as a freelancer for the Quaker Silver Company of North Attleboro, Massachusetts. In 1933 the enterprising and talented fledgling designer opened her own studio in New York City. Remarkably, by 1935 she numbered among her clients Ebeling and Reuss, Inc. for china, Warren Telechron Company for clock cases, and the Celluloid Corporation for vanity sets.[22] That year, under her own auspices, she displayed her products at the National Alliance of Art and Industry's *Industrial Arts Exposition* in Rockefeller Center in which International, Wallace, and the Poole silver companies were also represented.[23] For her numerous articles in trade journals and other publications on silverware, its proper usage, care, and stylistic trends, and her designs for Quaker, Reed & Barton, Towle, and Samuel Kirk & Son, of Baltimore, Maryland, Kogan was known in the field as "The Silver Lady."[24]

In retrospect, her most important work was done for Reed & Barton, especially the two groups that she designed in 1936 in the modern classic idiom, with the ornament wedded to the form for a functional purpose.[25] This was most forcefully expressed in the silverplated group. On uncovered pieces the only decoration consisted of a reeded panel centered lengthwise that unfurled over the rims to serve as curved handles. The best example is the large "meat dish" (fig. 6.15).[26] The most developed piece in the group is the double vegetable dish, an artistic triumph for which the designer used a limited palette of line and form to merge the modern classic and streamline styles (fig. 6.16). The reeded band and handles were retained for the interior of the dish. The hard edge of the rectangular rim contrasts with the curved contours of both the dish and cover, which when inverted serves as another dish. Exterior reeded bands unify the two components by sweeping over the cover and up the shorter sides of the dish to meet at

FIGURE 6.13 Salad serving fork, 1937. Tiffany & Co. Gilded silver. DMA, JSASC, cat. 242

the handles. Each end of the cover band is intersected by a straight row of five connected balls that evokes machine precision. The placement and contrast of the small spherical elements with the dominant parallels in a composition otherwise devoid of ornamentation was a simple, brilliant strategy to punctuate and anchor the design. A barely visible narrow reeded base provides a subtle classical reinforcement to the composition. Of all the silver objects that Kogan designed during her career, this covered vegetable dish represents the apogee of her power as a designer in the medium.

For the sterling holloware group, Kogan's approach was less restrictive and more ornate. Reeded panels that extended to form handles were carried over and were bracketed by decorative scroll and bead motifs, and the shallow bases were incised to suggest the triglyphs found in Doric architecture (see fig. 6.8, left). In 1937 Reed & Barton proudly loaned examples from these two groups by Kogan to the Brooklyn Museum for the exhibition *Contemporary Industrial and Handwrought Silver* (see fig. 8.9).

Streamlining: A Machine Aesthetic

> Machinery, a new factor in human affairs,
> has aroused a new spirit.
> —Le Corbusier

Whereas the skyscraper had provided an authentic symbol for American modernism in the 1920s, streamlining took its place in the 1930s as the ultimate modernist

FIGURE 6.14 Belle Kogan, 1940

statement and became a distinct style identifiable in architecture and product design. A scientific concept originally applied to hydrodynamics and later to aerodynamics, streamlining took its cues in product design from the innovative transportation vehicles of the time, the latest automobiles, trains, ships, and aircraft, which represented speed, efficiency, and progress. The new field of industrial design and its pioneers, Norman Bel Geddes, Henry Dreyfuss, Raymond Loewy, Walter Dorwin Teague, and Lurelle Guild, among them, had the most impact on the style. The utopian faith in

FIGURE 6.15 Meat dish, 1936. Reed & Barton, Belle Kogan, designer. Silverplate. DMA, JSASC, cat. 174

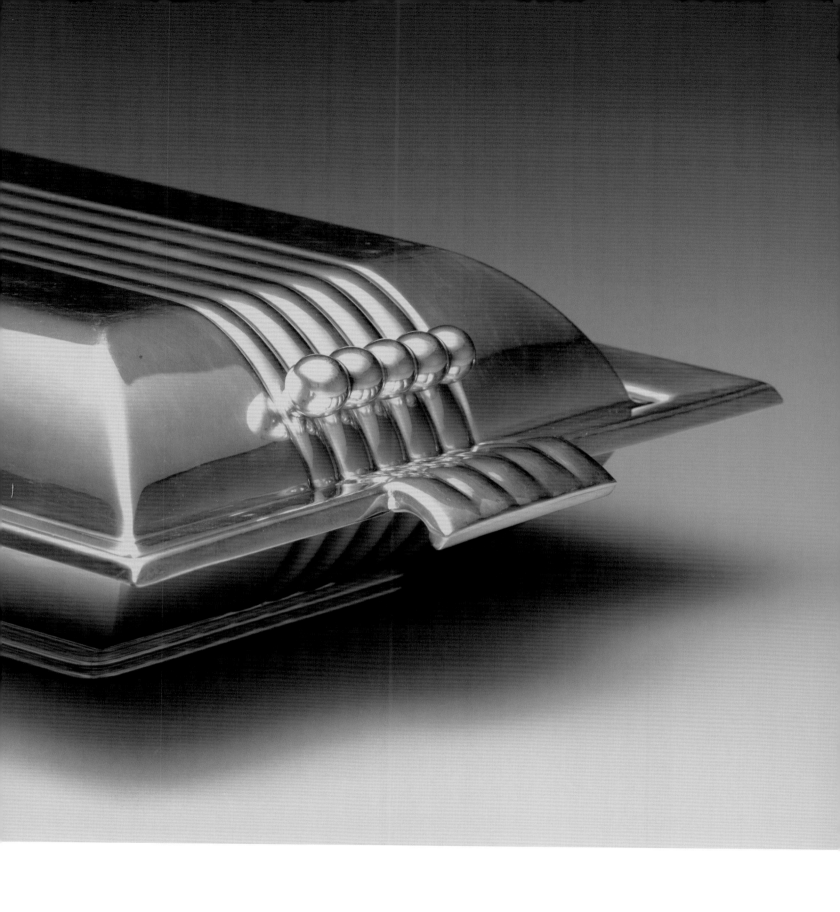

FIGURE 6.16 Double vegetable dish, 1936. Reed & Barton, Belle Kogan, designer. Silverplate. DMA, JSASC, cat. 173

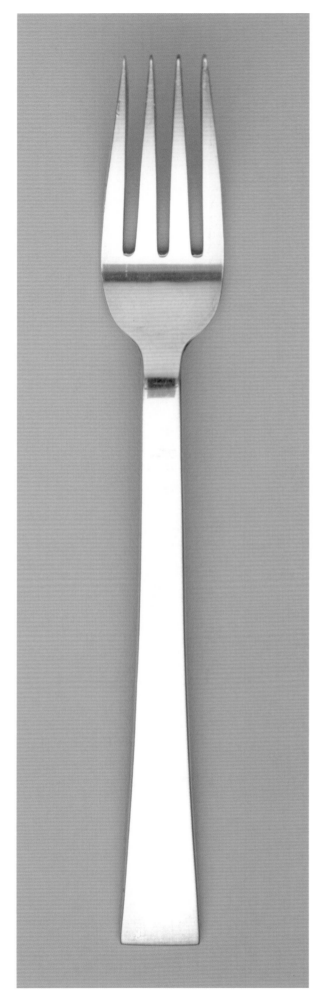

the unlimited potential of advances in science and technology would find its best expression at the New York World's Fair in 1939, with its optimistic theme: Building the World of Tomorrow.

The first wide-reaching public exposure to streamlining, however, occurred several years earlier, in 1933, at the *Century of Progress Exposition* in Chicago and was confirmed by three events at the exposition in 1934, during its second year: the debuts of the Chrysler Airflow automobile and of two streamliner trains. The exhibit of Union Pacific's new train, the City of Salinas, was visited by more than a million people, and the arrival of the Burlington Zephyr on its first run drew gaping sightseers as the Goodyear blimp floated over the crowds.[27] Meanwhile in New York the Museum of Modern Art had presented *Machine Art,* a seminal exhibition espousing an aesthetic of machine purity. That same year the Metropolitan Museum of Art mounted its thirteenth exhibition of *Contemporary American Industrial Art.* On the Co-operating Committee organizing the exhibits were the architects Ely Jacques Kahn and Ralph T. Walker, who had been involved in the planning and design of the *Century of Progress Exposition.* Not surprisingly, a sleek, streamlined Designer's Office and Studio by Lee Simonson and the industrial designer Raymond Loewy was one of the room displays at the Metropolitan. The influence of machine purity and the predilection for basic geometric forms, such as the sphere, were visible in commissioned designs fabricated by International Silver, especially Saarinen's tea urn and Lobel's tea service (see figs. 5.3, 5.6).

The prominent characteristics of the streamlined style were the simplification of form, sculptural plasticity, absence of surface ornament, and emphasis on flowing horizontal lines, often parallel, with rounded corners to express continuous movement and speed. Evoking the essential qualities of machines, streamlining eschewed traditional motifs and historical references. Like machines, it was impersonal and its imagery abstract. These features would be rapidly appropriated by manufacturers in their bid to lure consumers out of the spending doldrums of the Depression. Beginning in 1934, the silver industry tested the marketplace. International's sterling flatware pattern *Continental* by the German-born staff designer Frederick W. Stark (1885–1969), was introduced that year (fig. 6.17). Totally devoid of surface decoration, the austere lines of *Continental* would have been ideal for the *Machine Art* exhibition, but the pattern was not available so the Museum of Modern Art resorted to Gorham's *Covington Plain*

FIGURE 6.17 *Continental* luncheon fork, 1934. International Silver Company, Frederick W. Stark, designer. Silver. Dallas Museum of Art, cat. 108

FIGURE 6.18   Mayonnaise bowl, 1934. Gorham Manufacturing Company. Silver. DMA, JSASC, cat. 30

(1914) and *Dolly Madison* (1929), traditional sterling patterns lacking decoration, for the House Furnishings and Accessories section of the exhibition.[28] Alerted early to the aim of the exhibition, Gorham produced a mayonnaise bowl (fig. 6.18) that, in its simplicity, was an embodiment of the machine aesthetic.[29] The smooth, undecorated contours, the ring-shaped handle that punctuates the design and balances the pouring spout, and the overall precision contribute to the eloquence of this small object.

By the mid-1930s streamlining conveyed modernity and was applied to all kinds of static objects to evoke the speed, efficiency, and progress inherent in transportation symbols and to capitalize on their magnetism.[30] Streamlined merchandise became an asset, and other silver manufacturers eager to stimulate sales in a stagnant economy embraced the style. Napier responded with a number of designs including two silverplated cream and sugar sets. For one, a stacked, compact model (fig. 6.19, right) cleverly named *The Duplex* to associate it with sophisticated urban living and to appeal to apartment dwellers, the spherical shape favored by Saarinen and Lobel was adopted. Curved contours, clean unadorned, mirrorlike surfaces, and harmonious proportions informed this innovative design. Napier also suggested an alternative function for *The Duplex*:

with hot water in the sugar bowl and butter in the cream pitcher placed over the bowl, the set could be used for drawn butter. *The Duplex* was a model of efficiency, a value prized by industrial designers in the 1930s. For another set (see fig. 6.19, left), characterized by streamlined minimalism, the flattened spherical bodies and curved handles visually reinforce the contours. In 1936 Reed & Barton produced a pitcher on which, notwithstanding the retention of some classical detailing, aerodynamic force was expressed in the upward thrust of the spout and the curving handle (fig. 6.20).

THE HELEN HUGHES DULANY STUDIO

Like the trajectory of a comet, the career of the industrial designer Helen Hughes Dulany (1885–1968) of Chicago rose rapidly in the 1930s, blazed brilliantly but briefly, and burned out. Dulany (fig. 6.21) was the second wife of George W. Dulany Jr., a graduate of Yale University and an immensely successful lumberman, who was listed in *Who's Who in America* in the 1930s.[31] From a "hobby of modeling clay" while recuperating from a serious illness in about 1930 she reportedly "discovered her talent for design."[32] In 1931 the Helen Hughes Dulany

FIGURE 6.19 Left and center: Creamer and sugar bowl, c. 1936, cat. 143; right: *The Duplex* cream and sugar set, c. 1936, cat. 142. Napier Company. Gilded silverplate. DMA, JSASC

Studio was first listed in the Chicago city directory. By 1934 Dulany's stunning modernist table accessories in a variety of materials were featured in *House Beautiful, Arts and Decoration,* and *Country Life in America,* where she was depicted as a trendsetter.[33] She established a factory to produce her own designs and provided consulting and styling service to industry.[34] Her status was indicated by her inclusion along with Donald Deskey, Henry Dreyfuss, and others in *Creative Design*'s "Directory of Contemporary Designers" in 1934.[35]

Dulany was listed in the directory as a consultant with the Chicago architects Holabird & Root on interiors and table appointments for the new Burlington Zephyr train,[36] and it was noted that she was "making some designs for International Silver."[37] No record of her work for International has yet been found. A rare pair of triple candelabra in silverplate and stamped with her hallmark, "HHD STUDIO" (fig. 6.22), shows Dulany's appreciation of the machine aesthetic and her ability to convey it dramatically with the simplest forms, cylinders, circular cutouts, and flat rectangular planes. This intriguing design, in which the two bracketing candles have to be inserted in their sockets through circular

openings in an upper horizontal element, may have been an experiment.[38]

At the height of her career in 1935, Dulany and her husband separated. They were divorced in December 1936, the last year in which the Helen Hughes Dulany Studio was included in the Chicago city directory.[39] Her last published notice appeared in 1937, in an article in the *New York Times* about outstanding women industrial designers.[40] The divorce abruptly closed down her studio and terminated her business. Almost overnight, Dulany disappeared from the industrial design field.

LURELLE GUILD

Lurelle Guild (1898–1986), a prolific industrial designer with an affinity for household products, was ranked as one of the ten "most active and successful designers" in the country by the mid-1930s (fig. 6.23) and, unlike Dulany, had a long, illustrious career.[41] The extent of his creative gifts was demonstrated by the simultaneous production of new designs in tabletop accessories for clients that included the Kensington division of Alcoa, the Chase Brass & Copper Company, and the International Silver Company. As the Depression began to lift, the enterprising Guild sent a proposal to Horace C.

FIGURE 6.20 Pitcher, 1936. Reed & Barton. Silverplate. DMA, JSASC, cat. 167

FIGURE 6.21 Helen Hughes Dulany, *Chicago Daily Tribune*, 1936

FIGURE 6.22 Candelabra, c. 1935. Helen Hughes Dulany Studio, Helen Hughes Dulany, designer. Silverplate. DMA, JSASC, cat. 10

"Hod" Wilcox, the director of holloware sales for International: "In the past six months I have developed a new and practical plan for the designing of silverware which, to my knowledge, has never been used by any firm, and I feel that it has in it a definite progressive step forward for the promotion of selling. May I have a brief interview to show you this plan?"[42] Guild's designs for the *Gift Ware* silverplate line of coordinated holloware serving pieces that was introduced in early 1934 were the fruits of that interview. Helen Sprackling, the decorative arts correspondent for the *New York Herald Tribune*, lauded International for being the first manufacturer to offer "matched giftware in the modern form." She noted, too, that the signature of Lurelle Guild as the designer on each piece gave the line "a distinction hitherto found only in exclusive, custom-made work."[43] *Gift Ware* was announced in a full-page color advertisement (see fig. 7.3), and a catalogue exclusively for the line was published. A selection of almost every type of container was offered: trays, bowls, covered dishes, candlesticks, boxes, compotes, vases, cocktail shakers, a wine cooler, a pitcher, salts and peppers, and coffee sets. Sleek surfaces predominated and the emphasis was on shape, especially the octagon, a holdover from 1920s *art moderne*. The outstanding decorative elements were "thread borders," ribbed bases, and reeded handles that, in the catalogue, were described as "classical modern" in feeling.[44] Enamel finishes in a choice of several colors were offered in a number of items. Guild negotiated a royalty of 2½ percent of sales for his design of *Gift Ware*, receiving, for example, $235.47 on sales of $9,418.95 in the last quarter of 1934.[45] The volume of business generated quickly prompted International to develop a complementary signature line in *Gift Ware* named *The Contemporary Group*.

Throughout the design process Guild and Harrison Corbin, a principal in the holloware sales division, carried on a spirited correspondence, humorously addressing each other as "Major" and "General," respectively. Corbin, Guild's primary contact at International, anticipated a demand for a larger after-dinner coffeepot and suggested one for *The Contemporary Group*,[46] so Guild designed a coffee set named "His Royal Highness" (fig. 6.24) and described extravagantly in the catalogue: "Received with acclaim! An After Dinner Coffee Pot of truly majestic capacity that will eliminate for the embarrassed hostess those painfully obvious 'refill' trips to the culinary regions." The sales representatives were admonished to "demonstrate the capacity. More need not be said."[47] Guild's showmanship shines in this foot-high domed coffeepot in which 1920s stepped and layered details, a streamlined threaded base, a Jensenesque flourish for the naturalistic bud finial, and an ebony side handle all coexist harmoniously.[48] Enthusiasm for the

FIGURE 6.23 Lurelle Guild. "Tomorrow's products are designed by this genius and his pencil," Venus-Velvet Pencils advertisement, 1934

stylish *Gift Ware* lines began to fade late in 1935 and on December 31 several items were discontinued, including the *Column* compote (which had been used on the cover of the *Gift Ware* catalogue as the logo for the line) and the *Empire* bowl.[49] A handwritten memo in a salesman's catalogue noted the termination of the lines: "All Giftware Disc. Dec. 1936."[50]

SPEED LINES

Although Guild mixed decorative elements in some *Gift Ware* items, during the 1930s most industrial designers, intent on smooth contours and horizontal profiles, eliminated surface ornament except for narrowly spaced parallel bands that alluded to speed and were often grouped in units of three.[51] These serial bands, or speed lines, became the primary decoration on the vast majority of consumer goods from household appliances of all sorts to casings for radios, clocks, and cameras. Abundant evidence survives confirming the ubiquity of this motif in modern industrial silver holloware of the period, including exemplary designs by the Stieff Company of Baltimore, Maryland, Currier & Roby of New York, Napier, Reed & Barton, Rogers, Lunt & Bowlen, Weidlich Brothers, and International (fig. 6.25; see also fig. 7.12). Noteworthy in this group are accessories that reveal the growing social acceptance, especially for women, of smoking in public. The novel sterling and plastic humidor by Stieff was based on a patent filed in 1935.[52] A box that Reed & Barton promoted in its "New 1937 Christmas Folder" as generous in size could hold more than a hundred cigarettes.[53]

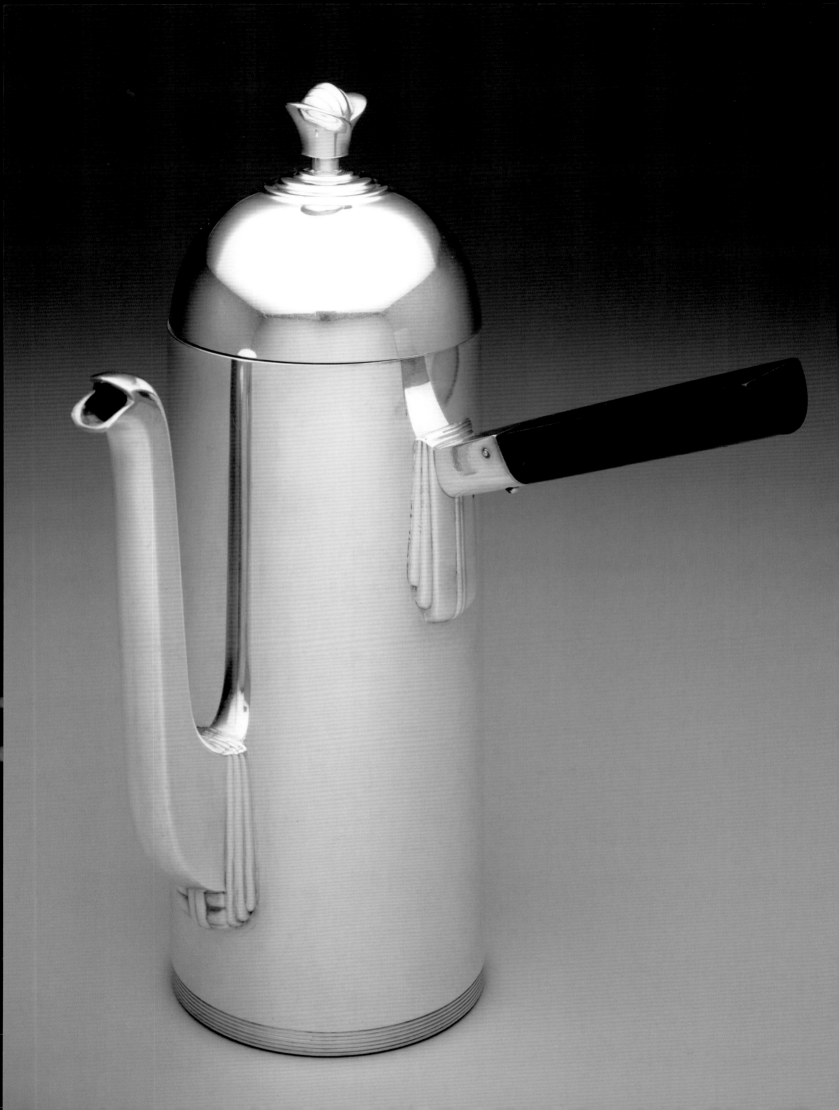

The most spectacular streamlined silver object made in the 1930s was the K. K. Culver Trophy for the Miami All American Air Maneuvers (fig. 6.26). Unequivocally one of the finest examples of twentieth-century modern presentation silver, the trophy embodied streamlining in a symbolic culmination of the aesthetic thrust of the decade. Named for the donor, Knight K. Culver, the president of Dart Air Craft Corporation in Columbus, Ohio, the trophy was commissioned from Viktor Schreckengost and executed in silverplate by the Bronze Division of Gorham in 1939. A prize for the winner of a fifty-mile straight course for women pilots, a competition inaugurated in 1939 and envisioned as being held annually for the next ten years, the trophy was awarded only once, to Edna Gardner of New Orleans, Louisiana. The panel for 1939 bears an inscription honoring her achievement.[54] From the prow of the base, which consists of three stacked and staggered blocks, a tapered shaft rises to support a partially draped female figure mounted horizontally in a sweeping pose, body arched upward and

FIGURE 6.25   Back left: Cigarette humidor, 1946. The Stieff Company. Silver, plastic, cat. 223; back, center: Cocktail shaker, c. 1936. International Silver Company. Silverplate, cat. 74; back, right: Candlesticks, c. 1935. Currier & Roby. Silver, cat. 7; front, left and center: Creamer and sugar bowl, 1936. Reed & Barton. Gilded silver, cat. 166; front, right: Cigarette box, 1937. Reed & Barton. Silverplate, cat. 172. DMA, JSASC

hair streaming, a gesture invoking aerodynamic flight. A miniature, gold-plated model of the winning airplane (a monocoupe in 1939) was to hang from the figure's hands for a year and then be presented to the pilot, together with a small replica of the trophy.[55] The design recalls the Rockefeller Center in New York City, an icon of the 1930s that may have inspired Schreckengost. The stylized female figure resembles Paul Manship's gilded *Prometheus* sculpture in the fountain of the sunken plaza in the Center and the floating figures in Robert Garrison's relief panels at the entrance to the original RKO Building on Sixth Avenue. The rounded corners and horizontal banding of the base echo elements of the marquee of Radio City Music Hall in Rockefeller Center and its interiors by Donald Deskey.

FIGURE 6.24   *Gift Ware,* "His Royal Highness" coffeepot, 1934. International Silver Company, Lurelle Guild, designer. Silverplate, ebony. DMA, JSASC, cat. 73

FIGURE 6.26 K. K. Culver Trophy, 1938. Gorham Manufacturing Company, Viktor Schreckengost, designer. Silverplated bronze. The Mitchell Wolfson Jr. Collection, cat. 31

GEORG JENSEN AND THE INFLUENCE OF SCANDINAVIA

Beginning in the early 1920s, Scandinavian silver, especially Danish and to some extent Swedish silver, exerted a pervasive influence on American industrial silver.[56] For the affluent customer the work of the Danish silversmith Georg Jensen (1866–1935) became a popular alternative to contemporary designs in *art moderne* and streamlining. Jensen's silver was heavy, had a rich look, and its smooth contours and naturalistic decoration made it acceptable to "traditional modernists." Scandinavian silver was included in many exhibitions that were not exclusively American during the interwar period. In her review of the *Exhibition of Swedish Contemporary Decorative Art* at the Metropolitan Museum of Art in 1927, the art critic Helen Appleton Read lauded Swedish design and reminded readers that "it was generally conceded by those who visited the International Exposition des Art Décoratifs, held in Paris year before last, that the Swedish Pavilion and the section of Swedish decorative arts in the Grand Palais were the most successful demonstrations of the coming of age of a modern style."[57]

In the American Federation of Arts traveling exhibition *Decorative Metalwork and Cotton Textiles* that toured major museums in Boston, New York, Chicago, and Cleveland in 1930 and 1931, more than seventy objects of Swedish silver occupied three cases in the exhibit and there was a smaller selection of Danish silver (see fig. 4.7). Swedish arts and crafts, including silverware, were shown in Chicago at the *Century of Progress Exposition* in 1933[58] and, in 1935, the Metropolitan Museum of Art exhibited its new acquisitions of contemporary French and Swedish applied arts.[59] Jensen was represented in the Brooklyn Museum's exhibition *Contemporary Industrial and Handwrought Silver* in 1937 and the company's *Blossom* teapot was illustrated in the catalogue. Several selections of Jensen's silver were included in the *Golden Gate International Exposition* in San Francisco in 1939.

The findings of a survey made in 1940 by the United States Tariff Commission indicated the inroads made by Danish silver into the American market. Exports of sterling silver from Denmark had almost tripled between 1926 and 1937, the United States was the leading foreign market, and the Georg Jensen firm was the principal supplier. The success of Danish silverware was attributed to the technical proficiency of its artisans, the "beauty of its plain surfaces . . . and the simplicity of its natural motifs of molded ornaments." Danish design, it was noted, reflected "the modern influence without departing from the best in traditional forms," and Danish artisans were described as practical, valuing the unity of beauty and utility, the keys to the viability of the style in the American market.[60]

American silver manufacturers were well aware of the appeal of Scandinavian modernism and, after 1925, beginning with Erik Magnussen at Gorham, tailored their goods to suit. In 1931, at the request of the manager of the new Waldorf-Astoria Hotel in New York City for a Scandinavian-style silverware service, the Danish-born silversmith Peer Smed was called in to collaborate with International's staff designer Frederick W. Stark (see figs. 7.10, 7.11). Typically, Scandinavian-influenced American flatware patterns showed the influence of traditional Jensen models in which scrolls, beads, buds, and leaves were the favored motifs. The Scandinavian origin of their inspiration was deliberately underscored by the names given to the patterns. One of the earliest in sterling flatware was *Copenhagen* (1936) from the Manchester Silver Company of Providence, Rhode Island (fig. 6.27). Later in the 1930s International cornered the domestic market with three modern Scandinavian-style sterling patterns: *Norse* and *Sonja* (1937), the latter a salute to the Norwegian Olympic ice skater Sonja Henie, whose first starring film, *Thin Ice*, premiered in 1937, and *Royal Danish* (1939), an almost identical copy

of Jensen's *Acorn* pattern, which had been designed in 1915 by Johan Rohde. In 1946 International followed up with *Northern Lights* (fig. 6.28).[61] Holmes & Edwards of Bridgeport, Connecticut, a division of International, produced the silverplate pattern *Danish Princess* in 1938, Wallace produced *Danish Queen* in 1944, and the National Silver Company of New York City produced *Astrid* in 1945.

One of the most refined designs in holloware to cater to the taste for Jensen's silver was Stark's sterling centerpiece designed for International and awarded a silver medal in the Paris exposition in 1937 (see fig. 8.7). The references to Danish silver were the subtle, smooth contours and harmonious proportions, the single bud motif that embellished each lilting, curvaceous handle, and the discrete fluting on the narrow base. A three-piece sterling tea service produced by Gorham in 1947 (fig. 6.29) was more direct in its quotation of Jensen's style, in particular two distinctive early services. The shape of the vessels and the wood side handles were similar to those of the *Number 80* coffee set designed by Georg Jensen in 1915 and the looped stem and floriated

FIGURE 6.27 *Copenhagen* salad fork, 1936. Manchester Silver Company. Silver. Dallas Museum of Art, cat. 135

FIGURE 6.28 *Northern Lights* luncheon fork, 1946. International Silver Company, Alfred G. Kintz, designer. Silver. Dallas Museum of Art, cat. 79

FIGURE 6.29 Tea service, 1947. Gorham Manufacturing Company. Silver, wood. Dallas Museum of Art, cat. 32

finials recalled those on the *Blossom* tea service he designed in 1905. Many watered-down, undistinguished versions of Scandinavian modern holloware flooded the middle market but International's centerpiece and Gorham's coffee set were among the finest examples of the American manufacturers' response to the taste for Jensen's silver in the 1930s.

THE ROMANCE OF THE TROPICS

By the 1940s, silver manufacturers were responding to the popular culture's fascination with the tropics, a fascination fueled by advances in air transportation, a presidential policy, Latin dance music, and Hollywood movies. By 1930, Pan American Airways had initiated routes to destinations as far south as Rio de Janeiro, Buenos Aires, and Santiago via its fleet of Flying Clipper Ships. Although the volume of passengers was small, the potential generated widespread excitement and was undoubtedly the catalyst in 1933 for the film *Flying Down to Rio*, the first Hollywood movie to star Fred Astaire and Ginger Rogers. In his inaugural address in 1933, President Franklin D. Roosevelt pledged that the United Stated would not intervene in South American affairs, an undertaking that became known as the Good Neighbor Policy. The mystique of countries "south of the border" was heightened in 1939 by the arrival in the United States of Carmen Miranda, the flamboyant singer known for her animated delivery, colorful costumes, and towering turbans piled high with fruit (fig. 6.30).[62]

FIGURE 6.30   Carmen Miranda, c. 1940

FIGURE 6.31   *"Tropical* by International Silver Company." Promotional brochure

FIGURE 6.32   *Tropical* platter, c. 1940. International Silver Company, Carl Conrad Braun, designer. Silverplate. DMA, JSASC, cat. 77

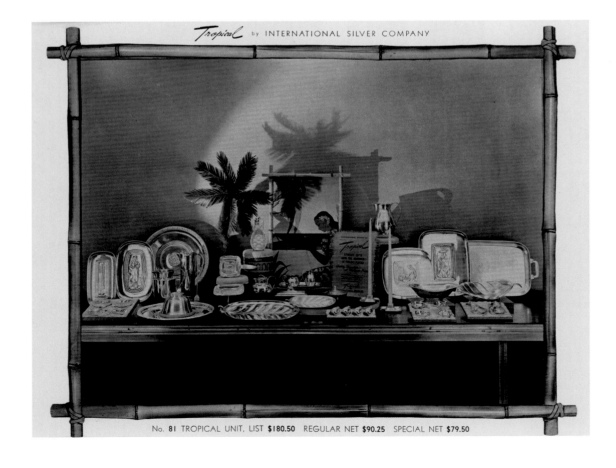

No. 81 TROPICAL UNIT, LIST **$180.50**   REGULAR NET **$90.25**   SPECIAL NET **$79.50**

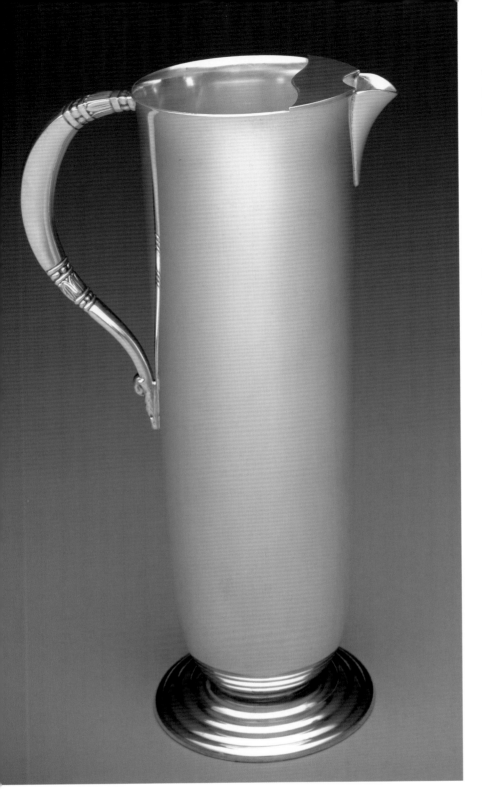

FIGURE 6.33 *Tropical* mixer, c. 1940. International Silver Company, Carl Conrad Braun, designer. Silverplate. DMA, JSASC, cat. 78

FIGURE 6.34 Hors d'oeuvres tray, 1936. Reed & Barton, Belle Kogan, designer. Silver. DMA, JSASC, cat. 171

"South American Way," her solo in the stage revue *The Streets of Paris*, became a hit song, in part because of its sensuous, upbeat lyrics:

> Ai, ai, ai, ai,
> Have you ever danced in the tropics?
> With that hazy lazy
> Like, kind of crazy
> Like South American Way[63]

The song, replayed and broadcast by radio stations across the country, caused Miranda's popularity to soar, as did her movies, *Down Argentine Way* in 1940 and *That Night in Rio* and *Weekend in Havana* both in 1941, which perpetuated the mystique of the tropics.

Around 1940, International Silver introduced a thematic giftware line designed by Carl Conrad Braun and named *Tropical*, an allusion to romantic fantasies of a natural, uninhibited, and idyllic existence in Latin America. A thinly veiled eroticism set the mood in the brochure: "Unusual gifts with the romance of far-off places. . . . New exotic beauty—the luxury of the tropics in stunning silverplate. Pagan Splendor hitherto found only in collectors pieces."[64] The line included twenty-four articles offered at moderate prices ranging from $2.50 to $11.50 (fig. 6.31). To enhance the desirability of the products and to guide hostesses, International used the captions to the illustrations in the promotional catalogue to suggest what might be served in each piece and included many contemporary favorites, such as canapés, bite-sized sausages, sandwich spreads, spiced fruits, and molded desserts.

Several pieces in the *Tropical* line were based on the shape of a fruit, for example, the pineapple, avocado, or pomegranate. Others took the form of a banana leaf, a "mangrove leaf," and one described as inspired by a "rare Amazon plant." Lush and leafy stylized environments were the settings for the central relief panels of four trays in which a voluptuous female figure was the focus. The representations of all four were erotically charged, with idealized breasts modeled in relief under clinging and draped garments. On the sandwich tray, a standing woman was depicted carrying a large bowl cradled in her right arm. On the luncheon tray a woman awaiting her guests sat beside a large bowl heaped with fruits. In the largest, the "palmetto" tray, a long-haired, seated beauty relaxed in a landscape heavy with vegetation. The platter, on which a female figure saucily balanced a fruit-filled tray on her head with her uplifted left arm while the other arm rested firmly on her hip (fig. 6.32), was touted in the catalogue for its usefulness: "The high-raised medallion of a lady of the tropics will inspire many new and original uses besides the serving of cold meats, fish, individual salads, chicken in pattie shells and, of

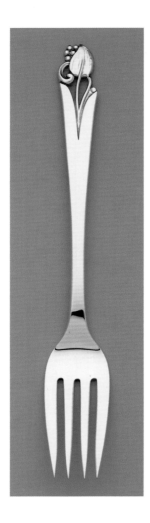

FIGURE 6.35 *Woodlily* salad fork, 1945. Frank W. Smith Silver Company. Silver. Dallas Museum of Art, cat. 221

NOTES

1. "Compotes," *International Sterling Hollow Ware*, catalogue (1929), 59–W (International Silver Company Archives, Meriden Historical Society, Meriden, Conn.; hereafter as International Silver Archives). Another example was Friedman's *To-Day* holloware line designed by Kem Weber in which classical reeded bases were the dominant element (see fig. 3.39).

2. Elizabeth Brown, "Contemporary Table Decoration," *Interior Decoration* 97 (Aug. 1937): 38.

3. "Announcing MODERN CLASSIC," Rogers, Lunt & Bowlen advertisement, *House Beautiful* 75 (May 1934): 24.

4. For example, at the same time that *Modern Classic* was introduced, plumbing fittings by George Sakier were described as "new classic" in "Art and Machines," *Architectural Forum* 60 (May 1934): 334.

5. Clipping, *Dover Democrat* (New Hampshire), Apr. 24, 1934 (Lurelle Guild Collection, Syracuse University Library, Box 9, International Silver folder; hereafter Guild Coll.). The clipping was attached to a letter from Harrison Corbin, International Silver Company, Meriden, Conn., to Lurelle Guild, New York City, May 15, 1934.

6. Margaret Moore Jacobs, "Ceremonial Tables for Holiday Festivities," *Arts and Decoration* 45 (Dec. 1936): 30.

7. A. Frederic Saunders, "Design Trend in Silverware," *Jewelers' Circular-Keystone* 106 (Jan. 1936): 28.

8. McCutcheon's, "McCutcheon's Presents the Masculine Slant on Smart Table Settings," n.d., n.p. (Dorothy Wright Liebes file, box 634, series 2, America at Home, 1939 New York World's Fair Coll., Manuscript and Archives Div., New York Public Library).

9. "Fascinating Dorian," Watson Company advertisement, *Vogue* 85 (Mar. 1, 1935): 14.

10. Robert E. Locher, "Silver—first among the bride's gifts," *Country Life* 68 (June 1935): 20.

11. Helen Bishop, "Silver—The Hostess' Great Heritage," *Arts and Decoration* 48 (Aug. 1938): 22; and "Sterling Plate," *Creative Design* 1 (spring 1935): 14.

12. "The Vogue," Wallace Luxor Plate advertisement, *Vogue* 85 (Apr. 15, 1935): 120. The identical pattern in chrome was advertised as *Ionian* by Mary Ryan, a representative of giftware manufacturers. It was presented as ideal for buffet and garden service and praised for not tarnishing (hence polishing was never required). The maker was not mentioned, but it would have been Wallace, as Wallace exhibited what was described as "chromium" flatware at the 1935 *Industrial Arts Exposition* sponsored by the National Alliance of Art and Industry in New York City. See "Ionian Pattern in Chrome; Style at a Price," Mary Ryan advertisement, *Gift and Art Buyer* 31 (Nov. 1935): 33; and "The Industrial Arts Exposition," *Jewelers' Circular-Keystone* 105 (May 1935): 65.

13. "'Classic Modern' Service No. N6700," *Wallace Silverplated Hollowware*, catalogue N-35, R. Wallace & Sons Mfg. Co., 1935. Another with classical allusions was *Ultra* (service No. N6704), in a Wallace holloware group that had the same applied wheat spray for decoration that was used on the *Ultra* flatware pattern of 1934 by the outside consultant John Vassos and may have been designed by him. The *Ultra* holloware was a hybrid, with rounded bodies and fluted bases. In the 1935 National Alliance of Art and Industry's *Industrial Arts Exposition*, Wallace showcased the work of Vassos in a special display; see illustration in "Industrial Arts Exposition, 65."

14. The prototype in the 1934 exhibition has not come to light and is known only from period photographs. Therefore, it is not possible to ascertain if the measurements of the parts that appear to be the same on both are in fact identical.

15. Gail S. Davidson, letter to author, Apr. 23, 1991.

16. For the service Hoffmann designed in 1928, see A. Krekel-Aalberse, J. R. ter Molen, and R. J. Willink, eds., *Silver of a New Era: International Highlights of Precious Metalware from 1880 to 1940*, exh. cat. Museum Boymans van-Beuningen, Rotterdam, and Museum voor Sierkunst, Ghent (Seattle: University of Washington Press, 1992), 271. For another of Hoffmann's teapots with a ponytail handle, see C. G. Holme, ed., *Decorative Art Year-Book* (London: The Studio, 1931), 158.

17. For the price of the International *Continental* tea service no. C342 and the other tea service, no. WC526, see pl. 522L and pl. 245W, respectively, in salesmen's catalogues, International Silver Archives. The less expensive five-piece service did not include a waste bowl.

18. "Jubilee, An Exquisite New Pattern in Sterling Silver by Reed & Barton," Reed & Barton advertisement, *Brides Magazine* 3 (winter 1936–37): 40.

course, hors d'oeuvres." In conformity with streamline design, the corners of this platter and of other rectangular and square servers in *Tropical* were rounded. The framing of the decorative panels in stepped layers was, however, a holdover from *art moderne*. Rounded forms and stepped layers were also characteristics of the tall *Tropical* mixer for "stirred drinks, concocted punches and the like" (fig. 6.33).[65]

In American industrial silver of the period, figuration was an uncommon expression of naturalism, which was primarily embodied in botanical forms. In 1936 for Reed & Barton Belle Kogan designed a sterling hors d'oeuvres tray (fig. 6.34) that has handles of overlapping stylized leaves in an openwork pattern that was quite unlike Scandinavian pieces. Always alert to currents in popular taste, Kogan may have anticipated the vogue for tropical imagery in this application of naturalism, an isolated, and perhaps experimental, motif in her oeuvre. More typical was the conservative and graceful *Woodlily*, an openwork sterling flatware pattern produced in 1945 by the Frank W. Smith Silver Company of Gardner, Massachusetts (fig. 6.35).

19. Carl Conrad Braun, telephone conversation with author, Apr. 8, 1992. Later in the 1930s Braun designed the *Tropical* holloware line for International Silver (see figs. 6.31–6.33).

20. The service consisted of a coffeepot, teapot, cream pitcher, sugar bowl, kettle and stand, and large oval tray.

21. Verso of Reed & Barton file card no. 635 for *Vogue* tea service, Reed & Barton Archives, Taunton, Mass..

22. Determined by author from design patents. My thanks to Helen Rice for sharing her pioneering research on Belle Kogan.

23. "Industrial Arts Exposition." For a photograph of Kogan's display, see Pat Kirkham, ed., *Women Designers in the USA 1900–2000* (New Haven: Yale University Press, 2000), 272.

24. Jane Eyre, "The Silver Lady," *American Life* 12 (June 1947): 5–6.

25. Kogan's strategy for these designs was noted in a contemporary periodical: "Ornament was kept simple and broad and used only when it could become a part of the form, or a natural development from it. Thus the flutes used are not only ornament, but an aid to strength and function" (caption, *Creative Design in Home Furnishing* 1 [fall 1936]: 34–35).

26. The centerpiece in the pattern, product number 1605, was included in the exhibition *Contemporary Industrial and Handwrought Silver* at the Brooklyn Museum in 1937.

27. John L. Wright, "The Beginning of the Streamlined Dream, 1919–1934," in *Streamlining America*, exh. cat. (Dearborn, Mich.: Henry Ford Museum and Greenfield Village, 1986), 14, 16. For a photograph of the Zephyr at the exposition, see Jeffrey L. Meikle, *Twentieth Century Limited: Industrial Design in America, 1925–1939* (Philadelphia: Temple University Press, 1979), 161.

28. *Machine Art*, exh. cat. (New York: Museum of Modern Art, 1934), n.p.

29. The first run of twenty-four mayonnaise bowls was made on March 2, 1934; the *Machine Art* exhibition opened March 6, 1934; Samuel J. Hough, "Report on Gorham Mayonnaise Bowl 43127," Nov. 13, 1988 (Jewel Stern Archives, Coral Gables, Fla.).

30. Donna R. Braden, "Selling the Dream," in *Streamlining America*, 56.

31. "Dulany, George William, Jr.," *Who's Who in America* 17 (1932–33): 740.

32. "Helen H. Dulany Seeks Divorce," *New York Times*, Dec. 6, 1936, 24; and Anne Petersen, "Women Rising Fast in Field of Design," *New York Times*, Jan. 24, 1937, sec. 5, p. 6.

33. For example, "Reminder List for August," *House Beautiful* 76 (Aug. 1934): 37; "A Truce With Formality," *Arts and Decoration* 41 (Sept. 1934): 47; and "High-Noon Sunday Breakfasts," *Country Life in America* 66 (Sept. 1934): 57.

34. "Helen H. Dulany Seeks Divorce."

35. "A Directory of Contemporary Designers," *Creative Design* 1 (fall 1934): 24.

36. See the HHD Studio stainless steel coffee set in J. Stewart Johnson, *American Modern, 1925–1940: Design for a New Age*, exh. cat. (New York: Abrams, in association with American Federation of Arts, 2000), 123. From a vintage photograph of the Solarium-Observation car of the Burlington Zephyr showing a table setting, it appears that the coffee set illustrated in Johnson is identical to the one designed for the Zephyr and may have been the prototype for the train service; photograph courtesy of the Museum of Science and Industry, Chicago.

37. "Directory of Contemporary Designers."

38. Objects designed by HHD Studio are extremely rare. A chromium-plated caviar server (accession number 84.124.13) is in the Brooklyn Museum of Art. In addition to the stainless steel coffee set illustrated in Johnson (see note 36, above), see a stainless steel and Lucite serving tray in Phillips de Pury & Luxembourg, *20–19th Century Design Art*, auction cat., New York, Dec. 11, 2002, lot 60. Dulany used a variety of materials in her designs, silverplate, brass, copper, wood, and glass among them. Dulany also designed hotel tableware for Buffalo Potteries; see "Bulletin of the Fall Table Market," *Creative Design* 1 (fall 1935): 15.

39. "Divorces: G. W. Dulany Jr.; Wife, an Industrial Designer, in Chicago Action Charges Desertion," *New York Times*, Dec. 13, 1936, 2.

40. Petersen, "Women Rising Fast."

41. Harry V. Anderson, "Contemporary American Designers," *Decorators Digest* 4 (Feb. 1935): 85.

42. Lurelle Guild, New York City, letter to H. C. Wilcox, Meriden, Conn., Oct. 31, 1932 (Guild Coll.).

43. Helen Sprackling, "What's New in Decoration," *New York Herald Tribune*, Mar. 11, 1934, 16.

44. "Thread border" described in International Silver Company General Offices, Meriden, Conn., unsigned letter to Lurelle Guild, New York City, Jan. 11, 1934 (Guild Coll.). For example, see *Bacchanal* punch bowl and *Globes* and *Regency* salts and peppers for bases described as "ribbed" in *International Gift Ware*, catalogue no. 192, n.d., n.p. (International Silver Archives).

45. International Silver Co. Credit Memorandum, Dec. 31, 1934 (Guild Coll.).

46. Harrison Corbin, Meriden, Conn., letter to Lurelle Guild, New York City, Mar. 8, 1934 (Guild Coll.).

47. "His Royal Highness Coffee Set," *The Contemporary Group*, catalogue no. 193, 5, (International Silver Archives).

48. A punch bowl, caviar dish, ice bowl, and chafing dish were other new items.

49. "No. 5841 bowl and No. 5834 compotier," "Plate 4440," Wilcox Silver Plate Company sales catalogue (International Silver Archives).

50. "Plate 4431," Wilcox Silver Plate Company sales catalogue (International Silver Archives). In the 1930s, Guild also designed dresserware for International's La Pierre line, trophies, and a silver chest (Guild Coll.). International engaged Guild again as a consultant in 1958 to develop the Lurelle Originals Decorator Line of solid brass wall decorations made with holloware parts. When Guild's concept was weakened and diluted, he withdrew his name from the line, which was later abandoned; John B. Stevens, Meriden, Conn., letter to Lurelle Guild, New York, Feb. 16, 1962 (Guild Coll.).

51. Donald J. Bush, *Streamlined Decade* (New York: George Braziller, 1975), 172.

52. For the humidor patent, see Jim Linz, *Art Deco Chrome* (Atglen, Pa.: Schiffer 1999), 145.

53. "New 1937 Christmas Folder," Reed & Barton Archives.

54. Information on K. K. Culver Trophy from Jewel Stern, "Supplement for Object Number 83.6.5," Collection Records, Wolfsonian–Florida International University, Miami Beach, Fla.; see also Henry Adams, *Viktor Schreckengost and 20th-Century Design*, exh. cat. (Cleveland: Cleveland Museum of Art, 2000), 71.

55. Although the trophy was awarded only once, there was a provision in the regulations to the effect that, if a pilot won the race three years in succession, she was entitled to keep the large trophy. The trophy does not have the miniature monocoupe attached and its location is unknown.

56. See chapter 1 for discussion on the emergence of Georg Jensen in the United States.

57. Helen Appleton Read, "Swedish Decorative Art Display at the Metropolitan Museum," *Brooklyn Daily Eagle*, Jan. 16, 1927 (Archives of American Art, Helen Appleton Read Papers, reel N736, frame 166).

58. Arna Otte Skold, "Swedish Arts and Crafts at the Chicago Fair," *London Studio* 6 (July–Dec. 1933): 96–99.

59. R. Craig, Miller, *Modern Design in the Metropolitan Museum of Art 1890–1990* (New York: Metropolitan Museum of Art and Abrams, 1990), 305.

60. United States Tariff Commission, *Silverware Solid and Plated*, report no. 139, 2nd series (Washington, D.C.: United States Government Printing Office, 1940), 100, 103. The value of Danish so-called solid-silver silverware exported to the United States in 1926 was $186,000; in 1937 the value was $542,000.

61. *Sonja*, *Royal Danish*, and *Northern Lights* were designed by Alfred G. Kintz, a staff designer at International.

62. The title song of the 1939 movie *South of the Border (Down Mexico Way)* starring Gene Autry, the "singing cowboy," became one of the top ten hit songs of the year.

63. The composer of "South American Way," 1939, was Jimmy McHugh, the lyrics were by Al Dubin.

64. *Tropical by International Silver Company*, brochure cover (International Silver Archives).

65. *Tropical*, n.p.

CHAPTER SEVEN

NOVELTIES AND NECESSITIES

PROHIBITION AND COCKTAIL SHAKERS

The era of Prohibition, the years that for the most part coincided paradoxically with the flamboyant Roaring Twenties, was the catalyst for the glamour and novelty that became attached to the cocktail shaker in popular culture. Motivated by the idealistic goal of reducing or eliminating alcohol abuse and its deleterious effect on family life and fueled by the temperance movement, the Eighteenth Amendment to the Constitution was ratified on January 16, 1919, and went into effect a year later. It ushered in "the noble experiment," a term that became synonymous with Prohibition, and is derived from the campaigning of Herbert Hoover, the "dry" candidate, who opposed the repeal of Prohibition in his successful bid for the presidency of the United States in 1928. The manufacture, sale, and transportation of intoxicating liquor became illegal in 1920. Although liquor stores and saloons were shut down, hidden speakeasies sprang up in urban centers. There alcoholic beverages were served to those who knew the password to be whispered to the bouncer. Many wealthy people continued to drink high-quality spirits that had been stockpiled in their cellars before Prohibition; ordinary people with limited resources resorted to brewing "bathtub gin" in their homes. "Moonshine" was made in illicit stills, and bootlegging, the clandestine trafficking in the banned spirits, became big business, especially for organized crime. The poor quality of contraband liquor was frequently masked and its scarcity stretched by flavorful additions that contributed to the rise in popularity of the mixed cocktail. The inability of the government to control the production and consumption of alcohol, and the view in the early Depression years that legalizing breweries would create new jobs, led the newly elected president, Franklin Delano Roosevelt, to support the repeal of Prohibition. The Twenty-first Amendment, which was ratified on December 5, 1933, ended the idealistic experiment.

In chic urban circles during Prohibition the home cocktail party became a badge of transgression and a glamorous way to entertain. It was legal to produce and sell accessories for serving mixed alcoholic drinks and, for some people, these became quite fashionable. Silver manufacturers were quick to respond, offering an array of stylish cocktail shakers, many with matching goblets and a tray in what were called "beverage sets." The word *cocktail* was discreetly avoided in promotions. Instead, advertisements referred to "beverage mixers," "mixers," or "beverage shakers." In 1928 Reed & Barton, for example, described goblets for mixed drinks as "cocktail cups" in a salesman's catalogue, but omitted the word *cocktail* from a similar advertisement in 1928, coyly showing six "cups" in a row on a "serving tray" (see fig. 1.27). Propriety may have prevented the company from producing a modernist cocktail shaker in the late 1920s, nonetheless two sterling cocktail cups in the mode were offered. Although both have the same shaped cup,

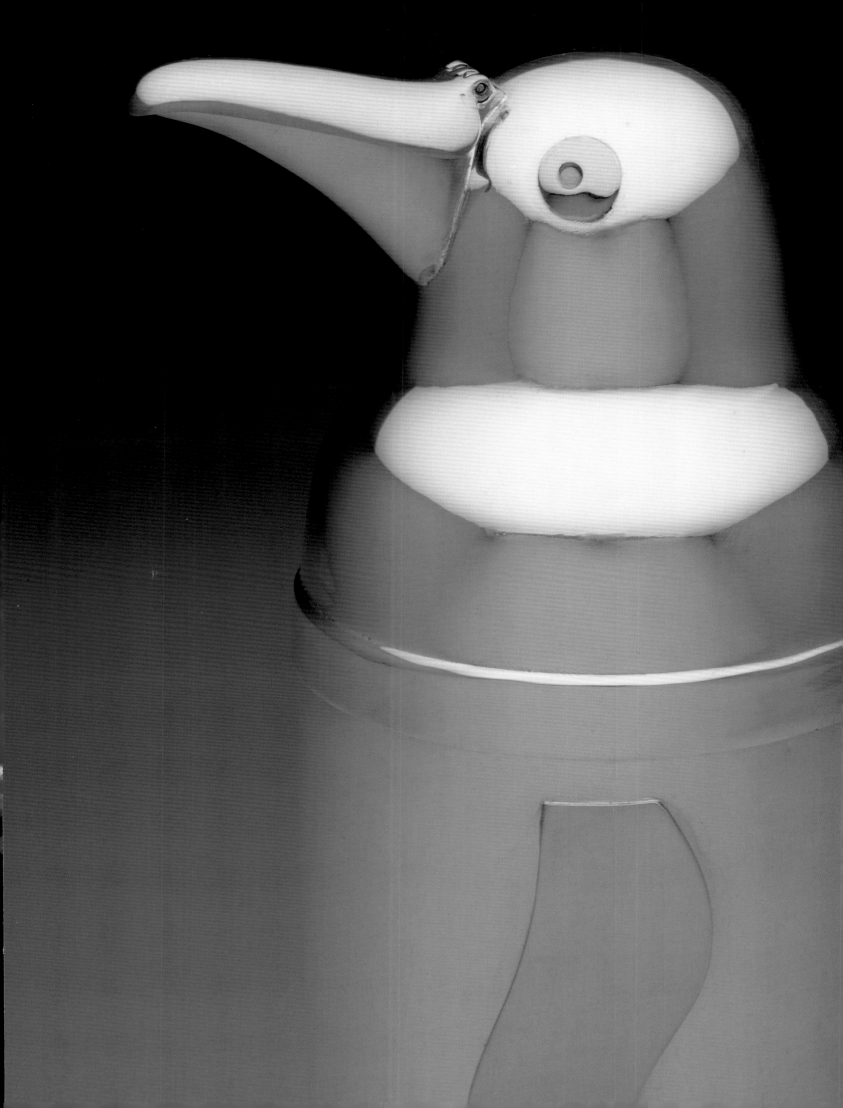

each has a different style foot. The model illustrated in that advertisement has a rectangular foot and no ornamentation (fig. 7.1, right); the other (fig. 7.1, center) has a domed foot and was incised on all its components with an angular pattern to approximate cubist planes.

A more strident three-dimensional expression of planarity was a silverplated "iced-drink set" of triangular form with gilded panels, part of a holloware group patented by Elsa Tennhardt for E. & J. Bass, that was shown in *Harper's Bazaar* in 1928 as a Christmas gift that would "solve the man problem." The jazzy set came with six "glasses" that had swaying stems—perhaps to set the mood for the anticipated libation—an ice bowl, and a serving tray with a black glass center.[1] Less lively than Tennhardt's cups but equally in tune with the zeitgeist was Erik Magnussen's *Modern American* design for Gorham. Magnussen drew his inspiration from Manhattan's iconic setback skyscrapers for the foot of his sterling martini glass–shaped cocktail cups (fig. 7.1, left) that are more commodious than the cups by Reed & Barton and E. & J. Bass. In contrast to the latter, Magnussen used linear chasing in horizontal and vertical patterns for decoration. The chasing on the *Modern American* cocktail shaker echoed that of the cocktail cups but the base of the shaker was flat, not stepped.[2] Of all these cocktail shakers, the most luxurious of the Prohibition era was

FIGURE 7.1 Left: *Modern American* cocktail cup, 1928. Gorham Manufacturing Company, Erik Magnussen, designer. Silver. DMA, JSASC, cat. 24; center: Cocktail cup, 1928. Reed & Barton. Silver. Dallas Museum of Art, cat. 161; right: *Modernist* cocktail cup, 1928. Reed & Barton. Silver. DMA, JSASC, cat. 154

the elegant red and black enameled shaker produced by divisions of International (see fig. 3.56).

After the repeal of Prohibition in 1933, cocktail shakers proliferated. Their use in films as props to depict the sophistication of café society added to their cachet and popularity. Several shakers introduced in 1934 demonstrated a new simplicity in design and a predilection for basic, static geometric forms, especially the sphere, cylinder, and cone, that resulted in objects quite unlike the cubist-inspired wares of the 1920s that had relied on fractured planes for effect. A sleek sterling "mixer" introduced in 1934 by the Wilcox & Evertsen Fine Arts Division of International sported a spherical finial emblematic of the new geometry (fig. 7.2).[3] The base has the undisputedly machine-made "narrow ribbed" or "reeded band" that figured strongly in International's holloware in the 1930s and for the most part replaced

FIGURE 7.2 Cocktail shaker, 1934. Wilcox & Evertsen Fine Arts. Silver. DMA, JSASC, cat. 123

FIGURE 7.3 "Smart Gifts for Smart People," International Silver Company advertisement, 1934

the stepped bases ubiquitous in the 1920s. However, a subtly stepped cover was retained.[4] The unusual finial pierced by a tiny fluted rod brings to mind the motif on the *Empire* bowl in International's silverplate *Gift Ware* line designed by Lurelle Guild and also introduced in 1934, and suggests that he had a hand in the design of this shaker.[5] For *Gift Ware* Guild designed a striking, enamel-trimmed sixteen-inch-high cocktail shaker with matching cups in two versions, appropriately named the *Tall Boy* and the *Slim Jim.* A ball-shaped stopper and reeded bands were features of the *Tall Boy,* which was offered in Mandarin Red, Mediterranean Blue, Eden Green, and Ebony Black enamel (fig. 7.3).[6] The softly rounded shoulders, spherical finial, horizontal bands, and elongation of these cocktail shakers made them quintessential, early streamlined objects. In fact, in the *Gift Ware* catalogue, the *Tall Boy* was described as a streamlined "projectile."[7]

Another shaker, unmarked, gives the impression of an artillery shell (fig. 7.4, center). It bridged the decades with dramatic 1920s telescoping imposed on a tapered Machine Age form reminiscent of German Zeppelin

airships and the American Goodyear blimp.[8] More rigorous is a silverplated conical shaker introduced in 1934 by Napier (fig. 7.4, left). Patented by the staff designer Emil A. Schuelke as assignor to Napier, it is an exercise in pure form and proportion. The only decoration consists of a band that metaphorically delineates the base.[9] George A. Henckel of New York City was a manufacturer that looked to Paris for inspiration in the 1930s, producing an almost identical copy (fig. 7.4, right) of the classic shaker that Christofle had produced for the renowned ocean liner *Normandie,* the pride of the French Line, which made her maiden voyage in 1935.

During the 1920s and 1930s cocktail shakers were often given novel and humorous shapes. Whimsical shakers took the form of animals, bowling pins,

FIGURE 7.4 Left: Cocktail shaker, 1934. Napier Company, Emil A. Schuelke, designer. Silverplate, cat. 140; center: Cocktail shaker, c. 1928. Unknown maker. Silverplate, cat. 279; right: Cocktail shaker, c. 1935. George A. Henckel & Co. Silver, cat. 69. DMA, JSASC

FIGURE 7.5 Cocktail shaker and cups, c. 1928. R. Wallace & Sons Manufacturing Company. Silverplate, glass. Dallas Museum of Art, cat. 281

dumbbells, hourglasses, lighthouses, and golf bags, the latter two produced in silverplate by divisions of International.[10] By 1928 Wallace made a silverplated shaker in the shape of a rooster with matching cups (fig. 7.5). The rooster, either as the shape or as a decorative motif, was frequently employed as a pun on the syllables that comprise the word *cocktail*. The penguin, too, was a popular zoomorphic form for shakers. Schuelke patented a statuesque, contoured *Penguin* shaker with a prominent pouring beak that was introduced in 1936 and touted playfully as the "master of ceremonies at successful parties." Napier's *Penguin* was available in two finishes, one in silverplate, and the other a deluxe model with gilded wings, beak, eyes, feet, and handle (fig. 7.6). At twice the price of the plain silverplated version, the gold-trimmed *Penguin* was an extravagance at the time and is consequently extremely rare.[11] The novelty design with the longest record of production was Reed & Barton's silverplated *Milk Can* cocktail shaker, introduced no later than 1935 and available in two sizes. The *Milk Can*, dearly beloved for almost fifty years, and consistently advertised by Reed & Barton, was finally retired from production in June of 1983 (fig. 7.7).[12]

The most opulent statement in cocktail ware during the interwar period was unequivocally Tiffany's cocktail service that was created especially for the House of Jewels display at the New York World's Fair in 1939 (see fig. 8.12). One hundred and thirty-six pale green cabochon emeralds were lavished on the service, which was designed by Arthur Leroy Barney (1884–1955). The fourteen-inch-high lighthouse-shaped mixer was described in a company memo as having a "tall tapering faceted body," the cover as having vertical rows of "alternating silver flutes and pale cabochon emeralds," and the cap as having a "crown of the same stones."[13] The stems of the eight faceted, cone-shaped cups, set on slightly stepped bases, had vertical rows of alternating emeralds and silver fluting. The fluted handles of the elongated oblong tray had panels inset with emeralds. In 1939 this elaborate cocktail service cost $1,700.[14]

SILVER BEYOND THE HOME

In the twentieth century, commercial tableware for public facilities such as hotels, restaurants, private clubs, railroads, steamships, and ocean liners, and, from the 1930s on, airlines, became a significant source of revenue for major silver manufacturers. Competition in these new markets was aggressive. International and Reed & Barton, for example, had separate departments for this trade, often called the Hotel Division, even

THE MILK CAN: TO SHAKE UP A PARTY, BRIGHTEN A BAR
Cocktail shaker in heavy silverplate. 32 oz. capacity, $75.00;
64 oz. capacity, $85.00. At finer silverware stores.

REED & BARTON
SILVERMASTERS SINCE 1824 · TAUNTON, MASSACHUSETTS

FIGURE 7.7 "The Milk Can: To Shake Up a Party, Brighten a Bar," Reed & Barton advertisement, 1934

though production was not exclusively for hotels. Orders for silverplated holloware and flatware services in large quantities and reorders occasioned by losses from theft and damage were lucrative. At International and Reed & Barton the hotel divisions accounted for much of each company's sales and profits.[15] The potential expanded dramatically as more and more Americans traveled across the continent by rail, on newly minted highways by automobile, and to distant destinations by air. Hotels sprang up to accommodate vacationing travelers. Not surprisingly, Reed & Barton experienced record sales between 1900 and 1929.[16]

Gorham also had a specialized commercial division. One example of the silverware it provided was the silverplate for the Master Apartment Building at 310 Riverside Drive in New York City. Designed by two local architectural firms, Corbett, Harrison & MacMurray with Sugarman & Berger, the building, erected in 1929, had the unusual distinction of housing a museum and art institute named for the charismatic Russian-born painter Nicholas Roerich. The project was planned as an elite cultural center, where residents lived independently but dined together in a ground-floor restaurant.[17] From a surviving teapot (fig. 7.8) with a stepped lid and spout opening, it is apparent that the design of the original service by Gorham was an echo of the setback massing of the Master Building

FIGURE 7.6 *Penguin* cocktail shaker, 1936. Napier Company, Emile A. Schuelke, designer. Gilded silverplate. DMA, JSASC, cat. 141

FIGURE 7.8 Master Building teapot, 1929. Gorham Manufacturing
Company. Silverplate. DMA, JSASC, cat. 28

and other skyscrapers built in the city during the 1920s. Louis Horch, an ardent supporter of Roerich's work and philosophy, was a major investor in the enterprise and nothing was spared to outfit the building. From the *art moderne* furniture created for the restaurant (fig. 7.9) to the cast doorknobs throughout the building, everything was reportedly custom designed.[18] Judging from the eccentric details of the teapot, this must have been true of the silverware for the restaurant as well.

The design process for an extensive custom-order flatware and holloware service is illustrated by International's work for the Waldorf-Astoria Hotel in New York City, which opened in 1931. Lucius Messenger Boomer, the managing director of the hotel, made the final selection. Invited to submit proposals, Frank N. Wilcox, the head of International's hotel division, and the staff designer Frederick W. Stark first examined the architectural drawings at the Schultze & Weaver firm and then proposed a modernist theme compatible with the style of the building.[19] Stark recalled that Boomer, however, wanted something more "provincial," rejected the modern design, and suggested that Wilcox and Stark meet with Peer Smed, a Danish silversmith in Brooklyn, whose handwrought works Boomer had previously acquired. Stark called on Smed, who made some rough sketches of the type of ornament he thought Boomer would like. In order to secure the job, International engaged Smed as a consultant. At the Meriden factory he made additional sketches that Stark developed and polished for the designs, patented by both Smed and Stark, that were accepted by Boomer and the Waldorf-Astoria's board of directors. Smed's contribution, the dominant bead, scroll, and floral motif (figs. 7.10, 7.11), was emphatically Danish in style and reflected Boomer's conservative taste rather than the architects' modernist vision for the luxury hotel. In more congenial circumstances International had no qualms about producing

FIGURE 7.9 Restaurant, Master Building, 310 Riverside Drive, New York, c. 1929

FIGURE 7.10 Waldorf-Astoria Hotel compote, 1931, International Silver Company, Peer Smed and Frederick W. Stark, designers. Silverplate. DMA, JSASC, cat. 71

FIGURE 7.11 Waldorf-Astoria Hotel luncheon fork, 1931. International Silver Company, Peer Smed and Frederick W. Stark, designers. Silverplate. DMA, JSASC, cat. 70

FIGURE 7.12   Cocktail shaker, c. 1936. International Silver Company. Silverplate. DMA, JSASC, cat. 76

FIGURE 7.13   Coffeepot, c. 1933. International Silver Company, Frederick W. Stark, ornament designer. Silverplate. Dallas Museum of Art, cat. 72

spirited modern hotel ware. A prime example is a softly rounded, stepped cocktail shaker with a jaunty spherical finial and three incised linear bands for decoration, an omnipresent 1930s streamline motif (fig. 7.12).[20] This chic bar accessory has a dial that enables the server to dispense the appropriate mix for ten popular cocktails including martinis, manhattans, and gibsons.

International's hotel division actively pursued commissions from transportation industries and outfitted many passenger ships, airlines, and railways. For example, International equipped the SS *Washington*, a transatlantic ocean liner of the United States Lines that made its maiden voyage in the spring of 1933.[21] A side-handled coffeepot in silverplate and stamped "United States Lines" may have been for the *Washington* (fig. 7.13). The shell motif border on its base was patented by Stark in 1932, but the body of the pot was derived from an earlier design of his.

International and Reed & Barton were major suppliers of modern silverware for the dining cars of trains launched in the 1930s. The most celebrated train equipped by Reed & Barton was the New York Central Mercury (a streamlined design by Henry Dreyfuss), which was completed in 1936 and operated between Cleveland and Detroit (fig. 7.14). The speed lines that wrapped around the exterior of the engine doubtless were an inspiration for the decorative elements of the Mercury's silver service. Reed & Barton also supplied the silverware for the Southern Pacific Company's Daylight train, which ran between San Francisco and Los Angeles, and for the Atchison, Topeka & Santa Fe

Railway Company's trains.[22] International took special pride in the silverware it produced in 1938 for the dining, night club, and lounge cars of the famous 20th Century Limited, another streamlined train designed for New York Central by Dreyfuss.[23] By 1948, International was supplying silverware to fifty American railroads.[24]

Airlines were a pioneering sector of development for International in the 1930s. When a full-course meal with table service was included in the fare and "dinner aloft" was an advertised inducement (fig. 7.15),[25] the company produced a signature flatware service for the American Airlines DC-3 Flagship fleet. On each side of the sculptural handles the nose, fuselage, and a propeller of the aircraft were rendered abstractly in profile and the word "Flagship" was stamped (fig. 7.16). Aerodynamic speed was conveyed through the elongation and curve of unbroken lines directed outward in relief to the end of each handle.

Commercial ware continued to be important after World War II. The production of airline flatware became big business as air travel expanded dramatically, and International secured the lion's share of that business. The firm's roster included United Airlines, Pan American Airlines, and Trans World Airlines; Eastern Airlines contracted with Reed & Barton. John Prip's sterling *Dimension*, designed in 1961, served as the pattern for the Eastern Airlines silverplated flatware (see fig. 12.9). For the three-piece place setting Reed & Barton retained the *Dimension* teaspoon and salad fork, but produced a smaller knife. The airline's logo, an abstract line drawing of an aircraft in profile within a circle, was stamped on each handle.[26] A profitable area for International was the production of "box top" patterns, that is, silverware that breakfast cereal producers such as Kellogg's and C. W. Post gave away as premiums.[27] In a novel product promotion, Clorox bleach rewarded its customers with a gift set composed of six miniature flatware servers made by the Meriden Silverplate Company, a division of International. The pattern adopted for the set was *First Lady* (1960), a design with contours characteristic of the 1950s. One recipient of the set was Elma Lamonds of Star, North Carolina, whose unused gift in its original box has come to light (fig. 7.17).

THE "TRAIN OF TOMORROW"

IS EQUIPPED WITH

REED & BARTON
Silverware

New York Central's sensational new stream-lined Mercury is so luxurious, so ultra modern that it is called the "train of tomorrow". It plies between Cleveland and Detroit. The superb dining car is of course equipped with Reed & Barton Silverware. The pattern was chosen because of its elegant smartness, so perfectly in keeping with the unique arrangement and stunning appointments of the Mercury's triple-division diner.

Besides supplying the silverware for crack stream-line trains, Reed & Barton likewise equips exclusive clubs, sumptuous liners, fashionable restaurants, And, of course, Reed & Barton has for many years furnished distinctive flatware and smartly matching hollowware to the leading hotels from Manhattan to Market Street.

Reed & Barton hotel silver is the finest in weight, workmanship, design, and finish that can be purchased. And there's a very complete range of patterns made specifically by Reed & Barton for hotel use.

We shall be happy to submit samples of flatware or hollowware, special sketches, or detailed information to you upon request.

FIGURE 7.14 "The Train of Tomorrow," Reed & Barton advertisement, c. 1936

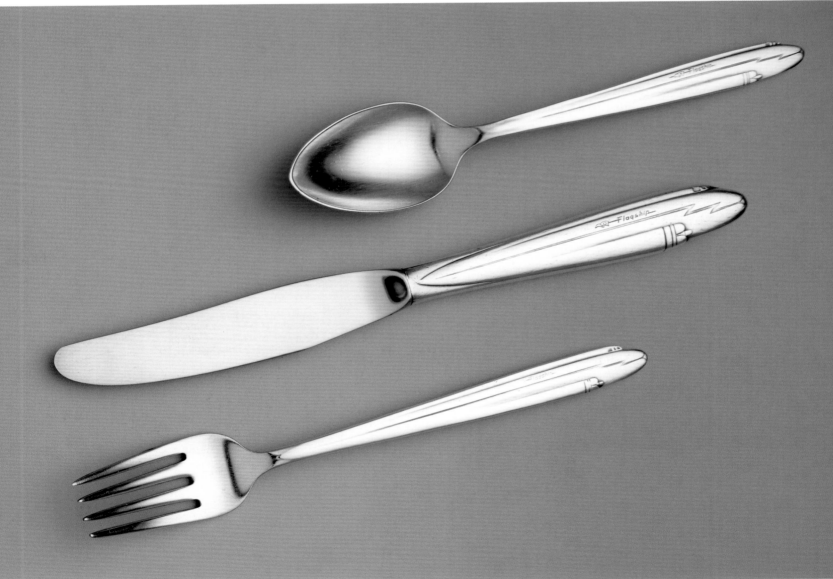

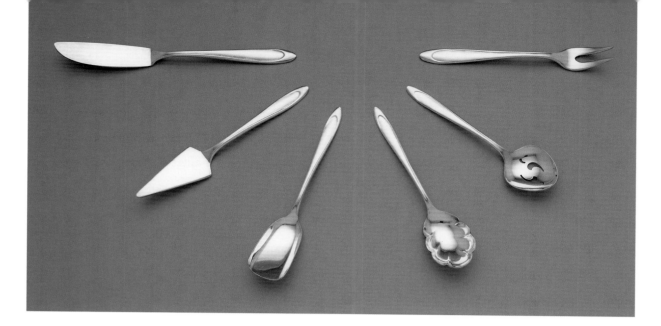

FIGURE 7.17 Clorox promotional flatware, c. 1960. Meriden Silver
Plate Company. Silverplate. DMA, JSASC, cat. 94

NOTES

1. "Gifts That Solve the Man Problem," *Harper's Bazaar* 63 (Dec. 1928): 92.

2. For an illustration of the *Modern American* cocktail shaker, see Janet Kardon, ed., *Craft in the Machine Age, 1920–1945: The History of Twentieth-Century American Craft*, exh. cat. (New York: Abrams, in association with the American Craft Museum, 1995), 175.

3. Around the same time, in its commercial hotel division, International produced two silverplated cocktail shakers on which spherical finials and linear banding were dominant elements (see figs. 6.25, 7.12).

4. For an illustration of the "mixer" in a set with matching cocktail cups and tray, see International advertisement, "Contenders for Your Christmas List," *Town and Country* 91 (Dec. 1936): 57. International offered a much less successful variation of the mixer (product no. WM225) that was smaller and had a slightly different base. Geared to a more conservative market, it was offered with cocktail cups of a traditional shape and a plain, round tray; illustration of variation from International Silver Company Archives, Meriden Historical Society, Meriden, Conn. (hereafter, International Silver Archives), courtesy of Stephen Visakay.

5. For the *Empire* bowl, see *International Gift Ware*, sales catalogue (International Silver Archives).

6. The *Slim Jim* was not offered in black enamel.

7. For the *Tall Boy* shaker, see *International Gift Ware* (International Silver Archives).

8. Some German-made cocktail shakers were upright replicas of Zeppelin airships.

9. See "Serving Accessories," *Gift and Art Buyer* 30 (Oct. 1934): 12; "The Male Box," *Vogue* 84 (Dec. 1, 1934): 71; and "For Indoor Sports," Marshall Field Co., *Fashions of the Hour*, Christmas number, 1934, 18.

10. For a variety of examples, see Stephen Visakay, *Vintage Bar Ware: Identification and Value Guide* (Paducah, Ky.: Collector Books, 1997).

11. "Meet the Penguin! A Bird of a Shaker," Hammacher Schlemmer advertisement, *New Yorker* 12 (Sept. 19, 1936): 61. My thanks to W. Scott Braznell for bringing this advertisement to my attention. See also "Gifts in Decorative Metals," *Arts and Decoration* 45 (Oct. 1936): 45.

12. The *Milk Can* shaker was listed in the 1935 Reed & Barton catalogue, but not in 1931. There are no catalogues at Reed & Barton for the years 1932, 1933, and 1934. The 1983–1984 catalogue indicates that the shaker was discontinued in June 1983 (Reed & Barton Archives, Taunton, Mass.).

13. Computed from "Articles of Silverware to be exhibited by Tiffany & Co. at their exhibit in the House of Jewels New York World's Fair," memorandum, 1939 (Tiffany & Co. Archives, Parsippany, N.J.).

14. Tiffany & Co. advertisement, *New Yorker* 15 (Dec. 16, 1939): 1. In 1989 Tiffany reproduced a cocktail set that was based on the 1939 service but embellished with moonstones instead of with emeralds; see Tiffany & Co., *Blue Book* (New York, 1989–90), 105.

15. Edmund P. Hogan, *An American Heritage: A Book About the International Silver Company* (Dallas, Tex.: Taylor Publishing, 1977), 63; and George S. Gibb, *The Whitesmiths of Taunton: A History of Reed & Barton, Silversmiths, 1824–1943* (Cambridge, Mass.: Harvard University Press, 1943), 218.

16. Gibb, *Whitesmiths of Taunton*, 329.

17. Robert A. M. Stern, Gregory Gilmartin, and Thomas Mellins, *New York 1930: Architecture and Urbanism Between the Two World Wars* (New York: Rizzoli, 1987), 400.

18. Daniel Entin, director, Nicholas Roerich Museum, New York City, e-mail to author, Oct. 2, 2003.

19. Frederick W. Stark (memo to Earl Chapin May, June 24, 1946 [inter-office correspondence, International Silver Archives]) and Earl Chapin May (*A Century of Silver, 1847–1947: Connecticut Yankees and a Noble Metal* [New York: Robert M. McBride, 1947], 276–78) are the sources for the development of the Waldorf-Astoria service.

20. See "Practical Hints on the Care of Silver," *Hotel Management* 33 (Feb. 1938): 145.

21. Hogan, *American Heritage*, 65.

22. Everett L. Maffett, *Silver Banquet* (Eaton, Ohio: Silver Press, 1990), 29, 208; and "Train of Tomorrow," Reed & Barton advertisement in *Latest Fashions for the Well Dressed Table* (New York: Ahrens, n.d.) (Reed & Barton Archives).

23. "The New Streamlined 20th Century Limited," International Silver Company advertisement, *Hotel Management* 34 (Sept. 1938): 5.

24. Hogan, *American Heritage*, 66.

25. "Did you ever wonder what people do on a Flagship?" American Airlines, Inc., advertisement, *New Yorker* 16 (Mar. 30, 1940): inside front cover.

26. "Reed & Barton Silverware to Be Part of Eastern Airlines 'New Look.' 'Famous Restaurants' Flights to Feature Our Flatware and Holloware," *The Silver Lining* (Reed & Barton newsletter) 23 (Mar./Apr. 1965): 7.

27. Siro Toffolon, telephone conversation with author, June 11, 2000. Toffolon, who began work in 1951 and was a prolific designer of flatware patterns for International, claimed that premium silverplate patterns were even more profitable than sterling patterns were in the regular line.

CHAPTER EIGHT

THE EXHIBITIONS CONTINUE, 1937–1940

For the decade, the year 1937 witnessed an unparalleled cultural emphasis on American silver. Interest in modern American industrial silver during the first half of the century reached its apogee that year with two exhibitions in America and one in Paris. It would have been difficult for viewers and reviewers of those exhibitions to envision the diminution of silver in American life that was ahead. Presaged by socioeconomic change, the inevitable trend toward informality was in an early stage in 1937. It would flower after World War II, much to the disadvantage of silverware manufacturers.

A Trio of Exhibitions

In the spring of 1937 the Metropolitan Museum of Art opened a special gallery, E15, for small exhibitions of contemporary design and limited to objects in a single material or of one type. The first was *Silver: An Exhibition of Contemporary American Design by Manufacturers, Designers and Craftsmen,* which was the fourteenth in the *Contemporary Industrial Art* series (fig. 8.1). In his introductory essay for the catalogue, Richard F. Bach noted that "quantity products . . . depend on design as a primary appeal to the consumer."[1] Bach and the museum hoped that the exhibition would give "some indication of present trends in design, specifically of current tendencies in the interpretation of what is now generally called the modern style"[2]—a hope that was fulfilled.

A reviewer for *House and Garden* asserted that the exhibit "notably achieved its purpose of demonstrating the steady improvement of art in industry and illustrating the consistent formulation of a contemporary style."[3] Helen Johnson Keyes declared that the exhibition "bears witness not only to an awareness of today's manner of living and feeling, but of courage in accepting and interpreting it." Keyes commended Percy B. Ball for his modern classic interpretation of "fluted shafts without any ornaments" in the *Dorian* pattern for the Watson Company. Several pieces of *Dorian* holloware, including a coffeepot and bowl, accompanied the flatware in the exhibition (fig. 8.2; see also fig. 6.6). Frederick W. Stark, a staff designer for International Silver Company, was applauded for being "felicitous in curving plain surfaces," a reference to the Scandinavian-inspired naturalistic motifs and subtle contours of his centerpiece bowl (see fig. 8.7). Keyes singled out Tiffany & Co.'s contribution as "a fine example of modern treatment." Of the *Century* flatware and holloware by the staff designer Arthur Leroy Barney produced to commemorate the company's hundredth anniversary in 1937, she wrote, "their square service plate is satisfyingly proportioned, and the flat pieces are smart in their simplicity. Decorated only with incised parallel lines and square studs, the beauty of this table setting is that of restraint and elegance" (fig. 8.3).[4] Keyes also admired a sleek, compact coffee set introduced by Tiffany in 1934:[5] "The forms are clean-cut,

dramatic and full of style. They are designed with understanding of what machines do best and with respect for the material, whose softly gleaming texture is allowed to express itself instead of being smothered under a screen of heavy ornament."[6] The most "clean-cut"[7] example in Tiffany's display was a rectilinear vanity case designed by Barney in 1934 (fig. 8.4). Devoid of ornament and handsomely organized into taut compartments, it was a quintessential 1930s Machine Age object.

Another reviewer, Elizabeth MacRae Boykin, recognized the exhibition as "a survey of the best things that are being done in silver designing." An outspoken admirer of the modernity and "flowing graciousness" of Swedish and Danish silver, she felt strongly that contemporary American silver had been influenced more by the warmth of Scandinavian modern silver than by the "harsh severity of most Continental silver." Boykin noted that "more softly flowing lines than straight or geometrically curving ones" were in evidence, a "different story than we would have had to tell in similar exhibits of a few years back."[8] She could well have been referring to objects such as Stark's centerpiece bowl (see fig. 8.7), or a "Nordic bowl" by Harold E. Nock, the chief designer at Towle (fig. 8.5).[9] Boykin ranked American industrially produced objects above those by craftsmen, praising manufacturers for coordinating varying influences to achieve distinctive flatware and holloware and for producing "pieces that have wider adaptability for use with other things in the American background."[10] The exhibit ran from April 11 to May 23 and attracted a modest attendance of 11,388 people.[11] Details of the installation that drew notice were the use of yellow instead of traditional black velvet for the background of display cases, the evenly distributed lighting in the cases, and the spacious arrangement of objects.[12]

Visitors to the *Exposition Internationale des Arts et des Techniques dans la Vie Moderne* who were interested in American silver would find examples in two places: the best representation of industrial objects in the official United States Pavilion and handcrafted objects in the Palais de l'Artisanat, the main building of an annex situated between the portes Maillot and Dauphine.[13] The United States Pavilion, designed by Paul Wiener, Julian Clarence Levi, and Charles H. Higgins, was located on the Left Bank of the Seine across from the Trocadero and on the axis of the avenue de Suffren near the Eiffel Tower. The sleek façade facing the Seine had ribbon

FIGURE 8.3   *Century* soup spoon, 1937. Tiffany & Co., Arthur Leroy Barney, designer. Silver. Dallas Museum of Art, cat. 240

windows that were split at the entrance by a nine-story, glass-enclosed cylindrical tower that afforded sweeping views (fig. 8.6).[14]

The Society of Designer-Craftsmen, a group organized in New York City in 1936, had been requested by Frederick A. Sterling, the American Commissioner to the exposition, to select works for display. From photographs submitted by craftsmen throughout the country a committee of five chose the works, one per exhibitor.[15] Forty objects from the Metropolitan Museum of Art's silver exhibition that had closed on May 23 were added.[16] Ultimately, some two hundred objects in a variety of materials, including metal, were sent to Paris.[17] Although the exposition was open from May 25 through November 2, the United States Pavilion was late, not opening until Independence Day, July 4.[18] Of the industrial silver entries, three by staff designers received silver medals: Frederick W. Stark for a centerpiece bowl (fig. 8.7) produced by International Silver Company; William S. Warren for a flatware prototype produced by R. Wallace & Sons; and Arthur Leroy Barney for his *Century* flatware produced by Tiffany & Co. (see fig. 8.3).[19] Except for the omission of the Ionic capital at the tip of the handles, Wallace's flatware entry appears to have been almost the same as the firm's fluted *Vogue* pattern produced in silverplate in 1935 (fig. 8.8). While *Vogue* reflected the influence of 1930s modern

FIGURE 8.1   Gallery view, *Silver: An Exhibition of Contemporary American Design by Manufacturers, Designers and Craftsmen*, at The Metropolitan Museum of Art, 1937

FIGURE 8.2   Left: *Dorian* bowl, 1935, cat. 303; right: *Dorian* coffeepot, 1935, cat. 302. Watson Company, Percy B. Ball, designer. Silver. DMA, JSASC

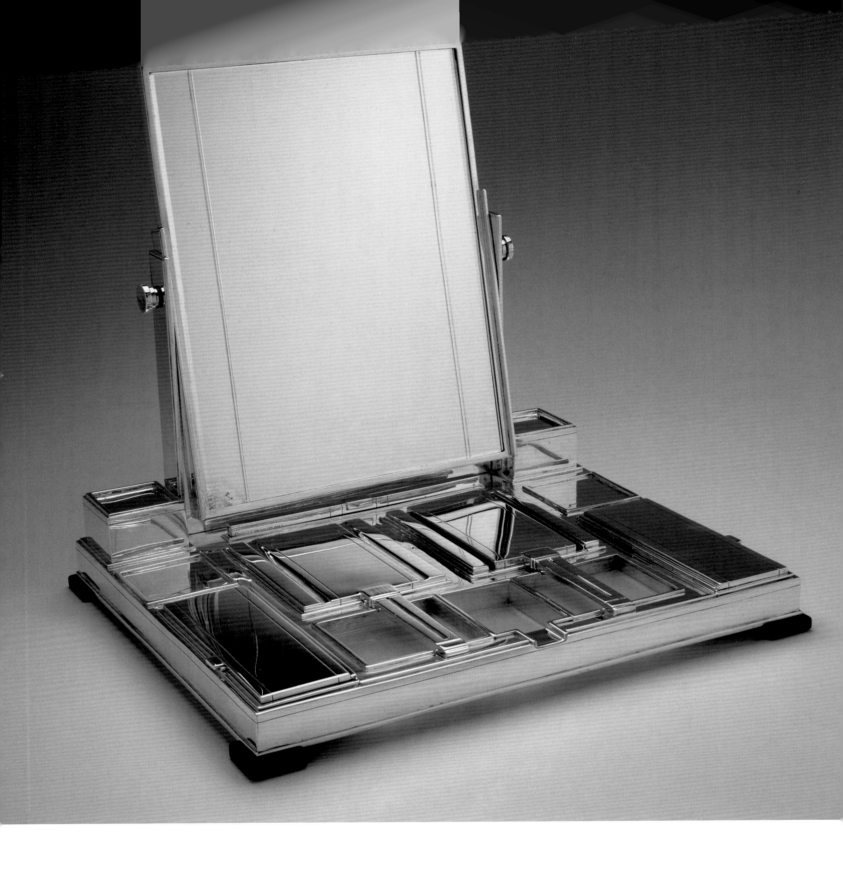

FIGURE 8.4   Vanity set, 1934. Tiffany & Co., Arthur Leroy Barney, designer. Silver, mahogany, glass, velvet. The John P. Axelrod Collection, Boston, Mass., cat. 239

classicism, *Century* retained the stacked and layered geometric motif ubiquitous in the late 1920s. In advertising, International proudly celebrated Stark's award-winning bowl, an example of the appreciation of Scandinavian taste in American silver.[20]

The other American exhibit, in the Palais de l'Artisanat, was assembled by the American Federation of Arts and organized with the aid of a Rockefeller Foundation grant.[21] The United States was one of a number of nations, including Great Britain, Austria, Finland, and Switzerland, invited by France to exhibit in this pavilion.[22] The American exhibit was derived from the *American Contemporary Crafts Show* mounted by the Art Alliance of Philadelphia in the spring of 1937,[23] and augmented by examples of southern mountain and American Indian crafts. Documentation from the American Federation of Arts unfortunately has not survived, nor has a copy of the catalogue, which was printed in Paris, been located.[24] However, contemporaneous accounts indicate that industrial silver was not included.[25] After the exposition closed, the American Federation of Arts included selected works in a traveling exhibition, *American Handicrafts from the Paris Exposition—1937.*[26]

The third notable exhibition of the year, *Contemporary Industrial and Handwrought Silver,* which opened on November 20 at the Brooklyn Museum, was more comprehensive, educational, and ambitious than the Metropolitan's exhibition. As in the latter, the focus was contemporary production, but eighteenth-century English and American examples were included to provide

FIGURE 8.5 Bowl, c. 1937. Towle Silversmiths. Silver. DMA, JSASC, cat. 255

historical context and as an introduction to the subject. Although differences between handwrought and mechanically spun or die-stamped silver were pointed out, especially in the appearance of surfaces, an objective, nonjudgmental stance was taken on aesthetics and fabrication. The interrelation of skilled manual work and machine production was stressed, while each method was allowed to stand on its "own merits."[27] Unusual were the demonstrations of various techniques of handwork and industrial processes throughout the course of the exhibition.[28] The Handy & Harman Company of New York, refiners and dealers in precious metals, supplied photographs showing the preparation of silver for industrial use, and the International Silver Company loaned a series of photographs illustrating the steps in the manufacture of silverplated flatware. Ten of these photographs appeared in the exhibition catalogue.[29] In addition International set up an electroplating bath in one gallery.[30] Also unlike the Metropolitan's exhibition, Mexican, American Indian, and Danish silver objects were included,[31] and the strong influence of "Danish and some Mexican silver" was cited in the catalogue.[32] The effect of Scandinavian-born American silversmiths on contemporary silver design was also mentioned in the press.[33]

Organized by Louise W. Chase, the director of the Brooklyn Museum's industrial art department, the

vignettes, and no two cases were alike. Because almost every case in the exhibition was devoted entirely to an individual silversmith or to a specific manufacturer, the production of each could be elucidated, compared, and evaluated.

The exhibition was staged in four galleries. As described by a reviewer for *Jewelers' Circular-Keystone,* the visitor, on entering the first small room, encountered examples of the work of colonial American silversmiths including a cup by John Coney made in 1701 and an engraved mug by Paul Revere. The visitor then proceeded past a Napoleonic dinner service borrowed from Cartier to the largest gallery, which was devoted to contemporary work in sterling silver by individual silversmiths and manufacturers. (A separate gallery contained industrial electroplated silver.) On one side of the large gallery were showcases of works by many American silversmiths of Scandinavian origin, including Peer Smed, Erik Magnussen, and Laurits Christian Eichner; on the other were sterling objects from American silver manufacturers. Keyes singled out the industrial examples: "The industrial designer, his genius trained to express itself within the exactions set up by machines, has perhaps even more adequately than the handworker made permanent in concrete images the temperament of our era. A visitor from Mars, set down before the display cases of commercial firms, would inevitably gain some impression of our homes and our customs."[35]

Outstanding showcases among the industrial firms represented were those of International and Reed &

installation was overseen by Christine Krehbiel, who was the daughter of Edward Krehbiel, the vice-president and general manager of Black, Starr & Frost-Gorham's store on Fifth Avenue in New York City,[34] and the presentation bore his aesthetic imprint. At the Metropolitan Museum, objects had been arranged uniformly on two levels; at the Brooklyn Museum, rectilinear bases in varying heights and widths were used. The effect was of

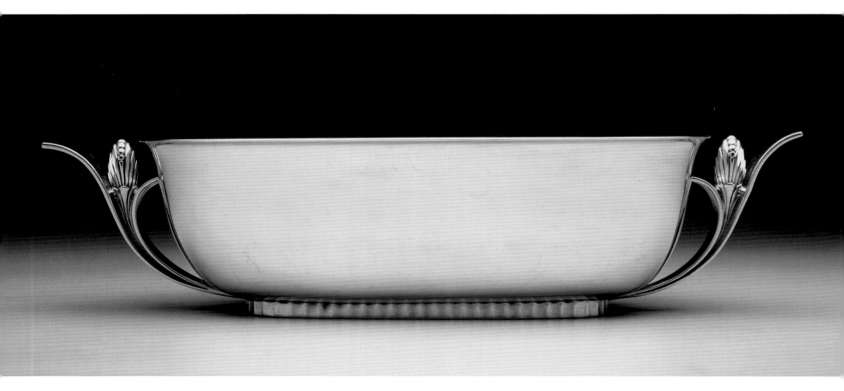

Barton. In the former, Frederick W. Stark demonstrated opposing sources of influence, nature and the machine. Naturalistic motifs embellished an ensemble in sterling comprising the centerpiece (see fig. 8.7) shown earlier in the year at the Metropolitan Museum and at the Paris exposition and its matching candelabra.[36] In contrast to this Scandinavian-inspired console set, and positioned adjacent to it, was a sterling place setting of *Continental* (see fig. 6.17), a severe, undecorated Machine Age pattern that Stark had designed in 1934, shown with its rectilinear service and bread and butter plates. Keyes made a connection between the geometry of this pattern and modern architecture.[37] Accenting the display was a sleek, stepped sterling cocktail shaker with a spherical finial that stood on an elevated base (see fig. 7.2).

The highlight of Reed & Barton's sterling silver showcase was the work of Belle Kogan: an oval sandwich tray (fig. 8.9) and a salad bowl in a design of adapted classical motifs (see fig. 6.8, left), an hors d'oeuvres tray with openwork handles of stylized overlapping leaves (see fig. 6.34), and a silverplated centerpiece in the same design as her double vegetable dish (see fig. 6.16).[38] Keyes lauded Kogan for evolving a "simple style of adornment."[39]

Rogers, Lunt & Bowlen loaned several pieces of *Modern Classic,* a sterling holloware and flatware pattern by Robert E. Locher, a prominent designer of interiors and decorative art, that was introduced in 1934. The "dignified simplicity" of *Modern Classic,* its lack of ostentation, and the emphasis on expansive surfaces were admired.[40] Those qualities are embodied in the formidable floral centerpiece with a geometric mesh cover and tray (see fig. 6.5) that is part of the service but was not, however, exhibited.

Golden Gate International Exposition

The completion of the San Francisco–Oakland Bay Bridge and of the Golden Gate Bridge in 1936 and 1937, respectively, occasioned the celebratory *Golden Gate International Exposition,* which opened on February 18, 1939, ran through October 29, and was revived in 1940 for a shorter run from May through September. Access to Treasure Island, the artificially created site of the exposition in San Francisco Bay, was via the Bay Bridge or by ferry.

Modern silver was exhibited in the Palace of Fine and Decorative Arts overlooking San Francisco Bay. In her catalogue essay, Elisabeth Moses, the curator of decorative arts of the M. H. de Young Memorial Museum in San Francisco, reflected: "If we use the catchword 'streamlined' for the style of the present day, we discover a close formal relationship between a building, a train and a teapot—model 1939. The architect, the engineer, and the silversmith follow the same determinants

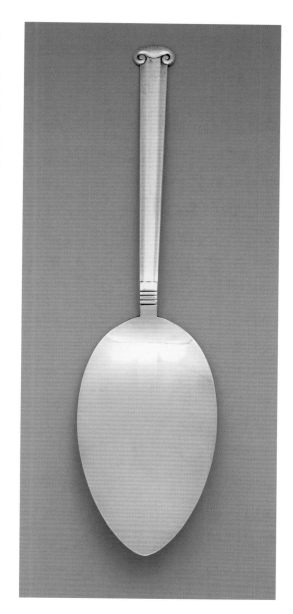

FIGURE 8.8 *Vogue* pie server, 1935. R. Wallace and Sons Manufacturing Company, William S. Warren, designer. Silverplate. DMA, JSASC, cat. 294

of form." Continuing, she praised silver objects that derived their beauty from line and smooth surfaces rather than from applied ornament. Of flat silver in the exhibit she observed that it "breaks away from tradition, repeating the characteristics of the larger silver objects. It is held to straight and rectangular lines, to massiveness of form, to restraint in ornamentation." Danish work was singled out for the highest accolade, a harbinger of Scandinavian dominance in design after World War II: "When the Danish artist designs with one bold stroke, he, of necessity, achieves a verve and a dynamic quality in the outline of his object. Simplicity, beauty of line, and quality—these are the criteria of style for all modern objects which surround us in everyday life."[41]

Denmark, Sweden, France, Mexico, and the United States contributed to the Modern Silver section. Georg Jensen Sølvsmedie, the Danish firm, sent designs by

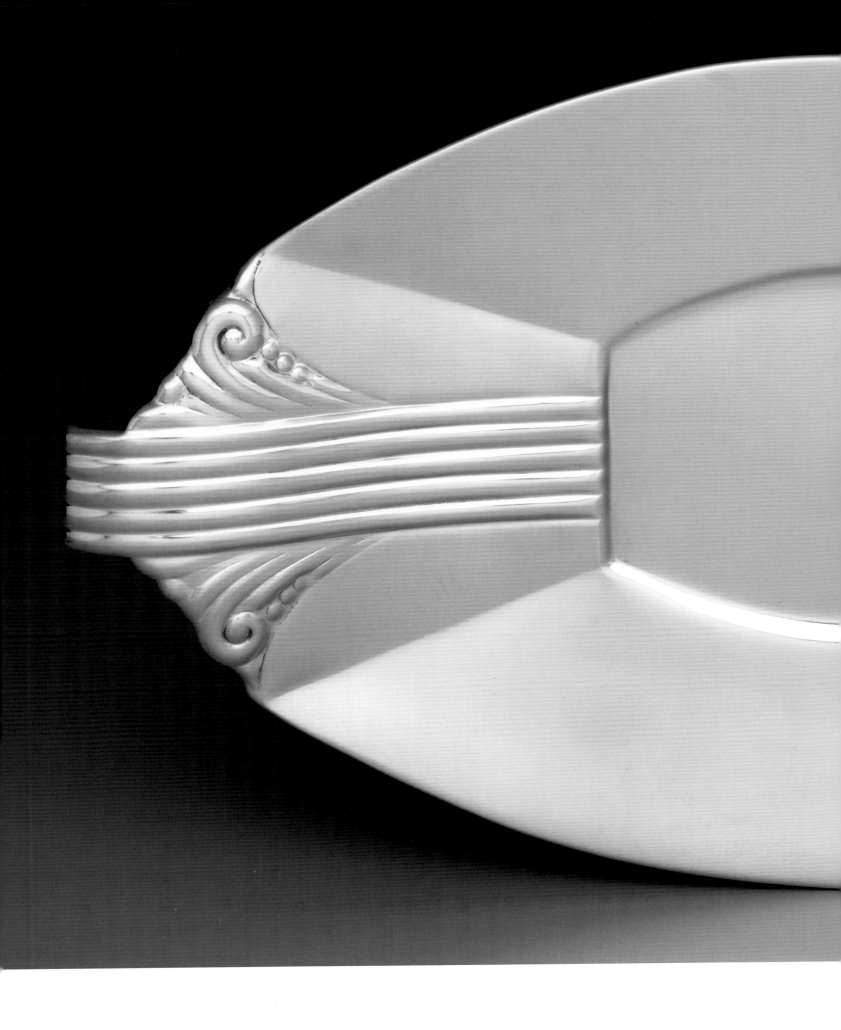

FIGURE 8.9   Sandwich tray, 1936. Reed & Barton, Belle Kogan,
designer. Silver. DMA, JSASC, cat. 170

Johan Rohde, Harald Nielsen, Just Anderson, the Swede Sigvard Bernadotte, and the American Henry Pilstrup.[42] Baron Erik Fleming represented Sweden. Puiforcat of France showed the largest group of silverware and it was extensively illustrated in the catalogue. William Spratling, an American working in Mexico, exhibited jewelry, flatware, and holloware. Handwrought and industrially produced silverware were exhibited together. Among the Americans exhibiting handwrought objects were Porter Blanchard, Margret Craver, Laurits Christian Eichner, and Peter Mueller-Munk.[43] The sole American manufacturer was the International Silver Company, represented by three services listed in the catalogue, the *Arcadia* and *Modern Colonial* silverplated services and the sterling *Continental* service, designed by and credited to E. J. Conroy, L. V. M. Helander, and Frederick W. Stark, respectively. The *Modern Colonial* service by Lillian Helander, a staff designer and one of the first women to be employed in that position, was as its name implied a hybrid, with traditional spouts and handles joined to triangular vessels with stepped bases, lids, and finials. As described in one of the company's sales catalogues, "this finest quality set is reminiscent of the colonial silver that graced the side-boards of our early American aristocracy and is blended with the modern in lovely combination."[44] Although the *Arcadia* service had smooth undecorated bodies, ovoid for the tea and coffeepots and creamer and spherical for the covered sugar and waste bowls, the design, which had been introduced in 1934, was a somewhat awkward attempt at "streamlining."[45] The rigid lines of *Continental* were a sharp contrast to those of the other two services. Lent by S. & G. Gump, the exclusive San Francisco department store, the *Continental* service in this exhibit consisted of the place setting in the pattern (see fig. 6.17) together with the severe rectilinear service plate designed to coordinate with the flatware.[46] This sophisticated

Machine Age ensemble by Stark had been shown two years earlier on the East Coast in the Brooklyn Museum's silver exhibition. The talented and versatile Stark, whose designs ranged from Scandinavian naturalism to geometric minimalism, produced silver of refinement and distinction regardless of the style he worked in (see figs. 6.17, 7.10, 7.11, and 8.7).

New York World's Fair, 1939–1940

Paying tribute to design movements that were symbolic of the decade and of the vision of a better future through science, industry, and business, the New York World's Fair opened in 1939 in a setting that expressed both modern classicism and streamlining. The most spectacular presentation of American industrial silver at the fair was unequivocally that of Tiffany & Co. in the House of Jewels. Located at Hamilton Place and Constitution Mall, the building (fig. 8.10), called "a jewel of modern architecture" in the official guidebook, was a collaboration between the designer Raymond Loewy and the architect J. Gordon Carr and was erected as a joint venture of De Beers Consolidated Mines Ltd. of South Africa, the Diamond Corporation Ltd., Tiffany & Co., Black, Starr & Frost-Gorham, Cartier, Marcus and Company, and Udall and Ballou.

The primary exhibitors of silverware were Tiffany & Co. and Black, Starr & Frost-Gorham.[47] Aside from a coffee set and cocktail shaker set that were fussy reversions to late-1920s design, Gorham concentrated heavily on period revival styles (fig. 8.11). The selections reflected the company's retreat from modernism after the lukewarm responses to Magnussen's designs and the

FIGURE 8.10   House of Jewels, New York World's Fair, 1939

FIGURE 8.11   Display case, Black, Starr and Frost-Gorham, House of Jewels, New York World's Fair, 1939

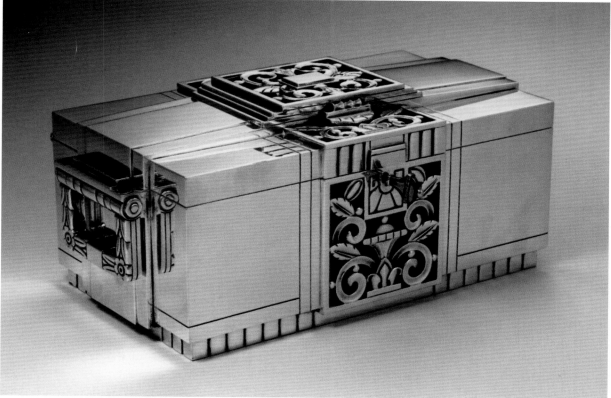

FIGURE 8.12   Display case, Tiffany & Co., House of Jewels,
New York World's Fair, 1939

FIGURE 8.13   Photograph: Box, 1938. Tiffany & Co., Arthur Leroy
Barney, designer. Silver. Exhibited in the House of Jewels, New York
World's Fair, 1939

FIGURE 8.14   Water pitcher and tumbler, 1938. Tiffany & Co., attributed to Arthur Leroy Barney, designer. Gilded silver. Dallas Museum of Art, cat. 246

onset of the Depression. Unwilling to take further risks, and with William Codman, an outspoken opponent of innovation, at the helm of the design department until 1938, Gorham had positioned itself conservatively in the marketplace and produced few modern designs in the 1930s.[48] Tiffany, in contrast, adhered to a robust, if late, interpretation of *art moderne* ornament (fig. 8.12). Prominent motifs were stylized leaves, scrolls, flutes, and layered stepping, clearly apparent on the large rectangular jewelry box (fig. 8.13) that rests on a base of convex flutes and has centered, openwork relief panels on the front, back, and cover in a stylized leaf and scroll design. Subtle layering occurs longitudinally across the top and sides to the handles embellished with rosettes and leaves. Similar are the pitcher and tumbler (fig. 8.14) from an exhibited service that originally had a matching tray and second tumbler (see fig. 8.12, extreme left). For these objects floral motifs were eschewed in favor of classical motifs. The pitcher and tumbler are supported on flat, square bases that are tied like a gift package to

the vessels by four vertical, layered bands that extend from the bottom of the bases to the rims, and are fluted horizontally. The fluting terminates at a delicate incised frieze above which the bands are accented by flat rectangular plaques that step up slightly above the rims. The pitcher handle arcs boldly to meet the rim with decorative flat volutes. Of the objects exhibited, a tea service that emphasized elliptical form was the most expressive of 1930s streamlining.[49]

Tiffany's display was a considerable investment on the part of the company, as well as the tour de force of its chief silver designer, Arthur Leroy Barney.[50] Cautious in adopting new trends in design during the late 1920s and especially during the economic recession of the 1930s, Tiffany & Co. used the opportunity of the World's Fair to ensure its leading position in the luxury trade. Although

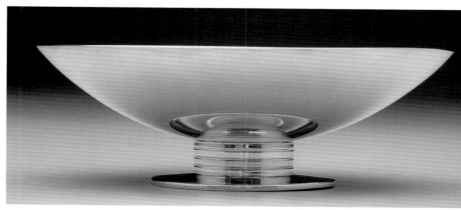

FIGURE 8.17   Compote, 1935. Tiffany & Co. Silver. DMA, JSASC, cat. 238

FIGURE 8.15   Salad serving set, 1937. Tiffany & Co., Olaf Wilford, designer. Gilded silver. DMA, JSASC, cat. 241

FIGURE 8.16   Salad bowl, 1940. Tiffany & Co., attributed to Olaf Wilford, designer. Silver. DMA, JSASC, cat. 241

highly sought after now, many of the pieces were too expensive for most consumers and were returned to the company unsold.[51] In 1940 Tiffany added several objects to its House of Jewels display that were more attuned to the marketplace, among them a production-line salad bowl with applied bands in a naturalistic motif that was executed in 1940 to match and accompany a set of gilded servers designed in 1937 by the Norwegian staff designer Olaf Wilford (1894–1980) (figs. 8.15, 8.16).[52] Although not given a formal pattern name by Tiffany, the motifs are commonly referred to by the public as tomato or pumpkin vine. The few flatware serving pieces and limited holloware made in this pattern were among the most popular from the period and remained in production until the early 1950s.[53] In contrast to the Scandinavian-influenced naturalism of the salad ensemble, a low compote (fig. 8.17) produced in 1935 and added to the display in 1940, was, with its sole decoration being horizontal incised lines on the foot, more evocative of austere 1930s minimalism.

Elsewhere at the fair, objects in silver were part of exhibitions in the United States Government Building

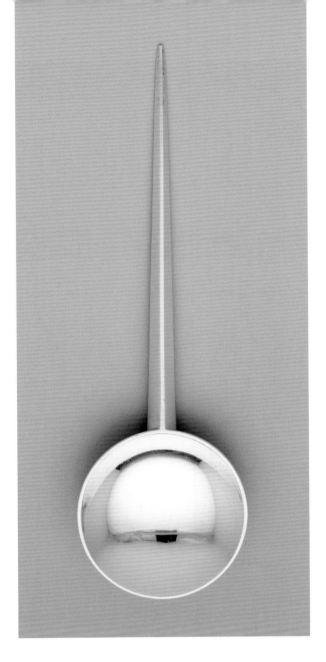

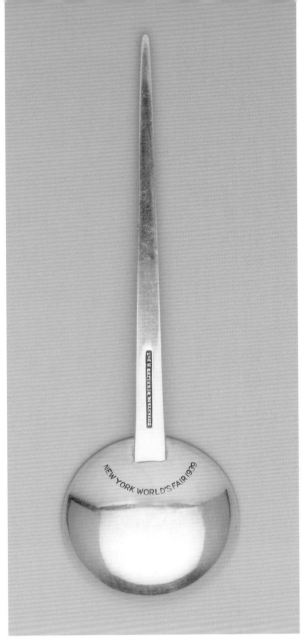

FIGURES 8.18, 8.19   1939 New York World's Fair spoon, 1937
(front and back views). Tiffany & Co., Arthur Leroy Barney, designer.
Silver. The Jewel Stern American Silver Collection, cat. 245

and the New York State Building. The Society of
Designer-Craftsmen was designated by the World's
Fair Commission to organize an open competition for
submission of furniture, textiles, and other crafts to be
exhibited in the United States Government Building.[54]
Neither prizes nor cash were awarded to successful
competitors, but each received a citation of excellence.[55] Peter Bittermann, the vice president and later
the president of the society, was the coordinator of the
project.[56] Francisco Rebajes, Kenneth Bates, and Laurits
Christian Eichner, all metalsmiths, contributed works
to the United States Government Building exhibits.[57] In
the New York State Building, the New York Society of
Craftsmen was one of the exhibitors.[58] Unfortunately,
no list of silversmiths whose work was shown in this
venue has come to light. A plan for an arts and crafts

exhibit in the America at Home Building, to be organized by Dorothy Wright Liebes, who had organized the
decorative arts at the *Golden Gate International Exposition* in San Francisco, was later abandoned.[59]

In addition to its exhibits in the House of Jewels, Tiffany & Co. produced a sterling souvenir spoon
(figs. 8.18, 8.19) designed by Barney in both tea and
demitasse sizes to commemorate the fair's theme building, the towering trylon and perisphere. The prismatic
handle and circular bowl of this abstract form elegantly
evoked the powerful symbol of the fair and was the epitome of 1930s streamlining.[60] International and Wallace
offered less expensive souvenir spoons in silverplate.
The handle of Wallace's spoon, a superb melding of
1930s streamlining and modern classicism, curves aero-
dynamically around the tip to embrace a trylon and perisphere set in a field of cobalt blue enamel punctuated
with a single star and supported by an abstract depic-
tion of classical columns. Stamped on the face of the
handle are the words "New York World's Fair . . . World
of Tomorrow 1939" (fig. 8.20). International's spoon was

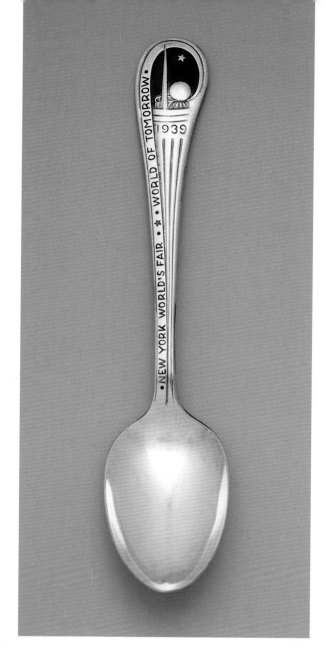

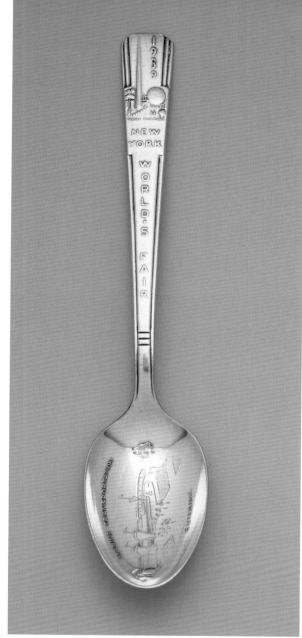

patented by Lillian Helander (1899–1973), a graduate of the Rhode Island School of Design, who began working at International in the early 1930s. Helander, a pioneering woman in the field, reportedly designed souvenir flatware for both the *Century of Progress Exposition* in Chicago in 1933 and the *Golden Gate International Exposition* in San Francisco in 1939.[61] Her design for New York included the emblematic trylon and perisphere stamped on a stepped-back and layered handle, a reprise of 1920s imagery (fig. 8.21). According to a history of the company that was published in 1947, "For nearly a year Miss Helander studied its ultra-modern architecture, poured [*sic*] over the files of the World's Fair Committee, studied drawings, photographs and ornamental decorations, until she had assimilated the spirit of the enterprise. Then she designed a World's Fair spoon which International distributed by the millions through a New York City daily paper."[62] The bowls of the spoons were decorated with images of prominent buildings at the fair, and the souvenirs could be purchased singly so that the buyers could select their favorite or assemble

FIGURE 8.20   1939 New York World's Fair spoon, 1939. R. Wallace & Sons Manufacturing Company. Enameled silverplate. DMA, JSASC, cat. 296

FIGURE 8.21   1939 New York World's Fair spoon, 1938. William Rogers Manufacturing Company, Lillian V. M. Helander, designer. Silverplate. The Jewel Stern American Silver Collection, cat. 100

FIGURE 8.22 Centerpiece and candelabra, 1949. Tiffany & Co.,
Oscar Riedener, designer. Silver. Dallas Museum of Art, cat. 247

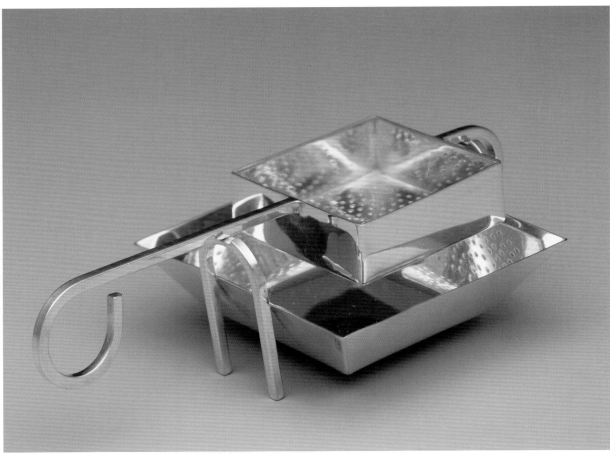

FIGURE 8.23 Display, Metals and Glass, Ely Jacques Kahn, architect. Exhibit in *Contemporary American Industrial Art,* the Metropolitan Museum of Art, 1940

FIGURE 8.24 Tea strainer with caddy, c. 1938–1939. Leonore Doskow, Inc., Leonore Doskow, designer. Silver. DMA, JSASC, cat. 9

a collection. International's William Rogers division manufactured these spoons as well as a flatware service in the pattern, but with plain bowls.[63] Unlike Tiffany's expensive spoon in sterling, International's popular, mass-produced spoon and flatware and Wallace's souvenir spoon, all in economical silverplate, were intended for the average consumer.

A quintessential example of the lingering influence of Tiffany's House of Jewels tour de force is a lavish ensemble created in 1949 by the Swiss-American Oscar Riedener (1901–2000), a staff designer. Consisting of a floral centerpiece and pair of candelabra on a regal scale (fig. 8.22), the set has a remarkable affinity with Tiffany's spectacular display. Not surprisingly, Riedener had assisted Barney on the silver made especially for the 1939 New York World's Fair.[64] A single naturalistic motif, the pyramidal pinecone, was chosen as the finial of the centerpiece and enlarged as low finials for the four-branched candelabra. The naturalism brings to mind Scandinavian silverware. However, Riedener retained the overall preciousness of the fair work and its French *art moderne* stylistic character, especially in the fluted supports of the centerpiece and the subtly notched octagonal bases, and he introduced softer curves in the contours, scallops, and loops of the components, artfully playing curve against curve for contrast. The upward curve of the centerpiece bowl complements the downward curve of the domed bases of the candelabra. The trumpet-shaped branches of the candelabra activate the ensemble and contrast effectively with the solidity of the centerpiece.

The set was extremely expensive to produce because of the enormous amount of hand labor involved. Karl A. Danielson, one of Tiffany's silversmiths, spent seven hundred hours on the three pieces, and he was only one of the fabricators. The cost of production, including 285 troy ounces of silver, was thirty-nine hundred dollars and the retail price was seventy-eight hundred dollars, a huge sum at the time.[65] This post–World War II ensemble appears to be unique and may have been a special order from an affluent customer with a fond recollection of the prewar Tiffany display in the House of Jewels. Or it could have been a commission in which Riedener finally had the opportunity and freedom to match his mentor Arthur Leroy Barney.

Contemporary American Industrial Art

As the New York World's Fair entered its second season in the spring of 1940, the Metropolitan Museum of Art mounted its fifteenth exhibition of *Contemporary American Industrial Art*. The events ran simultaneously through the summer. The format of the Metropolitan's exhibition was similar to that held in 1934, and Ely Jacques Kahn, Ralph Walker, and Eugene Schoen, all

veterans of the exhibitions in 1929 and 1934, headed three of the four sections. In his catalogue essay Richard F. Bach asserted that "the exhibition of 1940 shows together, as they are used in daily life, the products of craftsmen and those of quantity-producing industry."[66] However, in contrast to 1929 and 1934, the silver industry was represented only with a minor contribution by Samuel Kirk & Son in the Room for a Five-year-old Child by Raymond Loewy.[67] The International Silver Company, which had had sizeable displays in 1929 and 1934, did not participate in 1940. The silverware entries were skewed in favor of craft, seemingly a reaction against mass-produced, machine-made goods and a revaluing of the unique handmade object. It was a harbinger, too, of the studio movement that would take off in the 1950s. This was evident in the groupings of Metals and Glass (fig. 8.23) under the direction of Ely Jacques Kahn, leader of the North Section, and of Metals and Synthetic Textiles in the East Section, overseen by the architect Harvey Wiley Corbett. Kahn selected the work of the silversmiths Rebecca Cauman, Leonore Doskow, Laurits Christian Eichner, Harold Tishler, and Peter Reimes, the latter working with the enamelist William Stark to produce a candelabrum designed by Tommi Parzinger.[68] The silver objects in Corbett's exhibit were a vase by Tishler and a tea service by Harry Bertoia.[69] Leonore Doskow (born 1910) was the only maker who developed quantity production lines.[70] Her geometrical cream and sugar set with a tray was similar in shape to another of her pieces from the same period, a square tea strainer, with circular perforations and a curved handle, that rested on a square and angled floating caddy with U-shaped supports (fig. 8.24), an innovative interpretation of a traditional object. The designer's company, Leonore Doskow, Inc., specialized in jewelry and small novelties on which geometric openwork monograms became a hallmark.[71]

The focus on individual silversmiths and the corresponding neglect of silver manufacturers in this exhibition can be attributed in part to the concentration of accomplished silversmiths in metropolitan New York in the late 1930s and to the recognition accorded them by their contemporaries in design. Many had previous exposure in important exhibitions such as the expositions in Paris in 1937 and in San Francisco in 1939.[72] Another factor was the close association of the influential Society of Designer-Craftsmen with the Architectural League of New York.[73] A lack of innovation from the silver industry, in part an effect of changing markets during the closing years of the decade, can be discerned from periodicals and may have contributed to the omission of manufacturers. In addition, a significant shift in mood and mode from the sleek glamour associated with 1930s streamlined design, epitomized by Deskey's

FIGURE 8.25 Dining Room, Donald Deskey, designer. Exhibit in *Contemporary American Industrial Art,* the Metropolitan Museum of Art, 1934

FIGURE 8.26 Prefabricated Cabin Interior, Donald Deskey, designer. Exhibit in *Contemporary American Industrial Art,* the Metropolitan Museum of Art, 1940

dining room in 1934 (fig. 8.25), to an informal idiom was apparent throughout the exhibition. Nowhere was this more evident than in the replacement of curvilinear tubular metal, a highlight in 1934, with straight-legged, light wood furniture (fig. 8.26).[74] Another contrast was in the attendance: the exhibition in 1934 had attracted twice as many visitors.[75] In a sense, the 1940 exhibition anticipated post–World War II casual lifestyles and the consequential move away from formal entertaining for which silver was a vital element.

Notes

1. Richard F. Bach, "Contemporary American Design in Silver," in *Silver: An Exhibition of Contemporary American Design by Manufacturers, Designers and Craftsmen,* exh. cat. (New York: Metropolitan Museum of Art, 1937), 5. The principal silver manufacturers exhibiting were: International Silver Company, Graff, Washbourne & Dunn, Samuel Kirk & Son Inc., Rogers, Lunt & Bowlen, Tiffany & Co., Towle Manufacturing Company, Tuttle Silver Company, Inc., R. Wallace & Sons Manufacturing Company, Gorham, and The Watson Company; see "Firms, Designers, and Craftsmen . . . ," in ibid., 11.

2. Ibid., 8.

3. "Exhibition Silver at the Metropolitan Museum," *House and Garden* 72 (July 1937): 58.

4. Helen Johnson Keyes, "Contemporary American Silver," *Christian Science Monitor,* May 1, 1937, sec. 10, p. 6.

5. For a photograph of the set, see Augusta Owen Patterson, "Silver Ritual from Nine to Five," *Town and Country* 89 (Oct. 15, 1934): 46. The price of the coffee set and tray was $350; see Tiffany & Co. advertisement, *Town and Country* 91 (June 1936): 1.

6. Keyes, "Contemporary American Silver."

7. Ibid.

8. Elizabeth MacRae Boykin, "Modern Silver Put on Display; Metropolitan Museum Has Contemporary Showing," *New York Sun,* Apr. 10, 1937 (newspaper clipping, Brooklyn Museum of Art Archives, Brooklyn, New York).

9. For the "Nordic bowl," see Elisabeth Brown, "Contemporary Table Decoration," *Interior Decorator* 97 (Aug. 1937): 41; "The Art of American Silversmiths Today," *Art News* 35 (Apr. 17, 1939): 12; and "Exhibition Silver at the Metropolitan Museum," *House and Garden* 72 (July 1937): 58.

10. Boykin, "Modern Silver."

11. Exhibition file, Metropolitan Museum of Art Archives, New York (hereafter Metropolitan Museum Archives).

12. "For This Day and Age," *Jewelers' Circular-Keystone* 107 (May 1937): 106.

13. For an overview of the 1937 Paris exposition, see John E. Findling and Kimberly D. Pelle, eds., *Historical Dictionary of World's Fairs and Expositions, 1851–1988* (New York: Greenwood Press, 1990), 288–89; for a detailed report, see Edmond Labbe, *Exposition internationale des arts et techniques dans la vie moderne (1937): rapport général,* 11 vols. (Paris: Imprimerie nationale, 1939–40).

14. *International Exhibition Paris 1937: Arts and Crafts in Modern Life: Official Guide,* May–November, English ed. (Paris: Editions de la société pour le développement du tourisme, 1937), 113.

15. The committee of five included Peter Bittermann, Maurice Heaton, and D. Adelbert Hoerger.

16. Exhibition file, Metropolitan Museum Archives.

17. "Paris Judgment: World Fair to See America's Products of Living Craftsmanship," *Literary Digest* 123 (May 8, 1937): 33. In the exposition catalogue, American silver was listed in the category of *Orfèvrerie. Coutellerie* (silverware and flatware), and assigned to *Groupe IX, Classe 44* (Labbe, *Exposition internationale,* 678).

18. "Craftsmen of U.S. to Exhibit in Paris," *New York Times,* July 3, 1937, 17. The pavilion closed the next day, and reopened on August 2.

19. "Rapport présenté à M. Le Ministre du Commerce par le rapporteur général près le jury supérieur de L'Exposition Internationale de Paris 1937 sur les opérations du jury," *Journal Officiel de la République Française* (July 22, 1938), 889–90. For R. Wallace & Sons flatware, see Brown, "Contemporary Table Decoration," 41; and "Exhibition Silver at the Metropolitan," 58. The International Silver bowl by Stark had been exhibited in 1937 in both the Metropolitan Museum and the Brooklyn Museum; the flatware by Tiffany & Co. (*Century*) and by R. Wallace & Sons had been exhibited only at the Metropolitan.

20. "A Christmas Bough by International Sterling," International Silver Company advertisement, *House Beautiful* 79 (Dec. 1937): 3. The bowl and matching candelabra were illustrated, the bowl priced at $150, the pair of candelabra at $175, and it was observed in the text that the bowl had been exhibited at the Metropolitan Museum of Art and at the Paris exposition.

21. The exhibit in the Palais de l'Artisanat (*Groupe II, Classe 9*) was the seventeenth international exhibition under the direction of the American Federation of Arts. The amount of the Rockefeller grant was $4,200 (Harold Oakhill, archivist, Rockefeller Archive Center, New York, letter to author, June 20, 1990). See also "Events Here and There," *New York Times,* June 20, 1937, 10: 7; and "American Crafts at the Paris Exposition," *Magazine of Art* 30 (June 1937): 350–51.

22. *International Exhibition Paris 1937,* 145.

23. Field Notes, *Magazine of Art* 30 (May 1937): 324. The Philadelphia Art Alliance show closed on April 10, 1937.

24. Annie Raulerson, exhibitions assistant, American Federation of Arts, letter to author, May 18, 1990.

25. "American Crafts," 350–51; and "Events Here and There," 7.

26. See Circulating Exhibition Number A-85, in National Exhibition Service, Handbook No. 2, Apr. issue, season 1937–38: 26; and "American Arts and Crafts as Exhibited at L'Exposition Internationale, Paris, 1937," in Modern Crafts, exh. cat. (New York: Baltimore Museum of Art, 1938), n.p. In addition to the Baltimore Museum of Art, the University of Pittsburgh and the George Walter Vincent Smith Art Gallery, Springfield, Mass., were venues in 1938; see Florence N. Levy, ed., American Art Annual 34 (1937–38), 257, 431.

27. Foreword, Contemporary Industrial and Handwrought Silver, exh. cat. (New York: Brooklyn Museum, 1937), n.p.

28. "New York Silver Yesterday & Tomorrow," Art News 36 (Dec. 11, 1937): 15.

29. Contemporary Industrial and Handwrought Silver.

30. "Museum Shows Commercial Silver," Jewelers' Circular-Keystone 108 (Feb. 1938): 71.

31. One case was devoted to contemporary Navajo work; See Helen Johnson Keyes, "Contemporary American Silverware," Christian Science Monitor (Nov. 27, 1937), 13.

32. Contemporary Industrial and Handwrought Silver.

33. Keyes, "Contemporary American Silverware"; and idem, "Creating Mass Appeal for Silver," Jewelers' Circular-Keystone 108 (Jan. 1938): 62.

34. "Museum Shows Commercial Silver," 72.

35. Keyes, "Creating Mass Appeal," 62–63.

36. For the console set by Stark, see Window Shopping, House Beautiful 179 (Nov. 1937): 12; and Barbara Hill, "Choosing the Bride's Silver," Country Life 74 (May 1938): 77. The bowl was illustrated in Marshall Field & Company, Fashions of the Hour (autumn 1937), 21.

37. "Creating Mass Appeal," 62.

38. The centerpiece was Reed & Barton's product number 1605.

39. "Creating Mass Appeal," 63.

40. Ibid.

41. Elisabeth Moses, "Modern Silver," in Official Catalog: Department of Fine Arts Division of Decorative Arts, Golden Gate International Exposition, San Francisco, 1939 (San Francisco: H. S. Crocker; Schwabacher-Frey, 1939), 81.

42. The work of Frantz Hingelberg and H. P. Jacobson, two other Danes, was also in the exhibit.

43. The jeweler Margaret De Patta and the Stone Associates firm exhibited their work.

44. Quoted from "No. 9300 Tea and Coffee Set," in 1847 Rogers Bros. Wm. Rogers & Son Hollowware, sales catalogue (n.d.), n.p. (International Silver Company Archives, Meriden Historical Society, Meriden, Conn.; hereafter International Silver Archives).

45. Official Catalog, 82–83. The Arcadia service, which was introduced in 1934 in the 1847 Rogers Bros. line, is illustrated in International Silver Service 3 (Sept. 1934): 16 (International Silver Archives).

46. From notes in a scrapbook at Gorham Archive (John Hay Library, Brown University, Providence, R.I.), it is apparent that what was described in the exhibition catalogue as the Continental "service" (i.e., a tea and coffee service) was in fact a service plate and place setting. A bread and butter plate in Continental was also designed and these two pieces appear to be the only ones that International produced to coordinate with the flatware pattern.

47. Official Guide Book: New York World's Fair, 1939 (New York: Exposition Publications, 1939), 76; and "Greater Jewel Exhibit Planned," New York Times, Mar. 28, 1940, 12.

48. Two known exceptions were the art moderne–inspired Franconia holloware pattern that was introduced by Gorham in the spring of 1930 but was probably on the drawing board in 1929 (see fig. 3.44) and a minimal, geometric mayonnaise bowl of 1934 (see fig. 6.18). For a history of the financial vicissitudes of Gorham in the 1920s and 1930s, see Charles L. Venable, Silver in America, 1840–1940: A Century of Splendor (Dallas, Tex.: Dallas Museum of Art, 1994), 228–29, 237–42.

49. Ibid., 287, fig. 9.32.

50. John Loring, Magnificent Tiffany Silver (New York: Abrams, 2001), 240–47. Barney was the chief silver designer from 1919 to 1955.

51. Ibid., 242. An exception was the tea set purchased at the 1939 New York World's Fair by Melvina Schulz Raymer; see Christie, Manson, and Woods International,

Inc., Important 20th Century Decorative Arts, sale catalogue, New York, Dec. 12 1992, lot 274A.

52. House of Jewels 1940 Inventory List (Tiffany & Co. Archives, Parsippany, N.J.; hereafter Tiffany Archives). Oscar Riedener, a designer for Tiffany, identified Wilford as the designer (Riedener, Irvington-on-Hudson, N.Y., letter to author, undated but 1992).

53. For a bowl with matching pastry server and berry spoon, see "Gifts from Tiffany" (1953), 16 (Tiffany Archives). For a ten-inch sandwich plate, see Tiffany & Co. sterling silverware catalogue (1954), 7 (Tiffany Archives). A pierced vegetable spoon and a cold meat fork were also produced in this pattern.

54. "Philippines Sign for Space at Fair," New York Times, May 25, 1938, 21; Levy, ed., American Art Annual 34, 362; and idem, American Art Annual 35 (New York: Macmillan, 1940), 345.

55. "Temple of Religion Is Started at Fair," New York Times, Nov. 24, 1938, 16.

56. Ibid.

57. United States Government Building; New York World's Fair 1940 (booklet), 20, 23 (courtesy of Queens Museum of Art, Queens, N.Y.).

58. "World's Fair Exhibits," New York Times, July 21, 1940, sec. 2, p. 7.

59. "Louise and Shep, telegram to Dorothy Wright Liebes Mar. 24, 1940 (Dorothy Wright Liebes file, box 364, series 2, America at Home, 1939 New York World's Fair Coll., Manuscripts and Archives Div., New York Public Library). The focus of the America at Home Building became the Living in America exhibit, sixteen model rooms by leading designers. Although industrial silver was probably displayed, no records have been found.

60. The demitasse spoon was reissued in 1989 to commemorate the fiftieth anniversary of the fair.

61. "Miss Lillian Helander: Pioneer in Industrial Design," Morning Record (Meriden, Conn.), Feb. 9, 1963, n.p. (newspaper clipping, International Silver Archives).

62. Earl Chapin May, A Century of Silver, 1847–1947: Connecticut Yankees and a Noble Metal (New York: Robert M. McBride, 1947), 309.

63. For Helander's flatware service, see Jeannine Falino, "Women Metalsmiths," in Pat Kirkham, ed., Women Designers in the USA, 1900–2000 (New Haven: Yale University Press, 2000), 234.

64. Loring, Magnificent Tiffany Silver, 247.

65. Information from Tiffany & Co. Archives in object file 1995.72.1–3, Dallas Museum of Art, Dallas, Tex.

66. Richard F. Bach, "Contemporary American Industrial Art: 1940," in Contemporary American Industrial Art, exh. cat. (New York: Metropolitan Museum of Art, 1940), 9.

67. Ibid., 38.

68. Ibid., 13.

69. Ibid., 22.

70. For the only known image of Doskow's cream and sugar set, see Alfred Auerbach, "New Materials in Decoration," Retailing, Home Furnishings 12 (May 6, 1940): 9.

71. At its peak in the 1970s, seventy-five people were employed. A family enterprise, it has continued into the twenty-first century under the name Croton Crafts in Westchester County, New York; see "Six Decades of Smithery," Bryn Mawr Alumni Bulletin (spring 2001): 39.

72. For example, Cauman, Tishler, and Eichner exhibited in the 1937 Paris exposition and in the 1937 Brooklyn Museum silver exhibition. Eichner and Parzinger exhibited in the 1939 Golden Gate International Exposition in San Francisco.

73. Waylande Gregory, "Attention, Designer-Craftsmen," Decorator Digest 6 (June 1936): 40–41. The organization also contributed to the 1939 New York World's Fair.

74. For example, in 1934 exhibits of work by Gilbert Rohde, Lee Simonson and Loewy, Lescaze, and Brown included tubular metal furniture. In 1940 exhibits of work by Loewy, Deskey, Lescaze, and Teague included furniture with straight legs and light wood finishes, and the exhibits of work by Russel Wright and Edward Durell Stone included furniture with wicker or rattan elements; see also "Home," Architectural Forum 73 (October 1940): 258.

75. In 1940 the turnout, 69,847, was half that of 1934, which was 139,261, and less than one-fourth if averaged per day of the respective runs.

CHAPTER NINE

WORLD WAR II: THE SILVER INDUSTRY

ON THE HOME FRONT

On December 7, 1941, Japan attacked the American naval base at Pearl Harbor, Hawaii, and the nation was thrust into World War II, a protracted struggle that ended with the surrender of Japan on VJ-Day, August 15, 1945. The silver industry, affected immediately by mobilization, would contribute to the war on the home front. In January 1942 the War Production Board was established and granted sweeping powers to control, convert, and expand the peacetime economy to maximum war production. Priorities were set for scarce materials, and nonessential industrial activity was prohibited. The government imposed restrictions, for civilian goods, on copper and its alloys, materials essential for plated silver, and limited the availability of solid silver. Creativity and innovation came to a halt. Between 1943 and 1945 no new patterns were introduced by any of the major producers of sterling flatware and none, it appears, in holloware either.[1] Moreover, the modern design movements of the 1930s—stripped classicism and streamlining, at their apogee in the New York World's Fair in 1939 and 1940—were sidelined and not revived. When the war ended in 1945, organic or biomorphic modernism, which had been quietly incubating in the 1930s, would become the relevant symbol of modernity.

Notwithstanding the crisis, a number of manufacturers prospered by negotiating munitions contracts with the government and converting their factories to wartime production. The largest manufacturers were Gorham, International Silver, Tiffany & Co., and Reed & Barton. At Gorham the manufacture of bronze and brass goods and all plated wares ceased, and the entire bronze division was converted to war work. Toilet ware and most ecclesiastical articles were discontinued. Holloware production was cut by 70 percent. Sterling flatware was produced only in six-piece place settings in the thirteen most popular patterns, and a rationing program was inaugurated for it in June 1942. During the war Gorham produced more than thirty kinds of material for the military, including steel cartridge cases, tank bearings, torpedo components, and small-arms parts.[2]

International became an important producer of armaments and supplies, and almost 100 percent of its huge capabilities were employed to equip the armed forces. Silverplate of all kinds was discontinued in April 1942, although a very small amount of sterling was made throughout the war. International handled 447 prime contracts and 1,450 separate subcontracts for at least 30 categories of equipment that ranged from identification tags and mess-kit flatware to bullet cores, shell cases, and metallic links for machine guns, the latter representing the greatest output at more than 216 million pieces.[3]

Tiffany & Co.'s Forest Hill plant was converted to war production to supply precision parts for anti-aircraft guns and fitting blocks for airplanes. The production of sterling silverware was

BACK HOME FOR KEEPS

You'll *feel his hand* closing tight over yours . . . you'll *hear* his voice speaking straight to your heart . . . you'll *know* this is not just for an hour, just for a day, *this is for keeps.*

For keeps, too, you'll choose your Community. See it *soon* at your jeweler's!

Community is the silverware craftsmen created for a lifetime of loving wear. Each fork, each spoon, has an overlay of solid silver at the points of greatest wear, each is *balanced* in the finest silverware tradition. And the patterns are enduring . . . like your love, they grow dearer through the years. Choose Community . . . you'll be thankful *for keeps.*

Community
THE FINEST SILVERPLATE

If its Community * . . . *its correct*

* TRADE MARK   COPYRIGHT 1945 ONEIDA LTD.

FIGURE 9.1   "Back Home for Keeps," Community, a division of Oneida, Ltd. advertisement, 1945

Tools and machinery that could be used only for silverware production were placed in storage, and production departments such as white-metal rolling, chasing, and sterling flatware were suspended. Late in 1942 when copper became unavailable and the nickel silver supply was shut off, the government selected Reed & Barton to develop a method of plating silver directly on steel. The company was successful and by the end of the war had produced more than twenty-nine million forks and spoons for the armed forces. At its height production amounted to two hundred and ten thousand forks and spoons per week. The peacetime work for the navy was expanded and more than three-quarters of its silver holloware was made by Reed & Barton. The company also manufactured surgical instruments for the Army Medical Corps, producing more than one million instruments in about thirty different categories.[6]

The formidable achievement of the silver industry during World War II was recognized by the Army-Navy "E" award for excellence and high achievement in production of war materials, an honor bestowed on Reed & Barton, Gorham, International, and others.[7] Charles L. Venable has commented on the achievement:

Even in the 1930s, the majority of silverware produced in this country required much hand labor in its creation and was made in relatively small batches. Consequently, to shift to the high volume production of thousands if not millions, of identical objects must have been difficult for workers who were used to a slower, more craft-oriented work routine. It is also ironic that in the end this transformation was made in two brief years, since countless managers, accountants, and efficiency experts had been trying to accomplish the same task for over half a century.[8]

Although restrictions were severe during the war, silver manufacturers continued to advertise so as to retain their prewar customers, Reed & Barton used a patriotic slogan printed in the center of a graphic V for Victory: "In peace, fostering a high standard of gracious living . . . Today, defending that standard by war production." Typically, an advertisement focused on the future. One advertisement, with the headline "As Lovely as Tomorrow," showed a young couple, the man in uniform, standing with their backs turned toward the reader as they gazed at a distant suburban dream house, presumably in their future. The copy noted the current situation but anticipated a return to peace and availability: "War means that silver manufacture is confined to the most commonly used pieces, such as knives, forks, spoons, and butter spreaders . . . which are available today. But remember that when war is over, you can complete your service and add all those pieces which are temporarily unobtainable."[9]

In the fall of 1945 after the victory over Japan, the tone of the advertisements was understandably optimistic. In *Glamour*, Gorham showed a photograph of a young smiling couple, the man still in uniform, and the headline "Honey . . . can you believe it?" Gorham assured readers that "Soon, we hope, there will be plenty of everything."[10] In the same issue of *Glamour*, Oneida Silversmiths of Sherrill, New York, advertised its Community silverplated flatware with a painting by the well-known illustrator Jon Whitcomb (1906–1988) of a beautiful young blonde passionately embracing her newly returned husband (fig. 9.1). Under the headline "Back Home for Keeps," the text breathlessly exclaimed: "You'll *feel* his hand closing tight over yours . . . you'll *hear* his voice speaking straight to your heart . . . you'll *know* this is not just for an hour, just for a day, *this is for keeps*" [emphasis in original]. And so, by association, would Community silverware be "for keeps." Whitcomb became associated with a series of illustrations he created on the theme "Back Home for Keeps" directed to women deprived by the war of their husbands and sweethearts. In the same advertisement, Oneida offered a free full-color reproduction, without the advertising copy, of this popular painting.[11]

After World War II ended in August 1945, the job of converting the production lines back to manufacturing silverware was tremendous. Salesmen were rehired and retrained, machines, tools, and equipment used for war work had to be removed, and both new and old machinery for silverware production installed. A backlog of orders had built up and included many from new brides.[12] Indicative of the difficulties in reorganizing was the manufacturers' slow start in introducing new flatware patterns. For example, Gorham's first new pattern, *Melrose,* was not introduced until 1948, as was Towle's *French Provincial.* Reed & Barton introduced *Burgundy* in 1949, but Wallace waited until 1950 to produce its first new postwar pattern, *Romance of the Sea.* The exception was International. The firm rebounded rapidly, producing *Northern Lights* in 1946 and a new sterling pattern for every year through the rest of the 1940s.[13]

Significantly, the new postwar sterling patterns in the 1940s were traditional revivals or Scandinavian influenced. The era of streamlining and modern classicism so brilliantly manifested in the 1930s was no longer appropriate. A return to tradition was the comfort Americans needed after the ordeal of war. By 1950, however, a new aesthetic based on organic forms, which had been evolving since the 1930s, would spawn a fresh international movement and reinvigorate design in the silver industry.

Significant changes occurred in the silver industry after the war, entailing new merchandising policies, new channels of distribution, and new approaches to design and production. Marketing through advertising was updated from black and white to full color in print (fig. 9.2), and from radio to television. In 1949, International, for example, made the transition from radio advertising, which had started in 1937, to the new medium of television.[14] Firms such as Gorham broadened their base of operations by door-to-door selling, which became an extremely successful method of marketing sterling flatware, to the consternation of resentful retail jewelers, the traditional source for silverware. As sterling moved from the "classes" to the "masses," it was sold by mail order, and department stores became more important than jewelry stores in the distribution chain.[15] The place setting emerged as the basic sales unit for flatware (previously individual pieces had been sold by the dozen or half dozen), and production was streamlined by eliminating highly specialized serving pieces.[16] A huge consumer boom after the war created

FIGURE 9.2 "Come live with me and bring your Reed & Barton sterling." Reed & Barton advertisement, 1957

new markets for products, and the profits permitted manufacturers to invest in new designs. The new, asymmetrical shapes of organic modernism that, for many young consumers, represented a release from the austerity of the war years fueled a surge of products with a new aesthetic.[17]

Notes

1. The major producers were Gorham, International, Reed & Barton, Tiffany, Towle, and Wallace.

2. Information on wartime production as supplied in Charles H. Carpenter Jr., *Gorham Silver, 1831–1981* (New York: Dodd, Mead, 1982), 265.

3. Edmund P. Hogan, *An American Heritage: A Book About the International Silver Company* (Dallas, Tex.: Taylor Publishing, 1977), 58, 60; and Charles L. Venable, *Silver in America, 1840–1940: A Century of Splendor,* exh. cat. (Dallas, Tex.: Dallas Museum of Art, 1994), 231.

4. All information on Tiffany & Co. from Venable, *Silver in America,* 230.

5. George S. Gibb, *The Whitesmiths of Taunton: A History of Reed & Barton, 1824–1943* (Cambridge, Mass.: Harvard University Press, 1943), 376–77.

6. Renee Garrelick, *Sterling Seasons: The Reed & Barton Story* (Taunton, Mass.: Reed & Barton, 1998), 66–71.

7. For Reed & Barton, see Gibb, *Whitesmiths of Taunton,* 381; for Gorham, see Carpenter, *Gorham Silver,* 265; for International, see Hogan, *American Heritage,* 60.

8. Venable, *Silver in America,* 231.

9. Garrelick, *Sterling Seasons,* 72.

10. "Honey . . . can you believe it?" Gorham advertisement, *Glamour* 14 (Nov. 1945): 51.

11. "Back Home for Keeps," Community, Oneida Ltd. advertisement, ibid., 6.

12. Hogan, *American Heritage,* 62.

13. For example, in the fall of 1947 International embarked on a six-month advertising campaign in part to commemorate the hundredth anniversary of the Rogers Brothers' contribution to the silverplate industry; "Record Silverware Campaign," *New York Times,* June 17, 1947, 42. For the conversion of International Silver's factories after World War II, see also Earl Chapin May, *A Century of Silver, 1847–1947: Connecticut Yankees and a Noble Metal* (New York: Robert M. McBride, 1947), 345–46.

14. Hogan, *American Heritage,* 72–73. In 1954 International discontinued television advertising in favor of printed media.

15. "Sterling Flatware Shifts from Classes to Masses," *Business Week,* Nov. 24, 1951, 150.

16. Ibid., 149.

17. Alexander R. Hammer, "Silverware Boom Forecast for '58," *New York Times,* Feb. 2, 1948, sec. 3, p. 10. This forecast was based on the "anticipated rise in nuptials."

PART TWO A NEW LOOK IN SILVER, 1950–2000

CHAPTER TEN

FREE FORM DESIGN IN THE 1950S

Organic modernism, an international movement, revolutionized the mainstream design aesthetics of the 1950s. In Paris, Christian Dior's 1947 Spring Collection, dubbed the "New Look" (fig. 10.1), in which he transformed the square-shouldered wartime silhouette into a shape resembling an hourglass (and often described as "pinched-in waist" or "wasp-waist"), was a turning point. The New Look brought about a fundamental change in the conception of the female form that was not merely a reaction against wartime austerity, nor simply a whim of fashion. It heralded a widespread change in design, including that of silver (fig. 10.2; see also fig. 13.18).[1]

Organic or biomorphic modernism in which amoeboid, boomerang, and kidney shapes proliferated, became an enormously popular style. But the groundwork for the style was laid in the decades preceding World War II. The pioneers of organic modernism sought a new design aesthetic that would obviate the severity of functional modernism. Biomorphic design softened the ascetic and rectilinear aspects of interwar modernism and machine-based imagery and was strongly influenced by aspects of contemporary painting and sculpture.[2] In France it was Jean Arp, influenced by Constantin Brancusi, who prefigured in his wood relief sculptures of the 1920s and 1930s the postwar adoption of biomorphic line (fig. 10.3).[3] Arp's amorphous shapes were influenced by landscape, the contours of the human body, and microscopic organisms that appeared abstract in their natural form. Arp in turn influenced Isamu Noguchi, Alexander Calder, and other artists. However, it was the Finnish architect Alvar Aalto who was the critical connection between Arp and 1950s organic modernism.[4] In the interplay between technology and nature, Aalto found an expressive form of modernism that was functional. He demonstrated it in objects such as the *Savoy* bowl (fig. 10.4), designed in 1936 and one of a series said to have been inspired by the shapes of Finnish lakes.[5] In 1938 his work was recognized in a one-man exhibition, *Alvar Aalto: Architecture and Furniture*, at the Museum of Modern Art in New York, and visitors to the Finnish Pavilion at the 1939 New York World's Fair were greeted by an undulating Aalto interior.

The American industrial designer Russel Wright also prefigured post–World War II modernist design in 1935 with the organic shapes of his *Oceana* wood serving pieces and in 1937 with his *American Modern* dinnerware, which was produced in 1939 (fig. 10.5). Unlike the industrial designer who had a kinship with the engineer, the organic modernist was often inspired by the dreamlike, psychological themes of surrealist painters such as the Armenian-born Arshile Gorky, who expressed them in his *Garden in Sochi* (fig. 10.6). Frederick Kiesler, an Austrian émigré architect and designer, had experimented with organic forms as early as 1935 in furniture, but his most influential work was the interior

that he designed in 1942 for Peggy Guggenheim's Art of This Century Gallery in New York City—a surreal setting in harmony with the work of the artists she exhibited: curving walls and idiosyncratic amoeboid pedestals, tables, and chairs made of plywood and covered with linoleum (fig. 10.7). In American architecture the most fully developed expression of organic modernism would occur in the mid-1950s in Eero Saarinen's design for the Trans World Airlines Terminal, at Idlewild (now the John F. Kennedy International) Airport (fig. 10.8).

World War II had affected the values of a younger generation, especially the men and women who had served in the armed forces. Some in this group who were creative turned to crafts as a way of life. Those who became metalsmiths, such as Ronald Hayes Pearson and Robert J. King, were responsive to the resurgence of Scandinavian design. In silverware this was the work of Henning Koppel (1918–1981), an innovative Danish designer who worked for Georg Jensen. During the war, Koppel had been an assistant to the Swedish sculptor Carl Milles and, like Aalto, he was strongly influenced

FIGURE 10.1   *Bar* suit, Christian Dior, 1947

FIGURE 10.2   *Trend* coffee service, 1952. Gorham Manufacturing Company. Silver, ebony. DMA, JSASC, cat. 33

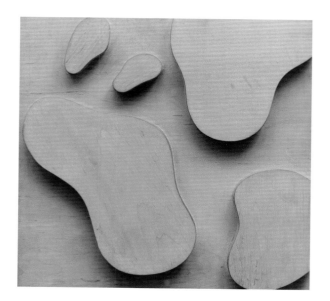

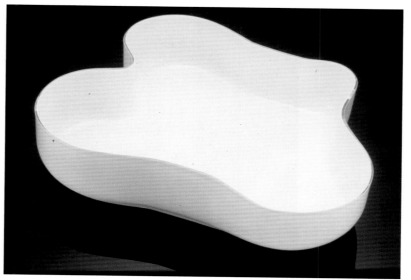

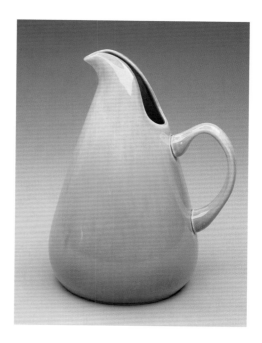

FIGURE 10.3   Jean (Hans) Arp, *Relief*, 1938–1939 (after a relief of 1934–1935). Wood. Museum of Modern Art, New York, gift of the Advisory Committee (by exchange)

FIGURE 10.5   *American Modern* pitcher, 1937. Steubenville Pottery, Russel Wright, designer. Earthenware. Dallas Museum of Art, General Acquisitions Fund

FIGURE 10.4   Alvar Aalto, *Aalto* (*Savoy*) bowl, c. 1936. Musée des Arts décoratifs de Montréal

FIGURE 10.6   Arshile Gorky, *Garden in Sochi*, 1941. Oil on canvas. Museum of Modern Art, New York. Purchase Fund and gift of Mr. and Mrs. Wolfgang S. Schwabacher (by exchange)

FIGURE 10.7 The Abstract Room, Frederick Kiesler, designer. Exhibit in Art of This Century Gallery, New York, c. 1942

FIGURE 10.8 Interior of Trans World Airlines (TWA) Terminal, Idlewild Airport (now John F. Kennedy International Airport), New York, 1956–1962. Eero Saarinen, architect

FIGURE 10.9 Photograph: Bowl, 1948. Georg Jensen, Henning Koppel, designer. Silver

by art. Soon after his association with Jensen began in 1945, Koppel introduced highly sculptural, expressive, abstract forms with irregular, biomorphic contours that broke with convention. Asymmetry was often associated with a newfound freedom. Referred to as *free form* or *free flow*, this aesthetic was perceived as expressing greater individuality and a sense of liberation from rational order and is exemplified in a bowl, one of his most sculptural, that Koppel designed in 1948 (fig. 10.9). Koppel's influence spread after he won gold medals in the Milan Triennales of 1951 and 1954, the years in which Scandinavian design achieved world leadership. The holloware of the distinguished American silversmith Frederick A. Miller (see fig. 13.7) was rooted in the Scandinavian ideas of form and function as expressed by Koppel and the Swedish silversmith Baron Erik Fleming, who taught Miller in 1948 in a workshop held by Handy & Harman in New York City. Miller's work, in turn, influenced designers for industry. The contributions of the craftsmen Pearson and King (who developed Towle's

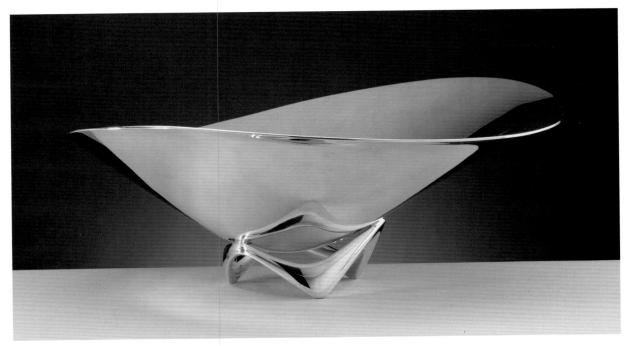

FIGURE 10.10   John Van Koert, c. 1970

groundbreaking *Contour* pattern of 1950) to the silver industry would also reflect the widespread appeal of naturalistic abstraction in modern Scandinavian design during the 1950s and 1960s.

TOWLE LEADS WITH CONTOUR

With the encouragement of his wife, the metalsmith Margret Craver, Charles Withers, the president of Towle, hired John Van Koert (1912–1998; fig. 10.10) in 1948 as director of design to develop a progressive line of sterling flatware and holloware. In 1951 Towle introduced the first American postwar flatware pattern to respond to the new aesthetic. Aptly named *Contour*, the flatware (fig. 10.11) was introduced in *Knife, Fork, and Spoon,* an exhibition co-sponsored in 1951 by Towle and the Walker Art Center in Minneapolis. The catalogue highlighted three departures from traditional form in *Contour*: the knife blade was smaller, the tines of the fork were less pronounced and shaped more like a spoon, and the bowl of the spoon was smaller.[6] These modifications were said to have been made partly to accommodate the contemporary tendency to serve food in smaller and softer pieces.[7] In a review for *Craft Horizons* magazine, the director of the Walker Art Center defended the absence of traditional decoration: "Contour is not plain. The play of concave and convex surfaces and the pattern of reflections in those surfaces are as ornamental as any carved silver garland . . . the flowing quality of silver is expressed. The objective of ornament is achieved by the modeling of the basic form."[8]

Although Van Koert filed the patent as the designer of *Contour* flatware, Robert J. King (b. 1917), a modest in-house designer and a former student of John Prip, had designed it and the matching holloware under the supervision of Van Koert, who assumed credit for the line. King, a trained silversmith who designed for

FIGURE 10.11   *Contour* place knife, place fork, and teaspoon, 1950. Towle Silversmiths, Robert J. King and John Van Koert, designers. Silver, stainless steel. Dallas Museum of Art, cat. 256

FIGURE 10.12 *Contour* beverage set, 1951–1952. Towle Silversmiths, Robert J. King and John Van Koert, designers. Silver, plastic. DMA, JSASC, cat. 257

FIGURE 10.13 Photograph: Teapot, 1951–1952. Gerald Gulotta, designer. Silver, wood

FIGURE 10.14 *Contour* candleholders, 1953. Towle Silversmiths, Robert J. King and John Van Koert, designers. Silver. DMA, JSASC, cat. 258

industry, first at Towle, and later for International Silver, also received many awards in competitions for his independent silver designs (see fig. 13.17), and together with Frederick Miller's, his work was represented in the Brussels World's Fair in 1958. The manipulation of the basic shape of an object into an attenuated or distorted form was one of the hallmarks of 1950s design. In silver, bodies were swollen, handles raised, and spouts drawn out beyond their expected length. The refinement in design and technique that King achieved in this idiom was clear in the *Contour* three-piece beverage set (fig. 10.12). The server has an affinity with a teapot (fig. 10.13) that was designed by Gerald Gulotta (b. 1921) as a prototype for a tea and coffee service (and raised by King), during Gulotta's brief association with Towle after graduating from Pratt Institute in 1950. Gulotta's design may have figured in the development of the *Contour* beverage set after he had left Towle in 1952, but Gulotta was not directly involved in the design of *Contour*.[9] Candleholders (fig. 10.14), salt and pepper shakers, and accessory dishes were also made in *Contour*.

Another source of talent at Towle in the 1950s was Marion Anderson Noyes (1907–2002), a metalsmith and designer who had worked intermittently at the firm since the 1930s. She was a student at the University of Wisconsin in the early 1930s when Harold Nock, Towle's head designer, visited the campus for market research and encountered her metalwork. He was so impressed that he recruited her for a position in the Towle design department.[10] Although she stayed at Towle for only a year after her graduation, Noyes (fig. 10.15) was a freelance consultant between 1944 and 1955. Her 1950s

modern holloware designs were a success in the marketplace. The most outstanding is a pair of serpentine candlesticks in sterling with black plastic tips that are of different heights and interact sensuously (fig. 10.16). Another item that sold well was a round trivet (fig. 10.17) that came in three sizes and had a contemporary loop and dot design. Noyes was also involved in the design of flatware at Towle and contributed to *Southwind*, a sterling flatware and holloware pattern produced in 1952.[11] *Southwind* was featured with *Contour* holloware on a buffet illustrated in *Sterling to Live With*, a promotional booklet published by the Sterling Silversmiths Guild of America in 1954 (fig. 10.18).

THE CONTEMPORARY GROUP AND REED & BARTON

Concurrent with the development of *Contour* at Towle, a modern holloware line in sterling and silverplate was developed at Reed & Barton by a young generation of designers trained at the Rhode Island School of Design in Providence, Rhode Island, and Pratt Institute in Brooklyn, New York. In 1950 a color brochure announced *The Contemporary Group* (fig. 10.20). The catalyst was the collaboration of the firm with the Design in Industry program initiated by the Institute of Contemporary Art in Boston in 1948 to revitalize industrial products by bringing talented young individuals into the design process.[12] Reed & Barton was one of the first manufacturers to associate itself with this endeavor. Of the five men selected by the Institute for monthlong internships at Reed & Barton, three would enter the company's design department: Milton P. Hannah (b. 1927) and Donald Pollard (1924–1994), who were graduates of the Rhode Island School of Design, and Robert H. Ramp (b. 1920), an industrial design graduate of Pratt Institute. All three contributed to *The Contemporary Group*. James S. Plaut, the director of the Institute of Contemporary Art, gave his imprimatur

FIGURE 10.15 Marion Anderson Noyes, 1937

to the collection in a statement for the promotional brochure: "With the release of its newly designed silverware, Reed & Barton joins the ranks of those forward-looking manufacturers who are attempting to provide the consumer with distinguished products in the spirit of contemporary American Life."[13]

The designs most influenced by organic modernism were those of Robert H. Ramp, who was hired early in 1949 as a staff designer. His radical interpretation of a triple-branch candelabrum in silverplate that rotates through 360 degrees on its base to form varied configurations when paired (fig. 10.19), bears a resemblance to the twisted candelabrum designed by Henning Koppel for Jensen in 1946 (fig. 10.21). Two other free form designs by Ramp are a swirling silverplate centerpiece bowl (fig. 10.22), and a sterling bonbon dish described in the brochure as "geometric fantasy . . . akin to sculpture" (fig. 10.23). Ramp's sterling cream and sugar dessert set (see fig. 10.20), noted as "classic in line, contour, and opposition of shapes" is more conservative.[14] The subtly contoured dessert set was the only one of Ramp's designs that were shown in the brochure to be featured as a full-page advertisement in upscale magazines such as *Gourmet*.[15]

While Ramp had four of his designs represented in the brochure, his colleagues from the Institute's program each had one. The design of Pollard's asymmetrical triangular bonbon dish in sterling was also used later for a *Contemporary Group* bowl and for a sandwich plate (see fig. 10.59). Touted in the brochure as a "simple, yet vital, free form elliptical design," Pollard's dish, like Ramp's dessert set, was promoted with a full-page advertisement.[16] The dish was revived briefly in the *Color-Glaze* silverplate line in 1969, and in the early

FIGURE 10.17 Trivet, 1954. Towle Silversmiths, Marion Anderson Noyes, designer. Silver, plastic. DMA, JSASC, cat. 259

FIGURE 10.18 Table setting, buffet supper, *Southwind* flatware and *Southwind* and *Contour* holloware, "Sterling to Live With" booklet, 1954

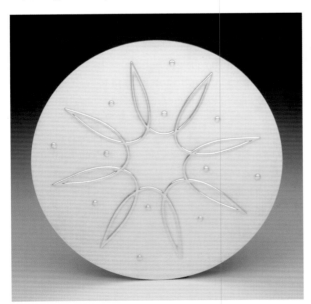

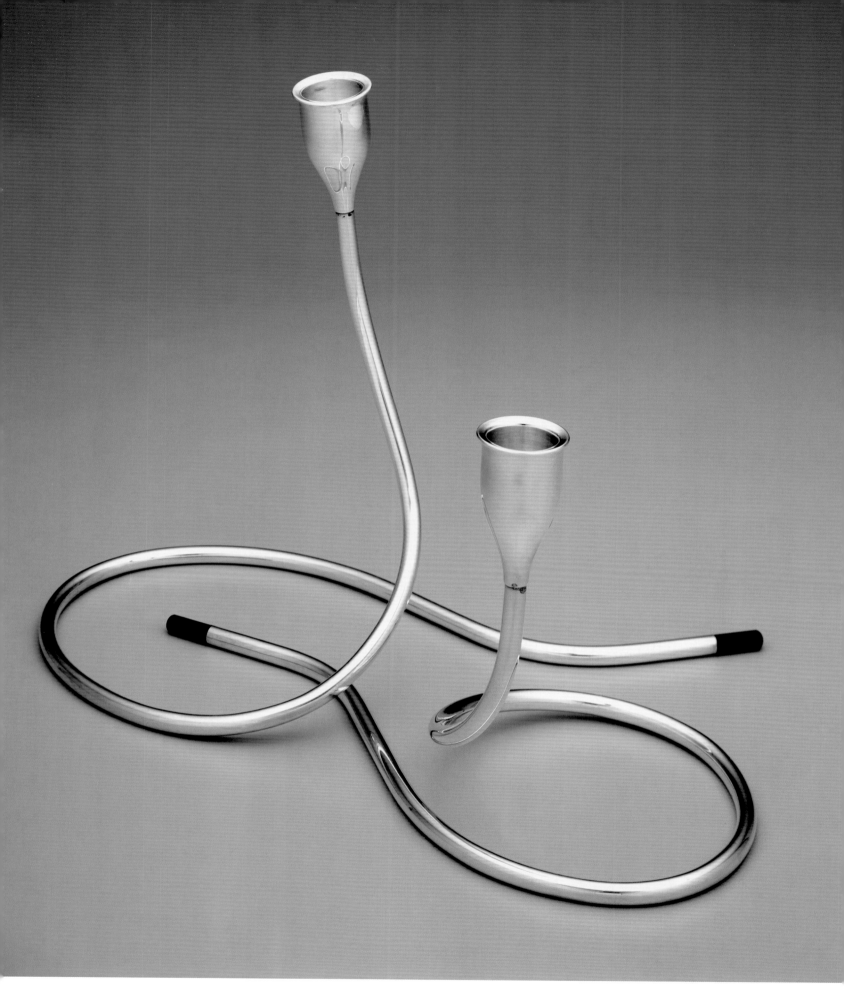

FIGURE 10.16   Candlesticks, c. 1957. Towle Silversmiths, Marion
Anderson Noyes, designer. Silver, plastic. DMA, JSASC, cat. 270

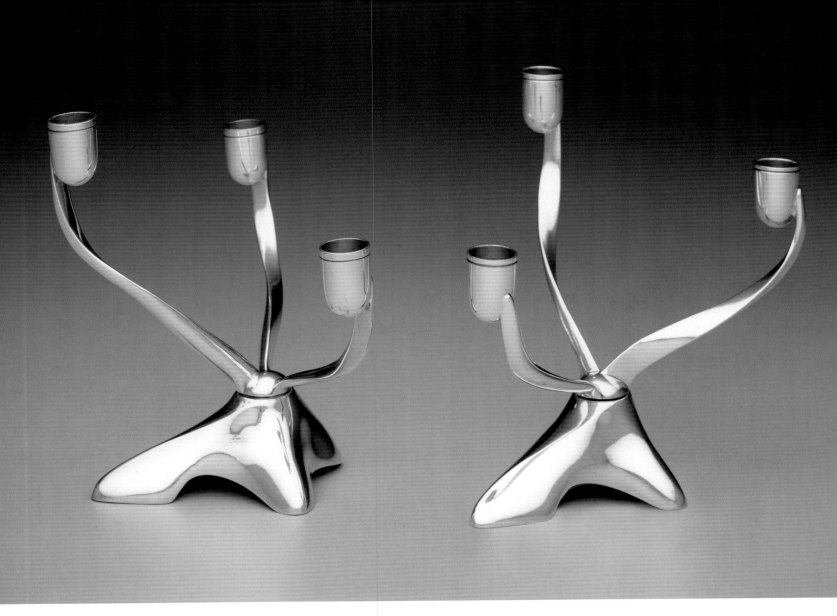

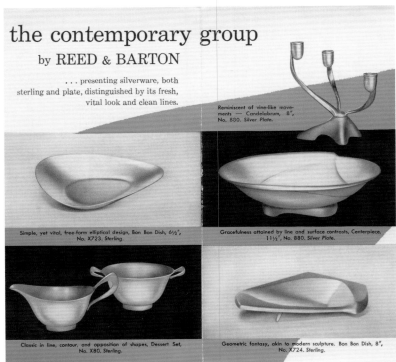

FIGURE 10.19 *Contemporary Group* candelabra, 1950. Reed & Barton, Robert H. Ramp, designer. Silverplate. DMA, JSASC, cat. 177

FIGURE 10.20 *Contemporary Group* brochure (detail), Reed & Barton, 1950

1970s the shape was reinterpreted for a silverplated bowl that came in three sizes, and was also offered with *Color-Glaze* interiors as a "serving dish" (see fig. 13.25).[17] Although praised in the brochure as the "purest of designs . . . elegant, light and direct," Hannah's sterling bonbon dish, a round shallow form with a distinctive base of crisscrossed straps, did not fare as well. Short lived, it was discontinued after 1952.[18] However, two of Hannah's free form silverplated designs from 1958 lasted longer, a bread tray (see fig. 10.60), and a bonbon dish that was later made in many shades of *Color-Glaze* (see fig. 13.25). The five other pieces shown in the brochure, the work of the experienced staff designer Theodore Cayer (1907–1969), were not technically *Contemporary Group* items but undoubtedly were included to appeal to conservative consumers. The three pieces in sterling by Cayer were from the *Classic American* group; the two in silverplate were from the *Gallery* group.[19] For marketing purposes the cover of the brochure showed a line drawing of the *Classic American* centerpiece superimposed on a drawing of a progressive molded plywood chair by Ray and Charles Eames.

To compete with Towle's *Contour* flatware, Reed & Barton introduced *Silver Sculpture*, a sterling silver pattern designed by Ramp, in 1954 (fig. 10.24). In an advertisement for the pattern (fig. 10.25) a parallel was drawn between *Silver Sculpture* and the figures in Carl Milles's Orpheus Fountain at Cranbrook Academy, a ploy to put the pattern on an equal footing with the fine arts. The text extolled this aspect of the design: "'Silver Sculpture' is Reed & Barton's answer to 'free taste' in American table settings. Its soft, sculptural beauty is fresh, new-looking. To create this unique pattern, silver artists shaped a 'figure' as a sculptor would in stone or bronze."[20] Ramp has described his inspiration differently:

Designing *Silver Sculpture* was an object of determination because it was believed to be too extreme. However in surveys it was either extremely liked or extremely disliked. Because of these extremes, it was deemed worthy of production. Even though it was named *Silver Sculpture*, my theme was the movement of the sea, the cresting of the waves and the returning flow under the surface. The sales promotion minds won the name, but I had the design accepted.[21]

A few pieces of holloware, including a free form bowl that embodies Ramp's theme (fig. 10.26), were designed by him to match the flatware.

One of the most striking free form holloware designs of the 1950s is the bean-shaped dish, offered by Reed & Barton in three sizes, the largest called a "salad dish" (see fig. 10.59). A single long and narrow curved foot with two points on which the dish rests was attached to the dish at the smaller end, an innovative element that added to the asymmetrical New Look of the dish. This foot also occurs on Hannah's bread tray (fig. 10.60) and his *Color-Glaze* bonbon dish (see fig. 13.25). An atypical mid-1950s product was the short-lived *Far East* holloware, an anomaly in which the bodies were studded with tiny stylized chrysanthemums (fig. 10.27).

INTERNATIONAL HAS FLAIR

In its outreach to contemporary consumers International cast a wide net to enhance sales at every level. Like its competitors, Towle and Reed & Barton,

FIGURE 10.21   Photograph: Candelabrum, 1946. Georg Jensen, Henning Koppel, designer. Silver

FIGURE 10.22 *Contemporary Group* centerpiece, 1950. Reed &
Barton, Robert H. Ramp, designer. Silverplate. DMA, JSASC, cat. 176

International employed asymmetry in its early 1950s sterling flatware, for example, *Silver Rhythm* (1953), *Torchlight* (1954), and *Silver Melody* (1955). Early in 1955 the 1847 Rogers Bros. division of the firm launched a silverplate flatware pattern, *Flair,* by the staff designer Robert L. Doerfler (1916–2004). Produced for the middle market, the pattern became a best-seller. To motivate retailers, *Flair* flatware and holloware was aggressively promoted in *Jewelers' Circular-Keystone,* the principal trade publication, with a sixteen-page insert.[22] For an introductory advertisement to the public, the name *Flair* was emblazoned across the page in lipstick red with the headline "new, new Flair so modern . . . it sets a new tradition."[23] Indeed, in *Flair* contemporary contours were mated with subtle touches of traditional Scandinavian motifs, leafy scrolls and beads (fig. 10.28). The following year *Flair* holloware was the focus of an intense advertising campaign (fig. 10.29) concentrated in *Life* magazine, which had at the time more than five and a half million readers each week.[24] The allusions to Scandinavian tradition were carried over in the finials of the contoured hot beverage set (fig. 10.30). Plastic strips in a color to suggest natural raffia and wicker were wrapped around the handle of the beverage server, used as decorative accents on the chafing dish and double vegetable dish, and to girdle the triple candelabrum.

For higher priced holloware, plastic strips in the same color were adopted. A carafe-style beverage server in sterling has a narrow neck encircled with the material (fig. 10.31, left). Although primarily for insulation, the treatment added a decorative note, as did the spherical finial. A creation of the staff designer Edward S. Buchko (1929–1997), it was part of an all-purpose three-piece beverage set with cream pitcher and open sugar bowl. A sterling pitcher with a similar pinched-in waist (fig. 10.31, right), another design that originated in-house, has a lyrical, looping handle that is wrapped in the plastic. Five versions of this pitcher with slight variations designed by Curtis Rittberg (1902–1973) were made in different sizes.[25] Also in 1955 an elegant sterling water pitcher (fig. 10.32) with subtle biomorphic contours and a contrasting arc-shaped handle was produced. The only decoration is an incised line that follows the gentle curve of the pouring rim to form a visual border.

In another progressive endeavor, the firm engaged the Danish émigré silversmith Kurt Eric Christoffersen (1926–1981; fig. 10.33) to design a signature collection for the International Sterling Craft Associates, a separate production line of craft-oriented holloware and jewelry established with the late Alphonse La Paglia (1907–1953). La Paglia, a Sicilian-born silversmith who had studied in Denmark with Georg Jensen, had originated the special line with International in 1952, the year before his premature death. Christoffersen and La Paglia were the recognized "craft associates" and each of their pieces bore the stamp Christoffersen Designed or La Paglia Designed.

Christoffersen's extreme reductive aesthetic and predilection for conical forms were articulated throughout his holloware group. The promotional brochure vividly described the Christoffersen Designed holloware:

Styled in superb weight . . . with a fresh approach in functional design . . . this selection of lovely holloware is for those whose preference is for the sophisticated. Sleek lines as crisp as icy crystals accentuate the bold spherical and conical shapes

FIGURE 10.23 *Contemporary Group* bonbon dish, 1950. Reed & Barton, Robert H. Ramp, designer. Silver. DMA, JSASC, cat. 178

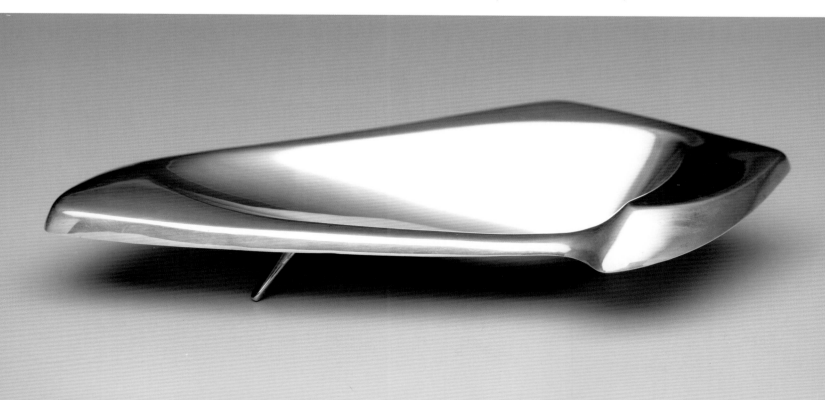

TOTALLY NEW! "SILVER SCULPTURE"
BY REED & BARTON

FIGURE 10.24   Robert Ramp working on *Silver Sculpture*
flatware model, 1953

FIGURE 10.25   "Totally New! 'Silver Sculpture' . . . ," Reed &
Barton advertisement, 1954

FIGURE 10.26   *Silver Sculpture* bowl, 1954. Reed & Barton,
Robert H. Ramp, designer. Silver. DMA, JSASC, cat. 180

offering intriguing reflecting surfaces. Each piece is characterized by a deceptive simplicity that is as ageless as the Pyramids
and as modern as Tomorrow. For the home where the unusual
in the very finest sterling artistry and craftsmanship are
appreciated.[26]

Christoffersen's innovative coffee service (fig.
10.35), a study in contrasts with an economy of means,
introduced the holloware line in the brochure and was
the only item illustrated on a full page. The tall coffeepot
in the service, his most complex holloware design, is
conical in shape and tapers to a narrow contoured lid
punctuated by a prominent finial in the reverse shape
of the pot (perhaps an abstract allusion to the New
Look's wasp waist). A tapered spout springs boldly
from the base to the height of the lid, as does a slender
tapered and sharply angled handle wrapped (except
for its "elbow" and points of attachment to the pot) in
black plastic strips to give the effect of raffia. Both elements balance and dramatize the object compositionally. The sugar bowl lid echoes that of the coffeepot but
Christoffersen reversed the shape for the bowl. The
creamer is the same shape as the coffeepot, but is sharply
angled at the top to mimic the slope of the coffeepot
handle. A projecting, partly wrapped handle extends the
line of the angle, emphasizing lift and energizing the
form. This stellar achievement by Christoffersen invites
comparison with Gorham's *Modern American* coffee
set designed in 1928 (see fig. 1.17) by Erik Magnussen,
who, like Christoffersen, was a talented Danish émigré
silversmith and had contributed significantly to modern
American industrial silver during the 1920s. Although
each of these objects is a prime example of its type, the
contrast in the two designers' interpretation of the same
forms is striking and epitomizes the evolving concept of
modernity in the twentieth century.

In a radical departure from tradition, Christoffersen
designed a stark centerpiece bowl totally devoid of ornament in an ensemble with cone-shaped candlesticks
(fig. 10.34). The power of the pared-down form stems
from the proportions of the bowl and the smooth,
subtle contours of the shallow interior surface, which
contrasts with the bowl's deeper, angled profile. These
formal strategies make International's Christoffersen
Designed bowl a masterpiece of minimalism. In contrast
to Christoffersen's work, La Paglia's designs for Crafts
Associates were strongly influenced by Jensen's early
pieces and hence were more conservative.[27] Typical is
a flared centerpiece bowl with an openwork pedestal of
bold balls, loops, and a floral collar (fig. 10.36).

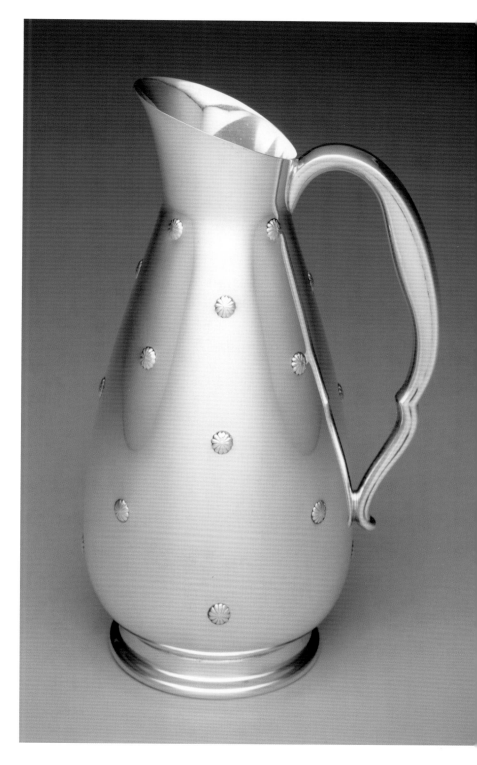

FIGURE 10.27 *Far East* water pitcher, 1956. Reed & Barton. Silver.
Dallas Museum of Art, cat. 186

In the new Flair design: 18" serving tray, $17.50. 14" roll tray, $10.00. Candelabrum, $17.50. Hot beverage server (10 cups), $37.50. Covered sugar, $13.00. Cream, $14.50. Sauce bowl and tray (12 oz.), $15.00. All holloware prices subject to Federal tax. Ladle, $3.50.

International sets the loveliest tables in America...

FIGURE 10.28   *Flair* place knife and fork, 1954. 1847 Rogers Brothers, Robert L. Doerfler, designer. Silverplate, stainless steel. Dallas Museum of Art, cat. 96

FIGURE 10.29   "International sets the loveliest tables in America . . . ," International Silver Company advertisement, 1956

FIGURE 10.30   *Flair* hot beverage service and serving tray, 1954. 1847 Rogers Brothers. Silverplate, plastic. DMA, JSASC, cats. 97, 98

FIGURE 10.31 Left: Carafe, 1955. Edward S. Buchko, designer. Silver, plastic, wood, cat. 111; right: Pitcher, c. 1955. Curtis Rittberg, designer. Silver, plastic. Simpson, Hall, Miller and Company. Dallas Museum of Art, cat. 112

FIGURE 10.32 Pitcher, 1955. Simpson, Hall, Miller and Company. Silver. DMA, JSASC, cat. 113

The burgeoning studio jewelry movement in the 1940s and the status given to it by the Museum of Modern Art with the exhibition *Modern Handmade Jewelry* in 1946 may have spurred International's pursuit of production-line jewelry. Georg Jensen's successful marketing of jewelry—in addition to holloware and flatware—and La Paglia's input may also have been factors. Another model was the Danish émigré silversmith Peer Smed, who had been a consultant at International in the 1930s and who, independently, had made hand-wrought jewelry in addition to holloware and flatware until the early 1940s. Although brief, International's showcasing of designer jewelry in Craft Associates was seminal for the silver industry in the second half of the twentieth century. In the 1970s, Tiffany & Co. and Reed & Barton would follow suit.

The Christoffersen Designed jewelry collection included matched sets of bracelets, earrings, brooches, cuff links, tie bars, and a few necklaces. More than fifteen predominantly abstract designs were offered, their names, such as *Summer Ivy, Wheat, Freeform,*

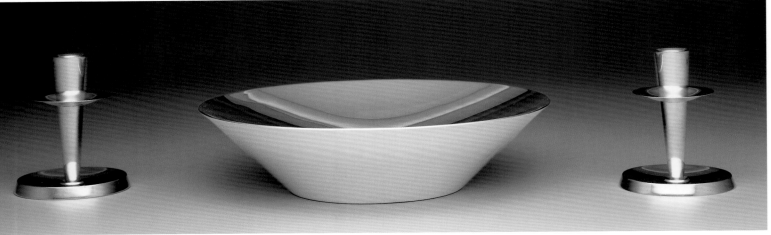

FIGURE 10.33   Kurt Eric Christoffersen in the International Sterling Crafts Associates workshop, c. 1955

FIGURE 10.34   Centerpiece bowl and candlesticks, 1955. International Sterling Crafts Associates, Kurt Eric Christoffersen, designer. Silver. The Jewel Stern American Silver Collection, cat. 89, and DMA, JSASC, cat. 90, respectively

FIGURE 10.35   Coffee service, 1955. International Sterling Crafts Associates, Kurt Eric Christoffersen, designer. Silver, plastic. The Jewel Stern American Silver Collection, cat. 91

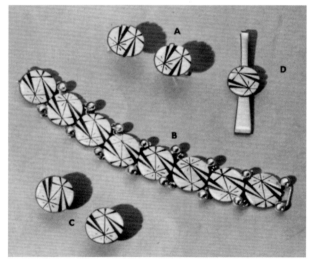

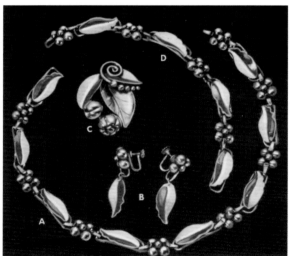

FIGURE 10.36 Centerpiece bowl, c. 1952. International Sterling Crafts Associates, Alphonse La Paglia, designer. Silver. The Jewel Stern American Silver Collection, cat. 88

FIGURE 10.37 Illustration of *Fireworks* pattern jewelry, 1955. International Sterling Crafts Associates, Kurt Eric Christoffersen, designer

FIGURE 10.38 Illustration of *Leaf and Blossom* pattern jewelry, 1955. International Sterling Crafts Associates, Alphonse La Paglia, designer

Snowflake, and *Fireworks* (fig. 10.37), corresponding to the motifs of the pieces. With the exception of the *Scroll* pattern, the motifs of La Paglia's matched jewelry sets were exclusively naturalistic, the *Leaf and Blossom* design (fig. 10.38) being an example. In these works, the contrast between Christoffersen's rigorous purity of line and La Paglia's decorative volumes, each a response to an aspect of Scandinavian design, was pronounced.

ONEIDA'S ACHIEVEMENT

Noting an increased demand for holloware driven by a surge in casual home entertaining, Oneida Silversmiths introduced three innovative contemporary holloware lines in silverplate in the mid-1950s.[28] The first, a high styled collection from the Heirloom division named *Heirloom "700,"* was introduced in 1955 and promoted for buffet-style dining (fig. 10.39). During the cost-conscious years of the Depression, buffet-style dining became more acceptable for informal middle-class socializing. After World War II the style became popular and gained the imprimatur of the tastemaker and designer Russel Wright, who championed a casual, modern lifestyle and informal hospitality in his popular *Guide to Easier Living*, which was published in 1950. For his *American Modern* dinnerware introduced in 1939 and in production through the 1950s, Wright had designed easily stacked, rimless coupe-shaped dishes for buffet service.[29] Although *Heirloom "700"* was advertised under the banner of Oneida, further research has revealed that the collection was contracted from Dorlyn Silversmiths of New York, a company known primarily for producing the designs of the German émigré Tommi Parzinger (1903–1981; fig. 10.40).[30] Indeed, *Heirloom "700"* bears a strong resemblance—with slight modifications—to brass and silverplated objects made by Dorlyn and bearing Parzinger's hallmark (figs. 10.41, 10.42).

A year later, in 1956, Oneida's Community division aggressively launched a contemporary collection called *Achievement,* with trays and dishes described as "sculptured oval" in form.[31] The introductory advertisement emphasized versatility and multipurpose capability, a competitive theme throughout the silver industry in the 1950s.[32] The "5-way" serving dish (fig. 10.43, left) was shown as a casserole with and without its ovenproof glass liner, as an open bowl for fruit and snacks, as a floral centerpiece, and with the handle detached from the cover, as a roll or bread tray. In a memorandum to the trade Oneida represented *Achievement* as the epitome of the "practical American imagination," proclaiming the line to be distinctively "American."[33] Although the hot beverage server was said to be in the "boot shape,"[34] an association with earlier Americana, its graceful contours betrayed its debt to contemporary Scandinavian sources. The handles and finial were of Durez, a tough

FIGURE 10.39   *Heirloom "700"* catalogue cover, Oneida Ltd. Silversmiths, 1955

FIGURE 10.40   Tommi Parzinger, 1939

FIGURE 10.41 *Heirloom "700"* covered compote, 1955. Heirloom, Tommi Parzinger, designer. Silverplate, plastic. DMA, JSASC, cat. 148

FIGURE 10.42 *Heirloom "700"* candelabrum, 1955. Heirloom, Tommi Parzinger, designer. Silverplate. DMA, JSASC, cat. 147

FIGURE 10.43   Left: *Achievement* "5-way" serving dish, 1956. Silverplate, glass, plastic, cat. 145; right: *Achievement* coffeepot, 1956. Silverplate, plastic, cat. 146. Community. DMA, JSASC

thermosetting phenolic resin that eliminated the need for insulators.[35] The form of the three-light candelabrum with jet-black tips and wide-edged cups (fig. 10.44) was atypical in the collection and alluded to both space age and biomorphic imagery. One of the most innovative designs of the 1950s, it was the only *Achievement* item carried over into the 1960s as part of Oneida's Heirloom *Decorator* group.[36] A year or so after its introduction, the *Achievement* collection was marketed at reduced prices in the Wm. A. Rogers division of Oneida, suggesting that it was not very successful.[37]

The third contemporary holloware group, named *Decorator*, was an offshoot of *Achievement*, but the marketing focus for this line was contemporary Scandinavian, especially Danish, design, rather than the "American imagination." The reference was clear in the catalogue description of the coffee service (fig. 10.45): "Here in a smart Danish Modern styling is the dramatic new look in silver—[with] the rich warmth of walnut. . . ." The *Achievement* boot-shaped body was retained for coffeepot, creamer and sugar bowl. All the lids, finials, and handles were, however, redesigned—the black Durez replaced with wood in a warm brown finish—and the handles of the creamer and sugar bowl were primarily of wood. The coffeepot was made available in two versions, one with a vertical wood handle attached to the body of the vessel on metal extensions; the other with a wood side handle that was described

FIGURE 10.44   *Decorator* candelabrum, 1956. Heirloom division, Oneida Ltd. Silversmiths. Silverplate, plastic. DMA, JSASC, cat. 149

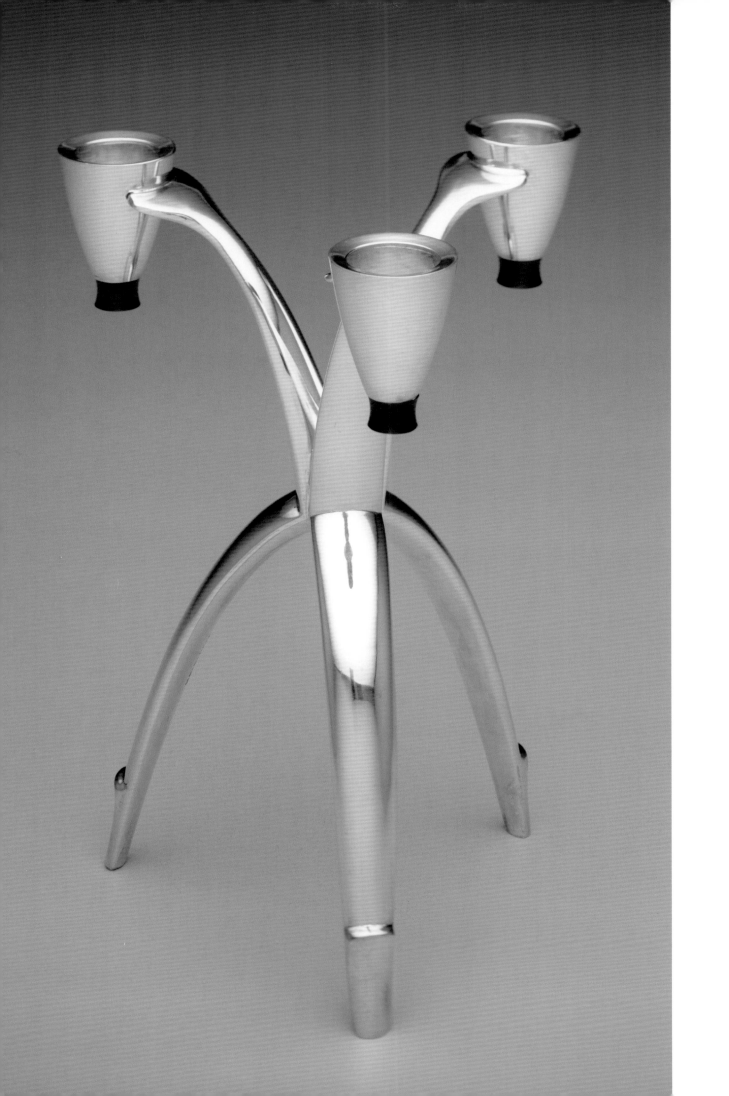

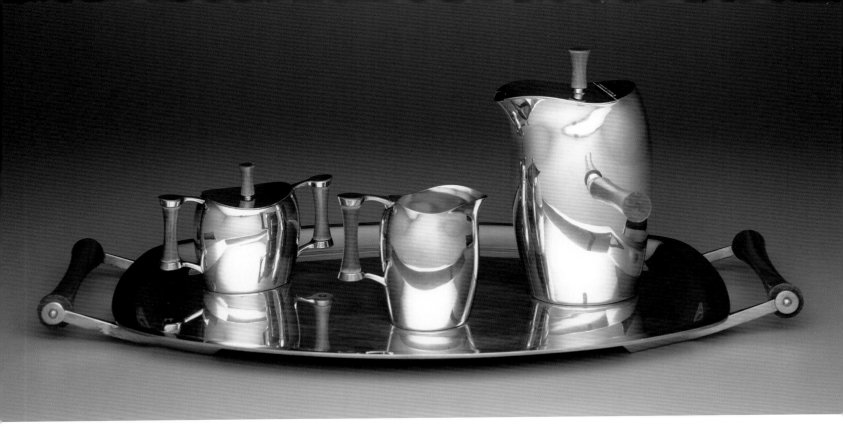

FIGURE 10.45 *Decorator* coffee service, c. 1960. Heirloom. Silverplate, walnut. DMA, JSASC, cat. 150

in the catalogue as the horizontal "continental style."[38] The holloware may have been influenced by the *Design in Scandinavia* exhibition that toured the nation in 1954. Illustrated in the exhibition catalogue was a coffeepot with a side handle and a hinged, contoured lid designed by Thor Lie-Jorgensen and executed by the Norwegian maker A. David-Andersen.[39] Although the shape of the vessels differed, the lid and side handle of the "continental style" *Decorator* model resemble the Norwegian example.

Gorham's Trend

Gorham was another major company galvanized by both the new design aesthetic and by consumers' desire for versatility. In the 1950s Gorham produced two contemporary holloware lines in sterling, *Trend*, the earlier of the two, and *Directional*. In an advertisement that appeared in numerous periodicals and in a photograph in the 1953–1954 *Studio Yearbook*, the concave, reel-shaped *Trend* candlesticks (fig. 10.46) were shown stacked in multiples, and it was pointed out in the advertisement that, with a "made-to-fit" mechanism inserted, they could be converted into a table lighter.[40] The salt and pepper shakers (fig. 10.47) have solid white and black plastic tops and a patented device by which the contents can be dispensed from below when the containers are shaken up and down. Touted in advertisements as a new method for sealing out moisture and keeping salt "free-flowing" and pepper "fragrant and fresh," the device also prevented the interiors and shaker caps from corroding.[41] The *Trend* coffeepot (see fig. 10.2, center), conceived in the hourglass, or pinched-in-waist shape, has a removable lid so that the

FIGURE 10.46 *Trend* candlesticks, 1952. Gorham Manufacturing
Company. Silver. DMA, JSASC, cat. 34

FIGURE 10.47 "Introducing the first free-flowing sterling salt and
pepper set," Gorham Company advertisement, 1954

DIRECTIONAL

1301 COFFEE SET AND TRAY
Sterling Silver - Butler Finish
Ebony handles and finials

THE GORHAM COMPANY
Providence, R. I.

1301 Coffee, Capacity 2¼ pints, Height 8¾ inches
1303 Sugar with Cover
1304 Cream, Sterling handle, Capacity ⅜ pint
1064 Gallery Tray, Trend, Black Formica center,
Diameter 12¾ inches

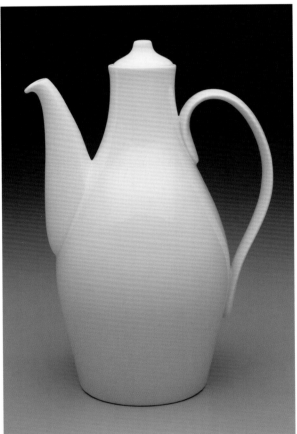

The talented guest gives Gorham Sterling

Years after the rice has been swept away, this smart guest will be remembered for her taste and thoughtfulness.

She thought enough of the bride and groom to give one of the world's most welcome gifts—Gorham sterling.

Gift-givers display their talents by adding to the Gorham sterling service already chosen by the delighted recipient. The pieces added may be practical—like extra

teaspoons—or something for special, magnificent occasions—a punch ladle, for example. Your choice of a gift is limited only by your imagination and sense of appropriateness. Illustrated here are a few such gifts, at various prices, to give singly or in combinations.

Remember, sterling is for now and forever...one of the loveliest and most complimentary gifts you can give.

Gorham STERLING
America's Leading Silversmiths Since 1831

FIGURE 10.48   Illustration of "Directional 1301 Coffee Set and Tray," salesman's catalogue, Gorham Company, 1957

FIGURE 10.50   "The talented guest gives Gorham Sterling," Gorham Company advertisement, 1958

FIGURE 10.49   *Museum* coffeepot. 1946. Shenango Pottery Company, Eva Zeisel, designer. Porcelain. Dallas Museum of Art, 20th-Century Design Fund

pot could be used as a pitcher or cocktail mixer, another example of versatility.

The teardrop form of Gorham's *Directional* coffee service (fig. 10.48) echoed that of Eva Zeisel's *Museum* dinnerware (fig. 10.49) introduced in 1946 at an exhibition at the Museum of Modern Art. The service was prominent among a display of wedding gifts in a Gorham advertisement, one in a thematic series revolving around life style that appeared in upscale magazines between 1955 and 1959 (fig. 10.50). The *Directional* pitcher, cream and sugar set, and the "Tri-round" bowl gently express the undulating free form line with smooth, unadorned surfaces (10.51; see also fig. 13.20). The cream pitcher by the staff designer Phillip B. Johnson (1899–1992) has a black plastic handle that sweeps up with élan and curves back. Although holloware was rarely patented and precedents existed in European silver for similarly shaped handles, Gorham deemed Johnson's pitcher unique enough in American silver to warrant one. To a small group of sterling holloware, Richard L. Huggins, assistant director of design, contributed the designs for candlesticks and salt and pepper shakers that coordinate with the flowing *Sea Rose* flatware that he had designed in 1958. The items were available with or without the decorative rose spray.[42] The shakers have canted bodies with wide, button-shaped brimmed tops that recall the pinched-in waist of the New Look as do the candlesticks, which flare out even more emphatically.[43]

FIGURE 10.51   Left and center left: *Directional* creamer and sugar bowl, 1955. Phillip Bernard Johnson, designer. Silver, plastic, cat. 36; center right: *Directional* "Tri-round" bowl, 1955. Silver, cat. 38; extreme right: *Directional* pitcher, 1955. Silver. Gorham Manufacturing Company. DMA, JSASC, cat. 37

FIGURE 10.52 "Beautiful and so Versatile," *Gorham 1959 Silver-plated Holloware Catalog,* 1959

FIGURE 10.53 *Modern* "Decorator" bowl, c. 1959. Gorham Manufacturing Company. Silverplate, plastic. DMA, JSASC, cat. 44

Pieces from Gorham's extensive contemporary *Modern* line in silverplate were illustrated on the cover of the company's 1959 catalogue. One of two coffee sets in the pattern was touted as "Beautiful and so Versatile" (fig. 10.52). The coffeepot was shown as a beverage pitcher or flower vase, the sugar bowl lid turned over on its handle became a candy dish, and it was suggested that the cream pitcher would be useful for syrup and sauces.[44] The "Decorator" bowl (fig. 10.53), which has an adjustable wing nut on its underside that allows the bowl to be set at various angles on the black plastic base, was also noted for its versatility. The elongated *Modern* pitcher (fig. 10.54, left) has the fluid contours of Scandinavian ware and a surprising, uncanny resemblance to a pre–World War II handwrought pitcher designed by Tommi Parzinger.[45] Automobile tail fins, especially those on Cadillacs in the 1950s, likely inspired the sleek, pointed twin handles of the *Modern* double vegetable dish (fig. 10.54, right, and fig. 10.55), which contrast effectively with the softly rounded profiles of the dish and its cover. The two arcing feet that face each other resonate with the curved ends of the dish. The same configuration informs the bases of the *Tira* centerpiece, celery or bread tray, and bonbon dish, items originally in the *Modern* line that were later renamed and advertised separately.[46] Another centerpiece in the *Modern* line was modeled on the shapely and exotic avocado fruit and named for it. The exaggeration of its organic lines heightens the sensuality of the form (see fig. 10.59).[47]

FIGURE 10.54 Left: *Modern* pitcher, c. 1955, cat. 40; right: *Modern* double vegetable dish, c. 1959. Gorham Manufacturing Company. Silverplate. DMA, JSASC, cat. 42

FIGURE 10.55 *Executive Rule* letter opener/ruler, c. 1953. Samuel Kirk & Son, Inc. Silver. DMA, JSASC, cat. 131

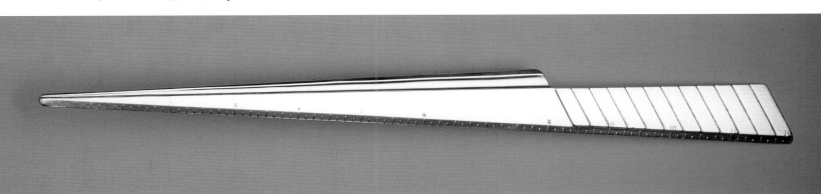

New tablele brilliance . . . the Bateau by Gorham

GcGorham creates a fascinating new form . . .
an intriguingng contemporary concept — the Bateau centerpiece.
Add canandles and your table sparkles with excitement . . .
for a lovely higinghlight, fill the Bateau with colorful flowers or fruit.
In In Gorham's lastingly lovely silverplate.
Commmplete, $13.50° . . . without candleholder, $10°

GORHAM

AMERICA'S LEADING SILVERSMITHS SINCE 1831

*PRICES INCLUDE FEDERAL TAX, SUBJECT TO CHANGE WITHOUT NOTICE

FIGURE 10.56 "New table brilliance
. . . the Bateau by Gorham," Gorham Company advertisement, 1960

FIGURE 10.57 *Bateau* double vegetable dish, 1959. Gorham Manufacturing Company, Alexandra C. Solowij (Watkins), designer. Silverplate. DMA, JSASC, cat. 53

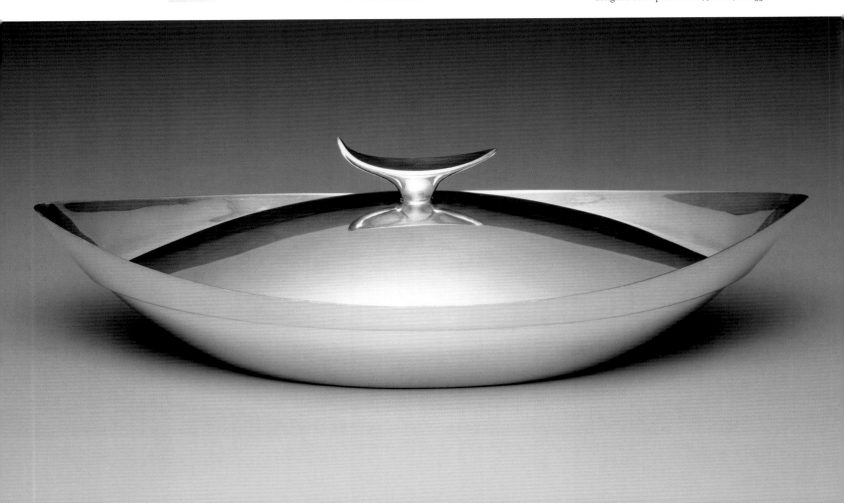

Gorham introduced the *Bateau* centerpiece in 1960 as "an intriguing contemporary concept" (fig. 10.56)[48]— the piece could be used simply as a centerpiece or with an insert for three tapers. In another version and size, a lid with a buoyant, contoured finial was added to transform the centerpiece into the *Bateau* double vegetable dish (fig. 10.57).[49] The pieces were the creation of a talented young Polish-born silversmith and jeweler, Alexandra Solowij (b. 1933), who had emigrated to Canada as a teenager in 1948 and ten years later graduated from the School of the Museum of Fine Arts in Boston. Her exhibited work at the school was discovered shortly afterward by Richard T. Hopcraft, Gorham's general merchandising manager, who induced her to leave Montreal and join the firm's design staff.[50] According to Solowij, her concept evolved from the shape of a dory, a typical New England flat-bottomed fishing boat with high flaring sides and a sharp prow, but the marketing department gave her design the French name for a boat, *bateau*.[51]

Free Form at Tiffany

Although it remained a generally conservative firm, Tiffany & Co. produced some handsome modernist silver holloware in the 1950s after Walter Hoving had assumed control of the company. The head staff designer Oscar Riedener created a competitive contemporary group with free form lines that was on display at the company's flagship store on Fifth Avenue in New York City in an exhibition that opened in the fall of 1955, reportedly the first of its kind in the firm's history.[52] Riedener's contemporary holloware was the subject of an illustrated review in the *New York Times Magazine*.[53] Among

FIGURE 10.59   Top left: Salad dish, 1959. Reed & Barton. Silver-plate, cat. 195; top right: *Flair* roll tray, 1954. 1847 Rogers Brothers. Silverplate, cat. 99; bottom left: Sandwich plate, 1955. Reed & Barton. Silver, cat. 184; bottom right: *Modern* "Avocado" centerpiece, c. 1955–1960. Gorham Manufacturing Company. Silverplate. DMA, JSASC, cat. 41

FIGURE 10.60   Top left: *Free-form* bowl, c. 1959. Gorham Manufacturing Company, Donald H. Colflesh, designer. Silverplate, cat. 46; top right: Bowl ("Viking"), c. 1959. F. B. Rogers Silver Company. Silverplate, cat. 212; center left: Centerpiece, c. 1955. W. & S. Blackinton & Company. Silverplate, plastic, cat. 6; bottom right: Bread tray, 1958. Reed & Barton, Milton P. Hannah, designer. Silverplate. DMA, JSASC, cat. 191

the items in the collection were a cocktail shaker set with a snowflake motif, a low triangular triple candelabrum, and a related seed-shaped, vaguely naturalistic centerpiece. The centerpiece (fig. 10.58) was balanced on four pointed feet undoubtedly inspired by Scandinavian examples and those made by studio silversmiths. Riedener's centerpiece was one of a number of distinctive silver holloware objects with an unequivocal 1950s "look" produced by Tiffany during the decade. One of the smartest 1950s designs, an hourglass mixer cinched at the waist with a hobnail-patterned band, was introduced in a cocktail set for Christmas 1958.[54] The stirring spoon had an allied finial, and the narrow bases of the cocktail cups matched the hobnail band exactly. An undecorated, low-slung, oblong bowl with a simple foot, designed by Riedener in 1937, but not produced until 1951, was the only silver object from Tiffany & Co. that was included in a traveling exhibition *20th Century Design U.S.A.*, mounted in 1959.[55] In a photograph of the exhibition installation at the Cleveland Museum of Art (see fig. 14.1), the bowl is in a case to the left of a pitcher by Reed & Barton.

NOTES

1. Lesley Jackson, *The New Look: Design in the Fifties* (New York: Thames and Hudson, 1991), 7, 8.

2. Lisa Phillips et al., *High Styles: Twentieth-Century American Design*, exh. cat. (New York: Whitney Museum of American Art in association with Summit Books, 1985), 112.

3. Jackson, *New Look*, 25.

4. Ibid.

5. Ibid., 26.

6. *Knife, Fork and Spoon*, exh. cat. (Minneapolis: Walker Art Center and Towle Silversmiths, 1951), 48–49.

7. D. S. Defenbacher, "Knife, Fork and Spoon," *Craft Horizons* 11 (summer 1951): 21.

8. Ibid.

9. The whereabouts of Gulotta's prototype service is unknown. (Robert J. King, telephone conversation with author, Feb. 3, 2004).

10. Marion Anderson Noyes, telephone conversation with author, Dec. 18, 1991.

11. Ibid., July 20, 2001. The patent holder for *Southwind* flatware was John Van Koert. The sterling *Southwind* celery dish, Towle product number 439, is typical of the holloware. Noyes designed two items for Towle in which she combined sterling silver and ceramic: a black ceramic jam jar with sterling cover, spoon, and saucer, and a black ceramic casserole dish with a sterling cover that had a black plastic finial. For the jam jar, see "Good things in Towle Sterling come in all shapes and prices," Towle Silversmiths advertisement, *House Beautiful* 97 (Nov. 1955): 15; and "Towle Gifts," Towle Silversmiths advertisement, *New Yorker* 33 (May 11, 1957): 123.

12. For a detailed history, see W. Scott Braznell, "A 'New Way of Life': A Candelabrum from Reed & Barton's 'Contemporary Group,'" *Yale University Art Gallery Bulletin* (1997–98): 76–83.

13. "Contemporary Group" brochure, n.p. (Reed & Barton Archives, Taunton, Mass.).

14. Ibid.

15. "Sterling silver dessert set from the Contemporary Group," Reed & Barton advertisement, *Gourmet* 16 (May 1956): 1.

16. "Contemporary Bonbon Dish in Sterling Silver," Reed & Barton advertisement, *New Yorker* 29 (Feb. 21, 1953): 18. The product number for the bonbon dish is X723.

17. "Gifts For a Lifetime: Reed & Barton Color Glaze," Reed & Barton promotional pamphlet (Apr. 1970) (Reed & Barton Archives). The product numbers of the bowls were 267, 268, and 269. In *Color-Glaze* these were described as "serving dishes," but the numbers remained the same.

18. The Reed & Barton product number for Hannah's bonbon dish is X721.

19. The sterling pieces from the *Classic American* holloware group were a sauce boat with attached plate (X242), a centerpiece (X244), and a candlestick, (X244). The silverplated pieces from the *Gallery* holloware group were a bread tray and compote, both with the number 1133.

20. "Totally New! 'Silver Sculpture' by Reed & Barton," Reed & Barton advertisement, *House Beautiful* 96 (Oct. 1954): 47.

21. Robert H. Ramp, letter to author, Sept. 20, 1991.

22. "Flair is Sweeping the Country," *Jewelers' Circular-Keystone* 125 (Mar. 1955): sixteen-page insert.

23. "New, new Flair," International Silver Company advertisement, *Brides Magazine* 21 (summer 1955): 39.

24. "National Advertising," International Silver Company *Annual Report* (1955).

25. A similar version of this pitcher was included in the *Living Today* exhibition of contemporary architecture, furniture, and interior decoration at the Corcoran Gallery of Art in Washington, D.C. in 1958; see entry 162 in Tableware in *Living Today: An Exhibition of Contemporary Architecture, Furniture, Interior Decoration*, exh. cat. (Washington, D.C.: Corcoran Gallery of Art, 1958), n.p.

26. International Silver Company, *International Sterling Craft Associates,* catalogue (n.d.), n.p. (International Silver Company Archives, Meriden Historical Society, Meriden, Conn.). See also Dorothy T. Rainwater, "Kurt Eric Christoffersen, Designer and Silversmith," *Silver* 28 (July/Aug. 1995): 10–12.

27. Dorothy T. Rainwater, "Alphonse La Paglia, Silversmith and Designer," *Silver* 28 (May/June 1995): 8–11.

28. "Silverware News you can use to increase sales," Oneida Ltd. advertisement, *Jewelers' Circular-Keystone* 126 (Aug. 1956): 172.

29. Charles L. Venable, *China and Glass in America 1880–1980: From Tabletop to TV Tray* (Dallas, Tex.: Dallas Museum of Art, 2000), 63–64.

30. Frank Perry, telephone conversation with author, July 28, 2000. Perry was formerly a vice president of design at Oneida.

31. Oneida Ltd. Silversmiths, *Achievement: New Design in Community* (1956), n.p. (Jewel Stern Archives, Coral Gables, Fla. [hereafter Stern Archives], courtesy of Oneida Ltd.).

32. "The new 5-way Serving Dish and Hot Beverage Server in *Achievement* pattern in *Community*," Oneida Ltd. advertisement, *New Yorker* 33 (Oct. 5, 1957): 5.

33. "Achievement: The New American Holloware by Community," memorandum (Stern Archives, courtesy of Oneida Ltd.); and "Achievement: the new pattern in Community," Oneida Ltd. advertisement, *Jewelers' Circular-Keystone* 126 (Sept. 1956): 161.

34. Maria Haar, Design Department, Oneida Ltd., letter to author, July 12, 2000.

35. "Achievement" memorandum, 4.

36. Oneida Ltd. Silversmiths, "Decorator Pieces" in Heirloom Silverplate Price List, June 15, 1964, n.p. (Stern Archives, courtesy of Oneida Ltd.). The *Achievement* candelabrum was priced $17.50 in 1956; $15.00 in Wm. A. Rogers in 1957; and $22.73 in the *Decorator* line in 1964; prices courtesy of Oneida Ltd.

37. Oneida Ltd. Silversmiths, *Presenting Achievement: New Design in Wm. A. Rogers Hollowware* (1957), 28 (Stern Archives, courtesy of Oneida Ltd.).

38. Oneida Ltd. Silversmiths, "Decorator" in *Heirloom Silverplate*, catalogue, 6 (Stern Archives, courtesy of Oneida Ltd.).

39. *Design in Scandinavia: An Exhibition of Objects for the Home*, exh. cat. (Oslo: Kirstes boktr., 1954), 71.

40. See, for example, "New Design for Giving: Gorham Original 'Trend' Candlesticks in Finest Sterling Silver," Gorham advertisement, *New Yorker* 29 (Sept. 12, 1953): 64; and "Wedding Gifts to Love, To Use, To Cherish For Years," *Brides Magazine* 21 (summer 1955): 144.

41. Instructions on how to fill and use the shakers were included with each set; see "Introducing the First Free-Flowing Sterling Salt and Pepper Set," Gorham advertisement, *New Yorker* 30 (Oct. 23, 1954): 59.

42. "Beauty wears a rose," Gorham advertisement, *New Yorker* 37 (Dec. 2, 1961): 46. In addition to the candlesticks and salt and pepper shakers, which were the only ones by Huggins, a compote, cream and sugar, and sauce boat with attached tray were illustrated. Huggins later designed the USS *Long Beach* service; see chapter 13.

43. The Gorham product number of Huggins's salt and pepper shakers is 1167; the product number of the candlesticks is 1155.

44. The Gorham product numbers for the other *Modern* coffee set are: coffeepot, YC851; covered sugar bowl, YC853; and creamer, YC854. The coffeepot has the pinched-in-waist shape and bowed walnut-color wood handle and finial. The model was also offered as a five-piece tea service with tray. For the coffeepot, see "You'll adore the Duchess," Gorham advertisement, *New Yorker* 38 (May 26, 1962): 49.

45. E. Bell, "Tommi Parzinger: Designer of Modern Interiors and Silver," *Studio* 123 (Jan. 1942): 37.

46. For the full-page Gorham advertisement of *Tira*, see "Gorham finds three new ways to grace a table," *New Yorker* 37 (May 13, 1961): 59. The Gorham product number of the *Tira* centerpiece is YC679 and that of the celery or bread tray, YC898.

47. Among other items in the *Modern* line are an open sugar bowl, YC943, and creamer, YC944, and a covered butter dish, YC775. See design patent 186,679 for another butter dish, Richard Thomas Hopcraft, assignor to Gorham Manufacturing Company, filed July 14, 1959, granted Nov. 17, 1959.

48. "New table brilliance . . . the Bateau by Gorham," Gorham advertisement, *House Beautiful* 102 (Oct. 1960): 3.

49. The *Bateau* centerpiece came in a twelve-inch length, YC689, and a larger size, more than fourteen inches in length, YC691.

50. Alexandra Solowij Watkins, telephone conversation with author, July 23, 2003. She freelanced for Gorham in 1958 while living in Montreal. In 1959 she moved to Providence to become a full-time designer at Gorham. Solowij left Gorham in June 1960. While she was there, Richard L. Huggins headed the design department.

51. Alexandra Solowij Watkins, telephone conversation with author, Aug. 30, 2003. A *Bateau* centerpiece (accession number 2004.205) is in the collection of the Museum of Fine Arts, Boston, as are examples of Solowij's studio work made at the Museum School, including a three-piece tea set (accession number 2004.203.1–3), a small chocolate pot (accession number 2004.204), and her later jewelry (accession number 1995.749).

52. Harriet Morrison, "Tiffany to Open Silver Show Today," *New York Herald Tribune*, Nov. 14, 1955, sec. 2, p. 8.

53. Betty Pepis, "New Character for Sterling," *New York Times Magazine*, Nov. 13, 1955, sec. 6, p. 55.

54. "Christmas Ideas From Tiffany," 1958 (Tiffany & Co. Archives, New York).

55. William Friedman, ed., *20th Century Design: U.S.A.*, exh. cat. (Buffalo, N.Y.: Albright Art Gallery, Buffalo Fine Arts Academy, 1959), 63. Annamarie Sandecki, e-mail to author, Oct. 12, 2001, Tiffany Archives. In the exhibition catalogue the date of design was erroneously given as 1957.

During the postwar decades of the 1950s and 1960s the use of silver in combination with materials, such as wood, plastic, enamel, and glass, was different conceptually from earlier manifestations in the 1920s and 1930s and was largely experimental. The use of wood was shaped by the dominance of Scandinavian modern design as was traditional decorative enameling. The glamour of the stark black contrasts effected with new plastics eclipsed the earlier taste for lively colored accents in Bakelite and Catalin. Towle experimented with stainless steel and sterling, and with enamel, and included ceramic parts in modern silver holloware. Gorham used colored glass and bits of colored plastic to suggest glass.

WOOD: THE INFLUENCE OF SCANDINAVIAN MODERN

The ascendance of modern Scandinavian design in the 1950s altered the use of wood in combination with silver. In 1920s modernist silver holloware, wood, especially rare macassar ebony, had been used for pot and tray handles and finials to emulate elements of French *art moderne* in expensive sterling holloware, and occasionally, in moderately priced silverplate lines. International, for example, used ebony in coffee sets made by its Wilcox & Evertsen and Barbour Fine Arts divisions (see fig. 2.8) and in the *Ile de France* silverplated holloware group. Diverse producers for the luxury market, such as A. L. Wagner in New York City and Marshall Field & Company in Chicago, also used exotic wood to accent costly goods (see figs. 2.14 and 3.7). In the 1930s, as *art moderne* was overtaken by a streamlined machine aesthetic, this treatment waned. In the modern classic idiom a holdover in the use of wood was the *Dorian* sterling tea service made by Watson (see fig. 8.2).

As early as 1946 the Metropolitan Museum of Art in New York City had showcased Scandinavian design in the exhibition *Modern Swedish and Danish Decorative Art*.[1] The influx of Scandinavian furniture in the 1950s and the illustrations in prominent shelter magazines of interiors filled with simple, wood-framed Danish Modern furniture signaled a radical shift in design. One of the finest versions of the style by an American was that designed by Paul McCobb (1917–1969) for the Directional Furniture Company (fig. 11.1).[2] Touted as the new contemporary trend, the interiors required compatible accessories in natural materials, often wood and ceramic. In 1954 a special section devoted to wood objects for table service was a part of the landmark exhibition of home furnishings, *Design in Scandinavia*, which received extensive coverage in *House and Garden*.[3] A collaborative venture, with organizing committees from Denmark, Finland, Norway, and Sweden and from more than twenty-five American and Canadian museums and the American Federation of Arts, the influential exhibition traveled across the continent between 1954 and 1957.[4] Dansk International Designs, Ltd., an American enterprise founded in 1954, engaged the versatile Danish designer Jens Quistgaard to

FIGURE 11.1 "A Permanent Contribution to American Design by Paul McCobb," Directional Furniture Company advertisement, 1954

FIGURE 11.2 Left: Ice bucket, c. 1964. International Silver Company. Silverplate, teak, cat. 81; center: Bowl, c. 1960. Wilcox Silver Plate Company. Silverplate, wood, cat. 129; right: Pitcher, 1965. International Silver Company. Silverplate, teak, cat. 82. DMA, JSASC

FIGURE 11.3 Top left: Candlesticks, 1966. The Stieff Company. Silver, rosewood, cat. 224; center right: Butter dish, c. 1965. Gorham Manufacturing Company. Silverplate, walnut, glass, cat. 61; bottom left: Salad fork and spoon, c. 1960. Napier Company. Silverplate, teak. DMA, JSASC, cat. 144

create a line of tableware in teak that included carving and cheese boards, trays, ice buckets, and pepper mills, as well as the teak-handled stainless flatware pattern *Fjord*. Dansk wares were introduced in the late 1950s, and Scandinavian imports became increasingly popular. In an effort to compete for customers enamored with contemporary Scandinavian design, silver manufacturers began using wood, especially teak, walnut, and rosewood, as the defining stylistic element for part of their production. International, Gorham, Stieff, Napier, Towle, and Reed & Barton were the most innovative manufacturers.

Among the earliest objects to demonstrate the trend was a salt shaker and pepper mill set in walnut and sterling with an enamel finial on the mill. The set was designed by Earl B. Pardon in about 1954 for Towle.[5] Another was a sterling bonbon dish with black walnut base and center, part of a small group that Reed & Barton introduced in 1959.[6] More evolved and stylish were objects by International in silverplate: a swooping bowl supported on a crossed wood base from the Wilcox Silver Plate Division of International, and a softly curvaceous pitcher with an assertive winglike walnut wood handle (fig. 11.2). An ice bucket, part of a Gourmet Line, with wood elements, that was featured in drawings in the firm's brochure for the New York World's Fair in 1964, has an onion-shaped lid articulated by a teak rim and finial (fig. 11.2, left).[7] Other makers, too, offered designs incorporating wood: in silverplate Napier produced salad servers with teak handles and Gorham produced a covered butter dish with an oiled walnut base and finial (fig. 11.3). Stieff produced a pair of flaring sterling and rosewood candlesticks (fig. 11.3). By the early 1970s, to compete with Dansk, a wine cooler made in Germany

for Towle was primarily of teak with only a silverplated collar and handles (see fig. 13.22).

A hallmark of the work of the studio silversmith Frederick A. Miller of Cleveland, Ohio—pointed, wood-tipped feet for supporting contoured bowls—was adopted by Reed & Barton as early as 1954 for a centerpiece bowl with Australian beefwood feet (see fig. 13.8). This novel application of wood for silverware achieved maximum refinement in Gorham's *Circa '70* triangular "Delta" centerpiece bowl and a matching candelabra, each supported by three angled, ebony-tipped feet (see fig. 13.6).

PLASTIC: SILVER AND BLACK

The use of plastic in combination with silver in the postwar period changed significantly. Colored Bakelite and Catalin, ubiquitous in the late 1920s and 1930s, was replaced by black plastic used only as a focal accent. In flatware, Lunt's *Contrast* by Nord Bowlen (1909–2001), the company's head designer and the son of William Bowlen, a founder of Rogers, Lunt & Bowlen, is a prime example.[8] When it was introduced in 1956, it was hoped that this bold, contemporary pattern (fig. 11.4), in which sterling silver was combined with black, injection-molded nylon handles, would compete with informal, imported stainless steel cutlery. Although enjoying a revival now, it was not commercially successful. The introduction of the domestic dishwasher by KitchenAid in 1949 and its increased presence in the American home by the late 1950s was undoubtedly a factor because, unlike stainless steel cutlery, flatware in this pattern had to be washed by hand.

In holloware, examples in which plastic and silver were mixed abounded in the 1950s.[9] Towle, Gorham, and Oneida were the most prolific exponents. A seminal application was the assertive handle of Towle's *Contour* beverage server (see fig. 10.12). On other objects, the accents were minimal, for example, the tips of Towle's sinuous sterling candlesticks by Noyes (see fig. 10.16) and the stopper bases of the individual *Columnesque* sterling salt and pepper shakers also by Towle that were sold in clear Lucite boxed sets of four.[10] For its *Modern* line in silverplate, Gorham used black plastic for the emphatic handle of the beverage server (see fig. 13.19) and for the base of the "Decorator" bowl (see fig. 10.53). For Oneida's *Achievement* line in silverplate, black plastic was used for the finials, larger handles, and the tips of the candelabra (see figs. 10.43, 10.44) and for the finials in the company's *Heirloom "700"* group (see fig. 10.41). Reed & Barton attached solid black Bakelite feet to a sterling bonbon dish[11] and, in an unusual treatment, the three feet of a free form silverplated centerpiece by W. & S. Blackinton of Meriden, Connecticut (see fig. 10.59), were partially wrapped in black plastic sleeves.

FIGURE 11.4 *Contrast* salad fork and spoon, 1956. Lunt Silversmiths, Nord Bowlen, designer. Silver, nylon (Zytel). Dallas Museum of Art, cat. 216

FIGURE 11.5 *Contempra House* spoons, 1955. Contempra House, Earl Pardon, designer. Silver, stainless steel, enamel. DMA, JSASC, cats. 274–276

FIGURE 11.6 *Contempra House* salad serving set, 1955. Contempra House, Earl Pardon, designer. Silver, enamel, plastic. DMA, JSASC, cat. 277

Some manufacturers used strips of plastic to imitate traditional woven raffia or wicker for insulating handles and for decoration. Foremost among these were Reed & Barton and International. In all three of the services that John Prip designed for Reed & Barton, the handles of the hot beverage servers were wrapped in plastic, black or a color to suggest natural raffia or wicker, for *The Diamond* service, black for the *Denmark* and *Dimension* services (see figs. 12.5, 12.7, and 12.8). International preferred natural raffia-colored plastic for various objects, including some in its highly successful *Flair* line (see figs. 10.30, 10.31).

ENAMEL, STAINLESS STEEL, AND CERAMICS

Towle was one of the earliest manufacturers to mix materials, experimenting with enamel in the 1950s. William DeHart, the director of design, invited the jeweler

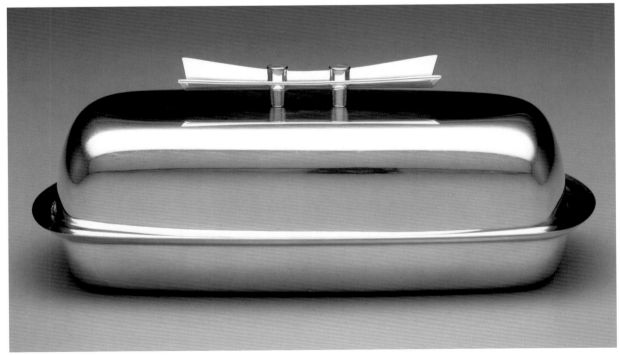

and enamelist Earl B. Pardon (1926–1991), his former student, to work with the company as an in-house consultant, to invigorate design. In 1954 Pardon took a year's leave of absence from Skidmore College in Saratoga Springs, New York, where he taught. Pardon's novel flatware pattern, in which the tines, blades, and bowls were of stainless steel for utility and the handles of jade green enamel-tipped sterling for elegance, was patented in 1955 and introduced in 1956. The design was made by a new division of Towle, Contempra House, which was established to compete with producers of stainless steel. Pardon's design was made in two versions with enamel tips in jade green, one with the handle scored vertically on the front side. Each version was also available with a rounded point instead of the enamel tip (figs. 11.5, 11.6). These four variations, all commonly referred to as Contempra House from their impressed mark, were the only patterns issued by the division. The combination of stainless steel and sterling did not sell well, very little was produced, and the concept was abandoned. The firm then converted the Contempra House division to Towle Stainless Steel.[12]

While developing the Contempra House division, Towle and Lenox joined forces to create a cream and covered sugar set and another related covered container, perhaps for an artificial sugar substitute such as saccharin. The containers are of Lenox's ivory-colored porcelain. Onion-shaped, each sterling lid has a finial with an enamel tip in jade green and the open porcelain creamer has a band of silver encircling it that both suggests a base and balances the lidded sugar bowl (fig. 11.7). The similarity of these enameled tips to those on Pardon's Contempra House flatware and salt and pepper sets for Towle that can be documented suggest an association with Pardon. In 1955 House and Garden published an illustration of Towle's sterling silver butter dish with enameled "studs" that terminate the supports of the cover's elevated handle (fig. 11.8).[13] The enameled accents are further evidence of Pardon's involvement in design at Towle from 1954 to 1955, the period in which he was an in-house consultant.

During those years Towle also offered a number of novel, informal holloware items in which sterling silver was combined with black ceramic and black plastic elements. Among these were a ceramic jam jar with a sterling cover that had a plastic finial and a ceramic casserole dish with a similar, but much larger cover, both by Marion Anderson Noyes.[14] In a variation, the casserole came with a warming stand and had a terraced sterling cover with a decorative enamel finial designed by Pardon.[15] Another item in the line is a black ceramic butter dish with a silver cover. The cover has a simple, subtly curved black plastic handle that mirrors the shape of the dish and unifies the components (fig. 11.9). In 1962, perhaps in emulation of Towle, Reed & Barton introduced a decorative black ceramic trivet with a sterling rim and three gold motifs in the ceramic, one floral and the other two resembling snowflakes.[16]

FIGURE 11.7   Left and center: Creamer and sugar bowl, c. 1955, cat. 268; right: Covered pot, c. 1955. Towle Silversmiths and Lenox China. Porcelain, silver, enamel. Dallas Museum of Art, cat. 269

FIGURE 11.8   Butter dish, c. 1955. Towle Silversmiths. Silver, enamel, ceramic. DMA, JSASC, cat. 267

FIGURE 11.9   Butter dish, c. 1955. Towle Silversmiths. Silver, plastic, ceramic. DMA, JSASC, cat. 266

FIGURE 11.10 Candy jars, 1963–1972. Gorham Manufacturing Company. Silver, glass. DMA, JSASC, cat. 60

FIGURE 11.11 *Ring* basket, c. 1968. Gorham Manufacturing Company. Silverplate, plastic. DMA, JSASC, cat. 63

GLASS AT GORHAM

In the 1960s Gorham used clear and colored glass for an assortment of centerpieces, vases, and hurricane lamps with silver bases, and for glass mustard and jam pots with silver lids. The most aesthetically satisfying item of this type is a candy jar made of amethyst glass by the Lindshammar Glasbruk in Sweden in 1963, for which Gorham provided a sterling cover with an elegant crystal ball finial. The stylish contemporary candy jar proved to be a brisk seller and, within a year, it was available in emerald green and cobalt blue glass as well (fig. 11.10).[17] In 1967, the design was offered for the first time in a rippled gray glass called "smoke optic," a version that was produced until 1972 (fig. 11.10, second from left). Gorham achieved the effect of glass with inexpensive inserts of colored plastic in a silverplated ring basket, described as a "fruit basket of silverplated rings jeweled here and there with blue and orange disks with the glow of stained glass" (fig. 11.11).[18] Gorham's ring basket and the candy jar in four colors demonstrate the appeal of color in the 1960s, an infatuation that inspired Reed & Barton to introduce its *Color-Glaze* line in 1961.

Notes

1. R. Craig Miller, *Modern Design in the Metropolitan Museum of Art 1890–1990* (New York: Metropolitan Museum of Art and Abrams, 1990), 305. The Metropolitan had mounted an *Exhibition of Swedish Contemporary Decorative Arts* in 1927, and in 1935 exhibited its new acquisitions of contemporary French and Swedish applied arts.

2. "A Permanent Contribution to American Design by Paul McCobb," Directional Furniture Company advertisement, *House and Garden* 106 (Dec. 1954): 7. Other American furniture lines influenced by the Danish Modern style were "Perspective" by Drexel, 1952, and "Dunbar for Modern," 1953.

3. *Design in Scandinavia: An Exhibition of Objects for the Home,* exh. cat. (Oslo: Kirstes boktr., 1954), 84–89; and "The Scandinavian Way," *House and Garden* 109 (Mar. 1956): 88.

4. *Design in Scandinavia,* 5–7. The Metropolitan Museum of Art in New York presented *The Arts of Denmark: Viking to Modern* in 1960, an exhibition that toured the United States; in 1962, the Cooper Union Museum showed *Creative Craft in Denmark.* See David Revere McFadden, ed. *Scandinavian Modern Design, 1880–1980,* exh. cat. (New York: Abrams and Cooper-Hewitt Museum, 1982), 21–22.

5. Salt shaker and pepper mill, Towle product number 32.

6. Reed & Barton bonbon dish, product number X51. Also in this group was an eight-inch bowl, X52; a sandwich plate, X53; and candlesticks, X50.

7. "Presenting the International Silver Company Exhibit at the New York World's Fair 1964–1965," n.p. (Jewel Stern Archive, Coral Gables, Fla.).

8. From 1935 on, Rogers, Lunt & Bowlen of Greenfield, Mass., used the trade name Lunt Silversmiths.

9. One of the most common applications of black plastic was for the bottom of trays that were given silver rims. Another was for salad bowls that had narrow ring bases of silver.

10. *Columnesque* shakers, Towle product number 12.

11. Reed & Barton product number X145.

12. Edward Mulligan, telephone conversation with author, Apr. 27, 2003. Mulligan was formerly the president of Towle Silversmiths. The Towle hallmark was not stamped on the flatware, only the words "Contempra House."

13. "Last-Minute Gift Guide for Armchair Shoppers," *House and Garden* 108 (Dec. 1955): 101. This butter dish was also made without enameled accents. The Towle product number, 53, was the same for both butter dishes.

14. Towle illustrated holloware pamphlet (1955), courtesy of Noyes, who identified her designs.

15. Towle casserole with heating stand illustrated in "Gourmet Goes Christmas Shopping," *Gourmet* 15 (Dec. 1955): 24.

16. Reed & Barton trivet, product number X118.

17. David Rogers, telephone conversation with author, Feb. 10, 1997.

18. "Gifts: Little Luxuries Under $35," *House and Garden* 134 (Nov. 1968): 98.

CHAPTER TWELVE

INNOVATION: THE REED & BARTON

DESIGN PROGRAM

In 1957, under the leadership of Roger Hallowell, its progressive president, who had assumed the position in 1953 and was a forceful advocate for modernity through the 1960s, Reed & Barton embarked on a dynamic campaign, called the "Design Program," to enhance the firm's status as the design leader in the industry.[1] By encouraging the exploration and creation of new shapes and forms in silver, and by stimulating the public interest in good industrial design, the firm hoped to achieve its goal. Gio Ponti was engaged to create a flatware pattern, and the firm instigated a Silver Design Competition in Italy, participated in museum exhibitions, and sponsored lectures by experts in art, architecture, and design at colleges. The most significant decision, however, would be to bring the master silversmith John Prip, a former teacher at the School for American Craftsmen in Rochester, New York, to Reed & Barton to become craftsman-in-residence.

GIO PONTI AND *THE DIAMOND*

The mid-1950s was a heady time full of optimistic experimentation in the silverware industry. The jeweler and enamelist Earl Pardon, a consultant at Towle between 1954 and 1955, designed *Contempra House* flatware, a combination of sterling, stainless steel, and enamel. Nord Bowlen's *Contrast* with its striking black plastic handles was introduced in 1956, and Wallace's *Discovery* pattern unveiled in 1957 was promoted under the name of its celebrated designer Raymond Loewy and later by provocative advertising (fig. 12.1). Reed & Barton contributed to this ferment in design. Early in 1954 as *Silver Sculpture* was launched, the firm decided to develop another dynamic contemporary pattern, one that would bring prestige to its name and distinguish the company from its competitors. Gio Ponti (1891–1979), an internationally renowned Italian architect and designer, was approached to create the new pattern.[2] Ponti agreed and proposed six possible designs, of which one was chosen. It would take several iterations over four years of development by Reed & Barton's design staff before Ponti's design evolved into *The Diamond* pattern of 1958. Photographs of the drawings at Reed & Barton document the course of the design process. Ponti's first elaboration shows a knife, fork, and spoon of equal size and a handle faceted like a diamond, unprecedented ideas for industrially produced American flatware (fig. 12.2). In the first stage of development at Reed & Barton, Robert H. Ramp, the staff designer who was primarily responsible for adapting Ponti's proposal, reduced the size and slightly lengthened the knife, but retained the original shape of each piece.[3] In the next stage the size of the fork and spoon were reduced again to proportions considered more compatible with American usage, a diamondlike facet was introduced at the tip of each piece, and the knife blade—though still short—was completely modified to a conventional shape.[4] In the final, produced version the seam

Wouldn't you like to sit down and...eat with Wallace Sterling every day!

You can! That's the beauty of Wallace Sterling. It's always at home with pottery and cotton or linen and limoges. ■ Of course, when you see Wallace Sterling, it does look more expensive than other sterling. But it isn't! It's just that Wallace, alone, is sculptured all around. ■ Pick it up and see the flow of design. Hold it in the warmth of your hand and feel its perfect balance. ■ When you eat with Wallace every day, it needs no more than soap and water care. It wears forever. Its lustre grows as your pride in it will. In use: Discovery, $37.50

WALLACE
STERLING

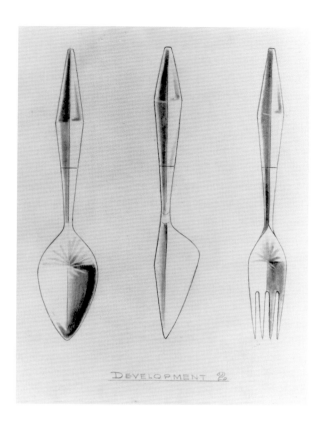

DEVELOPMENT 2

across the handles was eliminated, the knife blade was lengthened, and the transition from the handle to the blade was changed to conform with the point at the neck of the spoon and fork (fig. 12.3). Looking back, Ramp recalled, "I knew that Ponti would not be happy with our solution but I feel, we maintained the essence of his concept."[5] Reed & Barton had no reservations at the time: "In its final form The Diamond Pattern retains the character of Ponti's original concept, yet it has been skillfully refined to meet American preferences."[6]

The manufacturing challenges presented by the design were one reason for the delays in producing the pattern. Even after the final design was approved there was some doubt about whether it could be produced. The wedge shape of the handles posed a host of problems and a new stainless steel knife blade had to be created especially for the pattern. The company credited the success of the undertaking to the teamwork of its die cutters, stampers, cutlery assemblers, polishers, buffers, and finishers who perfected new techniques to produce the pattern.[7] To introduce *The Diamond*, Reed & Barton organized the "biggest 'new pattern' advertising promotion in company history." This was the heyday of the company's "grand media opening night events" to introduce new patterns and early in January 1958, a special reception was held at the Plaza Hotel in New York City to introduce the pattern to publishers, editors, and other representatives of leading magazines, newspapers, and radio and TV stations.[8] Ponti flew in to attend the event and mingle with guests, among them, Henry Luce, the publisher of *Life* and *Time*.[9] In a lavish

FIGURE 12.1   "Wouldn't you like to sit down and . . . ," Wallace Silversmiths advertisement, 1957

FIGURE 12.2   Drawing, "Development 2," Gio Ponti, c. 1954–1955

FIGURE 12.3   "Are you ready for it? . . ." Reed & Barton advertisement, 1958

ARE YOU READY
FOR IT?
THE MOST
ADVANCED
STERLING OF OUR
GENERATION

THE DIAMOND
PATTERN
BY REED & BARTON

two-page advertisement (fig. 12.3), the company issued the challenge: "Are you ready for it? The most advanced sterling of our generation."[10]

SILVER DESIGN COMPETITION IN ITALY

In 1959, as part of its Design Program, Reed & Barton invited several distinguished Italian designers to enter a competition to create a sterling flatware pattern. This project became known as the Silver Design Competition in Italy. The company articulated its aim as one "consistent with a long-standing company policy of instilling in its own American design team a sense of sustained curiosity and unhampered invention."[11] The designers were Franco Albini, Achille and Pier Giacomo Castiglioni, Constantino Corsini, Angelo Mangiarotti and Bruno Morassutti, Carlo Mollino, Roberto Mongo, Bruno Munari, Carlo Scarpa, Ettore Sottsass, and Marco Zanuso.[12] The idea had been broached as early as 1953 but was postponed in favor of engaging Ponti.[13] The reception for *The Diamond* and the fanfare surrounding its introduction revitalized interest in the design competition.[14] According to Reed & Barton, Ponti's "aid, advice and encouragement were vital influences in both the concept and organization" of the competition.[15]

The designs were fabricated in silver as prototypes and a panel of five experts was organized to judge the entries. The jury consisted of Ponti, the sculptor Isamu Noguchi, James S. Plaut, director emeritus of the Institute of Contemporary Art in Boston, James C. Raleigh, the head of the silverware department of Marshall Field & Company in Chicago, and William T. Hurley, Jr., the vice president of Reed & Barton.[16] The Castiglionis were awarded first prize in the competition and Corsini and Scarpa placed second and third, respectively. In October 1960 the winners were announced at a gala exhibition opening at the Institute of Contemporary Art in Boston, which was attended by the consul general of Italy in New England. In December the exhibit moved to the Columbia University School of Architecture in New York City, and in the spring of 1961 the prototypes were displayed for a month in the show windows of the Italian State Tourist Office on Fifth Avenue.[17] *Interiors* magazine described the "ten passionately individualistic Italian designers" as of "one mind in their collective concept of silver flatware as sculpture with a purpose," a concept manifested by their unanimous rejection of surface decoration. The reviewer cited the Castiglionis' winning knife for echoing the curve of the hand, Corsini's design for the balance of concave and convex surfaces, and Mollino's for its "wire slim shank in profile."[18] Although Reed & Barton took pride in its effort to explore new concepts and shapes in silver and in having interested "design-conscious Americans," none of the experimental designs was produced.[19]

JOHN PRIP: A CRAFTSMAN IN INDUSTRY

For three years beginning early in 1957 until 1960, after which he became an outside design consultant until 1970, John Prip (b. 1922) was craftsman-in-residence at the Reed & Barton plant. He had the full support of Hallowell, who firmly believed that "the craftsman has a place in industry, and that place is one of leadership."[20] Prip was given "carte blanche to work in a totally unfettered atmosphere" in his own private workshop.[21] Hallowell was a realist and knew that, in a company that employed nine hundred people, practicality had to prevail and products had to sell.[22] Prip was sympathetic to this pragmatism, a key to his rapport with Hallowell:

I learned an awful lot there. I learned to respect what they were doing. I guess I came to Reed and Barton with a certain superior feeling, but I was rather impressed with the integrity with which they approach their job. It's a very honest sort of game to be in, in a way, because no one makes any bones about it. Either it sells or it doesn't. You can argue forever about the merits of a painting, but in a sense the merit of something done for industry, aside from whatever aesthetic judgment you may pass on it, is very easily evaluated. It shows up either in black ink or red ink.[23]

The confidence Hallowell placed in Prip was rewarded with outstanding performance in design. The critic Rose Slivka may well have been referring to Reed & Barton and Prip when she observed in an editorial in *Craft Horizons* magazine in 1959 that "the silver holloware

FIGURE 12.4 John Prip attaching the cover to a coffeepot in *The Diamond* pattern, 1958

industry is making great strides to produce fresh designs evolved by metal craftsmen."[24]

In addition to his background in Scandinavian design and his mastery of technique, Prip brought a rich vocabulary of sculptural form and a refined sensitivity for detail to his work. No other craftsman contributed more to the silver industry in the second half of the twentieth century than Prip did. One of his earliest assignments (fig. 12.4) was a sterling tea and coffee service to coordinate with the *The Diamond* flatware pattern that was evolving from Ponti's design. First the coffee set was introduced in 1958 and later the line was extended to a full tea and coffee service. *The Diamond* vessels (fig. 12.5), smooth-surfaced and based on reversed conical forms that subtly echo the wedge-shaped flatware handles, were spun over collapsible chucks.[25] The handles, spouts, and elongated diamond-shaped finials were angled in planes to harmonize with the flatware. Originally, natural rattan or woven black plastic was used to wrap and insulate coffee and teapot

FIGURE 12.5   *The Diamond* tea and coffee service, 1958. Reed & Barton, John Prip, designer. Silver, plastic. DMA, JSASC, cat. 193

FIGURE 12.6 "'The Diamond' Pepper and Salt Set . . . ," Reed & Barton advertisement, 1961

FIGURE 12.7 *Denmark* tea and coffee service, 1958. Reed & Barton, John Prip, designer. Silverplate, plastic. DMA, JSASC, cat. 192

handles. Later the rattan was replaced with colored plastic.[26] A tray was not produced to match the service. Well received, the three-piece coffee set was advertised as late as 1976 with the headline "The Diamond Is Forever."[27] To coordinate with both the flatware and the tea and coffee services, Prip designed two sets of salt and pepper shakers as miniature versions of the teapot form. In a dramatic black-and-white full-page advertisement published in 1961 (fig. 12.6), Reed & Barton extolled the shakers as a "brilliant new facet in table settings."[28] In 1958 Prip's *Denmark* service in pewter was introduced, and two years later it was available in silverplate as well. In this service Prip was not constrained by a matching flatware pattern. Consequently, the rounded lines of the vessels were more fluid as they tapered at the necks and bases (fig. 12.7). Except for the flat lid punctuated by an abstract birdlike finial, the teapot bore a resemblance to the one that the Danish silversmith Henning Koppel had designed for Jensen and which had been awarded a gold medal at the Milan Triennale in 1954.[29]

Prip's handwrought *Onion* teapot of 1954, now in the collection of the Museum of Fine Arts, Boston, was the prototype for the *Dimension* tea and coffee service (fig. 12.8), the last of his three. The swelling teardrop form with lids tapering in one piece to form the finials has a vague Middle Eastern flavor and calls to mind Russian onion domes such as those of the sixteenth-century Church of St. Basil in Moscow. The unusual folded and cantilevered hinges of the *Onion* were retained for the pots, as were the looping handles, and their shape, echoed in the curving spouts, creates the effect of continuous flow, a metaphor of their function.[30] The service has a matching tray with a removable black Formica insert to coordinate with the black plastic–wrapped pot handles. Although the service carried the name of Prip's *Dimension* flatware pattern of 1961 and was introduced the same year, the character of each differed. The flatware (fig. 12.9) has a rigid linear quality with a sharp profile. To improve its function the knife was turned 90 degrees from its traditional position, and when set on the table the blade is upright.[31]

In addition to *Dimension*, Prip designed two other sterling patterns in which he abandoned the asymmetrical contours that had proliferated in the 1950s in favor of slender elongation. In *Lark* (1960), a recessed canoe-shaped handle tapers to a severely attenuated shaft (see fig. 14.6). Prip did not endorse the embellishment of *Lark* with motifs to become *Star*, a decision imposed by management to broaden its appeal. The patterns were advertised in tandem in a two-page spread headlined "Reed & Barton sterling captures the changes in the air" in "a new concept in form: the one pure, the other adorned. Both for the young and aware."[32] Although the shape of Prip's *Tapestry* pattern (1964) was derived from *Dimension*, it was embellished with deeply carved decoration that is difficult to define, and this indefinability, accentuated in the promotion, calls attention to a post–World War II eclecticism and the marketing of such products (see fig. 14.7): "The spare and slender shape of today—entwined with a million yesterdays. The form still startling a decade from now. The design as ancient as the thread of the first love story ever told. Mediterranean? Scandinavian? Modern? Medieval? Yes and no. Tapestry is all of them and none of them. It is whatever you want it to be."[33]

Among the holloware pieces that Prip designed during his association with Reed & Barton was a serving dish introduced in 1963 and advertised as "The Complete Casserole," to "inspire chefs and encourage show-offs."[34] In the early 1980s, shortly before being retired from production, it was deemed "The Connoisseur Casserole" (fig. 12.10).[35] The server consists of three parts: a round white ovenproof liner by Hall China Company of East Liverpool, Ohio, a silverplated frame in which to insert the liner, and a silverplated cover. The smooth, clean surfaces are devoid of decoration except for the elegantly modeled finial, a minimal sculpture in its own right, and the uplifted handles. Prip designed several silverplated bowls, including a triangular one available

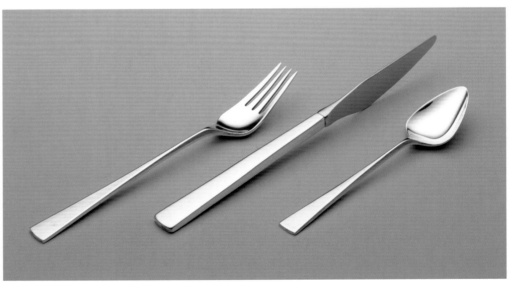

FIGURE 12.8 *Dimension* tea and coffee service, 1961. Reed & Barton, John Prip, designer. Silverplate, plastic. Dallas Museum of Art, cat. 199

FIGURE 12.9 *Dimension* place knife, place fork, and teaspoon, 1961. Reed & Barton, John Prip, designer. Silver, stainless steel. Dallas Museum of Art, cat. 200

FIGURE 12.10 *Connoisseur* casserole, 1963. Reed & Barton, John Prip, designer. Silverplate, ceramic. DMA, JSASC, cat. 201

in silverplate and with *Color-Glaze* interiors and in three sizes,[36] and a silverplated ashtray in *Color-Glaze* (see fig. 13.25). Although Prip's contribution to the firm's quest for good design was stellar and his relationship with the company satisfactory, the realities of the marketplace led him to acknowledge some frustration and disappointment: "I wish I could say that I came in and completely revolutionized Reed and Barton, and they discovered that with my designs they'd sell twenty times as much. This just isn't so. The traditional patterns still account for the majority of sales."[37]

Nonetheless, Prip's work was recognized in two exhibitions at the Museum of Contemporary Crafts in New York City in the early 1960s. The first, *A Craftsman's Role in Modern Industry* in 1962, explored new trends in contemporary silver and pewter exclusively through the work of Prip at Reed & Barton. More than fifty examples—one-of-a-kind experimental pieces and items that had been successfully produced and marketed—were shown.[38] To promote the company as well as the exhibition and to reinforce Reed & Barton's progressive position in the industry, Hallowell presided over a preview for more than 250 editors and radio-television personalities.[39] In 1964 Prip's work for the company was honored again in *Designed for Production: The Craftsman's Approach*, a nationwide survey, organized by the Museum of Contemporary Crafts, in which he was one of six featured designers in a field of sixty-six. On display were his five-piece *Dimension* tea service without the tray, his three-piece *The Diamond* coffee set, the smallest triangular bowl in *Color-Glaze*, a silverplated centerpiece bowl, *The Diamond* salt and pepper shakers in the taller size, pewter salt and pepper shakers, and *Tapestry* flatware.[40] The importance of the exhibition was underscored in a special issue, "The Craftsman in Production," published by *Craft Horizons* magazine. Looking back on their collaboration, Hallowell was complimentary: "In the last seven years we have been very fortunate in having with us John Prip, who has brought us the originality and ingenuity of a true craftsman-designer, but who has also learned what can and cannot be done by machine."[41]

THE REED & BARTON DESIGN LECTURE

In another phase of the outreach program to enhance its status, the firm sponsored an annual lecture to foster a greater appreciation of good design in industry and the arts. The first lecture in 1962 was held at Wellesley College in Wellesley, Massachusetts, and was given by Sir Kenneth Clark, the renowned English art historian and a former director of the National Gallery of Art

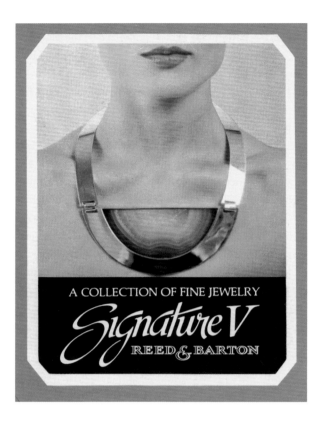

FIGURE 12.11 Agate neckpiece, Mary Ann Scherr. Cover, Reed &
Barton, *Signature V* brochure, 1977

in London. That a capacity audience of almost fifteen hundred people, including students, art critics, the press, and representatives of museums, turned out for the lecture, "The Blot and the Diagram: An Historian's Reflection on Modern Art," indicated a considerable public relations effort.[42] At the University of Michigan in Ann Arbor, the following year, the German émigré architect Marcel Breuer delivered the second lecture, "Matter and Intrinsic Form," in which he defined space as "having again become 'the sculpture into which one enters.'"[43] In 1964 at Sarah Lawrence College in Bronxville, New York, Sigvard Bernadotte, the Swedish designer who worked for Georg Jensen and was at the time the chief designer of the Swedish Pavilion at the New York World's Fair, gave the third and last lecture, "The Designer's Responsibility to His Time."[44] As the cultural climate changed in the 1960s, the firm's commitment to progressive design waned. Prip terminated his role as consultant in 1970, and Hallowell's tenure as president ended in 1971.

THE *SIGNATURE V* JEWELRY COLLECTION

In 1977 in an unusual move to boost business, and to capitalize on the vogue for silver jewelry that was being designed by Elsa Peretti and Angela Cummings for Tiffany, and by other well-known designers, Reed & Barton launched *Signature V,* a collection of sterling silver and vermeil jewelry designed by five outstanding studio jewelers. The undertaking had parallels with the jewelry line designed by Kurt Eric Christoffersen and Alphonse La Paglia for International's Craft Associates venture in the mid-1950s. Reed & Barton hoped to expand the market for jewelry with "something different" following the success of the *Damascene* line introduced in 1970, in which an ancient technique of layering colored metals was revived for decorative effect.[45] The idea for *Signature V* originated with Hallowell (now chairman of the board) after he met Arline Fisch at Boston University, where she taught a summer course in jewelry making. Hallowell asked Fisch to design jewelry suitable for quantity production and to find other accomplished craft artists to join her in creating a contemporary collection of fashion jewelry with a bold "one-of-kind" look.[46] In addition to pieces by Fisch the *Signature V* collection included work by Glenda Arentzen, Ronald Hayes Pearson, Lynda Watson, and Mary Ann Scherr, whose agate neckpiece appeared on the brochure cover (fig. 12.11). In order to appeal to women with different personal styles, the jewelry designers were chosen for the distinctive character of their work. The original collection consisted of twenty-five designs and each of the necklaces, bracelets, pins, and earrings was signed with the hallmark of its creator and packaged in a specially designed gift box. The retail prices ranged from fifteen to three hundred dollars.[47] Although embarked upon optimistically and widely advertised with a striking two-page spread that illustrated a necklace by each of the five, the venture had limited success.[48] *Signature V* marked the end of an era of bold experiment and creative risk taking by Reed & Barton.

NOTES

1. Hallowell's reign as president of Reed & Barton ended in 1971.

2. "Dynamic New Idea in Sterling, The Diamond Pattern is the Result of Italian Inspiration and Real American Ingenuity," *The Silver Lining* (Reed & Barton newsletter) 16 (May 1958): 2.

3. Photograph of drawing "Development 3" and all development drawings in Reed & Barton Archives, Taunton, Mass.

4. Photograph of drawing "Development 4" (Reed & Barton Archives).

5. Robert H. Ramp, letter to author, Sept. 20, 1991. John Prip confirmed that it was not, as erroneously reported, he who reworked Ponti's flatware design that ultimately became *The Diamond*, but Ramp (Prip, telephone conversation with author, Mar. 11, 2002).

6. "Dynamic New Idea in Sterling," 3.

7. "The Problem: To Translate Unprecedented Shapes Into Sterling—Many Said it Couldn't Be Done," *The Silver Lining* (Reed & Barton newsletter) 16 (May 1958): 4.

8. For marketing at Reed & Barton in the 1950s and 1960s, see Renee Garrelick, *Sterling Seasons: The Reed & Barton Story* (Taunton, Mass.: Reed & Barton, 1998), 87–101, 109–10.

9. "250 Guests Acclaim the Diamond Pattern at New York Press Party," *The Silver Lining* (Reed & Barton newsletter) 16 (May 1958): 8–9.

10. "The Diamond Pattern by Reed & Barton," *House Beautiful* 100 (May 1958): 16–17. The advertisement also appeared in the *New Yorker* and *Town and Country*.

11. Reed & Barton, "Silver Design Competition in Italy" exhibition wallboard (Reed & Barton Archives).

12. "Winners of R&B's Silver Design Competition in Italy Announced at Premiere of Exhibit at Art Institute," *The Silver Lining* (Reed & Barton newsletter) 18 (Nov. 1960): 1.

13. Ibid.

14. Ibid.

15. "Winners of R&B's Silver Design."

16. B. B. P. "Design Renascence in Silver," *Interiors* 120 (Dec. 1960): 97.

17. "R&B's Silver Design Competition in Italy Exhibit Opens in New York; Press Reception attended by over 100 Guests," *The Silver Lining* (Reed & Barton newsletter) 19 (May 1961): 1.

18. "Design Renascence," 97.

19. "Winners of R&B's Silver Design." See also Marco Ferreri, ed. *Cutlery* (Mantua, Italy: Corraini Edittore, 1997), 64–69.

20. Jan McDevitt, "The Craftsman in Production," *Craft Horizons* 24 (Mar./Apr. 1964): 22.

21. "A Craftsman's Role in Modern Industry: The Story of John Prip at Reed & Barton," in *A Craftsman's Role in Modern Industry*, exh. cat. (New York: Museum of Contemporary Crafts, 1962), n.p.; see also Thomas S. Michie and Christopher P. Monkhouse, eds., *John Prip: Master Metalsmith*, exh. cat. (Providence, R.I.: Rhode Island School of Design; New York: American Craft Museum, 1987).

22. McDevitt, "Craftsman in Production," 23.

23. John Prip, "John Prip and Reed & Barton ' . . . it's been a good relationship . . . ,'" *Craft Horizons* 24 (Mar./Apr. 1964): 52.

24. Rose Slivka, "U.S. Crafts in This Industrial Society," *Craft Horizons* 19 (Mar./Apr. 1959): 17.

25. Arthur J. Pulos, "John Prip's Odyssey in Metal," *American Crafts* 48 (Aug./Sept. 1988): 52. Prip's *The Diamond* service was recognized early on in two museum exhibitions, *The New England Silversmith* (the five-piece service)—and *Silver in American Life* (the teapot); see *The New England Silversmith: An Exhibition of New England Silver from the Mid-Seventeenth Century to the Present*, exh. cat. (Providence: Museum of Art, Rhode Island School of Design, 1965); and Barbara McLean Ward and Gerald W. R. Ward, eds., *Silver in American Life: Selections from the Mabel Brady Garvan and Other Collections at Yale University*, exh. cat. (Boston: David R. Godine, in association with Yale University Art Gallery and the American Federation of Arts, 1979), 88.

26. In the *Reed & Barton Sterling Silver Holloware Catalog Supplement—October 1, 1958*, *The Diamond* coffee set was shown with a black plastic–wrapped handle. On the cover of the November 1959 issue of *House Beautiful*, the coffee set appeared with a handle wrapped in natural raffia or wicker. The variety—three different wrappings, one in a natural material and two in plastic, one of which was black and the other a color that imitated the natural material—was unusual.

27. "The Diamond is Forever," Reed & Barton advertisement, *New Yorker* 52 (Dec. 13, 1976): 5.

28. "'The Diamond' Pepper and Salt Set," Reed & Barton advertisement, *New Yorker* 37 (Mar. 18, 1961): 5. The advertisement also appeared in *Gourmet*.

29. Graham Hughes, *Modern Silver throughout the World: 1880–1967* (New York: Crown Publishers, 1967), 19.

30. The distinctive hinges by Prip were discontinued within a year, because so many pots were returned for repair. They were replaced with more practical ones that compromised the aesthetics of the pots.

31. Pulos, "John Prip's Odyssey," 52. The *Dimension* knife had a precedent in the designs of two finalists in the 1960 International Design Competition for Sterling Silver Flatware exhibited in *Designed For Silver*, those of Franck Ligtelijn of Holland and Arthur J. Pulos; see *Designed for Silver: An Exhibition of Twenty-two Award-Winning Designs from the International Design Competition for Sterling Silver Flatware*, exh. cat. (New York: Museum of Contemporary Crafts of the American Craftsmen's Council and The International Silver Company, 1960), 37, 47.

32. "The Lark and the Star," Reed & Barton advertisement, *House Beautiful* 102 (Apr. 1960): 6. *Lark* proved the more successful; according to Prip, "*Star* laid an egg" (John Prip, telephone conversation with author, Mar. 12, 2004).

33. "Reed & Barton bring you a TAPESTRY in solid silver," Reed & Barton advertisement, *Town and Country* 118 (May 1964): 13.

34. "The Complete Casserole," Reed & Barton advertisement, *New Yorker* 46 (Feb. 24, 1968): 109.

35. "A Classic Is Art You Use," Reed & Barton advertisement, *New Yorker* (Sept. 7, 1981): 93.

36. Among other silverplated bowls by Prip are the almond-shaped bowl, product number 252, introduced in 1958 and in production until 1969 (also as a bonbon dish, number 242), and the ovoid bowl with squared ends, product number 253, introduced in 1958 and in production until 1962 (also as a bonbon dish, number 243).

37. McDevitt, "Craftsman in Production," 26.

38. Examples of experimental holloware by Prip at Reed & Barton are illustrated in Tim McCreight, "Master Metalsmith: John Prip," *Metalsmith* 3 (fall 1983): 6.

39. "R&B's Special Exhibit—'A Craftsman's Role in Industry Today'—Opens in New York City; Press Reception is Attended by More than 250 Guests," *The Silver Lining* (Reed & Barton newsletter) 19 (Feb. 1962): 5.

40. Reed & Barton pewter salt and pepper shakers by John Prip, DMA 2003.34.18.1–2.

41. McDevitt, "Craftsman in Production," 23.

42. "Reed & Barton's 1st Annual Design Lecture at Wellesley College," *The Silver Lining* (Reed & Barton newsletter) 20 (Apr. 1962): 3; and "Noted Art Authority Sir Kenneth Clark Delivers First Annual Reed & Barton Design Lecture to 1,400 at Wellesley College on April 3rd," *ibid.* 20 (May 1962): 1.

43. "Reed & Barton Design Lecturers, Breuer and Clark, Will Receive Nationwide Recognition," *ibid.* 21 (May 1963): 3.

44. "Count Sigvard Bernadotte, World-Famed Industrial Designer, Delivers Third Annual Reed & Barton Design Lecture Oct. 13," *ibid.* 22 (Nov.–Dec. 1964): 3.

45. Annalee Gold, "Reed & Barton Goes Crafty," *Jewelers' Circular-Keystone* 147 (July 1977): 318. Reed & Barton's *Damascene* line entailed a patented process of selective etching and plating of silver and 24-karat gold over brass ("History of Damascene," Reed & Barton Archives). The contrasting colors and variety of decorative motifs in *Damascene* contributed to its success. Towle's earlier attempt to market jewelry had proved disappointing. In 1965 the company had introduced a line of informal sterling jewelry inspired by the dense floral decoration on its then-new pattern *Contessina*. Advertised as "gifts for her" and "gifts for him," the group included matching bracelet and earrings for women, and for men, a tie bar, cuff links, tie tack, and money clip; "Towle introduces Contessina jewelry in sterling silver," Towle Silversmiths advertisement, *House and Garden* 128 (Oct. 1965): 12. According to Colin Richmond, the designer of *Contessina* flatware, the jewelry line "lasted five minutes" (Richmond, telephone conversation with author, July 12, 2000).

46. Gold, "Reed & Barton Goes Crafty," 318–19.

47. *Signature V* order form, fall 1977 (Reed & Barton Archives). Arentzen supplied seven designs, Fisch supplied three, Pearson supplied four, Scherr supplied five, and Watson supplied six.

48. "Reed & Barton premieres SIGNATURE V . . . a unique collection of sterling silver and vermeil jewelry," *Vogue* 167 (Nov. 1977): 86–87.

CHAPTER THIRTEEN

SPACE AGE SILVER

Space Age imagery entered the cold war design vocabulary after the Soviet Union launched the satellite Sputnik in 1957. A short time afterward formal and metaphoric references to the zeitgeist began to appear in American industrial silverware and other products. The fascination with space in popular culture grew in the years between Sputnik and the moon landing in 1969. During this period silver manufacturers continued to incorporate elements into their designs that resonated with space imagery or suggested it. Gorham and International seized the moment and produced the most spectacular silver by their staff designers. They were Gorham's atomic-inspired USS *Long Beach* service and International's cosmic Moon Room display, aglow with unique pieces of futuristic silver, at the New York World's Fair in 1964. In production silver, pitchers for stirring drinks eclipsed the cocktail shaker and became *the* Atomic Age party accessory. Another shift in silver design was the introduction in the 1960s of brightly colored finishes to the interior surfaces of holloware, a phenomenon prompted by contemporary Scandinavian imports, and one that persisted until the early 1980s at Reed & Barton, the innovator in the field.

A Galaxy of Silver

As early as 1957, the year of Sputnik, Gorham introduced a star-studded sterling flatware pattern designed by Richard L. Huggins and aptly named *Stardust* (fig. 13.1).[1] In the late 1950s the star was ubiquitous in the names of sterling flatware patterns, such as Wallace's *Dawn Star* (1958), Stieff's *Diamond Star* (1958), Alvin's *Star Blossom* (1959), Reed & Barton's *Star* (1960), and Towle's *Vespera* (1961), named for the Evening Star.

The infatuation with the stars continued into the 1960s, when Gorham introduced *Starburst*, a candleholder for six candles with a Space Age look (fig. 13.2). Modeled on a candleholder designed by Jens Quistgaard for Dansk, the *Starburst* came boxed singly with a set of twelve tapers, six white and six red. A silverplated chafing dish by Fisher Silversmiths of Jersey City, New Jersey, and New York City, has legs with an insectlike quality and spring to them that have subtle references to spacecraft (fig. 13.3). In the late 1960s as domestic production costs rose, Towle reached across the Atlantic to an old-line German silver manufacturer, P. Bruckmann & Sohne, of Heilbronn, to fabricate a group of stylish holloware objects.[2] Among these was a silverplated sectional candlestick with spherical brass fittings (fig. 13.4) by which the candlestick could be adjusted to four different heights, up to sixteen inches.[3] When staggered in a group of three, the effect of these candlesticks was striking (fig. 13.5).

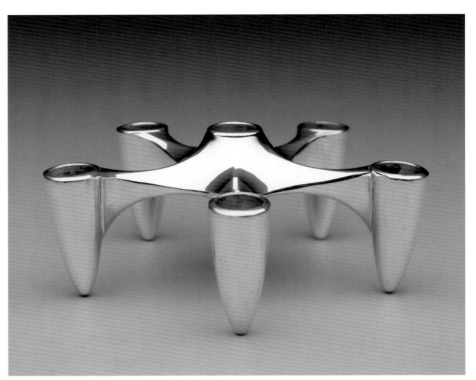

FIGURE 13.1 *Stardust* teaspoon, 1957. Gorham Manufacturing Company, Richard L. Huggins, designer. Silver. Dallas Museum of Art, cat. 45

FIGURE 13.2 *Starburst* candleholder, c. 1967. Gorham Manufacturing Company. Silverplate. DMA, JSASC, cat. 62

FIGURE 13.3 Chafing dish, c. 1965. Fisher Silversmiths, Inc. Silverplate, wood. DMA, JSASC, cat. 14

FIGURE 13.4   Table setting for a buffet, with candlesticks by Towle Silversmiths, 1969

FIGURE 13.5   Candlesticks, c. 1969. Towle Silversmiths. Silverplate, brass, DMA, JSASC, cat. 272

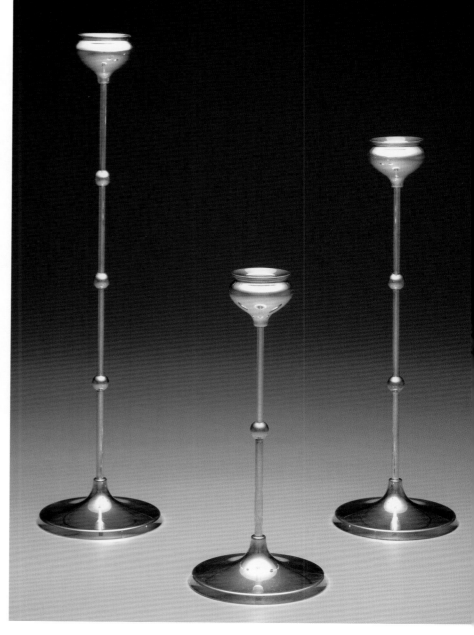

GORHAM'S *CIRCA '70* AND THE USS LONG BEACH SERVICE

In 1960 Gorham introduced *Circa '70*, a contemporary sterling holloware collection and an exemplar of advanced styling. The tiny pamphlet that accompanied pieces suggested that space travel was a source of inspiration, the design expressing "a feeling of flowing vertical motion . . . the upward look to space."[4] The concept was prescient: within a year at a joint session of Congress President John F. Kennedy issued a bold challenge to the nation to send a man to the moon and return him safely by the end of the decade. *Circa '70* was the conception of the staff designer Donald H. Colflesh (b. 1932), a native of Cleveland and graduate of Pratt Institute, who has acknowledged the influence of the studio silversmith Frederick A. Miller (1913–2000), one of his teachers at the Cleveland Institute of Art.[5] This connection is most apparent in the "Delta" triangular bowl and the candelabrum (fig. 13.6; see also fig. 13.7), each poised on three feet with pointed ebony tips. (An earlier example of Miller's influence on industrial silver was Reed & Barton's silverplated centerpiece [fig. 13.8] with gently flowing contours and pointed Australian beefwood feet that was produced in 1954.)

The refined execution of detail in the *Circa '70* group, especially the finish of the ebony finials and handles of the tea and coffee service, was exceptional for

midcentury American industrial holloware (fig. 13.9). The unique, concave modeling of the elongated, outward curving spouts makes them appear twisted in profile yet gives the impression of upward movement or lift.[6] Delicate ribbed and tapered silver settings hold the plume-shaped ebony finials that recall similar flourishes on early twentieth-century silverware by Josef Hoffmann at the Wiener Werkstätte.[7] The piece best resolved sculpturally in the service is the exquisitely proportioned, ovoid covered sugar bowl with its shallow concave lid that adds another highly reflective and contrasting surface to the squat, contoured form punctuated by assertive, arc-shaped handles. The round, oversized tray with a black Formica center frames and contains the service in a dramatic equilibrium. The shape of the large silver handles, sensitively designed to echo those of the sugar bowl, subtly unites the ensemble. The tray was not, however, designed by Colflesh and was added to the line after he left the company.[8] Other pieces in the *Circa '70* line include a pitcher-mixer with spoon (fig. 13.10) and the "Contour" bowl on a pedestal (fig. 13.11).[9] *Circa '70*

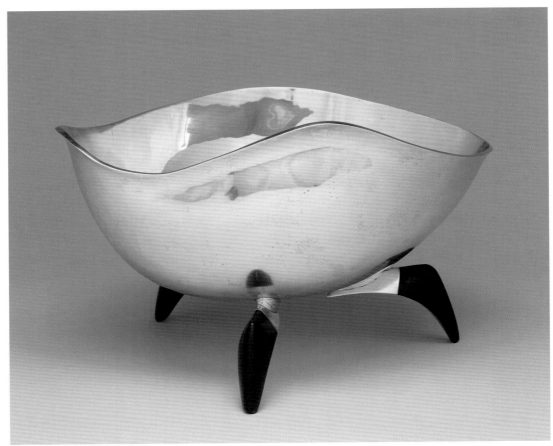

FIGURE 13.8 Centerpiece, 1954. Silverplate, beefwood. Reed & Barton. DMA, JSASC, cat. 179

was the last major contemporary holloware group to be produced by Gorham in the twentieth century.

The most extraordinary example of the Space Age idiom in silverware was the sterling silver service that the city of Long Beach, California, presented to its namesake, the USS *Long Beach*, the navy's first nuclear-powered missile cruiser. The service celebrated the commissioning of the ship in early September 1961.[10] Among the half dozen or so traditionally oriented designs submitted by Gorham to the Long Beach City Council was an avant-garde proposal by Richard L. Huggins (b. 1929), the firm's young director of design who, like the innovative silver designers Robert Ramp and Donald Colflesh, was a graduate of Pratt Institute. His theme, inspired by atomic and space travel imagery, resonated with the ship's source of power and the tempo of the time, characteristics that contributed to the selection of his design.[11] Gorham described Huggins's service as "the essence of the atomic age, captured in sterling silver." The designer was credited with giving "body to the elusive atom" by molding traditional shapes into

FIGURE 13.6 Left: *Circa '70* candelabrum, 1960. The Jewel Stern American Silver Collection, cat. 50; right: *Circa '70* "Delta" bowl, 1960. Gorham Manufacturing Company, Donald H. Colflesh, designer. Silver, ebony. DMA, JSASC, cat. 49

FIGURE 13.7 *Free form* fruit bowl, 1955. Frederick A. Miller, designer. Silver, ebony. The Cleveland Museum of Art, Silver Jubilee Fund, 1956.116; cat. 137

FIGURE 13.9 *Circa '70* tea and coffee service, 1958. Silver, ebony. Gorham Manufacturing Company, Donald H. Colflesh, designer. Dallas Museum of Art, cat. 47. *Circa '70* tray, 1963. Silver, Formica. Gorham Manufacturing Company. Dallas Museum of Art, cat. 48

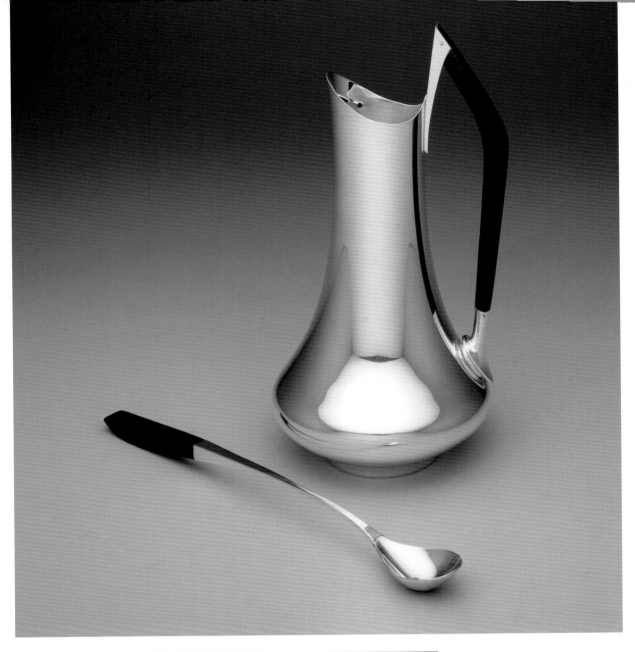

FIGURE 13.10 *Circa '70* pitcher-mixer with mixer spoon, 1960. Gorham Manufacturing Company, based on a design by Donald H. Colflesh. Silver, ebony. DMA, JSASC, cat. 52

FIGURE 13.11 *Circa '70* "Contour" bowl, 1958. Gorham Manufacturing Company, Donald H. Colflesh, designer. Silver. The Jewel Stern American Silver Collection, cat. 51

FIGURE 13.12 USS *Long Beach* service, candelabra, and electric coffee urn and tray, 1961. Gorham Manufacturing Company, Richard L. Huggins, designer. Silver, cats. 55, 56

forms associated with "known atomic expressions such as the mushroom cloud" produced by a detonated atomic bomb and which symbolized the "tremendous power of the atom." The upward sweep of line was said by Gorham to suggest "man's search into space for new horizons." The swirled six-light candelabra (fig. 13.12) was cited for the "graceful upward and outward curve of the arms" that expressed "mankind's eternal search for peace and the hope that the atom may be used to achieve this goal."[12] The finials, based on a model of an atom with circling electrons, alluded to the Atomium, a sculptural representation of the atom that had dominated the Brussels World's Fair in 1958 and became a symbol of the Atomic Age. A historian of Gorham cited the unusual stiltlike legs that supported most pieces, especially the coffeepot, cream pitcher, and sugar bowl, for giving the objects the appearance of "imaginary Martians or creatures from other galaxies."[13]

FIGURE 13.13   Architectural rendering of the Pavilion of American Interiors, New York World's Fair, 1964

FIGURE 13.14   Moon Room (detail). Exhibit by the International Silver Company at the New York World's Fair, 1964

Fly me to the moon
and let me play among the stars
let me see what spring is like
on Jupiter and Mars[14]
—*"Fly Me to the Moon," Bart Howard*

President Kennedy's mission in 1961 to reach the moon culminated in the successful voyage of the Apollo 11 spacecraft in 1969. The exploration of space and the efforts of the National Aeronautics Space Administration (NASA) to accomplish this objective exerted a powerful influence on the decade. This was formidably demonstrated in 1964 at the New York World's Fair, where the United States government had a Space Park with exhibits that included a full-scale model of the Saturn V rocket. The primary theme of the fair was Peace Through Understanding, but another that referred to space exploration was added: Man's achievements on a shrinking globe in an expanding universe. Walter Dorwin Teague's design for the fair's visual symbol, Journey to the Stars, which was rejected, reflected the latter. Ultimately, a huge 140-foot-high spherical steel armature, an open grid of meridians and parallels with superimposed shapes of the continents that was encircled by three rings representing the first man-made satellites launched into space, was chosen and named the Unisphere.

Although the American Craftsmen's Council did exhibit photographs of the work of five craftsmen, among them John Prip, International was the sole silverware manufacturer displaying its products at the fair.[15] International's exhibit was installed in the Pavilion of American Interiors, a four-story building on the Avenue of Progress devoted exclusively to home furnishings (fig. 13.13). The dazzling Moon Room, inspired by the possibility of interplanetary space travel, was the highlight of International's exhibit. The focus of the display, designed by the New York firm of Ellen Lehman McCluskey, was the suspended table and floating chairs of clear plastic, which were bathed in lighting to suggest twinkling galaxies (fig. 13.14). The custom-made holloware for the Moon Room, almost all sterling silver, was the company's in-house tour de force. Robert J. King, who started at International in 1962 after leaving Towle, where he had designed *Contour*, was the designer of the *Celestial Centerpiece* (fig. 13.15), a circle of six candleholders enclosing a brilliant silver "flowerburst"

FIGURE 13.15 *Celestial Centerpiece*, 1964. International Silver Company, Robert J. King, designer. Silver, spinel sapphires. DMA, JSASC, cat. 80

FIGURE 13.16   *Lunar* coffee service, 1963. International Silver Company, Stuart A. Young, designer. Silver, ebony. DMA, JSASC, cat. 115

FIGURE 13.17   Robert King with the coffee service he designed and the second-place award he won in the Sterling Today Student Design Competition, sponsored by the Sterling Silversmiths Guild of America, 1958

tipped with 133 spinel sapphires. King also designed a pair of tapered conical candlesticks with blue enamel trim and a pair of five-light candelabra with spherical elements to evoke the planets. The *Nova* tureen with matching spoon by Milton Gonshorek and the *Venus* water pitcher by Edward Buchko were displayed in wall niches. So, too, was the *Lunar* coffee service designed by Stuart Young (b. 1924) in an experimental three-sided form (fig. 13.16) unique in American post–World War II industrial silver.[16] Like Gorham's *Cubic* service by Erik Magnussen in the 1920s, the *Lunar* service was a show-piece prototype that was either too avant-garde or too expensive to put into mass production. Although the shape of the pouring vessels of the *Lunar* service may recall to some the triangular iced-water jug by Sigvard Bernadotte for Jensen, which was illustrated and listed erroneously as a coffeepot in the catalogue for the *Design in Scandinavia* exhibition in 1954, Young's design differed in significant ways.[17] The elongated spout of his pot is an independent element; the spout of Bernadotte's jug is integral; the *Lunar* handle is angled and faceted; Bernadotte's handle is vertical and rounded; the *Lunar* has an angled and faceted finial; Bernadotte's jug has none; the *Lunar* has a recessed base, Bernadotte's piece has no base. Moreover, the edges of the triangular *Lunar* are crisp folds in contrast to the fluid curving edges of Bernadotte's jug.

A more likely and important source of inspiration for the coffee set and other pieces in the Moon Room would have been the annual Sterling Today competitions sponsored by the Sterling Silversmiths Guild of America (a trade association of silver manufacturers founded in 1919). The competitions encouraged innovation by students and craftsmen and recruited potential designers for the industry. Buchko, for example, received an award in the first competition in 1957, and King received awards in 1957 and 1958 (fig. 13.17). The carafe on the Moon Room table was, however, made independently by King in the early 1950s, but it fit the theme and was deemed an appropriate addition. No doubt, its voluptuous biomorphic shape was a factor (fig. 13.18). The *Vision* pattern, also designed earlier, was similarly selected as the Moon Room flatware. The designer of *Vision* was the metalsmith Ronald Hayes Pearson (1924–1996), a finalist in the 1960 International Design Competition for Sterling Silver Flatware, and the prototype was produced in 1961 by International (see fig. 14.5). The name given to the pattern was indeed visionary and may have been inspired by Kennedy's vision that year of reaching the moon.

COCKTAILS FOR THE ATOMIC AGE

The cocktail shaker in all its ebullient iterations was not resurrected after World War II. By and large, labor-saving devices such as electric blenders and battery-operated cocktail mixers usurped the privileged place that the colorful shakers had previously enjoyed. For the home cocktail party, a sophisticated yet relatively easy way of entertaining in the 1950s and 1960s, especially in suburbia, multiuse pitchers for mixing drinks rather than shaking them became a smart accessory. Gorham, for example, produced versions in sterling and silverplate. The *Modern* beverage server in silverplate by the staff designer Donald H. Colflesh is a simple cylinder with a barely discernable spout and a bold, black plastic, serpentine handle. It was priced moderately at $17.95, and there was an optional "stir-up" spoon to accompany it for $2.00 (fig. 13.19).[18] A sterling liquor mixer in the *Directional* holloware pattern cost $79.50. In contrast to the *Modern* beverage server, the *Directional* liquor mixer

FIGURE 13.18 Carafe, c. 1952–1953. Robert J. King. Silver. DMA, JSASC, cat. 130

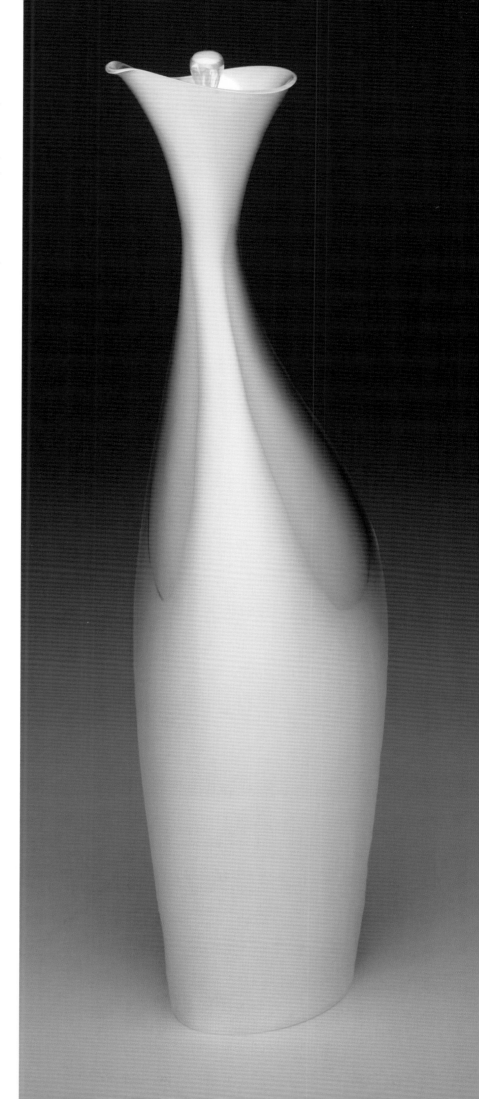

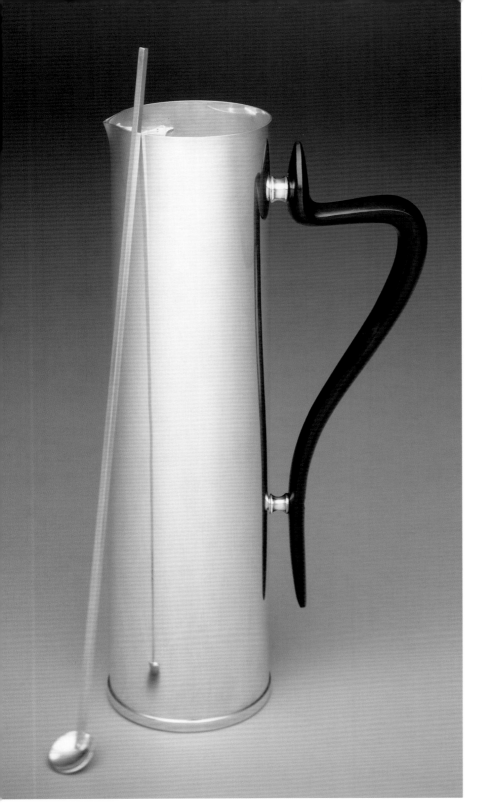

FIGURE 13.19   *Modern* beverage server and "stir-up" spoon, c. 1959. Gorham Manufacturing Company, Donald H. Colflesh, designer. Silver-plate, plastic. DMA, JSASC, cat. 43

FIGURE 13.20   *Directional* liquor mixer, 1955. Gorham Manufacturing Company. Silver, ebonized wood. DMA, JSASC, cat. 39

FIGURE 13.21   *Stoplight* jigger, c. 1961. Gorham Manufacturing Company, Howard A. Tarleton, designer. Enameled silver. DMA, JSASC, cat. 54

flares upward from its base to a wide, curving mouth and has an elongated comma-shaped, ebonized mahogany handle that is attached to the vessel by curved silver extensions. The effect of flow was embodied in the form itself (fig. 13.20). The witty *Stoplight* jigger in sterling (fig. 13.21), a novelty of the early 1960s, was another of Gorham's accoutrements for cocktails. The patented jigger has three levels, each embellished with an enameled circle to correspond to a typical traffic light. The 1-ounce level has a green enameled circle, the 2½-ounce level is yellow, and the topmost level at 3½ ounces is red.

The insulated ice bucket had became essential for serving drinks "on the rocks." Dorlyn Silversmiths produced an ice bucket in silverplate (and in brass), designed by Tommi Parzinger, that was a triumph of simplicity and proportion (fig. 13.22, left). A less severe example by the English Silver Manufacturing Corporation of Brooklyn has a decorative enameled cover (fig. 13.22, center). The wood trim of an ice bucket by International (see fig. 11.2) shows Scandinavian influence, and the distinctive onion-dome form of Reed & Barton's *Dimension* tea and coffee service of 1961 was adopted for the cover. By the early 1970s, as more Americans began drinking wine at dinner parties, Towle, asserting that "there's a difference between eating and dining," advertised a teak and silverplate wine cooler (fig. 13.22, right) that, like the firm's adjustable candlesticks, was made in Germany.[19]

The service of after-dinner cordials was another aspect of formal home entertaining addressed by silver manufacturers. Many produced traditional cordial cups; few made modern sets with decanters. A rare example by Kurt Eric Christoffersen (fig. 13.23) from International's Craft Associates division was advertised in 1958. The sterling decanter with matching cordial cups is a radical geometric design based on the cone and recalls Napier's cone-shaped cocktail shaker of the 1930s (see fig. 7.4). International called the set "uncompromising in its sophistication" and the "newest of the for-tomorrow designs."[20] Although a decanter by La Paglia was not included in the Craft Associates catalogue, cordial cups with his traditional Jensen-style ornamentation were available in a boxed set of eight or individually. An idiosyncratic cordial decanter, Middle Eastern in character, was part of Gorham's *Circa '70* sterling holloware

FIGURE 13.22 Left: Ice bucket, c. 1955. Dorlyn Silversmiths, Tommi Parzinger, designer. Silverplate, cat. 8; center: Ice bucket, c. 1965–1970. English Silver Manufacturing Corp. Silverplate, enamel, cat. 12; right: Wine cooler, c. 1969. Towle Silversmiths. Silverplate, teak, cat. 273. DMA, JSASC

FIGURE 13.23 "Sophistication in Sterling," International Silver Company advertisement, 1958

Continental Decanter Set . . . A Christoffersen Original

Sophistication in Sterling
by International

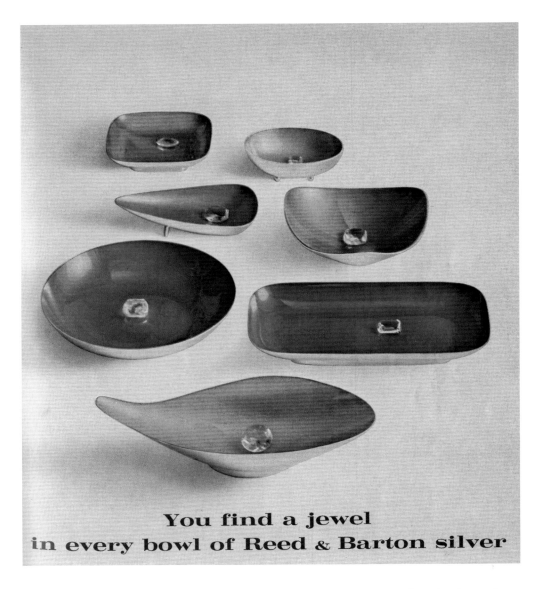

**You find a jewel
in every bowl of Reed & Barton silver**

group of 1960. The conical cordial cups that were intended to be part of the set looked incongruous with the decanter and, oddly, none of the pieces bore a relationship to the formal elements of other objects in the *Circa '70* pattern.

A Craze for Color

The 1960s witnessed an explosion of color in combination with silver, a phenomenon precipitated by the proliferation in the 1950s of contemporary Scandinavian enameled metalware in bright colors. Among the precedents was the multicolor cookware with decorative naturalistic motifs in the *Lotus* pattern by Grete Korsmo for the Norwegian firm Cathrineholm and the Krenit bowls, which had solid color interiors, by Herbert Krenchel for the Danish firm Torben Ørskov. Although American craftsmen and women had been covering silver and copper objects with glass enamels since the 1920s, enamel in colors had been used in industrial silver only for the discrete articulation of motifs (see figs. 3.56–3.58). The

application of solid color to the entire interior surface of holloware was new for silverware manufacturers. John Prip, as craftsman-in-residence at Reed & Barton, was aware of the popularity of imported Scandinavian enameled bowls, and proposed a similar effect. He helped to develop the technology to produce the finish that became *Color-Glaze,* an enamel-like translucent painted finish that Reed & Barton introduced in 1961.[21] The company claimed that *Color-Glaze* was the "result of six years of experimentation and research to develop a tough, wear-resistant color lining. . . . 'Color-Glaze' will not mar, stain or blister under normal home use, and it is impervious to sulphur, cigarettes, extreme temperatures."[22] An ambitious advertising campaign, under the title "The time is ripe for color," introduced the new line in fashionable magazines.[23] Three advertised "jewel tones"—ruby red, sapphire blue, and emerald green—were initially offered. The popularity of *Color-Glaze* was greater than expected and, when sales reportedly reached forty thousand dollars in a three-week period, the firm's concern became one of production, not sales.[24] By 1963 additional colors were available and the advertisement "You find a jewel in every bowl of

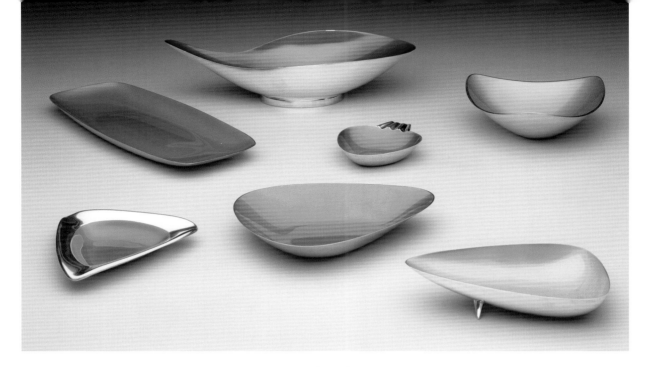

Reed & Barton silver" (fig. 13.24) highlighted the new colors and shapes, including the *Free Form* centerpiece in "burnt orange" pictured in the foreground and Prip's *Triangle* bowl in "purple."[25] At least fourteen colors, including avocado green, topaz yellow, chartreuse, cinnamon, moonstone, coral, aquamarine, pearl blue, turquoise, and amethyst, were offered at various times and applied to more than three dozen items (figs. 13.25, 13.26). The *Color-Glaze* line proved extremely popular, became widely emulated, and was produced by Reed & Barton until the early 1980s.

Scandinavian modernism in home furnishings was widespread in the 1950s, and most major silver manufacturers followed Reed & Barton's lead in the early 1960s. Wallace, for example, produced a version called *Color-Clad*, for which an enamel-like finish in

six "decorator-coordinated colors" was applied to the interiors of compotes, assorted trays, and bowls.[26] A green *Color-Clad* bowl (fig. 13.27, right) in an elongated ovoid that tapers to spoutlike points at each end was a copy of a stainless steel relish dish (without ball feet) by the German maker WMF (Württembergische Metallwerkenfabrik) and distributed in the United States

FIGURE 13.25 Back left: *Party* dish, 1965, cat. 198; back center: *Free Form* centerpiece, 1960, cat. 197; back right: *Triangle* bowl, 1958, John Prip, designer, cat. 188; center: ashtray, 1958, John Prip, designer, cat. 187; front left: Ashtray, 1958, Milton P. Hannah, designer, cat. 190; front center: Serving dish, c. 1969–1970, cat. 203; front right: Bonbon dish, 1958, Milton P. Hannah, designer, cat. 189. All Reed & Barton. Silverplate with applied color. DMA, JSASC

FIGURE 13.26 Assorted works from Reed & Barton, Wallace, and Towle. Silverplate with applied color and enamel. DMA, JSASC

FIGURE 13.27 Left: Centerpiece, c. 1970. Reed & Barton. Silverplate with applied color, cat. 204; right: Bowl, c. 1963. R. Wallace & Sons Manufacturing Company. Silverplate with applied color. DMA, JSASC, cat. 299

during the 1950s by William Fraser.[27] Gorham, in its Newport division, devised an iridescent finish for a group of footed triangular bowls, which the company described as *Tri-round*, in colors flowing from red to blue and blue to red (fig. 13.28) and green to yellow. In 1962, Oneida introduced *Silver Hues*, a "heat-treated, durable color coating" that the company claimed would not crack, craze, or chip. Collaboration with an upscale shelter magazine was a marketing strategy to associate the line with the latest in home décor. The *Silver Hues* finish that was offered in two of *House & Garden*'s annual color selections for stylish interiors—Bristol Blue (1961) and Tangerine (1956)—was applied to the interior of *Decorator* bowls (fig. 13.29) and so-called servettes, low-slung, contoured candy dishes.[28] F. B. Rogers

Silver Company of Taunton, Massachusetts, chose to import holloware with color finishes. A compote with a green interior on a cone-shaped pedestal bears the manufacturer's mark as well as the imprint "Made in Denmark," one of the earliest examples of outsourcing (fig. 13.30).

Most of these color applications were not true vitreous enamel, but a painted finish. At Towle, however, Charles Withers, the president, was motivated by the enamelwork of his wife Margret Craver and that of the virtuoso enamelist and jeweler Earl Pardon, a consultant. Towle, more than any other silver manufacturer, would have been better attuned to the work and writings of Edward Winter, an American craftsman, pioneer in decorative enameling as an artistic expression, and an influence on the home accessories market.[29] For four

FIGURE 13.28 Left: Dish, c. 1963, cat. 59; right: *Tri-round* bowl, c. 1963, cat. 58. Newport. Silverplate with applied color. DMA, JSASC

FIGURE 13.29 "Introducing Lovely Silver Hues," catalogue, *Heirloom Silverplate by Oneida Silversmiths*, 1962

FIGURE 13.30 Compote, c. 1962–1965. F. B. Rogers Silver Company. Enameled silverplate. DMA, JSASC, cat. 213

different, but related silverplated tazzas with enameled interiors, an allover decorative design was stamped on the color fields and encircled with a black border at the rim for accent (fig. 13.31). The motifs that enlivened the tazzas (shallow dishes with a short foot), especially the starbursts, seed forms, and loops, had precedents in contemporary ceramics, textiles, and glass. In interviews with retired staff members, it was learned that a Japanese girl named "Julie" from a school in Boston had worked as an intern in product development at Towle with Ross Pollard, a staff designer, and may have contributed to these decorative enamels.[30] Research has identified Juliette Fukuoka, who attended the Museum

School of the Museum of Fine Arts, Boston, from 1954 to 1955, as the intern.[31]

Towle also produced a sterling tazza with an enameled interior that has, instead of an allover decorative design, a stamped central motif (fig. 13.32) that is reminiscent of the village drawings of the Swiss modernist artist Paul Klee during the 1920s and of the early 1950s works of the Egyptian-American sculptor Ibram

FIGURE 13.31 Top left: Tazza, c. 1955, cat. 262; top right: Tazza, c. 1955, cat. 263; bottom left: Tazza, c. 1955, cat. 260; bottom right: Tazza, c. 1955, cat. 261. Towle Silversmiths. Enameled silverplate. DMA, JSASC

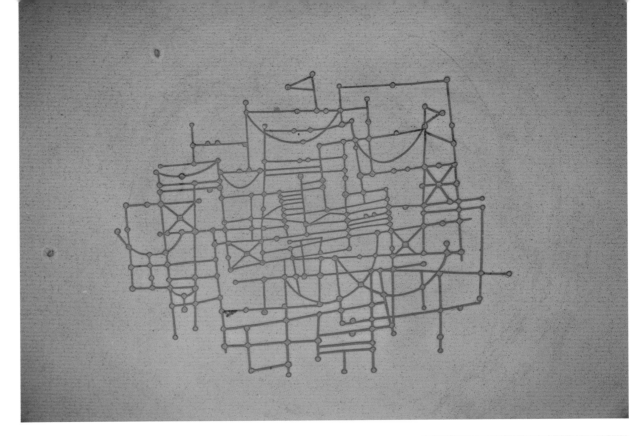

FIGURE 13.32   Tazza (detail), c. 1955. Towle Silversmiths, attributed
to Earl Pardon, designer. Enameled silverplate. DMA, JSASC, cat. 264

FIGURE 13.33   Bowl, c. 1955. Towle Silversmiths. Enameled silver.
DMA, JSASC, cat. 265

Lassaw.[32] The interlocking, linear structure of the design strongly suggests the hand of Earl Pardon, whose jewelry and a cloisonné enamel plaque on a presentation cigar box that he made at Towle for Sir Winston Churchill, has similar scaffolding and connecting elements.[33] As such, Pardon may have been the catalyst for the entire group of tazzas.

Even more experimental, and quite rare, is a bowl with a playful, abstract design of multicolor wiggling shapes embedded in the enameled interior (fig. 13.33). Unlike the designs for the tazzas that were duplicated, the floating, confetti-like relief decoration of this bowl was random and is unique. Towle also produced various sterling items enameled in solid colors. The most common were conservative, Paul Revere–style bowls, and among the most exuberant is a set of coasters in six different colors—red, yellow, blue, purple, green, and black.[34]

NOTES

1. Huggins also designed the *Stardust* bowls and sandwich plates (Richard L. Huggins, telephone conversation with author, Feb. 24, 2000).

2. Edward Mulligan, telephone conversation with author, May 7, 2003; Mulligan was formerly the president of Towle.

3. Among other items made for Towle in Germany were a wine cooler (see fig. 13.22) and a cocktail shaker.

4. Gorham, "Circa '70," pamphlet, n.p., quoted in Sotheby's, auction 5771, Nov. 17, 1988, lot 26. The name may have been copied and updated from a collection of modern furniture by the Henredon Furniture Company of North Carolina, introduced in 1953 and called "Circa '60"; see "Henredon Presents Circa '60, a New Collection of Modern Furniture," *House and Garden* 103 (Mar. 1953): 139.

5. Donald H. Colflesh, telephone conversation with author, June 26, 2000.

6. However, the spouts proved difficult to clean (David Rogers, conversation with author, Smithfield, R.I., May 29, 1991).

7. See, for example, the coffeepot designed by Hoffmann in 1905, which is illustrated in Annelies Krekel-Aalberse, *Art Nouveau and Art Deco Silver* (London: Thames and Hudson, 1989), 203.

8. Colflesh, telephone conversation.

9. A cordial decanter with cordial cups was the only other item in the line.

10. David B. Warren, Katherine S. Howe, and Michael K. Brown, *Marks of Achievement: Four Centuries of American Presentation Silver*, exh. cat. Museum of Fine Arts, Houston (New York: Abrams, 1987), 171. The service had been ordered through a local store, C.C. Lewis Jewelry Company, which was the liaison between the navy and Gorham. See also Charles H. Carpenter, *Gorham Silver 1831–1981* (New York: Dodd, Mead, 1982), 267–68; and Martin Filler, "Architecture, Ceramics, and Metalwork in the 1940s and 1950s," in Brook Kamin Rapaport and Kevin L. Stayton, *Vital Forms: American Art and Design in the Atomic Age, 1940–1960*, exh. cat. Brooklyn Museum of Art (New York: Abrams, 2001), 150.

11. Warren, Howe, and Brown, *Marks of Achievement*. The USS *Long Beach* service consists of two coffeepots, a sugar bowl, a cream pitcher, two large trays, two punch bowls, two punch ladles, an electric coffee urn, candelabra, three serving platters, and three covered vegetable dishes ("U.S.S. Long Beach Atomic Cruiser—Vital Statistics," Gorham memo, Sept. 7, 1961; courtesy of Richard L. Huggins).

12. "Sterling Silver Service Presented by the Citizens of Long Beach, California to the Atomic Cruiser U.S.S. Long Beach," Gorham public relations memo, n.d., courtesy of Richard L. Huggins.

13. Carpenter, *Gorham Silver*, 268.

14. The song "Fly Me to the Moon," with words and music by Bart Howard, was written in 1954 and originally titled "In Other Words." It became a hit after Joe Harnell recorded an instrumental version around 1962. The popular singers Perry Como and Tony Bennett, in 1963 and 1965, respectively, were among those who recorded the song.

15. "Pavilion of American Interiors," *Interiors* 123 (Mar. 1964): 105. Prip's designs for Reed & Barton were shown in the photographs; see "Reed & Barton Honored by Special Displays at New York World's Fair American Crafts Exhibit, and at the Museum of Contemporary Crafts," *The Silver Lining* (Reed & Barton newsletter) 22 (Apr. 1964): 1.

16. Other pieces specially created for the Moon Room were a silver and rosewood salad bowl and salad servers by Siro R. Toffolon, a celery tray by Robert L. Doerfler, an olive dish with sapphires by John L. Czanonis, a bread tray by Victor B. Fusco, and salt and pepper shakers by Milton Gonshorek. These objects and the others from the Moon Room appeared in the exhibition *Good Design for Christmas* at the Wadsworth Atheneum, Hartford, Conn., from November 23, 1964 through January 3, 1965, but have not yet come to light. Neither have King's candlesticks and candelabra. A "heroic" nine-quart size Peace Chalice in sterling silver designed by Fusco (and with the words of the theme of the fair, Peace Through Understanding, inscribed on its rim) was placed on a pedestal at the entrance to the International exhibit. The chalice was later sold, the inscription having been altered, as a corporate trophy to the Times Wire Company of Wallingford, Conn. (Victor B. Fusco, telephone conversation with author, Feb. 17, 2004).

17. *Design in Scandinavia: An Exhibition of Objects for the Home* (Oslo: Kirstes boktr., 1954), 72.

18. Another economical cocktail server was the "MacMixer" produced by Oneida in the late 1960s.

19. "There's a Difference between Eating and Dining," Towle Silversmiths advertisement, *New Yorker* 47 (May 22, 1971): 50. At about the same time, in perhaps the last gasp for cocktail shakers, Towle briefly marketed an austere shaker in silverplate, product number 4109, that like the wine cooler and adjustable candlesticks, was made in Germany.

20. "Sophistication in Sterling by International," International Silver Company advertisement, *New Yorker* 34 (Dec. 6, 1958): 75.

21. Renee Garrelick, *Sterling Seasons: The Reed & Barton Story* (Taunton, Mass.: Reed & Barton, 1998), 99.

22. "'Color-Glaze' Plated Holloware," *Reed & Barton 1962–1963 Holloware Catalogue*, 6 (Reed & Barton Archives, Taunton, Mass.); and John Prip, telephone conversation with author, Oct. 25, 2004. Milton P. Hannah, a designer for Reed & Barton, recalled that special dust-free cubicles were installed at the factory in Taunton to apply the sprayed and baked *Color-Glaze* finish (Hannah, telephone conversation with author, Oct. 27, 2004).

23. "The time is ripe for color in silver by Reed & Barton," Reed & Barton advertisement, *New Yorker* 37 (Nov. 11, 1961): 86.

24. Garrelick, *Sterling Seasons*, 99.

25. "You find a jewel in every bowl of Reed & Barton silver," Reed & Barton advertisement, *House Beautiful* 105 (Nov. 1963): 26. Hannah's no. 94 bonbon dish is to the left of Prip's *Triangle* bowl.

26. "Some colors shout, but . . . Color-Clad by Wallace speaks like a lady," Wallace advertisement, *House and Garden* 124 (Dec. 1963): 63; see also "R.S.V.P. with Counter Points," *Town and Country* 117 (Oct. 1963): 91.

27. For Fraser's relish dish, see "What makes it gleam so?" Calgonite advertisement, *House and Garden* 113 (Mar. 1958): 36.

28. "Introducing Lovely Silver Hues in Decorator Bowls," *Heirloom Silverplate by Oneida Silversmiths* (1962), n.p. (courtesy of Paul Gebhardt, vice president of design, Oneida Ltd.). In about 1965 Oneida offered another line, *Silver and Color*, for which two of the colors were "royal burgundy" and "antique yellow."

29. Winter was a prolific contributor to trade publications; see Edward Winter, *Enamel Art on Metals* (New York: Watson-Guptill, 1958), 150. For mid-century enamelware, see Alan Rosenberg, "Alluring Enamel," *Modernism Magazine* 6 (spring 2003): 68–73.

30. Donald Roaf, telephone conversation with author, Feb. 9, 2000; and Arthur Roy, telephone conversation with author, Feb. 9, 2000.

31. Museum School Archive, Museum of Fine Art, Boston. Fukuoka was twenty-nine years old when she enrolled at the Museum School.

32. For example, Klee's *Chosen Site* (1927) and Lassaw's *Kwannon* (1952).

33. The cigar box was commissioned by the Ancient and Honorable Artillery Company of Boston as a presentation piece on the occasion of its first official visit to London in 316 years, as was a silver bowl for Queen Elizabeth with emerald green *pliqué à jour* enamel accents. Both were made by Pardon in 1954. See Kathryn C. Buhler, "The Silversmiths' Art in America," *American Architect* 44 (spring 1956): 54. Pardon's necklace is illustrated in Toni Greenbaum, *Messengers of Modernism: American Studio Jewelry 1940–1960*, exh. cat. Montreal Museum of Decorative Arts (Paris: Flammarion, 1996), 152–53.

34. Towle enameled coasters, product number 101.

CHAPTER FOURTEEN

EXHIBITION SILVER IN

THE 1950s AND 1960s

After World War II exhibition venues of modern manufactured goods changed significantly. The Metropolitan Museum of Art ceased sponsoring the *Contemporary American Industrial Art* exhibitions that had defined modernism from the 1920s to 1940. Nor were there parallels to the comprehensive silver exhibitions at the Metropolitan and the Brooklyn Museum in 1937. The rise of the studio movement after the war was a factor. Symptomatic was the Metropolitan's exhibition *Form in Handwrought Silver* in 1949–1950 and the Brooklyn Museum's *Designer-Craftsmen U.S.A. 1953* exhibition.[1] Indicative of change, too, was the conspicuous neglect of industrial silver in the *Good Design* exhibitions, a joint program of the Museum of Modern Art in New York and the Merchandise Mart in Chicago between 1950 and 1955. Directed by Edgar Kaufmann Jr., the intention was to stimulate excellence in the design of modern home furnishings through annual exhibitions vetted by a selection committee. The only industrial silver in any of the *Good Design* shows was an exhibit of ten pieces of *Contour* flatware by Towle in 1951.[2]

Of all the silver manufacturers, it was Towle, led by its president Charles C. Withers, who promoted silver through exhibitions in the 1950s. No doubt, his activist wife, the talented metalsmith Margret Craver, was a strong influence. *Knife, Fork, and Spoon*, in 1951, an exhibition that was sponsored by the firm and held at the Walker Art Center in Minneapolis, was an historical survey of cutlery that culminated with *Contour*, Towle's new flatware pattern.[3] In 1953, the same year in which Craver was a "consulting silversmith" for *Designer-Craftsmen U.S.A. 1953*, Towle established a permanent gallery for changing exhibitions of early and contemporary silver at its plant in Newburyport, Massachusetts.[4] In 1955, in collaboration with the American Federation of Arts, the firm sponsored the exhibition *Sculpture in Silver from Islands in Time*, a project that sought to link the firm with modernism in the fine arts and to bring prestige to the material of silver. Eight contemporary American sculptors were commissioned by Towle to create unique, experimental works of art in sterling silver that were neither functional nor decorative. The invited sculptors were Jose de Creeft, Cecil Howard, Ibram Lassaw, Oronzio Maldarelli, Richard Lippold, Jose de Rivera, David Smith, and William Zorach. A small group of objects lent by museums was added to provide an historic reference and as a background against which to evaluate the new work. The exhibition opened at the Brooklyn Museum and traveled to the J. B. Speed Art Museum, Louisville, Kentucky, the Dallas Museum of Art, M. H. de Young Memorial Museum, San Francisco, and the Seattle Art Museum.[5]

In the spring of 1958 the Corcoran Gallery of Art in Washington, D.C., presented *Living Today: An Exhibition of Contemporary Architecture, Furniture, Interior Decoration*. The exhibition was national in scope and most objects were manufactured and designed in the United States. Although they were selected for

their aesthetic merit, attention was paid to function, and price was also a consideration. Industrially produced silver figured in the Tableware category. Flatware was represented by Nord Bowlen's *Contrast* (see fig. 11.4) from Lunt (1956), and surprisingly by International's *1810* (1930), an interwar version of the traditional fiddleback pattern.[6] The one piece of holloware, also from International, was a smooth-surfaced sterling pitcher of swelling bulbous form with a looping handle wrapped in woven plastic to imitate natural raffia or wicker, for which contemporary Scandinavian silver would have been a source of inspiration.[7] Several versions of the pitcher by the staff designer Curtis Rittberg were introduced around 1955 (see fig. 10.31).[8] The World's Fair in Brussels also opened in the spring of 1958. The exhibit *Industrial Design, Interior Design and Crafts* organized for the United States Pavilion did not include industrially produced silverware, an indication of the growth and influence of the postwar studio movement. However, two craftsmen who also designed for industry, Robert J. King at Towle and John Prip (at the time the craftsman-in-residence at Reed & Barton), were represented by examples of their handwrought work.[9]

The broadest exposure for contemporary industrial silver in exhibitions during the 1950s and 1960s materialized the following year in the survey *20th Century Design: U.S.A.* organized by the Albright Art Gallery of the Buffalo Fine Arts Academy. During 1959 and 1960 the exhibition traveled to seven venues, the Cleveland Museum of Art, Dallas Museum of Art, Dayton Art Institute, Minneapolis Institute of Arts, Portland Art Museum, St. Louis Art Museum, and the San Francisco Museum of Art. Although almost eleven hundred

objects were catalogued, relatively few examples were by designer-craftsmen. The emphasis in this exhibition was on machine-made articles and the beauty derived from precision in this method of production.[10] To facilitate identification of the pieces for potential sales, the maker's product number was included in each catalogue entry. In the Metal Ware and Cutlery section, Gorham and Reed & Barton were the largest contributors, with eleven and nine objects, respectively. International, Towle, Lunt, Kirk, Tiffany, and Wallace and its division, Smith & Smith, were represented with fewer pieces, between one and four entries each. The designers were listed in the catalogue and in an index that also gave their addresses, a rare instance in the silver industry of recognition for in-house staff.

An installation of the Metal Ware and Cutlery section at the Cleveland Museum of Art was a stunning asymmetrical arrangement with, in the foreground, a lounge table by Isamu Noguchi and a molded plywood dining chair with metal legs by Ray and Charles Eames (fig. 14.1). Behind the furniture, low-slung containers rested on a long shelf. A panel on the wall above it displayed six place settings of cutlery. In the case at one end, several objects by Reed & Barton and the sterling *Trend* candlesticks by Gorham (see fig. 10.46) can be distinguished, all designed between 1952 and 1957. Those of Reed & Barton were a pitcher by Cayer, a relish tray by Ramp, both in silverplate, and sterling candlesticks by Hannah (fig. 14.2). The silver holloware exhibited had clean undecorated surfaces and swelling

FIGURE 14.1   Installation view, *20th Century Design, U.S.A.* exhibition, Cleveland Museum of Art, 1959

volumes or was low and sleek. The aesthetic impact was dependent on the shape and the machine fabrication was undisguised.

Two exhibitions in the 1960s gave industrial silver some visibility, but it was minimal. In 1965 the Museum of Art of the Rhode Island School of Design in Providence presented *The New England Silversmith: An Exhibition of New England Silver from the Mid-Seventeenth Century to the Present.* In the exhibition were Reed & Barton's five-piece *The Diamond* tea and coffee service by Prip and the three-piece *Lunar* coffee set by Young from International's Moon Room at the recent New York World's Fair.[11] In 1966 the American Heritage Foundation sponsored *American Showcase,* a traveling exhibition shown at more than forty shopping centers throughout the country that paid tribute to American industry and its contribution to the nation's high standard of living. Reed & Barton, although one of twenty-three companies selected, was the silver industry's only representative. The exhibit *Silverware . . . Where the Past and Present Meet* depicted the history of silver design in America from the colonial period to the present. For the modern age Prip's work at Reed & Barton, both experimental and for mass production, was featured in a showcase against a graphic Mondrianesque background with a photograph of Prip at his workbench.[12] In holloware, his three-piece *Dimension* coffee set was on display, as was the largest of the *Free Form* bowls (see fig. 13.25), a staff design that was popular in *Color-Glaze* until the line was discontinued in 1983.

In the early 1960s the Museum of Contemporary Crafts actively advocated the collaboration of craftsmen and industry with the goal of improving design in manufactured wares and expanding opportunities for craftsmen. It was a means, too, of partly filling the voids left when the Metropolitan Museum of Art and the Museum of Modern Art discontinued their design exhibitions, *Contemporary Industrial Art* and *Good Design,* respectively. Three of the exhibitions held at the Museum of Contemporary Crafts, *Designed for Silver* in 1960, *A Craftsman's Role in Modern Industry* in 1962, and *Designed for Production: The Craftsman's Approach* in 1964, were the most relevant for the silver industry. International and Reed & Barton forged productive relationships with the museum, International for The International Design Competition for Sterling Silver Flatware, which was the catalyst of the exhibition *Designed for Silver,* and Reed & Barton for the exhibition in 1962 (which was a one-man show of John Prip's work at the company) and for Prip's contribution to the group exhibition in 1964. The association of these projects with the earlier programs of design exhibitions by the Metropolitan and the Museum of Modern Art was alluded to by John B. Stevens, the vice president of International, when he

FIGURE 14.2   Front: Relish tray, 1955. Reed & Barton, Robert H. Ramp, designer. Silverplate, cat. 182; center: Candlesticks, 1956, Reed & Barton, Milton P. Hannah, designer. Silver, cat. 185; back: Pitcher, 1955. Reed & Barton, Theodore E. Cayer, designer. Silverplate, cat. 183. DMA, JSASC

framed the firm's objective as one "to marry art and industry in an attempt to bring good design into the American home."[13]

The flatware competition cosponsored by International was a vast project. A committee composed of representatives of the visual arts, industrial design, and creative merchandising[14] extended invitations to 107 participants from seventeen countries. Each of the designers received an honorarium, but only 22 of the 206 designs submitted would be chosen for further development and execution in model form. No doubt as an incentive to participants, International agreed to produce at least one pattern and to provide royalties to the designer. The twenty-two models, five of which were cited for awards, were showcased in the exhibition *Designed for Silver* at the Museum of Contemporary Crafts in the fall of 1960.[15] Nine designs were from the United States;[16] ten countries were represented by the other thirteen. Only Sweden, Holland, and Israel had more than one finalist, and of the five recipients of awards, two were Swedish, two Israeli, and one Finnish.[17]

Perhaps in competition with International for leadership and prestige, the designs of the finalists in Reed & Barton's Silver Design Competition in Italy were exhibited at the Institute of Contemporary Art in Boston at the same time. The international competition was, however, the more influential, introducing trends in the design of silver and stainless steel flatware that were apparent for more than a decade. The results of

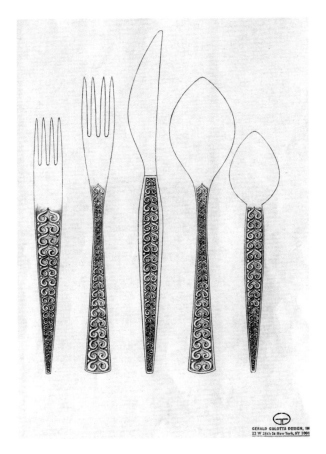

GERALD GULOTTA DESIGN, IN
12 W 24th St New York, NY 1001

the competition demonstrated the international rather than the regional character of design, and the existence of two opposing tendencies: an insistence on simplicity and modulation of form as the foremost expression of design; and a renewed interest in surface enrichment. Meyric R. Rogers, the curator of the Garvan collection at the Yale University Art Gallery and director of the entire competition, noted the latter as an incipient and potentially important direction in silver design, a theme that was underscored by others in the exhibition catalogue as well:

The models representative of this second tendency deserve our closest consideration for they brave the most difficult design problem of our time. . . . We have cast aside an outworn and trite traditional ornamental vocabulary in order to emphasize basic structure. We are now faced with the problem of finding new symbols for development and enrichment of form in order to satisfy what is apparently an inherent need for the humanization of this basic abstraction. Awkward and stumbling as these first tentative efforts must be, they are nevertheless the bridge to the future though it may be difficult to recognize them as such.[18]

Stevens did not hesitate to register his defense of decoration: "And may I add a personal opinion that ornament and decoration in silver are not in bad taste as

some modernists would have us believe? Contemporary artists are often too adamant in their insistence that we must address ourselves entirely to form and that any ornamental adornment is garbage."[19] The designer John Van Koert, who was a consultant to the exhibition, was more outspoken. He accused modernists of attributing "superior moral stature to barrenness" and asserted that silver is a material that should not be held to the "rigid, ideological disciplines that control the character of many mass-produced articles." In conclusion, he asked, "Aren't we entitled to some aesthetic experience divorced from utilitarianism?"[20]

The decorative trend was manifested in the designs of only six of the twenty-two finalists, yet the contrast with the majority of abstract, ornament-free designs was apparently striking. Of the six, three were accented with a single motif, while those by the Americans Samuel Ayres, Robert A. Von Neumann, and Gerald Gulotta (fig. 14.3), had an allover decorative pattern. It was the patterned effect that became the alternative stream to purism. A critic of the exhibition noted the two sharply defined groups and recognized the challenge by "a few rambunctious upstarts who preach the gospel of 'textural enrichment in harmony with our times and our tastes.'"[21] This was not true of the Design Competition in Italy in which decoration was unanimously rejected by a like-minded group of architects. The inclusion of

FIGURE 14.4 Ronald Hayes Pearson in his workshop, c. 1956

1. A HILLSIDE HOUSE IN CALIFORNIA

For Sale: This stunningly modern 1-to-5-room home, designed in 1956 by one of America's outstanding architects for her own use. Flexible floor plan allows owner to shift room areas by means of movable closets. House is perched on hillside for a sweeping view of Beverly Hills and Pacific Ocean. Cantilevered construction makes it seem to float in space...slim steel supports emphasize its airy silhouette. Outside walls are clear glass, alternating with panels painted yellow, aqua, grey, white. Graveled terrace in rear. $69,500.

2. VISION STERLING BY INTERNATIONAL

For Sale: This stunningly modern 5-piece place setting, designed in 1961 by one of America's outstanding designers. Its space-age lines are cue to a new way of construction. Handles are turned at right angles—to make VISION simpler to hold, better balanced, more graceful to look at. Slim silhouette echoes the slender steel supports of contemporary architecture. Only the Soaring '60s could produce such a knife blade. Gives any home a modern touch...makes a modern home ultra-modern. Single 5-piece place setting, incl. Fed. Tax, $50.

women judges in the international design competition may have been a factor. The silversmith Virginia Cute participated in the initial selection, and Dorothy Draper, the interior decorator, and Mrs. Robert Wadsworth, a past president of the Junior League of America, were in the jury to determine the finalists. The international competition differed also in that it drew from a broader group that included silversmiths, industrial designers, craftsmen, architects, professors, and jewelers, some famous, others little known.[22] Another reviewer noticed the similarity of certain elements in the designs of the finalists to characteristics of contemporary stainless steel flatware, especially in the knife and fork.[23] In many, but not all, of the designs, knife blades were shortened and reshaped, and the join between handle and blade was disguised to give the impression of the continuity that was possible in stainless steel knives. Forks tended to have shorter tines and longer and deeper bowls.

International lived up to its word in producing one of the designs by a finalist, but not, however, that of any of the five award winners. The design chosen was the work of the American Ronald Hayes Pearson (fig. 14.4), and the pattern, *Vision*, was introduced in 1961 in a double-page advertisement in which it was romanticized as having been shaped "proud and pure" into new forms for a "skyward age," and the designer lauded as the "laureate" of the competition.[24] Of note was the name of the pattern, an allusion to both designer and maker as visionaries and trendsetters. This theme was reflected in International's innovative 1962 advertising campaign

FIGURE 14.5 "Two things to own," International Silver Company advertisement, 1962

FIGURE 14.6 Left: *Lark* place knife, 1959. Reed & Barton, John Prip, designer. Silver, stainless steel, cat. 196; center: *Soliloquy* place knife, 1963. R. Wallace & Sons Manufacturing Company, Clark L. Lofgren, designer. Silver, stainless steel, cat. 298; right: *Classique* place knife, 1961. Gorham Manufacturing Company, Burr Sebring, designer. Silver, stainless steel, cat. 55. Dallas Museum of Art

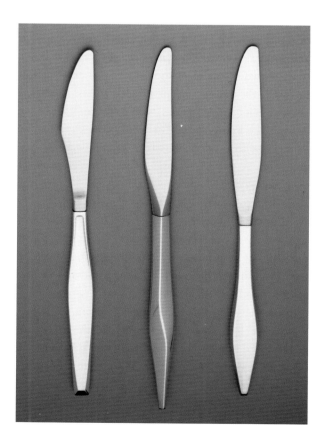

FIGURE 14.7 Left: *Contessina* dinner fork, 1965. Towle Silversmiths. Silver, cat. 271. right: *Tapestry* place fork, 1964. Reed & Barton, John Prip, designer. Silver, cat. 202. Dallas Museum of Art

FIGURE 14.8 Left: *Spanish Tracery* place fork, 1970. Gorham Manufacturing Company. Silver, cat. 64; right: *Tradewinds* dinner fork, 1975. International Silver Company. Silver, cat. 83. Dallas Museum of Art

FIGURE 14.9 *Royal Satin* place fork, 1965. R. Wallace & Sons Manufacturing Company, David B. Hoover, designer. Silver. Dallas Museum of Art, cat. 300

"Two things to own," a pairing of residences in various architectural styles with a compatible International sterling pattern. For "Two things to own in Extreme Modern," *Vision* was paired with a house perched dramatically on a hillside in California (fig. 14.5).[25] Indeed, *Vision* was the most radical, innovative production-line sterling pattern offered by a major manufacturer during the century. When viewed from above, the plain surfaces of the crisp, wafer-thin upright handles of the spoons and forks flowed uninterruptedly into rounded bowls to accentuate their elongation. Flow was expressed in profile by the undulating curve of the arched handles, a sensuous element integrated with the clean lines of the design. The join between the solid silver knife handle and its slightly triangulated blade was subtle. Appropriately, the "skyward age" *Vision* pattern was used to set the Moon Room table in International's exhibition at the 1964 New York World's Fair (see fig. 13.14).

Like *Vision*, Reed & Barton's *Lark* (1960) and *Dimension* (1961; see fig. 12.9) by John Prip were sterling patterns in the minimalist stream of flatware rooted in post–World War II Scandinavian modern silverware and exhibited in *Designed for Silver*. In the 1960s, other firms who competed in this mode were Gorham with *Classique* (1961) by the staff designer Burr Sebring (b. 1928), and Wallace with *Soliloquy* (1963) by the staff designer Clark L. Lofgren (b. 1936) (fig. 14.6).[26] Notwithstanding the advent of these progressive unornamented patterns, Meyric Rogers had correctly predicted the success of the other stream of contemporary flatware,

which was characterized by its decoration. Within a few years a revitalized decorative vocabulary evolved in no small measure from the response to the international design competition. A characteristic of this new vocabulary was the application of decorative patterning to contemporary instead of traditional shapes. Early experiments were Reed & Barton's *Tapestry* (1964) and Towle's *Contessina* (1965), a modern reprisal of Kirk's dense nineteenth-century repoussé patterns (fig. 14.7). One of the first contemporary shaped handles to have an allover pattern like those shown by Ayres and Gulotta in *Designed for Silver* was International's *Valencia* (1964). Among others that followed were Towle's *Meadow Song* (1967), Reed & Barton's *Renaissance Scroll* (1969), and Oneida's *Rubaiyat* (1969). The predilection for decorative patterning continued into the 1970s with Gorham's *Spanish Tracery* (1970) and International's *Tradewinds* (1975) (fig. 14.8).[27]

Another aspect of this new direction in decoration was the texturing of surfaces to add richness to the clean lines of contemporary shapes. In a survey of flatware published in 1965 by the periodical *Modern Bride*, patterns with textured surfaces were featured.[28] Alert to this trend, Wallace had introduced early in 1964 a textured surface it called "Firenze" that was available in two versions of *Soliloquy*, and later in the year *Spanish Lace*, a new allover decorative pattern, was added to comprise a group with the Firenze finish. Designed specifically to showcase the finish, and introduced in 1965, the star of the Firenze collection was *Royal Satin* by the staff designer David B. Hoover (1928–2002), an elegant patented pattern with an elongated, tapered shaft and sculpted tip (fig. 14.9). Wallace associated *Royal Satin* with both Italian craftsmanship in Renaissance Florence and the modern "shape of today."[29] Described as "misted silver" by Wallace to denote its matte finish, Firenze paralleled the fashion in the 1960s for gold jewelry with Florentine-style brushed surfaces.[30] Competitors quickly followed suit. By texturing the surface Gorham turned *Classique* (1961) into *Damascene* in 1964, and *Esprit* (1963) into *Gossamer* in 1965. Similarly, Towle transformed *Vespera* (1961) into *R.S.V.P.* in 1965. International, however, like Wallace with *Royal Satin*, conceptualized *Dawn Rose* (1969) with a textured surface. The two tendencies that had crystallized in the *Designed for Silver* exhibition, pure abstraction and a new model of decoration, persisted into the early 1970s. However, they lost momentum as the nation prepared to celebrate its bicentennial in 1976, an event that ushered in a revival of early American and other traditional silver patterns.

Notes

1. For the Metropolitan Museum of Art, "Silver for the Artist," *Art Digest* 24 (Jan. 1, 1950): 21; and *Designer-Craftsmen U.S.A. 1953* (Brooklyn, N.Y.: American Craftsmen's Educational Council, 1953).

2. "Objects 136–145 in Tableware" in *Good Design 1951: An Exhibition of Home Furnishings Selected by The Museum of Modern Art, New York, for The Merchandise Mart, Chicago* (New York: Museum of Modern Art, 1951), n.p. See also Terence Riley and Edward Eigen, "Between the Museum and the Marketplace: Selling Good Design," in Museum of Modern Art, *The Museum of Modern Art at Mid-Century: At Home and Abroad*, Studies in Modern Art 4 (New York: Museum of Modern Art; 1994), 150–75.

3. *Knife, Fork, and Spoon*, exh. cat. Minneapolis: Walker Art Center, 1951, 18–21.

4. For Towle, see "Exhibitions," *Craft Horizons* 13 (Oct. 1953): 44. For Craver, see *Designer-Craftsmen*, 61.

5. *Sculpture in Silver from Islands in Time*, exh. cat. American Federation of Arts and Towle Silversmiths, 1955, n.p.

6. Henri Dorra, Introduction, in *Living Today: An Exhibition of Contemporary Architecture, Furniture, Interior Decoration* (Washington, D.C.: Corcoran Gallery of Art, 1958), n.p. See also, ibid., List of Objects, under Tableware, entry 161 for *1810* flatware and entry 167 for *Contour* flatware.

7. Ibid., entry 162, pitcher, product no. E112.

8. "Corcoran Gallery Exhibits Silver by International," unidentified newspaper clipping, May 10, 1958, n.p. (International Silver Archives, Meriden Historical Society, Meriden, Conn.).

9. "Industrial Design, Interior Design and Crafts Exhibits; U.S. National Pavilion, Brussels World's Fair 1958," Object List (Jewel Stern Archives, Coral Gables, Fla.). The listing for Prip's three salt and pepper shaker sets acknowledged his association with Reed & Barton. King's six-piece place setting was listed independently. His buffet server and ladle were loans from the St. Paul Gallery and School of Art, St. Paul, Minn.

10. William Friedman, "Notes on the Exhibition," in William Friedman, ed., *20th Century Design: U.S.A.*, exh. cat. (Buffalo, N.Y.: Albright Art Gallery, Buffalo Fine Arts Academy, 1959), 15.

11. *The New England Silversmith: An Exhibition of New England Silver from the Mid-Seventeenth Century to the Present* (Providence: Museum of Art, Rhode Island School of Design, 1965), n.p.; for Prip's tea and coffee service, see fig. 82; for Young's coffee set, see fig. 84.

12. "Reed & Barton Selected to be One of Twenty-three Exhibitors in 'American Showcase,' a National Traveling Historical Exhibition," *The Silver Lining* (Reed & Barton newsletter) 24 (May–June 1966): 1.

13. John B. Stevens, "Industry and the Designer," in *Designed for Silver: An Exhibition of Twenty-two Award-Winning Designs from the International Design Competition for Sterling Silver Flatware*, exh. cat. (New York: Museum of Contemporary Crafts of the American Craftsmen's Council and The International Silver Company, 1960), 8.

14. The five members of the selection committee were: Meyric R. Rogers, the director of the competition; John B. Stevens, the vice president of International; John Van Koert, a consultant to the competition; David R. Campbell, the president of American Craftsmen's Council; Elliot V. Walter, the retired president of R. H. Macy & Company; and Virginia Cute, a silversmith and the chairman of the design committee of the Philadelphia Art Alliance.

15. Those on the jury of award were Dorothy Draper, the interior decorator; Mrs. Robert C. Wadsworth, the past secretary of the Junior League of America; Joseph P. Kasper, chairman of the board of Associated Merchandising Corporation; Edward Durell Stone, the architect; and Walter Dorwin Teague, the industrial designer. Statements by each of the five jurors were published in the exhibition catalogue. See *Designed for Silver*, 10–12. *A Survey of Implements of Eating*, comprising more than one hundred historical examples of cutlery borrowed from several museums and International accompanied the exhibit of the work of the twenty-two finalists. Helen Sprackling, the decorative arts critic, wrote a catalogue essay entitled "A Brief History of the Knife, Fork and Spoon" (ibid., 59–63). Virginia W. Cute wrote another, "The Care and Use of Sterling Silver Flatware" (ibid., 63–65).

16. The Americans were: Samuel Ayres Jr., Boston; D. Lee DuSell, Syracuse, N.Y.; Gerald Gulotta, New York; Allison R. Macomber, Segreganset, Mass.; Ronald Hayes Pearson, Victo, N.Y.; Arthur J. Pulos, Syracuse, N.Y.; Olaf Skoogfors, Philadelphia; Robert A. Von Neumann, Champaign, Ill.; and Lewis A. Wise, Calabasas, Calif.

17. From Sweden were Ainar Axelsson and Sven Arne Gillgren; from Israel, Menahem Berman and David H. Gumbel; and from Finland, Tapio Wirkkala.

18. Meyric R. Rogers, "The Results of the Competition," in *Designed for Silver*, 6.

19. Stevens, "Industry and the Designer," 8.

20. John Van Koert, "Simplicity Versus Decoration," in *Designed for Silver* 1960, 9.

21. B. B. P., "Design Renascence in Silver," *Interiors* 120 (Dec. 1960): 98.

22. Ibid.

23. Greta Daniel, "Sterling Silver for the Sixties," *Craft Horizons* 20 (Sept./Oct. 1960): 21; see also "Silver Designs for the Sixties," *House and Garden* 118 (Oct. 1960): 190.

24. "Vision," International Silver Company advertisement, *New Yorker* 37 (Oct. 7, 1961): 18–19.

25. "Two things to own in Extreme Modern," International Silver Company advertisement, *House Beautiful* 104 (Apr. 1962): 14–15. Other pairings included American Romantic: an antebellum plantation in the Old South with *Prelude*; Polynesian-Oriental: a small island in the South Pacific with *Swan Lake*; Scandinavian: a castle in Denmark and *Royal Danish*; French Classical: a Louis XIV chateau on Long Island and *Joan of Arc*; French Formal: a nobleman's residence in Paris and *Angelique*; Late Italian Renaissance: a baroque villa on Lake Maggiore and *Rhapsody*; and New Romantic: a fairytale manor in the Connecticut woods and *Rose Ballet*.

26. Towle's *Vespera* (1961), Gorham's *Esprit* (1963) and *Gossamer* (1965), both by Burr Sebring, and International's *Crystal* and *Snowflake* (1966), both by the staff designer Siro R. Toffolon, were other examples.

27. These patterns were all sterling. Examples in silverplate were *Esperanto* (1967) and *Silver Lace* (1968), from International's 1847 Rogers Bros. Division, and *Silver Sands* (1966) and *Tangier* (1969), from Oneida's Community division.

28. "Sterling and Stainless," *Modern Bride* 16 (Dec. 1964/Jan. 1965): 126–29.

29. "Royal Satin in Firenze by Wallace," Wallace advertisement, *House and Garden* 128 (Nov. 1965): 12.

30. "Look closely. This is misted silver and we call it Firenze," Wallace advertisement, *New Yorker* 40 (Nov. 14, 1964): 164.

CHAPTER FIFTEEN

A SEA OF CHANGE, 1960s–1980s

The 1960s began brimming with hope for the silver industry. Reed & Barton was in the midst of its ambitious Design Program, and International was riding high on the reception of its flatware competition and the exhibition *Designed for Silver,* events that were lauded in the media. Social forces beyond the control of the industry, however, provoked an upheaval that would undermine such progressive efforts. Many young prospective brides, who constituted the principal market for flatware, were caught up in the hippie movement of the early 1960s, which inspired a stream of youths to cross the continent in 1967 to attend the Monterey Pop Festival, making the hit song of the year, "If you're going to San Francisco," the movement's unofficial anthem. The impact of the cultural revolution and its free and easy lifestyle on home furnishings was captured that year in an advertisement in the *New Yorker* for Bonniers, an emporium of trendsetting home accessories on Madison Avenue and the destination of 1960s design cognoscenti. In the advertisement (fig. 15.1), a group of young men and women with long shaggy hair and beaded necklaces, the sooty-eyed women sitting cross-legged or in a yoga position and looking "spaced out" on drugs, were situated among objects sold at the store, most in Lucite, some with psychedelic patterns. Silver was nowhere in sight and by association no longer "The American Thing" at Bonniers.[1] The contrast between that image and an advertisement for Gorham published in the mid-1950s (fig. 15.2) was striking. Under the headline "They picked it above all others," Gorham showed a cluster of smiling, neatly coifed and conservatively dressed coeds being polled by market researchers about their preferences in sterling.[2] Creative strategies were certainly needed to offset the effects of increasingly casual lifestyles. In an advertisement for Oneida sterling flatware in 1967, a young bride with flowing blond hair, bangs over her brows, and heavy eye makeup, wore a veil with "flowers in her hair" and had a *First Frost* sterling spoon in her mouth (fig. 15.3). The headline, "Clarissa was born with an Oneida spoon in her mouth," was an attempt to make sterling appeal to a bride on the edge of the counterculture.[3]

This approach was insufficient, and other measures were implemented to sustain the industry: a venture into the stainless steel market, a return to the safety of traditional patterns, the reintroduction of the "Midas touch" (gilded accents on flatware), partnerships with art museums, and creative advertising campaigns. These efforts were, however, severely undermined by the

Bonniers. The American Thing.

They picked it above all others...

FIGURE 15.1 "Bonniers. The American Thing," Bonniers, Inc. advertisement, 1967

FIGURE 15.2 "They picked it above all others," Gorham Company advertisement, 1955

Clarissa was born with an Oneida spoon in her mouth.

Clarissa's mother has sterling by Oneida. Clarissa's grandmother has sterling by Oneida. Clarissa's great-aunt has sterling by Oneida. So making tasteful choices comes naturally to Clarissa.

She breezed through her choice of patterns as merrily as she breezed down the aisle. Leaning on Oneida all the way, Clarissa selected "First Frost," from Oneida's Heirloom®

Sterling collection. (That's it, above. $36.50 per four-piece place setting. Or save as much as $107 with the Heirloom Sterling Dividend Plan. Ask your dealer.)

On the following pages, for all the other beautiful brides, is the Oneida Silversmiths guide to a treasure-chest of tableware. A high, wide and handsome collection of sterling, silverplate and stainless.

FIGURE 15.3 "Clarissa...," Oneida Ltd. advertisement, 1967

collapse of the American silver market in 1980–1981 and by the success of imports from old line European silver firms. Understandably, American silver manufacturers let innovation slide in their struggle for survival.

CULTURE AND COMPETITION

As if the influences of the counterculture were not enough, the silver industry faced social change in the mainstream as well: the increasing numbers of women in the workplace and the concomitant relaxation in home entertaining increased the demand for low-maintenance stainless steel cutlery and holloware. As early as 1950, B. Altman & Co., a prominent department store in New York and a leader in sales of tabletop accessories, organized an exhibition of table settings that included three stainless flatware patterns imported from Denmark.[4] By 1955, a trade publication survey indicated that stainless steel flatware and holloware sales had risen rapidly.[5] Threatened, American silver manufacturers created their own competition by entering the stainless market. The following year *Modern Bride* published an article on stainless steel, describing the material as "handsome as it is up-to-the-minute."[6] In addition to imports from Germany and Scandinavia, domestic stainless by Wallace and Gorham was pictured. Japan, however, quickly became the greatest source of competition to American stainless steel producers, and pressure by the industry led to tariff restrictions in 1959 on imported Japanese stainless steel flatware.[7] The International Silver Company entered the stainless market in the 1960s with advertisements intended, somewhat paradoxically, to elevate the status of stainless. One raised the question, "How come brides are now registering stainless?" implying that stainless was on par with the sterling that was, traditionally, registered for wedding gifts.[8] Another asserted, "We think stainless should look like stainless," a criticism of makers who copied their old-fashioned sterling patterns for stainless flatware. International positioned itself on the high ground with "clean, simple lines that add to the modern look and contemporary feeling of the material itself,"[9] reinforcing the point by illustrating three modern stainless patterns, *Saturna*, *Astra*, and *Today*. Implying that stainless steel was the equivalent of sterling, International advertised that "it takes 35 steps to make sterling. We use 34 of them to make stainless," an assurance to consumers that the company's stainless was executed with the same meticulous care as was its sterling.[10]

The two trends in design that characterized contemporary sterling flatware after the 1960 *Designed for Silver* exhibition carried over into stainless production. Stainless patterns by the staff designer Milton Gonshorek (1918–1998) for International illustrate the contrasting aesthetic positions. The name of *Astra*, a sleek, complex sculptural form that was introduced in 1963 (fig. 15.4), alluded to celestial bodies, astronauts, and outer space, a connection that was emphasized in promotional literature. *Geometric*, designed in 1970, was an allover decorative pattern in a contemporary rectangular shape (fig. 15.5). By 1970, the *Jewelers' Circular-Keystone* annual *Flatware Pattern Directory* listed 324 current patterns of "jewelry-store quality" stainless steel, both domestic and imported, available from American suppliers. The market for silverplate in the price range of stainless had dwindled to only 53 active patterns by the American producers, International, Oneida, Reed & Barton, and Towle. In the sterling category, 339 patterns were noted. Except for 25 by Georg Jensen, the Norwegian Silver Corporation, and Worcester Silver combined, all were from American makers.[11]

As higher quality stainless became an acceptable alternative to sterling, the industry resorted to a new tactic in promotion, focusing on a specific decorative element to emphasize the richness of detail associated with most traditional flatware and to distinguish it from contemporary, plainer stainless. Reed & Barton pioneered this approach in the early 1960s.[12] Towle adopted the strategy for *Contessina* in 1965, with an advertisement picturing a handle the full height of the page to magnify the encrusted decorative surface.[13] Tiffany used a similar effect to highlight the fine relief ornamentation of its nineteenth-century patterns, especially *Audubon* and *Chrysanthemum*.[14] The most extreme example was one of International's advertisements for *Royal Danish*

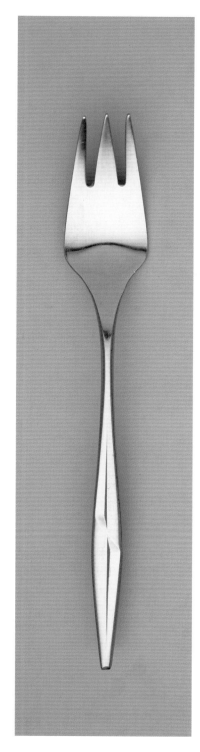

FIGURE 15.4 *Astra* salad fork, 1963. International Silver Company (International Stainless Deluxe), Milton Gonshorek, designer. Stainless steel, cat. 116. The Charles L. Venable and Martin K. Webb Collection

FIGURE 15.5 Drawing for *Geometric* fork. International Silver Company, by Milton Gonshorek, 1970

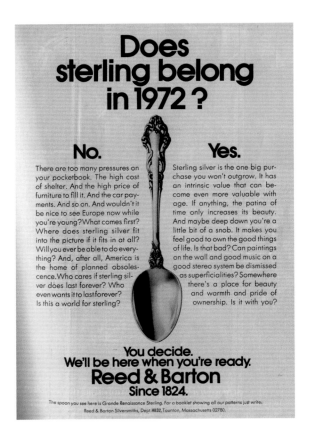

FIGURE 15.6 "Does sterling belong in 1972?" Reed & Barton advertisement, 1972

in 1968: the image of the decorative tip alone filled an entire page.[15]

Strategies for Survival

In the face of a shrinking market caused by the cultural changes of the 1960s, the replacement of silver in the home with stainless steel and other lower maintenance materials, competition from abroad, and limited success with contemporary designs, many American silver manufacturers went out of business in the 1970s. Those that survived had largely withdrawn to the safety of tradition and would remain there. The dire situation was addressed head on in an advertisement (fig. 15.6) in which Reed & Barton asked readers of magazines such as *House and Garden* and *House Beautiful,* "Does sterling belong in 1972?" Tellingly, the pattern illustrated was the firm's ornate *Grande Renaissance* (1967). The taste for traditional period-revival styles was reinforced by the 1976 bicentennial, which precipitated a colonial revival and a brief resurgence of pewter. In the late 1970s, Gorham's best-selling pattern was *Chantilly* (1895), Reed & Barton's, *Francis I* (1907), Wallace's, *Grand Baroque* (1941), Towle's, *Old Master* (1942), all traditional patterns.[16] In 1979, Edward Mulligan, the president of Towle Silversmiths, would aptly describe the situation in an interview: "Every time a contemporary pattern comes out everyone gets excited. But it doesn't sell. . . . Even people in those modern houses in California put traditional patterns on their tables," or they chose to entertain without silver.[17]

With a very few exceptions, the 1970s represented a retreat from modernism. To entice consumers, the industry changed its tactics. Reverting to an idea that had been abandoned in the early 1950s, silver flatware was ornamented with electroplated gold accents. Wallace revived the fashion with *Golden Aegean Weave* in 1971. The pattern, by the staff designer Charlotte Schwarz Hallet (b. 1943) and first introduced as *Aegean Weave* (1970), is difficult to categorize. The pieces have smooth, straight, pencil-slim handles and decorative panels in a textured basket weave at the tips and joins (fig. 15.7). In promoting the pattern, Wallace announced that it was acknowledging the desire of "a new generation" to "create its own traditions," and thus recognizing the "generation gap" that had opened up in the anti-establishment 1960s. It was hoped that the images in the advertisements of robust, earthy Mediterranean workers harvesting bushels of red ripe tomatoes would appeal to sensuous nonconformists who wanted to express their individuality and to "establish their own traditions."[18] The next year the pattern was issued as *Golden Aegean Weave,* with the four narrow bands that bordered the basketry now goldplated.

The precedent for accenting modern postwar sterling flatware with gold was set in 1952 when, in a lavish advertising campaign, Gorham inaugurated *Thread of Gold,* a sterling flatware pattern in five variations with hand-applied 18-karat-gold decoration. The name of each denoted its ornamental motif, *Gold Tip, Stardust, Snowflake, Gold Cipher,* and *Golden Wheat.* The flatware was costly. A place setting of *Gold Tip,* the least expensive of the five at $65, was more than twice as expensive as the equivalent in Gorham's plain sterling, which cost $29.75. The price of *Golden Wheat,* the most expensive of the five at $110, was almost four times higher.[19] That early application of gold to sterling flatware, referred to as the "Midas touch," was a concept that soon died out. In 1964, Gorham made another foray. The pattern *Damascene* by the staff designer Burr Sebring was also offered as *Golden Damascene.* This experiment, too, was an isolated occurrence and was not emulated in the industry. Wallace's *Golden Aegean Weave* was successful, and the idea was copied by every major producer of sterling flatware in the 1970s: International with *Golden La Strada* (1972), Lunt with *Golden Columbine* (1973), Towle with *Danish Baroque Gold,* Reed & Barton with *Golden Tree of Life* (1974), Gorham with *Golden Scroll* (1977), and Towle with *Celtic Weave Gold* (1979).[20] With the exception of Lunt's *Golden Columbine,* a copy of *Aegean Weave* by Nord Bowlen, all were highly decorative revivals.

In 1975, Kirk introduced the sterling pattern *Selene* (fig. 15.8), named for the mythological Greek goddess of the moon, in all silver and with gold. *Selene* was one of the last purely sculptural, clean-lined, undecorated contemporary patterns, a late bloomer influenced by International's flatware competition in 1960 and, thus, unusual for American industrial silver in the 1970s. Kirk optimistically promoted *Selene* and *Golden Selene* to customers described as "classic contemporaries," who, it was hoped, longed for a sterling pattern "full of history and part of this age, steeped in tradition yet part of the 80s."[21] The golden version of *Selene* was cited in 1979 as the exception to the rule that traditional silver sells the best; it reportedly did remarkably well, especially in western states. By then industry leaders knew the combination of sterling with gold was the "coming thing," as indeed it would be.[22] In 1980 Oneida published a pamphlet offering seven stainless patterns in the Golden Accents Collection and four in Community Gold Electroplate, a group entirely goldplated and traditional in styling.[23] In its catalogues, Reed & Barton presented consumers with "24-karat gold electroplated flatware" in four traditional patterns in 1985 and two years later Gorham offered a group of five stainless patterns with gold details, all traditional with the exception of *Golden Swirl*.[24] The popularity of gold decoration and goldplated flatware continued through the 1990s.

Mobilized by the 1976 bicentennial and a desire to enhance its prestige and invigorate sales, Stieff developed a distinctive pattern identified with eighteenth-century traditions. The firm negotiated with the Smithsonian Institution to issue a design based on the historic French silverware owned by John Quincy Adams, the sixth American president (1825–1829). To reinterpret the original, which is held by the Smithsonian, Stieff engaged as a consultant the designer-craftsman Ronald Hayes Pearson. The result was the *Smithsonian* sterling pattern introduced in 1978.[25] Stieff

FIGURE 15.7 "A new generation should create its own traditions," Wallace Silversmiths advertisement, 1971

FIGURE 15.8 *Selene* teaspoon, 1975. Samuel Kirk & Son, Inc. Silver. Dallas Museum of Art, cat. 133

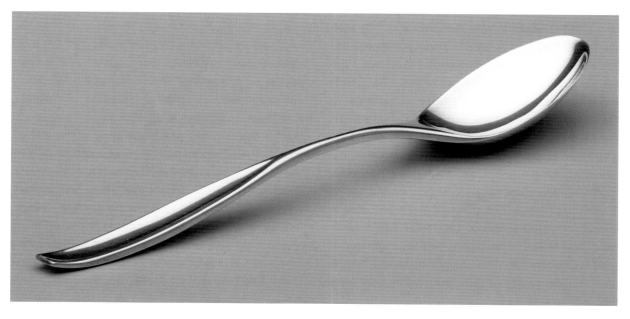

FIGURE 15.9 "Good grief, Frank," Reed & Barton advertisement, 1984

Good grief, Frank. They took the Reed & Barton Stainless.

set an example that other manufacturers copied to give their wares the imprimatur of a prestigious art museum. In 1980 Gorham licensed the use of paintings from the Metropolitan Museum of Art in New York for an advertising campaign titled "Consider them signed originals," in which such masterpieces as August Renoir's *By the Seashore* and Francisco de Goya's *Don Manuel Osorio de Zuniga* were reproduced.[26] Not to be outdone, in 1982 Reed & Barton introduced *Winterthur,* a silverplated adaptation of the colonial shell pattern from the collection of the Henry Francis du Pont Winterthur Museum in Wilmington, Delaware. Opportunely for Reed & Barton, Winterthur at the time was interested in expanding its name recognition and income through licensing arrangements with manufacturers. Because the museum was renowned for its extraordinary collection of early American decorative arts, Reed & Barton proudly identified itself and the pattern with the institution. To assure the survival of the flatware as a family heirloom, purchasers were offered an unprecedented hundred-year guarantee.[27]

Reed & Barton had already anticipated the revival of period styles, having produced *Eighteenth Century* in 1971 and advertising the pattern as an indication of the beginning of a "new romantic age."[28] In 1976, the firm introduced *Sterling II,* a line of flatware that had sterling handles in period revival styles and stainless steel blades, bowls, and tines. Towle had briefly experimented with the combination of materials in *Contempra House* in 1956, but unlike that pattern, Reed & Barton's was traditional in style. *Sterling II* was a measure to boost sales by making a concession to affordability; the price was about half that of an entirely sterling pattern. The sales pitch, "Contemporary. Yet Traditional. The best of all possible worlds," was an appeal to a wider spectrum of the market.[29] Around this time Reed & Barton positioned itself as a purveyor of what it described as "The Classic American Silver" in an advertising campaign that continued into the 1980s with various headlines:

A classic is original no matter how often it's imitated.
A classic has nothing to do with fashion. And everything to do with style.
A classic never looks old. Or new.
A classic achieves a perfect balance between form and function.
A classic becomes a tradition the moment it's created.
A classic makes its statement with understatement.[30]

Not one contemporary pattern was featured.

In competition with itself, the firm, as International had done earlier, promoted stainless as having status equivalent to sterling. In 1984 an advertisement depicted the silhouetted cartoon of a horrified woman making a startling discovery in the dining room: "Good grief, Frank. They took the Reed & Barton Stainless" (fig. 15.9).[31] In another advertisement, the glamorous hostess at a black-tie dinner party declares, "Nobody leaves this room . . . there's a teaspoon missing from our Reed & Barton Stainless."[32] That same year Towle proclaimed its stainless flatware as the "Sterling of Stainless," an indication of the exploding market for stainless in the 1980s.[33]

To raise sagging sales of sterling in the late 1970s, the Sterling Silversmiths Guild of America sponsored a series of advertisements in upscale magazines under the slogan "Sterling says it all," a message directed to affluent consumers concerned with status.[34] Under the headline, "Tsk, tsk. You have a St. Laurent, a Cuisinart, and no sterling?" the copy ran:

A St. Laurent and a Cuisinart say something about what goes on in your head. Tiny, revealing parts of a whole attitude and life style. That logically should include sterling silver flatware. Because sterling is nothing out of the ordinary for you. It goes with what you already have and do. And how you show yourself to the world. . . . It's surprising you don't already have it. But no one will be surprised when you do.[35]

In advertisements published during the 1980s the guild adopted the theme "Sterling silver, it nourishes your sense of elegance" for a series of illustrations of one pattern by each of the six members of the guild, Kirk Stieff, Lunt, Oneida, Reed & Barton, Towle, and Wallace-International (the name given to the merged firm after the two companies were acquired by Katy Industries).[36] In a subsequent series of advertisements, "Sterling Silver: The Eternal Element of Style," which continued until at least 1990, the pleasures of companionship were the focus.[37] People were photographed together enjoying breakfast in bed, lunch, dinner, or a lawn party, always in a setting replete with traditional silver. This was the last hurrah for the guild, which ceased operation in 1990.[38]

In 1979 *Silver in American Life,* an exhibition of selections from the Yale University Art Gallery's fine collection, began a three-year tour organized by the American Federation of Arts. Included were a few modern twentieth-century industrial objects, for example, *The Diamond* teapot designed by John Prip for Reed & Barton (see fig. 12.5), and a La Paglia Designed bowl from International's Craft Associates division (see fig. 10.36).[39] The exhibition stirred interest again in American silver and occasioned an extensive essay in *Town and Country* in which the author related the exhibition to the present state of the silver industry. Featured were the heads of the "six silversmithing dynasties," Reed & Barton, Lunt, Tiffany, Oneida, Kirk, and Stieff, as well as the presidents of Wallace, Towle, Gorham, and International.[40] John Ambrose, then vice president of the Sterling Silversmith's Guild of America, enumerated the ways in which changes in American lifestyles affected the industry:

People are getting married later, their tastes are more set. There is less advice coming from mothers and aunts. Then there is the revolution in the dining room, fewer servants, the growing trend in buffet entertaining that has changed the types of bowls, serving platters and other holloware people select. Then there is a big post-marriage market. Young couples, especially when both husband and wife work, keep adding to their silver on their own. Many successful single career people now will invest in silver in their thirties and forties. And another big recent fashion is silver for the second home.[41]

In light of the realities in the industry, it appears that Ambrose expressed what silver manufacturers *hoped* the future would hold. It is noteworthy, too, that the exhibition fostered an interest in nineteenth-century antique silver that would blossom in the late 1980s and early 1990s with the collecting of old, not new, silver.[42]

Meanwhile, the Hunt brothers, who had cornered the market in the metal, precipitated a mercurial rise in the price of silver, which had been about $1.95 an ounce in 1973, from about $5 dollars an ounce as 1979 began to more than $50 an ounce early in 1980. During the 1970s Nelson Bunker Hunt and William Herbert Hunt, businessmen from an immensely wealthy family in Dallas, Texas, had legally accumulated silver in huge quantities as a hedge against inflation. Investors following the Hunts' example caused havoc in the commodities market for silver. Families lined up to sell their sterling to be melted down and as prices for sterling flatware escalated, brides switched to silverplate or stainless steel.[43] The Federal Reserve Bank intervened

to stabilize the market, and the price of silver dropped drastically, the collapse causing tremendous losses for all the speculators, especially the Hunts.

This crisis marked a turning point in the decline of the already troubled silver industry. As early as 1981, the relationship between the soaring price of silver and the dramatic increase in demand for stainless steel tableware had been the subject of another lively essay in *Town and Country.* Noting that "from Bloomingdale's to Bullocks, from Marshall Field's to Burdine's, U.S. department store aisles are overflowing in galaxies of fine stainless," the author went on to quote a government survey: "higher quality stainless product increased at least 15 percent in unit sales with imports in the same area rising by 60 percent last year [1980] over 1979." A stainless steel knife in a new pattern, *Iona* (fig. 15.10), a modernist design by Gerald Gulotta for the H. E. Lauffer Company, was prominently illustrated.[44] Professionals in the tableware industry were quoted as reporting

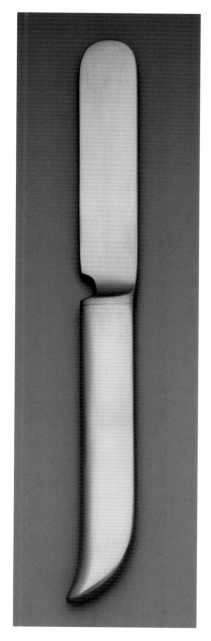

FIGURE 15.10 *Iona* place knife, 1980. H. E. Lauffer, Gerald Gulotta, designer. Stainless steel. Dallas Museum of Art, cat. 134

FIGURE 15.11   Candleholders, c. 1970. Samuel Kirk & Son, Inc. Silver. DMA, JSASC, cat. 132

that fashion-conscious consumers did not mind mixing higher quality stainless flatware with fine china and crystal. This was the attitude that provoked the Sterling Silversmiths Guild's ambitious advertising campaigns in the 1980s.

The downhill slide of the silver industry, which became precipitous in the 1980s, can be charted by calculating the number of new sterling flatware patterns introduced by each of the six major manufacturers—Gorham, International, Lunt, Reed & Barton, Towle, and Wallace—in each decade beginning with the 1950s.[45] The trajectory is clear. In the 1950s and 1960s, these companies introduced between seven and ten new patterns in each decade. The decline began in the 1970s, when Wallace introduced only three and Lunt and Towle only seven. In the 1980s the numbers dropped to between zero (for International) and five (for Lunt). Although Wallace had produced only three new patterns in the 1980s, one of those, *Caribbean,* with a graceful, overlapping, asymmetrical wave motif, was the company's contribution to modern design, the last it would make. Perhaps inspired by a similar pattern designed by the Italian architect Paolo Portoghesi in 1983, *Caribbean* was emulated by two competitors.[46] In 1986 Gorham introduced *Sea Sculpture* and Kirk Stieff, *Dancing Surf,* both iterations of *Caribbean.* These three and Kirk Stieff's *Paramount* in 1987 were the last contemporary patterns in sterling to be introduced by the silver industry in the twentieth century. In the 1990s the sterling flatware business worsened. Reed & Barton introduced only *Ashmont,* in 1990; Kirk Stieff, only *Veranda,* in 1993; and Lunt introduced *Quintessence* in

1990, *Holmes* in 1992, and *Golden Soleil* in 1995.[47] All were traditional.

In general the holloware sector of the industry was in worse straits. Innovation was rare and had nearly come to a halt in the 1970s. In 1976 International stopped producing any sterling holloware, and in 1981 sold its silverplated holloware business to Oneida.[48] There was little incentive to take risks on new designs during a period when traditional styles were enjoying a revival and the bicentennial had bolstered the market for colonial reproductions. A rare exception early in the 1970s was the pronged sterling candleholder made by Kirk for pillar-style candles (fig. 15.11), but even that design looked back to seventeenth-century European candlesticks.[49] Another was Gorham's silverplated "candelabra centerpiece" with curvaceous tubular elements for nine slim tapers, which was advertised in a Space Age context as a "galaxy of lights."[50] Designed for versatility and multiple usage, characteristics of mid-century Gorham holloware, this object, which functioned as both centerpiece and candelabra, came apart into two units.

Reflecting the lack of incentive to invest in new contemporary designs in the 1970s is Reed & Barton's decision to produce John Prip's holloware designs (see figs. 12.5, 12.7, and 12.10)—*The Diamond* (1958) and *Denmark* (1960) tea and coffee services, and the *Connoisseur* casserole (1963)—until the early 1980s rather than develop new ones. For that reason, and because of its

FIGURE 15.12 *Plank* vase, 1989. Reed & Barton, Clark L. Lofgren, designer. Silverplate. Dallas Museum of Art, cat. 205

popularity, the *Color-Glaze* line, which had been created in the early 1960s, was not discontinued until 1983.[51] The company's spring 1985 catalogue showed only one holloware item that had a modern look, a newly designed gift-boxed pair of V-shaped champagne flutes from the Sheffield Silverplate division.[52] Not until 1989 did Reed & Barton again risk an innovative modern design, a group of three related *Plank* vases (fig. 15.12), contemporary studies in pure form by the design director Clark L. Lofgren.

Although the mood of the silver manufacturers who had been interviewed by *Town and Country* in 1979 had appeared buoyant on the surface, they did mention their concern about the increasing influx of silverware from foreign manufacturers. The threat of competition from firms abroad who used less expensive Asian labor was voiced by "Pete" Noyes, the chairman of the board of Oneida, and Sinclair Weeks Jr., the president of Reed & Barton.[53] A symptom, too, of a growing taste among Americans for European flatware was the introduction of "continental-size" stainless by International in 1977.

FIGURE 15.13 "Skylines." Kirk Stieff advertisement, 1987

In the advertisement for this new line, the differences between European and American silver were pointed out and the former connected to enhanced status: "The knives and forks and spoons wealthy Europeans use are not like the ones you use. They are larger. Heavier. Somehow, they just look and feel better."[54] This was a far cry from Reed & Barton's determination in the 1950s to reduce the European scale of Ponti's flatware design for *The Diamond* pattern to suit American taste.

What was a concern turned out to have been a prediction. By the early 1980s prominent Italian and French silver houses, perceiving an opportunity, began to compete aggressively for a share in the market for expensive flatware and holloware, most, but not all, in quality silverplate. This was evident from the roster of French firms advertising in upscale magazines: Ercuis, Christofle, Cardeilhac, Puiforcat, Cartier, and Christian Dior.[55] The presence of goods from Italian firms such as San Lorenzo, Alessi, Mazzucato, Ricci, Bulgari, and Buccellati, was felt, too.[56] Soon Christofle had a foothold in its own outlet on Madison Avenue in New York City, and Puiforcat followed suit. In 1990 Christofle introduced *Atlantide Gold*, a pattern intended to challenge a profitable sector of the American flatware market, and Cartier announced a new collection of china, crystal, and silver called Les Maisons de Cartier.[57] As more Americans traveled abroad, the connotation of European, and especially French, silver with Old World status gained cachet. Gorham attempted to compete in 1991 with the *Terrassa* silverplate holloware collection that had green and black marble accents modeled on similar decoration used by French makers such as Puiforcat. However, instead of promoting the collection for its overt French connection, Gorham described *Terrassa* as derived from the "Greco-Roman period," and pointed out that the "step and dome design" had the same architectural elements as did the Jefferson Memorial in Washington, D.C.[58] In fact, *Terrassa* had a classical Art Deco revival look. By avoiding a reference to its French precedents, Gorham may have sabotaged the experiment. In the end the collection failed to sell well.[59]

Terrassa reflected the popular revival in the last quarter of the twentieth century of 1920s French *art moderne*. The catalyst for the revival was an exhibition, *The World of Art Deco*, at the Minneapolis Institute of Arts in 1971, the first comprehensive American survey of *art moderne,* then a largely devalued style. *Art Deco,* the newly coined name for the style, was an abbreviation of the title of the exhibition held in Paris in 1925: *Exposition Internationale des Arts Décoratifs et Industriels Modernes,* which had brought the style into focus. The seminal exhibition in Minneapolis precipitated a revival of the style that lasted for several decades and was manifest in a stream of publications on the subject, the enthusiastic collecting of period artifacts of every kind, and the selective adaptation of the earlier design elements to new consumer goods. The silver industry was slow to respond even though authentic sterling and silverplate objects from the 1920s and 1930s were appearing in fashionable interiors in shelter magazines and becoming potential competitors. An exception in the early 1980s was Towle, who engaged Larry Laslo, an interior and product designer, to create a signature line of holloware in silverplate and brass that dramatically incorporated Art Deco motifs, primarily layered setbacks, telescoping, and in plates, the octagonal shape. Items included in the line introduced in 1984 were a coffee set with tray, a beverage mixer with matching stirrer, tall cocktail flutes, a standing champagne bucket, and a vase with a stacked disk base. Tags attached to the pieces carried, above the Towle hallmark, the comment: "Larry Laslo brings his inimitable sense of luxury and style to the elegant tradition of silverplated holloware."[60] Often mistaken as vintage objects, the pieces are all stamped LASLO FOR TOWLE and have his own hallmark, a column of geometric shapes—a square, circle, and at the top, a triangle—all drawn in outline. As yet another example of overseas outsourcing, the Laslo line was fabricated mainly in India and Italy and the objects were marked accordingly. In *Futura,* another group that was made for Towle in Italy, Laslo combined wood and stainless steel for a spherical ice bucket with a swinging, hinged handle and red enamel details. It was clearly derived from a bun warmer that was designed by Russel Wright in the 1930s and fabricated in spun aluminum and wood.

American Art Deco architecture was a strong influence as well, and Kirk Stieff seized on that reference for the design motif and promotion of *Paramount* sterling flatware. For the introductory advertisement in 1987, the stepped handles were set in a cityscape of skyscrapers, one suggesting New York's iconic 1920s Chrysler Building (fig. 15.13). The text cleverly played on the skyline theme: "Paramount. Masterfully constructed lines that turn artistic texture into sterling architecture. We've taken elegance to its greatest height and kept it well within your reach."[61] Notwithstanding these revivals,

the silver industry could not compete with the fashion for collecting authentic Art Deco silver objects.

Lifestyles were changing and for some the collecting and display of expensive antique silver became a statement of status. Emblematic of the return in the early 1980s to opulent entertaining and glamour was an advertisement for Estée Lauder perfume in which an exquisitely gowned, patrician hostess (the model Karen Graham) was depicted awaiting her guests in front of an elegant sideboard laden with expensive, apparently antique traditional silver holloware.[62] In this rarified environment, not only was modern silverware out of place, but so also was any notion that an upwardly mobile middle class might acquire the industrially produced traditional revivals in silverware that were on the market. The industry was not helped by the prevalence of divorce in the closing decades of the century. No longer were these hostesses filling out their collections of silverware by acquiring additional pieces as their repertoires expanded. One of the consequences of divorce, the division of property, was the thrust of an advertisement that Kirk Stieff addressed to the same sector of the market that Estée Lauder had envisioned a year earlier, the people who, traditionally, valued sterling silver. In a cartoon depicting the affluent country club set (fig. 15.14), in which wives drove expensive German-made cars, vacationed in second homes, relaxed over lunch after a vigorous set of tennis, and discussed their divorce settlements, a woman reports triumphantly, "Richard got the BMW and the condo, but at least he didn't get the Kirk Stieff sterling."[63] Although the intent of the advertisement was to bolster the prestige of those who owned silver, it was unlikely that the divorcee would be contemplating the new purchases critical to the survival of the industry.

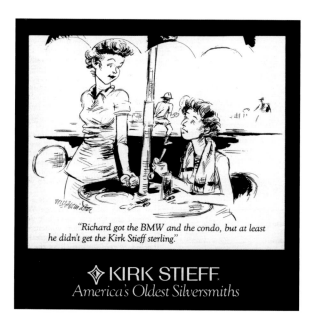

"Richard got the BMW and the condo, but at least he didn't get the Kirk Stieff sterling."

◆ KIRK STIEFF.
America's Oldest Silversmiths

FIGURE 15.14 "Richard got the BMW . . . ," Kirk Stieff advertisement, 1983

NOTES

1. "Bonniers. The American Thing," Bonniers advertisement, *New Yorker* 43 (Dec. 9, 1967): 189.

2. "They picked it above all others," Gorham advertisement, *House Beautiful* 97 (Oct. 1955): 35.

3. "Clarissa was born with an Oneida spoon in her mouth," Oneida advertisement, *Modern Bride* 19 (June/July 1967): 80. The flowers in her hair associated the pattern, via the model with the opening line, "If you're going to San Francisco be sure to wear some flowers in your hair," of the song "If you're going to San Francisco," which was a hit in 1967.

4. "Silver of 50 Years Will Be Exhibited," *New York Times,* Mar. 10, 1950, 30.

5. "Stainless steel: the retailer's point of view," *Crockery and Glass Journal* 157 (Aug. 1955): 28.

6. "Stainless Steel . . . as handsome as it is up-to-the-minute," *Modern Bride* 8 (summer 1956): 116–17.

7. "U. S. Tightens Tariff on Japanese Flatware," *New York Times,* Oct. 22, 1959.

8. "How come brides are now registering stainless?" International Silver Company advertisement, *Modern Bride* 16 (June/July 1964): 1.

9. "We think stainless should look like stainless," International Silver Company advertisement, *New Yorker* 42 (June 4, 1966): 20.

10. "It takes 35 steps to make sterling. We use 34 of them to make stainless," International Silver Company advertisement, *New Yorker* 43 (Apr. 15. 1967): 65.

11. *Jewelers' Circular-Keystone, Flatware Pattern Directory* (1970), 423–46.

12. See, for example, Reed & Barton advertisements: "The Lark," *House and Garden* 122 (Apr. 1960): 6; and "We are Incorrigible Moderns," *New Yorker* 39 (May 4, 1963): 22–23. Here, however, the enlargements were meant to show off the distinctive forms.

13. "Towle Introduces Contessina," Towle Silversmiths advertisement, *House and Garden* 128 (Oct. 1965): 13.

14. "Tiffany sterling is a work of art," Tiffany & Co. advertisements, *New Yorker* 41 (Oct. 16, 1965): 12; and 43 (Apr. 29, 1967): 9.

15. "International Sterling. Because you don't just buy it, you marry it," International Silver Company advertisement, *House Beautiful* 110 (Apr. 1968): 62–63.

16. Kathryn Livingston, "Silver: A Sterling American Obsession," *Town and Country* 133 (May 1979): 194.

17. Ibid., 197.

18. "A new generation should create its own traditions, Introducing Aegean Weave," Wallace advertisement, *New Yorker* 46 (Feb. 13, 1971): 58.

19. For pricing, see "Thread of Gold," Gorham advertisement, *New Yorker* 28 (Oct. 11, 1952): 9.

20. In 1973 International introduced *Golden Centennial* in silverplate from its 1847 Rogers Bros. division. The edges were electroplated with 24-karat gold.

21. "Selene," Kirk advertisement, *New Yorker* 54 (Nov. 13, 1978): 125.

22. Livingston, "Silver: A Sterling," 197.

23. *Oneida Silverplate, Gold Electroplate, Stainless,* flatware pamphlet (June 1, 1989) (Jewel Stern Archives, Coral Gables, Fla.; hereafter Stern Archives).

24. *Reed & Barton, The Classic American Silver* catalogue (spring 1985), 5; and *Gorham China Crystal Silver* catalogue (1987) (Stern archives).

25. "Introducing sterling from the Smithsonian Institution," Stieff advertisement, *New Yorker* 54 (May 8, 1978): 67.

26. For Renoir, see "Consider them signed originals," Gorham advertisement, *House Beautiful* 122 (Oct. 1980): 7; for Goya, see ibid. (Dec. 1980): 1.

27. "Introducing Winterthur. An exquisite pattern in silverplate inspired by a great museum," Reed & Barton advertisement, *House and Garden* 154 (Oct. 1982): 119.

28. "A new romantic age in sterling begins with Eighteenth Century by Reed & Barton," Reed & Barton advertisement, *House and Garden* 139 (Apr. 1971): 9.

29. "Sterling II by Reed & Barton," Reed & Barton advertisement, *House Beautiful* 118 (Apr. 1976): 2.

30. For example, see "A Classic Never Looks Old. Or New," Reed & Barton advertisement, *New Yorker* 54 (Nov. 6, 1978): 90. A triad of images in a bar across the top of the advertisement was the hallmark of the series. For this one, the patchwork quilt, a scene from the film *Gone With the Wind,* and a jeep were illustrated to make the point of the headline.

31. "Good grief, Frank. They took the Reed & Barton Stainless," Reed & Barton advertisement, *New Yorker* 59 (Jan. 16, 1984): 15.

32. "Nobody leaves this room . . . there's a teaspoon missing from our Reed & Barton Stainless," Reed & Barton advertisement, *New Yorker* 60 (Sept. 10, 1984): 65.

33. "Towle, the Sterling of Stainless," Towle advertisement, *New Yorker* 60 (June 4, 1984): 138.

34. The organization was founded in 1919 as The Sterling Silverware Manufacturers Association. In 1926, the name was changed to The Sterling Silversmiths Guild of America.

35. "Tsk, tsk. You have a St. Laurent, a Cuisinart, and no sterling?" Sterling Silversmiths Guild of America advertisement, *House and Garden* 150 (Mar. 1978): 6.

36. See, for example, "Sterling Silver: It Nourishes Your Sense of Elegance," Sterling Silversmiths Guild of America advertisement, *House and Garden* 157 (Nov. 1985): 60.

37. See, for example, "The Joy in Every Moment. The Pure Pleasure of Sterling," Sterling Silversmiths Guild of America advertisement, *HG* [House and Garden] 162 (Sept. 1990): 29.

38. The expense of maintaining the guild was the reason. An effort by the president of Reed & Barton, Tim K. Riddle, who has an interest in the history of silver, to revive the guild was in process in 2005 (Susan Kindberg-MacKenzie, Reed & Barton, e-mail to author, Oct. 5, 2004, and Feb. 28, 2005).

39. See Barbara McLean Ward and Gerald W. R. Ward, eds., *Silver in American Life: Selections from the Mabel Brady Garvan and Other Collections at Yale University,* exh. cat. (Boston: David R. Godine, in association with Yale University Art Gallery and the American Federation of Arts, 1979), 88 (for Prip), 186 (for La Paglia); also, 122 (for Ronald Hayes Pearson) and 89 (for Mary Ann Scherr).

40. Livingston, "Silver: A Sterling," 152–53, 194.

41. Ibid., 197.

42. For example, in the 1980s Sam Wagstaff assembled an extensive collection of nineteenth-century American silver that was exhibited at the New-York Historical Society in 1987. For the silver collection of the Dallas Museum of Art, see Charles L. Venable, *Silver in America, 1840–1940: A Century of Splendor,* exh. cat. (Dallas, Tex.: Dallas Museum of Art, 1994) and his introduction in the present catalogue.

43. This was later characterized by Jeffrey M. Christian, the managing director of the CPM Group, a precious-metals consulting company that was based in New York, as "another nail in the coffin" of the silverware industry; see Jonathan P. Hicks, "With the Price Right, the White Metal Heads for a Rebound," *New York Times,* Jan. 6, 1991, 11.

44. Linda Marx, "Stainless Steel Shows its Mettle," *Town and Country* 135 (June 1981): 167, 168.

45. Determined by the author from *Jewelers' Circular-Keystone, Sterling Flatware Pattern Index,* 2d ed. (1995).

46. For Portoghesi, see Marco Ferreri, ed., *Cutlery* (Mantua, Italy: Corraini Edittore, 1997), 25.

47. Lunt also introduced *Golden Embassy Scroll* (1991), a variation of *Embassy Scroll* (1981).

48. Dorothy T. Rainwater, *Encyclopedia of American Silver Manufacturers,* 3rd rev. ed. (West Chester, Pa: Schiffer, 1986), 91.

49. Candleholder illustrated in "Sweetness & Light," Kirk advertisement, *Town and Country* 124 (Nov. 1970): 52.

50. "Galaxy of Lights," Gorham advertisement, *New Yorker* 49 (Oct. 29, 1973): 121.

51. Prip's *Dimension* tea and coffee service (1961) had been retired in the late 1970s as were his triangle bowls in *Color-Glaze.* By 1985 all Prip's holloware was discontinued, as were the entire *Color-Glaze* line and *Free Form* bowls, a staff design from the 1950s.

52. *Reed & Barton, The Classic American Silver* catalogue (spring 1985), 28 (Stern Archives).

53. Livingston, "Silver: A Sterling," 155.

54. "Introducing International's New Continental-Size Stainless," International Silver Company advertisement, *House Beautiful* 119 (June 1977): 29.

55. For Christofle silverplate, see "The Elegant Alternative," *New Yorker* 57 (Nov. 30, 1981): 7; "French couture pour la Table," *New Yorker* 58 (Dec. 27, 1982): 3; and "Introducing Atlantide. A New Wave in French Couture pour la Table," *House and Garden* 160 (Nov. 1988): 10. See also "Ercuis: The fine silverplate of France," *New Yorker* 57 (Mar. 30, 1981): 28; "Even in France Only a Few Own Cardeilhac Sterling," *New Yorker* 59 (Apr. 18, 1983): 7; "The Art of Giving by Cartier," *Town and Country* 138 (Nov. 1984): 62; "Puiforcat Silversmith in Paris Since 1820," *House and Garden* 157 (Oct. 1985): 36; and "Christian Dior Art de la Table Collection," *HG* [House and Garden] 163 (Oct. 1990): 23.

56. See "The Pride of Italy Comes to America; Mazzucato. Fine Art in Sterling," *Town and Country* 134 (Sept. 1980): 51; "Presenting Ricci Silverplate, Classics From Italy," *New Yorker* 59 (Feb. 13, 1984): 1; and "The New Age of Elegance . . . Buccellati," *New Yorker* 61 (Dec. 9. 1985): 19.

57. "Atlantide Gold," *HG* [House and Garden] 162 (Apr. 1990): 71; and "Cartier: The Art of Being Unique," Cartier advertisement, *HG* [House and Garden] 162 (May 1990): 25.

58. *Gorham Silver Holloware Catalog* (1991), 4 (Stern Archives). The *Terrassa* collection included bowls, candlesticks, trays, an ice bucket, and a covered box.

59. David Rogers, telephone conversation with author, Feb. 24, 2004. Syratech, the parent company of Wallace, was more successful with three flatware collections, issued by the Wallace division in 1998, that capitalized on the cachet of European silver. The Italian Collection patterns, *Venezia, Giorgio, Barocco,* and others, were new and had been designed in house. The English Collection included *English Onslow, Queens, William and Mary,* and others—patterns designed by the C. J. Vander Company of Sheffield, England, and acquired by Wallace. For the La Preference Collection several of International's existing designs were recycled, including *Pantheon* (1920), *Trianon* (1921), and others. Patterns from these three collections are still available (Brian Cohen, Syratech Corp., conversation with author, October 19, 2004).

60. "Laslo for Towle," tag (Stern Archives).

61. "Skylines," Kirk Stieff advertisement, *HG* [House and Garden] 159 (May 1987): 107.

62. Estée Lauder advertisement, *New Yorker* 58 (May 10, 1982): 5.

63. "Richard got the BMW," Kirk Stieff advertisement, *New Yorker* 59 (Oct. 17, 1983): 165.

CHAPTER SIXTEEN

A FINAL FLOURISH, 1980–2000

Notwithstanding the precipitous decline of the silver industry in the last quarter of the century, some exceptional modernist silverware was created during that time. These innovations sprang from diverse, atypical sources. The new wave of design emanating from Italy in the early 1970s was influential. Under the aegis of Tiffany & Co., independent talents breathed new life into silver collections. Designers associated with the fashion industry extended their domain into home accessories. Swid Powell, a creative partnership that emerged in the 1980s in New York brilliantly commissioned, produced, and showcased tabletop accessories designed by prominent postmodern architects.

THE ITALIAN CONNECTION

By the 1970s, Italy had wrested the world leadership in design away from Scandinavia. The hegemony of organic modernism was over and the influence of the free form style on home furnishings had waned. Postmodernism was now on the rise. Stirrings in Italy early in the decade would affect American silverware in the last quarter of the twentieth century. Among the developments were the silverware projects initiated by Cleto Munari, a wealthy industrialist based in Vicenza, the engagement of the postmodern Italian architect Ettore Sottsass in 1972 by Alessi, a mass producer of metal tableware located near Milan, and the establishment, in Milan, of San Lorenzo, an enterprise that exported silverware to the United States as early as 1972.[1] Common to all of these ventures was the influence of architects as designers of objects for the table.

San Lorenzo was founded in 1970 by Ciro Cacchione, a manufacturer who was determined to create sterling silver of the highest quality in a modern idiom. Cacchione brought together a close-knit group of talented architects that included Antonio Piva and Massimo and Lella Vignelli (b. 1931 and 1934, respectively), with a team of experienced craftspeople to create and produce their exclusive designs. Although silver flatware and holloware was the main thrust of the operation, jewelry and some objects in porcelain, glass, and aluminum were produced in the studio. The Vignellis had established ties in the United States in 1957, and in 1965 Massimo with other American designers formed Unimark International, a firm that had offices in Milan, Chicago, and New York. The Vignellis moved to New York the following year, but maintained their professional relationships in Italy, where they became affiliated with the young, dynamic firm of San Lorenzo, a relationship that continued into the 1990s.

In 1971 they established Vignelli Associates, which distinguished itself as one of the most influential design offices in the United States. In her first design for San Lorenzo that year, Lella Vignelli created a carafe of exquisite form and finish (fig. 16.1), which was part of a bar ensemble of strong architectonic character. Its unique spout has been described as a "simple

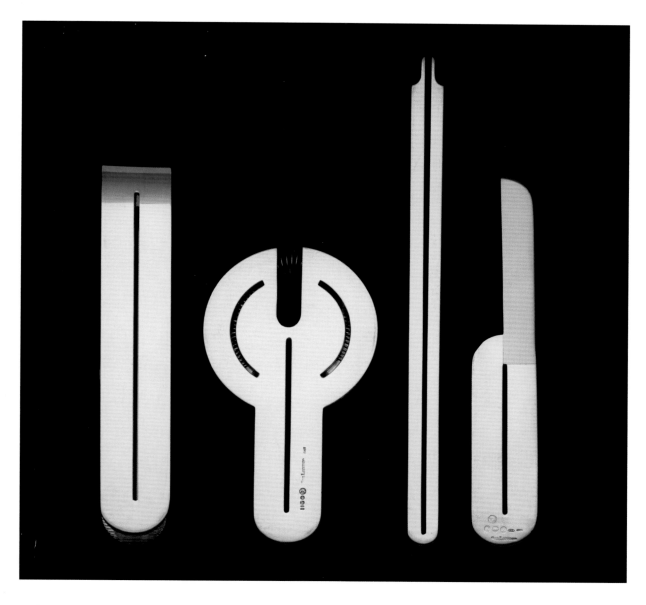

V-shaped section cut from the flat inverted rim" that "guides the liquid in a perfect arc from the vessel to the glass." The unusual exterior surface has a "finely striated texture of closely set vertical furrows, each minutely differing from the other in both width and depth." Referred to as a "metallic bark," the surface was described as unexpectedly "soft to the touch."[2] In fact, the bark of a tree had inspired Vignelli.[3] The following year Massimo and Lella added a set of four bar tools (fig. 16.2) to coordinate with the carafe and other objects in the group. The finish on these was smooth and the handles were modeled on the curved, bisected, and folded carafe handle. In 1972 the Vignellis' bar accessories, described as "the most elegant Christmas gift of Christmas 1972,"[4] were available at Cartier in New York, for affluent, sophisticated American shoppers in search of ultramodern sterling holloware and serving pieces.

DESIGNERS FOR TIFFANY

Another resource for contemporary silverware in the 1970s and later, some produced abroad in a trend that gained momentum at this time, was Tiffany & Co.[5] An impressive aspect of the firm in the second half of the twentieth century was its engagement of talented, independent designers, some of whom it recognized by name. Elsa Peretti, Ward Bennett, Victor Carranza, and the sculptors Charles O. Perry and Tom Penn were among them. There had been isolated instances in the silver industry of signature collections before, but they had been rare. Those that stand out were Gorham's decision to mark Erik Magnussen's designs in the 1920s; International's *Gift Ware* by Lurelle Guild in the 1930s and its Christoffersen Designed and La Paglia Designed lines in the 1950s, and Reed & Barton's *Signature V* in the 1970s. Occasionally, name recognition was exploited to enhance the promotion of sterling flatware patterns.

FIGURE 16.1 *Striated* carafe, 1971. San Lorenzo, Lella Vignelli, designer. Silver. The Jewel Stern American Silver Collection, cat. 217

FIGURE 16.3   Bowl, c. 1970–1980. Ward Bennett Design, Ward Bennett, designer. Silverplate. DMA, JSASC, cat. 5

This was true of Wallace's *Discovery* pattern of 1957, which was designed by the internationally renowned, French-born American industrial designer Raymond Loewy, and of Reed & Barton's collaboration with Gio Ponti on the *The Diamond* pattern introduced the following year. Although Tiffany tended to be a conservative firm, it is apparent that from the 1960s on it became more adventurous, a consequence of the strong leadership of the design directors Van Day Truex and John Loring.[6] The designer collections that resulted from their planning were the exception in the conservative silver industry during the last quarter of the twentieth century.

One of Tiffany's first experiments in engaging a noted outside designer was for the prototype of the flatware pattern named for its creator, the minimalist designer Ward Bennett (1917–2003). Tiffany retained Bennett in the 1960s to design china, glassware, and silver. His sterling flatware and accessories, ashtrays, salt and pepper shakers, and coasters for candles were introduced on table settings at the store in New York City in the fall of 1972 and in the company's catalogue, the *Blue Book*, for that year. Unfortunately, difficulties in executing the flatware pattern according to Bennett's precise

specifications and his inflexibility over revisions led to its demise before it was made available to consumers, an embarrassing moment for the firm.[7] A silverplated bowl (fig. 16.3) with the hallmark "Ward Bennett Design," produced independently, reveals the skillful modeling of form stripped of superfluous ornament and the clean lines for which he was known.

Results were different for the work of Elsa Peretti (b. 1940). An Italian-born, high fashion model and accessory designer for the American designer known as Halston (Roy Halston Frowick) and others, Peretti began designing jewelry for Tiffany in 1974. Four years later she created a small, sensuous holloware group that included a tray with her signature indented thumbprint for handles, and a tall, *Bone* candlestick of organic inspiration. In 1984 Tiffany introduced Peretti's *Padova*, a smooth, contoured flatware pattern with asymmetrical flowing lines and looped openwork handles (fig. 16.4). Peretti's aesthetic was powerfully expressionistic and sensual and can be compared to Henning Koppel's designs of sculptural holloware for Jensen. The most complex three-dimensional realization was Peretti's covered tureen of 1986 with a platter (fig. 16.5) that exhibited the refinement of form characteristic of all her work. Peretti evoked the free form, 1950s style, especially in the asymmetrical platter that had a precedent in this work in the *Flair* pattern by International (see fig. 10.29). As was becoming more common throughout the industry, the tureen and platter were made abroad, produced by the Pampaloni Company in Florence, Italy.[8] Other pieces of note in the collection were a water pitcher, carafe, candleholder, and wine goblet.

Charles O. Perry (b. 1929) designed three intricate nonfunctional objects that could be used as centerpieces or for display. Derived from his monumental sculptures, the objects were named *Thrice, Cassini,* and *Elipsoid* (a pair of interlocking pentagonal bowls that formed a centerpiece). He also designed a small "seed-shaped" box with a vermeil lining.[9] Perry's designs were executed by the Italian-American master silversmith Ubaldo Vitali, and bore his hallmark in addition to Tiffany's. A special event, Breakfast at Tiffany's, was arranged in October 1979 at the store on Fifth Avenue so that customers could meet Perry and see his collection of objects and jewelry.[10] With the exception of the "seed box," Perry's sterling pieces, extremely heavy and a challenge to produce, were expensive. *Elipsoid,* the interlocking centerpiece, was the most expensive, costing $12,600.

FIGURE 16.4 "Design by Elsa Peretti," Tiffany & Co. advertisement for *Padova* flatware, 1993

FIGURE 16.5 Tureen with platter, 1986. Tiffany & Co., Elsa Peretti, designer. Silver. Dallas Museum of Art, cat. 250

In 1980 Tiffany's design director, John Loring (b. 1939), created a small group of objects with an all-over surface decoration that was based on the tread-plate pattern used for manufactured aluminum and steel flooring to prevent skidding. Loring took a high-tech industrial product and transformed it into a witty commentary on elegance. According to Tiffany, the box (fig. 16.6) was "not chased with the traditional hammers or dies, but with a more recent process that uses compressed air to chase the low-relief pattern."[11]

Several years later, the Mexican-born, multifaceted designer Victor Carranza (b. 1951) began his association with Tiffany and created his *Bow* collection, a group consisting of picture frames, a bud vase, box, tray, and candlesticks made in his workshop in Mexico City, that was first advertised in the *Blue Book* for 1987–1988.[12] In the early 1990s, the firm took another innovative step in making an exclusive arrangement with the sculptor Tom Penn (b. 1952), the son of Irving Penn, the photographer. For Tiffany Penn designed five pieces, *Ribbon* and *Wing* candleholders, a *Wind* tray, an *Olive* dish, and the *Twisted* vase. At first these were handwrought by the Scottish silversmith Alan Place at Old Newbury Crafters of Amesbury, Massachusetts, and those pieces bear its marks as well as the hallmarks of Place and of Tiffany. Later, Ubaldo Vitali fabricated Penn's designs and those have Vitali's mark. In the unusual, canti-levered *Olive* dish (fig. 16.7), Penn contrasted clean sweeping curves with crisp straight and angled planes to animate this small but complex form. For the *Twisted*

FIGURE 16.6   *Tread Plate* box, 1980. Tiffany & Co., John Loring, designer. Silver. The John Loring Collection, cat. 249

FIGURE 16.7   *Olive* dish, c. 1990. Tiffany & Co., Tom Penn, designer. Silver. The Peter Forss Collection, cat. 251

FIGURE 16.8   *Twisted* vase, c. 1990. Tiffany & Co., Tom Penn, designer. Silver. The Jewel Stern American Silver Collection, cat. 252

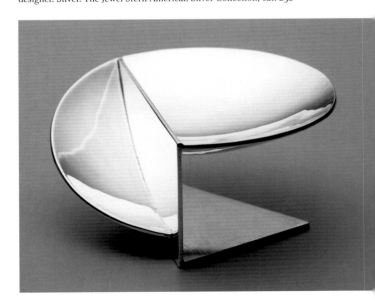

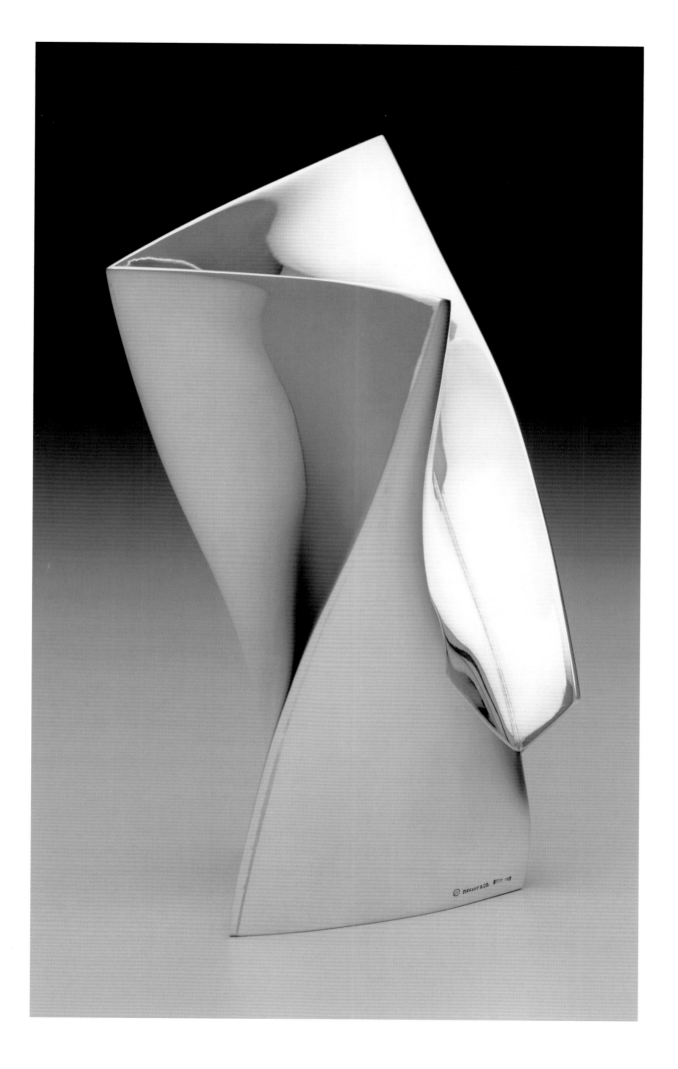

vase (fig. 16.8), he manipulated a thick sheet of the metal to form a dramatic torqued shape. Of all these designer collections, Peretti's was the most successful and her work is still produced.

FASHION CONSCIOUS SILVERWARE

The influence of fashion on the silver industry had been apparent since the arrival of the New Look in the late 1940s after World War II. It was manifested in the jewelry designed by Christoffersen and La Paglia for International's Sterling Craft Associates in the 1950s, in Reed & Barton's *Signature V* by studio jewelers in the 1970s. By the 1980s, with the exception of Peretti's silver collections for Tiffany, silver manufacturers rarely, if ever, turned to fashion for inspiration. In a reversal in the 1980s, the fashion industry turned to silver as it broadened its business beyond clothing to home accessories. Two jewelers, Stephen Dweck (b. 1960), who began his career with the fashion designer Geoffrey Beene, and Ted Muehling (b. 1952), who has been recognized by the fashion industry with American Fashion Coty awards in 1978 and 1982, designed sterling silver tableware that was produced in small quantities. By 1990 they were not alone, a phenomenon that was the subject of an article in *House and Garden* magazine:[13] "While the worlds of fashion and interior design enjoy a mutual attraction as powerful as gravity, innovative jewelry designers are mining the give-and-take of ideas, materials, and applications to create objects for the house, or 'accessories' as they are known."[14] Of the

FIGURE 16.9 Serving set, 1986. Stephen Dweck Design, Stephen Dweck, designer. Silver, bronze. Stephen Dweck, cat. 11

work illustrated, only that by Dweck and Muehling was in silver.

Each took nature as his model, but the expression of it varied. Intertwined vines with grape leaves and his trademark beetle often embellished the romantic objects in Dweck's Home Collection, which was launched in 1988 and included in 1989 a three-piece serving set (fig. 16.9) consisting of a pastry server, spoon, and fork in silver and bronze, with a bronze beetle ensconced on each piece. Dweck brought the intricate delicacy of his jewelry to a collection that also included a centerpiece fruit bowl, candleholders, napkin rings, picture frames, and small dishes with matching serving pieces, as well as larger serving spoons and forks, demitasse spoons, and cocktail forks. Natural mother-of-pearl, exotic woods, and semiprecious stones such as azurite were combined with silver. Although the pieces were lavish, simple organic forms were their inspiration. "Brooklyn, believe it or not," he said in 1990, "still has a ton of nature."[15] Interviewed the next year by *Harper's Bazaar*, he commented that "with tableware, I have finally found a functional medium for my art."[16] In the early 1990s, the Home Collection was mentioned in many stylish publications including *Mirabella* and *Bon Appetit*. Sold at Bergdorf Goodman and Neiman Marcus, among the most exclusive department stores in

FIGURE 16.10   *Queen Ann's Lace* tea strainer, 1999. Silver, cat. 138; *Concave* cup and *White Coral* spoon, 2000. Porcelain by Porzellan-manufaktur Nymphenburg. Ted Muehling Inc., Ted Muehling, designer. Dallas Museum of Art, cat. 139

the country, the objects were expensive. Production was limited and ceased after about eight years.

Ted Muehling has a different sensibility. A graduate with a degree in industrial design from Pratt Institute, where he was mentored by Gerald Gulotta (who had been a finalist in the international competition for flatware and whose submission was exhibited in the associated *Designed for Silver* exhibition in 1960; see figs. 10.13, 14.3), Muehling nevertheless found his métier in jewelry design, although he did acknowledge Gulotta's influence on his work.[17] In the mid- to late 1980s, Muehling began making objects for his own use and as gifts for friends, experiments that led to the very limited production of silver objects for the table.[18] The shapes were restrained and abstract while still capturing the essential grace of a shell, a branch, or a stone, all natural forms that Muehling recalled from summers spent on the beach in Nantucket when he was a child and later explored further in making jewelry.[19] Dishes in the shape of a shell, a spoon with a twig handle, another with a petal-shaped bowl, a twisted fork, and a cream pitcher, all subtly modeled and exquisitely proportioned and balanced without an extraneous detail, are typical of his tableware. In the early 1990s descriptions of these objects began appearing in articles in the *New York Times Magazine, House and Garden, Harper's Bazaar,* and other publications.[20] Muehling's table accessories were sold primarily in his own shop in New York City, in art galleries in the United States and abroad, and, like Dweck's Home Collection, in Bergdorf Goodman. For his evanescent sterling *Queen*

Ann's Lace tea strainer designed in 1999, Muehling used a computer to create a template for etching the intricate patterning (fig. 16.10).[21] Muehling's interpretation merged his experience of industrial design, craft, nature, fashion, and technology.

Two widely marketed and internationally renowned fashion designers in the late twentieth century, Calvin Klein and Ralph Lauren, entered the home furnishing market in the 1990s with coordinated designs for linens, tabletop ware, and other accessories. The Ralph Lauren Home collection embodied Lauren's genteel upper-class American imagery and in 1993 he offered *New Kings,* an elaborate, traditional flatware pattern. Four years later *Chain Link,* with bold linked handles, except for the knives, was added to the collection. Both patterns, made by Reed & Barton, were of sterling and available in vermeil. Lauren also designed a large, and competing, selection of stainless steel flatware.

In the early 1990s, in what appears to have been exclusive arrangements in some cases, several department stores offered unusual flatware by designers who had established their reputations in the 1980s. After leaving Tiffany & Co., the jeweler Angela Cummings opened her own business in 1984 and secured a special boutique in Bergdorf Goodman in New York City, where *Shore Line,* her sterling flatware pattern

FIGURE 16.11   Nan Swid and Addie Powell with some of the architects who designed for Swid Powell, 1984. Left to right: Richard Meier, Nan Swid, Andrée Putman, Arata Isozaki, Robert Siegel, Stanley Tigerman, Addie Powell, Robert A. M. Stern, Charles Gwathmey, Frank Gehry, and James Stewart Polshek

with seashell motifs, was sold.[22] At Barney's New York, another trendsetting retail establishment, a silverplated flatware pattern with a lacy medallion on the handle tips designed by Marisa Osorio-Farinha Chupin for Siècle, a fashionable jewelry and silver shop established in Paris in 1983 by Chupin and her husband, was available to order.[23] The Neiman Marcus stores offered its patrons a silverplated pattern called *Twiggy*, one of the earliest works by Michael Aram, an American designer who has produced silverware in India since the late 1980s.[24] Although the volume of sales was small, such department store boutiques were another source of competition for the silver industry.

Swid Powell: Postmodernism in Silver

Unexpectedly, the strongest competition for the silver industry's modernist ware in the mid-1980s and 1990s came from a pair of savvy, ambitious American women, Nan Swid and Addie Powell. Both had been associated with Knoll International, a well-known manufacturer of modern furniture and textiles, Swid as design director for product development and Powell as a vice president for sales. They recognized a demand for higher quality design in contemporary tableware and were familiar with the Italian makers, San Lorenzo, Cleto Munari, and Alessi, who had commissioned modern silver designs by architects. (Alessi, for example, had introduced, in 1983, in an experimental division named Officina Alessi, a collection of eleven postmodern silver services, published in *Tea & Coffee Piazza*, each designed by a well-known architect, among them, the Americans Michael Graves, Richard Meier, Stanley Tigerman, and Robert

Venturi. The objects were produced in numbered, limited editions.)[25]

"I realized," said Swid, "that beautiful things for contemporary homes were missing from the market. . . . I found I was buying fine old things when I am really a Modernist at heart. What I wanted was a portrait of my generation. I also knew that very few people would ever live in houses designed by Richard Meier or Robert Venturi, but I thought they would like to experience that aesthetic level."[26] Swid and Powell also foresaw the nascent trend toward an international design culture that would flower more fully in the 1990s and promoted the popularity of objects designed by famous architects and designers who were increasingly becoming celebrities. In 1982 Swid and Powell established their company, Swid Powell, and assembled a group of designers (fig. 16.11) to create the inaugural collection of architect-designed crystal, china, and silver. Among those Swid Powell initially extended commissions to were eight architects, Charles Gwathmey, Robert Siegel, Arata Isozaki, Richard Meier, Laurinda Spear, Robert A. M. Stern, Stanley Tigerman, and Robert Venturi.[27] Never before in the United States had such a program been implemented for product development. When the first collection was unveiled at Marshall Field's department store in Chicago in 1984, some of the silverware was reported to have sold out within four days, and

the store's buyer Robert Doerr exclaimed, "It's been a long time since the tabletop has had this kind of excitement."[28] Swid and Powell were shrewd marketers and their goal was to reach upscale department and specialty lifestyle stores. They selected their retailers "as carefully as we selected our architects," noted Powell.[29] As Rosenthal had required with its Studio-Line in Europe, each store had to buy the entire collection and devote a special section to it.[30] Within a few years the partners were credited with having "a perspective that turned the tabletop market upside down."[31] Swid and Powell benefited from the economic boom years of the mid-1980s, when many wealthy Americans rediscovered the joys of nesting and of dining at home and would buy domestic accessories to enhance the experience.[32] Intuitively, their timing was ahead of the wave. By 1990, when the company's products were sold in five hundred American stores and in others abroad, the architecture critic Paul Goldberger wrote:

The Swid Powell objects forge a new point of intersection between architecture and the realm of consumer products—a point of intersection that could not have existed a few years ago. They find this point not at the lowest common denominator of fashion but at a higher, more serious level—not by bringing architecture down to the level of commercial products, but by bringing commercial products up to the level of architecture."[33]

FIGURE 16.12 *King Richard* bowl, 1983. Swid Powell, Richard Meier, designer. Silverplate. The Jewel Stern American Silver Collection, cat. 226

Swid and Powell had stated their mission in the brochure that introduced their first collection: "We are not," said Swid, "interested in producing artifacts, nor are we looking for sculptures or one-of-a-kind museum pieces"; rather, continued Powell, "we wanted, and succeeded in producing beautiful, functional pieces that can be lived with and used."[34] The firm's values were rooted in the historical link between architecture and the decorative and applied arts as epitomized earlier in

FIGURE 16.13 Display window in the Bergdorf Goodman department store, New York, 1988; the floor of the window was filled with Richard Meier's *King Richard* bowls

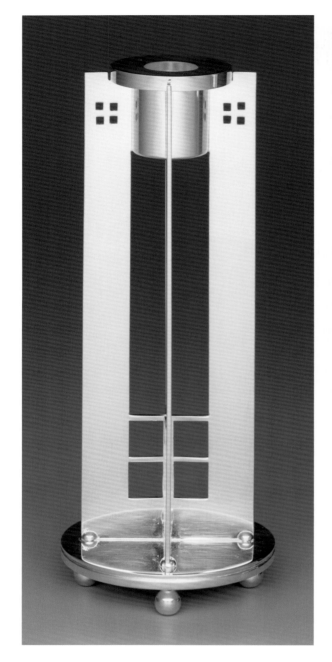

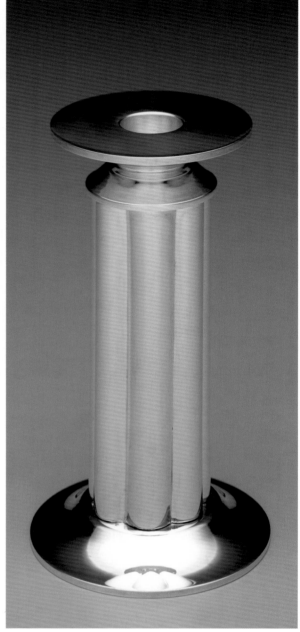

FIGURE 16.14 *King Richard* candlestick, 1983. Swid Powell, Richard Meier, designer. Silverplate. The Jewel Stern American Silver Collection, cat. 225

FIGURE 16.15 *Century* candlestick, 1983. Swid Powell, Robert A. M. Stern, designer. Silverplate. DMA, JSASC, cat. 227

FIGURE 16.16 Pitcher, 1985. Swid Powell, Robert A. M. Stern, designer. Silverplate. DMA, JSASC, cat. 228

the century by the Wiener Werkstätte, the Bauhaus, and Cranbrook Academy. Unlike the objects produced by those institutions, which were available only to a "privileged few," Swid Powell's wares were meant for a "widespread and discerning market."[35] The *King Richard* bowl (fig. 16.12) designed by Richard Meier (b. 1934) for the inaugural collection, was described as "a shallow silver basin rimmed with a chaste band of openwork squares," considered to be "superbly proportioned" and of the silver objects in the collection, the piece "destined to become" a classic.[36] The border of openwork squares revived a motif favored by Josef Hoffmann and the Wiener Werkstätte, a strong influence on Meier, as was the Scottish architect Charles Rennie Mackintosh. Many of these bowls, which were made by Lunt, the first fabricator of holloware for Swid Powell,[37] were displayed in one of Bergdorf Goodman's windows (fig. 16.13) during the American Institute of Architects convention in

Like Tiffany and other competitors, Swid Powell quickly began outsourcing silverplated holloware abroad. Cleto Munari in Italy made Meier's candlestick and Stern's pieces. Later, less expensive makers were found in Argentina, Hong Kong, and Korea. As for American makers, Swid Powell's foremost relationship was with Reed & Barton.

In 1989 Swid Powell entered into a licensing agreement with Reed & Barton to market a "flatware accessory collection" by Meier, Venturi, Graves, and David Palterer, an Israeli architect working in Florence, Italy.[39] Each example articulated its designer's distinctive sensibility. Meier's salad serving set was in stainless steel with black epoxy inlay in a row of squares on the handles; the other three designers worked in silverplate.[40] Later Meier designed a more formal salad serving set (fig. 16.17) in silverplate with classical fluting and a grid of squares that clearly referred to Hoffmann. The ovoid spoon bowl, horizontally positioned, also had a precedent in Hoffmann's flatware.[41] Graves (b. 1934) designed a salad serving set with an allover, stylized floral pattern (fig. 16.18). The squared handles were

New York in 1988. Meier's debt to Hoffmann was even more pronounced in a candlestick of formal complexity and precision that was also in the inaugural collection (fig. 16.14). Meier, the most prolific designer of silver objects for Swid Powell, would ultimately create more than forty pieces for the firm.[38] Stern (b. 1939), an outspoken postmodern advocate of historicism, designed three candlesticks, the *Century,* the *Metropolitan,* and the *Harmonie,* that took their cues from traditional architectural elements. For the *Century* candlestick (fig. 16.15), Stern quoted the classical reeded column. Like the *King Richard* bowl, these candlesticks were initially available in sterling as well as in silverplate. However, after testing the market, the firm soon withdrew the sterling version. In 1985 Stern designed an exquisitely proportioned pitcher (fig. 16.16) with allusions to seventeenth- and nineteenth-century American silver. The lip recalled those of tankards of the seventeenth century, but for his pitcher Stern inverted the shape of the historic vessel. The exaggerated, looped handle reflected early nineteenth-century classical taste and added a note of buoyancy to the otherwise austere form.

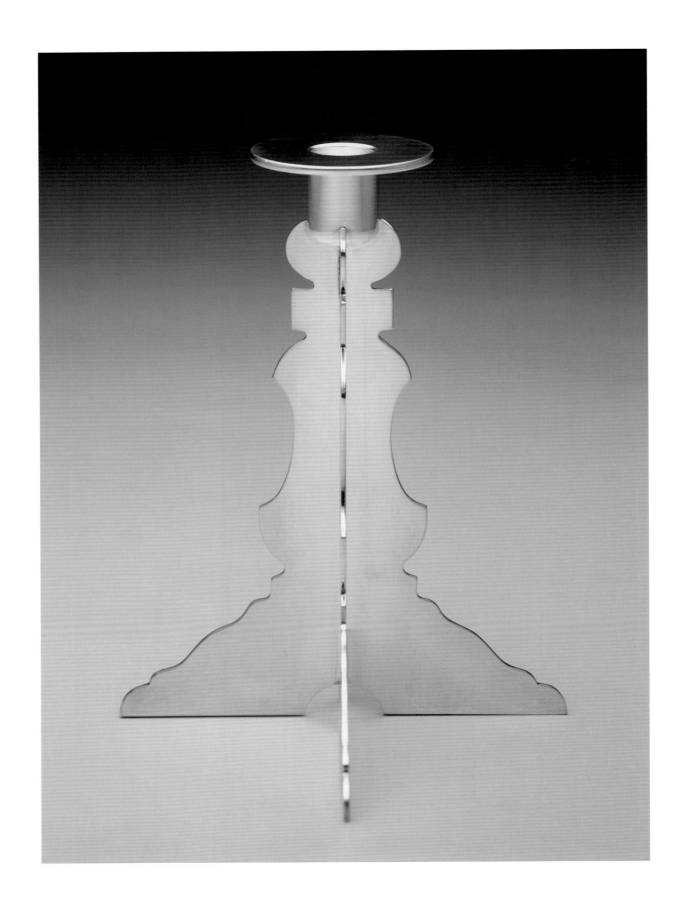

FIGURE 16.21 Candlestick, 1986. Swid Powell, Robert Venturi, designer. Silverplate. DMA, JSASC, cat. 229

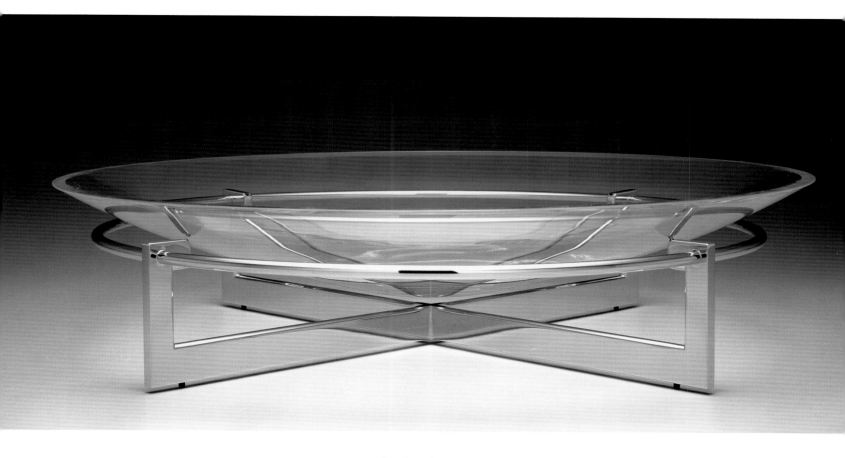

FIGURE 16.22 *Framed* bowl, 1994. Steuben Glass Works, Richard Meier, designer. Glass, silverplated nickel. Dallas Museum of Art, cat. 222

counterpoints to the round bowls, and one was jauntily notched in an abstract keyhole shape to serve as the fork (fig. 16.19). Venturi (b. 1925) interpreted two classical orders of architecture, the Doric and Ionic, for the handles of his carving set (fig. 16.20). He subsequently designed an elongated platter spoon, with a handle derived from the Corinthian order, as a witty complement to the carving set. His most innovative silver design for Swid Powell was the candlestick designed in 1986. Venturi cleverly intersected two flat cutouts of his Chippendale-style shape at right angles to make a three-dimensional standing object (fig. 16.21). Like the candlesticks designed by Meier and Stern and Stern's pitcher, Venturi's candlestick was made in Italy by Munari.

The popularity of these objects inspired Steuben to engage two members of the Swid Powell team to create signature works that combined glass with metal. In 1989 the Archaic Vessel Collection, designed by Michael Graves and consisting of a bowl and two vases supported on bronze stands in the manner of ancient vessels, was introduced. The Framed Vessel Collection by Richard Meier followed in 1994. Meier's collection was described in Steuben's catalogue as "an exploration of contrasting materials and shapes, harmonized by the brilliant reflective surfaces of glass and metal . . . the essence of Meier's architectural aesthetic."[42] For his

bowl and two vases, Meier reinterpreted in his own modernist idiom Graves's historical interpretation of the ancient vessel type, a bold, competitive rejoinder. The large shallow bowl (fig. 16.22) and the glass vases, which were flared at the top and capsule-shaped at the bottom, were held in a rigid geometric framework based on the right angle, a characteristic element of Meier's architectural and design vocabulary. In contrast to Graves's bronze, the metal scaffolding was sleek, modern silverplate. Two master silversmiths were instrumental in fabricating Meier's designs: Ubaldo Vitali executed the prototypes and Michael Brophy produced the line for Steuben.[43]

Flushed with the success of their mass-produced lines, and to celebrate and coincide with the publication by Rizzoli International in 1990 of a monograph on the company, Swid and Powell undertook a limited edition series of expensive objects called the Architects' Collection. According to Marc Hacker, the exceptionally gifted vice president of design and development from 1983 to 1998, the company's intention, in giving the architects an opportunity to "fantasize a little" and to "stretch their imaginations," was to say thank you for their cooperation in working within unaccustomed parameters.[44] In the group of twelve were some of the inaugural architects, Meier, Spear, Stern, Tigerman, and Venturi, together with the later contributors, Graves and Palterer, and Peter Eisenman, Frank Gehry, Robert and Trix Haussmann, Ettore Sottsass, and George Sowden.[45] They all worked in the idiom of late

FIGURE 16.23 Photograph: Tureen, Architects' Collection, 1990. Swid Powell, Stanley Tigerman, designer. Silver, rose quartz

FIGURE 16.24 Photograph: Ice bucket, Architects' Collection, 1990. Swid Powell, Robert A. M. Stern, designer. Silver, gold, glass

twentieth–century postmodernism, but it was their diverse, individualistic viewpoints and strategies, ranging from Meier's cool, elegant, reworked modernism to Stern's historical musings and Tigerman's outrageous playfulness, that were represented in the collection. All were reacting against the stark functionalism of International Style modernism. For the mass-produced objects, the architects had been given strict guidelines about the types of items desired and the specific price for which they would be sold.[46] For this luxurious series the architects were free to choose from an array of precious materials and make whatever kind of object they desired. Silver, ebony, porcelain, lead crystal, onyx, and polished chrome were employed and often combined in the pieces. Embellishments of mother-of-pearl, semiprecious stone, and gilding served as decorative accents. An oval sterling tray by Spear (b. 1950), for example, was formed in three asymmetrical tiers. The surface of the lowest was given a simple, hand-hammered finish, the middle tier was engraved with radiating lines of varying lengths, and the top tier, the rim border, was smooth and set with alternating stones of lapis lazuli, coral, and onyx. One of the most expensive and grandest objects in the collection was a fluted and domed tureen (fig. 16.23) by Tigerman (b. 1930) that was supported by a row of rose quartz spheres strung like pearls along the outer edge. The wing shape of the handles

FIGURE 16.25 *Wing vase,* 1991–1992. Swid Powell, Elsa Rady, designer. Silverplate. DMA, JSASC, cat. 230

on the cast lid is an iconic motif of Tigerman's work, and he used variations of it in a silverplated picture frame and a footed, white porcelain fruit bowl.[47] Stern designed an ice bucket (fig. 16.24) as a replica of a classical Athenian monument with Doric columns on a stepped base, an object that perpetuated a tradition dating back to the Renaissance of conceiving decorative objects as miniaturized buildings.[48] Meier produced a mantel clock with a movement that was housed in a sterling case decorated with black cloisonné squares, which, together with onyx, were repeated on the base. The clock face was embellished with mother-of-pearl inlaid in enamel and lapis lazuli.[49] The nervousness that both Swid and Powell had expressed in an interview about introducing the expensive Architects' Collection

FIGURE 16.26 Left: Candlesticks, c. 1995. The Jewel Stern American Silver Collection, cat. 232; right: Teapot, c. 1995, cat. 231. Swid Powell (Nan Swid Design), Calvin Klein, designer. Silverplate. DMA, JSASC

in the midst of a recession unfortunately turned out to have been justified.[50] Although the mass-produced lines had been extremely profitable, the distressed economy militated against the financial success of this extravagant venture.[51]

In the early 1990s, as the company sought to catch the next wave, Swid Powell expanded its portfolio to include designers from the worlds of fashion, contemporary art, and studio craft. The fashion designer Geoffrey Beene, the photographer Robert Mapplethorpe, the

FIGURE 16.27 *Ellipse* dinner fork, dinner knife, soup spoon, 1995. Swid Powell (Nan Swid Design), Calvin Klein, designer and producer. Silverplate, stainless steel. DMA, JSASC, cat. 233

painter Donald Sultan, the jeweler Robert Lee Morris, and the ceramist Elsa Rady were invited to work with the company. The drift away from the original model of the partnership was articulated in a promotional handout, "Swid Powell Stories," an envelope containing a set of postcard-sized enclosures on which the current offerings were illustrated in line drawings and photographs. The text card read: "The initial collection was instantly a design success and accepted universally by leading retailers as well as introduced into modern design collections of numerous international museums. Updating its alternative approach to design, Swid Powell has created a new grouping for the next generation of retail by combining high style and accessible pricing."[52] "Accessible pricing" would be a key factor for the company's expansion in the 1990s. In continuing to offer designs by Meier, a lively holloware group by the architect Calvin Tsao, and other designs by Rady and Morris, Swid Powell was competing with the silver industry.[53] A leading figure in the American studio craft movement, Elsa Rady (b. 1943) designed dinnerware and a group of silverplated objects for Swid Powell, the latter from prototypes modeled in clay. The first

silverplated object, a "four winged" bowl based on the porcelain pieces she was making in the 1980s, was an immediate success. A tall vase (fig. 16.25) with a single wing, sharply cut away to a point to appear unfurled, was the most striking. Rady's inspiration for this soaring form was the renowned *Bird in Space* (1926) by the sculptor Constantin Brancusi. The vases were produced in Argentina by Plata Lappas S. A., but after fewer than 150 vases were produced, the design was abandoned: the execution of the wing required costly hand cutting, which slowed down production, and the vases tended to crack during fabrication.[54]

The jeweler Robert Lee Morris, who bridged the worlds of fashion and art, was recruited to design a holloware group in harmony with more casual contemporary lifestyles. The group was produced in a material that Swid Powell referred to as "alternative metal."[55] The material was actually Wilton Armetale, a metal alloy made by the Wilton Company of Lancaster County, Pennsylvania. Wilton Armetale and tableware of a similar material called Nambé became popular in the 1990s as easily maintained, stylish alternatives to silver and stainless steel. Wilton Armetale began competing for a share in the silver holloware market as early as 1981 with an advertisement in the *New Yorker* that carried the headline, "Who said your silver had to be silver?"[56] The designs illustrated in the advertisement were, however, not contemporary, unlike those that Morris produced for Swid Powell a decade later.

In 1993 Powell left the company and Swid assumed command. The Swid Powell mark continued for about a year until it was changed to read "Nan Swid Design." The business entered a new phase when Swid signed a licensing agreement with the fashion designer Calvin Klein (b. 1942) to produce and distribute all the tabletop accessories and giftware, regardless of the material, for the Calvin Klein Home collection, which was introduced in 1995. Klein insisted on maintaining the Swid Powell name along with his on the hallmark, and the holloware was stamped accordingly, a tribute to the recognition achieved earlier by the partners.[57] A few silverplated pieces were produced that reflected Klein's modern reductive aesthetic, among them a teapot and candlesticks (fig. 16.26) with the clean, strong lines and proportions associated with his apparel. Also introduced in 1995 was Klein's *Ellipse* (fig. 16.27), a minimalist silverplated flatware pattern, made in Korea, that has slim, elongated handles and a shape somewhat reminiscent of the cutlery that Antonio Piva had designed for San Lorenzo in 1970.[58]

Conditions in the marketplace were changing. In America Swid Powell had stood alone in championing modernist design during the 1980s. Although mass-produced, the objects had a connotation of exclusiveness and were marketed to a discriminating clientele that made its purchases in small lifestyle shops run by people who zealously promoted modernist design and in boutique sections of department stores.[59] In the 1990s established and more moderately priced chain stores, such as Pottery Barn and Crate and Barrel, expanded dramatically and, recognizing that good design was good business, offered their mainstream customers stylish contemporary wares that were affordable.[60] These products were, moreover, accepted by affluent sophisticates for casual entertaining because they were so well designed. The chain stores offered serious competition for department stores. The era of designers' Home Collections was in full swing, too, by the late 1990s. In 1997, Kmart, a discount store leader, announced the Martha Stewart Everyday Home Collection, designed by the noted diva of domesticity, and the following year the fast-growing Target discount retail chain profitably introduced household wares designed by Michael Graves, who had once worked with Swid Powell. The original Swid Powell vision of a small coterie of outstanding architects creating refined, well-designed tabletop accessories had been compromised by the constantly shifting exigencies and requirements of the marketplace. Symptomatic was the oversimplification of Meier's silver objects, for example, so as to reduce their production costs and to make them attractive for middle-market retail chains and department stores.[61] In addition, the Calvin Klein Home collection, which required enormous runs and global distribution, had monopolized Nan Swid Design. This culture was not conducive to Swid's strengths nor did it satisfy the passion for design that had fueled the phenomenal synergy between Swid Powell and its founding architects. Perhaps burned out by then, Swid decided to close the company in 2000 and, in choosing not to sell her name, ended at the millennium a unique and fertile chapter in twentieth-century American decorative and applied arts.

NOTES

1. Alberto Alessi, the third-generation scion of the family and a champion of progressive design, assumed leadership of the company in 1970.

2. Eric Turner, "The Silversmith's Studio San Lorenzo," in *The Work of the Silversmith's Studio San Lorenzo, Milano, 1970–1995,* exh. cat. Victoria and Albert Museum, London (Milan: Electa, 1995), 20; see also Jeannine Falino, "Women Metalsmiths," in Pat Kirkham, ed., *Women Designers in the USA, 1900–2000* (New Haven: Yale University Press, 2000), 240, 243.

3. Angela Vettese, "Silver: Forms for Today," in *Work of the Silversmith's Studio,* 24.

4. Susan Grant Lewin, "Gifts for Christmas: Come Shop with Us!" *House Beautiful* 114 (Nov. 1972): 138. The carafe was priced at $250. Vignelli's bar tool set was soon recognized in the twentieth-century survey exhibition *For the Tabletop* at the American Craft Museum in New York City. Also featured was flatware by Charles Rennie Mackintosh and Josef Hoffmann, as pioneers of modernism, and the contemporary masters John Prip (Reed & Barton's *Dimension*) and Tapio Wirkkala; see *For the Tabletop,* exh. cat. American Craft Museum of the American Craft Council, New York (1980), 35. In 1983 the bar tool set was included in the Philadelphia Museum of Art's exhibition *Design Since 1945;* see Kathryn B. Hiesinger and George H. Marcus, *Design Since 1945,* exh. cat. Philadelphia Museum of Art (1983), 162.

5. In fact, San Lorenzo in Milan, Italy, produced holloware for Tiffany; one example is a sleek, contemporary coffee and tea service; MaryAnn Aurora, Tiffany & Co., letter to author, Apr. 16, 2002; for the service, see Tiffany & Co., *Blue Book* (1983–84), 98.

6. While living in Provence from 1967 to 1979, Van Day Truex, who had been design director since 1955, was a co-director of design and a consultant. George O'Brien was design director from 1967 to 1978. Loring has been the design director since 1979.

7. John Loring, telephone conversation with author, Apr. 5, 2002.

8. John Loring, *Magnificent Tiffany Silver* (New York: Abrams, 2002), 257.

9. "Charles Perry Design in Sterling Silver," Tiffany & Co. advertisement, *Town and Country* 134 (Apr. 1980): 1; and Tiffany & Co., *Blue Book* (1979–80), 138–39.

10. Invitation, courtesy of Charles O. Perry.

11. John Loring, *Magnificent Tiffany Silver* (New York: Abrams, 2001), 249.

12 Victor Carranza, telephone conversation with author, May 25, 2004. Carranza has designed and had made in his workshops in Mexico a *Rose* and a *Woven* collection for Tiffany as well as jewelry.

13. Wendy Goodman, "New Settings: Jewelry Designers Apply Their Artistry to Gracious Objects for the Home," *HG* [House and Garden] 162 (Aug. 1990): 134–37. The other jewelers represented were Izabel Lam, Lisa Jenks, and Robert Lee Morris. See also idem, "Stephen Dweck Domesticates the Great Outdoors," *HG* [House and Garden] 164 (Feb. 1992): 52.

14. Goodman, "New Settings," 136.

15. Ibid., 137.

16. Anne Rosenblum, "Table Manners," *Harper's Bazaar* 124 (Jan. 1991): 123. In 1990 as a result of his Home Collection, Dweck signed a licensing agreement with Sasaki, the prominent Japanese tabletop ware manufacturer, for a line of china.

17. Ted Muehling, "Biographical Notes," n.p. (courtesy of Ted Muehling).

18. Loring McAlpin, letter to author, Jan. 3, 2002.

19. Simone Girner, "Practical Magic," *Departures Magazine* 73 (Oct. 2001): 139.

20. See Amy Sullivan, "Down to Earth," *Harper's Bazaar* 126 (Apr. 1993): 260–63; Julie V. Iovine, "Curves Ahead," *New York Times Magazine*, Sept. 5, 1993, 31; "Liquid Assets Silver," *House and Garden* 168 (Dec. 1996): 89; and "Silver Streak," *New York Times Magazine*, Dec. 21, 1997, 57.

21. Muehling, "Biographical Notes."

22. Notes, *HG* [House and Garden] 164 (July 1992): 22.

23. Notes, *HG* [House and Garden] 162 (Mar. 1990): 52.

24. Notes, *HG* [House and Garden] 163 (Nov. 1991): 47.

25. Officina Alessi, *Tea & Coffee Piazza* (Rome: Shakespeare & Company², 1983). The services were available at the Max Protech Gallery in New York City. In 1988 the Cleto Munari Collection of over thirty postmodern silver holloware and flatware objects, most of them designed by European architects and designers, would be distributed in the United States by Domus, Inc., of New York. Swid and Powell would also have been aware of the progressive Studio-Line china and glassware produced by the Rosenthal China Corp.; see also note 30, below.

26. Annette Tapert, *Swid Powell: Objects by Architects* (New York: Rizzoli, 1990), 17.

27. "Swid Powell Introduces Architect-Designed Objects for the Home," brochure (1984). The architects were remunerated with royalties on sales (Addie Powell, telephone conversation with author, Apr. 23, 2004).

28. J. D. Reed and William Tynan, "Their Plates Are Smashing," *Time* 124 (Dec. 17, 1984): 90.

29. Tapert, *Swid Powell*, 27.

30. In addition, stores were expected to give an opening party for Swid Powell (ibid., 27–28). For the Rosenthal Studio-Line, see Charles L. Venable, *China and Glass in America 1880–1980: From Tabletop to TV Tray*, exh. cat. (Dallas, Tex.: Dallas Museum of Art, 2000), 239, 242–43.

31. Heather Smith MacIsaac, "Coming Home," *HG* [House and Garden] 161 (Dec. 1989): 36.

32. Marc Hacker, telephone conversation with author, Apr. 20, 2004.

33. Tapert, *Swid Powell*, 12.

34. "Swid Powell Introduces Architect-Designed Objects for the Home" (New York: Swid Powell, 1984), 1–2.

35. Tapert, *Swid Powell*, following p. 17.

36. Martin Filler, "The Architectural Tabletop," *House and Garden* 156 (Oct. 1984), 96. Filler found the bowl "unfortunately named." Swid Powell subsequently dropped the name.

37. Alessi made the prototype for Meier's bowl, but would have charged too much to produce it, so Swid and Powell took the prototype to Lunt (Powell, telephone conversation).

38. *Richard Meier: The Architect as Designer and Artist*, exh. cat. Museum for Applied Arts, Frankfurt, Germany (New York: Rizzoli, 2003), 102.

39. "Reed & Barton Introduces the Swid Powell Flatware Accessory Collection," Reed & Barton press release, Oct. 16, 1989 (Jewel Stern Archives, Coral Gables, Fla.). Lunt and Reed & Barton were the only American silver manufacturers that produced objects for Swid Powell.

40. Later Reed & Barton and Swid Powell added five-piece place settings and a matching five-piece Hostess Set in a stainless pattern by Meier and one by the jeweler Robert Lee Morris. Meier's pattern featured a repetitive square motif. A Dessert Serving Set by Ettore Sottsass, consisting of a pie server and an ice cream scoop, was another addition in stainless to the joint venture.

41. See, "Tabletop, Desktop, and Personal Accessories," in *Richard Meier: The Architect*, 102–107.

42. "The Richard Meier Collection," Corning, Inc., *Steuben*, sales catalogue, 2001, 26.

43. Vitali, a fourth-generation silversmith from Rome, Italy, is based in Maplewood, N.J.; Brophy works in Carlyle, Mass.

44. Hacker, telephone conversation. The collection was unveiled at the book party at the Four Seasons Restaurant in New York City. The Peter Joseph Gallery in New York City represented the collection. The objects ranged in price from five thousand to thirty-five thousand dollars.

45. Each of the objects was offered in editions of 20, with the exceptions of Meier's clock (30), Palterer's candelabra (25), Eisenman's candelabra (5), and Gehry's lead-crystal goblets (sold in sets of 6 in an edition of 250).

46. Suzanne Slesin, "Architects Show How to Set a Grand Table," *New York Times*, Nov. 29, 1990, sec. C, p. 6.

47. Like Meier's Framed Vessel Collection for Steuben, the tureen and other silver objects in the Architects' Collection were crafted by Brophy.

48. Lois E. Nesbitt, *Architects' Collection* (New York: Swid Powell, 1990), n.p. Stern's ice bucket, but not the lid or the liner, was stolen from Swid Powell. For Stern's drawing of the ice bucket, see Tapert, *Swid Powell*, 104.

49. Meier's clock was stolen.

50. Slesin, "Architects Show How."

51. According to Addie Powell, the business of selling the mass-produced objects was "extremely profitable" before she left the company in 1993 (Powell, telephone conversation).

52. "The Swid Powell Story," in "Swid Powell Stories," Swid Powell promotional handout (c. 1993) (Stern Archives).

53. The silverplated objects sold as TsAO designs in the early 1990s and designed by Calvin Tsao of the architectural firm Tsao & McKown, included a pitcher, a *Dimple* bowl, a bonbon bowl, *Flip Flop* and *Lantern* candlesticks, and picture frames named *Flip Flop*, *Ripple*, and *Wave*.

54. Elsa Rady, telephone conversations with author, Apr. 18 and 26, 2004.

55. Stanley Tigerman was the only other person to design objects in so-called alternative metal for Swid Powell.

56. "Who said your silver had to be silver?" Wilton Armetale advertisement, *New Yorker* 57 (Nov. 16, 1981): 229.

57. Powell, telephone conversation.

58. *Work of the Silversmith's Studio*, 85. Another Calvin Klein Home flatware pattern, *Triangular*, was a replay of an earlier, forgotten 1950s modernist pattern, *Avanti*, by the Mexican maker Celsa; See "avanti!" Celsa advertisement, *House Beautiful* 101 (June 1959): 91.

59. The independent lifestyle stores were major outlets for the early collections of architect-designed, upscale wares. According to Addie Powell, most of these stores, such as the legendary D. F. Sanders on Madison Avenue in Manhattan and The American Hand in Washington, D.C., were owned and operated by knowledgeable gay men who enthusiastically represented Swid Powell objects and sold significant numbers of them. The AIDS epidemic of the 1980s cast an unexpected shadow on Swid Powell's business as these men succumbed to the disease and their stores closed (Powell, telephone conversation).

60. For Crate and Barrel, see Venable, *China and Glass*, 297, 321–22.

61. Meier continued designing for Swid well into the late 1990s.

CONCLUSION

SILVER AT THE DAWN OF A NEW CENTURY

In the second half of the twentieth century, changes in the fabric of society eroded the time-honored place of silver in the American home.[1] Although informality and casual living had made inroads in the 1930s, the culturally turbulent 1960s accelerated the trend as many members of a younger generation rejected traditional values. Feminism drew more women into the workplace, divorce became commonplace, and households headed by a single parent no longer had the resources nor the luxury of time for elegant dinner parties. The disappearance of servants from most homes made simplified entertaining more appealing even for traditionally minded, affluent families. At all levels of society, formality was relaxed. In this environment the maintenance of silverware became a burden, and goods in materials such as glass, plastic, wood, ceramic, and stainless steel that were easier to care for were preferred. In the 1990s purchases of sterling flatware declined by nearly 50 percent,[2] most brides and others setting up their first households choosing stainless steel for their flatware. A string of newspaper articles in 1994 attested to the status achieved by stainless: "Stainless steel joins the upper crust," "A sterling notion: stainless flatware now adds glamour to tables," and "Best-dressed tables are wearing stainless."[3] Succumbing to the marketplace, Tiffany & Co., the hallowed name in sterling silver, announced its first line of stainless flatware in the year 2000.[4]

In sum, the effect on the silver industry was catastrophic. The high cost of domestic labor encouraged production overseas and further diminished the battered industry through globalization from expanded outsourcing. At the sophisticated, stylish end of the spectrum, the popularity of expensive imported flatware in silverplate, especially from France, continued to grow in the 1990s. Other factors that dampened creativity in designs for industrially produced American silver were the dominance of conservative taste in sterling flatware and the persistence of a strong market for Jensen's silverware. It became fashionable to collect eighteenth- and nineteenth-century antique silver, a development that further depressed the market for holloware. With the exception of objects commissioned by Swid Powell, the production of modernist silver holloware was at a standstill at the end of the 1990s.[5]

An inventory of the major silver manufacturers at the close of the century reveals a complex of mergers, consolidations, and leveraged buyouts—all attempts to survive and make a profit—and illustrates the dire situation in the 1980s and 1990s. In 1983 Katy Industries of Boston purchased Wallace Silversmiths and began negotiating to buy the International Silver Company, which was a subsidiary of Insilco Corporation.[6] In the following year, Katy merged the two manufacturers as Wallace-International Silversmiths. The combined company performed poorly, and in 1986 was sold to Syroco, a company owned by Leonard Florence, the former chairman of Towle, who had been forced to resign shortly

before that company filed for protection from creditors under Chapter 11 in 1985.[7] Towle limped along until 1990, when it did declare bankruptcy, was bought by Syratech (ironically, a company that had been started by Florence), and shut down,[8] a sad end for a company that had been a vital part of Newburyport, Massachusetts, and of the silver industry, for more than two hundred years.

The situation at Gorham and Kirk Stieff was similarly tangled. In 1979 the Stieff Company in Baltimore purchased Samuel Kirk & Son, also in Baltimore, and the merged companies became the Kirk Stieff Corporation. Textron, a conglomerate headquartered in Providence, Rhode Island, had (through its then-subsidiary Lenox China) acquired Gorham in 1982. Four years later, in 1986, when Gorham was moved from Providence to a new plant in Smithfield, Rhode Island, the work force numbered eleven hundred people; in contrast, four thousand people had been employed at the Providence plant early in the century.[9] Textron retained its Gorham division until 1989, when it was sold to Dansk International Designs of Mt. Kisco, New York. In the meantime, Lenox China had been sold to Brown-Forman of Louisville, Kentucky, in 1984, and in 1990 Lenox acquired Kirk Stieff and downsized the company. In 1991, Brown-Foreman acquired Dansk and its subsidiary Gorham. Neither of the conglomerate's silver companies thrived. In October 1998, Brown-Forman announced the termination of Kirk Stieff (a company whose origins can be traced back as far as 1815) and closed its landmark factory in Baltimore in January 1999.[10] By then, employment at Gorham in Smithfield was down to 150 workers.[11] At the end of 2002, Lenox (still a subsidiary of Brown-Forman) announced that the Gorham plant would be closed and that sterling flatware would be produced in Lenox's factory in Pomona, New Jersey, yet another humbling finale for one of the most prestigious American silver manufacturers, whose roots dated back to the early nineteenth century.

By 2000 only four of the major old line silver manufacturers were still in business. These were Reed & Barton (est. 1824) and Lunt Silversmiths (est. 1880), both family owned, Oneida (est. 1877), a public company that had become the dominant American producer of stainless flatware, and Tiffany & Co. (est. 1837), primarily a retailer of silverware now, with more than three dozen company-owned branches. Each firm still maintained an in-house design department, but only part of Oneida's flatware and holloware in silverplate was produced domestically, although all of its sterling flatware was still made in Sherrill, New York, near Oneida.[12] Lunt continued to produce sterling flatware and holloware in Greenfield, Massachusetts, at its home plant; Reed &

Barton, led by descendents of Henry Reed, maintained its production facilities in Taunton, Massachusetts.[13]

In the year 2000, when sterling comprised only 22 percent of the flatware market, who was buying it and what were the criteria for selection?[14] In general, brides picked new patterns that looked like the designs they grew up with or they expanded inherited sets of sterling. They were choosing conservative, traditional patterns that dated from between the end of the nineteenth century and the mid-1940s: Gorham's *Chantilly* (1895), Tiffany's *Shell and Thread* (1905), Reed & Barton's *Francis I* (1907), Durgin's (a subsidiary of Gorham) *Fairfax* (1910), International's *Royal Danish* (1939), Wallace's *Grande Baroque* (1941), Towle's *Old Master* (1942), and Oneida's *Damask Rose* (1946).[15]

In the 1990s, a revival of interest in the modernist patterns of the 1950s and 1960s was propelled by a general growing interest in midcentury taste, exemplified by, for instance, the postwar suburban ranch house and furniture by Charles and Ray Eames. Many in the younger generation sought flatware with sleek, undecorated, sculptural patterns that would be compatible with the architectural style and interior décor of their newly acquired midcentury homes and turned to the antiques market, where they bought used sets of flatware and holloware of the period.[16] The bride who desires sterling for special occasions still registers for the silver that is familiar to her.

At the dawn of a new century, the spirited objects in the exhibition *Modernism in American Silver: 20th-Century Design* have become precious artifacts to be collected by museums and cherished at home as stunning embodiments of our recent past. We are indebted to the bold designers who interpreted the zeitgeist in silver and to the intrepid silver manufacturers who produced this brilliant legacy.

NOTES

1 Gerald W. R. Ward, "'An Handsome Cupboard of Plate': The Role of Silver in American Life," in Barbara McLean Ward and Gerald W. R. Ward, eds., *Silver in American Life: Selections from the Mabel Brady Garvan and Other Collections at Yale University*, exh. cat. (Boston: David R. Godine, in association with Yale University Art Gallery and the American Federation of Arts, 1979), 33–38.

2. Kathleen Yanity, "Gorham Regaining Its Luster," *Providence Journal*, Dec. 29, 1998, sec. E, p. 1.

3. Elaine Markoutsas, "Stainless Steel Joins the Upper Crust," *Chicago Tribune*, Nov. 13, 1994, 1; "A Sterling Notion/Stainless Flatware Now Adds Glamour to Tables" *Minneapolis Star Tribune*, Nov. 19, 1994, 1E; and Elaine Markoutsas, "Best-dressed Tables Are Wearing Stainless," *Houston Chronicle*, Dec. 31, 1994, 4.

4. Julie Dear, "Stainless Flatware Available at Tiffany's for the First Time," *Houston Chronicle*, Nov. 30, 2000, 4. Tiffany's stainless was made in France.

5. The void would be partially filled early in the first decade of the twenty-first century from various venues. Calvin Klein under his own label introduced a limited number of sterling holloware items including a three-piece tea set. E. R. Butler of New York produced a group of silverplated brass candlesticks designed by and produced in collaboration with Ted Muehling. Tiffany & Co. introduced an *Arts and Crafts* holloware collection, an elegant, contemporary interpretation of the early twentieth-century style. In 2004 the fashion designer Vera Wang designed a gift collection of modern silverplated tabletop accessories and flatware, which was produced by the Towle division of Syratech.

6. "Katy Industries: Why It Wants Insilco's Silver," *Business Week*, Oct. 3, 1983, 96.

7. Gregory A. Patterson, "Towle Ex-Owner to Buy Another Silver Maker," *Boston Globe*, Sept. 20, 1986, 33. Through the acquisition Katy gained a share in Syroco.

8. David Mehegan, "Towle Mfg.'s 300-Year Tie to Newburyport Nearing End," *Boston Globe*, July 26, 1990, 33.

9. Yanity, "Gorham Regaining."

10. Nancy Kercheval, "Baltimore's Kirk Stieff Silver Firm Will Cease Operations in January," *Baltimore Daily Record*, Oct. 22, 1998, 5A.

11. Yanity, "Gorham Regaining."

12. Constance L. Hays, "Why the Keepers of Oneida Don't Care to Share the Table," *New York Times*, June 20, 1999, 3.1; and David Gymburch, telephone conversation with author, Sept. 21, 2004. Gymburch is Oneida's public relations manager.

13. No silverplate was manufactured by Lunt in 2000. Reed & Barton's silverplated flatware and holloware was produced domestically.

14. Dear, "Stainless Flatware."

15. Joseph P. Brady, telephone conversation with author, July 26, 2004. Brady, an independent appraiser, is affiliated with the Beverly Bremer Silver Shop, Atlanta, Ga.

16. Ibid.

FORGING THE MODERN: BEYOND INDUSTRY

Kevin W. Tucker
The Margot B. Perot Curator of
Decorative Arts and Design
Dallas Museum of Art

Any study that purports to reveal the origins and scope of modernist design in American silver should be positioned to confront a complex subject laden with preconceptions and inherent contradictions. The exploration that frames *Modernism in American Silver: 20th-Century Design* not only reveals the achievements of the American silver manufacturers and designers, but also charts the difficulties that they met in anticipating the desires of a changing market and in challenging the profoundly historic legacy of silverware in the decades following the *Exposition Internationale des Arts Décoratifs et Industriels Modernes* held in Paris in 1925. Eschewing tradition to offer bold visions of the present and future, the resulting works offer testimony to the most progressive impulses of the industry during the past century. As presented within the opening chapter, the pursuit by American silver manufacturers of novel alternatives to the colonial revival styles that dominated the market for silverware in the 1920s was largely prompted by the growing interest in Danish silver and French *art moderne* design. Emerging in the midst of an American market seeking refuge in expressions of traditional taste, modernism in American silver, as in other media, did not arise as a simple, transient fashion for any one style of silverware. The singular trend of *art moderne* yielded to other realizations of modernism's ideals, reflective of the codification of "modern" as an evolving movement that offered alternatives to conservative work and helping to sustain the importance of silver design throughout the twentieth century. Nevertheless, in recent decades, social changes that have recast our ideal of luxury, and the role of newer, surrogate materials in usurping silver's place and, prior to the revelations of *Modernism in American Silver* and other recent studies, relative unfamiliarity with these aspects of modernist design have altered our perception of silverware and have raised questions about its relevance to contemporary life.[1] In addition, the antimodernist elements of ornamental lavishness with which manufactured silver has customarily been allied have nurtured lingering philosophical challenges to any closer association of silver with expressions of modernity. In many regards, the purportedly democratizing and purifying tenets of modernism, the espousing of unadorned forms, simplified shapes, and machine production, suggest the antithesis of silverware's historically held raison d'être—to offer a continuum of tradition, craftsmanship, and material and decorative sumptuousness. Sustained by the promotional efforts of manufacturers as well as those of individual craftspeople, the image of the silversmith laboring to create a distinctive work by hand remains an indelible, often nostalgic link with the past, a rejection of modernism's regard for technology and model of mass production in favor of a consuming veneration for the precious, handmade object. That within this milieu American silver manufacturers made significant contributions to the realm of

modernism is nothing less than remarkable. Capable of simultaneously evoking potent notions of tradition, modernity, craft, and design, silver of the past century is a complex subject that reflects the creative tensions of a rapidly changing world.

Whereas, in organizing *Modernism in American Silver*, the Dallas Museum of Art has provided an understanding of how modernist ideals realized their fullest expression through the means of industrial production, the study of progressive design in twentieth-century silver can benefit from explorations beyond the domain of the manufacturer. From the Arts and Crafts movement's celebration of the handmade object at the turn of the twentieth century to contemporary work, craftspeople have remained a vital force in shaping the aesthetic development of American silver over the past century. Freed from the manufacturer's constraints of mass production and broader market demands, independent silversmiths could readily pursue their creative impulses for a clientele eager for the individualistic expression such works provided. Essays by Scott Braznell for *The Ideal Home, 1900–1920: The History of Twentieth-Century American Craft* (1993) and Jewel Stern for *Craft in the Machine Age: The History of Twentieth-Century American Craft, 1920–1945* (1995) framed the importance of studio silver from the first half of the century and the broader significance of handmade silverware.[2] Even so, comprehensive studies of American studio silverwork after 1945—an era equally marked by a renewed interest in craft—or over the entirety of the twentieth century have yet to be undertaken. In addition, although singular examples of silver have been included in publications surveying craft of the past century, relatively few silversmiths of the era have been the focus of detailed scholarly examination. In a recently published monograph on the work of William Waldo Dodge, Bruce Johnson offers a greater appreciation of the achievements of one self-taught silversmith working in the 1920s and 1930s, who developed new, patented working techniques and simple forms occasionally suggestive of modernity. But Dodge's sensibilities fully embraced the association with colonial silversmiths and the handmade ideals of the Arts and Crafts movement, and his work presumably appealed to those desirous of finding in it "something in common with fine old silver wrought in earlier times."[3] Suggesting the dichotomy between early modernist concepts and the lingering preindustrial spirit of the Arts and Crafts movement, Dodge's silver was emblematic of the unresolved dialogue between inventive forays in shaping new work and preferences for the familiar that characterized even the most progressive American metalwork in the first decades of the twentieth century.

The museum's previous examination of the industry, *Silver in America, 1840–1940: A Century of Splen-* dor, revealed the technological and cultural changes that shaped the high achievements of late nineteenth-century silverware. Within a vast array of designs available at the turn of the twentieth century, one concept of modern was approached by assimilating the characteristics of what was called "New Art" from Europe. The Art Nouveau styling of the *Martelé* line with which Gorham sought to revitalize the industry presented American consumers with lavish, organic forms expressing a fashionable sympathy with French design. Gorham, however, in an apparent contradiction of its aesthetic, also promoted *Martelé* as the realization of the English Arts and Crafts movement's principles supporting handcrafted goods and the unity of designer and silversmith, noting the laborious handmade method of production and dubbing the line with the French word for "hammered."[4] Even within this attempt to draw on associations with reformist ideals championing the individual, the extravagantly chased naturalistic surfaces and luxurious forms more effectively marked the culmination of the American silver industry's nineteenth-century ornamental achievements rather than serving as an introduction to the ideal of simplicity to which Arts and Crafts reformers aspired. In 1900, as the line was introduced, the American Arts and Crafts movement had already begun to encourage a shift away from the use of decorative techniques and materials that embodied the opulence of the previous century. Within this new appreciation of largely unadorned forms, material properties, and evident construction, the seeds of modernist ideology began to take root.

From the earliest exhibitions of Arts and Crafts metalwork in 1897 at Hull House in Chicago and Copley Hall in Boston, alternatives to commercial silverwork were created by means of a series of societies or guilds formed to provide outlets for amateur craftspeople to exhibit and sell their work.[5] Across the country, the celebration of the handmade was embodied within the membership of these groups, and the rallying call for their efforts was sounded in periodicals published by leading reformers. In his periodical *The Craftsman*, Gustav Stickley, the furniture producer and proselytizer of the Arts and Crafts movement, offered a proclamation "to express function frankly; above all, to be modern." Through a sensitivity to elemental material and structural qualities, the resulting objects could reveal a "vital power" and "promise of progress."[6] Even though there was little ambiguity in portrayals of the inherent value of craft, articles offered viewpoints that illustrated the ongoing challenges in recognizing nascent modernism as a movement based upon principles when many critics considered the concept of the modern to be an essentially European style defined by particular formal properties. The artist Charles Shean presented the dilemma by lauding the series of progressive German interiors at the 1904 *Louisiana Purchase International Exposition* as "wholly modern," and of "New Art" and noting that "it is anything but a simple matter to define the style at the present time, so varied and often so contradictory are its performances; or to predict what its final characteristics will be, or what will be the future scope of its influence." Shean observed that the "ardent search for modernism" was as yet incomplete. "It is not necessary," he said, "nor is it particularly desirable, to have a definition now. We are only witnessing the first experiments—the childhood of a style which is still in its formative period. When the movement can be defined with any approach to scientific accuracy, when its features and characteristics have become set, the work of evolution and growth will have reached its term."[7]

Although the relevance of craft and declarations of its association with modern life were championed within reformist publications, most, including *The Craftsman*, essentially neglected contemporary American silver, praising instead the efforts of individuals in America and Europe who "restored to dignity many materials not heretofore considered costly enough in themselves for objects of luxury."[8] Iron, copper, and brass, carrying evident hammer marks of their working and a warm patina evocative of the dim glow of the forge and hearth, appealed to the romantic, democratic sensibilities imbued in the movement's elevation of common materials and were, unlike silver, suggested as inexpensive and readily available metals for amateur metalsmiths. Finished vessels, lamps, and other articles were offered to consumers through Stickley's catalogues. Similarly, Elbert Hubbard's Roycrofters in East Aurora, New York, produced and sold handmade metal objects to support their own efforts in extolling the virtues of simplicity, work, and individualism. Alongside unsophisticated, quasi-medieval works were designs that in their strikingly architectonic forms, geometric nickel silver detailing, and jade cabochons clearly denoted the influence of European modernist design. Karl Kipp, the leader of the Roycroft Copper Shop after 1909, and his fellow Roycrofter, Dard Hunter, drew heavily from the Wiener Werkstätte for their inspiration, but used silver sparingly.[9] Although silver and silverplate were minor elements or concessions to conventional taste introduced late into the Roycrofters' repertoire—and neither Hubbard's nor Stickley's enterprises were principally dedicated to the production of metalware—their publications and products were among the best-known vehicles for the dissemination of reformist principles and, through marginalization and omission, illustrated the absence of a broader endorsement of silver as a medium of modern expression. Philosophically, silver

FIGURE 1   Bowl, 1907. The Handicraft Shop, Karl F. Leinonen with Mary C. Knight. Silver. Dallas Museum of Art, Discretionary Decorative Arts Fund

too readily recalled the devalued ornamental excesses of previous decades.

Nonetheless, in Boston, Chicago, Cleveland, Detroit, Minneapolis, Pasadena, and elsewhere, smaller collaborative organizations and some individuals, including former employees of leading silver manufacturers, found no such difficulties in producing silverware reflecting Arts and Crafts sensibilities. The quest for simplicity in design encouraged some silversmiths in traditional East Coast centers such as Boston to fashion works that evoked America's colonial past. A punch bowl by the Handicraft Shop (fig. 1) may have appealed to reformist sensibilities in its straightforward handwrought forms and unusual stylized punchwork decoration, but it remained equally recognizable as sympathetic to the larger, more conservative market for colonial revival wares. Other makers rejected historicism in favor of works that drew from the stylization of nature and from England, the spiritual home of the reform movement. Established in 1900, Clara Barck Welles's Kalo Shop in Chicago began, after 1905, to produce copper and silver objects, the earliest of which alternate between boldly angular, paneled forms and wares that recall the English Arts and Crafts silver and pewter sold by Liberty & Co. or works by the designer Charles Robert Ashbee.[10] Within a few years, Kalo's holloware was largely characterized by softly lobed, segmented forms offering, in their most restrained incarnations, an aesthetic that presaged the modernity of a future age and helped sustain the firm's relevance decades beyond the zenith of the American Arts and Crafts movement (fig. 2). Through the efforts of these smaller concerns as well as those of

independent craftspeople, silver as a medium of progressive expression quietly endured during the first three decades of the twentieth century amidst the dominant market for colonial revival style wares.

The Arts and Crafts movement upheld the ideal of handwork as an antidote to what was cast as the soulless, mechanized nature of commercially produced objects and shaped the romanticized image of an individualistic artist-craftsperson who rejected the excesses of revivalist styles as inappropriate to the new century. That the works produced by this generation of disillusioned former silver industry workers and amateur metalworkers varied in style, execution, and resonance with concepts of modernism is hardly unexpected. What was encouraged by their efforts was an entirely new approach to metalware that questioned silver's cherished image through a new reductivist aesthetic and appreciation of functional concerns and anticipated the advent of modernism in the 1920s and 1930s. As silver manufacturers had earlier appropriated the characteristics of Arts and Crafts wares in offering simplified forms bearing evident, if at times machine-applied, hammer marks, studio silversmiths began to be equally willing to produce objects that engaged the stylistic vocabulary of industry. In 1936, within a year after establishing her studio in San Francisco, Margaret De Patta departed from her earlier experiments and began to create jewelry that exhibited the influence of streamlined design in the use of layered, banded metals and elongated, curvilinear forms. With her adoption of this new aesthetic came a highly sophisticated design for silver and copper flatware that, in visual purity and refined form, evoked the image of the machine age as well as any mass-produced object

(fig. 3). De Patta's interests were not limited to the appearance of industry; after World War II she began to experiment with the fabrication of multiples from her jewelry designs. The celebrations of mechanization in the 1930s and 1940s collided with a renewed interest in craft and individualistic expression which intensified in the late 1940s and early 1950s. Silversmiths such as John Prip, Robert King, and Alexandra Solowij entered the industry as designers and, with a craftsperson's understanding of material, adapted their personal vision to the requirements of production. Conventions recalling traditional silver were disregarded as the machine became an accepted part of the craftsperson's world, as much as craft remained a part of industry. Throughout the twentieth century, what was at first offered as a balm for the impersonal nature of production forged its own contributions to the evolving natures of modernism and American silver.

The Dallas Museum of Art's realization of an unparalleled collection of manufactured American silver of the nineteenth and twentieth centuries has placed it in a unique position to transform the understanding of these works and their meaning within the context of two centuries of domestic and commercial change, the rise of industrial design and, in this exhibition, modernism within the American silver industry. Even so, the subject of studio silver offers another rich perspective to explore. From the earlier, provocative dialogue with factory work and contributions to the visualization of proto-modernist principles to the affirmation of personal expression, such work established a significant lineage within the evolution of progressive twentieth-century metalware. Now, as the boundaries of art, craft, and design are debated anew, an understanding of the relationships among these realms will be crucial to our awareness of the meaning and continued relevance of silver.

Although the Arts and Crafts movement yielded to changes in taste and fashion, its works spawned an acceptance of individual expression that helped sustain studio craft throughout the last century. So too does modernism transcend its time. Without the conceptual meaning that context once provided, its realizations have also been neatly categorized by their visual characteristics as styles, and history has assumed them to be confident standard-bearers of another era. Even so, the word *modern* retains an uncanny ability to invade our consciousness and defy attempts to confine it wholly to an earlier age. Modernism's principles will remain its legacy, just as the renewed appreciation for and enduring validation of studio work remain that of design reformers of the turn of the twentieth century. Regardless of the claims of superceding fashions and styles, these values remain today as elements whose

tensions resonate with our fundamental hopes for the future and need for a meaningful past. As creative individuals engage silverwork in new ways, and as manufacturers are challenged to seek new ways to reinvigorate the market, the question is rightly raised, what will the ever-shifting intersections of craft and industry, modern and old bring to silver of the twenty-first century?

FIGURE 3   Flatware, 1936. Margaret De Patta. Silver, copper, stainless steel. Dallas Museum of Art, the Patsy Lacy Griffith Collection, gift of Patsy Lacy Griffith by exchange

NOTES

1. Herbert Muschamp, "Silver's Shiny Journey from Craft to Art," *New York Times*, Oct. 24, 2003, 31. For a discussion of the perception of modernism as viewed through Viennese silver, see Christopher Wilk, "Looking at the Past Through Modernist Eyes," in Michael Huey, ed., *Viennese Silver: Modern Design, 1780–1918*, exh. cat. (Ostfildern-Ruit: Hatje Cantz Verlag, 2003), 363–67.

2. W. Scott Braznell, "Metalsmithing and Jewelrymaking, 1900–1920," in Janet Kardon, ed., *The Ideal Home, 1900–1920: The History of Twentieth-Century American Craft*, exh. cat. (New York: Abrams, in association with the American Craft Museum, 1993), 55–63; Jewel Stern, "Striking the Modern Note in Metal," in Janet Kardon, ed., *Craft in the Machine Age, 1920–1945: The History of Twentieth-Century American Craft*, exh. cat. (New York: Abrams, in association with the American Craft Museum, 1995), 122–34.

3. William W. Dodge Jr., *Maker of Hand Wrought Silver* (Asheville, N.C., 1935), brochure, reproduced in Bruce E. Johnson, *Handwrought Silver and Architecture: The Artistry of William Waldo Dodge*, exh. cat. (Asheville, N.C.: Asheville Art Museum, 2005), 36.

4. Charles L. Venable, *Silver in America, 1840–1940: A Century of Splendor*, exh. cat. (New York: Dallas Museum of Art, 1994), 257–58.

5. For a survey of the leading schools and societies supporting handmade metalwork at the turn of the twentieth century, see Braznell, "Metalsmithing and Jewelrymaking," 55–63.

6. Gustav Stickley, "Thoughts Occasioned by an Anniversary: A Plea for a Democratic Art," *The Craftsman* 3, no. 1 (October 1904): 46.

7. Charles M. Shean, "The New Art: A Personal and Creative Art," *The Craftsman* 8, no. 5 (August 1905): 609.

8. Ibid., 608.

9. Beginning in their catalogue of metalwork in 1919, Roycroft offered selected copper wares with a silverplated finish, though some works were produced in silverplate several years prior to this date. Sterling silver was rarely used, but notably in jewelry made by Dard Hunter; see Robert Rust, et al., "Alchemy in East Aurora: Roycroft Metal Arts," in Marie Via and Marjorie B. Searl, eds., *Head, Heart and Hand: Elbert Hubbard and the Roycrofters*, exh. cat. (Rochester, N.Y.: University of Rochester Press, 1994), 75–96.

10. Sharon S. Darling, *Chicago Metalsmiths* (Chicago: Chicago Historical Society, 1977), 45.

BIOGRAPHIES OF SELECTED DESIGNERS

Of the numerous designers of silverware in America since 1925, those who have made important contributions to the silver industry but are less well known have been included here. Designers whose lives and careers have been extensively documented in other publications have been omitted, as have those whose major work has already been addressed in this book. Here the emphasis is on illuminating the careers of the unknown and augmenting the information on the known. These biographies have been pieced together over many years and result from an intricate web of research that includes hundreds of telephone calls and voluminous correspondence, interviews with living designers, with family members of those deceased, and with retired employees of silver manufacturers, research in company archives, and the perusal of wills and probate documents as well as of social security and cemetery records. Persistence played a large part in this quest, as did serendipity. The records of this pursuit form a part of the Jewel Stern Archives, which will be given to the Dallas Museum of Art.

Ward Bennett (1917–2003)
b. Washington Heights, New York

Bennett was reaching the apex of his varied career in fashion, architectural, interior, and product design in the 1960s when he was engaged by Tiffany & Co. to design tableware. A maverick and adventurer who left home and school at the age of thirteen, Bennett first worked in the fashion industry. In the late 1930s in Paris, the friendship he formed with the sculptor Constantin Brancusi influenced Bennett's reverence for "the pure line." Another role model was Le Corbusier: "From Corbu—whose great thing," said Bennett, "was the cube, the cone, the cylinder, the spiral—I learned that vocabulary in design is invariable." Returning to New York from Paris, he shared studio space for a time with the sculptor Louise Nevelson, made ceramic sculpture that was exhibited in the Whitney Annual of 1944, and studied painting with Hans Hofmann. In 1946 the brass and silver jewelry that he had made in Mexico the previous year was included in the exhibition *Modern Handmade Jewelry* at the Museum of Modern Art in New York. Bennett gradually became known for his minimalist and high-tech interiors and furniture design, and he was a prodigious designer of objects. Summing up his philosophy, Bennett said: "In life and design, try to pull it all down to a minimum." His tableware in silver for Tiffany embodied this ideal, as did his production-line, independently marketed bowl in silverplate of about 1980, created at the time when Bennett was considered "the father of minimalism" in design.

Nord Bowlen (1909–2001)

b. Mansfield, Massachusetts

Nord Bowlen was the son of William C. Bowlen, one of the founders of Rogers, Lunt & Bowlen Silversmiths, a company that has marketed its products under the name of Lunt Silversmiths since 1935. He graduated from the Rhode Island School of Design in 1930 and entered the firm. Bowlen, who was the design director for twenty-six years, created *Eloquence* (1953), which ranked, in 1974, as Lunt's all-time best-selling sterling pattern. Although most of his flatware was conservative, in the mid-1950s he did design an innovative pattern for which he combined sterling with molded handles of DuPont's black Zytel nylon. Appropriately called *Contrast* (1956), the flatware was intended to fit in with the casual lifestyle that gained acceptance after World War II, but it did not sell well. *Raindrop* (1959) was an undecorated sculptural pattern of Bowlen's that was more typical of the 1950s.

Carl Conrad Braun (1905–1998)

b. Joliet, Illinois

An architect and industrial designer, Carl Conrad Braun graduated from the University of Illinois in 1927 and became an assistant professor in architecture and design at the school. In the early 1930s he traveled in Europe for a year studying design before moving to New York City, where he worked for three years for the architects of the Rockefeller Center. In 1936, as a result of his own initiative, Braun was engaged by Reed & Barton as an outside consultant. He designed the *Jubilee* sterling flatware pattern in 1936 and in the same year he began his twenty-year-long architecture practice in New York City. For Reed & Barton he also designed the elaborate *Vogue* sterling tea service for which he used the *Jubilee* handle motif. In 1939 he approached the International Silver Company and was engaged to design a contemporary stainless steel pattern as well as the extensive *Tropical* holloware line in silverplate. While practicing architecture, Braun was a consultant for twenty years in the design of hearing aids for the Sonotone Corporation of Elmsford, New York. A hearing aid that he had designed in 1957 was included in the traveling exhibition *20th Century Design: U.S.A.* (1959–1960). Braun moved to Greenwich, Connecticut, in the mid-1950s and continued practicing architecture there until his retirement. He was a member of the Architectural League of New York and of the American Institute of Architects.

Kurt Eric Christoffersen (1926–1981)

b. Ringsted, Denmark

A severe injury to his throat at the age of two from accidentally swallowing a toxic substance in the family kitchen led Christoffersen to Boston in 1947 for surgery to remedy the residual damage. It was a positive experience and he was determined to return to the United States. Christoffersen had been trained as a gold- and silversmith during a five-year apprenticeship in Copenhagen at the renowned firm of A. Michelsen, jewelers to the Royal Danish Court. In 1949 he graduated from the Academy of Arts and Crafts in Copenhagen and, at a ceremony attended by King Frederik IX and Queen Ingrid of Denmark, Christoffersen received a Silver Medal for Excellence, the highest award granted by the Danish gold- and silversmiths guild. The award included a scholarship to study in the United States and Christoffersen left for Boston soon after graduation. In Boston he became a salesman for Shreve, Crump & Low, an exclusive jewelry store, and learned about American taste and the marketplace. During his five-year association with the firm, Christoffersen worked nights as a waiter in order to fund his independent ventures in silverware and jewelry, which he exhibited in local libraries and in a large savings institution in downtown Boston. A representative of the International Silver Company happened to see these exhibited pieces and was impressed. As a result Christoffersen was engaged in January 1955 to invigorate the International Sterling Craft Associates division, which had languished after the untimely death of Alphonse La Paglia (1907–1953), with whom the division had been organized in 1952. Christoffersen was installed in La Paglia's former studio on Colony Street in Meriden, Connecticut, and, as International had acquired the rights to La Paglia's designs, those were offered jointly with Christoffersen's under the umbrella of Sterling Craft Associates. In contrast to La Paglia's naturalistic decoration in the Jensen taste, Christoffersen's holloware was abstract, predominantly conical in form, and devoid of decoration. Although prized now, in the 1950s his designs had little popular appeal.

By 1958 Christoffersen was no longer working at International. For the next seven years he was the chief designer of the Artistic Wire Products Company in nearby East Hampton, and later in Norwich and Taftville, Connecticut. This firm specialized in housewares and giftware and, from 1960 through 1964, Christoffersen applied for six design patents, which were assigned to Artistic Wire Products, among them designs for a rack for trays, a bowl caddy, a holder for a carafe, and two baker's cooking racks. He also designed decorative planters and a wide assortment of wire accessories, including small furniture. Compared to his aesthetic accomplishments while working for International's Craft Associates, these wares, although creative, were mundane. Christoffersen left Artistic Wire Products in 1965 to work for the fledgling United States Agency for International Development (USAID, instituted 1961) as a consultant to modernize the national silver industries of Peru and Bolivia, *Artesanías del Peru* and *Artesanías Bolivianas*. He left South America in 1968 for the U.S. Virgin Islands, a former Danish colony, where he was briefly associated with the Glass Slipper, a store in St. Thomas that specialized in Danish silver, Swedish crystal, English china, and other imports. Later in 1968 he returned permanently to Ringsted, Denmark, with his Peruvian wife and their infant daughter Lisa, thus ending a two-decades-long adventure in the Americas.

Donald H. Colflesh (b. 1932)
b. Cleveland, Ohio; lives in New York City

Donald Colflesh studied at the Cleveland Institute of Art for two years and was influenced in his design studies by members of the faculty: John Paul Miller, Frederick Miller, and William DeHart. Afterward he entered the Pratt Institute in Brooklyn, New York. For the summer of his first year he attended the Hans Hofmann School of Fine Arts in Provincetown, Massachusetts. While he was at Pratt, the Gorham Company recruited him, and in 1956, a year after he received a bachelor of arts degree in industrial design, he began working as a holloware designer at Gorham. According to Colflesh, his "purpose for being there" was to provide a "contemporary dimension." Hence, early in the course of his employment he was sent, at Gorham's expense, to study design in France, Italy, and England. In 1959, he designed a sleek cylindrical beverage mixer and a free form bowl, both in silverplate. His most significant creation was the sterling silver *Circa '70* holloware line, which he had designed in 1958 but was not marketed until 1960. None of his flatware designs was produced. Colflesh left Gorham and silverware design in 1962. He worked for Walter Dorwin Teague Associates (from about 1963 until 1969) and for other companies, mainly in graphics and packaging design, until opening his own firm, Donald Colflesh Design. Among his principal clients was Procter and Gamble, for whom he designed a squeeze bottle.

Helen Hughes Dulany (1885–1968)
b. Bismarck, North Dakota

Helen Hughes Dulany was the only daughter and one of five children of Alexander Hughes, the first attorney general of North Dakota. Her father became a multimillionaire in the electric utility business, which he had entered in the early 1900s. In about 1910, her older brother George developed the electric range, the first home stove to use electricity, and by the end of the decade his company had merged with Hotpoint and General Electric. Helen Hughes was living in Minneapolis, Minnesota, when she married George W. Dulany Jr. (1877–1959), a wealthy, divorced lumberman, in 1913. The couple moved to Chicago in 1920, and Helen Dulany embraced the life of a socialite.

In 1931 she became seriously ill and was considered a hopeless invalid. Although she had never studied art, she began modeling clay as a hobby and discovered her talent for design. She recuperated and later that year she founded the Helen Hughes Dulany Studio from the Dulanys' penthouse apartment at 936 Shore Drive. By 1934 her striking, modern table accessories in chromium, glass, brass, wood, and stainless steel were being noted in chic magazines such as *House Beautiful, Arts and Decoration,* and *Country Life in America.* That same year she was listed in a "Directory of Contemporary Designers" in the periodical *Creative Design* as "perhaps the first person in America to design and fashion stainless steel for use in table appointments." At the time she was a consultant with the Chicago architectural firm Holabird & Root on interiors for the Burlington Railroad; she also designed tableware for the new Burlington Zephyr train and hotel dinnerware for Buffalo Potteries. Dulany designed holloware in silverplate and these pieces, as well as her other metalware, carried her mark: HHD STUDIO. In 1939, in an installation of streamlined furniture and decorative arts, the San Francisco Museum of Art included a sleek vase and covered dish by Dulany, and she gave a lecture there on industrial design. During this period her marriage collapsed and the Dulanys divorced at the end of 1936. In the *New York Times* notice of the divorce proceedings, it was reported that she owned "a factory, manufacturing household accessories and [was] retained as a designer by many large firms." Ironically, the last time her name was mentioned in print as a designer was in an article, "Women Rising Fast in Field of Design," by the journalist Anne Petersen, which was published in the *New York Times* in January 1937: Dulany was recognized as "the inventor of a new method of backing glass with metal," and as "the first woman to design stoves, having restyled the General Electric line." The divorce ended her brilliant, meteoric career as an industrial designer. In January 1938, after touring around the world, a journey that was followed in the society columns of the *Chicago Daily Tribune*, she married Atherton Richards, a prominent businessman in Honolulu. The Japanese attack on Pearl Harbor, Hawaii, in 1941 prompted their move to Washington, D.C., and Helen Hughes Dulany Richards began a new career as a "roving editor" for the Reader's Digest Association. She died in New York City in 1968 at the age of eighty-four. A brother was her only survivor.

Merle Fenelon Faber (1891–1980)
b. Carpinteria, California

In the 1930s, Merle F. Faber, a mechanic by trade and a manufacturer of tools and dies, operated a company in Milbrae, California, that produced pressed metal parts for model railroads. In 1943 the business was moved to San Francisco, where Faber did government work for the war effort. After World War II, he began making silverplated holloware and accessories as Merle F. Faber Products, San Francisco. The holloware line may have continued into the early 1950s. According to a niece, Faber did not attend a design school, nor did he employ staff designers. Instead, he adapted the ideas of others from books and catalogues. Because many of his collectible objects have the sleek, streamlined look of the 1930s and are trimmed with black or white plastic, they are mistakenly dated from that decade. The Merle F. Faber Manufacturing Company for pressed metals was last listed in the San Francisco city directory in 1960. Faber, a Christian Scientist, was married, but had no children.

Virginia Hamill (1898–1980)
b. Chicago, Illinois

Virginia Hamill was born into a socially prominent family in Chicago. An uncle was on the board of the Art Institute of Chicago. Her mother, the independent daughter of a newspaper editor, was widowed young and took the ten-year-old Virginia, an only child, to Europe, where she attended schools in Switzerland, Italy, and France and mastered several languages. After returning to America at the age of sixteen to make her social debut, she was enrolled in Mt. Vernon Junior College in Washington, D.C. and, later, in Parsons School of Design in New York City. She soon became an advisor on merchandising and the styling of home furnishings. An early client was the Lord & Taylor department store. Hamill made her mark as the executive director of Macy's two groundbreaking exhibitions, *Exposition of Art in Trade* in 1927 and *International Exposition of Art in Industry* in 1928. At about the time of the latter exhibition, the International Silver Company engaged Hamill as a product stylist to modernize holloware. She is best known for her styling of silverplated dinette sets by the staff designer Jean G. Theobald. International is her only recorded client in the silver industry. By 1929 she established her own business as a "decorative art consultant" to manufacturers. Among her early clients was Cannon Mills, for whom she introduced the first colored bath towels and linens. In 1935 she designed the general background of the *Industrial Arts Exposition* at the Rockefeller Center, and from 1935 to 1944 she was the interior decoration editor of *Woman's Home Companion*. She was also a contributing editor to *House and Garden* for many years. Hamill married the banker and businessman Lincoln Johnson in 1930. In 1953 the couple moved to Tucson, Arizona, where Hamill was active in the arts community and served as a board member of the Tucson Museum of Art.

Lillian V. M. Helander (1899–1973)
b. Providence, Rhode Island

The daughter of Swedish immigrants, Lillian Valborg Mariea Helander was a graduate of the Rhode Island School of Design. There her talent for fine detail was recognized by an instructor who encouraged her to enroll in an evening class in silverware design. Helander became a pioneering woman designer in the male-dominated silver industry. Her major work was at the International Silver Company, where she designed flatware and holloware from 1932 to 1962. Among her many sterling flatware patterns were *Serenity* (1940), *Spring Glory* (1942), *Processional* and *Tranquility* (1947), and *Queen's Lace* (1949); Holmes & Edwards's *Danish Princess* (1938) in silverplate was another. Helander designed International's souvenir flatware for the *Century of Progress Exposition* in Chicago in 1933, the *Golden Gate International Exposition* in San Francisco in 1939, and the 1939 New York World's Fair, and she designed a spoon to commemorate the visit of the king and queen of England to the United States and Canada in 1939. Her *Modern Colonial* tea and coffee service, designed for 1847 Rogers Bros., was exhibited at the *Golden Gate International Exposition*. Earlier in her career, between 1925 and 1931 and before she joined International, Helander worked for Gorham and for Oneida, designing, for example *Avion,* silverplated flatware in 1929 for Oneida. Helander was listed in *Who's Who in American Women, Who's Who in American Art,* and *Who's Who in the East.*

Richard L. Huggins (b. 1929)

b. Vigo County (outside Terra Haute), Indiana; lives in Avon, New York

In 1955 Huggins graduated from Pratt Institute in Brooklyn, New York. An industrial designer, not a craftsman, he worked as a staff designer for Gorham from 1955 to 1957 and, for the next two years, taught in the industrial design department of the University of Illinois-Urbana. In 1959, he returned to Gorham as assistant director of design and later became director. He is best known for the holloware service he designed in 1961 for the USS *Long Beach*, the United States Navy's first nuclear-powered cruiser. Huggins designed three modern sterling flatware patterns, *Stardust* (1957) and *Sea Rose* (1958) with matching holloware, and *Firelight* (1959). He also designed ten stainless steel patterns for Gorham. In 1962, Huggins left both Gorham and his career in silver design to become the director of design for Bausch and Lomb, a position he held until 1976.

Robert J. King (b. 1917)

b. Madison, Wisconsin; lives in Wallingford, Connecticut

Robert King graduated in 1941 from the University of Wisconsin, where he was a student of John Van Koert's. From 1939 to 1941 he worked in Van Koert's commercial studio, making jewelry and small novelties using the lost-wax process. During World War II King served in the Army Air Forces from 1943 to 1946. Soon after he was discharged in 1946, he entered the School for American Craftsmen in Alfred, New York, studying enameling and metalwork. Among the faculty there were Mitzi Otten, Lauritz Christian Eichner, and John Prip. In 1949 King joined the design department of Towle Silversmiths, initially under Van Koert. A consummate craftsman, King himself made the models for *Contour* flatware (1950) and afterward for the holloware. Following a suggestion made to Van Koert by a museum curator, King's pistol grip knife became the prototype for the flatware. Independent of Towle, King worked in silver and enamel and, during the 1950s, received awards for pieces included in such exhibitions as *Designer-Craftsmen U.S.A. 1953*, the *Wichita Decorative Arts Annual* in 1954, *Fiber, Clay, Metal* in 1957, and those sponsored by the Sterling Silversmiths Guild of America in 1957 and 1958, all arising from competitions. His handmade work was exhibited in the American Pavilion at the Brussels World's Fair in 1958. After thirteen years with the company, King left Towle in 1962 to become a staff designer at International Silver. For International's Moon Room exhibit at the 1964 New York World's Fair, King designed the unique *Celestial Centerpiece*, candelabra, and candlesticks, and his earlier carafe was also displayed. King's work appeared in the prestigious traveling exhibitions, *Objects USA* in 1970 and *Forms in Metal, 275 Years of Metalsmithing in America* in 1975. He retired from International in 1977. In 1983 his *Contour* flatware appeared in the Philadelphia Museum of Art exhibition *Design Since 1945* and his work is in the collections of the Museum of Modern Art, in New York, the Museum of Fine Arts in Boston, and the Museum of Arts & Design (formerly the American Craft Museum) in New York, the St. Paul Gallery and School of Art, and the Memorial Art Gallery, University of Rochester.

Belle Kogan (1902–2000)

b. Ilyashevka, Russia (Ukraine)

Belle (Bella) Kogan, the oldest of eight children, emigrated with her family from Russia in 1906, when she was four years old. The family settled in Bethlehem, Pennsylvania, where her father had a jewelry store and sold silverware. Kogan's first art teacher recognized her potential and directed her to a mechanical drawing class in which she was the only girl. She excelled in the subject and was invited to teach the course after graduating from high school in 1920. With the money earned she entered Pratt Institute in Brooklyn, but left shortly afterward when her family moved to New York City and her father needed her help in operating the new store. During the eight years she spent working at the store, she honed her business skills and designed settings for jewelry. Simultaneously she pursued her dream of becoming a portrait painter by studying with Boardman Robinson at the Art Students League and at the Winold Reiss Art School. In 1929, at the onset of the Depression, her father's business failed and an unexpected opportunity for Kogan to design industrial silver materialized. While she was dining at a restaurant, a stranger at a nearby table asked to see her sketchbook. The stranger was James W. Jennings, the co-owner of the Quaker Silver Company of Attleboro, Massachusetts. Coincidentally, Kogan had sold many of Quaker's salt and pepper shakers at her father's store. Impressed with her drawing, Jennings persuaded a reluctant Kogan to design a line of pewter and, later, silver. She was invited to visit the factory and then offered a studio on the premises. The inducement was a paid summer course in design at New York University as a prelude to employment. In Attleboro she learned manufacturing from the ground up and attended night school at the Rhode Island School of Design on a scholarship arranged by Jennings. In 1930 she was sent abroad by Quaker for over a year to study silverware design at the Kunstgewerbeschule in Pforzheim, Germany. During her sojourn in Europe, Kogan traveled to Czechoslovakia, Austria, northern Germany, and Paris, absorbing design. Although she continued to design for Quaker intermittently through the 1950s, she grew restless not long after her return and left for New York to expand her scope of industrial design and the roster of her clients. In 1933, during the Depression, she opened an office. An early client was the Keystone Silver Company of Philadelphia, Pennsylvania, for whom she designed pewter holloware in 1934. With perseverance Kogan secured enough work to have her own showcase of objects at the *Industrial Arts Exposition* at the Rockefeller Center in 1935. She was in good company. Nearby was a display of John Vassos's *Streamline* chromium-plated flatware and *Ultra* silverplated holloware produced by R. Wallace & Sons. Other designers exhibiting works in silverplate were Alfons Bach for Keystone and Peter Mueller-Munk for Poole Silver; International Silver, too, had a large display. Although Kogan did not exhibit silver, she was contacted by Reed & Barton for a "special assignment" to meet the "growing demand for modern design in silverware." Introduced in 1936, Kogan's holloware designs in sterling and silverplate, the most outstanding a mesh of modern classicism and streamline, were selected for an influential exhibition of silver at the Brooklyn Museum in 1937. In January 1937, Kogan's first essay into what was to become a passionate public advocacy of silver in the home, an article entitled "Modern Trend in Silverware Design," was published in the trade periodical *Jewelers' Circular-Keystone*. Kogan wrote a sophisticated appreciation of the development of contemporary silverware in the years between the Metropolitan Museum's two industrial art exhibitions in 1929 and 1934. Dozens of enthusiastic articles followed on the heels of her first; in many she stressed the importance of consumer education and in all she proved a boon to the industry. Holding that sterling was "the symbol of fine living in America," she frequently remarked that "silver is the jewelry of the table." She foresaw the trend toward Scandinavian design and made a pilgrimage to those countries in 1937. Her next silverware commission came from Samuel Kirk & Son, of Baltimore, for whom she designed *Severn* in 1940, in essence a traditional sterling flatware and holloware pattern that was, nonetheless, considered modern for the conservative firm. Her *Cedric* and *Windsor* sterling holloware lines for Quaker in the 1940s were influenced by Scandinavian silverware, as was her *Rope* line for Towle (1948). In 1946 the Philadelphia Art Alliance gave Kogan a solo exhibition that highlighted her work in five media, silver, glass, ceramics, wood, and plastics. In her silverware designs Kogan never surpassed the modernist

lines that she had developed for Reed & Barton in the 1930s. Surmounting the obstacles inherent in a male-dominated field, Kogan succeeded as a contract product designer and contributed to several professional organizations beginning with the American Designers Institute (Industrial Designers Society of America). Devoted to her career, Kogan did not marry until her early fifties. In 1970 Belle Kogan-Watman retired to Israel.

Paul A. Lobel (1899–1983)
b. Baku, Romania

When he was an infant, Paul Lobel's family immigrated to the United States and settled on Manhattan's Lower East Side. He studied commercial art at the Pratt Institute in Brooklyn and illustration with Boardman Robinson at the Art Students League. The turning point in Lobel's career was the encounter in his mid-twenties with sculptural *art moderne* at the *Exposition Internationale des Arts Décoratifs et Industriels Modernes* in Paris in 1925. On his return home he allied himself with exponents of the modern movement in decorative art such as Eugene Schoen, who exhibited his early metalwork. In 1929 he and Leo J. Uris formed Lobel-Uris, a studio workshop with Lobel as designer for the production of contemporary metal and glass furnishings and accessories, among them, lamps, andirons, screens, and doorstops, some in whimsical linear shapes, others severely modern. Lobel-Uris worked in a variety of metals including cold rolled steel, bronze, chromium, and brass. In 1931, Lobel's designs were included in four exhibitions: *Decorative Metalwork and Cotton Textiles: The Third International Exhibition of Contemporary Industrial Art,* organized by the American Federation of Arts; the Metropolitan Museum of Art's *Twelfth Exhibition of Contemporary American Industrial Art;* an exhibition sponsored by the American Union of Decorative Artists and Craftsmen at the Brooklyn Museum; and the annual exhibition of the Architectural League of New York. Although Lobel did not specialize in tableware, a dramatic coffee service of cylindrical form with rectilinear handles that appeared to slice into the vessels, which he designed in 1931, may have been the catalyst for a commission from International Silver for a service to be included in the exhibition *Contemporary American Industrial Art* in 1934. In addition to the brilliantly conceived spherical coffee service, Lobel designed a cocktail shaker that was also executed by International for the exhibition. Somewhat modified, both prototypes went into production. The only other documented industrial silver tableware that Lobel designed for International was a child's three-piece silver set that was included in the *Industrial Arts Exposition* sponsored by the National

Alliance of Art and Industry at Rockefeller Center in 1935. In the early 1940s, Lobel's work shifted away from large forged pieces to independently made small-scale sculpture and jewelry.

Robert Evans Locher (1888–1956)
b. Lancaster, Pennsylvania

Robert Locher was an architect before establishing himself in New York City as a set designer, first with the Washington Square Players, and later in London. In Paris he worked for the influential couturier Paul Poiret. Inspired by the *Exposition Internationale des Arts Décoratifs et Industriels Modernes* in 1925, Locher became an active participant in the milieu that advanced modernism in the United States. He exhibited a mirror in Macy's *Exposition of Art in Trade* in 1927 and a lamp in Macy's *International Exposition of Art in Industry* in 1928, and he was a founding member of the American Designers' Gallery. For that group's first exhibition in 1928, he designed a foyer described in *Arts & Decoration* as a "fairy story" of crystal and glass, with black and gold mirrors and small ottomans upholstered in yellow leather. Locher also exhibited in the group's second and last exhibition in 1929 and was commissioned to design glamorous public spaces for the Hotel Nacional in Havana, Cuba, which opened in 1930. Locher joined the American Union of Decorative Artists and Craftsmen (AUDAC), and his chromium-plated and frosted glass dressing table lamp was illustrated in the union's *Annual of American Design 1931*. On the editorial staff of *House and Garden*, Locher also wrote for other prominent shelter magazines such as *Vogue, Home and Field, Country Life, Interior Architecture and Decoration*, and *Vanity Fair*, illustrated books, and designed book jackets. At one time he taught at the New York School of Fine and Applied Art.

A colorful man of many talents, Locher was the inspired choice of Rogers, Lunt & Bowlen Silversmiths to design a new sterling flatware and holloware pattern during the Depression. Hoping to stimulate sales, the manufacturer capitalized on Locher's international renown in the advertisement that announced, in 1934, *Modern Classic* flatware, Locher's first industrial silver commission, and included his signature in the hallmark of all *Modern Classic* holloware. A photograph of Locher appeared in the advertisement with a caption extolling his career as "one of America's most important contemporary designers."

Tommi Parzinger (1903–1981)
b. Munich, Germany

A prolific and versatile designer of furniture, fabrics, wallpapers, lighting fixtures, tableware, porcelain figures, perfume bottles, posters, ecclesiastical vessels and vestments, and interiors, Parzinger also designed modern silverware. His precocious bent for design manifested itself early. He attended the Kunstgewerbeschule in Munich and later studied in Berlin and Vienna. A prize in a poster competition brought him to the United States for the first time in 1932 or 1933 and, prompted by the political situation in Germany, he returned permanently to New York City in 1934 or 1935. Like that of many other creative European émigrés in the decorative arts, Parzinger's work was introduced to Americans by Rena Rosenthal, the sister of the architect Ely Jacques Kahn, in her decorative and applied arts shop on Madison Avenue and Forty-ninth Street. Some of his early work in silver for Rosenthal was shown in silver exhibitions mounted in 1937 at the Metropolitan Museum of Art and the Brooklyn Museum, and his enamel and pewter work was shown in the *Golden Gate International Exposition* in San Francisco in 1939. As a result of his meteoric success and favorable notice in the media, Parzinger had his own home furnishings business by 1939. At the end of that year, his line of handwrought silver was featured in "Silver in Modern Dress," an illustrated profile in *Life Magazine*. In the Metropolitan Museum of Art's *Contemporary American Industrial Art* exhibition in 1940, Parzinger showed enameled silver candelabra.

Parzinger's major American silver designs can be divided broadly into two periods: from 1939 through 1942, he was designing handwrought sterling holloware and accessories that were produced in very small numbers, with a few in silverplate and enameled; in the 1950s he was designing primarily objects in silverplate to be produced in quantity by Dorlyn Silversmiths and Mueck-Cary of New York City and Oneida Silversmiths. Almost all of the handwrought silver was made by the silversmith Peter Reimes, a German émigré who had attended art school with Parzinger. Otto Rasmussen, a Dane who had learned the craft from his father, also executed silver for Parzinger. As an apprentice Felix Balbo assisted both silversmiths. William Stark, another German émigré who later worked for the jeweler David Webb, was Parzinger's enamelist. Parzinger's designs from each period can be distinguished by their marks. Handwrought silver that has come to light is stamped "Parzinger" in script and has a conjoined "RP" in which the "R" was reversed. The initials stand for Reimes and Parzinger. In about 1952 or 1953, Parzinger designed an extensive line of holloware in brass, with some objects being made in silverplate, for Dorlyn Silversmiths, 383 Lafayette Street, New York. These were distributed by the Vincent Lippe Company, 225 Fifth Avenue, New York. The pieces for Dorlyn were marked "Made by Dorlyn Silversmiths" with a conjoined "PR" in a V-shape with the P reversed. The "R" here probably referred to Rasmussen, as Reimes had committed suicide in the early 1940s. The Oneida *Heirloom "700"* line, contracted from Dorlyn in the mid-1950s, was not identified by Oneida as Parzinger's design, nor was the work he did for Mueck-Cary. Many of the pieces were, however, identical or very similar to the brass and silverplate objects that had been executed by Dorlyn and bore Parzinger's mark. Since Parzinger's holloware became collectible in the 1990s, some of the brass pieces that Dorlyn made have reappeared on the market with new silverplating over the brass.

Robert H. Ramp (b. 1920)
b. Cincinnati, Ohio; lives in Newville, Pennsylvania

While in high school, Ramp attended night classes in the fine arts department of the Cincinnati Art Academy. During World War II he served in the U. S. Army Medical Corps, retiring as a major. Soon after the war he entered Pratt Institute in Brooklyn, New York, and in 1949, after three years of study, he received a certificate in industrial design. (There was no degree in industrial design at the time.) According to Ramp, he was recruited at Pratt by Reed & Barton to design contemporary silverware. Married and with a child, Ramp accepted the offer and became a staff designer in 1949. With his peers from the Rhode Island School of Design, Milton P. Hannah and Donald Pollard, who had also joined the design department under the same program, Ramp contributed most of the forward-looking holloware to Reed & Barton's innovative *Contemporary Group* of 1950. Ramp designed the *Silver Sculpture* sterling flatware and holloware pattern, Reed & Barton's answer, in 1954, to Towle's *Contour*. He adapted Gio Ponti's prototype designs that were produced as *The Diamond* sterling flatware in 1958. Ramp's celery, bread, or relish tray, which he designed in 1955, was included in the exhibition *20th Century Design: U.S.A.* (1959–1960). Although Ramp primarily designed holloware and sterling flatware, he is credited with the *Safari* and *Style* (both 1957) and *Seascape* (1958) stainless patterns. In 1960 Ramp left Reed & Barton to design eyewear at Bausch and Lomb in Rochester, New York. Coincidentally, Richard L. Huggins, who had been the director of design at Gorham, became the director of design at Bausch and Lomb in 1962, and the two former silver designers worked together until 1976, when

Huggins left the company. In Rochester, Ramp belatedly studied silversmithing with Ronald Hayes Pearson and began making commemorative pieces, primarily for local corporations and colleges. He retired from Bausch and Lomb in 1989.

Louis W. Rice (dates unknown)
Birthplace not known

Louis W. Rice and his brother Jacques B. Rice were the sons of the silver manufacturer Bernard Rice, who had founded a silver company with his brother in 1861. In 1867 the business moved to New York. After Bernard Rice died in 1896, Louis and Jacques formed a partnership. By 1906 the business had grown to the point where the factory was moved from Manhattan to Brooklyn. In 1922 the company was incorporated as Bernard Rice's Sons and operated under that name as well as under the names of its subsidiaries, the Apollo Silver Company and Apollo Studios. Production consisted of silverplated holloware, novelties, dresser sets, candy and cigarette boxes, and smokers' articles, which were sold to gift shops, jewelers, silverware and toilet goods departments, and specialty shops throughout the United States. From 1912 through the 1930s, the company maintained a showroom and offices at 325 Fifth Avenue. Louis W. Rice was the gifted designer of Bernard Rice's Sons' patented *Sky-scraper* line of silverplated holloware (1928). In its Apollo Gift Lines, Bernard Rice's Sons produced and marketed *Shadowardt* holloware (1928), a design inspired by Erik Magnussen's *Cubic* coffee service for Gorham, which had been dubbed "Lights and Shadows of Manhattan."

Burr Sebring (b. 1928)
b. Dundee, New York; lives in Barrington, Rhode Island

Sebring attended the School for American Craftsmen at the Rochester Institute of Technology and studied there with the metalsmiths John Prip and Hans Christensen. He received a bachelor of fine arts degree in 1958 and joined the design department at Gorham. In 1959 he received Honorable Mention in the Sterling Today competition sponsored by the Sterling Silversmiths Guild of America. Among his modern flatware patterns, for which he also made the models, were *Classique* (1961), *Aspen* (1963), and *Esprit* (1963). Sebring left Gorham in 1982.

Frederick William Stark (1885–1969)
b. Germany

Stark came to the United States as a boy with his mother, who settled in the vicinity of Providence, Rhode Island, and later remarried. His career began in 1902 as an apprentice in the design department of the Gorham Company in Providence. He enrolled at the Rhode Island School of Design for a short time and also studied life drawing and painting with Herbert Cyrus Farnum, a local artist who had trained in Paris. Stark worked for Gorham until 1923, when he moved to the International Silver Company in Meriden, Connecticut. At International he designed sterling holloware, trophies, and hotel and ecclesiastical silver. The designs for which Stark is known were created for International in the 1930s. These are the rigorously minimal *Continental* sterling flatware pattern (designed in 1934 and illustrated in *Art and the Machine* by Sheldon and Martha Candler Cheney, which was published in 1936), the Waldorf-Astoria Hotel flatware and holloware service designed with Peer Smed, and a Scandinavian-influenced centerpiece bowl that was awarded a silver medal at the *Exposition Internationale des Arts et des Techniques dans la Vie Moderne* in Paris in 1937. According to his son, Stark worked with Henry Dreyfuss on the service for the New York Central's 20th Century Limited streamliner train in 1938. In fact, several patents were filed with Stark as designer of holloware pieces used by the New York Central Line. He retired from International in 1950.

Elsa Tennhardt (1889–1980)
b. Bucheim, Germany

Fragments of information gathered from relatives are the main source of information about Elsa Tennhardt, a painter and art instructor who designed modernist silver in 1928 for E. & J. Bass of New York. Born Gertrud Elsa Tennhardt in the village of Bucheim near Leipzig, she was one of four siblings. She had a sister and two brothers, one of whom died in World War I. Her educational background is not known. Reportedly, at some time between 1910 and 1913, she traveled to the United States as a nanny with an English family. In 1914 a postcard was addressed to her in New Brunswick, New Jersey. By the end of the decade Tennhardt had become acquainted with members of the Austro-German émigré artists' colony in New York City and had become a close friend of Winold Reiss and his family. Their six-year-old son Tjark stayed with Tennhardt in Rowayton, Connecticut, during the summer of 1920.

Tennhardt was part of the circle of artists around Reiss that included Ilonka Karasz, and she maintained contact with Reiss's first wife Henriette into the 1960s. A ledger begun in October 1925 by the Winold Reiss Art School, 4 Christopher Street, documents Tennhardt's employment from that date until June 1926. In a letter of June 4, 1972, to a friend, she recalled replacing Ernst

Geidlinger, painter and art educator from Munich, as a teacher at Reiss's school and her encounter with another painter from Munich, Carl Link, an associate of Reiss. Surviving photographs of studio classes at the school show that Tennhardt had studied drawing from life there prior to 1925. In the 1920s, before returning to Germany on a family visit in 1926 that included France, Tennhardt married out of her religion to Jerome Rosenthal, a Jewish Lithuanian-born philosopher, author, and critic, who had earned a master's degree in German literature from Columbia University. Tennhardt's introduction to E. & J. Bass to design silverware in 1928 may have been through the Viennese émigré Otto J. Baumgarten, who operated the exclusive restaurants Le Voisin, Crillon, and Elysée in New York City, and with whom Reiss had a long-standing relationship. Surprisingly, in the annual exhibition of the Architectural League of New York in 1931, Tennhardt exhibited two curtains, one in "silver and gold," that she had designed for Temple Emmanu-El in New York. For the rest of her life Tennhardt primarily painted and taught drawing and painting, usually for adult education night classes, at times at Cooper Union and New York University. She exhibited at the Montross Gallery in 1934 and with the Municipal Art Committee in 1937. A positive review of her abstract paintings at the Modern Art Studio appeared in the *New York Times* in 1945. Rosenthal died in 1952 and Tennhardt moved to Southampton in the mid-1960s. She was described as tall and gaunt with piercing blue eyes, a heavy smoker, imperious, demanding, and extraordinarily proud. Although she was barely surviving economically, she turned down an opportunity to exhibit her paintings at the Parrish Museum one November because it was the off-season in Southampton. Tennhardt had a hard life. Her husband was paralyzed in the early 1930s, and she was frustrated in her career as a painter. Her foremost achievement was her brief flirtation with the design of modernist silver in the late 1920s for which she is recognized today.

John O. Van Koert (1912–1998)
b. St. Paul, Minnesota

John Van Koert, a painter, graduated from the University of Wisconsin at Milwaukee in 1934 and received a master's degree from Columbia University in 1935. Although not trained in the craft, he taught an art and metalwork course at the University of Wisconsin at Madison and revived the study of the lost-wax process. In the late 1930s, he opened a shop and workroom nearby where he employed his students, among them Robert J. King. The advent of World War II closed the venture. After the war Van Koert briefly worked in the office of the industrial designer Henry Dreyfuss in New York City and designed jewelry for Harry Winston. During a chance meeting between the metalsmith Margret Craver and Robert King at Handy & Harman in New York City, King recommended Van Koert to Craver, who was the wife of Charles Withers, the chief executive officer of Towle Manufacturing Company. This led to Van Koert's appointment as Towle's director of design in 1948. The next year Van Koert brought King to Towle. Under Van Koert's leadership King designed and made the models for the groundbreaking *Contour* sterling flatware and holloware. Van Koert, a self-assured promoter, arranged for the flatware to be featured in the exhibition *Knife, Fork, and Spoon*, which was co-sponsored, in 1951, by Towle Silversmiths and the Walker Art Center. Conflicts with Craver, who acted as a consultant at Towle, ultimately caused Van Koert to leave the company in about 1953. After serving as the American exhibition director of *Design in Scandinavia* in 1954 and as consultant to the International Silver Company's International Design Competition for Sterling Silver Flatware that resulted in the exhibition *Designed for Silver* in 1960, Van Koert's professional life was centered in furniture design.

CATALOGUE OF
SELECTED WORKS

In an effort to provide an expanded reference for future scholars, the following catalogue includes all works in the exhibition and a selection of modernist silver from the Jewel Stern American Silver Collection at the Dallas Museum of Art that is illustrated in the catalogue. The entries are organized alphabetically by the manufacturer's name and the division name, chronologically by date of design (as in the captions), and by the designer's name or the pattern name, where known. Designers, patent dates, and related details are provided when known. As far as possible, marks are recorded in their entirety, as they appear, with the original capitalization and punctuation retained. For loans for which the exact configuration and appearance of the marks has not been provided, exceptions do occur. Dimensions for most works are provided in the order of overall height, width, and depth. Some works have only two dimensions provided: height and diameter. All silver is considered sterling grade unless otherwise noted. Information referenced within entries is, unless otherwise cited, provided by courtesy of Jewel Stern and the Jewel Stern American Silver Archives.

Objects included in the exhibition are denoted by asterisks.

E. & J. Bass
NEW YORK, NEW YORK
ACTIVE 1890–c. 1930

1. Creamer and sugar bowl, 1928*

Elsa Tennhardt

American (b. Germany), 1889–1980

Patent 75,939 (for a dish or article of analogous nature) filed May 23, 1928, granted July 31, 1928. Silverplate with traces of original gilding. Creamer 4 × 5¼ × 3 in. (10.2 × 13.3 × 7.6 cm); sugar bowl 2½ × 4 × 4 in. (6.4 × 10.2 × 10.2 cm). Marked (each): *E. & J. B*

Dallas Museum of Art, The Jewel Stern American Silver Collection, acquired through the Patsy Lacy Griffith Collection, gift of Patsy Lacy Griffith by exchange, DMA 2002.29.44.1–2

Although this creamer and sugar bowl set has no pattern name, E. &. J. Bass produced a holloware series in this triangular design that included a cocktail shaker set with matching cups, ice tub and tray, vase, candlesticks and bowls in two versions, salt and pepper shakers, and individual almond dishes (see chapter 3).

2. Vanity set, 1928*

Elsa Tennhardt

American (b. Germany), 1889–1980

Patent 76,361 (for a mirror back or similar article) filed May 23, 1928, granted Sept. 18, 1929; patent 75,937 (frame for trays or similar article) filed May 23, 1928, granted July 31, 1928. Silverplate, glass. Tray 1¼ × 14½ × 7 in. (3.2 × 36.8 × 17.8 cm); mirror 11 × 7 in. (27.9 × 17.8 cm); brush 9 × 4½ in. (22.9 × 11.4 cm); box 4⅝ × 5⅜ × 5⅜ in. (11.7 × 13.7 × 13.7 cm); comb 8 in. (20.3 cm); perfume vessel 7 × 3 × 2⅝ in. (17.8 × 7.6 × 6.7 cm)

The Mr. and Mrs. Roger D. Redden Collection

In keeping with Tennhardt's other silver designs for E. & J. Bass, which are reminiscent of the faceted geometry of cubism, the triangle becomes a dramatic leitmotif for the forms and zigzag ornament of this rare vanity set. Although other makers such as Bernard Rice's Sons produced modernist dressing articles with geometric surface decoration, Tennhardt's bold, assertive design is aesthetically unified to the degree that the handles of the brush and mirror eschew practical considerations in favor of the dominant triangular theme.

BENEDICT MANUFACTURING CORPORATION
EAST SYRACUSE, NEW YORK
ACTIVE 1894–1953

3. *Modernistic plate* tray, 1928

Albert F. Saunders

American, 1877–1964

Patent 74,990 (for a cake stand) filed Jan. 31, 1928, granted Apr. 24, 1928. Silverplate, plastic. 2¼ × 7½ in. (5.7 × 19.1 cm). Marked: [within a hexagon] *BENEDICT/modernistic/PLATE,* [underneath hexagon] *E.P.N.S./B.M.M./558*

Dallas Museum of Art, The Jewel Stern American Silver Collection, acquired through the Patsy Lacy Griffith Collection, gift of Patsy Lacy Griffith by exchange, DMA 2002.29.144

The tray is one of the objects in a holloware group based on design patents for a cake stand and for a cake plate (Patent 75,655) by Albert F. Saunders (see chapter 1). Saunders, a craftsman and the art director of Benedict from 1907 to 1946, was the chief designer at the George W. Shiebler silverware firm in New York City for three years before joining Benedict.[1] Although without a pedestal, the tray has the elongated hexagonal shape of the patented cake stand and has similar, cubist-inspired angular decoration. The red plastic handles add a lively accent. The tray was one of the items featured in an introductory advertisement that invited dealers to become "style leader[s]" by offering "benedict modernistic plate."[2]

1. "Albert Frederick Saunders," in Anita Jacobsen, *Jacobsen's Biographical Indexes of American Artists* (Carrollton, Tex.: A. J. Publications 2000), vol. 1, bk. 4, 2832.
2. "The Period Silver of Tomorrow," "benedict modernistic plate" advertisement, *Keystone* 56 (Nov. 1928): 25.

4. *Modernistic plate* pitcher, 1928

Albert F. Saunders

American, 1877–1964

Designer of border pattern

Patent 75,654 (for a border strip for a dish) filed Jan. 31, 1928, granted June 26, 1928. Silverplate. 8⅜ × 8¾ × 5½ in. (21.3 × 22.2 × 14 cm). Marked: [within a hexagon] *BENEDICT/modernistic/PLATE,* [underneath hexagon] *E. P. N. S.* [each in a square] *B. M. M./562*

Dallas Museum of Art, The Jewel Stern American Silver Collection, gift of Jewel Stern, DMA 2003.34.12

The *art moderne*–inspired border strip at the shoulder of this pitcher was designed and patented by Saunders. It is not known if he designed this pitcher, which has a beaklike spout and an angular handle modeled on Erik Magnussen's *Cubic* service for Gorham. The jaunty pitcher was the focus of one advertisement for "benedict modernistic plate," a multi-design line of modern holloware enthusiastically introduced in 1928.[1]

1. "Smart as the day after tomorrow," "benedict modernistic plate" advertisement, *Keystone* 56 (Dec. 1928): 25.

WARD BENNETT DESIGN
NEW YORK, NEW YORK
ACTIVE c. 1980

5. Bowl, c. 1970–1980

Ward Bennett

American, 1917–2003

Silverplate. 3¼ × 4¼ × 4¼ in. (8.3 × 10.8 × 10.8 cm). Marked: *Ward Bennett Design* [in script]

Dallas Museum of Art, The Jewel Stern American Silver Collection, gift of Jewel Stern, DMA 2005.25.12

Although little is known about this bowl, Bennett, who designed silver for Tiffany & Co. in the 1960s, appears to have created his own line of holloware for a short while in the 1970s and perhaps early 1980s. The larger prototype of this bowl was fabricated in India.[1] The bowl in this size was reportedly available in a "cool contemporary shop" in the Century City Shopping Center in Los Angeles in the early 1980s.[2] The design was made in at least one larger size. The subtle, sophisticated modeling of form, stripped of all decoration, shows the influence of Bennett's earlier experience in ceramics and sculpture as well as his predilection for minimalism.

1. David McCorkle, telephone conversation with Jewel Stern, June 14, 2004.
2. Candace Koval, e-mail to Jewel Stern, June 14, 2004.

W. & S. BLACKINTON & COMPANY
NORTH ATTLEBORO, MASSACHUSETTS
ACTIVE 1865–1967

6. Centerpiece, c. 1955

Silverplate, plastic. 2¾ × 12½ × 6¼ in. (7.0 × 31.8 × 15.9 cm). Marked: [stamped] *W & S BLACKINTON/FINE SILVER PLATE/Since 1865/40.* Paper label: *SILVER PLATE ON THIS PIECE IS/Unconditionally Guaranteed* [in script]/*FOR THE LIFE OF THE ARTICLE/W. & S. BLACKINTON CO./SINCE 1865*

Dallas Museum of Art, The Jewel Stern American Silver Collection, gift of Jewel Stern, DMA 2005.25.11

The centerpiece is a variant of the popular triangular free form shape of the 1950s. Three angled feet taper to tiny balls and have conical black plastic partial "sleeves" that accent and emphasize the feet as well as the triangular shape of the piece. Blackinton also made a smaller dish in this design.

CURRIER & ROBY
NEW YORK, NEW YORK
ACTIVE 1900–1940

7. Candlesticks (pair), c. 1935

Silver. Each 4⅛ × 3 in. (10.5 × 7.6 cm). Marked (each): *STERLING 291 CR* [entwined]

Dallas Museum of Art, The Jewel Stern American Silver Collection, acquired through the Patsy Lacy Griffith Collection, gift of Patsy Lacy Griffith by exchange, DMA 2002.29.57.1–2

These streamlined, cone-shaped candlesticks are simply decorated with two incised bands, one with three lines at the wide end, the other with two lines at the narrow end. The ample, slightly domed bases stabilize the flaring objects. Versatile, the candlesticks were designed to be used upside down as well. In this position the cones taper upward and the bases become wide saucer-like bobeches. For the conservative Currier & Roby firm, these candlesticks were a rare foray into modernism.

DORLYN SILVERSMITHS
NEW YORK, NEW YORK
ACTIVE C. 1945–1970

8. Ice bucket, c. 1955*

Tommi Parzinger
American (b. Germany), 1903–1981

Silverplate. 9 × 9½ × 7½ in. (22.9 × 24.1 × 19.1 cm). Marked: *Made by / dorlyn-silversmiths* [in arc] / [conjoined P (reversed) and R mark]
Dallas Museum of Art, The Jewel Stern American Silver Collection, Decorative Arts Fund, DMA 2002.29.91.A–B

The quiet elegance of the form is an effect of its harmonious proportions and the subtle contours, which are minimally accented by looped handles and a small corseted finial. This model was also produced by Dorlyn in brass and was adapted as well for the Oneida *Heirloom "700"* line in silverplate by the addition of scored, radiating lines from the finial outward to the edge of the cover, and by garnishing the finial with a black plastic disk. The reversed P and R conjoined is a Parzinger mark. The "P" represents Parzinger; the "R," Peter Reimes, the German émigré metalsmith who first crafted Parzinger's sterling silverware in the late 1930s. Although Reimes had died in the 1940s, Parzinger retained the mark. Among other silverplated objects that Parzinger designed for Dorlyn are candlesticks and a footed tazza.

LEONORE DOSKOW, INC.
NEW YORK, NEW YORK
ACTIVE 1934–1941

MONTROSE, NEW YORK
ACTIVE 1941–1985

9. Tea strainer with caddy, c. 1938–1939

Leonore Doskow
American, b. 1910

Silver. 1¾ × 6½ × 3¼ in. (4.4 × 16.5 × 8.3 cm). Marked: *LEONORE DOSKOW / HANDMADE STERLING*
Dallas Museum of Art, The Jewel Stern American Silver Collection, Decorative Arts Fund, DMA 2002.29.298.A–B

In 1934, together with her husband, the newlywed Leonore Doskow, a self-taught silversmith who had had her own Silver Craft Studio in Philadelphia, went into a small production-line business of handmade sterling silver giftware and novelties in New York City, where the couple then lived. Smoking accessories, jewelry, and small serving pieces, many with bold geometric monograms supplied to order, were featured in her 1939 catalogue, and her silverware was recognized in the exhibition *Contemporary American Industrial Art* at the Metropolitan Museum of Art in 1940 (see chapter 8). Inspired by the geometric forms of 1930s modernism, Doskow created this square tea strainer and caddy in which the concentric perforations in the strainer form a perfect circle. In Doskow's sketchbook the tea strainer is no. 6542 and the tea caddy is no. 6543. According to Doskow, about six were made and the design was discontinued after World War II because it was too expensive to produce.

HELEN HUGHES DULANY STUDIO
CHICAGO, ILLINOIS
ACTIVE MID-1930S

10. Candelabra (pair), c. 1935*

Helen Hughes Dulany
American, 1885–1968

Silverplate. Each 5 × 9 × 1¾ in. (12.7 × 22.9 × 4.4 cm). Marked (each): *HHD* [conjoined] / *STUDIO*
Dallas Museum of Art, The Jewel Stern American Silver Collection, Decorative Arts Fund, DMA 2002.29.100.1–2

For this Machine Age design, Dulany employed the simplest geometric forms, circles, cylinders, planes and bars, and by organizing these elements on different levels and in units of twos and threes, she created a unique arrangement in which two of the three candles penetrate the upper plane of each candelabrum (see chapter 6).

STEPHEN DWECK DESIGN
(DWECK INDUSTRIES, INC.)
BROOKLYN, NEW YORK
ACTIVE 1980–PRESENT

11. Serving set, 1989 (designed 1986)*

Stephen Dweck
American, b. 1960

Silver, bronze. Knife 12 × 2 in. (30.5 × 5.1 cm); spoon 10 × 2¾ in. (25.4 × 7 cm); fork 10¼ × 2¾ in. (26 × 7 cm). Knife marked: [fish] [lizard] © 1989 © *Stephen Dweck* [in script] ® / *STERLING* / 01. Fork / spoon marked: © 1989 / [fish] © *Stephen Dweck* [in script] ® [lizard] / *STERLING* / 001
The Stephen Dweck Collection

Although Stephen Dweck began his artistic journey in painting and sculpture, he found his métier as a fashion jeweler. In 1981 he created his first collection, which was launched by the fashion designer Geoffrey Beene. For almost a decade Dweck designed jewelry for Beene's runway shows while expanding his own business. His interests extended to objects for the table and in 1988 he produced the Stephen Dweck Home Collection of serving pieces and accessories. His lavish use of naturalistic decoration and silver primarily, but also rare wood with bronze, vermeil, abalone, mother-of-pearl, and semiprecious stones, was an extension of his design aesthetic in jewelry.

For the Home Collection Dweck made molds from real grape leaves, which he cast afterward for the "meandering vines" he employed in an openwork arrangement for the handles of these three serving pieces. His trademark beetle, here in bronze, that appears to alight on the jagged serving portion of each piece was molded and cast from an actual beetle he found in his garden. Dweck associated the beetle with ancient Egyptian scarabs and the vines with classical laurel victory wreaths. Dweck considers "giving a new life to old styles" his forte.[1] An example is this late twentieth-century interpretation of traditional flatware in which the lyrical delicacy of the intertwined vine and twig openwork handles, with their spiraling tendrils, imparts a lush, romantic quality to the pieces. The set, comprising a pie server and a salad serving spoon and fork, was originally made in all silver by Lunt Silversmiths for the 1988 Home Collection. It was the only item in the collection that was not made in-house. This set in mixed metals was introduced in the second collection in 1989 and it was made in-house. Both versions were packaged in a specially fitted box and about fifty of each were produced (see chapter 16).

1. "The World of Stephen Dweck," Dweck Industries Inc. public relations biography, 1989, n.p. (courtesy of Stephen Dweck).

ENGLISH SILVER MANUFACTURING
CORPORATION
BROOKLYN, NEW YORK
ACTIVE C. 1950–1976

12. Ice bucket, c. 1965–1970

Silverplate, enamel. 8¾ × 10 in. (22.2 × 25.4 cm). Marked (on one side): ∫ M R S [in shield] / *ENGLISH SILVER MFG CORP / MADE IN U.S.A.* / [bust of man]
Dallas Museum of Art, The Jewel Stern American Silver Collection, Decorative Arts Fund, DMA 2002.29.287.A–D

The colored enamel on the lid of the ice bucket is an example of the influence of post–World War II Scandinavian metalware on American silverware in the 1960s.

MERLE F. FABER PRODUCTS
SAN FRANCISCO, CALIFORNIA
ACTIVE 1943–1960

13. Candlesticks (pair), c. 1943–1950*

Merle Fenelon Faber
American, 1891–1980

Silverplate. Each: 4¾ × 2³⁄₁₆ in. (12.1 × 5.6 cm). Marked (each): [in circle] *MERLE F. FABER/ PRODUCTS/ S.F./ 11662* [scratched] / [outside circle] *417* [scratched]
Dallas Museum of Art, The Jewel Stern American Silver Collection, acquired through the Patsy Lacy Griffith Collection, gift of Patsy Lacy Griffith by exchange, DMA 2002.29.171.1–2

The setback construction of 1930s skyscrapers such as those of New York's Rockefeller Center was the inspiration for these candlesticks by Faber, a small San Francisco manufacturer of high-styled tableware and accessories in silverplate. Faber also applied this design to salt and pepper shakers. Another item in the line was a cream and sugar set with geometric accents in black or white plastic. A small cylindrical coffeepot to match has a sharp angular spout, a plastic cube finial, and a ponytail handle at a right angle to the pot (see chapter 3).

FISHER SILVERSMITHS, INC.
JERSEY CITY, NEW JERSEY
NEW YORK, NEW YORK
ACTIVE C. 1936–1970

14. Chafing dish, c. 1965*

Silverplate, wood. 10½ × 16¼ × 12¾ in. (26.7 × 41.3 × 32.4 cm). Marked: *FISHER/* [crown] *EPC* [shield] / *K300*
Dallas Museum of Art, The Jewel Stern American Silver Collection, gift of Jewel Stern, DMA 2003.34.19.A–F

Of the modern lines produced by Fisher in New York in the 1950s and 1960s, this chafing dish is the most impressive object in scale and resolution of design. A fusion of Scandinavian styling, especially in its wood elements, and Space Age imagery, embodied in its three arching legs and disk-shaped bowl that recall spacecraft, the chafing dish, like Oneida's *Decorator* candelabrum which is also in the collection of the Dallas Museum of Art, are reminders of America's fascination with space exploration in the late 1950s and 1960s.

FRIEDMAN SILVER COMPANY
BROOKLYN, NEW YORK
ACTIVE 1908–1960

15. Creamer and sugar bowl, 1928*

Howard L. Budd
American, dates unknown

Patent 75,411 (for a pitcher or similar article) filed Mar. 16, 1928; granted June 5, 1928. Silverplate, painted wood. Creamer 2½ × 5¼ × 3¾ in. (6.4 × 13.3 × 9.5 cm); sugar bowl 2½ × 5¼ × 3¾ in. (6.4 × 13.3 × 9.5 cm). Marked (each): *J* [within an equilateral triangle] [crown within a diamond] *F* [within an equilateral triangle] / *E. P.–N. S./ 7688/ 1984* [scratched]
Dallas Museum of Art, The Jewel Stern American Silver Collection, acquired through the Patsy Lacy Griffith Collection, gift of Patsy Lacy Griffith by exchange, DMA 2002.29.142.1–2

The dark blue wood handles add contrast, and the notched rims, reminiscent of crenellations, add visual interest to the cubist geometry of this cream and sugar set in one of two holloware lines by Howard L. Budd, a talented designer living in New York City.

16. Vase, 1928

Howard L. Budd
American, dates unknown

Patent 75,825 (for a vase or similar article) filed Apr. 9, 1928, granted July 24, 1928. Silverplate, plastic. 13⅜ × 6⁵⁄₁₆ × 4½ in. (34.0 × 16.0 × 11.4 cm). Marked: *J* [within an equilateral triangle] [crown within a diamond] *F* [within an equilateral triangle] / *E. P.–N. S./ 7154*
Dallas Museum of Art, The Jewel Stern American Silver Collection, gift of Jewel Stern, DMA 2003.34.9

The tall slender vase is from one of two holloware lines designed and patented by Budd for Friedman. The folding of the metal was meant to convey the cubist angular planarity that prevailed at the 1925 Paris exposition. The green plastic handles added another note of modernity.

17. *Silver Style* cocktail shaker, 1928*

Kem (Karl Emmanuel Martin) Weber
American (b. Germany), 1889–1963

Silverplate, rosewood. 10¼ × 7 × 4½ in. (26.0 × 17.8 × 11.4 cm). Marked: *SILVER STYLE/ A/ Kem Weber* [in script] / *DESIGN/ J* [within an equilateral triangle] [crown within a diamond] *F* [within an equilateral triangle] / *E.P.–N. S./ 8E4/ D* [in circle]
Dallas Museum of Art, gift of the Decorative Arts Guild of North Texas, 1994 Midwest Trip, DMA 1994.52.A–C

The Friedman Silver Company commissioned Kem Weber to design avant-garde silverplated holloware in 1928. Two modernist lines, *Silver Style* and *To-Day*, were the result. This cocktail shaker possesses the telescoping and stepped details characteristic of all objects in the *Silver Style* pattern. Many original drawings of his designs for Friedman, some never executed, are in the Kem Weber Archive at the University Art Museum, University of California, Santa Barbara.

GORHAM MANUFACTURING COMPANY
PROVIDENCE, RHODE ISLAND
ACTIVE 1831–PRESENT

18. Candy jar, 1926*

Erik Magnussen
Danish, 1884–1961

Silver, ivory. 6⅝ × 8¾ in. (16.8 × 22.2 cm). Marked: *GORHAM/* [lion] [anchor] *G/ STERLING/ EHH* [and] *MADE FOR SPALDING & COMPANY/ EM* [stylized and overlapping]
Dallas Museum of Art, gift in memory of Ethyl Carradine Kurth, DMA 1990.230.A–B

This candy jar is an exceptional example of Magnussen's handcrafted work from the year following his arrival at Gorham. Raised traditionally from sheet silver, the surface retains subtle planishing marks from hammering. The ivory pedestal and washer under the finial were carved in Gorham's ivory workshops. The use of scrolls and beads, characteristic of Danish silverware, reveals the strong influence his Scandinavian training had on Magnussen's American designs.

19. Bonbon dish, 1927*

Erik Magnussen
Danish, 1884–1961

Silver, carnelian. 4¼ × 5½ in. (10.8 × 14.0 cm), Marked: *GORHAM EM* [stylized and overlapping] / [lion] [anchor] *G/ 63/ STERLING*
Dallas Museum of Art. The Jewel Stern American Silver Collection, acquired through the Patsy Lacy Griffith Collection, gift of Patsy Lacy Griffith by exchange, DMA 2002.29.28

A trio of giraffes in silhouette and resting on carnelian spheres serve as legs to support the dish. Magnussen created a number of similar pieces with figures of birds or animals, among them the toucan, stork, hawk, deer and buffalo. The use of carnelian in the piece adds to its richness and relates the piece to contemporary European silver in which semiprecious stones were often incorporated. Gorham's records indicate that eight dishes were registered in December 1927 and twelve more in March 1928, making a total of twenty produced in this design.[1]

1. Samuel J. Hough, "Report on Gorham Sterling Bon Bon Dish designed by Erik Magnussen E. M. 63," Feb. 22, 1989.
Reference: Helen Appleton Read, "Twentieth-Century Decoration: The Modern Theme Finds a Distinctive Medium in American Silver," *Vogue* 72 (July 1, 1928): 94.

20. Candlesticks and vase, 1927*

Erik Magnussen
Danish, 1884–1961

Silver. Candlesticks 11 × 5 in. (27.9 × 12.7 cm); vase 14½ × 5 in. (36.8 × 12.7 cm). Candlesticks marked: *GORHAM/* [lion] [anchor] *G/ STERLING/ A14004/ CEMENT LOADED*. Vase: *GORHAM/* [lion] [anchor] *G/ A14007/ STERLING*
Dallas Museum of Art, 20th-Century Design Fund, DMA 2001.283.1–3

This fluted vase and matching candlesticks are typical of Magnussen's more conservative early modern work for Gorham.

21. *Cubic* coffee service and tray, 1927*

Erik Magnussen
Danish, 1884–1961

Silver with patinated and gilt decoration, ivory. Coffeepot 9¾ × 9⅛ × 4 in. (24.8 × 23.2 × 10.2 cm); tray 22 × 13⅝ in. (55.9 × 34.6 cm). Marked (each): *GORHAM/EM* [stylized and overlapping]/[lion] [anchor] *G/28/ STERLING/DESIGNED AND EXECUTED BY ERIK MAGNUSSEN*
Museum of Art, Rhode Island School of Design, Providence. The Gorham Collection, gift of Textron, Inc.

No other American silver object expresses the impulse of modernity and the influence of cubism as emphatically as Erik Magnussen's *Cubic* coffee service. A flamboyant proclamation of Gorham's foray into modernist design, the service, along with a matching bowl and a pair of serving spoons, were promoted as objects evocative of the spirit of the age, but the *Cubic* holloware pattern was never serially produced. Imaginatively dubbed the "Lights and Shadows of Manhattan" after being introduced, Magnussen's service combines brightly polished faceted surfaces with those of oxidized and gilded silver, providing "sharp angles and sharp variation of light and shade, which are clearly the product of those phenomena found in our skyscraper civilization."[1] The current whereabouts of the matching bowl and serving spoons are unknown.

1. Elizabeth Lounsbery, "Modernistic Influence on Sterling Silver; The Lights and Shadows of a Skyscraper are Reflected in this New Table Silver," *Arts and Decoration* 28 (Apr. 1928) 52.

22. *Modern American* coffee service, 1928*

Erik Magnussen
Danish, 1884–1961

Silver, ivory, ebony. Coffeepot 8 × 8¼ in. (20.3 × 21.0 cm); sugar bowl 2¾ × 6³⁄₁₆ in. (7.0 × 15.7 cm); creamer 4½ × 6⅝ in. (11.4 × 16.8 cm). Coffeepot marked: *EM* [stylized and overlapping]/*14051/ STERLING/ GORHAM/*[lion] [anchor] *G*. Sugar bowl: *EM* [stylized and overlapping]/*14052/STERLING/GORHAM/*[lion] [anchor] *G*. Creamer/ sugar bowl: *EM* [stylized and overlapping] /*14053/STERLING/GORHAM/*[lion] [anchor] *G*
Dallas Museum of Art, 20th-Century Design Fund, DMA 1997.146.1–3

A Gorham advertisement in the July 9, 1928, issue of *Jeweler's Circular* announced the *Modern American* holloware line by Erik Magnussen and illustrated this three-piece coffee set. The unusual "feet" of the set call attention to the linear details at the base of the simple cylindrical bodies. The carved ivory finials atop the coffeepot and sugar bowl and the solid ebony handles are traditional elements in Magnussen's eclectic interpretation of a modern coffee set. In this respect the coffee set differs from other holloware pieces in the *Modern American* pattern. According to Gorham's records, thirteen production-line sets were made from one prototype, which had black Bakelite handles. The three pieces, designated as "black coffee set," originally retailed for $250. These were discontinued on January 24, 1931. A matching tray (of which thirteen were produced) was offered at $125.[1]

1. Samuel J. Hough, "Report on Gorham Coffee Set A14051," Sept. 1, 1993.

23. *Modern American* bowl, 1928*

Erik Magnussen
Danish, 1884–1961

Patent (for a bowl or similar article) filed Aug. 18, 1928, granted Dec. 4, 1928. Silver. 6⅝ × 9¼ × 9¼ in. (16.8 × 23.5 × 23.5 cm). Marked: *EM* [stylized and overlapping] *14066 STERLING* [lion] [anchor] *G GORHAM*
Dallas Museum of Art, The Jewel Stern American Silver Collection, acquired through the Patsy Lacy Griffith Collection, gift of Patsy Lacy Griffith by exchange, DMA 2002.29.29

In addition to the coffee set, this bowl was illustrated in the Gorham advertisement that introduced the *Modern American* pattern in the *Jeweler's Circular*. Samuel J. Hough notes that twenty-four bowls were made and, in contrast to many other Magnussen pieces, this bowl "sold right out." It was priced initially at $115, but production costs were reduced and, in the *Sterling Silver by Gorham* catalogue for 1929, the bowl, described as "hand chased," was listed at $100.[1]

1. Samuel J. Hough, "Report on Gorham Bowl A14066," n.d.

24. *Modern American* cocktail cup, 1928*

Erik Magnussen
Danish, 1884–1961

Silver. 5¼ × 4 in. (13.3 × 10.2 cm). Marked: *EM* [stylized and overlapping] *14083 STERLING* [lion] [anchor] *G GORHAM*
Dallas Museum of Art, The Jewel Stern American Silver Collection, acquired through the Patsy Lacy Griffith Collection, gift of Patsy Lacy Griffith by exchange, DMA 2002.29.299.1

The stepped base of this cocktail cup echoes the form of the bowl Magnussen designed in the same pattern. In the *Sterling Silver by Gorham* catalogue for 1929, the cups were offered in units of a dozen at $210. A popular barware item, these cups remained in production until the end of February 1936.[1]

1. Samuel J. Hough, "Report on Gorham Modern American Cocktail Cup A14083," Sept. 23, 1993.

25. *Modern American* teaspoon, 1928*

Erik Magnussen
Danish, 1884–1961

Silver. ¾ × 1¼ × 5⅞ in. (1.9 × 3.2 × 14.9 cm). Marked: H [in diamond] [lion] [anchor] *G STERLING GORHAM, INC.*
Dallas Museum of Art, The Jewel Stern American Silver Collection, gift of Jewel Stern, DMA 2003.34.8

Magnussen designed a little-known sterling flatware pattern to match the *Modern American* holloware. To a traditional shape of flatware, he applied an incised motif based on the strict linear banding prominent in the holloware. The flatware was not successful in the marketplace.

26. Console set, 1928

Silver. Compote (made in 1929) 2¾ × 11½ in. (7.0 × 29.2 cm); candlesticks (2002.29.120.2 made in 1928; 2002.29.120.3 made in 1929) 10½ × 4 in. (26.7 × 10.2 cm). Candlestick 2002.29.120.2 marked: *GORHAM/*[lion] [anchor] *G/STERLING/ A13749/CEMENT-LOADED/*[zeppelin, the 1929 year symbol]. Compotier marked: *GORHAM/*[lion] [anchor] *G/STERLING/A13748/*[zeppelin, the 1929 year symbol]. Candlestick 2002.29.120.3 marked: *GORHAM/*[lion] [anchor] *G/STERLING/ A13748/CEMENT-LOADED/*[haystack, the 1928 year symbol]
Dallas Museum of Art, The Jewel Stern American Silver Collection, acquired through the Patsy Lacy Griffith Collection, gift of Patsy Lacy Griffith by exchange, DMA 2002.29.120.1–3

This hand-chased console ensemble in the Arts and Crafts style consists of a compote and a pair of candlesticks. Sold separately, the retail price of a compotier was $75, the same as a pair of candlesticks. Gorham records indicate that only six compotes were produced, and the item, reduced in price by a third, was discontinued on November 12, 1932, whereas fifty candlesticks were made (see chapter 3).[1]

1. Samuel J. Hough, "Report on Gorham sterling compotier A13748," June 2, 1988; and idem, letter to Jewel Stern, June 20, 1988.

27. Cigarette box, c. 1928*

Enameled silver. 2½ × 6 × 3¾ in. (6.4 × 15.2 × 9.5 cm). Marked: [lion] [anchor] *G STERLING 173 C 60 / E9864* [scratched in and scratched out] *E13084* [scratched]
Dallas Museum of Art, The Jewel Stern American Silver Collection, acquired through the Patsy Lacy Griffith Collection, gift of Patsy Lacy Griffith by exchange, DMA 2002.29.40

The enamel design on this box features the stepped motifs associated with the ubiquitous 1920s setback skyscrapers. The colors, black and red, were a popular combination in modern enameled silverware at the end of the decade.

28. Master Building teapot, 1929*

Silverplate. 5¼ × 6¼ × 3⅛ in. (13.3 × 15.9 × 7.9 cm). Marked: *MASTER BUILDING/GORHAM/7 E* [anchor in shield] *P* [zeppelin, the 1929 year symbol]/*SILVER SOLDERED/014052/10 OZ*
Dallas Museum of Art, The Jewel Stern American Silver Collection, acquired through the Patsy Lacy Griffith Collection, gift of Patsy Lacy Griffith by exchange, DMA 2002.29.140

An example of Gorham's Hotel Division commercial silverware, this lively teapot was part of the service for the modernist restaurant of the Master Apartment Building that housed the Roerich Museum in New York City (see chapter 7).

29. *Franconia* **sandwich plate, 1930***

Silver. ⅞ × 13¾ × 11¼ in. (2.2 × 34.9 × 28.6 cm). Marked: *GORHAM /* [lion] [anchor] *G / STERLING / A 14115 / 1 /* [elephant, the 1930 year symbol] */ FRANCONIA*

Dallas Museum of Art, The Jewel Stern American Silver Collection, acquired through the Patsy Lacy Griffith Collection, gift of Patsy Lacy Griffith by exchange, DMA 2002.29.27

In April 1930, Gorham introduced a line of holloware named *Franconia* that included sandwich plates, chop dishes, relish dishes, and a bowl with flower holder. Pieces in the line were produced with and without handles and with and without a foot. This sandwich plate is the version with handles and without a foot. Thirty-six were made. The retail price was $45.[1]

1. Samuel J. Hough, "Report on Two Pieces of Gorham Sterling Holloware 'Franconia,'" June 2, 1988.

30. Mayonnaise bowl, 1934*

Silver. 20¼ × 6⅛ × 4¼ in. (5.7 × 15.6 × 10.8 cm). Marked: *GORHAM /* [lion] [anchor] *G / STERLING / 43127*

Dallas Museum of Art, The Jewel Stern American Silver Collection, acquired through the Patsy Lacy Griffith Collection, gift of Patsy Lacy Griffith by exchange, DMA 2002.29.5

The mayonnaise bowl was introduced in 1934 in four runs of twenty-four each. Two dozen more were produced in 1936 and another two dozen in 1937. The number in the last run in 1940 was not recorded. This design appears unique as no others related to it have been identified by Hough in the Gorham Archives at Brown University (see chapter 6).[1]

1. Samuel J. Hough, "Report on Gorham Mayonnaise Bowl 43127," Nov. 13, 1998.

31. *K. K. Culver Trophy,* **1938***

Viktor Schreckengost
American, b. 1906

Silverplated bronze. 40 × 14 × 9 in. (101.6 × 35.6 × 22.9 cm). Engraved: [on front] *K K CULVER* [in raised letters] / *Trophy / Miami / All American / Air Maneuvers.* [on stepped block] *WON BY / EDNA GARDNER KIDD, R. N. / Plane / MONOCOUPE*
The Mitchell Wolfson Jr. Collection

Completed at the end of 1938 for a new women's race in the Miami All-American Air Maneuvers competition, the Culver trophy features a soaring recumbent female representing the spirit of flight. Schreckengost's figure recalls the smooth, rounded forms of his ceramics and its prow-like pylon and stepped base evoke the image of aerodynamic speed suggested by his similarly streamlined industrial designs such as that for the Limoges China Company's *Triumph* china and Murray's "Mercury" bicycle (see chapter 6).

32. Tea service, 1947*

Silver, wood. Teapot 6½ × 8¾ × 5¼ in. (16.5 × 22.2 × 13.3 cm); sugar bowl 3¾ × 3⅝ in. (9.5 × 9.2 cm); creamer 2¾ × 4¾ × 2⅞ in. (7.0 × 12.1 × 7.3 cm). Teapot marked: *GORHAM /* [lion] [anchor] *G / STERLING / 791 / 7* [in a square, the 1947 year symbol] */ 1½ PINT / 6.* Teapot lid: *STERLING 6.* Creamer: *GORHAM /* [lion] [anchor] *G / STERLING / 792 / 7* [in a square, the 1947 year symbol] */ 1½ PINT / 6.* Sugar bowl: *GORHAM /* [lion] [anchor] *G / STERLING / 793 / 7* [in a square, the 1947 year symbol] */ 15⁄16 PINT.* Sugar bowl lid: *STERLING 2*
Dallas Museum of Art, gift of Marie and John Houser Chiles on the occasions of their Anniversary, February 4, 1997 through the 20th-Century Design Fund, DMA 1997.3.1–3

Gorham's tea service reflects Danish design in the Jensen taste in mid-century American silver holloware.

33. *Trend* **coffee service, 1952**

Silver, ebony. Coffeepot 8 × 7¼ in. (20.3 × 18.4 cm); creamer 4¾ × 4¼ in. (12.1 × 10.8 cm); sugar bowl 5¼ × 3½ in. (13.3 × 8.9 cm). Coffeepot marked: *GORHAM /* [lion] [anchor] *G / STERLING / 1061 / 2* [in pentagon, the 1952 year symbol] */ 2⅜ PINT / 51.2 / 51.* Creamer: *GORHAM /* [lion] [anchor] *G / STERLING / 1063 / 2* [in pentagon, the 1952 year symbol] */ ⅝ PINT.* Sugar bowl: *GORHAM /* [lion] [anchor] *G / STERLING / 1062 / 2* [in pentagon, the 1952 year symbol] */ 10*
Dallas Museum of Art, The Jewel Stern American Silver Collection, Decorative Arts Fund, DMA 2002.29.182.1–3

Trend, Gorham's first modern post–World War II sterling holloware line, was influenced by the pinched-in-waist shape of the New Look in fashion as well as contemporary Scandinavian silverware. The versatile coffeepot can double as a pitcher for water and mixed drinks.[1]

1. "Silver Leads a Double Life," *House and Garden* 105 (Feb. 1954): 77; see also, "Piece by Piece," *House and Garden* 111 (May 1957): 93.

34. *Trend* **candlesticks (six), 1952***

Silver. 1¾ × 3⅜ in. (4.4 × 8.6 cm). Marked (each): *GORHAM / STERLING / CEMENT REINFORCED / 829.* Paper label (on 2002.29.74.1): *GORHAM* [in script] */ STERLING / PYRAMID / CANDLESTICK*
Dallas Museum of Art, The Jewel Stern American Silver Collection, Decorative Arts Fund, DMA 2002.29.73–75.1–2

The *Trend* candlesticks were designed to stack and create multi-tiered arrangements. In an advertisement in the *New Yorker,* the price was listed as $15 for two, and it was suggested that buyers might "use the pair singly for contemporary good looks or buy several to pyramid together for tall sticks of unusual drama."[1] A pair of the *Trend* candlesticks was exhibited in *20th Century Design: U.S.A.,* a traveling exhibition in 1959 and 1960, although only one was listed in the catalogue (see chapter 14).

1. "Console Candlesticks, circa 1953 . . ." Gorham advertisement, *New Yorker* 29 (May 2, 1953): 67.

35. *Trend* **salt and pepper shakers, c. 1954***

Silver, Styron. 2¾ × 1¾ in. (7.0 × 4.4 cm). Marked (each) [molded in relief]: *GORHAM STERLING / ON / STYRON / LICENSED UNDER / PAT. 2644616,* [scratched] *H1–7441.* Paper label (on pepper shaker): *GORHAM / STERLING /* [lion] [anchor] *G*
Dallas Museum of Art, The Jewel Stern American Silver Collection, Decorative Arts Fund, DMA 2002.29.181.1–2

Instructions included with this salt and pepper set described its novel design: "Pick up as you would a conventional salt or pepper shaker, *but don't turn over*—simply shake up and down. Spices will spray from bottom." The Gorham advertisements in the *New Yorker* and *House Beautiful* in 1954 heralded the item as "the First Free Flowing Sterling Salt and Pepper Set."[1] The black (for pepper) and white (for salt) Styron (polystyrene) caps, which had no holes, may be unscrewed to allow the shakers to be filled.

1. "Introducing the First Free Flowing Sterling Salt and Pepper Set," Gorham advertisement, *House Beautiful* 96 (May 1954): 139.

36. *Directional* **creamer and sugar bowl, 1955**

Phillip Bernard Johnson
American, 1899–1992

Patent (for a creamer) filed Oct. 19, 1955, granted Oct. 23, 1956. Silver, plastic. 4½ × 5 in. (11.4 × 12.7 cm), Marked (each): *GORHAM /* [lion] [anchor] *G / STERLING / 5* [in shield, the 1955 year symbol] */ 1310* [on creamer], *1309* [on sugar bowl]
Dallas Museum of Art, The Jewel Stern American Silver Collection, acquired through the Patsy Lacy Griffith Collection, gift of Patsy Lacy Griffith by exchange, DMA 2002.29.179.1–2

Directional and *Trend,* the earlier of the two, were Gorham's 1950s modern sterling holloware lines. This *Directional* creamer was the only patented piece in the line and is different from the creamer of the coffee set (see chapter 10). The shape of this creamer and sugar bowl is similar to that of the *Directional* "liquor mixer," which may also have been the work of Johnson, the staff designer who filed for the patent on this creamer. Although the upward curving black plastic handle was innovative in American silver, there were similar European precedents.

37. *Directional* **pitcher, 1955**

Silver. 8 × 5½ in. (20.3 × 14.0 cm). Marked: *GORHAM /* [lion] [anchor] *G / STERLING / 1312 / 5* [in shield, the 1955 year symbol] */ 2¼ PINT*
Dallas Museum of Art, The Jewel Stern American Silver Collection, acquired through the Patsy Lacy Griffith Collection, gift of Patsy Lacy Griffith by exchange, DMA 2002.29.178

In addition to the coffee set creamer, at least two pitchers including this one were made in the *Directional* pattern. The fluid contours and sculptural purity of the coffee set creamer were retained for this pitcher (see chapter 10). A larger version of this pitcher was also produced.

38. *Directional* "Tri-round" bowl, 1955

Silver. 2¼ × 7½ × 6¾ in. (5.7 × 19.1 × 17.1 cm). Marked: *GORHAM* / [lion] [anchor] *G* / *STERLING* / *958* / *5* [in shield, the 1955 year symbol] Dallas Museum of Art, The Jewel Stern American Silver Collection, Decorative Arts Fund, DMA 2002.29.180

The triangular "Tri-round" *Directional* bowl was made in two sizes. This example is the smaller of the two. The larger size (no. 959) was ten inches in diameter.

39. *Directional* liquor mixer, 1956 (designed c. 1955)*

Silver, ebonized wood. 9 × 7¼ × 4¾ in. (22.9 × 18.4 × 12.1 cm). Marked: *GORHAM* / [lion] [anchor] *G* / *STERLING* / *1308* / *6* [in shield, the 1956 year symbol] / *2 PINT* Dallas Museum of Art, The Jewel Stern American Silver Collection, acquired through the Patsy Lacy Griffith Collection, gift of Patsy Lacy Griffith by exchange, DMA 2002.29.67

The contours of the *Directional* liquor mixer, especially the pouring rim, were emphasized by a cantilevered, curved, and tapered ebonized wood handle.

40. *Modern* pitcher, c. 1955*

Silverplate. 12 × 6¾ × 5 in. (30.5 × 17.1 × 12.7 cm). Marked: *E* [in rounded square] [anchor in shield] *P* [in rounded square] / *GORHAM* [in rounded rectangle] / *YC888* / *3¾ PINT* Dallas Museum of Art, The Jewel Stern American Silver Collection, gift of Jewel Stern, DMA 2004.13.2

Gorham's contemporary 1950s silverplated holloware line was named *Modern* in the firm's catalogues. The smooth contours and looping handle of this tall pitcher in the *Modern* group owes a debt to mid-century Scandinavian design. It was produced in four sizes; this twelve-inch size is the largest. Other *Modern* items are a beverage server with "stir-up" spoon, a double vegetable dish, a three-piece coffee set, an "Avocado" centerpiece, a "Decorator" bowl, a covered butter dish, a five-piece tea service on matching tray, a cream and sugar set, and the *Tira* centerpiece and bread tray.

References: "Make it a Christmas with a Silver Lining," *House and Garden* 108 (Dec. 1955): 130; "Holloware brimming with new ideas," *Bride's Magazine* 32 (winter 1965): 155.

41. *Modern* "Avocado" centerpiece, c. 1955–1960

Silverplate. 1¾ × 16 × 5¾ in. (4.4 × 40.6 × 14.6 cm). Marked: *Gorham* [in script] / *E* [in rounded square] [anchor in shield] *P* [in rounded square] / *YC844* Dallas Museum of Art, The Jewel Stern American Silver Collection, Decorative Arts Fund, DMA 2002.29.276

The sinuous, organic shape of the *Modern* "Avocado" centerpiece was also applied to an eight-inch bonbon dish.

42. *Modern* double vegetable dish, c. 1959*

Silverplate. 4 × 11 × 7 in. (10.2 × 27.9 × 17.8 cm). Marked: *E* [in rounded square] [anchor in shield] *P* [in rounded square] / *GORHAM* [in rounded rectangle] / *C847* Dallas Museum of Art, The Jewel Stern American Silver Collection, Decorative Arts Fund, DMA 2002.29.85.A–B

The fluid shape of this double vegetable dish and the crisp curves of its twin handles recall sleek 1950s automobiles and the rise of the tail-fin motif.

43. *Modern* beverage server and "stir-up" spoon, c. 1959*

Donald H. Colflesh
American, b. 1932

Silverplate, plastic. Beverage server 11⅛ × 6⅜ × 3 in. (28.3 × 16.2 × 7.6 cm); spoon ¾ × ¹³⁄₁₆ × 12¾ in. (1.9 × 2.1 × 32.4 cm). Pitcher marked: *Gorham* [in script] / *E* [anchor in shield] *P* / *YC845* / *CAP. 40 OZS* / [scratched] *TSBS*. Spoon: *GORHAM E* [anchor in shield] *P N13* Dallas Museum of Art, The Jewel Stern American Silver Collection, Decorative Arts Fund, DMA 2002.29.86.A–B

The *Modern* beverage server and "stir-up" spoon, which was offered separately, appeared on the cover of the *Gorham 1959 Silverplated Holloware Catalog*. The slender height of the cylindrical vessel is striking in its simplicity and elegance, while the bold organic curve of the black plastic handle provides a dynamic counterpoint. By 1969, Gorham had discontinued almost the entire *Modern* line, yet this stylish beverage server remained in production.

44. *Modern* "Decorator" bowl, c. 1959*

Silverplate, plastic. 6½ × 10¾ × 9½ in. (16.5 × 27.3 × 24.1 cm). Marked (on bowl): *E* [anchor in shield] *P* / *GORHAM* [in rounded rectangle]. On base [molded in relief]: *Gorham* [in script] Dallas Museum of Art, The Jewel Stern American Silver Collection, Decorative Arts Fund, DMA 2002.29.87

Introduced in the late 1950s, this bowl was one of many items in Gorham's *Modern* line of silverplated holloware. By means of a wing nut on the underside of the base, the bowl can be made to rotate through 360 degrees to create a variety of asymmetrical free form shapes. Gorham suggested the bowl for "imaginative floral arrangements," hence the "Decorator" designation. In line drawings in the catalogue the bowl was shown in three positions and buyers were advised that "any non-tarnishing florist putty will hold glass or metal flower arranger in place."[1] These drawings were replicated on the original paper label affixed to each bowl.

1. *Gorham 1959 Silverplated Holloware Catalog*, 10.

45. *Stardust* flatware, 1957*

Richard L. Huggins
American, b. 1929

Silver, stainless steel knife blade. Place knife ¾ × 8⅞ in. (1.9 × 22.5 cm); place fork ⅞ × 7½ in. (2.2 × 19.1 cm); salad fork 1 × 7 in. (2.5 × 17.8 cm); teaspoon 1¼ × 6 in. (3.2 × 15.2 cm). Fork / salad spoon / teaspoon marked: *GORHAM STERLING*. Knife (on handle): *GORHAM*. Knife (on blade): *STAINLESS* Dallas Museum of Art, gift of Beverly Hart Bremer, 1998.163.1–4

Gorham's *Stardust* flatware was aptly named, for its tapered handles are stamped with asterisk-like stars made up of four intersecting lines. Only the handle of the knife shows the design on both front and back. Huggins also designed two bowls and a sandwich plate in this pattern.

46. *Free-form* bowl, c. 1959

Donald H. Colflesh
American, b. 1932

Silverplate. 6 × 10½ × 8⁹⁄₁₆ in. (15.2 × 26.7 × 21.8 cm). Marked: *GORHAM* [in script] *E* [anchor in shield] *P* / *YC663* / *197–05–1281* [scratched] Dallas Museum of Art, The Jewel Stern American Silver Collection, gift of Jewel Stern, DMA 2004.13.4

The swooping *Free-form* footed bowl stood in profile in the cover photograph of the *Gorham 1959 Silverplated Holloware Catalog*. The shape of the bowl bears a resemblance to Colflesh's "Contour" bowl in the *Circa '70* group. This bowl was an item selected for Gorham's *Giftware*, a line of holloware with a brass-color lacquer finish and color applied to the interiors to emulate enamel. On the *Giftware* label Gorham declared that its new finish prevented tarnish and discoloration, and consumers were cautioned not to use polish.

47. *Circa '70* tea and coffee service, 1963 (designed 1958, introduced 1960)*

Donald H. Colflesh
American, b. 1932

Silver, ebony. Coffeepot 11½ × 6¾ × 5¾ in. (29.2 × 17.1 × 14.6 cm); teapot 9¼ × 6¾ × 5¾ in. (23.5 × 17.1 × 14.6 cm); creamer 6½ × 3⅝ × 3½ in. (16.5 × 9.2 × 8.9 cm); sugar bowl 4½ × 6⁹⁄₁₆ × 4¾ in. (11.4 × 16.7 × 12.1 cm). Teapot marked: *Gorham* [in script] / *STERLING* / [lion] [anchor] *G* / *1462* / *3* [in hexagon, the 1963 year symbol] / *2¾ PINT* / *23*. Teapot lid: *STERLING 23* [and] *STERLING 8*. Coffeepot: *Gorham* [in script] / *STERLING* / [lion] [anchor] *G* / *1461* / *3* [in hexagon, the 1963 year symbol] / *3 PINT* / *2*. Coffeepot lid: *STERLING 23* [and] *STERLING 8*. Creamer: *Gorham* [in script] / *STERLING* / [lion] [anchor] *G* / *1464* / *3* [in hexagon, the 1963 year symbol] / *¾ PINT*. Sugar bowl: *Gorham* [in script] / *STERLING* / [lion] [anchor] *G* / *1463* / *3* [in hexagon] / *1*. Sugar bowl lid: *STERLING 4* Dallas Museum of Art, 20th-Century Design Fund, DMA 1997.2.1–4

Circa '70 was a line marketed in 1960 as the wave of the future. In this set, the elongated shape of the vessels, the vertical thrust of the handles that appear to soar upward, and the attenuated finials were the designer's formal means of suggesting the race into space that mesmerized Americans in the late 1950s. At the time it was introduced this four-piece service cost $650. It was initially offered with either a round silverplated tray or a sterling tray with a black Formica center.[1]

1. "Circa '70 by Gorham," Gorham advertisement, *New Yorker* 37 (Apr. 8, 1961): 27.

48. *Circa '70* tray, 1963*

Silver, Formica. 5 × 27 × 25 in. (12.7 × 68.6 × 63.5 cm). Marked: *GOR-HAM* [lion] [anchor] *G / STERLING 1468*
Dallas Museum of Art, The Patsy Lacy Griffith Collection, gift of Patsy Lacy Griffith by exchange, DMA 2004.21

In 1963 a matching tray for the *Circa '70* service was made available. It was not by Donald Colflesh, the designer of the service, as he had left Gorham in 1962. The wing form of the handle of the sugar bowl was enlarged and adapted by the design department for the handles of the circular tray, which has a black Formica center mounted within a dramatically curved, saucer-like silver rim.

49. *Circa '70* "Delta" bowl, 1960 (designed 1958)*

Donald H. Colflesh
American, b. 1932

Silver, ebony. 5⅛ × 11⅞ × 10⅞ in. (13.0 × 30.2 × 27.6 cm). Marked: *GORHAM / STERLING / [lion]* [anchor] *G / 1457 / [hexagon, the 1960 year symbol] / ME [scratched]*
Dallas Museum of Art, The Jewel Stern American Silver Collection, Decorative Arts Fund, DMA 2002.29.69

This triangular bowl seems to hover above its striking feet, which have ebony tips. An advertisement for the *Circa '70* "Delta" bowl and candelabra appeared in both the *New Yorker* and *Town and Country* in November 1960.[1] A month later, the bowl was illustrated, in an article by Poppy Cannon, as an example of fine design."[2] The retail price of the "Delta" bowl was $185 in 1960.

1. "Circa '70: Created for today, tomorrow, forever in precious Gorham sterling," Gorham advertisement, *New Yorker* 36 (Nov. 19, 1960): 16.
2. Poppy Cannon, "Great Day in the Morning," *Town and Country* 114 (Dec. 1960): 137.

50. *Circa '70* candelabrum, 1960 (designed 1958)*

Donald H. Colflesh
American, b. 1932

Silver, ebony. 8¼ × 9¼ in. (21.0 × 23.5 cm). Marked: *Gorham* [in script] / *STERLING / [lion]* [anchor] *G 1458 / [hexagon, the 1960 year symbol]*
The Jewel Stern American Silver Collection, promised gift of Jewel Stern, DMA 5.2003.16

The triangular, three-light *Circa '70* candelabrum has three ebony-tipped feet like those of the *Circa '70* "Delta" bowl with which it is coordinated to make an ensemble (in a pair). The ebony finial is the finishing touch of enrichment. The price of a pair was $400 in 1960.

51. *Circa '70* "Contour" bowl, 1960 (designed 1958)

Donald H. Colflesh
American, b. 1932

Silver. 7½ × 7⅞ × 6⁷⁄₁₆ in. (19.1 × 20.0 × 16.4 cm). Marked: *Gorham* [in script] / *STERLING / [lion]* [anchor] *G / 1455 / [hexagon, the 1960 year symbol]*
The Jewel Stern American Silver Collection, promised gift of Jewel Stern, DMA 5.2003.17

As its name implied, contour was the essence of this curving bowl that tapers to a flared pedestal. It has no decoration to distract from its form, which is similar to that of the *Free-form* bowl Colflesh designed for Gorham in silverplate.

Reference: Poppy Cannon, "Great Day in the Morning," *Town and Country* 114 (Dec. 1960): 137.

52. *Circa '70* pitcher-mixer with mixer spoon, 1960

Silver, ebony. Pitcher 11¾ × 6¾ × 5¾ in. (29.8 × 17.1 × 14.6 cm); spoon 1 × 1¾ × 12½ in. (2.5 × 4.4 × 31.8 cm). Pitcher-mixer marked: *Gorham* [in script] / *STERLING / [lion]* [anchor] *G / 1460 / [hexagon, the 1965 year symbol] / 3 PINT*. Spoon: *GORHAM STERLING*
Dallas Museum of Art, The Jewel Stern American Silver Collection, Decorative Arts Fund, 2002.29.68.A–B

The pitcher-mixer was adapted by the Gorham design department from the *Circa '70* coffeepot that had been designed by Donald Colflesh before he left Gorham in 1962. The mixer spoon with an ebony handle was a staff design made to coordinate with the pitcher-mixer.

53. *Bateau* double vegetable dish, 1960 (designed 1959)

Alexandra C. Solowij (Watkins)
American (formerly Canadian) (b. Poland), 1933

Patent 188,731 (for a bowl) filed Mar. 31, 1960, granted Aug. 30, 1960. Silverplate. 4 × 13⅛ × 6⅝ in. (10.2 × 33.3 × 16.8 cm). Marked: *Gorham* [in script] / *E* [anchor in shield] *P / YC694*
Dallas Museum of Art, The Jewel Stern American Silver Collection, gift of Jewel Stern, 2003.34.17.A–B

A design for what was referred to as a "covered dish with handles" in a group of drawings submitted by Solowij, then a Canadian citizen, to Gorham after graduating from the School of the Museum of Fine Arts, Boston in 1958, was the prototype for the *Bateau* double vegetable dish. The skills that Solowij demonstrated in the drawings led to a position in the Gorham design department from 1959 to 1960. Shortly after she arrived at Gorham, her covered dish was earmarked for production in two versions. Without the lid, it became the vigorously marketed twelve-inch *Bateau* centerpiece available with an optional three-light insert for tapers (see chapter 10). This model also was produced in a fourteen-and-a-quarter-inch size and as a bonbon dish. With a lid, and without the handles, the original design was transformed into the *Bateau* double vegetable dish. A pointed asymmetrical finial on the lid sweeps upward with panache as it echoes the points of the dish, yet it capably balances the piece when the lid is turned over to function as a second serving dish. Of all the items in the group, the smaller, twelve-inch *Bateau* centerpiece and the bonbon dish were in production the longest.[1]

1. *Gorham Silverplated Holloware Catalog,* March 1969, 10, 20.

54. *Stoplight* jigger, c. 1961

Howard A. Tarleton
American, dates unknown

Patent (for a jigger) filed Sept. 30, 1961, granted May 29, 1962. Enameled silver. 2½ × 2¼ in. (6.4 × 5.7 cm). Marked: *GORHAM / STERLING / 354 / STOPLIGHT JIGGER / 3½* [underlined] / *2½* [underlined] / *1 oz* [underlined]
Dallas Museum of Art, The Jewel Stern American Silver Collection, Decorative Arts Fund, DMA 2002.29.204

See chapter 13.

55. *Classique* flatware (knife), 1961*

Burr Sebring
American, b. 1928

Silver, stainless steel. Place knife ⅜ × ¾ × 9 in. (1.0 × 1.9 × 22.9 cm); place fork ½ × 1 × 7⅜ in. (1.3 × 2.5 × 18.7 cm); salad fork ½ × 1 × 6⅝ in. (1.3 × 2.5 × 16.8 cm); teaspoon ⅜ × 1¼ × 6 in. (1.0 × 3.2 × 15.2 cm). Knife marked (on blade): *GORHAM / STERLING HANDLE / STAINLESS BLADE*. Fork / salad fork / teaspoon: marked: *GORHAM / [lion]* [anchor] *G* [in circle] / *STERLING*
Dallas Museum of Art, gift of Beverly Hart Bremer, DMA 2000.401.1–4

Sebring, a staff designer, gave *Classique* a diamond-shaped handle with angled planes that terminate in a faceted tip. The planarity of these elements contrasts with the otherwise subtle contouring of the form.

56. USS *Long Beach* service candelabra (pair), 1961*

Richard L. Huggins
American, b. 1929

Silver. 25½ × 18 in. (64.8 × 45.7 cm). Both unmarked.
Property of the U.S. Navy, donated by the City of Long Beach, Calif.

A stylized atomic motif serves as decorative finials for these two six-light candelabra, part of an eighteen-piece presentation service for the navy's first nuclear-powered missile cruiser, the USS *Long Beach*. In recognition of the pioneering nature of its namesake ship's propulsion system, the City of Long Beach, California, selected Huggins's dramatic but controversial proposal from among several more conservative services offered by Gorham's designers—and those submitted by two other silver manufacturers. The candelabra's elongated, wasp-waisted candleholders secured by exuberantly curved arms appear to hover atop a circular platform, which in turn is supported by upswept stilt-like legs. Reminiscent of the soaring, flared forms of Gorham's *Circa '70* line, the details of the various trays, platters, dishes, and bowls included in the service evoke futuristic images of flying saucers and orbiting electrons, all in lavish celebration of the Atomic Age. A company memorandum noted the pair required 160 hours to fabricate and were assigned a combined retail value of $5,000 (see chapter 13).

References: "U.S.S. *Long Beach* Atomic Cruiser—Vital Statistics," Gorham memorandum, Sept. 7, 1961, courtesy Richard L. Huggins; David B. Warren, Katherine S. Howe, and Michael K. Brown, *Marks of Achievement: Four Centuries of American Presentation Silver*, exh. cat. Museum of Fine Arts Houston (New York: Abrams, 1987), 170–71.

57. USS *Long Beach* service electric coffee urn and tray, 1961*

Richard L. Huggins
American, b. 1929

Silver. Coffee urn 22 × 16½ × 18¾ in. (55.9 × 41.9 × 47.6 cm); tray 28½ × 20⅝ in. (72.4 × 52.4 cm). Both unmarked.
Property of the U.S. Navy, donated by the City of Long Beach, Calif.

A company memorandum indicates this "thermostatically controlled" coffee urn from the USS *Long Beach* presentation service required 177 hours to fabricate and was assigned a retail value of $4,500.

Reference: "U.S.S. Long Beach Atomic Cruiser—Vital Statistics," Gorham memorandum, Sept. 7, 1961, courtesy Richard L. Huggins.

58. *Tri-round* bowl, c. 1963*

Silverplate with applied color. 2½ × 8¼ in. (6.4 × 12.0 cm). Marked: G [in octagon] / NEWPORT / SILVERPLATE / N [in shield] [tower in shield] / YB2
Dallas Museum of Art, The Jewel Stern American Silver Collection, Decorative Arts Fund, DMA 2002.29.266

The silverplated exterior of this rounded triangular bowl on three stubby feet is in sharp contrast to the vibrant red and blue of its interior. *Tri-round* bowls were produced in three sizes and offered in gradations of red, blue, and green. This predominantly blue bowl is in the medium size. The company assured its customers that the translucent colors lining the interiors were of a "superior dyed enamel . . . that will not crack, stain or blister with normal use," and is "impervious to salt, sulphur and concentrated heat from cigarettes."[1]

1. "Newport: A Distinguished Line of Silverplated Holloware," Gorham trade brochure (Jan. 1964), n.p.

59. Dish, c. 1963

Silverplate with applied color. 1½ × 9½ × 5 in. (3.8 × 24.1 × 12.7 cm). Marked: G [in octagon] / NEWPORT / SILVERPLATE / [anchor in shield] N [in shield] [tower in shield] / YB97
Dallas Museum of Art, The Jewel Stern American Silver Collection, Decorative Arts Fund, DMA 2002.29.264

This free form dish has the same color finish as the Newport *Tri-round* bowl, but is flat and sleeker. It was not illustrated in the January 1964 brochure.

60. Candy jar, 1963*

Silver; green and colorless glass. 5¾ × 5½ in. (14.6 × 14.0 cm). Marked (lid): GORHAM / STERLING / 893
Dallas Museum of Art, The Jewel Stern American Silver Collection, Decorative Arts Fund, DMA 2002.29.70.A–B

This glass and silver candy jar was made in four colors (see chapter 13) and introduced in 1963 in three of them, emerald green, amethyst, and cobalt blue. In this color, emerald green, it was produced until 1965; in amethyst and cobalt blue, until 1967. It was offered in smoke-gray Optic glass in 1967, and this version remained in the line until 1972. The jewel-like colors of the glass container seem appropriate to the form, which resembles the cut of a precious gem. For all the jars, the finial was made of clear glass, giving it the appearance of a drop of water that has just "splashed" onto the silver lid. The glass was produced by the Swedish firm Lindshammar Glasbruk.

61. Butter dish, c. 1965*

Silverplate, walnut, glass. 2⅝ × 9³⁄₁₆ × 3¹¹⁄₁₆ in. (6.7 × 23.3 × 9.4 cm). Marked: Gorham [in script] / E [anchor in shield] P / YC 75
Dallas Museum of Art, The Jewel Stern American Silver Collection, gift of Jewel Stern, DMA 2003.34.13.A–C

The influence of 1950s modern Scandinavian wood table accessories is apparent in this contoured, hand-rubbed and oiled walnut butter dish that has a glass liner and a silverplated cover with a simple walnut finial. By 1969 this model was no longer in production.

62. *Starburst* candleholder, c. 1967*

Silverplate. 2 × 4⅝ × 4⅜ in. (5.1 × 11.7 × 11.1 cm). Marked: GORHAM SILVERPLATE / YC-40
Dallas Museum of Art, The Jewel Stern American Silver Collection, Decorative Arts Fund, DMA 2002.29.95

When inserted into the radiating holder, the central taper stands straight while the other five tall tapers (the six included in a set with the candleholder) angled slightly outward, adding to the starburst effect for which the piece was named (see chapter 13). The price of the candleholder was $9.95.[1]

1. "12 new glimpses into the elegant world of silver," *Gift & Tableware Reporter* (Oct. 16, 1967): 10.

63. *Ring* basket, c. 1968

Silverplate, plastic. 3¾ × 9½ in. (9.5 × 24.1 cm). Marked: Gorham / E [anchor in shield] P / YC 744
Dallas Museum of Art, The Jewel Stern American Silver Collection, Decorative Arts Fund, DMA 2002.29.252

The openwork *Ring* basket was made in two variations, as in this example, with a number of inserted disks of colored translucent plastic in bright blue and orange, and with a clear red or blue glass liner (see chapter 11).

64. *Spanish Tracery* flatware (fork*), 1970

Silver, stainless steel knife blade. Place knife ¾ × 8¹⁵⁄₁₆ in. (1.9 × 22.7 cm); place fork ⅝ × ¹⁵⁄₁₆ × 7⁷⁄₁₆ in. (1.6 × 2.4 × 18.9 cm); salad fork 1¹⁄₁₆ × 6¹³⁄₁₆ in. (2.7 × 17.3 cm); teaspoon 1¼ × 6 in. (3.2 × 15.2 cm). Knife marked (on blade): © GORHAM STERLING HANDLE STAINLESS BLADE. Fork / salad fork: [lion] [anchor] G © GORHAM / STERLING SPANISH TRACERY
Dallas Museum of Art, gift of Beverly Hart Bremer, DMA 1998.178.1–4

Decorative patterns that evoked Spain enjoyed popularity around 1970. Gorham's *Spanish Tracery* was among these, as were its stainless patterns, *Spanish Scroll* and *Hacienda*. The use of dense decoration on simple handles of a contemporary shape was a design strategy of the 1960s and early 1970s. In *Spanish Tracery*, flowers, arches, and volutes fill the field of the square-tipped handles. The salad fork, pierced just beneath the prongs, is the most ornate piece.

ALVIN CORPORATION
PROVIDENCE, RHODE ISLAND
FOUNDED 1886

DIVISION OF GORHAM MANUFACTURING COMPANY AFTER 1928

65. *Gift Line* sandwich plate, 1930

Silver. ½ × 9 in. (1.3 × 22.9 cm). Marked: ALVIN / STERLING / H1508
Dallas Museum of Art, The Jewel Stern American Silver Collection, acquired through the Patsy Lacy Griffith Collection, gift of Patsy Lacy Griffith by exchange, DMA 2002.29.122

In 1930, Alvin released the extensive *Gift Line* holloware series, one of the last designs manufactured by the company. Among the many items in this moderately priced sterling group was this sandwich plate, of which 250 were made to sell for $10 each.[1]

1. Samuel J. Hough, "Report on Alvin sterling pieces from 'Gift Line,'" June 3, 1988.

66. Luncheon plate, 1930

Silver. 1¾ × 10½ in. (4.4 × 26.7 cm). Marked: ALVIN / STERLING / H90
Dallas Museum of Art, The Jewel Stern American Silver Collection, acquired through the Patsy Lacy Griffith Collection, gift of Patsy Lacy Griffith by exchange, DMA 2002.29.123

This pattern is more limited in variety and was more expensive than Alvin's *Gift Line* holloware. Other than the luncheon plate in this design, only a bowl has come to light and no record of other pieces has been found in the Gorham Archives at Brown University. The luncheon plate was introduced in 1930 for $25. Fifty examples were produced.[1]

1. Samuel J. Hough, "Report on Alvin sterling luncheon plate H90," June 3, 1988.

WILLIAM B. DURGIN COMPANY
CONCORD, NEW HAMPSHIRE
1853–1931

PROVIDENCE, RHODE ISLAND

DIVISION OF GORHAM MANUFACTURING COMPANY
AFTER 1905

67. Sandwich tray, 1928*
Silver, jade. 1¼ × 13 in. (3.2 × 33.0 cm). Marked: *GORHAM D* [in script in circle] *STERLING 92628*. Engraved: *CRA*
Dallas Museum of Art, The Jewel Stern American Silver Collection, acquired through the Patsy Lacy Griffith Collection, gift of Patsy Lacy Griffith by exchange, DMA 2002.29.31

The tray is among a group of expensive holloware objects enlivened with semiprecious stones to appeal to affluent consumers. A serving piece with matching jade finial was originally offered with this tray.

Reference: "Modern Design in Silver," *House and Garden* 54 (Sept. 1928): 86.

68. Tea caddy and spoon, 1928*
Silver, rose quartz. Tea caddy 4½ × 4½ in. (11.4 × 11.4 cm); spoon ¾ × 4 × 2½ in. (1.9 × 10.2 × 6.4 cm). Tea caddy marked: *GORHAM / D* [in script in circle] / *STERLING / 92637C*. Spoon: *STERLING*. Engraved: *FMH*
Dallas Museum of Art, The Jewel Stern American Silver Collection, acquired through the Patsy Lacy Griffith Collection, gift of Patsy Lacy Griffith by exchange, DMA 2002.29.30.1–2

A tea caddy and matching spoon are among the rarest holloware objects from the late 1920s. Like Durgin's sandwich tray embellished with jade, this ensemble was among the objects produced by the firm for the carriage trade. The whimsical rose quartz finial on the caddy is in the shape of an elephant. The tea caddy and spoon were also made with carved jade enrichments. For this version, the price in 1928 at Gorham's store on Fifth Avenue in New York was $107.[1]

1. "Stone Trimmed Sterling: The Newest Thing by Gorham," Gorham advertisement, *New Yorker* 4 (Apr. 21, 1928): 69; and "Modern Design in Silver," *House and Garden* 54 (Sept. 1928): 85.

GEORGE A. HENCKEL & CO
NEW YORK, NEW YORK
ACTIVE 1909–43

69. Cocktail shaker, c. 1935
Silver. 10¼ × 3 in. (26 × 7.6 cm). Marked: [stylized H with lines and circle] / *STERLING / 3 /* [scratched] *T*. Engraved: *MHH*
Dallas Museum of Art, The Jewel Stern American Silver Collection, acquired through the Patsy Lacy Griffith Collection, gift of Patsy Lacy Griffith by exchange, DMA 2002.29.157.A–C

The classic shape of this shaker recalls a shaker made by Christofle for the *Normandie*, the French ocean liner launched in 1932.

INTERNATIONAL SILVER COMPANY
MERIDEN, CONNECTICUT
ACTIVE 1898–PRESENT

70. Waldorf-Astoria Hotel flatware, 1931
Peer Smed
Danish, 1878–1943
and Frederick W. Stark
American (b. Germany), 1885–1969

Patent 86,553 (for a fork or other article of flatware) filed Mar. 23, 1931, granted Mar. 15, 1932. Silverplate, stainless steel knife blade. Tablespoon ⅝ × 1¼ × 6¼ in. (1.6 × 3.2 × 15.9 cm); soup spoon ¾ × 1⅝ × 6 in. (1.9 × 4.1 × 15.2 cm); fork ⅞ × ¾ × 6¹³⁄₁₆ in. (2.2 × 1.9 × 17.3 cm); knife ⁷⁄₁₆ × 1 × 9¹³⁄₁₆ in. (1.1 × 2.5 × 24.9 cm); butter knife ¾ × ⅞ × 6¹³⁄₁₆ in. (1.9 × 2.2 × 17.3 cm); teaspoon ⅝ × 1¼ × 6¼ in. (1.6 × 3.2 × 15.9 cm). Knife / butter knife marked (on handle): *WALDORF ASTORIA*; (on blade): *IPR STAINLESS*. Fork: *WALDORF ASTORIA*. Soup spoon / teaspoon (on handle): *INTERNATIONAL SIL-VER CO. / WALDORF ASTORIA*
Dallas Museum of Art, The Jewel Stern American Silver Collection, gift of Jewel Stern, DMA 2001.50.1–5

The flatware was designed for the new Waldorf-Astoria Hotel that opened on September 30, 1931 in New York City. The same decorative motif distinguishes both the flatware and the hotel's holloware service.

71. Waldorf-Astoria Hotel compote, 1939 (introduced 1931)*
Peer Smed
Danish, 1878–1943
and Frederick W. Stark
American (b. Germany), 1885–1969

Patent 86,554 (for a dish or other similar article) filed Mar. 23, 1931, granted Mar. 15, 1932. Silverplate. 3½ × 7 in. (8.9 × 17.8 cm). Marked: *THE WALDORF ASTORIA / 1939 / I* [in square] *S* [in square] / *INTER-NATIONAL SILVER CO. / SILVER SOLDERED / C05038 / 7 IN / PATENT 86554*
Dallas Museum of Art, The Jewel Stern American Silver Collection, acquired through the Patsy Lacy Griffith Collection, gift of Patsy Lacy Griffith by exchange, DMA 2002.29.173

This compote was part of a complete service made for the Waldorf-Astoria Hotel. The main decoration on the rim consists of a series of facing volutes and beads.

72. Coffeepot, c. 1933*
Frederick W. Stark
American (b. Germany), 1885–1969
Ornament designer

Patent for border 87,491 (for a dish or other similar article of holloware) filed Apr. 1, 1932, granted Aug. 2, 1932; patent for shape 83,580 (for a coffeepot or similar article) filed Dec. 29, 1930, granted Aug. 2, 1932. Silverplate. 8½ × 9 × 7 in. (21.6 × 22.9 × 17.8 cm). Marked (on bottom): *UNITED STATES LINES / I* [in square] *S* [in square] / *INTER-NATIONAL SILVER CO. / SILVER SOLDERED / 05044 / 48 OZ 34* [in square] / *PATENT 83580 / PATENT 1637853 / PATENT 87491* and 7 and 6. On lid: 7 and 6.
Dallas Museum of Art, 20th-Century Design Fund, DMA 1995.105

This side-handled coffee pot was designed for a transatlantic ocean liner of the United States Lines during the 1930s (see chapter 7). The design patent 87,491 for the decorative band encircling the base was filed by International's staff designer Frederick W. Stark. The body of the pot was derived from Stark's earlier design, patent 83,580 for a "coffee pot or similar article." The structural patent 1637853, for "a hollow-handle for metal vessels," was filed by the staff designer Leslie A. Brown, who was also involved in the evolution of this object. The horizontal handle splits into four petal-like sections at the point of contact with the pot, leaving small arched spaces in between. The finial echoes the stylized motif of the decorative band.

73. *Gift Ware* "His Royal Highness" coffeepot, 1934*
Lurelle Guild
American, 1898–1986

Silverplate, ebony. 12 × 9¼ × 6½ in. (30.5 × 23.5 × 16.5 cm). Marked: *Lurelle Guild* [in script] / *INTERNATIONAL* / [chalice in octagon] / *GIFT WARE]* [previous three lines within an octagon] / *EPNS* [each in a square] / *TRIPLE / I* [in square] *S* [in square] / *PLATE* [previous three lines within an octagon] / *5864*. (on lid): 33
Dallas Museum of Art, The Jewel Stern American Silver Collection, acquired through the Patsy Lacy Griffith Collection, gift of Patsy Lacy Griffith by exchange, DMA 2002.29.58

The coffeepot is part of a side-handled, three-piece coffee set in the *Contemporary Group*, an offshoot of International Silver's signature *Gift Ware* line by Lurelle Guild. In this tall cylindrical and domed coffeepot from "His Royal Highness" coffee set, Guild used an array of crowd-pleasing decoration that included details in the earlier *art moderne* style. The three-piece set sold for $35 (see chapter 6).

References: Sheila Hibben, "The One-piece Meal," *House Beautiful* 77 (Feb. 1935): 37; "Designer for Mass Production: Lurelle Guild develops mechanical improvement as well as eye-appeal," *Art and Industry* 24 (June 1938): 232.

74. Cocktail shaker, c. 1936
Silverplate. 9½ × 3½ in. (24.1 × 8.9 cm). Marked: *I* [in square] *S* [in square] / *INTERNATIONAL SILVER CO / SILVER SOLDERED / 030 / 32 OZ 40* [in square]
Dallas Museum of Art, The Jewel Stern American Silver Collection, acquired through the Patsy Lacy Griffith Collection, gift of Patsy Lacy Griffith by exchange, DMA 2002.29.167.A–B

The cylindrical form, smooth undecorated surfaces (except for two horizontal linear bands), a narrow ribbed base, and a spherical finial identify this object as quintessentially 1930s.

75. *Flagship* flatware, c. 1936*

Silverplate, stainless steel knife blade. Knife, ⅜ × ⅝ × 7 in. (0.9 × 1.6 × 17.8 cm); fork 6⅛ × ⁹⁄₁₆ × 1 in. (15.6 × 1.4 × 2.5 cm); teaspoon 5½ × 1⅛ × ½ in. (14.0 × 2.9 × 1.3 cm). Knife marked (on blade): INSICO [flag logo] / *Flagship* [in fuselage of aircraft]. Fork, teaspoon: [flag logo] / *Flagship* [in fuselage of aircraft] / *INTERNATIONAL SILVER CO.*
Dallas Museum of Art, gift of Kevin W. Tucker in honor of Jewel Stern, DMA 2005.22.1–3

The flatware was a custom design for the American Airlines DC-3 air-craft for the transcontinental routes that were inaugurated in 1936. Full table service was provided for passengers on these flights. The handles of the spoon and fork depict the fuselage and nose of the aircraft in relief. Two versions of the knife handle were produced—one in full relief, as in this setting, and the other with the design incised upon a ordinary, thin blank. All carry the thunderbolt design reflecting the livery of American's *Flagship* aircraft.

76. Cocktail shaker, c. 1936*

Silverplate. 8¼ × 2⅝ in. (21.0 × 6.7 cm). Marked: I [in square] S [in square] / *INTERNATIONAL SILVER CO.* / *SILVER SOLDERED* / *05049* / *16 OZ* / *34* [in square]. Engraved (circling top): *1—2—3—4—* / *DUBONNET* / *MARTINI* / *MANHATTAN* / *GIBSON* / *JACK ROSE* / *BRONX* / *LONE TREE* / *BACARDI* / *CLOVER CLUB* / *WALDORF*
Dallas Museum of Art, The Jewel Stern American Silver Collection, acquired through the Patsy Lacy Griffith Collection, gift of Patsy Lacy Griffith by exchange, DMA 2002.29.63.A–C

The curves, narrow bands and spherical element characteristic of 1930s streamlined design are harmoniously merged in this object. The finial spins to reveal quantities for mixing popular cocktails.

Reference: "Practical Hints on the Care of Silver," *Hotel Management* 33 (Feb. 1938): 145.

77. *Tropical* platter, c. 1940*

Carl Conrad Braun
American, 1905–1998

Silverplate. 1 × 15¾ × 12¼ in. (2.5 × 40.0 × 31.1 cm). Marked: *Tropical* [in script] / *by* [in script] / *INTERNATIONAL SILVER CO.* / *8166*
Dallas Museum of Art, The Jewel Stern American Silver Collection, acquired through the Patsy Lacy Griffith Collection, gift of Patsy Lacy Griffith by exchange, DMA 2002.29.7

International Silver produced an illustrated brochure featuring more than twenty-five items to promote the new moderately priced *Tropical* line released in about 1940 (see chapter 6). A central figurative panel is the primary decorative feature of this softly rounded rectangular plat-ter, one of the largest in the line and priced at $8.50.

78. *Tropical* mixer, c. 1940

Carl Conrad Braun
American, 1905–1998

Silverplate. 11 × 7 in. (27.9 × 17.8 cm). Marked: *Tropical* [in script] / *by* [in script] / *INTER-NATIONAL SILVER CO.* / *8143*
Dallas Museum of Art, The Jewel Stern American Silver Collection, acquired through the Patsy Lacy Griffith Collection, gift of Patsy Lacy Griffith by exchange, DMA 2002.29.172

Braun drew on several sources including the streamline style, classi-cism, and *art moderne* for this mixer. A tiny spout at the rim accentu-ates the height of this tall, subtly rounded pitcher, which holds a quart and a half. In contrast to the smooth body of the vessel, frieze-like bands in a classical leaf and bead pattern, vaguely Scandinavian in character, decorate the handle, an attempt, paradoxically, to give it a tropical look. The round stepped base is a reprise of a late 1920s design strategy.

79. *Northern Lights* flatware, 1946*

Alfred G. Kintz
American, 1884–1963

Patent 145,580 (for a spoon or other article of flatware) filed Apr. 6, 1946, granted Sept. 10, 1946. Silver, stainless steel knife blade. Place fork ⁹⁄₁₆ × 7⅛ in. (1.4 × 18.1 cm); salad fork ½ × 6⁵⁄₁₆ in. (1.3 × 16 cm); teaspoon ½ × 1¼ × 6⁷⁄₁₆ in. (1.3 × 3.2 × 16.4 cm). Marked, all (on back): [Native American head] / *NORTHERN LIGHTS* / *INTERNATIONAL STERLING*

Dallas Museum of Art, gift of Beverly Hart Bremer, DMA 1998.177.1–3

Six symmetrically divided spirals decorate the handle tips of this Scandinavian-influenced pattern, which was introduced one year after the end of World War II.

80. *Celestial Centerpiece*, 1964*

Robert J. King
American, b. 1917
Albert G. Roy, maker
Dates unknown

Silver, spinel sapphires. 9 × 14 in. (22.9 × 35.6 cm). Unmarked
Dallas Museum of Art, The Jewel Stern American Silver Collection, acquired through the Patsy Lacy Griffith Collection, gift of Patsy Lacy Griffith by exchange and gift of Jewel Stern in honor of Kevin W. Tucker, DMA 2005.24.1.A–B

Within International Silver's installation for the Pavilion of American Interiors at the New York World's Fair in 1964, a selection of specially created holloware, including the majestic *Celestial Centerpiece* designed by Robert J. King, presided over the elegantly futuristic Moon Room setting. The firm reveled in the allusions: "Come to our Moon Room. It is beautiful and strange. A moon dining room floating in cosmic space. . . . It is the most heavenly part of the International Silverware Exhibit at the World's Fair. Here by the light of the moon you will see Vision— sterling flatware ten light years ahead of its time. Find a silver coffee service you'd fly to the moon for. Water pitchers too ethereal for water. Futuristic design far too advanced to go on the market. (Although our culture is going at such a fast clip—who knows?)"[1]

Supported by six legs, which appear to continue through the body of the dish to become elongated trumpet-form candleholders, the base of the *Celestial Centerpiece* serves as a reflective dish for a starburst-like cluster studded with glittering gemstones. King originally conceived the idea for a large coupe-shaped centerpiece for tall candles after noticing a six-light candleholder in a store window in New York.[2] A proficient metalsmith, he fashioned a prototype cluster in silver with enameled cup tips (also in the DMA Collection). Following a review by International's management, the design of what was described as the "flowerburst" was revised to increase the centerpiece's radiance by incorporating cut gemstones. The second and final version, tipped by 133 spinel sapphires, was completed shortly before the fair opened. This centerpiece was included in the exhibition *Good Design for Christmas* at the Wadsworth Atheneum, Hartford, Connecticut, from Nov. 23, 1964 through Jan. 3, 1965.

In addition to production settings of Ronald Hayes Pearson's *Vision* flatware, more than a dozen other silver objects expressing the room's futuristic Space Age theme were presented, three of which are cur-rently in the Dallas Museum of Art's collection, including a carafe by King and Stuart Young's *Lunar* coffee service. King's work was repre-sented by the *Celestial Centerpiece*, his carafe, a pair of tapered conical candlesticks with blue enamel trim, and a pair of five-light candelabra with spherical planetary elements. The current whereabouts of King's candlesticks, candelabra, and other Moon Room works are unknown (see chapter 13).

1. "Have you ever been to a Moon Room?" International Silver Company advertise-ment, *Pavilion of American Interiors: New York World Fair 1964–65: Souvenir Journal* (n.p.), 14.
2. Robert J. King, telephone conversation with Kevin W. Tucker, November 22, 2004.

81. Ice bucket, c. 1964*

Silverplate, teak. 8¾ × 8 in. (22.2 × 20.3 cm). Marked: I [in square] S [in square] [diagonally within a four-pointed star] / *INTERNATIONAL* / *S3025*
Dallas Museum of Art, The Jewel Stern American Silver Collection, Decorative Arts Fund, DMA 2002.29.217.A–D

The ice bucket has a teak finial and cover rim. It was part of a line of holloware serving pieces with wood trim illustrated in the Inter-national Silver Company brochure for its exhibition in the Pavilion of American Interiors at the New York World's Fair in 1964.

82. Pitcher, 1965*

Silverplate, teak. 8½ × 7¼ × 4 in. (21.6 × 18.4 × 10.2 cm). Marked: I [in square] S [in square] [diagonally within a four-pointed star] / *INTERNATIONAL* / *S 3005*
Dallas Museum of Art, The Jewel Stern American Silver Collection, Decorative Arts Fund, DMA 2002.29.84

The undulating line that flows from the spout to the end of the comma-shaped wood handle energizes the form and contributes to the dynamism of this pitcher. A splendid example of post–World War II organic modernism executed with an economy of means, this pitcher was one of 175 new products from the design staff pictured in an in-house publication by the International Silver Company in 1966.

83. *Tradewinds* flatware (fork*), 1975

Silver, stainless steel knife blade. Teaspoon 1¼ × 6¼ in. (3.2 × 15.9 cm); place knife ¾ × 8⅝ in. (2.0 × 21.9 cm); place fork ½ × 1 × 7⅝ in. (1.3 × 2.5 × 19.4 cm); salad fork 1 × 6¾ in. (2.5 × 17.2 cm). Teaspoon / fork / salad fork marked: © INTERNATIONAL / STERLING. Knife marked: (on side) STERLING HANDLE.
Dallas Museum of Art, gift of Beverly Hart Bremer, DMA 1998.161.1–4

Oriental in character, the handles of this flatware, except for the knife, have a woven openwork pattern and are surrounded with a bamboo design border.

BARBOUR SILVER COMPANY
BARBOUR STERLING FINE ARTS
HARTFORD, CONNECTICUT
FOUNDED 1892
DIVISION OF INTERNATIONAL SILVER COMPANY

84. Coffee service, c. 1928–1929*

Silver, ebony. Coffeepot 7¼ × 5¾ × 3¼ in. (18.4 × 14.6 × 8.3 cm); creamer 3¼ × 4½ × 5⅝ in. (8.3 × 11.4 × 14.3 cm); sugar bowl 4⁵⁄₁₆ × 2¼ in. (11.0 × 5.9 cm). Coffeepot marked: B SC [S over C, all inscribed in square] / STERLING / 571 / 1¼ PINTS. Creamer / sugar bowl: B SC [S over C, all inscribed in square] / STERLING / 571. Engraved (each): HNE
Dallas Museum of Art, The Jewel Stern American Silver Collection, acquired through the Patsy Lacy Griffith Collection, gift of Patsy Lacy Griffith by exchange, DMA 2002.29.24.1–3

Stylistically, this sterling coffee set from the Barbour Sterling Fine Arts Division of the International Silver Company shows the influence of *art moderne*, especially in its staggered spouts and handle attachments, subtle stepped bases and finial, the stepped ebony handles of the sugar bowl, and the vertical flutes alluding to classicism. The carved handles of the open sugar bowl, coffeepot, and creamer and the finial knob of the pot are of macassar ebony. A matching tray was not offered.

BARBOUR SILVER COMPANY
HARTFORD, CONNECTICUT
FOUNDED 1892
DIVISION OF INTERNATIONAL SILVER COMPANY

85. Vase, c. 1929–1935*

Silverplate, plastic. 10 × 3½ in. (25.4 × 8.9 cm). Marked: BARBOUR S. P. CO. [curved] / INTERNATIONAL S. CO. / 6917
Dallas Museum of Art, The Jewel Stern American Silver Collection, acquired through the Patsy Lacy Griffith Collection, gift of Patsy Lacy Griffith by exchange, DMA 2002.29.46

This sleek conical vase with exuberant red and black geometric accents in plastic is rare and difficult to date as no record of it has been found in surviving catalogues of the International Silver Company at the Meriden Historical Society.

CHARTER COMPANY
WALLINGFORD, CONNECTICUT
ACTIVE C. 1930–1942
DIVISION OF INTERNATIONAL SILVER COMPANY

86. Cocktail shaker, 1928*

Enameled silver, wood. 14¹⁄₁₆ × 5 in. (35.7 × 12.7 cm). Marked: [oak leaf in rectangle] / STERLING / SM207–1 / 4½ PINTS
Dallas Museum of Art, The Jewel Stern American Silver Collection, acquired through the Patsy Lacy Griffith Collection, gift of Patsy Lacy Griffith by exchange, DMA 2002.29.2.A–C

This very tall stately cocktail shaker with elegant enamel decoration in bright red and black is the grandest object of its type to come to light from the late 1920s. It was offered separately and with optional matching cocktail cups and tray. The modern abstract colonnade motif that decorates the shaker was also applied to the cups, which had black stems and plain round bases, and to the rim of the serving tray, which had a black center (see chapter 3).

87. Centerpiece, c. 1929*

Eliel Saarinen
Finnish, 1873–1950

Silver. 3⅞ × 15⅛ in. (9.8 × 38.4 cm)
The John C. Waddell Collection

A massive prototype for this centerpiece, measuring twenty inches in diameter, was exhibited in the dining room designed by Saarinen for the Metropolitan Museum of Art's exhibition, *The Architect and the Industrial Arts* in 1929. Within the year, Arthur Nevill Kirk, the recently appointed head of Cranbrook's silver studio, fashioned at least one smaller variant (Cranbrook Art Museum Collection) and International created four production versions, of which this example is the largest. Others were produced in thirteen- and eleven-inch sizes, along with a compote that was seven inches in diameter. To reinforce the association of the design with the renowned architect, International took the unusual step of adding not only its company marks, but also a script "By Saarinen" mark, reflecting a form of recognition that manufacturers of other domestic articles were beginning to adopt as, increasingly, industrial designers became celebrated public figures. Saarinen's use of a similarly segmented, petal-like bowl form is repeated in his designs for the brass and copper lighting fixtures produced by Edward F. Caldwell and Company for Saarinen House in 1930.

References: "American Silver Achieves New Beauty," *House and Garden* 60 (Dec. 1931): 67; "Modern Art Expressed in Silver," *Jewelers' Circular* (Mar. 7, 1929): 55.

INTERNATIONAL STERLING CRAFT ASSOCIATES
MERIDEN, CONNECTICUT
FOUNDED 1952
DIVISION OF INTERNATIONAL SILVER COMPANY

88. Centerpiece bowl, c. 1952*

Alphonse La Paglia
American (b. Sicily), 1907–1953

Silver. 5¾ × 10 × 4¾ in. (14.6 × 25.4 × 12.1 cm). Marked: INTERNATIONAL / STERLING / La Paglia Designed [in script] / 139 14–1
The Jewel Stern American Silver Collection, promised gift of Jewel Stern, DMA 17.2004.16

In 1952, International established a craft shop that became known as International Sterling Craft Associates. La Paglia, who had been a student of the Danish silversmith Georg Jensen, and whose work shows his influence, was an active participant in the venture until his death a year later. Subsequently International acquired his designs for production. In 1955 Kurt Eric Christoffersen was hired by International to invigorate the undertaking and his work along with that of La Paglia was promoted in the catalogue *International Sterling Craft Associates* with La Paglia and Christoffersen as the exclusive Craft Associates (see chapter 10). Their works were distinguished by their mark, as La Paglia Designed or Christoffersen Designed.

The bold spherical and looped elements of the foot contrast with the gracefully flared bowl, while the delicate openwork band complements its shape. The price of this bowl in the late 1950s was $185. A matching pair of low candlesticks by La Paglia was also offered.

References: Barbara McLean Ward and Gerald W. R. Ward, eds., *Silver in American Life: Selections from the Mabel Brady Garvan and Other Collections at Yale University*, exh. cat. (Boston: David R. Godine, in association with Yale University Art Gallery and the American Federation of Arts, 1979), 186; Dorothy T. Rainwater, "Alphonse La Paglia: Silversmith and Designer," *Silver* 28 (May/June 1995): 8–11.

89. Centerpiece bowl, 1955*

Kurt Eric Christoffersen
Danish, 1926–1981

Silver. 3 × 12 in. (7.6 × 30.5 cm). Marked: INTERNATIONAL STERLING / Christoffersen Designed [in script] / CD600
The Jewel Stern American Silver Collection, promised gift of Jewel Stern, DMA 17.2004.14

This bowl from International's Sterling Craft Associates epitomizes Christoffersen's reductive aesthetic. Relying on shape, proportion, and smooth reflective surfaces with not an iota of decoration, he derived from the cone a radical bowl form that is solid in appearance and has a shallow concave area for containment. The Christoffersen Designed collection is notable for the weight of the silver. The price of the bowl was $160. A pair of candlesticks to match the bowl was designed.

90. Candlesticks (pair), 1955*

Kurt Eric Christoffersen
Danish, 1926–1981

Silver. Each 5 × 4 in. (12.7 × 10.2 cm). Marked (each): *INTER-NATIONAL STERLING / Christoffersen Designed* [in script] / *CN100*
Dallas Museum of Art, The Jewel Stern American Silver Collection, gift of Jewel Stern, DMA 2002.29.72.1–2

Designed for International's Sterling Craft Associates signature collection, these candlesticks are coordinated with the centerpiece bowl to make a table ensemble. The cone, a form rigorously employed by Christoffersen, was clearly enunciated in these candlesticks. All his objects were stamped Christoffersen Designed. The price of the candlesticks, sold as a pair, was $70.

Reference: Dorothy T. Rainwater, "Kurt Eric Christoffersen: Designer and Silversmith," *Silver* 28 (July/Aug. 1995): 10–12.

91. Coffee service, 1955*

Kurt Eric Christoffersen
Danish, 1926–1981

Silver, plastic. Coffeepot 13⅛ × 8½ × 5¾ in. (33.3 × 21.6 × 14.6 cm); creamer 4½ × 4 × 2½ in. (11.4 × 10.2 × 6.4 cm); covered sugar bowl 5 × 3¼ × 3¼ in. (12.7 × 8.3 × 8.3 cm). Coffeepot / creamer / sugar marked: *INTERNATIONAL STERLING / Christoffersen Designed* [in script] / *CC100*
The Jewel Stern American Silver Collection

Of all the Christoffersen Designed objects in the International Sterling Crafts Associates collection, the boldest expression of conical form was reserved for the tall coffeepot of the three-piece service, Christoffersen's crowning achievement for this luxurious holloware line (see chapter 10). The price of the three-piece set, fabricated in heavy-gauge silver, was $300. A simple twelve-inch diameter tray in the line was offered for the service and cost $125. In addition to the coffee service and centerpiece and candlesticks, the Christoffersen Designed collection included a sandwich server, salt and pepper shakers, open salts with spoons, a mustard jar with spoon, a decanter, cocktail and cordial cups, beakers, three vases, a jam jar and spoon set, mint dishes, and bowls and trays.

MERIDEN SILVER PLATE COMPANY
MERIDEN, CONNECTICUT
FOUNDED 1869

DIVISION OF INTERNATIONAL
SILVER COMPANY

92. *Vogue* centerpiece with flower frog, 1928

Silverplate, plastic. Centerpiece 14½ × 1½ in. (36.8 × 3.8 cm); flower frog 4⅛ × 4⅜ in. (10.5 × 11.1 cm). Centerpiece marked: *D / MERIDEN S.P. CO* [in curve of D] / *INTERNATIONAL S. CO.* [along flat part of D] / [lion inside D] / *2986*
Dallas Museum of Art, gift of the Alconda-Owsley Foundation, DMA 1995.19.A–B

In 1928 International Silver Company introduced a moderately priced holloware line called *Vogue*, a name implying that the pattern was in step with current fashion. Classical flutes, a stylized adaptation of *art moderne* classicism, constituted the dominant decorative motif in the *Vogue* line. Wide flutes girdled the upright forms and provided the border decoration of flat forms such as trays, as well as the rims of other dishes. Handles and finial tips of ivory-colored Catalin to emulate true ivory added a touch of luxury. The centerpiece's separate openwork flower holder rises from a fluted and notched base in two rounded tiers with intervening stepped bands to a bulbous and segmented triangular Catalin finial. Of all the items in the extensive *Vogue* line, this large centerpiece with flower holder is the most dramatic. The introductory price of the centerpiece and flower holder was $30.[1]

1. International Silver Company, Silver Plated Holloware; Supplement to Catalog No. 34, 1928, 2.

93. Water pitcher, c. 1928*

Silverplate. 7¾ × 7 × 6½ in. (19.7 × 17.8 × 16.5 cm). Marked: *MERIDEN S.P. CO.* (in arch surround) / [lion holding vase] / *INTERNATIONAL S. CO.* [at base of arch surround] / *986 / I* [in square] *S* [in square]
Dallas Museum of Art, The Jewel Stern American Silver Collection, acquired through the Patsy Lacy Griffith Collection, gift of Patsy Lacy Griffith by exchange, DMA 2002.29.41

The bulged telescoping form of this pitcher is unusual in late-1920s American silver. The shape was described as a "modern design, suggestive of pottery" in the trade periodical *Jewelers' Circular* (see chapter 2).[1]

1. A. Frederic Saunders, "Modernism in Silverware," *Jewelers' Circular* 100 (Feb. 27, 1930): 104.

94. Clorox promotional flatware, c. 1960

Silverplate. Butter knife ⅝ × 1⅝ × 5½ in. (1.6 × 4.1 × 14 cm); sugar spoon ⅞ × 1¼ × 6½ in. (2.2 × 3.2 × 16.5 cm); nut scoop ¾ × 1¼ × 6¼ in. (1.9 × 3.2 × 15.9 cm); cheese server ⅝ × 1 × 6⅝ in. (1.6 × 2.5 × 16.8 cm); spoon ¾ × 1½ × 5 in. (1.9 × 3.8 × 12.7 cm); pickle fork ½ × ⅝ × 5⅛ in. (1.3 × 1.6 × 13 cm). Marked (all): *MERIDEN SILVERPLATE CO.*
Dallas Museum of Art, The Jewel Stern American Silver Collection, gift of Jewel Stern, DMA 2004.13.7.1–6

The silverplated flatware pattern *First Lady* (1960) was miniaturized for the serving pieces of this promotional gift set offered by the manufacturers of Clorox bleach (see chapter 7).

1847 ROGERS BROTHERS
HARTFORD, CONNECTICUT
FOUNDED 1847

DIVISION OF INTERNATIONAL
SILVER COMPANY

95. *Silhouette* flatware (spoon*), 1930

Leslie A. Brown
American, active c. 1925–1935

Patent 81,521 (for a spoon or similar article) filed Apr. 18, 29, granted Aug. 8, 1930. Silverplate, stainless steel knife blade. Knife 9½ × ⅞ × ⅜ in. (24.1 × 2.2 × 1 cm); fork 7½ × 1⅛ × 1 in. (19.1 × 2.9 × 2.5 cm); spoon ⅞ × 6 × 1¼ in. (2.2 × 15.2 × 3.2 cm). Knife marked: *1847 ROGERS BROS.* (on blade): *INSICO / STAINLESS.* Fork/spoon: *1847 ROGERS BROS.*
Dallas Museum of Art, 20th-Century Design Fund, DMA 1995.102.1–3

The sterling flatware prototypes designed by Eliel Saarinen and included in the Metropolitan Museum of Art's exhibition *The Architect and the Industrial Arts* in 1929 had an unconventional long-handled, short-bladed knife. The International Silver Company quickly acquired a flatware patent from Saarinen for this styling and registered *Viande* as the trademark (see chapter 4). *Silhouette* in silverplate from its 1847 Rogers Bros. subsidiary was the pilot pattern for the *Viande* style, which was offered as an option. The layered and folded crisscrossed flowing lines of *Silhouette* are most effective in the *Viande* forks, where the design elements merge to become integral with the tines. International promoted *Silhouette* as "modern as a Paris gown, fit to compete in smartness with everything else on the table."[1]

1. "1847 Rogers Bros. Original and Genuine Rogers Silver plate," trade brochure, International Silver Co. Factory E, Meriden Conn., c. 1930, n.p.

96. *Flair* flatware, 1954

Robert L. Doerfler
American, 1916–2004

Patent 176,601 (for a spoon or other similar article of flatware) filed Oct. 17, 1954, granted Apr. 9, 1955. Silverplate, stainless steel knife blade. Place knife 9⅛ × ¾ × 5⁄16 in. (23.2 × 1.9 × 0.8 cm); place fork: 7⁷⁄16 × 1 × ¾ in. (18.9 × 2.5 × 1.9 cm). Knife marked (on blade): *STAINLESS.* Fork: *1847 ROGERS BROS. IS Flair* [in script]
Dallas Museum of Art, 20th-Century Design Fund, DMA 1995.104.1–2

The creation of a staff designer, the asymmetrical contoured and swirled *Flair* design, replete with leaf and bead motif, was one of the most successful flatware patterns to embrace the naturalistic and organic modern idiom from Scandinavia during the 1950s. An extensive holloware group was designed to coordinate with the flatware and was vigorously promoted by International (see chapter 10).

97. *Flair* hot beverage service (coffeepot*), 1954

Silverplate, plastic. Coffeepot 10½ × 7½ × 5¼ in. (26.7 × 19.0 × 13.3 cm); creamer 5 × 5¼ in. (12.7 × 13.3 cm); sugar bowl 5 × 4 in. (12.7 × 10.2 cm). Marked (all): *Flair* [in script] / *1847 ROGERS BROS.* / *I* [in square] *S* [in square]

Dallas Museum of Art, The Jewel Stern American Silver Collection, Decorative Arts Fund, DMA 2002.29.215.1–3

Advertising the new *Flair* design in its 1954 catalogue, the International Silver Company touted this service as "perfect in balance of design . . . the last word in modern holloware. Here is beauty, rhythm and flowing grace in silver. . . ."[1] Contour, asymmetry, and naturalism, the characteristics of *Flair* flatware, were adapted for the holloware line and are clearly evident in the elongated, melon-shaped vessels of this service and succinctly articulated in the spouts, handles, and finials. Another characteristic of the *Flair* line was the accenting of select elements, such as handles and finials, by wrapping them in plastic strips in a color that evokes natural raffia or wicker in order to lend an air of informality to the serving pieces.

1. "Flair" International Silver Company catalogue, 1954, n.p., International Silver Company Archives, Meriden Historical Society, Meriden, Conn.

98. *Flair* serving tray, 1954

Silverplate. 2¼ × 18½ × 13¼ in. (5.7 × 47.0 × 33.7 cm). Marked: *Flair* [in script] / *1847 ROGERS BROS.* / *I* [in square] *S* [in square]

Dallas Museum of Art, The Jewel Stern American Silver Collection, Decorative Arts Fund, DMA 2002.29.237

Designed to accompany the three-piece hot beverage service, this ovoid tray (the largest offered) has the asymmetrical sculptural rims that were typical of all the trays, bowls, and dishes in the *Flair* pattern.

99. *Flair* roll tray, 1954

Silverplate. 2 × 14 × 7 in. (5.1 × 35.6 × 17.8 cm). Marked: *Flair* [in script] / *1847 ROGERS BROS.* / *I* [in square] *S* [in square]

Dallas Museum of Art, The Jewel Stern American Silver Collection, Decorative Arts Fund, DMA 2002.29.221

WILLIAM ROGERS MFG. CO.

HARTFORD, CONNECTICUT
FOUNDED 1865

DIVISION OF INTERNATIONAL
SILVER COMPANY

100. 1939 New York World's Fair spoon, 1938

Lillian V. M. Helander
American, 1899–1973

Patent 113,866 (for a spoon or other article of flatware) filed Mar. 8, 1938, granted Mar. 21, 1938. Silverplate. ⅞ × 5 × 1¼ in. (2.2 × 12.7 × 3.2 cm). Inscribed (on front): *MARINE TRANSPORTATION BUILDING* / *1939 NEW YORK WORLD'S FAIR*. Marked (on back): *PAT. PEND.* / *WM ROGERS MFG CO. I* [in square] *S* [in square]

Dallas Museum of Art, The Jewel Stern American Silver Collection, gift of Jewel Stern

The stepped handle of the souvenir spoon features the iconic symbols of the fair, the trylon and perisphere. As a memento of the event, a replica of the Marine Transportation Building by Ely Jacques Kahn and William Muschenheim was stamped into the bowl of this spoon. The design was also offered with plain bowls as a flatware pattern (see chapter 8).

SIMPSON, HALL, MILLER
& COMPANY

WALLINGFORD, CONNECTICUT
FOUNDED 1866

DIVISION OF INTERNATIONAL
SILVER COMPANY

101. *Tropical Sunrise* bowl, 1928*

Alfred G. Kintz
American, 1884–1963

Patent 75,734 (for a dish or similar article) filed Apr. 28, 1928, granted July 10, 1928. Silver. 2½ × 12½ × 10 in. (6.4 × 31.8 × 25.4 cm). Marked: *INTERNATIONAL* / *S* [in shield surmounted by knight's helmet] *STERLING* / *D107A* / *Patent Pending*. Engraved: *IR*

Dallas Museum of Art, The Jewel Stern American Silver Collection, acquired through the Patsy Lacy Griffith Collection, gift of Patsy Lacy Griffith by exchange, DMA 2002.29.102

Tropical Sunrise was one of three patterns in the *Spirit of Today* holloware series designed by Kintz in 1928. More traditional than the other two patterns, *Ebb Tide* and *Northern Lights*, the predominant motifs of *Tropical Sunrise* are radiating lines resembling sun rays on its borders and stylized handles that suggest the leaves of tropical plants. A *Tropical Sunrise* bowl was exhibited in R. H. Macy's *International Exposition of Art in Industry* in 1928 and was illustrated in *Country Life* as an example of how "sterling silver goes modernist."[1] *Spirit of Today* patterns were offered in an array of serving pieces: luncheon plates, bonbon dishes, compotiers, almond dishes, napkin bands, relish dishes with glass liners, mayonnaise and whipped cream bowls, bread and butter plates, vases, salt and pepper shakers, centerpieces with mesh, and candlesticks in two sizes. Dishes and bowls were available with and without handles.

1. Lee McCann, "Sterling Silver Goes Modernist," *Country Life* 54 (May 1928): 90. References: Dudley T. Fagen, "Modernism: Its Possibilities in America," *National Jeweler* 25 (Jan. 1929): 26; Patricia F. Singer, "Alfred G. Kintz: An American Designer," *Silver* 19 (Sept./Oct. 1986): 18.

102. *Tropical Sunrise* compote, 1928

Alfred G. Kintz
American, 1884–1963

Silver. 6¼ × 7 in. (15.9 × 17.8 cm). Marked: *INTERNATIONAL S* [in shield surmounted by knight's helmet] *STERLING T107A* / *Patent Pending*

Dallas Museum of Art, The Jewel Stern American Silver Collection, acquired through the Patsy Lacy Griffith Collection, gift of Patsy Lacy Griffith by exchange, DMA 2002.29.103

The border decoration and handles of this compote, listed as a compotier in the *International Sterling Hollow Ware* catalogue for 1929, are the same as those of the *Tropical Sunrise* bowl, but smaller in scale. The radiating lines of the base echo the border. The compote was offered with and without handles.

103. *Ebb Tide* compote, 1928*

Alfred G. Kintz
American, 1884–1963

Patent 75,735 (for a dish or similar article) filed Apr. 28, 1928, granted July 10, 1928. Silver. 6⅜ × 7⅜ in. (16.2 × 18.7 cm). Marked: *INTERNATIONAL* / *S* [in shield surmounted by knight's helmet] *STERLING* / *T106A* / *Patent Pending*

Dallas Museum of Art, The Jewel Stern American Silver Collection, acquired through the Patsy Lacy Griffith Collection, gift of Patsy Lacy Griffith by exchange, DMA 2002.29.106

Ebb Tide was one of three patterns in the *Spirit of Today* holloware series designed by Kintz in 1928. The *Ebb Tide* compote, listed as a compotier in the *International Sterling Hollow Ware* catalogue for 1929, has a base of narrow concentric rings that step up to a slender stem. The entire well of the dish is treated in the same manner, with the addition of narrow wavelike terracing on the rim border, which is accented with sprightly quarter-round handles. The compote was offered with and without handles. In addition to the holloware, a perfume bottle in *Ebb Tide* has come to light.

Reference: Helen Appleton Read, "Twentieth-Century Decoration: The Modern Theme Finds a Distinctive Medium in American Silver," *Vogue* 72 (July 1, 1928): 59.

104. *Ebb Tide* candlesticks (pair), 1928

Alfred G. Kintz
American, 1884–1963

Silver. Each 7⅛ × 3¼ in. (18.1 × 8.3 cm). Marked (each): *INTERNATIONAL* / *S* [in shield surmounted by knight's helmet] *STERLING* / *N54* / *CEMENT-LOADED* / *Patented*

Dallas Museum of Art, The Jewel Stern American Silver Collection, acquired through the Patsy Lacy Griffith Collection, gift of Patsy Lacy Griffith by exchange, DMA 2002.29.107.1–2

The bases of the *Ebb Tide* candlesticks are the same as that of the *Ebb Tide* compote. Narrow concentric telescoping, a hallmark of the pattern, was adapted for the candle cups. A low, dome-shaped candlestick was also produced in the pattern.

105. *Northern Lights* whipped cream bowl and ladle, 1928*

Alfred G. Kintz
American, 1884–1963

Patent for bowl 75,733 (for a dish or similar article) filed Apr. 28, 1928, granted July 10, 1928. Patent for ladle 76,193 (for a spoon or similar article) filed June 9, 1928, granted Aug. 28, 1928. Silver. Bowl 3¼ × 5½ × 5½ in. (8.3 × 14.0 × 14.0 cm); ladle 1 × 1¾ × 5½ in. (2.5 × 4.4 × 14.0 cm). Bowl marked: *INTERNATIONAL / S* [in shield surmounted by knight's helmet] *STERLING / G11 / Patent Pending*. Ladle: *INTERNATIONAL S* [in shield surmounted by knight's helmet] *STERLING PAT. APPL'D FOR*
Dallas Museum of Art, The Jewel Stern American Silver Collection, acquired through the Patsy Lacy Griffith Collection, gift of Patsy Lacy Griffith by exchange, DMA 2002.29.22.1–2

Suggesting the spreading light of the aurora borealis, swirling motifs overlap, repeat, and radiate around the border of this *Northern Lights* whipped cream bowl and around the attached saucer base. The matching ladle is similarly embellished. *Northern Lights*, one of three *Spirit of Today* patterns, was offered in other pieces with wing-shaped handles that reinforced the effect of motion.

106. Bonbon dish, c. 1928*

Silver, rose quartz. 7¾ × 5 in. (19.7 × 12.7 cm). Marked: *INTERNATIONAL / S* [in shield surmounted by knight's helmet] *STERLING / B71*
Dallas Museum of Art, The Jewel Stern American Silver Collection, acquired through the Patsy Lacy Griffith Collection, gift of Patsy Lacy Griffith by exchange, DMA 2002.29.55.A–B

This covered bonbon dish is a modern interpretation of the classical urn shape. The rose quartz finial adds a touch of luxury and color contrast. International also employed rose quartz for the cylindrical foot of a compote.

107. Box, c. 1931*

Silver, mahogany. 3⅝ × 7¹⁄₁₆ × 5⅛ in. (9.2 × 17.9 × 13 cm). Marked (on bottom): *INTERNATIONAL / S* [in shield surmounted by knight's helmet] *STERLING / B74*. On lid: 3
Dallas Museum of Art, 20th-Century Design Fund, DMA 1994.230.A–B

The overall form of this rare box was derived from Chinese vessels, though the linear decorative elements suggest a more contemporary reference to the fluted Viennese boxes from the early 1920s and the similarly Chinese-inspired work of the metalsmith Marie Zimmermann. In keeping with these sources and with French *art moderne*'s incorporation of luxurious accents, this box bears a cylindrical mahogany finial (see chapter 3). Another example with a finial fashioned of rose quartz is also known.[1]

1. W. Scott Braznell, "The Advent of Modern American Silver," *The Magazine Antiques* 125 (Jan. 1984): 238.

108. *Continental* flatware, 1934*

Frederick W. Stark
American (b. Germany), 1885–1969

Patent 95,092 (for a spoon or other article of flatware) filed Jan. 29, 1935, granted Apr. 2, 1935. Silver, stainless steel knife blade. Luncheon fork ¾ × 1 × 7⅛ in. (1.9 × 2.5 × 18.1 cm); luncheon knife ½ × ¾ × 8⅞ in. (1.3 × 1.9 × 22.5 cm); butter knife ⅜ × ⅝ × 6⅞ in. (1.0 × 1.6 × 15.2 cm); soup spoon ¾ × 1⅞ × 6 in. (1.9 × 4.8 × 15.2 cm); teaspoon ½ × 1¼ × 6 in. (1.3 × 3.2 × 15.2 cm). Fork marked: *INTERNATIONAL /* [shield] *STERLING*. Knife: *INTERNATIONAL / STAINLESS*. Butter knife: [shield] *STERLING* [on blade]. Soup spoon: *INTERNATIONAL* [shield] *STERLING*. Tea spoon: *INTERNATIONAL* [shield] *STERLING E*
Dallas Museum of Art, gift of Beverly Hart Bremer, DMA 2000.400.1–5

This severe design epitomizes the 1930s machine aesthetic more than any other industrially produced pattern of the period. Austere rectangular service plates and bread and butter plates were produced to accompany *Continental* flatware (see chapter 6).

109. *Continental* coffee pot, c. 1935*

Silver, ivory. 7⅝ × 7⅜ × 4 in. (19.4 × 18.7 × 10.2 cm). Marked: *S* [in shield surmounted by knight's helmet]. Engraved: *GLG*
The Wolfsonian–Florida International University, Miami Beach, Florida. The Mitchell Wolfson Jr. Collection. XX1990.539.4

The rounded, ivory ponytail handles and finials lend the objects in the *Continental* service a graceful and especially lavish touch. The service was available as a complete six-piece set including a coffeepot, teapot, creamer, sugar bowl, waste bowl, and matching waiter. When first on the market, the service was offered for $750. The coffeepot was available individually for $175; this example is part of a four-piece service.

110. Centerpiece, c. 1937*

Frederick W. Stark
American (b. Germany), 1885–1969

Silver. 3½ × 11¼ × 6⅞ in. (8.9 × 28.6 × 17.5 cm). Marked: *INTERNATIONAL / S* [in shield, surmounted by knight's helmet] *STERLING / V132A*
Dallas Museum of Art, The Jewel Stern American Silver Collection, acquired through the Patsy Lacy Griffith Collection, gift of Patsy Lacy Griffith by exchange, DMA 2002.29.53

The centerpiece, part of a console set with a pair of double-branched candelabra, was exhibited at the *Exposition Internationale des Arts et des Techniques dans la Vie Moderne* in Paris in 1937. For his blend of Scandinavian naturalism and classicism in this bowl, Stark was awarded a silver medal. In 1937 the bowl was included in *Silver: An Exhibition of Contemporary American Design by Manufacturers, Designers and Craftsmen* at the Metropolitan Museum of Art, and the complete console set was exhibited in *Contemporary Industrial and Handwrought Silver* at the Brooklyn Museum (see chapters 6 and 8).

References: Barbara Hill, "Choosing the Bride's Silver," *Country Life* 74 (May 1938): 74; "A Christmas Bouquet by International Sterling," International Silver Company advertisement, *House Beautiful* 79 (Dec. 1937): 3; "Creating Mass Appeal for Silver," *Jewelers' Circular-Keystone* 108 (Jan. 1938): 62; "For This Day and Age," *Jewelers' Circular-Keystone* 107 (May 1937): 106; "Window Shopping," *House Beautiful* 79 (Nov. 1937): 12.

111. Carafe, 1955

Edward S. Buchko
American, 1929–1997

Silver, plastic, wood. 10 × 5¼ in. (25.4 × 13.3 cm). Marked on bottom: *INTERNATIONAL / S* [in shield surmounted by knight's helmet] *STERLING / C382 1/3 Pts*. Marked (side of stopper): *STERLING / 20 Z 10 Z*.
Dallas Museum of Art, gift of the Friends of the Decorative Arts, 1992 "Bikini-A-Go-Go" Miami Beach Trip, DMA 1992.16.A–B

Buchko, a staff designer from about 1949 until 1967, designed this carafe, which was part of an "All Purpose Beverage Set" introduced in 1955 that included a cream pitcher with a plastic-wrapped handle and an open sugar bowl.[1] The bulbous form of the carafe and the plastic-wrapped neck ally the object to the pitcher designed by Curtis Rittberg at about the same time. According to Buchko, the carafe did not "take off" and was in the line for only about two years. In 1957 Buchko won an honorable mention in the Sterling Today Student Design Competition sponsored by the Sterling Silversmiths Guild of America for a handmade water pitcher with a lilting serpentine handle, and in 1958 he won again for an "hors d'oeuvres scoop server."

1. International Silver Annual Report, 1955, n.p.

112. Pitcher, c. 1955*

Curtis Rittberg
American, 1902–1973

Silver, plastic. 8 × 6¼ × 4¾ in. (20.3 × 15.9 × 12.1 cm). Marked: *INTERNATIONAL / S* [in shield surmounted by knight's helmet] *STERLING / E111 / 3 Pts*
Dallas Museum of Art, 20th-Century Design Fund, DMA 1994.224

In about 1955, International Silver introduced a group of smooth, voluptuous sterling pitchers in different sizes and similar shapes influenced by modern Scandinavian silverware. These all had handles wrapped in strips of plastic that imitated natural raffia or wicker. The number E112 pitcher by the staff designer Curtis Rittberg, which is closely related to this one, was exhibited in *Living Today: An Exhibition of Contemporary Architecture, Furniture, Interior Decoration* at the Corcoran Gallery of Art, Washington, D.C., in 1958.

113. Pitcher, 1955

Silver. 10¼ × 7 × 5¼ in. (26.0 × 17.8 × 13.3 cm). Marked: *INTERNATIONAL / S* [in shield surmounted by knight's helmet] */ INTERNATIONAL STERLING / E106 / 4 Pts* [scratched]
Dallas Museum of Art, The Jewel Stern American Silver Collection, Decorative Arts Fund, DMA 2002.29.76.

The form of this smooth, undecorated pitcher gently swells to a pro-truding spout and is balanced by the bowed handle and the narrow band at the open rim. The pitcher is a subtle example of 1950s organic modernism.

Reference: "Let Silver Serve the Cool Course of Your Summer Barbeque Meals," *House and Garden* 107 (June 1955): 103.

114. *Vision* flatware, 1961 (designed 1959)*

Ronald Hayes Pearson
American, 1924–1996

Patent 191,010 (for a fork or similar article) filed Nov. 30, 1959, granted Apr. 5, 1960. Silver, stainless steel knife blade. Place knife ⅝ × 8⅝ × ¾ in. (1.6 × 21.0 × 1.9 cm); place fork ¾ × 7¾ × 1 in. (1.9 × 19.7 × 2.5 cm); salad fork ¾ × 6⅜ × 1 in. (1.9 × 16.2 × 2.5 cm); spoon ⅞ × 6⅜ × 1¼ in. (2.2 × 16.2 × 3.2). Knife marked (on handle): STERLING HANDLE. Fork / salad fork / teaspoon (on verso of handle): *INTER-NATIONAL S* [in shield surmounted by knight's helmet] *STERLING*
Dallas Museum of Art, 20th-Century Design Fund, DMA 1995.124.1–4

The *Vision* pattern arose out of the International Design Competition for Sterling Silver Flatware of 1960. This design by Pearson was one of the finalists and was selected for production by the International Silver Company (see chapter 14).

115. *Lunar* coffee service, 1963*

Stuart A. Young
American, b. 1924
Albert G. Roy, maker
Dates unknown

Silver, ebony. Coffeepot 11⅜ × 8⅜ × 4 in. (28.9 × 21.3 × 10.2 cm); creamer 6⅛ × 4¼ × 2⅝ (15.6 × 10.8 × 6.7 cm); sugar bowl with lid 5 × 7 × 3¼ in. (12.7 × 17.8 × 8.3 cm). Coffeepot marked: *S* [in shield surmounted by a knight's helmet] *STERLING / 166–01 / 033023040* [scratched]. Creamer: *S* [in shield surmounted by a knight's helmet] *STERLING / 166–04 / 033022049* [scratched]. Sugar bowl: *S* [in shield surmounted by a knight's helmet] *STERLING / 166–03 / 033023040* [scratched]
Dallas Museum of Art, The Jewel Stern American Silver Collection, Decorative Arts Fund, DMA 2002.29.80.1–3

The triangular *Lunar* coffee service was designed specifically for the Moon Room in the International Silver Company's exhibition in the Pavilion of American Interiors at the New York World's Fair in 1964 and was made by the company silversmith Albert G. Roy with the col-laboration of the designer (see chapter 13). The service was also exhib-ited in *Good Design for Christmas* at the Wadsworth Atheneum in late 1964 and in *The New England Silversmith* at the Museum of Art, Rhode Island School of Design in 1965. The only other known example of the *Lunar* coffee service is in the International Silver Company Archives at the Meriden Historical Society in Meriden, Connecticut.

Reference: *The New England Silversmith: An Exhibition of New England Silver from the Mid-Seventeenth Century to the Present,* exh. cat. Museum of Art (Providence, R.I.: Rhode Island School of Design, 1965), n.p.

116. *Astra* flatware (fork*), 1963

Milton Gonshorek
American, 1918–1998

Patent 195,889 (for a fork or similar article of flatware) filed Jan. 16, 1963, granted Sept. 6, 1963. Stainless steel. Knife ⅜ × 8¾ × ⅞ in. (1.0 × 22.2 × 2.2 cm); fork ⅞ × 8¾ × ⅞ in. (2.2 × 22.2 × 2.2 cm); spoon ¾ × 6¼ × 1¼ in. (1.9 × 15.9 × 3.2 cm). Knife marked: *Wilcox S.P.*; spoon / fork marked: *INTERNATIONAL STAINLESS DELUXE* [in rectangle]
The Charles L. Venable and Martin K. Webb Collection

In the mid-1950s, Milton Gonshorek graduated with a degree in indus-trial design from Pratt Institute, where he demonstrated a talent for innovative flatware. From 1960 to 1976 he was on the design staff of the International Silver Company. Modern stainless flatware became his specialty and *Astra*, his most sculptural pattern, referred directly to the Space Age. At the same time that *Astra* was introduced, the Inter-national design department began preparing for the Moon Room at the New York World's Fair in 1964, to which Gonshorek contributed hollo-ware. In addition to *Astra,* Gonshorek designed *Geometric, Cortez, Avant Garde, Calypso, Forecast, Navaho,* and *Youth* in stainless. Although his forte was abstract and sculptural patterns such as *Geometric* and *Astra,* he also designed the romantic sterling pattern *Dawn Rose* (1969).

References: "Practically a gift at $1," International Stainless Deluxe advertise-ment, *House Beautiful* 105 (May 1963): 62; "We think stainless should look like stainless," Stainless by International advertisement, *New Yorker* 42 (June 4, 1966): 20.

WILCOX & EVERTSEN FINE ARTS
NEW YORK, NEW YORK
1892–1896

MERIDEN, CONNECTICUT
1896–1929

WALLINGFORD, CONNECTICUT
1929–1968

DIVISION OF INTERNATIONAL
SILVER COMPANY

117. *Evening Sea* candelabra, 1928*

Silver. 7 × 7⅜ × 3¾ in. (17.8 × 18.7 × 9.5 cm). Marked: *INTERNATIONAL /* [winged creature] *STERLING / 494 / CEMENT FILLED*
Dallas Museum of Art, The Jewel Stern American Silver Collection, acquired through the Patsy Lacy Griffith Collection, gift of Patsy Lacy Griffith by exchange, DMA 2002.29.3.1–2

The *Evening Sea* candelabra and a bowl in the pattern were exhibited in R. H. Macy's *International Exposition of Art in Industry* in 1928. Interna-tional Silver described the candelabra as "modernistic as modernistic can be from its smart finial to its serrated base."[1] A candelabrum was illustrated and extolled for its "entirely new and original" ideas "free from tradition" and for "not in the least emulating anything previously done."[2] It was also illustrated in another trade periodical as a prime example of modern form.[3] The arms may be detached and the base used as a single candlestick.

1. "International Sterling Hollow Ware," International Silver Company catalogue, 1929, 55-W.
2. Dudley T. Fagen, "Modernism: Its Possibilities in America," *National Jeweler* 25 (Jan. 1929): 26.
3. A. Frederic Saunders, "Modernism in Silverware," *Jewelers' Circular* 100 (Feb. 27, 1930): 104.

118. *Evening Sea* luncheon tray, 1928

Silver. 1½ × 11½ in. (3.8 × 29.2 cm). Marked: [winged creature] *STER-LING / 108½*
Dallas Museum of Art, The Jewel Stern American Silver Collection, acquired through the Patsy Lacy Griffith Collection, gift of Patsy Lacy Griffith by exchange, DMA 2002.29.109

Various dishes and bowls with and without handles and with and without small feet were produced in the *Evening Sea* pattern. The most elegant is this luncheon tray with handles. Although the primary decoration consisted of classical fluting with a modicum of stepping at the rims and wells of the objects, International described *Evening Sea* as "a stunning modernistic design taking its inspiration from the gentle rhythmic ripples of the sea at evening."[1]

1. Dudley T. Fagen, "Modernism: Its Possibilities in America," *National Jeweler* 25 (Jan. 1929): 265

119. Cigarette container, 1928*

Enameled silver, jade. 4¼ × 3 in. (10.8 × 7.6 cm). Marked: *INTER-NATIONAL /* [winged creature] *STERLING / 360–1J*
Dallas Museum of Art, The Jewel Stern American Silver Collection, acquired through the Patsy Lacy Griffith Collection, gift of Patsy Lacy Griffith by exchange, DMA 2002.29.23.A–C

The rich enameling in black and red and the exotic jade finial knob of this cigarette container distinguish it as an object for the luxury market (see chapter 3).

120. Coffee service (coffeepot*), 1928

Silver, ebony. Coffeepot 7¼ × 6¼ × 3½ in. (18.4 × 15.9 × 8.9 cm); creamer 3 × 4 × 3 in. (7.6 × 10.2 × 7.6 cm); sugar bowl 2½ × 3½ in. (6.4 × 8.9 cm). Coffeepot marked: *11 / INTERNATIONAL /* [winged creature] *STERLING / 572 / 1 PINT*. Marked (coffeepot lid): *11*. Creamer / sugar bowl: *INTERNATIONAL /* [winged creature] *STERLING / 572*
Dallas Museum of Art, The Jewel Stern American Silver Collection, acquired through the Patsy Lacy Griffith Collection, gift of Patsy Lacy Griffith by exchange, DMA 2002.29.110.1–3

Only the coffeepot of this *art moderne* influenced three-piece set has a carved ebony handle. Two trays were available for the service, a simple round one and an elongated oval in rosewood with silver handles.

References: Lee McCann, "The Treasure Chest of Silver," *American Home* 2 (June 1929): 330; "Gifts of Sterling Silver," *House Beautiful* 64 (Dec. 1928): 700.

121. Compote, 1928–1929*

Silver. 6⅜ × 6 in. (16.2 × 15.2 cm). Marked: *INTERNATIONAL STERLING* [winged creature] *331*
The Jewel Stern American Silver Collection, promised gift of Jewel Stern, DMA 18.2003.19

Neoclassicism, an important thread in *art moderne,* inspired the shape of this compote, which alludes to an ancient Greek form. Harmonious stepped, layered, and telescoping elements contribute to the unity of this stylish object (see chapter 6).

122. *Empress* flatware, 1932*

Alfred G. Kintz
American, 1884–1963

Silver, stainless steel knife blade. Place knife ¾ × 8¹¹⁄₁₆ in. (1.9 × 22.1 cm), place fork 1¹⁄₁₆ × 7⁵⁄₁₆ in. (2.7 × 18.6 cm); salad fork 1 × 6⁷⁄₁₆ in. (2.5 × 16.4 cm); teaspoon: 1¼ × 5¹³⁄₁₆ in. (3.2 × 14.8 cm). Knife marked: *VIANDE* (on blade) *STAINLESS.* Fork / salad fork / teaspoon: *INTERNATIONAL* [winged creature] *STERLING*
Dallas Museum of Art, gift of Beverly Hart Bremer, DMA 1998.171.1–4

The *Empress* pattern, although elaborate, anticipated modern classicism of the mid-1930s.

123. Cocktail shaker, 1934*

Lurelle Guild (possibly by)
American, 1898–1986

Silver. 13½ × 4¾ in. (34.3 × 12.1 cm). Marked: [winged creature] *STERLING / WM226 / 3½ Pts.*
Dallas Museum of Art, The Jewel Stern American Silver Collection, gift of Jewel Stern, DMA 2002.29.54.A–B

The cocktail shaker was available as part of a complete beverage set that included twelve cocktail cups and a waiter and retailed for $240, a significant sum at the time. The mixer alone cost $55. The smooth undecorated lines of the body, the narrow ribbed base, and the spherical finial are elements that give the object a distinct 1930s modernist look. The well-publicized shaker appeared in the exhibition *Contemporary Industrial and Handwrought Silver* at the Brooklyn Museum in 1937 (see chapters 7 and 8). The similarity of the unusual finial of this shaker to the motif on Guild's *Empire* bowl in the 1934 *Gift Ware* group suggests his involvement in this design.

References: Dorothy Whitney, "Traditional Ceremony in the Contemporary Setting," *Arts and Decoration* 41 (Oct. 1934): 8; "Contenders for Your Christmas List," International Silver Company advertisement, *Town and Country* 91 (Dec. 1936): 57; "Creating Mass Appeal for Silver," *Jewelers' Circular-Keystone* 108 (Jan. 1938): 62; "Doubling in Silver," *Vogue* 81 (Aug. 15, 1936): 81; "Trophies," *House Beautiful* 76 (Aug. 1934): 42.

Wilcox Silver Plate Company

Meriden, Connecticut
active 1867–c. 1960

Division of International Silver Company

124. Dinette set, 1928*

Jean G. Theobald
American, active 1920s–1930s

Silverplate, wood. Teapot 4 × 7 × 4¼ in. (10.2 × 17.8 × 10.8 cm); creamer 2¼ × 4¼ × 3⅛ in. (5.7 × 10.8 × 7.9 cm); sugar bowl and lid 2¼ × 4¼ × 3⅛ in. (5.7 × 10.8 × 7.9 cm); tray 1 × 13¼ × 5¼ in. (2.5 × 33.7 × 13.3 cm). Marked teapot : *WILCOX S.P. CO.* [curved] [two crossed hammers in half circle] / *INTERNATIONAL S. CO* / 7037 / 2c. Creamer and sugar bowl: *WILCOX S.P. CO.* [curved] [two crossed hammers in half circle] / *INTERNATIONAL S. CO* / 7037 / A40. Tray: *WILCOX S.P. CO.* [curved] [two crossed hammers in half circle] *INTERNATIONAL S. CO* [bottom, across] / 7037
Dallas Museum of Art, The Jewel Stern American Silver Collection, acquired through the Patsy Lacy Griffith Collection, gift of Patsy Lacy Griffith by exchange, DMA 2002.29.43.1–4

In 1928, three fitted tea sets, later dubbed "dinette sets" in the firm's salesman's catalogue to denote their compact size and usage, were introduced by International Silver, all by Theobald. Although the only one of the three not patented, this set is documented as his design and was given further styling by Virginia Hamill (see chapter 1). The price of this silverplated four-piece set, the components of which were also offered individually, was $35. This design was also made in pewter.

References: "The Christmas Gift Parade," *Charm* 10 (Dec. 1928): 59; "New Sophistication in keeping with fine old traditions of silversmithing," International Silver Company advertisement, *Vogue* 73 (May 1929): 71.

125. Dinette set, 1928*

Jean G. Theobald
American, active 1920s–1930s

Patent 76,564 (for a table set) filed July 17, 1928, granted Oct. 9, 1928. Silverplate, lacquer, wood. Teapot 3½ × 4¼ × 3⅛ in. (8.9 × 10.8 × 7.9 cm); creamer 3½ × 4½ × 3⅛ in. (8.9 × 10.8 × 7.9 cm); sugar bowl 3½ × 4¼ × 2½ in. (8.9 × 10.8 × 6.4 cm); tray 3¼ × 6 × 4⅜ in. (8.3 × 15.2 × 11.1 cm)
The Wolfsonian–Florida International University, Miami Beach, Florida, The Mitchell Wolfson Jr. Collection

In the International advertisement promoting the three "dinette sets" introduced in 1928, this circular model was described as "compact to fit into the scheme of daily living" and forming "a striking and efficient unit."[1] It was the only one of the three that was illustrated in its tray, and the semicircular teapot and quarter-round sugar and cream holders were also shown removed as separate parts. The circular dinette set has an affinity with the other unnamed model, which has the separate components lined up in a row on its tray. Although more compact, the circular set has the same riveted wood handles and smooth, rounded surfaces, but unlike the flattened knobs and feet of the previous entry, those on the circular set are spherical. Both contrasted with a third dinette set, the sharply angular *Diament,* which had bold, staggered and layered forms. The cost of the circular set was $45. It was also available in pewter at $25.[2]

1. "New Sophistication in keeping with fine old traditions of Silversmithing," International Silver Company advertisement, *Vogue* 73 (May 11, 1929): 71.
2. "The Christmas Parade," *Charm* 10 (Dec. 1928): 59.

126. *Diament* dinette set, 1928*

Jean G. Theobald
American, active 1920s–1930s

Patent 76,434 (for a table set) filed June 29, 1928, granted Sept. 25, 1928. Silverplate, plastic. Teapot 7½ × 6⅝ × 3⅝ in. (19.1 × 16.8 × 9.2 cm); creamer 4½ × 4¼ × 3½ in. (11.4 × 10.8 × 8.9 cm); sugar bowl and lid 4½ × 4¼ × 3½ in. (11.4 × 10.8 × 8.9 cm); tray 1⅜ × 13½ × 4¾ in. (3.5 × 34.3 × 12.1 cm). Marked teapot: *WILCOX QUALITY / WILCOX S. P. CO.* [curved] / *EPNS* [each in a square in half circle] *INTERNATIONAL S. CO.* [at bottom, straight across] / *W.M. Mounts / 1982N / PAT. APPL'D FOR / 109.* Creamer: *WILCOX QUALITY / WILCOX S. P. CO.* [curved] *EPNS* [each in a square in half circle] *INTERNATIONAL S. CO.* [at bottom, straight across] / *W.M. Mounts / 1982N / PAT. APPL'D FOR /* A27. Sugar bowl: *WILCOX QUALITY / WILCOX S. P. CO.* [curved] / *EPNS* [each in a square in half circle] / *INTERNATIONAL S. CO.* [at bottom, straight across] / *W.M. Mounts / 1982N / PAT. APPL'D FOR /* A17. Tray: *WILCOX QUALITY / WILCOX S. P. CO.* [curved] / *EPNS* [each in a square in half circle] / *INTERNATIONAL S. CO.* [at bottom, straight across] / *W.M. Mounts / 1982N / PAT. APPL'D FOR*
Dallas Museum of Art, The Jewel Stern American Silver Collection, gift of Jewel Stern, DMA 2002.29.42.1–4

The boldest of the three fitted "dinette" sets designed by Theobald, the *Diament* is the only one named by International and was the most expensive at $75 (see chapters 1 and 3). A little-known console set, composed of stepped candlesticks and a flower holder fabricated with the tooling of the *Diament* tray, was also called *Diament.* Another item, a "cigarette set," was an exact replication, except for the internal fittings to contain them, of the *Diament* tray. A set containing only a sugar bowl, creamer, and tray was also available.

Reference: "Tea Service in the Modern Spirit," International Silver Company advertisement, *House and Garden* (Dec. 1928): 145

127. Tea urn, c. 1932–1933*

Eliel Saarinen
Finnish, 1873–1950

Silverplate. 14½ × 7¾ in. (36.8 × 19.7 cm). Marked: *WILCOX S.P. CO / EPNS* [each in square] / *INTL S. CO / N5873 / TS*
The Susan Saarinen Collection

The precise spherical form of Saarinen's stately tea urn, mounted on a pierced columnar base concealing an alcohol burner, is enlivened by its lobed plume-like finial and tapered, curving faucet handle. In 1934, a larger, twenty-six-cup production version of this urn (current whereabouts unknown) was included in the designer's Room for a Lady for the exhibition *Contemporary American Industrial Art* at the

Metropolitan Museum of Art. This example, as well as Saarinen's own urn with a tray and accompanying sugar bowl and creamer, now in the collection of the Metropolitan Museum of Art, appear to be early variants with their sixteen-cup capacity, insulators, ball feet, and attenuated slat-like elements in the base. Another sixteen-cup urn of similar design, but lacking insulators, is in the collection of the Cranbrook Art Museum. Two twenty-six-cup urns with thin slats and ball feet were ordered for the Cranbrook School for boys and the Kingswood School for girls (now Cranbrook Kingswood Middle School) in 1938. With the exception of Saarinen's own service in brass-plated nickel silver, all other known examples were executed in silverplate. In a 1935 International salesman's catalogue, a twenty-six-cup production version of the urn, lacking the ball feet and with wider slat-like elements, was priced at $80; an accompanying eighteen-inch-diameter circular tray was offered for $30. Examples of the production urn are in the collections of the British Museum and the St. Louis Art Museum. The paucity of extant examples suggests that relatively few were ever produced (see chapter 5).

References: "At Metropolitan Museum," *International Silver Service* (International Silver Company newsletter) 3 (Jan.–Feb. 1935): 6.
Our thanks to John C. Waddell for his insights on this work.

128. Coffee set, 1934*

Paul A. Lobel
American (b. Romania), 1899–1983

Silverplate, alpaca, Britannia pewter, wood. Tray 1⅛ × 18⅛ in. (2.9 × 46.0 cm); teapot 6 × 6 × 8⅛ in. (15.2 × 15.2 × 20.6 cm); sugar bowl 4⅛ × 4 × 5½ in. (10.5 × 10.2 × 14 cm); creamer 4¼ × 4 × 5½ in. (10.8 × 10.2 × 14 cm). Marked on underside (each): *WILCOX S.P. CO./ INTERNATIONAL S. CO.* [in D-shaped reserve with crossed hammers in center]/*N5873/I* [in square] *S* [in square]; sugar bowl: *45*; creamer: *E P W M* [each in square]
The John C. Waddell Collection

Lobel's spherical four-piece coffee set reigns as a masterpiece of 1930s American streamlined modernism. The prototype of this production-line set was included in the exhibition *Contemporary American Industrial Art* at the Metropolitan Museum of Art in 1934, described as a "tea service." In the Wilcox salesman's catalogue of the same date, this production model was labeled a "coffee set." The multiple layers of plating—including silver, alpaca, and Britannia pewter—suggest that this example was the subject of experiments to test the appearance of various metals.

References: J. Stewart Johnson, *American Modern 1925–1940: Design for a New Age* (New York: Abrams in association with American Federation of Arts, 2000); Richard Guy Wilson, Dianne H. Pilgrim, and Dickran Tashjian, *The Machine Age in America: 1918–1941*, exh. cat. Brooklyn Museum (New York: Abrams, 1986), 310; "At Metropolitan Museum," *International Silver Service* (International Silver Company newsletter) 3 (Jan.–Feb. 1935): 6.

129. Bowl, c. 1960*

Silverplate, wood. 4 × 11 × 6¾ in. (10.2 × 27.9 × 17.1 cm). Marked: *WILCOX/I* [in square] *S* [in square]/*INTERNATIONAL SILVER CO./ 6885*
Dallas Museum of Art, The Jewel Stern American Silver Collection, Decorative Arts Fund, DMA 2002.29.243

The crossed and pronged wood base of this swooping ovoid bowl was a creative treatment intended to attract customers with a penchant for the Danish Modern furniture and other Scandinavian modern accessories, many made of teak, that were flooding the marketplace in the 1950s and early 1960s.

Robert J. King
American, b. 1917

130. Carafe, 1952–1953*

Robert J. King
American, b. 1917

Silver. 14½ × 5 × 3½ in. (36.8 × 12.7 × 8.9 cm). Unmarked
Dallas Museum of Art, The Jewel Stern American Silver Collection, gift of Jewel Stern in honor of Robert J. King, DMA 2002.29.101.A–B

This attenuated, wasp-waist carafe with strong organic lines was designed and made independently by the silversmith Robert J. King and accepted for the competition and exhibition *Designer Craftsmen U.S.A. 1953*.[1] King received a $50 award in the Metals class for this carafe and it was illustrated in the catalogue. Described as "elegantly slender," the carafe was the prominent image in an article in *Glamour* magazine, and it appeared in an article in the *New York Times*, both published in 1953.[2] The contours of the carafe resemble those of a vase by the Finnish designer Tapio Wirkkala that was illustrated in *Craft Horizons* in 1955.[3] The carafe later joined one-of-a-kind pieces made by King and other staff designers expressly for the International Silver Company's Moon Room exhibit at the 1964 New York World's Fair, where it stood on a floating crystalline table adjacent to King's bejeweled *Celestial Centerpiece* (see chapter 13).

1. *Designer-Craftsmen U.S.A. 1953*, exh. cat. Brooklyn Museum of Art, 1953, 32.
2. "The Shape of Things," *Glamour* 30 (Dec. 1953): 108; and Betty Pepis, "Crafts of the U.S.A.," *New York Times*, Oct. 18, 1953, sec. 6, p. 50.
3. Annikki Toikka-Karvonen, "Design in Metal by Three Scandinavians," *Craft Horizons* 15 (Apr. 1955): 11.

Samuel Kirk & Son, Inc.
Baltimore, Maryland
active 1815–1979

131. *Executive Rule* letter opener/ruler, c. 1953

Silver. ⅛ × 12 in. (0.3 × 30.5 cm). Marked: *S. KIRK & SON/STERLING/6*
Dallas Museum of Art, The Jewel Stern American Silver Collection, Decorative Arts Fund, DMA 2002.29.190

The shape of this angular combination letter opener and ruler evokes racy 1950s automobile tail fins. Unusually modern for the conservative Kirk firm, the *Executive Rule* became a popular gift item and remained in the line for over twenty years.

References: "Give more than its weight in silver . . . give Kirk Sterling," Kirk advertisement, *House and Garden* 104 (Dec. 1953): 12; "Last minute shoppers' guide to the right gift," *House and Garden* 104 (Dec. 1953): 125; "Silver you'd love to collect," *House and Garden* 147 (Mar. 1975): 81.

132. Candlesticks (pair) c. 1970*

Silver. Each 4⅝ × 6½ in. (11.7 × 16.5 cm). Marked (each): *S KIRK & SON/STERLING/80*
Dallas Museum of Art, The Jewel Stern American Silver Collection, Decorative Arts Fund, DMA 2002.29.188.1–2

In an effort to attract Christmas shoppers in 1970, Samuel Kirk & Son advertised these pillar-style candlesticks in the November and December issues of *Town and Country*. The price of a single candlestick was $105.

133. *Selene* flatware (fork*), 1975

Silver. Place fork ⅝ × 15/16 × 7½ in. (1.6 × 2.4 × 19.1 cm); soupspoon 13/16 × 1⅜ × 7⅝ in. (2.1 × 3.5 × 19.4 cm). Marked (both): (stamped on back) *S. Kirk & Son STERLING ©*
Dallas Museum of Art, gift of Beverly Hart Bremer, DMA 2000.398.1–2

This gently contoured sterling pattern of 1975 was also offered, with gilded highlights, as *Golden Selene*.

H. E. Lauffer Company
Active early 1950s–1982

134. *Iona* flatware (fork*), 1980

Gerald Gulotta
American, b. 1921

Stainless steel. Knife ½ × ⅞ × 8⅝ in. (1.3 × 2.2 × 21.9 cm); dinner fork 15/16 × 1 × 7 15/16 in. (2.4 × 2.5 × 20.2 cm); salad fork ⅞ × ⅞ × 6⅞ in. (2.2 × 2.2 × 17.5 cm); teaspoon ¾ × 1¼ × 6¼ in. (1.9 × 3.2 × 15.9 cm); tablespoon ¾ × 1⅝ × 7⅞ in. (1.9 × 4.1 × 20.0 cm). Knife marked (on blade): *LAUFFER STAINLESS/JAPAN*. Fork/salad fork/teaspoon/tablespoon: *LAUFFER ® 18/8 JAPAN*
Dallas Museum of Art, gift of Gerald Gulotta, DMA 1999.154.1–5

The *Iona* stainless flatware of 1980 was designed by Gulotta for H. E. Lauffer and manufactured in Japan by Yamazaki Kinzoku Kogyo Co. Ltd. Standard place settings were available in boxes of four; serving utensils were priced separately. Except for the dinner knife, the pieces have elongated rectilinear handles rounded at one end and with ovoid bowls or shortened tines at the other. In contrast to these forms, the knife handle is wider and curves inward sharply, and the wide rounded blade is notched where it joins the handle.

MANCHESTER SILVER COMPANY
PROVIDENCE, RHODE ISLAND
ACTIVE 1887–1985

135. *Copenhagen* flatware, 1936*

Silver, stainless steel knife blade. Luncheon knife ¾ × 8¹¹⁄₁₆ in. (1.9 × 22.1 cm); luncheon fork 1 × 7 in. (2.5 × 17.8 cm); salad fork 1¹⁄₁₆ × 6¼ in. (2.7 × 15.9 cm); teaspoon 1¼ × 6¹⁄₁₆ in. (3.2 × 15.4 cm). Knife marked (on handle): *STERLING*; (on blade): *STAINLESS*. Fork/salad fork: [cross with crown and M] *STERLING.* Teaspoon: [cross with crown and M] *STERLING*
Dallas Museum of Art, gift of Beverly Hart Bremer, DMA 1998.169. 1–4

This early Danish-style pattern has a stylized bud and volutes for decoration at the end of its handles. Unlike many flatware patterns, *Copenhagen* was not patented.

MARSHALL FIELD & COMPANY
CHICAGO, ILLINOIS
ACTIVE 1852–PRESENT

136. Cream and sugar set with tray, c. 1929*

Silver, ebony. Creamer and sugar bowl 3½ × 5¾ × 2¾ in. (8.9 × 14.6 × 7 cm); tray ¾ × 12 × 5 in. (1.9 × 30.5 × 12.7 cm). Marked (on each): *MARSHALL FIELD & CO./STERLING*
Dallas Museum of Art, The Jewel Stern American Silver Collection, acquired through the Patsy Lacy Griffith Collection, gift of Patsy Lacy Griffith by exchange, DMA 2002.29.37.1–3

The weight, execution, and design of the cream and sugar set, part of a suite that included candlesticks, compotes, and castors, place it among the most luxurious silver objects of the period. Clearly meant for a discriminating client who appreciated sophisticated European *art moderne* silverware, the suite appears to have been custom made in the Marshall Field Craft Shop (see chapter 2).

FREDERICK A. MILLER
BRECKSVILLE, OHIO
FOUNDED 1948

137. *Free form* fruit bowl, 1955*

Frederick A. Miller
American, 1913–2000

Silver, ebony. 6½ × 10½ × 8¼ in. (16.6 × 26.8 × 21.0 cm). Marked: *Handwrought/FM/STERLING*
The Cleveland Museum of Art, Silver Jubilee Treasure Fund, 1956.116

More than any other object made by Miller, it is his free form bowls, such as this one on pointed wood (and occasionally ivory) feet and made by the stretching method (see below), for which he is best known. The first free form bowl that he entered into the Cleveland Museum of Art's May Show in 1949 was internationally recognized two years later in the *Studio Year Book,* an English publication.[1] For this particular bowl (in 1949) and for his silver objects included in the May Show in 1956, Miller won Horace E. Potter Memorial Awards for Excellence in Craftsmanship.[2] In contrast to other methods of fabrication, the stretching method using thick pieces of metal was ideal for the irregular free form shapes of post–World War II organic modernism because it made it possible to design and construct a piece in a fluid spontaneous manner.[3] Although examples of his holloware had some influence on the design of industrial silver, Miller's primary influence on production-line silver was through the students he taught at the Cleveland Art Institute. Many, such as Donald H. Colflesh, the designer of Gorham's *Circa '70* line, became associated with silver manufacturers (see chapter 13). Miller reportedly was "proud" that "at one time he had former students working as designers in every major silver company in North America."[4]

1. *Bulletin of the Cleveland Museum of Art* 36 (May 1949): n.p.; and "Silver and Tableware," in Rathbone Holme and Kathleen Frost, eds., *1951–52 Studio Year Book of Furnishings & Decoration* (London and New York: Studio Publications, 1952), 111.
2. *Bulletin of the Cleveland Museum of Art* 43 (May 1956): n.p.
3. "Fred Miller Makes a Bowl," *Craft Horizons* 16 (Dec. 1956): 37.
4. William Baran-Mickle, "Frederick A. Miller: A Precarious Balance," *Metalsmith* 13 (spring 1993): 36.

TED MUEHLING, INC.
NEW YORK, NEW YORK
ACTIVE 1979–PRESENT

138. *Queen Ann's Lace* tea strainer, 1999*

Ted Muehling
American, b. 1952

Silver. 4¼ × 4¼ × ½ in. (10.8 × 10.8 × 1.3 cm). Marked: T MUEHLING/ STERLING
Dallas Museum of Art, anonymous gift, DMA 2005.23.1

Muehling's aesthetic was indelibly shaped by his appreciation of the natural world, a perception formed in childhood and retained throughout his artistic career. He views his design process as embodying both "craftsmanship" and "intuition."[1] In this respect, Muehling was influenced by the industrial designer Gerald Gulotta, who taught at Pratt Institute, and from whom Muehling learned "model-making," how to "see purely," and to rely on his own intuition.[2] Although he mainly uses traditional techniques, for the *Queen Ann's Lace* tea strainer Muehling experimented with the computer to create the template for etching the intricate design derived from the flower for which it is named.[3] The "membrane-like delicacy" of the tea strainer was noted by an art critic, who aptly described the object as a "barely concave disc of silver that is more perforation than material."[4]

1. "Ted Muehling," biographical notes, n.d., n.p., courtesy of Ted Muehling.
2. Andrea Dinoto, "Ted Muehling," *American Craft* (Feb./Mar. 2001): 72.
3. Ibid.
4. Roberta Smith, "Design Review," *New York Times,* May 17, 2003, sec. B, p. 31.

139. *Concave* cup and *White Coral* spoon, 2000*

Ted Muehling
American, b. 1952

Porcelain. Cup 3⅛ × 3⅛ × 3½ in. (7.9 × 7.9 × 8.9 cm); spoon 5¾ × 1 × ½ in. (14.6 × 2.5 × 1.3 cm). Cup marked: [Nymphenburg mark] *Porcelain by Nymphenburg T Muehling* [in script]. Spoon marked: [Nymphenburg mark]
Dallas Museum of Art, anonymous gift, DMA 2005.23.2–3

Muehling's fascination with a porcelain figurine in the window of a pastry shop in Munich in 1998 led him to the local maker, the Porzellan-Manufaktur Nymphenburg, a small factory that was founded in the eighteenth century on the grounds of the Nymphenburg Palace.[1] Impressed with the ideals of the maker and having developed a rapport with the managing director,[2] Muehling designed a collection for the factory. His desire to "capture some essential and compelling quality found in nature," such as the "tactile texture of coral," was realized in the perforated *White Coral* spoon as well as in other objects in the collection.[3] The smooth porcelain *Concave* cup is a perfect foil for his *Queen Ann's Lace* tea strainer in silver.

1. "Ted Muehling," biographical notes, n.d., n.p., courtesy of Ted Muehling.
2. Simone Girner, "Practical Magic," *Departures Magazine* 73 (Oct. 2001): 142.
3. "Ted Muehling."
Reference: "A Pilgrim's Progress," *House and Garden* 172 (May 2000): 156.

NAPIER COMPANY
MERIDEN, CONNECTICUT
ACTIVE 1922–1999

140. Cocktail shaker, 1934*

Emil A. Schuelke
American, dates unknown

Patent 94,098 (for a shaker or similar article) filed July 18, 1934, granted Dec. 18, 1934. Silverplate. 9¼ × 3¾ in. (23.5 × 9.5 cm). Marked: *NAPIER/PAT. PEND*
Dallas Museum of Art, The Jewel Stern American Silver Collection, acquired through the Patsy Lacy Griffith Collection, gift of Patsy Lacy Griffith by exchange, DMA 2002.29.60.A–B

Singled out in *Vogue* as a "brilliant opportunity" for a man to "show his dexterity at mixing," as it was "shakable with one hand,"[1] this streamlined conical cocktail shaker by Emil A. Schuelke, a staff designer for Napier, was released in time to tempt Christmas shoppers in 1934. The shaker alone was priced at $5; the set with four matching cups and a tray cost $10. In *Fashions of the Hour,* Marshall Field & Company offered a version with two red bands at the base.[2]

1. "The Male Box," *Vogue* 84 (Dec. 1, 1934): 71.
2. Marshall Field & Company, *Fashions of the Hour,* Christmas number, 1934, 18; see also "Serving Accessories," *Gift and Art Buyer* 30 (Oct. 1934): 12.

141. *Penguin* cocktail shaker, 1936*

Emil A. Schuelke
American, dates unknown

Patent 101,559 (for a cocktail shaker or similar article) filed Aug. 22, 1936, granted Oct. 13, 1936. Gilded silverplate. 13 × 7¼ × 5 in. (33.0 × 18.4 × 12.7 cm). Marked: *NAPIER / PATENTS PEND.*
Dallas Museum of Art, The Jewel Stern American Silver Collection, gift of Jewel Stern, DMA 2002.29.8.A–B

A holiday advertisement in 1936 invited consumers to "Meet the Penguin: A Bird of A Shaker," which was offered in this "deluxe gold-trimmed" version for $25 and in plain silverplate for half the price. Adding whimsy to the shaker's streamlined form, the penguin's hinged beak serves as a spout. Cocktail shakers were emblems of the euphoric quest for pleasure that typified the Roaring Twenties. The repeal of Prohibition in 1933 bolstered the demand for stylish barware. Because of their tuxedo-like markings, penguins were often associated with success and affluence in the Depression era (see chapter 7).

142. *The Duplex* cream and sugar set, c. 1936*

Gilded silverplate. Creamer 1¾ × 3⅝ in. (4.4 × 9.2 cm); sugar bowl 1⅝ × 3⅝ in. (4.1 × 9.2 cm). Creamer marked: *NAPIER / PAT. PEND. /* [scratched] *1 × 29.* Sugar bowl: *NAPIER / PAT. PEND. /* [scratched] *1 × 2 ×*
Dallas Museum of Art, The Jewel Stern American Silver Collection, gift of Jewel Stern, DMA 2004.13.10.1–2

Cleverly named *The Duplex,* this two-piece set becomes a smooth spherical unit when stacked. The interiors of both creamer and sugar bowl are gilded. *The Duplex* was marketed to urban dwellers in small apartments, who would value its compactness. A small companion teapot was also available.

143. Creamer and sugar bowl, c. 1936

Silverplate. Creamer 6 × 1¾ in. (15.2 × 4.4 cm); sugar bowl 3¾ × 6 × 1¾ in. (9.5 × 15.2 × 4.4 cm). Marked (each): *NAPIER / SILVERPLATE*
Dallas Museum of Art, The Jewel Stern American Silver Collection, acquired through the Patsy Lacy Griffith Collection, gift of Patsy Lacy Griffith by exchange, DMA 2002.29.165.1–2

In the 1930s, Napier produced a number of sleek, modernist designs in silverplate. The designer of this stylized creamer and sugar set relied solely on rounded surfaces and a smooth flattening of form to express streamlining.

144. Salad serving set, c. 1960*

Silverplate, teak. Each ¾ × 3¼ × 12 in. (1.9 × 8.3 × 30.5 cm). Marked (each): *NAPIER ©*
Dallas Museum of Art, The Jewel Stern American Silver Collection, Decorative Arts Fund, DMA 2002.29.92.1–2

The pencil-thin handles of this salad set taper to set off the elliptical shape of the bowls. This set exemplifies the extreme attenuation of form characteristic of 1950s and 1960s organic modernism as well as the influence of imported Scandinavian accessories in wood, especially teak, on American tableware.

ONEIDA LTD. SILVERSMITHS
SHERILL, NEW YORK
ACTIVE 1877–PRESENT

COMMUNITY
DIVISION OF ONEIDA LTD. SILVERSMITHS

145. *Achievement* "5-way" serving dish, introduced 1956*

Silverplate, glass, Durez. 5¼ × 11½ × 8¾ in. (13.3 × 29.2 × 22.2 cm). Marked: *ACHIEVEMENT / COMMUNITY* [in two arched lines with twelve dots inset]
Dallas Museum of Art, The Jewel Stern American Silver Collection, Decorative Arts Fund, DMA 2002.29.273.A–C

The versatility of the "5-way" serving dish was the focus of advertisements for Oneida's *Achievement* line of holloware from its Community division (see chapter 10).[1] An ovenproof glass casserole liner was included.

1. "Silverware News," Oneida Ltd. advertisement, *Jewelers' Circular-Keystone* 126 (Aug. 1956): 172; and "The new 5-way Serving Dish and Hot Beverage Server in Achievement pattern in Community," Oneida Ltd. advertisement, *New Yorker* 33 (Oct. 1957): 5; see also, "House and Garden's Handbook of Holiday Entertaining," *House and Garden* 112 (Nov. 1957): 81.

146. *Achievement* hot beverage set (coffeepot*), introduced 1956

Silverplate, Durez. Coffeepot 8¼ × 7¼ × 3½ in. (21.0 × 18.4 × 8.9 cm); creamer 4 × 4½ × 2½ in. (10.2 × 11.4 × 6.4 cm); sugar bowl 4³⁄₁₆ × 2⅜ × 6 in. (10.6 × 6.0 × 15.2 cm). Marked (each): *ACHIEVEMENT / COMMUNITY* [in two arched lines with twelve dots inset]
Dallas Museum of Art, The Jewel Stern American Silver Collection, Decorative Arts Fund, DMA 2002.29.219.1–3

The subtly flowing contours of the *Achievement* hot beverage server are anchored and stabilized by the domed lid of this harmoniously proportioned and balanced vessel, sculpturally one of the most successful, aesthetically resolved objects of its type from the 1950s. The pierced and contoured black Durez plastic finial echoes the shape of the lid, complements the handle of the same material, and adds an elegant flourish.

HEIRLOOM
ACTIVE 1929–PRESENT
DIVISION OF ONEIDA LTD. SILVERSMITHS

147. *Heirloom "700"* candelabrum, 1955*

Tommi Parzinger
American (b. Germany), 1903–1981

Silverplate. 19½ × 13¾ × 8½ in. (49.5 × 34.9 × 21.6 cm). Marked: *HEIRLOOM / "700" / CRAFTED IN SILVERPLATE* [curved]
Dallas Museum of Art, The Jewel Stern American Silver Collection, Decorative Arts Fund, DMA 2002.29.9

In 1955 the Heirloom division of Oneida introduced a high-styled, glamorous contemporary line of holloware cryptically named *Heirloom "700."* The line was contracted (although this was not acknowledged by Oneida) from Dorlyn Silversmiths of New York, which adapted and modified its own line of brass and silverplated holloware by Tommi Parzinger for the *Heirloom "700"* line (see chapter 10). The tall, three-light candelabrum has a "bowl base," which, the catalogue noted, was "suitable for floral arrangements."[1] Radial scoring on circular elements is the main decorative device and was characteristic of other pieces in the line. A five-light candelabrum in the design was also offered, as was a low three-light candelabrum in a different style, but with the same candle cups and bobeches.

1. Oneida Ltd. Silversmiths, *Heirloom "700" Highly Styled Pieces in Contemporary Design,* Oneida Ltd. Silversmiths catalogue (1956), n.p.

148. *Heirloom "700"* covered compote bowl, 1955*

Tommi Parzinger
American (b. Germany), 1903–1981

Silverplate, plastic. 8 × 9½ in. (20.3 × 24.1 cm). Marked: *HEIRLOOM / "700" / CRAFTED IN SILVERPLATE* [curved]
Dallas Museum of Art, The Jewel Stern American Silver Collection, Decorative Arts Fund, DMA 2002.29.224.A–B

The footed square base of the elegantly proportioned covered compote bowl is a formal device frequently employed by Parzinger. The pierced black plastic disk finial was a feature of all cover lids in the *Heirloom "700"* line.

Reference: "Wedding Gifts Chosen for You and By You," *Bride's Magazine* 22 (spring 1956): 167.

149. *Decorator* candelabrum (one of pair), designed 1956*

Silverplate, Durez. 7¾ × 5½ in. (19.7 × 14.0 cm). Marked (on each leg): *HEIRLOOM*
Dallas Museum of Art, The Jewel Stern American Silver Collection, Decorative Arts Fund, DMA 2002.29.88.2

This candelabrum was introduced by the Community division of Oneida in 1956 in *Achievement,* a full line of holloware heralded by the company in its advertisements.[1] The *Achievement* candelabrum was retained for the early 1960s Heirloom division *Decorator* series and the mark changed from Community to Heirloom. Standing on a tripod of arched legs, the radial form splits into three arms that curve and spring outward to support suspended candle cups that appear weightless. The cups were emphasized by the addition of black Durez plastic tips (see chapter 10).

1. "Achievement the New Pattern in Community," Oneida Ltd. Silversmiths advertisement, *Jewelers' Circular-Keystone* 126 (Nov. 1956): 161.

150. *Decorator* coffee service, c. 1960

Silverplate, walnut. Coffeepot 9 × 8 × 5 in. (22.9 × 20.3 × 12.7 cm); creamer 4½ × 5 × 2¾ in. (11.4 × 12.7 × 7.0 cm); sugar bowl 4½ × 6¹⁄₁₆ × 2¾ in. (11.4 × 15.4 × 7.0 cm); tray 1½ × 23½ × 13½ in. (3.8 × 59.7 × 34.3 cm). Coffeepot / creamer / sugar bowl marked: *HEIRLOOM / EP* [in rounded triangle]. Tray: *HEIRLOOM / SILVER PLATE*
Dallas Museum of Art, The Jewel Stern American Silver Collection, Decorative Arts Fund, DMA 2002.29.232.1–4

To compete with imported and domestic tableware in the modern Scandinavian style, Oneida reinvented its *Achievement* line using many of its dies and adding walnut handles and finials to vessels to evoke the Danish Modern style, a broad term used during the 1950s and 1960s to describe contemporary Scandinavian furnishings. Of all the *Decorator* holloware pieces, this three-piece coffee service with matching tray has the most stylish wood trim (see chapter 10).

PAYE & BAKER MANUFACTURING COMPANY
NORTH ATTLEBORO, MASSACHUSETTS
ACTIVE 1901–1935

151. Tea ball and stand, 1928*

Ilonka Karasz
American (b. Hungary), 1896–1981

Silverplate. 4½ × 3¼ × 1¹⁵⁄₁₆ in. (11.4 × 8.3 × 4.9 cm). Marked: *EPNS* [each in a square] / *P* [in heart] *&* [in heart] *B* [in heart] / *562 IK*
The Jewel Stern American Silver Collection, promised gift of Jewel Stern, DMA 18.2003.16.A–B

In 1928 Paye & Baker produced small quantities of three modernist holloware groups designed by Karasz. This tea ball and stand is in the group that is distinguished by its cone shapes on finlike cruciform supports, reminiscent of Marianne Brandt's Bauhaus vessels (see chapter 3).

JEAN PUIFORCAT
FRENCH, 1897–1945

152. Tea and coffee service, designed 1925*

Jean Puiforcat
French, 1897–1945
(Dallas Museum of Art venue only)
Silver, rosewood. Kettle 8½ × 8¾ × 9½ in. (21.6 × 22.2 × 24.1 cm); teapot 4¾ × 7 × 4⅝ in. (12.1 × 17.8 × 11.7 cm); coffeepot 7¼ × 6 × 3¹³⁄₁₆ in. (18.4 × 15.2 × 9.7 cm); creamer 3⅜ × 3⅝ × 2 in. (8.6 × 9.2 × 5.1 cm); waste bowl 2⅝ × 4½ × 3¼ in. (6.7 × 11.4 × 8.3 cm); sugar bowl 3¾ × 4¾ × 3¹³⁄₁₆ in. (9.5 × 12.1 × 9.7 cm); tongs ⅞ × 1⅞ × 4 in. (2.2 × 4.8 × 10.2 cm). Marked (each): *jean e. puiforcat / france / saks fifth avenue*. Engraved (each): *LMW*
Dallas Museum of Art, the Patsy Lacy Griffith Collection, gift of Patsy Lacy Griffith by exchange, DMA 2002.17.1–7

The design of this boldly geometric tea and coffee service was first seen at the *Exposition Internationale des Arts Décoratifs et Industriels Modernes* in 1925 in Paris, where it was among the most popular services shown. As cubist-influenced silverware was essentially unknown in America, the dramatically faceted design was considered startling and extreme to most Americans. In the late 1920s, select department stores, including Saks Fifth Avenue, served as retailers for Puiforcat's silver, introducing modern French designs to their fashionable clientele. The purchaser, a salesman for Saks, acquired two services from Puiforcat: one for himself and his wife, and this example for his sister-in-law and brother, Lilly and Morris White. The addition of an electrified hot-water kettle reinforces the modern sensibilities of its maker and owners.

Reference: Gail S. Davidson, "Perfection: Jean E. Puiforcat's Designs for Silver," *The Magazine Antiques* 163 (Jan. 2003): 174–83.

REED & BARTON
TAUNTON, MASSACHUSETTS
ACTIVE 1824–PRESENT

153. *Modernist* coffee service, 1928*

Silver. Coffeepot: 9 × 2⅞ × 7½ in. (22.9 × 7.3 × 19.1 cm); creamer 3⅞ × 1¾ × 4 in. (9.8 × 4.4 × 10.2 cm); sugar bowl: 5½ × 5½ × 2⅛ in. (14.0 × 14.0 × 5.4 cm); tray: 1¼ × 13½ × 10½ in. (3.2 × 34.3 × 26.7 cm). Coffeepot marked: [eagle] *R* [in shield] [lion] / *STERLING / D1000 /* [eagle, the 1928 year symbol] / 27. Creamer / sugar bowl / tray: [eagle] *R* [in shield] [lion] / *STERLING / D1000 /* [eagle, the 1928 year symbol]
Dallas Museum of Art, The Jewel Stern American Silver Collection, acquired through the Patsy Lacy Griffith Collection, gift of Patsy Lacy Griffith by exchange, DMA 2002.29.25.1–4

In 1928 Reed & Barton introduced a line called *Modernist*, which was advertised as a "sensible," meaning conservative, interpretation of modernism.[1] This three-piece coffee set and matching ovoid waiter was illustrated in the advertisement. The price of the four-piece set was $150 and the pieces were also available individually. Not only were the shapes idiosyncratic for American silver of the period, but also the set was given a hand-hammered surface that is associated with the earlier Arts and Crafts movement. The creamer in this service is identical to the one in the introductory advertisement; however, another version of the creamer, the same height and shape as the open sugar bowl, was also produced. Although the set was popular in the media, appearing in *Good Furniture Magazine, Country Life, Vogue,* and *Jewelers' Circular,* as well as being exhibited in 1928 in Macy's *International Exposition of Art in Industry,* by 1931 it was out of production (see chapters 1 and 2).

1. "Sensibly Interpreting the Spirit of Modernism," Reed & Barton advertisement, *House and Garden* 53 (June 1928): 123.
References: Ella Burns Meyers, "Trends in Decoration," *Good Furniture Magazine* 31 (Sept. 1928): 130; Helen Appleton Read, "Twentieth Century Decoration: The Modern Theme Finds a Distinctive Medium in American Silver," *Vogue* 72 (July 1, 1928): 98; A. Frederic Saunders, "Modernism in Silverware," *Jewelers' Circular* 100 (Feb. 27, 1930): 105; "Gleaming Christmas Silver," Reed & Barton advertisement, *Vanity Fair* 31 (Dec. 1928): 120.

154. *Modernist* cocktail cup (one* of set of six), 1928

Silver. 5 × 2½ in. (12.7 × 6.4 cm). Marked: *REED & BARTON /* [eagle] *R* [in shield] [lion] / *STERLING / 50 /* [eagle, the 1928 year symbol]. Engraved: [reverse and forward K]
Dallas Museum of Art, The Jewel Stern American Silver Collection, acquired through the Patsy Lacy Griffith Collection, gift of Patsy Lacy Griffith by exchange, DMA 2002.29.117.1

Unlike other conservative holloware pieces depicted in Reed & Barton's advertisement under the heading "Sensibly Interpreting the Spirit of Modernism," the geometric form of this cocktail cup, one of a set of six, was truly "modernist" in 1928, when the set was offered for $50. Interior gilding was an additional $3. A narrow rectangular serving tray on which the cups stand in a single row was available with and without handles. The cocktail cups went out of production in 1936.

References: Isobel Torrington, "Simplicity and Elegance in Modern Silverware," *Arts and Decoration* 29 (Aug. 1928): 59; "Early American and Modernistic Christmas Gift Suggestions," *Arts and Decoration* 30 (Dec. 1928): 75.

155. *Modernist* vase, 1928

Silver. 9 × 5½ in. (22.9 × 14 cm). Marked: *REED & BARTON /* [eagle] *R* [in shield] [lion] / *STERLING / 990 /* [eagle, the 1928 year symbol]
Dallas Museum of Art, The Jewel Stern American Silver Collection, acquired through the Patsy Lacy Griffith Collection, gift of Patsy Lacy Griffith by exchange, DMA 2002.29.114

The unusual shape of this nine-inch vase was replicated and adapted for the candle cups of a pair of candlesticks (with the same product number, 990) introduced at the same time. The vase, originally priced at $40, was discontinued on Jan. 16, 1931.

References: Ella Burns Meyers, "Trends in Decoration," *Good Furniture Magazine* 31 (Sept. 1928): 130; "Sensibly Interpreting the Spirit of Modernism," Reed & Barton advertisement, *House and Garden* 53 (June 1928): 123.

156. *Modernist* vase, 1928

Silver. 4½ × 3½ in. (11.4 × 8.9 cm). Marked: *REED & BARTON /* [eagle] *R* [in shield] [lion] / *STERLING / I 985 /* [eagle, the 1928 year symbol]
Dallas Museum of Art, The Jewel Stern American Silver Collection, acquired through the Patsy Lacy Griffith Collection, gift of Patsy Lacy Griffith by exchange, DMA 2002.29.115

The vertical facets of this small vase provide contrasts of light and shadow. The vase, originally priced at $18, was discontinued at some time between 1931 and 1935.

References: Ella Burns Meyers, "Trends in Decoration," *Good Furniture Magazine* 31 (Sept. 1928): 130; "Sensibly Interpreting the Spirit of Modernism," Reed & Barton advertisement, *House and Garden* 53 (June 1928): 123.

157. *Modernist* compote, 1928*

Silver. 3¾ × 8 in. (9.5 × 20.3 cm). Marked: [eagle] *R* [in shield] [lion] / *STERLING / 983* / [eagle, the 1928 year symbol]
Dallas Museum of Art, The Jewel Stern American Silver Collection, acquired through the Patsy Lacy Griffith Collection, gift of Patsy Lacy Griffith by exchange, DMA 2002.29.113

This compote emulated an earlier design smaller in size by the French silversmith Jean Puiforcat. The last catalogue in the Reed & Barton archives in which the compote was offered is dated 1931.

Reference: "Modern Designs in Silver," *House and Garden* 54 (Sept. 1928): 86.

158. *Modernist* candlesticks (pair) and compote, 1928*

Silver. Candlesticks each 10½ × 3½ × 4½ in. (26.7 × 8.9 × 11.4 cm), compote 7½ × 3½ × 4½ in. (19.1 × 8.9 × 11.4 cm). Marked on one candlestick: *REED & BARTON* [in an arc] / [eagle] *R* [in shield] [lion] / *STERLING* [in an inverted arc] / *1020* / [eagle, the 1928 year symbol]. On second candlestick: [eagle] *R* [in shield] [lion] / *STERLING / 1020* / [eagle, the 1928 year symbol]. Compote: *REED & BARTON* [in an arc] / [bird] *R* [in shield] [lion] / *STERLING* [in an inverted arc] / *1020* / [eagle, the 1928 year symbol]
The John P. Axelrod Collection, Boston, Mass.

Within the *Modernist* holloware series introduced in 1928 was a distinct group of objects that had narrow, layered and overlapping geometric bands for its borders and rims. Several pieces in this group appeared in *Harper's Bazaar* in 1929. They included a gravy boat and stand, a large rectangular platter, an open vegetable dish, and these candlesticks and compote. Other objects in the group but not illustrated were a squared "entrée or chop dish" and a narrow cocktail tray that was produced with and without handles. Unique to this group and to American industrial silver of the period were the stems of the compote and candlesticks, which rose from small stepped pedestals in rectangular bases. Their structure was described in the magazine as having been derived from the steel framing used in skyscrapers. The horizontal bracing of the vertical bars at regular intervals suggests the similarity and this may have been the case. The name of the creator of these objects is not known, but it is likely to have been an innovative staff designer (see chapter 3).

Reference: "June . . . Weddings . . . And Silver . . . Now and Forever," *Harper's Bazaar* 64 (June 1929): 93.

159. *Modernist* gravy boat and tray, 1928*

Silver. Gravy boat 2¼ × 8 × 4¼ in. (5.7 × 20.3 × 10.8 cm); tray ¾ × 8 × 4¼ in. (1.9 × 20.3 × 10.8 cm). Gravy boat marked: [eagle] *R* [in shield] [lion] / *STERLING / 1020* / [eagle, the 1928 year symbol]. Tray: *REED & BARTON* / [eagle] *R* [in shield] [lion] / *STERLING / 1020* / [eagle, the 1928 year symbol]
Dallas Museum of Art, The Jewel Stern American Silver Collection, acquired through the Patsy Lacy Griffith Collection, gift of Patsy Lacy Griffith by exchange, DMA 2002.29.26.1–2

The trapezoidal shape, angular spout, and cantilevered handle of this gravy boat demonstrate the influence of cubist-inspired *art moderne*. The tray has the raised overlapping geometric border of a holloware group within Reed & Barton's *Modernist* pattern. The only example of a *Modernist* gravy boat and matching tray in sterling silver from the late 1920s that has come to light, it was first advertised in 1929. A casualty of the Depression, it was no longer in production by 1931.

References: Ella Burns Meyers, "Trends in Decoration," *Good Furniture Magazine* 31 (Sept. 1928): 130; "June . . . Weddings . . . And Silver . . . Now And Forever," *Harper's Bazaar* 64 (June 1929): 93; "Silver in the Spirit of Today," Reed & Barton advertisement, *House and Garden* 56 (Dec. 1929): 127.

160. Candlesticks (pair), 1928*

Silver. Each 10¼ × 4½ in. (26 cm × 11.4 cm). Marked (each): [eagle] *R* [in shield] [lion] / *STERLING / 990* / [eagle, the 1928 year symbol] / *CEMENT REINFORCED*
Dallas Museum of Art, The Jewel Stern American Silver Collection, acquired through the Patsy Lacy Griffith Collection, gift of Patsy Lacy Griffith by exchange, DMA 2002.29.116.1–2

These gracefully curving candlesticks were featured in the advertisement "Sensibly Interpreting the Spirit of Modernism." The stylized tulip shape of the candle cups was repeated for the stems of the candlesticks, which are linked in design to the no. 990 *Modernist* vase. In production only briefly, they were discontinued in May 1930.

Reference: Lee McCann, "Sterling Silver Goes Modernist," *Country Life* 54 (May 1928): 92.

161. Cocktail cup, 1928*

Silver. 5 × 2⅝ in. (12.7 × 6.7 cm). Marked: [eagle] *R* [in shield] [lion] / *STERLING / 60* [eagle, the 1928 year symbol]
Dallas Museum of Art, gift of Daniel Morris and Denis Gallion, Historical Design Collection, Inc., DMA 1994.239

With oxidized incised lines in an angular pattern, Reed & Barton attempted to give the impression of three-dimensional cubism in this cup, a variant of the *Modernist* cocktail cup no. 50 introduced in the advertisement "Sensibly Interpreting the Spirit of Modernism" in 1928. The rectangular stem was incised on all four sides with an elongated diamond, and the round base has a raised eight-pointed motif reminiscent of a starburst. Introduced in 1928, the cocktail cup was discontinued on May 15, 1930.

Reference: Ella Burns Meyers, "Trends in Decoration," *Good Furniture Magazine* 31 (Sept. 1928): 130.

162. Fruit dish, c. 1933*

Silver. 1¾ × 13½ × 7 in. (4.4 × 34.3 × 17.8 cm). Marked: [eagle] *R* [in shield] [lion] / *STERLING / 952A* / [duck, the 1934 year symbol]
Dallas Museum of Art, The Jewel Stern American Silver Collection, acquired through the Patsy Lacy Griffith Collection, gift of Patsy Lacy Griffith by exchange, DMA 2002.29.151

Called a "fruit dish" by Reed & Barton, this object appears to have been introduced in 1933. It was not in the 1931 catalogue and is unlikely to have been released in 1932 at the depth of the Depression. In late 1933 it was illustrated in *Arts and Decoration*, its "sweeping lines and curved handles" described as "strictly modern in feeling."[1] It was available at the Reed & Barton retail outlet at 4 Maiden Lane in New York City for $29. The dish was also sold at the American branch of the French jeweler Cartier in 1933 (see chapter 3).[2] The design was discontinued on May 20, 1940.

1. "From the Smart Shops and Galleries: Silver," *Arts and Decoration* 39 (Oct. 1933): 57.
2. A fruit dish marked Cartier with the 1933 symbol is in a private collection.

163. *Milk Can* cocktail shaker, c. 1935–1983 (designed c. 1935)*

Silverplate. 11½ × 8 × 5 in. (29.2 × 20.3 × 12.7 cm). Marked: *REED & BARTON / 25 / 64 OZ.*
Dallas Museum of Art, The Jewel Stern American Silver Collection, acquired through the Patsy Lacy Griffith Collection, gift of Patsy Lacy Griffith by exchange, DMA 2002.29.174.A–C

The *Milk Can* cocktail shaker can be documented as having been produced by Reed & Barton from 1935 until June 1983. Its record longevity in the line speaks to its popularity. In addition to this sixty-four-ounce size, the shaker was made in a smaller, thirty-two-ounce capacity. The shaker was accorded full-page advertisements during the 1950s, 1960s, and 1970s.

References: Elizabeth Sverbeyeff, "House Beautiful's Beautiful Boutique," *House Beautiful* 107 (Dec. 1965): 172; "For The Martini Man," *Town and Country* 120 (May 1966): 67; "The 'Milk Can' Cocktail Shaker in Silverplate," Reed & Barton advertisement, *New Yorker* 29 (Apr. 25, 1953): 17; "The Milk Can: To Shake Up A Party, Brighten A Bar," Reed & Barton advertisement, *New Yorker* 46 (June 27, 1970): 23.

164. *Maid of Honor* flatware, 1935*

Silverplate, stainless steel knife blade. Knife 9½ × 13/16 × 7/16 in. (24.1 × 2.1 × 1.1 cm); fork ½ × 1 × 7½ in. (1.3 × 2.5 × 19.7 cm); spoon ½ × 1 × 7⅜ in. (18.7 × 2.5 × 18.7 cm). Knife marked: *REED & BARTON / MIRRORSTELE.* Fork / spoon: *REED & BARTON / XXXX*
Dallas Museum of Art, The Jewel Stern American Silver Collection, gift of Jewel Stern, DMA 2005.25.15.1–3

Although commercial construction dwindled during the Depression, this pattern exemplifies the continuing influence of the stepped-back skyscraper motif on silverware design in the mid-1930s. No patent has been found for this pattern.

165. Bowl, 1936

Silver. 4 × 9 in. (10.2 × 24.1 cm). Marked: [eagle] R [in shield] [lion] / STERLING / X500 / [arrow in target, the 1936 year symbol]
Dallas Museum of Art, The Jewel Stern American Silver Collection, acquired through the Patsy Lacy Griffith Collection, gift of Patsy Lacy Griffith by exchange, DMA 2002.29.149

A stepped base rises to meet a decorative frieze, enlivening the bowl that flares above it. Divided into quadrants defined by four groups of "ribs" that suggest classical flutes, this bowl is a dignified, conservative example of the modern classic idiom of the mid-1930s (see chapter 6).

166. Creamer and sugar bowl, 1936

Gilded silver. Creamer 2½ × 4¼ × 2¼ in. (6.4 × 10.8 × 5.7 cm), sugar bowl 2½ × 4 × 2½ in. (6.4 × 10.2 × 6.4 cm). Marked (each): [eagle] R [in shield] [lion] / Sterling / X287 / [arrow in target, the 1936 year symbol]
Dallas Museum of Art, The Jewel Stern American Silver Collection, acquired through the Patsy Lacy Griffith Collection, gift of Patsy Lacy Griffith by exchange, DMA 2002.29.47.1–2

Called a "dessert set" in Reed & Barton's card file, this sterling creamer and sugar bowl have the rounded form and simple incised lines for decoration characteristic of 1930s streamlined modernism. The squared creamer spout adds a note of contrast while the gilded interiors of both objects connote luxury.

167. Pitcher, 1936*

Silverplate. 9 × 8 × 7 in. (22.9 × 20.3 × 17.8 cm). Marked: REED & BARTON / 5625 / [arrow in target, the 1936 year symbol]
Dallas Museum of Art, The Jewel Stern American Silver Collection, acquired through the Patsy Lacy Griffith Collection, gift of Patsy Lacy Griffith by exchange, DMA 2002.29.62

The sharp angle of the pitcher's projecting spout suggests the forward motion associated with 1930s streamlining. The pitcher was discontinued in 1939.

168. *Jubilee* flatware (teaspoon*) 1936

Carl Conrad Braun
American, 1905–1998

Patent 100,848 (for a spoon or similar article) filed Feb. 10, 1936, granted Aug. 18, 1936. Silver, stainless steel knife blade. Knife ¹³⁄₁₆ × 8¹³⁄₁₆ in. (2.1 × 22.3 cm); fork 7¼ × ¹³⁄₁₆ in. (18.4 × 2 cm); teaspoon 1¼ × 6 in. (3.1 × 15.2 cm). Knife marked: (on side) STERLING HANDLE (on blade) REED & BARTON / MIRRORSTELE. Fork: R. [eagle] R [in shield] [lion]. Teaspoon: H [eagle] R [in shield] [lion] / STERLING
Dallas Museum of Art, gift of Beverly Hart Bremer, DMA 1998.175.1–3

In 1934 Rogers, Lunt & Bowlen introduced *Modern Classic* flatware named for its reductive interpretation of classicism. Others followed suit, including Reed & Barton with *Jubilee*, which was less severe in its interpretation of classicism than were other patterns of the 1930s. Reed & Barton appealed to a wide spectrum of consumers by stressing this aspect of the design in its marketing.

Reference: "Jubilee: An Exquisite New Pattern in Sterling Silver," Reed & Barton advertisement, *Bride's Magazine* 3 (winter 1936–37): 40.

169. Salad bowl, 1937 (introduced 1936)*

Belle Kogan
American (b. Russia), 1902–2000

Silver. 3 × 14 × 8 in. (7.6 × 35.6 × 20.3 cm). Marked: [eagle] R [in shield] [lion] / STERLING / X353L / [sailboat, the 1937 year symbol] / J. E. CALDWELL & CO.
Dallas Museum of Art, The Jewel Stern American Silver Collection, acquired through the Patsy Lacy Griffith Collection, gift of Patsy Lacy Griffith by exchange, DMA 2002.29.147

The salad bowl was in one of two holloware groups (the other in silverplate) designed by Belle Kogan in 1936 in a modern classical idiom for Reed & Barton. An example of this salad bowl was exhibited in *Contemporary Industrial and Handwrought Silver* at the Brooklyn Museum in 1937 (see chapters 6 and 8). This salad bowl was sold by J. E. Caldwell, an exclusive jewelry store in Philadelphia, and bears its name. A cream and sugar set was also produced in this group. Other items in the design include a sandwich tray, model no. X352 and a narrow bread tray, model no. X351.

References: "Creating Mass Appeal for Silver," *Jewelers' Circular-Keystone* 108 (Jan. 1938): 63; *Creative Design in Home Furnishings* 1 (fall 1936): 34–35.

170. Sandwich tray, 1936 (introduced 1936)

Belle Kogan
American (b. Russia), 1902–2000

Silver. 1¼ × 15¾ × 8½ in. (3.2 × 40.0 × 21.6 cm). Marked: [eagle] R [in shield] [lion] / STERLING / X352. Engraved: *1936* / [arrow in target, the 1936 year symbol]
Dallas Museum of Art, The Jewel Stern American Silver Collection, acquired through the Patsy Lacy Griffith Collection, gift of Patsy Lacy Griffith by exchange, DMA 2002.29.146

Like the salad bowl in this pattern, the sandwich tray was exhibited in the exhibition *Contemporary Industrial and Handwrought Silver* at the Brooklyn Museum in 1937 (see chapters 6 and 8).

Reference: Belle Kogan, "Modern Trend in Silverware Design," *Jeweler's Circular-Keystone* 107 (Jan. 1937): 74.

171. Hors d'oeuvres tray, 1936 (introduced 1936)

Belle Kogan
American (b. Russia), 1902–2000

Silver. 1 × 14½ × 9½ in. (2.5 × 36.8 × 24.1 cm). Marked: [eagle] R [in shield] [lion] / STERLING / X1301 / RA [scratched] / 3117581 [scratched]
Dallas Museum of Art, The Jewel Stern American Silver Collection, acquired through the Patsy Lacy Griffith Collection, gift of Patsy Lacy Griffith by exchange, DMA 2002.29.148

The atypical handles of this ovoid tray are semicircular in shape and feature a pierced and overlapping stylized leaf motif, a departure by Kogan from neoclassicism. A bowl (model no. X1300) was also made in this design.

172. Cigarette box, 1937

Silverplate. 2½ × 7¼ × 3 in. (6.4 × 18.4 × 7.6 cm). Marked: REED & BARTON / 200 / [ship, the symbol for 1937]
Dallas Museum of Art, The Jewel Stern American Silver Collection, acquired through the Patsy Lacy Griffith Collection, gift of Patsy Lacy Griffith by exchange, 2002.29.170.A–B

The surface of this streamlined object was given a hand-hammered effect, an odd coupling in 1930s silverware. It was advertised as a container for cigarettes (see chapter 6).

173. Double vegetable dish, 1938 (introduced 1936)*

Belle Kogan
American (b. Russia), 1902–2000

Silverplate. 3¼ × 13½ × 9 in. (8.3 × 34.3 × 22.9 cm). Marked: E P N S [each within a shield] / REED & BARTON / 1605 / [trumpet, the 1938 year symbol]
Dallas Museum of Art, The Jewel Stern American Silver Collection, gift of Jewel Stern in honor of John C. Waddell, DMA 2002.29.59.A–B

This double vegetable dish, the quintessential 1930s example of streamlining merged with modern classicism, was part of a silver-plated holloware group designed by Belle Kogan for Reed & Barton (see chapter 6). The group was represented in the exhibition *Contemporary Industrial and Handwrought Silver* at the Brooklyn Museum in 1937 with a centerpiece (model no. 1605) (see chapter 8). Although a double vegetable dish was previously reported to have appeared in the exhibition, Brooklyn Museum archival records show that it was a different Reed & Barton double vegetable dish (model no. 6200), not designed by Kogan, that was exhibited. Other items in this design by Kogan were an uncovered vegetable dish (model no. 1610), a large "meat dish" (model no. 1610), a bread tray (model no. 1601), and a sandwich tray (model no. 1600).

References: W. Scott Braznell, "Sterling Character," *Spirit* (Aug. 1990): 47; Alastair Duncan, *American Art Deco* (New York: Abrams, 1986), 90; idem, *Modernism: Modernist Design 1880–1940; The Norwest Collection*, exh. cat. Minneapolis (Woodbridge, Suffolk: Antique Collectors' Club, 1998), 228; Jeannine Falino, "Women Metalsmiths," in Pat Kirkham, ed., *Women Designers in the USA 1900–2000* (New York: Bard Graduate Center for Studies in the Decorative Arts; New Haven: Yale University Press, 2000), 232.

174. Meat dish, 1938 (design introduced 1936)

Belle Kogan
American, (b. Russia), 1902–2000

Silverplate. 1¼ × 20 × 12 in. (3.2 × 50.8 × 30.5 cm). Marked: [eagle] R [in shield] [lion]/E.P.N.S. [in rectangle]/REED & BARTON/1610/ [trumpet, the 1938 year symbol]
Dallas Museum of Art, The Jewel Stern American Silver Collection, acquired through the Patsy Lacy Griffith Collection, gift of Patsy Lacy Griffith by exchange, DMA 2002.29.163

The model no. 1610 tray was designated a "meat dish" in Reed & Barton's illustrated object file cards and was the largest piece made in this silverplated holloware pattern, which was designed by Belle Kogan (see chapter 6).

175. Vogue coffeepot, 1938*

Carl Conrad Braun
American, 1905–1998

Silver, ivory. 10 × 9 × 5½ in. (25.4 × 22.9 × 14.0 cm). Marked: [eagle] R [in shield] [lion]/STERLING/635/9/Vogue [in script]/3 PTS/ [trumpet, the 1938 year symbol]
Dallas Museum of Art, The Jewel Stern American Silver Collection, acquired through the Patsy Lacy Griffith Collection, gift of Patsy Lacy Griffith by exchange, DMA 2002.29.48

Braun, the designer of Jubilee flatware, also designed Reed & Barton's extravagant classically inspired Vogue tea service. This coffeepot was part of the six-piece service that included a kettle and stand and a matching twenty-eight-inch waiter with handles. The tray was large enough to hold the weight of the entire service. The service was lavished with vertically ribbed, carved ivory handles and finials. Braun literally quoted his Jubilee flatware pattern for the applied decoration of all components in the service (see chapter 6).

Reference: A. Frederic Saunders, "Trends in Silver," Jewelers' Circular-Keystone 108 (Mar. 1938): 46.

176. Contemporary Group centerpiece, 1950

Robert H. Ramp
American, b. 1920

Silverplate. 3½ × 11¾ × 7¼ in. (8.9 × 29.2 × 18.4 cm). Marked: [drum, the 1950 year symbol]/E P [each in a shield] N S [each in a circle] REED & BARTON/880
Dallas Museum of Art, The Jewel Stern American Silver Collection, Decorative Arts Fund, DMA 2002.29.225

This free form sculptural centerpiece bowl was introduced in 1950 as part of Reed & Barton's landmark Contemporary Group and was one of four designs by Ramp for the collection (see chapter 10). The introductory brochure described the centerpiece as "gracefulness attained by line and surface contrasts."[1] This centerpiece and two other pieces by Ramp in the Contemporary Group, the three-branch rotating candelabrum and the free form bonbon dish, were the only ones from the collection illustrated in a French publication, where they were depicted as "the first expression of the so-called modern school to appear in American silversmithing."[2] The flowing form of the centerpiece anticipated Ramp's Silver Sculpture flatware and holloware pattern of 1954 (see chapter 10). The last Reed & Barton catalogue in which the centerpiece appeared was 1959.

1. The Contemporary Group, Reed & Barton Silversmiths brochure, Aug. 15, 1950, n.p.
2. Tony Bouilhet and Luc Lanel, Contemporary Silverware of Europe and America (Paris: privately published, 1954), n.p.

177. Contemporary Group candelabrum, 1950*

Robert H. Ramp
American, b. 1920

Silverplate. 8¼ × 6½ × 8 in. (21.0 × 16.5 × 20.3 cm). Marked: [drum, the 1950 year symbol]/ REED & BARTON/880
Dallas Museum of Art, The Jewel Stern American Silver Collection, Decorative Arts Fund, DMA 2002.29.83.A–B

A seminal example of post–World War II organic modernism in American holloware, the triple candelabrum, introduced in Reed & Barton's Contemporary Group, rotates through 360 degrees to make intriguing juxtapositions when used in a pair. In the firm's brochure the candelabrum's branches and form were described as "reminiscent of vine-like movements" (see chapter 10).[1] This piece was last offered in the 1960–1961 Reed & Barton catalogue.

1. The Contemporary Group, Reed & Barton Silversmiths brochure (Aug. 15, 1950), n.p.

References: Tony Bouilhet and Luc Lanel, Contemporary Silverware of Europe and America (Paris: privately published, 1954), n.p.; W. Scott Braznell, "A 'New Way of Life': A Candelabrum from Reed & Barton's 'Contemporary Group,'" Yale University Art Gallery Bulletin (1997–98): 76–81; "New Products," Crockery and Glass Journal 147 (Dec. 1950): 16.

178. Contemporary Group bonbon dish, 1950*

Robert H. Ramp
American, b. 1920

Silver. 1¼ × 8⅛ × 4⅝ in. (3.2 × 20.6 × 11.7 cm). Marked: [drum, the 1950 year symbol]/REED & BARTON/STERLING/X724
Dallas Museum of Art, The Jewel Stern American Silver Collection, Decorative Arts Fund, DMA 2002.29.65

Only one foot raises one side of this asymmetrical bonbon dish. The bonbon dish and the candelabrum by Ramp from the Contemporary Group show the influence on Ramp's work of the Danish silversmith Henning Koppel's free form sculptural holloware for Georg Jensen. The bonbon dish was in production for less than five years. It did not appear on the August 1955 price list.

179. Centerpiece, 1954

Silverplate, beefwood. 1½ × 9½ × 7½ in. (3.8 × 24.1 × 19.1 cm). Marked: [mortar and pestle, the 1954 symbol]/REED & BARTON/ 128/A [inscribed in C, a copper alloy mark]
Dallas Museum of Art, The Jewel Stern American Silver Collection, Decorative Arts Fund, DMA 2002.29.274

This curvaceous silverplated centerpiece with Australian beefwood–tipped feet was introduced in the "Supplementary Trade Price List" issued August 1, 1954, and cost $27.50. In production only briefly, the centerpiece was not on the corresponding price list of August 1, 1955.

180. Silver Sculpture bowl, 1954

Silver. 1¼ × 14 × 4 in. (3.2 × 35.6 × 10.2 cm). Marked: [mortar and pestle, the 1954 year symbol]/REED & BARTON/STERLING/X151/Silver Sculpture [in script]
Dallas Museum of Art, The Jewel Stern American Silver Collection, Decorative Arts Fund, DMA 2002.29.66

The Silver Sculpture bowl was part of a holloware group designed by Ramp to accompany his Silver Sculpture flatware, also introduced in 1954. The other pieces were a bonbon dish, a sandwich plate, salt and pepper shakers, individual nut dishes, and an ash tray. Although Ramp designed a prototype coffee service, it was not produced. The last catalogue in which the bowl appeared was 1960–1961.

181. Silver Sculpture flatware, 1954*

Robert H. Ramp
American, b. 1920

Patent 172,109 (for a spoon or similar article) for June 10, 1953, granted May 4, 1954. Silver, stainless steel knife blade. Teaspoon ½ × 1¼ × 6⅛ in. (1.3 × 3.2 × 15.6 cm); salad fork ⅝ × 1 × 6¾ in. (1.6 × 2.5 × 17.1 cm); place fork ⅝ × ⅞ × 7⅜ in. (1.6 × 2.2 × 18.7 cm); place knife ½ × ¾ × 9 in. (1.3 × 1.9 × 22.9 cm). Fork/salad fork/teaspoon marked: Reed & Barton [in script] STERLING. Knife: REED & BARTON/MIR-RORSTELE/STERLING HANDLE
Dallas Museum of Art, gift of Beverly Hart Bremer, DMA 1998.162. 1–3

Silver Sculpture was the first post–World War II flatware pattern produced by Reed & Barton to express the sculptural, asymmetrical free form style (see chapter 10). It followed other patterns in the mode such as Towle's Contour (1950), Wallace's Waltz of Spring (1952), International's Silver Rhythm (1953), and Gorham's baroque interpretation of free form, Décor (1953).

182. Relish tray, c. 1958–1969 (introduced 1955)

Robert H. Ramp
American, b. 1920

Silverplate. 2 × 9½ × 6 in. (5.1 × 24.1 × 15.2 cm). Marked: REED & BARTON/67/A [inscribed in C, a copper alloy mark]
Dallas Museum of Art, The Jewel Stern American Silver Collection, Decorative Arts Fund, DMA 2002.29.89

The tray was introduced in the 1955 Reed & Barton catalogue as a "bread, celery or olive tray." Like Wallace's green Color-Clad dish with ball feet (see chapter 13), this tray is similar in shape to a "relish dish" in stainless steel by the maker WMF (Württemburgische Metallwaren-fabrik), which may in turn have had a Scandinavian precursor.[1] In the catalogue for the traveling exhibition 20th Century Design: U.S.A., the

Reed & Barton piece was listed as a "relish tray" (see chapter 14).[2] In 1966, Reed & Barton changed the name to a "bread tray." It was discontinued on October 27, 1969. Because the last year in which Reed & Barton stamped a year symbol on holloware was 1957, it is not possible to assign a year of production to this example.

1. "What makes it gleam so?" Calgonite advertisement, *House and Garden* 113 (Mar. 1958): 36.
2. William Friedman, ed. *20th Century Design: U.S.A.*, exh. cat. Albright Art Gallery, Buffalo Fine Arts Academy, 1959, 64.

183. Pitcher, c. 1958 (introduced 1955)

Theodore E. Cayer
American, 1907–1969

Silverplate. 8¾ × 7½ × 5¼ in. (22.2 × 19.1 × 13.3 cm). Marked: *REED & BARTON / 5490 / 3½ PT.*
Dallas Museum of Art, The Jewel Stern American Silver Collection, Decorative Arts Fund, DMA 2002.29.242

This pitcher by Theodore Cayer, who had been a staff designer for Reed & Barton since 1926, was chosen for the 1959 traveling exhibition *20th Century Design: U.S.A.*, and was illustrated in the catalogue (see chapter 14).[1] A popular item that received a full-page advertisement, it remained in the line for over twenty years until it was discontinued in July 1977.[2]

1. William Friedman, ed., *20th Century Design: U.S.A.*, exh. cat. Albright Art Gallery, Buffalo Fine Arts Academy, 1959, 63.
2. "Water or Cocktail Pitcher in Silverplate," Reed & Barton advertisement, *New Yorker* 32 (Aug. 18, 1956): 5.

184. Sandwich plate, c. 1958–1962 (introduced 1955)

Silver. ½ × 11½ × 8⁵⁄₁₆ in. (1.3 × 29.2 × 21.1 cm). Marked: *REED & BARTON / STERLING / X727*
Dallas Museum of Art, The Jewel Stern American Silver Collection, gift of Jewel Stern, DMA 2004.13.14

On August 1, 1955, this smooth, elliptical free form sandwich plate was added to Reed & Barton's *Contemporary Group*, which originated in 1950. It was discontinued on February 5, 1962.

185. Candlesticks (pair), c. 1958–1974 (introduced 1956)

Milton P. Hannah
American, b. 1927

Silver. Each 4 × 3½ in. (10.2 × 8.9 cm). Marked (each): *REED & BARTON / STERLING / H41 / Weighted* [in script]. Paper label on (2002.29.194.1): *REED & BARTON* [in script] / *STERLING*
Dallas Museum of Art, The Jewel Stern American Silver Collection, Decorative Arts Fund, DMA 2002.29.194.1–2

These candlesticks by Hannah, who graduated with a degree in industrial design from the Rhode Island School of Design in 1949, were included in the traveling exhibition *20th Century Design: U.S.A.* in 1959 (see chapter 14). The candlesticks flare outward from a pinched-in waist recalling the fashionable post–World War II New Look. Hannah was one of the designers of the Reed & Barton *Contemporary Group*, introduced in 1950 (sterling bonbon dish no. X721). The last catalogue in which the candlesticks were offered was 1974.

186. *Far East* water pitcher, 1957 (introduced 1956)*

Silver. 10 × 6½ × 5 in. (25.4 × 16.5 × 12.7 cm). Marked: [arrow, the 1957 year symbol] / *REED & BARTON / STERLING / X426 / FAR EAST* [stylized]
Dallas Museum of Art, gift of the Friends of the Decorative Arts in honor of Marie Chiles, DMA 1997.96

The *Far East* sterling holloware group was introduced late in 1956 in the "Add On" to the Reed & Barton 1956–1957 catalogue. A pitcher, a three-piece coffee set with matching tray, a bowl, and a centerpiece were produced in *Far East*. As was often the case in holloware groups, the water pitcher was essentially adapted from the coffeepot. In production for only two years, the *Far East* pitcher was discontinued on October 15, 1958. Befitting the name of the group, the tiny stylized chrysanthemum flowers that serve as decorative bosses on the surface of the works suggest a connection with a familiar Japanese motif.

Reference: "New 'Far East' Coffee Service in Sterling Silver," Reed & Barton advertisement, *New Yorker* 32 (Nov. 3, 1956): 89.

187. Ashtray, c. 1962–1969 (shape introduced 1958)*

John Prip
American, b. 1922

Silverplate with applied color. 1 × 4¾ × 4 in. (2.5 × 12.1 × 10.2 cm). Marked: *REED & BARTON / 73 / A* [inscribed in C, a copper alloy mark]
Dallas Museum of Art, The Jewel Stern American Silver Collection, Decorative Arts Fund, DMA 2002.29.283

This ashtray was designed by John Prip for production in silverplate in 1958. When it was introduced in *Color-Glaze* in 1962, one of the colors offered was "ruby red." The ashtray was discontinued in 1969.

188. *Triangle* bowl, c. 1965 (shape introduced 1958)*

John Prip
American, b. 1922

Silverplate with applied color. 2½ × 7 in. (6.4 × 17.8 cm). Marked: *REED & BARTON / 251 / A* [inscribed in C, a copper alloy mark]
Dallas Museum of Art, The Jewel Stern American Silver Collection, Decorative Arts Fund, DMA 2002.29.238

The *Triangle* bowl shape in silverplate by Prip was introduced in 1958 in two sizes, a bonbon dish, no. 241, and a bowl, no. 251. In 1960 the largest size bowl, no. 261, was added to the line. The three sizes were offered in the introductory *Color-Glaze* line of 1961 (see chapter 13). This no. 251 *Triangle* bowl has a chartreuse interior, a color in production for a short time, and the bowl itself was discontinued on July 1, 1976. The no. 261 *Triangle* bowl was discontinued in 1970 and the bonbon dish, no. 241, in 1979.

189. Bonbon dish, c. 1965 (shape introduced 1958)*

Milton P. Hannah
American, b. 1927

Silverplate with applied color. 1½ × 7 × 4⅛ in. (3.8 × 17.8 × 10.5 cm). Marked: *REED & BARTON / 94*
Dallas Museum of Art, The Jewel Stern American Silver Collection, Decorative Arts Fund, DMA 2002.29.12

This bonbon dish, shaped as a rounded isosceles triangle, stands on a single curved and pointed foot positioned at its narrow end. It was designed by Hannah, a contributor to the *Contemporary Group* of 1950. The bonbon dish, initially released in 1958, was one of the first shapes introduced in *Color-Glaze* in 1961. In this example, the gold color of the interior adds a luminescent quality to the piece. The no. 94 bonbon dish in *Color-Glaze* was discontinued in 1973.

190. Ashtray, c. 1962–1972 (shape introduced 1958)*

Milton P. Hannah
American, b. 1927

Silverplate with applied color. ¼ × 6 in. (0.6 × 15.2 cm). Marked: *REED & BARTON / 88 / A* [inscribed in C, a copper alloy mark]
Dallas Museum of Art, The Jewel Stern American Silver Collection, Decorative Arts Fund, DMA 2002.29.279

This ashtray has an "emerald green" *Color-Glaze* interior. This color green was in the first group of colors offered in *Color-Glaze* and remained as a staple until *Color-Glaze* was discontinued in the early 1980s. The ashtray was introduced in silverplate in 1958, with color in 1962, and discontinued in 1972.

191. Bread tray, c. 1958–1969 (introduced 1958)

Milton P. Hannah
American, b. 1927

Silverplate. 2½ × 10¾ × 5⅝ in. (6.4 × 27.3 × 14.3 cm). Marked: *REED & BARTON / 87 / A* [inscribed in C, a copper alloy mark]
Dallas Museum of Art, The Jewel Stern American Silver Collection, Decorative Arts Fund, DMA 2002.29.288

Like the no. 94 bonbon dish of the same year by Hannah, the bread tray has one curved and pointed foot at is narrow end. The thrust of the elongated triangular free form shape conjures movement. Soon after it was released in the fall of 1958, Reed & Barton heightened that perception in a full-page advertisement.[1] The bread tray was discontinued as of October 27, 1969.

1. "Contemporary Bread Tray in a Sweeping Motion of Heavy Silverplate," Reed & Barton advertisement, *New Yorker* 35 (May 16, 1959): 5.

192. *Denmark* tea and coffee service (teapot*), 1960 (designed 1958)

John Prip
American, b. 1922

Silverplate, plastic. Coffeepot 10½ × 8 × 6½ in. (26.7 × 20.3 × 16.5 cm); teapot 6½ × 6 × 7 in. (16.5 × 15.2 × 17.8 cm); creamer 4½ × 4¼ × 3½ in. (11.4 × 10.8 × 8.9 cm); sugar bowl 4¼ × 4½ in. (10.8 × 11.4 cm). Coffeepot marked: *REED & BARTON / 1720 / DENMARK / 38*. Teapot: *REED & BARTON / 1721 / DENMARK*. Creamer: *REED & BARTON / 1723 / DENMARK*. Sugar bowl: *REED & BARTON / 1722 / DENMARK*. Paper label (on each): *Reed & Barton* [in script] / *THE WORLD'S FINEST SILVERPLATE*
Dallas Museum of Art, The Jewel Stern American Silver Collection, Decorative Arts Fund, DMA 2002.29.82.1–4

The *Denmark* service, one of three services designed by John Prip (see also *The Diamond* and *Dimension,* chapter 12), was introduced in pewter as a three-piece coffee set in 1958 and later made as a five-piece service. In 1960 it was offered in silverplate as a five-piece tea and coffee service. A matching tray was not produced for *Denmark.* This four-piece service does not include the waste bowl. The silverplated service was discontinued in 1983.

References: "Teapots to Make Pouring a Joy," *House and Garden* 130 (Sept. 1966): 32; "They're new . . . They're yours to profit by," *Jewelers' Circular-Keystone* 128 (Dec. 1958): 22.

193. *The Diamond* tea and coffee service (coffeepot*), 1958 (designed 1957–1958)

John Prip
American, b. 1922

Silver, plastic. Coffeepot 12 × 8½ × 5½ in. (30.5 × 21.6 × 14 cm); teapot 8 × 8½ × 6 in. (20.3 × 21.6 × 15.2 cm); creamer 4½ × 4½ × 3½ in. (11.4 × 11.4 × 8.9 cm); sugar bowl 5 × 4½ in. (12.7 × 11.4 cm). Coffeepot marked: *REED & BARTON / STERLING / 440 / 22 / THE DIAMOND.* Teapot: *REED & BARTON / STERLING / 440 / 4 / The Diamond.* Creamer, sugar bowl: *REED & BARTON / STERLING / 440 / THE DIAMOND.* Paper label (on each): *Reed & Barton* [in script] / *STERLING*
Dallas Museum of Art, The Jewel Stern American Silver Collection, Decorative Arts Fund, DMA 2002.29.71.1–4

The Diamond tea and coffee service was created by John Prip to coordinate with *The Diamond* flatware pattern (1958), and was the only one of the three services he designed that was made in sterling silver (see chapter 12). Introduced as a three-piece coffee set in the "Oct. 1, 1958 Sterling Silver Holloware Catalog Supplement," the five-piece service first appeared in the Reed & Barton 1960–1961 catalogue. A matching tray was not offered. *The Diamond* service was discontinued on June 15, 1984.

Reference: Thomas S. Michie and Christopher P. Monkhouse, eds., *John Prip: Master Metalsmith,* exh. cat. (Providence: Rhode Island School of Design; and New York: American Craft Museum and Museum of Art, 1987), 12.

194. *The Diamond* flatware (knife*), 1958 (designed 1954–1958)

Robert H. Ramp
American, b. 1920
adapted from a design by
Gio Ponti
Italian, 1891–1979

Silver, stainless steel knife blade. Place knife ¼ × 1 × 8⅞ in. (0.6 × 2.5 × 22.5 cm); place fork ¹⁵⁄₁₆ × ¹⁵⁄₁₆ × 7½ in. (2.4 × 2.4 × 19.1 cm); teaspoon 1¼ × ⅝ × 6⅛ in. (3.2 × 1.6 × 16.6 cm). Knife marked: *REED & BARTON / MIRRORSTELE / STERLING HANDLE.* Fork / teaspoon: *Reed & Barton* [in script] / *STERLING*
Dallas Museum of Art, 20th-Century Design Fund, DMA 1995.128.1–3

For the evolution of the design of *The Diamond* flatware pattern, see chapter 12. The flatware currently remains in production as one of more than forty-six patterns in Reed & Barton's Made-to-Order program.

195. Salad dish, c. 1959–1963 (introduced 1959)*

Silverplate. 2¼ × 13¼ × 9½ in. (5.7 × 33.7 × 24.1 cm). Marked: *REED & BARTON / 53 / A* [inscribed in C, a copper alloy mark]
Dallas Museum of Art, The Jewel Stern American Silver Collection, gift of Jewel Stern, DMA 2004.13.3

This dish is one of the most graceful examples of 1950s biomorphic design in silver and a precursor in shape to Elsa Peretti's celebrated "bean" designs for Tiffany & Co. from the 1970s and 1980s. It rests asymmetrically on one wide, double-pointed foot at its narrow end. The design was made in three sizes: a small bonbon dish, a slightly larger sandwich plate, and the largest, this salad dish. Introduced in the fall of 1959, the dishes were in production briefly. The 1962–1963 Reed & Barton catalogue was the last one in which they appeared.

196. *Lark* flatware, 1960 (designed 1959)*

John Prip
American, b. 1922

Patent 85,569 (for a spoon or similar article) filed Feb. 9, 1959, granted May 23, 1959. Silver, stainless steel knife blade. Place knife ¹³⁄₁₆ × 9 in. (2.1 × 22.9 cm); fork 7½ × 1 in. (19.1 × 2.5 cm); salad fork 7¹⁄₁₆ × 1¹⁄₁₆ in. (17.9 × 2.6 cm); teaspoon 6⁵⁄₁₆ × 1⅛ in. (16 × 2.9 cm). Knife marked: *REED & BARTON / MIRRORSTELE / STERLING HANDLE.* Fork / salad fork / teaspoon: *Reed & Barton* [in script] *STERLING*
Dallas Museum of Art, gift of Beverly Hart Bremer, DMA 1998.172.1–4

Lark was one of three sterling patterns designed by Prip for Reed & Barton (see chapters 12 and 14). The others were *Dimension* (1961) and *Tapestry* (1964).

197. *Free Form* centerpiece, 1960 (shape introduced 1957)*

Silverplate with applied color. 3½ × 13½ × 6½ in. (8.9 × 34.3 × 16.5 cm). Marked: *REED & BARTON / 68 / A* [inscribed in C, a copper alloy mark]
Dallas Museum of Art, The Jewel Stern American Silver Collection, Decorative Arts Fund, DMA 2002.29.290

The *Free Form* shape was introduced in 1957 as a silverplated bonbon dish, model no. 64. In 1958 the *Free Form* centerpiece, no. 65, was added to the line. This no. 68 *Free Form* centerpiece, the largest size, entered the line in 1960. All three sizes were available in the initial offering of *Color-Glaze* in 1961. The plum color interior of this example is unusual. The no. 68 centerpiece was discontinued in 1970. The last Reed & Barton catalogue to include the *Free Form* no. 64 bonbon dish and the no. 65 centerpiece was that for 1980–1983, the end of the *Color-Glaze* line.

198. *Party* dish, c. 1966–1983 (shape introduced 1965)*

Silverplate with applied color. 1 × 14 × 5½ in. (2.5 × 35.6 × 14 cm). Marked: *REED & BARTON / 1168*
Dallas Museum of Art, The Jewel Stern American Silver Collection, Decorative Arts Fund, DMA 2002.29.90

The low-slung, rounded rectangular *Party* dish was introduced in silverplate by Reed & Barton in 1965, and a year later it was first offered in *Color-Glaze.* The color interior of this dish is Reed & Barton's "pearl blue." Apparently a stock item, the dish was given stylish feet by Gorham and called *Tira* in its late-1950s *Modern* line. Wallace also used it with *Color-Clad.* The Reed & Barton *Party* dish remained in the line until *Color-Glaze* was discontinued in June 1983.

199. *Dimension* tea and coffee service, c. 1961–1977 (introduced 1961)*

John Prip
American, b. 1922

Silverplate, plastic. Coffeepot 8½ × 9½ × 6¼ in. (21.6 × 24.1 × 15.9 cm); teapot 6½ × 10 × 9 in. (16.5 × 25.4 × 22.9 cm); sugar bowl and lid 5 × 4¾ in. (12.7 × 12.1 cm); creamer 4¾ × 4½ in. (12.1 × 11.4 cm); waste bowl 2⅝ × 5 in. (6.7 × 12.7 cm); tray 1½ × 25¾ × 16 in. (3.8 × 65.4 × 40.6 cm). Coffeepot marked: *REED & BARTON / 1500 / DIMENSION.* Teapot: *REED & BARTON / 1501 / DIMENSION.* Sugar bowl: *REED & BARTON / 1502 / DIMENSION.* Creamer: *REED & BARTON / 1503 / DIMENSION.* Tray: *Reed & Barton / 1505 / 25*
Dallas Museum of Art, gift of Marie Chiles in honor of John Houser Chiles on their 40th Anniversary through the 20th-Century Design Fund, DMA 1995.17.1–6

Of the three Reed & Barton services designed by Prip, only *Dimension* had a tray designed to accompany it. The oval tray has a black Formica insert to coordinate with the black plastic–wrapped handles of the coffeepot and teapot (see chapter 12). Because they broke so easily, the original hinges, which had been modeled on those on Prip's handwrought *Onion* teapot, were modified; the new hinges, which did not have the refinement and distinction of the original design, first appeared on the teapot and coffeepot in the 1962–1963 catalogue. The *Dimension* service was discontinued in 1977.

References: "Dimension, An Interpretive Form of the Future, Now in a Tea Service of Heavy Silver plate," Reed & Barton advertisement, *New Yorker* 38 (Apr. 14, 1962): 137, and *New Yorker* 42 (Sept. 17, 1966): 111.

200. *Dimension* flatware, 1961*

John Prip
American, b. 1922

Patent 187,589 (for a knife or similar article) filed Nov. 30, 1959, granted Apr. 5, 1960. Silver, stainless steel knife blade. Place knife ⅞ × ¾ × 8⅞ in. (2.2 × 1.9 × 22.5 cm); place fork ⅞ × 1⅛ × 7½ in. (2.2 × 2.9 × 19.1 cm); teaspoon ½ × 1⅞ × 6 in. (1.3 × 4.8 × 15.2 cm). Knife marked: *REED & BARTON / MIRRORSTELE / STERLING HANDLE*. Fork / teaspoon: *Reed & Barton* [in script] *STERLING*
Dallas Museum of Art, 20th-Century Design Fund, DMA 1995.123.1–3

Launched in 1961 at $42.50 for a six-piece place setting, *Dimension* sterling flatware, totally devoid of decoration, was described by Reed & Barton as combining the "simplicity of classic lines with the freshness of contemporary design."[1] *Dimension's* subtly modeled, elongated triangular handles, which taper as narrowly as possible to rounded triangular bowls, demonstrated Prip's finesse as a sculptor and his assimilation of post–World War II Scandinavian modernism in flatware.

1. "Sterling Seen in a New Light," *The Silver Lining* (Reed & Barton newsletter) 19 (Sept. 1961): 5.
Reference: "This is Dimension, An Enlightened Design in Sterling Reflecting the Infinite Variety of Pure Planes," Reed & Barton advertisement, *New Yorker* 38 (July 7, 1962): 1

201. *Connoisseur* casserole, c. 1963–1984 (introduced 1963)*

John Prip
American, b. 1922

Silverplate, ceramic. Overall 6¼ × 10½ × 7½ in. (15.9 × 26.7 × 19.1 cm). Marked: *REED & BARTON / 1163*. Paper label: *Reed & Barton* [in script] / *THE WORLD'S FINEST SILVERPLATE*. On ceramic liner: *HALL / RB*
Dallas Museum of Art, The Jewel Stern American Silver Collection, gift of Jewel Stern, DMA 2002.29.19.A–C

In production from 1963 to 1984, this contemporary three-piece casserole ensemble, designed for an elegant presentation at the table, consists of a "silverplated frame and cover" for a white, three-and-a-half-pint-capacity "oven-proof china liner" made by Hall China Company. Initially advertised as the "Complete Casserole," it was dubbed the "Connoisseur Casserole" in 1981.[1] In 1963, it retailed for $29.75. The price escalated over the years and in 1981 it cost $145—almost five times the original price. In 1972 a five-pint-capacity version (no. 1164) was introduced. The larger version did not sell well and both versions were discontinued in 1984.

1. "The Complete Casserole," Reed & Barton advertisement, *New Yorker* 46 (Feb. 24, 1968): 109; and "The Connoisseur Casserole," Reed & Barton advertisement, *New Yorker* 58 (Nov. 8, 1982): 15.
References: "A Classic Is Art You Use," Reed & Barton advertisement, *New Yorker* 57 (Sept. 7, 1981): 93; "Service With A Style," *Bride's Magazine* 36 (Sept. 1969): 147; "Wedding Gifts," *Gourmet* 30 (May 1970): 40.

202. *Tapestry* flatware (fork*), 1964

John Prip
American, b. 1922

Silver, stainless steel knife blade. Place knife 9 × ⅞ in. (22.9 × 2.2 cm); place fork 1 × 7½ in. (2.5 × 19.0 cm); teaspoon 6 1/16 × 1¼ in. (15.3 × 3.2 cm). Knife marked: *REED & BARTON / MIRRORSTELE / STERLING HANDLE*. Fork / teaspoon: *Reed & Barton* [in script] *STERLING*
Dallas Museum of Art, gift of Beverly Hart Bremer, DMA 1998.166. 1–3

For *Tapestry* flatware, see chapters 12 and 14.

203. Serving dish, c. 1969–1972*

Silverplate with applied color. 1¼ × 8 × 5¾ in. (3.2 × 20.3 × 14.6 cm). Marked: *REED & BARTON / 268*
Dallas Museum of Art, The Jewel Stern American Silver Collection, Decorative Arts Fund, DMA 2002.29.17

This free form triangular dish is very similar in shape to two sterling dishes from the 1950s *Contemporary Group*—a bonbon dish, no. X723, and a sandwich plate, no. X726. The bonbon dish was designed by Donald Pollard, who may have designed all the iterations of it. Or, possibly, his bonbon dish was adapted later by the company's design staff. This serving dish, no. 268, was introduced in *Color-Glaze* in 1969. This example has a *Color-Glaze* interior in Reed & Barton's "burnt orange." The dish was discontinued in 1972.

204. Centerpiece, c. 1970

Silverplate with applied color. 2 × 13⅛ × 6½ in. (5.1 × 33.3 × 16.5 cm). Marked: *REED & BARTON / 247*
Dallas Museum of Art, The Jewel Stern American Silver Collection, gift of Jewel Stern, DMA 2005.25.8

The form of this centerpiece with an emerald green *Color-Glaze* interior is a hybrid, made with the die of the centerpiece, no. 259 (1960–1966), designed by John Prip, without its original base, but with new legs added. It was introduced in 1970 in *Color-Glaze* and was discontinued October 2, 1972.

205. *Plank* vase, 1989*

Clark L. Lofgren
American, b. 1936

Silverplate. 6⅝ × 6⅛ × 1¾ in. (16.8 × 15.6 × 4.4 cm). Marked: *REED & BARTON / ©*
Dallas Museum of Art, gift of Reed & Barton Silversmiths, DMA 2005.18

In 1989, Carl Lofgren, Reed & Barton's design director, created three contemporary *Plank* vases, flattened ovoid forms in different heights and widths that flared outward slightly at their narrowed openings. All decoration was eliminated. Lofgren relied on the shapes, proportions, and smooth reflective surfaces for aesthetic appeal. This *Plank* vase is the widest and most visually effective of the three forms. It was also the most expensive at $150. All three vases were discontinued in the spring of 1992.

DOMINICK & HAFF
NEW YORK, NEW YORK
FOUNDED 1872

DIVISION OF REED & BARTON

206. *Contempora* flatware (teaspoon*), introduced 1930 (designed c. 1928–1929)

Eliel Saarinen
Finnish, 1873–1950

Patent 79,854 (for a spoon or similar article) filed July 20, 1929, granted Nov. 5, 1929. Silver. Tablespoon 2 × 8½ in. (5.1 × 21.6 cm); teaspoon ¾ × 1¼ × 6 in. (1.9 × 3.2 × 15.2 cm); salad fork ½ × 1 1/16 × 6¼ in. (1.3 × 2.7 × 15.9 cm); dinner fork 1 × 1 1/16 × 7¾ in. (2.5 × 2.7 × 19.6 cm); dinner knife ¼ × ⅞ × 9¼ in. (0.6 × 2.2 × 23.5 cm); butter knife ⅛ × ⅝ × 6½ in. (0.3 × 1.6 × 16.5 cm). Tablespoon / salad fork marked: [rectangle-circle-diamond] *STERLING*. Teaspoon / dinner fork: *STERLING* [rectangle-circle-diamond] *R*. Dinner knife (on handle): [obscured] *NG HANDLE*. Butter knife (on blade): *STERLING* [rectangle-circle-diamond]
Dallas Museum of Art, gift of Sherry Hayslip and Cole Smith through the 20th-Century Design Fund in honor of Dr. Charles L. Venable, DMA 1995.18.1–6

For *Contempora* flatware, see chapter 4.

207. *Contempora* salad dish, 1930

Eliel Saarinen
Finnish, 1873–950

Silver. 2¾ × 10 in. (7.0 × 25.4 cm). Marked: [diamond] [circle] *DH* [in rectangle]/*STERLING*/*1053*/*10 IN*/[fleur-de-lis, the Reed & Barton 1930 year symbol]
Dallas Museum of Art, The Jewel Stern American Silver Collection, gift of Jewel Stern, DMA 2002.29.39

Contempora flatware and holloware were introduced to the trade under the banner of Dominick & Haff, a subsidiary of Reed & Barton, in a separate sales catalogue. It was claimed that *Contempora* expressed the "Spirit of American Life and Art" in sterling and the status of the designer, the architect Eliel Saarinen, was proudly invoked as "out-standing among the artistic geniuses of the day."[1] However, with the exception of this salad dish, which flares out gracefully to its rim and has a stylish stepped-back base, the full service was "conservatively modern." In 1931, a salad dish was illustrated in *House & Garden* and described as "a modern interpretation with sweeping lines."[2] It was available in sterling at least until 1935 (an undated record of this salad dish in silverplate has been found in the Reed & Barton Archives).

1. *Dominick & Haff Present a New Pattern Contempora; Sterling in the Contemporary Art*, promotional flatware and holloware catalogue (n.d.), courtesy of Reed & Barton.
2. "American Silver Achieves New Beauty," *House and Garden* 60 (Dec. 1931): 67. Reference: Other *Contempora* holloware is illustrated in Lee McCann, "Reflections on Silver," *Country Life* 58 (Oct. 1930): 96.

BERNARD RICE'S SONS
NEW YORK, NEW YORK
ACTIVE C. 1899–1959

APOLLO STUDIOS
NEW YORK, NEW YORK

DIVISION OF BERNARD RICE'S SONS

208. *Shadowardt* gravy boat, 1928*

Patinated silverplate. 2½ × 8¼ × 3¼ in. (6.4 × 21.0 × 8.3 cm). Marked: *APOLLO E.P.N.S.* [in rectangle]/*MADE BY*/*BERNARD RICE'S SONS INC.* [B, R, and S each in a square]/*5302*/*SHADOWARDT* [top line of stylized S sloping down over *HADOW* and under *ARDT*]
Dallas Museum of Art, The Jewel Stern American Silver Collection, acquired through the Patsy Lacy Griffith Collection, gift of Patsy Lacy Griffith by exchange, DMA 2002.29.143

The *Shadowardt* pattern in holloware was introduced in 1928 in an advertisement in *The Keystone* in which a four-piece tea and coffee service on a tray was illustrated.[1] The name of the pattern was a sly reference to Erik Magnussen's *Cubic* service, which had been dubbed "Lights and Shadows of Manhattan" (see chapters 1, 3).

1. Bernard Rice's Sons, Inc. advertisement, *Keystone* 56 (Nov. 1928): 31.

209. *Sky-scraper* three-piece tea set, 1928*

Louis M. Rice
American, dates unknown

Patent 75,387 (for a beverage pitcher or similar article) filed May 23, 1928, granted May 29, 1928. Patinated silverplate. Teapot 6¼ × 8¼ × 5 in. (15.9 × 21.0 × 12.7 cm); sugar bowl 4¼ × 5½ × 3¼ in. (10.8 × 14 × 8.3 cm); creamer 4¾ × 5 × 3 in. (12.1 × 12.7 × 7.6 cm). Marked (all): *SKY* [underlined] *SCRAPER* [vertical]/*DES. PAT. PENDING*/*APOLLO E.P.N.S.* [in rectangle]/*MADE IN U.S.A. BY*/*BERNARD RICE'S SONS, INC.* [B, R, and S each in a square]
The John P. Axelrod Collection, Boston, Mass.

Incorporating stepped lids upon towering trapezoidal forms and pro-vided with black patinated "smoke-stack" handles, Apollo's silverplated *Sky-scraper* line presents an unabashed assimilation of skyscraper forms as emblematic of modern design. Advertising for the line encouraged buyers to view the skyscraper as "the inspiration for Modernism" and by association, consider the forms of this holloware pattern an "expres-sion of our modern scheme of life" (see chapter 3).[1]

1. Bernard Rice's Sons, Inc. advertisement, *Keystone* 55 (May. 1928): 23.
Reference: Helen Appleton Read, "Twentieth-Century Decoration; The Filter of American Taste," *Vogue* 71 (June 1, 1928): 116.

ROCKWELL SILVER COMPANY
MERIDEN, CONNECTICUT
ACTIVE 1905–1978

LENOX CHINA
TRENTON, NEW JERSEY
FOUNDED 1906

DIVISION OF ROCKWELL
SILVER COMPANY

210. *Moderne* coffeepot with demitasse cup and saucer,* c. 1930 (cup and saucer shape introduced c. 1908; coffeepot shape introduced 1919)

Porcelain with silver overlay. Coffeepot 8½ × 8¼ × 4¾ in. (21.6 × 21.0 × 12.1 cm); cup 3 × 2 × 2⅛ in. (7.6 × 5.1 × 5.4 cm); saucer ⁷⁄₁₆ × 4¹¹⁄₁₆ in. (1.1 × 11.9 cm). Coffeepot marked: *L* [in wreath]/*LENOX*/*12 Moderne* [in script]/*R.S. Co. STERLING*. Cup/saucer: *L* [script, in circle, the Lenox palette]. Cup: *1306*/*LENOX*/*R.S. Co. STERLING* [on lid]
Dallas Museum of Art, 20th-Century Design Fund, DMA 1997.8.1–2

Although the shapes were designed and introduced earlier, the decora-tion on these porcelain pieces dates from about 1930 (see chapter 1).[1]

1. Charles L. Venable, *China and Glass in America 1880–1980: From Tabletop to TV Tray*, exh. cat. (Dallas, Tex.: Dallas Museum of Art, 2000), 161, 435.

PAIRPOINT MANUFACTURING COMPANY (ATTRIBUTED TO)
NEW BEDFORD, MASSACHUSETTS 1880–1937

DIVISION OF ROCKWELL
SILVER COMPANY

211. Plate, c. 1925–1935*

Glass with silver overlay. ⅞ × 10¾ in. (2.2 × 7.3 cm). Unmarked
Dallas Museum of Art, 20th-Century Design Fund, DMA 1999.47

The image of the leaping gazelle with stylized foliage, here in silver overlay on glass, was popular in mid-1920s French *art moderne* design (see chapter 1).[1]

1. Charles L. Venable, *China and Glass in America 1880–1980: From Tabletop to TV Tray*, exh. cat. (Dallas, Tex.: Dallas Museum of Art, 2000), 161, 435.

F.B. ROGERS SILVER COMPANY
TAUNTON, MASSACHUSETTS
FOUNDED 1883

212. Bowl ("Viking"), c. 1959*

Silverplate. 3¼ × 6¾ × 6¾ in. (8.3 × 17.1 × 17.1 cm). Marked: *TRADE MARK*/*1883* [crown between 8 and 8]/*F.B. ROGERS SILVER CO*/*437*
Dallas Museum of Art, The Jewel Stern American Silver Collection, Decorative Arts Fund, DMA 2002.29.281

Dubbed the "Viking" bowl in *House Beautiful*,[1] this triangular three-legged bowl came in at least three sizes and was, in fact, a copy of a contemporary Scandinavian bowl.

1. "Window Shopping with Peggy Ryan," *House Beautiful* 101 (Sept. 1959): 37.

213. Compote, c. 1962–1965

Enameled silverplate. 3½ × 4⅞ in. (8.9 × 12.4 cm). Marked: *TRADE MARK*/*18* [crown] *83*/*F.B. ROGERS*/*MADE IN DENMARK*/*454*
Dallas Museum of Art, The Jewel Stern American Silver Collection, gift of Jewel Stern, 2004.13.8

The conical pedestal base and green interior of this compote reflect an elegantly spare, colorful Scandinavian aesthetic. Marks indicate that the bowl was produced in Denmark, designating it an early example of an American manufacturer's outsourcing silverware production to an overseas concern. The design was also produced with a red interior and in a larger, six-and-one-quarter-inch diameter size.

214. *Modern Classic* spoon, 1934*

Robert E. Locher
American, 1888–1956

Patent 94,229 (for a spoon or similar article) filed Mar. 9, 1934, granted Jan. 1, 1935. Silver. ¾ × 1¼ × 6¼ in. (1.9 × 3.2 × 15.9 cm). Marked: *R B L* [each in a square with sides arranged to form an equilateral triangle]/*STERLING*
Dallas Museum of Art, gift of the Everts Jewelry Company, DMA 1952.65

Modern Classic was the first Depression-era sterling flatware pattern to reflect the new direction in architecture and design that became known as modern classicism or "stripped" classicism, an abstract, pared-down revival of classical form (see chapter 6). A place setting and other serving pieces of flatware were included in the exhibition *Contemporary Industrial and Handwrought Silver* at the Brooklyn Museum in 1937.

215. *Modern Classic* centerpiece, 1934*

Robert E. Locher
American, 1888–1956

Silver. Tray 1⅝ × 12 in. (4.1 × 30.5 cm); centerpiece 3⅞ × 9⅜ in. (9.8 × 23.8 cm); mesh 1½ × 9⅜ in. (3.8 × 23.8 cm). Marked: *51255485* [scratched] / *Treasure* [in script, maker's hallmark][1] / *STERLING* / *R B L* [each in a square with sides arranged to form an equilateral triangle] *Robert E. Locher* [in script]/*1674*
Dallas Museum of Art, The Jewel Stern American Silver Collection, acquired through the Patsy Lacy Griffith Collection, gift of Patsy Lacy Griffith by exchange, DMA 2002.29.56.A–C

Locher designed a signature line of holloware to accompany his *Modern Classic* flatware of 1934. These pieces were all stamped "Robert E. Locher" in script. The weight and size of this floral centerpiece with mesh and under tray made it very expensive during the Depression, and the severity of its sleek surfaces rendered it too radical for most consumers (see chapter 6). Both factors contributed to its rarity; this is the only example of its kind that has come to light.

The tea and coffee service (nos. 1600–1604), salt and pepper shakers (no. 1644), and candlesticks (no. 1685) were shown in the exhibition *Contemporary Industrial and Handwrought Silver* in 1937 at the Brooklyn Museum. A compote (no. 1619) is another *Modern Classic* object.

1. From 1921 to 1954, "Treasure" Solid Silver was a registered trademark of Rogers, Lunt & Bowlen.

216. *Contrast* salad serving set, 1956*

Nord Bowlen
American, 1909–2001

Patent 181,574 (for a spoon or similar article) filed Mar. 29, 1956, granted Dec. 3, 1957. Silver, nylon (Zytel). Fork 1¼ × 2¹⁄₁₆ × 9⅛ in. (3.2 × 5.2 × 23.2 cm); spoon 1¼ × 2¹⁄₁₆ × 9⅛ in. (3.2 × 5.2 × 23.2 cm). Marked (each): *LUNT*/*STERLING*
Dallas Museum of Art, the Patsy Lacy Griffith collection, bequest of Patsy Lacy Griffith, DMA 2001.122.1–2

It took Bowlen, the head designer at Lunt, over a year to investigate and test synthetic products for this informal contemporary flatware.[1] The result was the striking contrast of sterling combined with molded black DuPont Zytel nylon, which was used for the handles, in this pattern, named *Contrast*. The introductory advertisement described *Contrast* as "a bold new creation in sterling" that would set "a new vogue in smartness and style for today's dining."[2] The panel of the knife was shown engraved with a contemporary single-letter monogram. The price of a four-piece place setting was $18.75.

1. Jane Fiske Mitarachi, "Plastics and the Question of Quality," *Industrial Design* 3 (June 1956): 64.
2. "Contrast: Sterling with Ebony Nylon Created by Lunt," Lunt Silversmiths advertisement, *House Beautiful* 98 (June 1956): 7.
References: L. W., "Contrast: Essential Forms from Sensuous Elements," *Interiors* 115 (May 1956): 112–13; "Annual Design Review," *Industrial Design* 3 (Dec. 1956): 105.

217. *Striated* carafe, 1974 (designed 1971)*

Lella Vignelli
American (b. Italy), 1934

Silver. 6⅞ × 4½ × 4½ in. (17.5 × 11.4 × 11.4 cm). Paper label: [profile of face in crescent moon, the maker's mark]/*San Lorenzo/D* [in circle, the 1974 year symbol]/*925* [in oval]/*lmv* [in circle, the designer's mark]/[star] *859MI* [in hexagon]/*20215* [handwritten]/*836* [handwritten]/*MADE IN ITALY*/[all letters of the alphabet each in black circle]
The Jewel Stern American Silver Collection, promised gift of Jewel Stern, DMA 17.2004.13

Introduced in 1971 by the fledgling Milanese firm of San Lorenzo as part of a barware collection that included an ice bucket, cocktail shaker, ashtray, cigarette boxes, and salt and pepper shakers, the *Striated* carafe by Lella Vignelli became the most recognized object in the group. Although initially attributed to the design partners Lella and Massimo Vignelli, Lella later took sole credit for her design (see chapter 16). The carafe is no longer in production: the silversmith who originally crafted the engraved surface of irregular grooves that characterize the line has retired and the company has been unable to replace him. An example of the *Striated* carafe is in the collection of the Metropolitan Museum of Art (accession number 1990.288). For an explanation of the San Lorenzo marks, see Franco Rizzi, "Notes for the Collector," in *The Work of the Silversmith's Studio San Lorenzo, Milano 1970–1995*, exh. cat. Victoria and Albert Museum, London (Milan: Electa, 1995).

Reference: Jeannine Falino, "Women Metalsmiths," in Pat Kirkham, ed., *Women Designers in the USA, 1900–2000* (New York: Bard Graduate Center for Studies in the Decorative Arts; New Haven: Yale University Press, 2000), 240, 243.

218. Bar tools, introduced 1972*

Lella Vignelli
American (b. Italy), 1934
and
Massimo Vignelli
American (b. Italy), 1931

Silver. Ice tongs 2 × 7¼ × 1¼ in. (5.1 × 18.4 × 3.2 cm); olive tongs ¹⁄₁₆ × 9½ × ¾ in. (0.2 × 24.1 × 1.9 cm); strainer 1 × 5¾ × 3¼ in. (2.5 × 14.6 × 8.3 cm); bar knife ¹⁄₁₆ × 7½ × 1¼ in. (0.2 × 19.1 × 3.2 cm). Ice tongs marked: [star *859MI* in hexagon] *925* [in oval] [profile of face in crescent moon inscribed in a circle, the maker's mark, stamped over obscured mark] *J* [in circle, the 1980 year symbol] *lmv* [in circle, the designer's mark] *San Lorenzo, ITALY*. Olive tongs: *lmv* [in circle, the designer's mark] *B* [in circle, the 1972 year symbol] [profile of face in crescent moon inscribed in a circle, the maker's mark] *925* [in oval] *859MI* [in hexagon]. Strainer: [star *859MI* in hexagon] *925* [in oval] [profile of face in crescent moon inscribed in a circle, the maker's mark] *J* [in circle, the 1980 year symbol] *ap* [in circle stamped over partially obscured designer's mark] *San Lorenzo ITALY*. Bar knife: *YZ* [in circle within an octagon, the Jubilee year symbol][1] / *crescent moon* [inscribed in a circle, the maker's mark] *lmv* [in circle, the designer's mark] *Z* [in circle, the 1996 year symbol] *925* [in oval] [star *859MI* in hexagon]/*San Lorenzo ITALY*
Dallas Museum of Art, The Jewel Stern American Silver Collection, Decorative Arts Fund, DMA 2002.29.78.1–4

A year after the barware collection that included the *Striated* carafe was introduced in 1971, a set of four coordinated bar tools designed by Lella and Massimo Vignelli was first offered. The set consisted of ice tongs, a bar knife, a strainer, and olive tongs. The distinctive handle of the *Striated* carafe is the motif that the Vignellis employed for the sleek bar tools.

1. The Jubilee mark consists of the letters of both 1995 (Y) and 1996 (Z) as a means of celebrating the objects produced during the run of the exhibition *The Work of the Silversmith's Studio San Lorenzo, Milano 1970–1995* at the Victoria and Albert Museum in London and the twenty-fifth anniversary of the firm.
References: Kathryn Hiesinger and George H. Marcus, *Design Since 1945*, exh. cat. (Philadelphia: Philadelphia Museum of Art, 1983), 12; *For the Tabletop*, exh. cat., American Craft Museum of the American Craft Council, New York, 1980, 35.

SHEETS-ROCKFORD SILVER PLATE COMPANY

ROCKFORD, ILLINOIS
ACTIVE 1925–56

219. *Art Modernё* double vegetable dish, introduced 1928*

Silverplate, Catalin. 2¼ × 12½ × 9 in. (5.7 × 31.8 × 22.9 cm). Marked: [in circle] *S. ROCKFORD S. CO.*—[scales in center]/*E P N S* [each in a square]/*178*
Dallas Museum of Art, The Jewel Stern American Silver Collection, acquired through the Patsy Lacy Griffith Collection, gift of Patsy Lacy Griffith by exchange, DMA 2002.29.4.A–B

The green rectilinear accents in plastic add zest to the objects in *Art Modernё,* a jazzy holloware line with sharply angled and stepped elements. The line was rushed out in 1928 to attract consumers enamored with the latest French style. Wasting no time on research, the company embellished the pattern name with an accent over the "n" in *Moderne* (see chapter 3). The price for this double vegetable dish was $18.[1]

1. "Why Not Have the Newest Things," Sheets-Rockford advertisement, *Keystone* 56 (Sept. 1928): 198.

220. *Art Modernё* pitcher, introduced 1928

Silverplate, Catalin. 8⅛ × 7¼ × 6¾ in. (20.6 × 18.4 × 17.1 cm). Marked: [in circle] *S. ROCKFORD S. CO.*—[scales in center]/*E P N S* [each in a square]/*4790*
Dallas Museum of Art, The Jewel Stern American Silver Collection, acquired through the Patsy Lacy Griffith Collection, gift of Patsy Lacy Griffith by exchange, DMA 2002.29.141

The smooth canted body of the *Art Modernё* water pitcher contrasts with the stepped border of the rim and the inversion of the border on the spout. The motif was repeated for the cantilevered extensions that support the upright green Catalin handle (see chapter 3). The *Art Modernё* creamer, a smaller version of the water pitcher, was described in a contemporary trade journal as "modernistic" and an "extreme design."[1]

1. A. Frederick Saunders, "Modernism in Silverware," *Jewelers' Circular* 100 (Feb. 27, 1930): 105.

FRANK W. SMITH SILVER COMPANY, INC.

GARDNER, MASSACHUSETTS
ACTIVE 1886–1958

221. *Woodlily* flatware, 1945*

Silver, stainless steel knife blade. Place knife ⅞ × 8¹¹⁄₁₆ in. (2.2 × 22.1 cm); place fork ⅝ × 1¹⁄₁₆ × 7⁷⁄₁₆ in. (1.6 × 2.7 × 18.9 cm); salad fork 1¹⁄₁₆ × 6¹³⁄₁₆ in. (2.7 × 17.3 cm); teaspoon 1¼ × 6⅜ in. (3.2 × 16.2 cm). Fork/salad fork/teaspoon marked: [Frank Smith logo]/*STERLING.* Knife marked: *SMITH/STAINLESS*
Dallas Museum of Art, gift of Beverly Hart Bremer, DMA 1998.170. 1–4

Woodlily was among the earliest postwar patterns and shows the lingering influence of earlier Scandinavian naturalism (see chapter 6).

STEUBEN GLASS WORKS

CORNING, NEW YORK
FOUNDED 1903

222. *Framed* bowl, designed 1994*

Richard Meier
American, b. 1934
Michael Brophy (maker)
American, b. 1959

Glass, silverplated nickel. 3¾ × 16 in. (9.5 × 40.6 cm). Marked (on glass): *STEUBEN;* (on base): *STEUBEN/*[short and long undulating lines]
Dallas Museum of Art, Discretionary Decorative Arts Fund, DMA 2001.320

Designed by the architect Richard Meier and evidencing a highly formal modernist aesthetic, the curved glass bowl of this centerpiece balances on a refined, rectilinear metal frame. Although Meier's silver

designs for Swid Powell reflect openwork grid patterns reminiscent of the *gitterwerk* of the Wiener Werkstätte, the cruciform base of this work also emphasizes a precise clarity of form that is enhanced by the brilliant transparency of the glass bowl. The combination of a glass vessel, horizontal ring element, and structural pier is reminiscent of the architectonic glass and brass vessels of the early twentieth-century Belgian designer Gustave Serruier-Bovy. This model, no. 8765, was offered in Steuben's 1990 catalogue for $5,780.

THE STIEFF COMPANY

BALTIMORE, MARYLAND
FOUNDED 1892

223. Cigarette humidor, 1946

Silver, plastic. 5 × 3⁹⁄₁₆ in. (12.7 × 9.0 cm). Marked (on plastic): *PATENT 1,987.3737/JANUARY 8, 1935;* (on underside of lid): *STIEFF/STERLING/L/0811*
Dallas Museum of Art, The Jewel Stern American Silver Collection, acquired through the Patsy Lacy Griffith Collection, gift of Patsy Lacy Griffith by exchange, DMA 2002.29.159.A–B

Although this streamlined humidor to keep cigarettes moist looks as if it may have been designed during the 1930s, before World War II, the letter symbol in the mark indicates that it was made in 1946. Several variants of the mechanical invention for a humidor that was patented by Solomon Shapiro in 1934 are known. One of the earliest was an economical version made in chromium with a black Bakelite base. Called the "Humidaire," it was advertised to sell for one dollar.[1] This sterling and plastic humidor made by Stieff was in the luxury class, but appears to have been copied from a less expensive, unmarked, but well-designed one in bright red enamel, chromium, and black plastic.[2]

1. "Tops for Christmas! Humidaire Keeps Cigarettes Fresh," Artcraft Metal Products advertisement, *Gift and Art Buyer* 31 (Nov. 1935): 69.
2. Jim Linz, *Art Deco Chrome* (Atglen, Pa.: Schiffer, 1999), 145; Shapiro's mechanical patent 1,987,373 is illustrated on the same page.

224. Candlesticks (pair), 1966*

Silver, rosewood. Each 7¼ × 4½ in. (18.4 × 11.4 cm). Marked (each): *STIEFF/STERLING/015 8*
Dallas Museum of Art, The Jewel Stern American Silver Collection, Decorative Arts Fund, DMA 2002.29.185.1–2

These graceful bell-shaped candlesticks with rosewood stems and disk-shaped bobeches are a fine example of silver combined with wood, a trend current in the 1950s and 1960s and driven by the influx of contemporary Scandinavian furniture and accessories.

SWID POWELL

NEW YORK, NEW YORK
ACTIVE 1984–c. 1994

NAN SWID DESIGN
ACTIVE 1994–2000

225. *King Richard* candlesticks (pair), c. 1987 (designed 1983)*

Richard Meier
American, b. 1934

Silverplate. Each ¾ × 1⁹⁄₁₆ × 10 in. (1.9 × 4.0 × 25.4 cm). Marked (each): *Swid Powell © RM* [conjoined]/*MADE IN ITALY/SILVER/PLATED* [three stars over tail of elongated script *S*]
The Jewel Stern American Silver Collection, promised gift of Jewel Stern, DMA 17.2004.15.1–2

In this, the most sculptural candlestick designed by Meier for Swid Powell, the pierced square and the square grid are the motifs that animate the form. The contrast between the circular base and ball feet and the rectangular panels at right angles adds another layer of complexity. It was introduced in 1984 as the *King Richard* candlestick and priced $210. In 1990 this candlestick (model no. 3055), no longer named, was recognized as "Swid Powell's most successful silver piece."[1]

1. Annette Tapert, *Swid Powell: Objects by Architects* (New York: Rizzoli, 1990), 76–77.

226. *King Richard* bowl, c. 1986 (designed 1983, introduced 1984)*

Richard Meier
American, b. 1934

Silverplate. 14 × 4 in. (35.6 × 10.2 cm). Marked: *Swid Powell/© RM* [conjoined]
The Jewel Stern American Silver Collection, promised gift of Jewel Stern, DMA 15.2005

The *King Richard* bowl was introduced in Swid Powell's inaugural collection in 1984 in this size, product number 3051, at $350, and in a ten-inch size, product number 3052, at $225. A six-inch size, number 3050, was later added to the line. The name was dropped and in 1990 the object was referred to as Fruit Bowl in a publication in which Meier commented on the prominent design motif: "The intention of the cut-out squares is to break up the surface, to be reflective and decorative. It's a different scaling device."[1]

1. Annette Tapert, *Swid Powell: Objects by Architects* (New York: Rizzoli, 1990), 73, 76.

227. *Century* candlestick, c. 1984 (designed 1983, introduced 1984)*

Robert A. M. Stern
American, b. 1939

Silverplate. 6½ × 3½ in. (16.5 × 8.9 cm). Marked: *Swid Powell/* [calligraphic *M*, the designer's mark]/*MADE IN ITALY/SILVER/PLATED* [three stars over tail of elongated script *S*]
Dallas Museum of Art, The Jewel Stern American Silver Collection, gift of Jewel Stern, DMA 2004.13.1

Stern's passion for classicism (see chapter 16) is unabashed in this reeded *Century* candlestick, one of three he designed for Swid Powell's inaugural collection. The price of the *Century* candlestick (model no. 3057) was $145.

228. Pitcher, introduced 1985*

Robert A. M. Stern
American, b. 1939

Silverplate. 11½ × 9½ × 6 in. (29.2 × 24.1 × 15.2 cm). Marked: *MADE IN ITALY SILVER/PLATED* [three stars over tail of elongated script *S*]/© *Swid Powell/* [calligraphic *M*, the designer's mark]
Dallas Museum of Art, The Jewel Stern American Silver Collection, Decorative Arts Fund, DMA 2002.29.97

Stern, a postmodernist who designed houses "that would be familiar to a nineteenth-century client," brought "modern traditionalist" ideas to his objects for the table.[1] This pitcher is among the most elegant expressions of his advocacy of historicism. In 1986, the price of the pitcher (model no. 3062) was $250. It was raised to $300 in 1989.

1. Annette Tapert, *Swid Powell: Objects by Architects* (New York: Rizzoli, 1990), 100–101.

229. Candlestick, introduced 1986*

Robert Venturi
American, b. 1925

Silverplate. 8¾ × 6⅝ in. (22.2 × 16.8 cm). Marked: *Swid Powell/© R. Venturi* [in script]/*MADE IN ITALY/SILVER-PLATED* [three stars over tail of elongated script *S*]
Dallas Museum of Art, The Jewel Stern American Silver Collection, Decorative Arts Fund, DMA 2002.29.98

Venturi, the recognized patriarch of postmodernism, drew inspiration from diverse historical sources. For this candlestick, composed of two planar elements in a cruciform arrangement to form silhouettes, Venturi recycled the eighteenth-century Chippendale style. In 1986 the price of the candlestick (model no. 3069) was $150.

Reference: Annette Tapert, *Swid Powell: Objects by Architects* (New York: Rizzoli, 1990), 122–23.

230. *Wing* vase, introduced 1992 (designed 1991–1992)*

Elsa Rady
American, b. 1943

Silverplate. 13¾ × 6 in. (34.9 × 15.2 cm). Marked: © *Swid Powell/Elsa Rady* [in script]/*Silver Plate/Made in Argentina*
Dallas Museum of Art, The Jewel Stern American Silver Collection, gift of Jewel Stern, DMA 2005.25.7

Rady, an accomplished ceramist known for her ethereal winged bowls in thrown porcelain, was the designer of this single *Wing* vase

(no. 3225), the largest and most visually dramatic of the objects she produced for Swid Powell. She also designed a smaller vase with two "wings" (model no. 3318), a bowl with four wings (no. 3319), a shallow *Lily* large bowl with a single wing, a bowl with two wings that have wing-shaped cutouts (no. 3320), and a *Lily* candlestick (no. 3322) (see chapter 16). The *Lily* pieces were named for her mother, who had been a dancer in Martha Graham's company. Swid Powell's silver holloware is not itself stamped with product numbers; the numbers mentioned here are noted in "Swid Powell Stories," a promotional envelope of pictorial cards distributed in the early 1990s.

231. Teapot, c. 1995*

Calvin Klein
American, b. 1942

Silverplate. 6½ × 8¼ in. (16.5 × 21 cm). Marked: *Calvin Klein/Swid Powell.* Paper label: *MADE/IN/HONG KONG*
Dallas Museum of Art, The Jewel Stern American Silver Collection, gift of Jewel Stern, DMA 2003.34.4

The triangular spout provides the geometric counterpoint to the cylindrical body and finial and the semicircular handle of this teapot, which evokes the clarity and pared-down sophistication of Klein's designs for clothing. Although Calvin Klein Home, a collection of which this teapot was a part, was produced by Nan Swid Design, formerly Swid Powell, the original name of the firm was retained in the hallmark (see chapter 16). A creamer and sugar bowl to match the teapot were produced.

232. Candlesticks (pair), c. 1995*

Calvin Klein
American, b. 1942

Silverplate. Each 14½ × 3½ in. (36.8 × 8.9 cm). Marked (each on brown felt): *Calvin Klein/Swid Powell.* Printed on clear plastic: *MADE/IN/HONG KONG*
The Jewel Stern American Silver Collection, promised gift of Jewel Stern, DMA 17.2004.3.1–2

These tall candlesticks from Calvin Klein Home epitomize Klein's elegant simplification of form. They were also made in a smaller version, ten inches high.

233. *Ellipse* flatware, 2004 (designed 1995)

Calvin Klein
American, b. 1942

Silverplate. Knife ⅜ × 9 × ¾ in. (1.0 × 22.9 × 1.9 cm); fork ⅝ × 8 × ⅞ in. (1.6 × 20.3 × 2.2 cm); salad fork ⅝ × 6⅞ × ¾ in. (1.6 × 17.5 × 1.9 cm); teaspoon ¾ × 6⅝ × 1¼ in. (1.9 × 16.8 × 3.2 cm); tablespoon 1 × 8 × 1½ in. (2.5 × 20.3 × 3.8 cm). Marked (each): *Korea/Calvin Klein*
Dallas Museum of Art, The Jewel Stern American Silver Collection, gift of Jewel Stern, DMA 17.2004.2.1–5

Originally produced by Nan Swid Design for Calvin Klein Home, the *Ellipse* pattern was continued independently by Klein after Swid closed her business in 2000 (see chapter 16).

SWID POWELL
NEW YORK, NEW YORK
ACTIVE 1984–c. 2000

WITH

REED & BARTON
TAUNTON, MASSACHUSETTS
ACTIVE 1824–PRESENT

234. Carving set, introduced 1989*

Robert Venturi
American, b. 1925

Silverplate. Knife 1½ × 2 × 13 in. (3.8 × 5.1 × 33 cm); fork 1¼ × 2 × 9¾ in. (3.2 × 5.1 × 24.8 cm). Marked (each): *REED & BARTON/Swid Powell/© Robert Venturi* [in script]
Dallas Museum of Art, The Jewel Stern American Silver Collection, Decorative Arts Fund, DMA 2002.29.99.1–2

In a press release issued on October 16, 1989, Reed & Barton announced the "The Swid Powell Flatware Accessory Collection," a joint venture with Swid Powell to produce a line of serving pieces initially designed by four architects (see chapter 16). Venturi, one of the four, applied his witty version of the classical Greek orders of architecture to the handles of this carving set and later to the handle of a companion platter spoon, all of which he treated as columns terminated by capitals. The early austere Doric order was the foil for the fork handle; the voluptuous volutes of the Ionic order embraced the knife handle. When it was introduced, the price of the carving set was $150.

235. Platter spoon, c. 1990*

Robert Venturi
American, b. 1925

Silverplate. ½ × 14 × 2¾ in. (1.3 × 35.6 × 7 cm). Marked: *REED & BARTON / Swid Powell / ©Robert Venturi*
Dallas Museum of Art, The Jewel Stern American Silver Collection, gift of Jewel Stern, DMA 2004.13.5

To complete the trio of classical orders, Venturi playfully interpreted the Corinthian for the handle of the long platter spoon that was produced after the carving set.

236. Salad serving set, 1990 (designed 1989)*

Michael Graves
American, b. 1934

Silverplate. Each ¾ × 3 × 11 in. (1.9 × 7.6 × 27.9 cm). Marked (each): *REED & BARTON / Swid Powell / © Graves* [in script] / *'90*
Dallas Museum of Art, The Jewel Stern American Silver Collection, Decorative Arts Fund, DMA 2002.29.21.1–2

The bold, modern geometric shapes of the servers contrast with the decoration of the entire upper surface of the handles, a sentimental, stylized floral pattern that recalls traditional fabrics and wallpapers. The price of the servers was initially $85.

Reference: Annette Tapert, *Swid Powell: Objects by Architects* (New York: Rizzoli, 1990), 43.

237. Salad serving set, 1991*

Richard Meier
American, b. 1934

Silverplate. Fork ¾ × 1⁹⁄₁₆ × 10 in. (1.9 × 4.0 × 25.4 cm); spoon: 1¼ × 3 × 9½ in. (3.2 × 7.6 × 24.1 cm). Marked (each): *REED & BARTON / SWID POWELL © RM* [conjoined]
Dallas Museum of Art, The Jewel Stern American Silver Collection, gift of Jewel Stern, DMA 2004.13.9.1–2

Meier had designed a stainless steel salad serving set inset with black cloisonné enamel for the first collection produced by Reed & Barton for Swid Powell in 1989. Two years later these more formal salad servers were added to the line. Like his earlier candlesticks in this exhibition, these servers have classical lines and grids of squares that reflect the influence of progressive early twentieth-century Austrian design, especially that of Josef Hoffmann and the Wiener Werkstätte (see chapter 16).

Tiffany & Co.

New York, New York
active 1837–present

238. Compote, 1935

Silver. 2 × 6 × 6 in. (5.1 × 15.2 × 15.2 cm). Marked: *TIFFANY & Co. / MAKERS / STERLING SILVER / 22140 / M*
Dallas Museum of Art, The Jewel Stern American Silver Collection, acquired through the Patsy Lacy Griffith Collection, gift of Patsy Lacy Griffith by exchange, DMA 2002.29.49

This compote was added to Tiffany's display in the House of Jewels in 1940 for the second year of the New York World's Fair. It was described in the firm's inventory list as a "plain, shallow bowl with turned lines on stem of foot."[1] In the 1950s the design was enlarged and produced in a twelve-and-three-quarter-inch bowl, which was sold singly and offered with candlesticks to match.

1. "Articles of Silverware to be exhibited by Tiffany & Co. at their exhibit in the House of Jewels New York World's Fair," 1940 memorandum, Tiffany & Company Archives, Parsippany, N.J.; hereafter Tiffany Archives.

239. Vanity set, 1934*

Arthur Leroy Barney
American, 1884–1955

Silver, mahogany, glass, velvet. 16⅝ × 15⅝ × 13⅛ in. (42.2 × 39.7 × 33.3 cm). Marked (each): *TIFFANY & Co. 22099 / Makers / 2423 / STERLING SILVER / 925–1000 / M* [in script]
The John P. Axelrod Collection, Boston, Mass.

This vanity set was touted as a supremely fashionable accessory for the young lady. In *Vogue* it was described as "the latest luxury to put on your dressing-table—a glorious vanity-box that's completely equipped with all the beauty necessities: bottles, cold-cream and powder containers, brush, comb, mirror, jewel-case, et al."[1] Unlike some of Barney's other designs, which incorporate stylized classical elements, this vanity set was unornamented, the emphasis placed on its sleek, geometric lines and subtle layered edge detail. The various components of the vanity rest neatly within the base, imposing a controlled pattern of rectilinear shapes seemingly machinelike in their efficient precision.

1. "Current Attractions," *Vogue* 68 (July 15, 1936): 44.
References: Charlotte Benton, Tim Benton, and Ghislaine Wood, eds., *Art Deco: 1910–1939*, exh. cat. Victoria and Albert Museum, London (Boston: Bulfinch Press, 2003), 346; John Loring, *Magnificent Tiffany Silver* (New York: Abrams, 2001), 241.

240. *Century* flatware (soup spoon*), 1943–1945 (designed 1937)

Arthur Leroy Barney
American, 1884–1955

Patent 105,193 (for a spoon or similar article) filed May 19, 1937, granted July 6, 1937. Silver, stainless steel knife blade. Luncheon knife ⁷⁄₁₆ × 8½ × ¾ in. (1.1 × 21.6 × 1.9 cm); luncheon fork ½ × 7¼ × ¹⁵⁄₁₆ in. (1.3 × 18.4 × 2.4 cm); soup spoon ⁹⁄₁₆ × 6¾ × 1¹³⁄₁₆ in. (1.4 × 17.1 × 4.6 cm); teaspoon ½ × 1⁵⁄₁₆ × 6 in. (1.3 × 3.3 × 15.2 cm). Knife marked: *TIFFANY & Co. / MAKERS / STERLING / M* [star]; (blade stamped): *TIFFANY & Co.* Fork / soup spoon / teaspoon: *TIFFANY & Co. STERLING M PAT.* [star]. Engraved (each): *R*
Dallas Museum of Art, 20th-Century Design Fund, DMA 1995.120.1–4

For the *Century* flatware pattern designed to commemorate the one-hundredth anniversary of Tiffany & Co. in 1937, Barney alluded to classical columns on the handle by using vertical engraved lines that terminate in a stepped and staggered panel, an allusion to a capital and an ideal place for a monogram. The original soup spoon had a distinctive round bowl (see chapter 8). For an explanation of the impressed star in the mark, which dates the production of this flatware to 1943–1945, see chapter 9.

241. Salad bowl with serving set: salad fork and spoon, 1937; bowl 1940*

Olaf Wilford (bowl attributed to)
American (b. Norway), 1894–1980

Silver; gilded silver servers. Bowl 3⅝ × 11⁵⁄₁₆ × 11⁵⁄₁₆ in. (9.2 × 28.7 × 28.7 cm); fork 1 ⁵⁄₁₆ × 2¹⁄₁₆ × 9⅞ in. (3.3 × 5.2 × 25.1 cm); spoon 1⅜ × 2³⁄₁₆ × 9¾ in. (3.5 × 5.6 × 24.8 cm). Bowl marked: *TIFFANY & CO. / MAKERS / STERLING SILVER / 22888 / M.* Spoon / fork: *TIFFANY & Co. STERLING PAT. M*
Dallas Museum of Art, The Jewel Stern American Silver Collection, acquired through the Patsy Lacy Griffith Collection, gift of Patsy Lacy Griffith by exchange, DMA 2002.29.50.1–3

The fork and spoon were introduced in 1937 and the matching bowl in 1940 (see chapter 8). The Scandinavian-inspired decorative motif on the handles of the servers was replicated on the vertical panels of the bowl. The design was not given a pattern name by Tiffany, but was referred to in-house as a "modern fruit and leaf decoration."[1] A sandwich plate was also made in holloware. Five flatware serving pieces, a cold meat fork, a vegetable spoon, a berry spoon, a tomato server, and a pastry server, were also produced.

1. "Articles of Silverware to be exhibited by Tiffany & Co. at their exhibit in The House of Jewels New York World's Fair," 1940 memorandum, Tiffany Archives.

242. Salad serving fork, 1937*

Gilded silver. ⅞ × 2½ × 10¼ in. (2.2 × 6.4 × 26.0 cm). Marked: *TIFFANY AND CO. STERLING M*
Dallas Museum of Art, The Jewel Stern American Silver Collection, acquired through the Patsy Lacy Griffith Collection, gift of Patsy Lacy Griffith by exchange, DMA 2002.29.52

This partly gilded fork is an elegant embodiment of 1930s modern classicism for the luxury market. A salad serving spoon to match this fork, a berry spoon, and a pastry server were among the pieces made in this design (see chapter 6).

243. Cigarette box, c. 1937*

Enameled silver. 2 × 6 × 4½ in. (5.1 × 15.2 × 11.4 cm). Marked (on lid): *TIFFANY & Co. STERLING*
Dallas Museum of Art, The Jewel Stern American Silver Collection, gift of Jewel Stern, DMA 2002.29.6

Green and black enamel delineate the abstract modern classic decoration on this cigarette box, which was offered in two other color combinations, cobalt blue and red, with the black. The cigarette box was advertised in the late 1930s for $63.[1] It was reissued briefly in 1989 with red and black enamel for $3,000.

1. Tiffany & Co. advertisements, *Harper's Bazaar* 20 (Sept. 1, 1937): 1; and *New Yorker* 15 (Dec. 16, 1939): 1.

244. Sandwich tray, 1939

Silver. ¼ × 9 in. (0.6 × 23.5 cm). Marked: *TIFFANY & Co./MAKERS* [scratched] *2377/STERLING SILVER/22801/M*
Dallas Museum of Art, The Jewel Stern American Silver Collection, acquired through the Patsy Lacy Griffith Collection, gift of Patsy Lacy Griffith by exchange, DMA 2002.29.152

This tray, a refined example of 1930s modern classicism (see chapter 6), was available in a twelve-inch size.[1] A footed compote was also made in this design.

1. Tiffany & Co. advertisement, *New Yorker* 17 (Nov. 29, 1941): 36.

245. 1939 New York World's Fair spoon, 1937*

Arthur Leroy Barney
American, 1884–1955

Patent 105,193 (for a spoon or similar article) filed May 19, 1937, granted July 6, 1937. Silver. ⅜ × 5⅜ × 1⅝ in. (1.0 × 13.7 × 4.1 cm). Marked: *NEW YORK WORLD'S FAIR 1939* [curved on back of spoon bowl] *TIFFANY & Co. STERLING M PAT.* [back of handle]
The Jewel Stern American Silver Collection, promised gift of Jewel Stern, DMA 27.2004

For the form of this souvenir spoon in sterling silver, Barney cleverly integrated the iconic symbols of the 1939 New York World's Fair, the trylon and perisphere. The trylon is represented in the elongated, obelisk-shaped handle. The round bowl of the spoon is an allusion to the globe-shaped perisphere. Stamped in an arc on the back of the spoon bowl are the words "New York World's Fair 1939." A smaller version of the spoon, four inches long in the demitasse size, was also produced. The two spoons were reissued for the 1940 fair and were dated accordingly. To celebrate the fiftieth anniversary of the event in 1989, Tiffany reproduced the smaller spoon with a change in the juncture of the handle to the bowl and without the date of the fair impressed. These were offered in sets of six (see chapter 8).

246. Water pitcher and tumbler, 1939 (designed 1938)*

Arthur Leroy Barney (attributed to)
American, 1884–1955

Gilded silver. Pitcher 9½ × 8¾ × 7 1/16 in. (24.1 × 22.2 × 18.0 cm); tumbler 4⅞ × 3½ in. (12.4 × 8.9 cm). Pitcher marked: *TIFFANY & Co./22640.* Tumbler: *TIFFANY & Co.*
Dallas Museum of Art, gift of Jolie and Robert Shelton, DMA 2001.308.1–2

This pitcher and tumbler, along with a companion tumbler and matching waiter, comprised a unique water service that was included in Tiffany & Co.'s modernist display at the House of Jewels pavilion of the 1939 New York World's Fair. Bound by a series of ornamental fluted bands, the square bases and rounded forms echo the circle-within-a-square motif of the tray. These fluted details and the stylized volute of the pitcher's handle reflect the integration of classical motifs in *art moderne* designs—an approach evident in nearly all of Tiffany's lavishly worked objects for the fair. Barney, who designed the similarly inspired *Century* flatware in 1937, worked on the firm's display for the fair and likely oversaw the creation of this water service.

247. Centerpiece and candelabra, 1949*

Oscar Riedener (designer)
American (b. Switzerland), 1910–2000
Karl A. Danielson (maker)
Dates unknown

Silver, wrought. Centerpiece 10 × 14 × 9½ in. (25.4 × 35.6 × 24.1 cm); candelabra 8½ × 10¾ × 9 in. (21.6 × 27.3 × 22.9 cm). Centerpiece marked: *TIFFANY & Co./MAKERS/STERLING SILVER/23274/M.* Candelabra: *TIFFANY & Co. MAKERS STERLING SILVER 23275 M.* Bobeches and corresponding candle sockets: [numbers 1 through 8]
Dallas Museum of Art, gift of the 1995 Silver Supper, DMA 1995.72.1–3

This magnificent flower bowl and accompanying candelabra, with their pinecone finials and elegantly curvilinear design, reflect the

influence of Scandinavian design in the years following World War II. The graceful openwork swags of the flower frame mesh echo the fluted corners of each piece, providing a rich, ornamental pattern and unified design. Tiffany & Co.'s production works of the late 1940s were largely conservative, suggesting this set was created as a private commission or for exhibition purposes. Underscoring the importance of the pieces, drawings of the set are kept in the company archives, and accompanying notations indicate that the silversmith Danielson labored for seven hundred hours to fabricate the three pieces. Karl Danielson worked for Tiffany & Co. between 1909 and 1950 (see chapter 8).[1]

1. Mary Mancuso Klindt, Tiffany Archives, New York, letter to Charles Venable, May 9, 1995.

248. Centerpiece, 1955*

Oscar Riedener
American (b. Switzerland), 1910–2000

Silver. 2¾ × 18¾ × 11¼ in. (7.0 × 47.6 × 28.6 cm). Marked: *TIFFANY & Co. MAKERS STERLING SILVER 23417 M*
Dallas Museum of Art, The Jewel Stern American Silver Collection, Decorative Arts Fund, DMA 2002.29.177

The rim of this centerpiece turns down and widens to sharply pointed and folded ends that continue the line that bisects this seed-shaped form. The bowl stands on four 1950s-style pointed feet, which echo the shape of the rim. Other items in this design group were a bonbon dish in the same shape as the centerpiece, a low, triangular three-light candleholder, and a dish in the shape of the candleholder.

249. *Tread Plate* box, 1980*

John Loring
American, b. 1939

Silver. 3⅜ × 10½ × 7⅛ in. (8.6 × 26.7 × 18.1 cm)
The John Loring Collection

Beginning in the late 1970s, the overt expression of structural and mechanical elements, epitomized in architecture by Renzo Piano's and Richard Rogers's Centre Pompidou in Paris, suggested a new Machine Age of gritty, urban-industrial chic. The design of this box, with its chased surface emulating commercial tread-plate flooring, cleverly transforms the relief of a mundane building material into an ornamental pattern for a luxurious silver object. Loring has served as design director for Tiffany & Co. since 1979. The box was offered in Tiffany's catalogue of 1989 at a price of $7,200; a similarly patterned frame was listed for $1,725.

Reference: John Loring, *Magnificent Tiffany Silver* (New York: Abrams, 2001), 249.

250. Tureen with platter, designed 1986*

Elsa Peretti
American, b. 1940
Pampaloni s.r.l. (mfg. for Tiffany & Co.)
Florence, Italy, active 1902–present

Silver. Tureen 11¼ × 11¾ × 10¾ in. (28.6 × 29.8 × 27.3 cm); platter 2 × 16½ × 15½ in. (5.1 × 41.9 × 39.4 cm). Tureen and platter marked: *Tiffany & Co./Elsa Peretti* [in script]/*925* [in oval] *ITALY*
Dallas Museum of Art, gift of Tiffany & Co., DMA 2005.20.A–C

The fluid, undulating lines of Peretti's sculptural tureen and platter, suggesting an elaboration of midcentury biomorphic design, reflect the dynamic qualities of her jewelry designs. Rather than offer overt references to natural forms or traditional metalwork, the tureen provides a highly original organic expression declaring the plasticity of silver as if in its molten state. A related pitcher, carafe, candleholder, and wine goblet were also produced.

Reference: John Loring, *Magnificent Tiffany Silver* (New York: Abrams, 2001), 256–57.

251. *Olive* dish, 1991 (designed c. 1990)*

Tom Penn
American, b. 1952
Alan Place (maker)
British, b. 1929
Old Newbury Crafters (mfg. for Tiffany & Co.)
Newburyport, Massachusetts, 1932–c. 1970
Amesbury, Massachusetts, c. 1970–present

Silver. 4½ × 4½ × 2 in. (11.4 × 11.4 × 5.1 cm). Marked: *TIFFANY & Co./AP* [in quatrefoil, mark for Alan Place, the maker]/*O.N.C./Hand-wrought/STERLING*
The Peter Forss Collection

In December 1990, Tiffany & Co.'s plan to produce the sculptor Tom Penn's first collection of sterling silver tabletop objects was announced in *Connoisseur*.[1] By the spring of 1992, this *Olive* dish and the expressionistic *Wind* tray from the Tom Penn Collection, exclusively at Tiffany & Co., were pictured in the *New York Times Magazine*'s "Home Design" issue.[2] The *Olive* dish was priced at $625, the *Wind* tray at $3,750. In addition, a *Twisted* vase, and *Ribbon* and *Wing* candlesticks were in the collection. Initially the pieces in the Penn Collection were raised and fabricated by the silversmith Alan Place at Old Newbury Crafters of Amesbury, Massachusetts. Like this *Olive* dish, the pieces made by Place bear his "AP" hallmark as well as that of Old Newbury Crafters and Tiffany & Co. Later, Ubaldo Vitali produced the pieces for Tiffany and these have his mark (see chapter 16).

1. Ann Dermansky, "Penn's purposeful sculpture," *Connoisseur* 220 (Dec. 1990): 74.
2. Carol Vogel, "Personal Statements," *New York Times Magazine*, pt. 2, "Home Design," Apr. 5, 1992, 11–15.

252. *Twisted* vase, 1991 (designed c. 1990)*

Tom Penn
American, b. 1952
Ubaldo Vitali, maker

Silver. 6¾ × 4 × 3 in. (17.1 × 10.2 × 7.6 cm). Marked: *UV* [in oval, mark for Ubaldo Vitali, the maker] *TIFFANY & CO. STERLING*
The Jewel Stern American Silver Collection

The shape of Penn's *Twisted* vase suggests a work made from a simply folded and torqued sheet of silver, belying the actual process and inherent difficulty in realizing the object's dramatically contorted form.

References: Ann Dermansky, "Penn's purposeful sculpture," *Connoisseur* 220 (Dec. 1990): 74; and Carol Vogel, "Personal Statements," *New York Times Magazine*, pt. 2, "Home Design," Apr. 5, 1992, 11–15.

TOWLE SILVERSMITHS
NEWBURYPORT, MASSACHUSETTS
ACTIVE 1882–PRESENT

253. *Ritz* almond set, 1929*

Harold E. Nock
American (b. England), 1876–1952

Patent 78,585 (for a compote or analogous article) filed Apr. 1, 1929, granted May 21, 1929. Silver. Large compote 3 × 6 in. (7.6 × 15.2 cm); small compotes (each) 1⅛ × 3 in. (2.9 × 7.6 cm). Large compote marked: *By Towle* [in script]/[lion in script *T*]/*STERLING*/48290. Small compotes: [lion in script *T*]/*STERLING*/96290
Dallas Museum of Art, The Jewel Stern American Silver Collection, acquired through the Patsy Lacy Griffith Collection, gift of Patsy Lacy Griffith by exchange, DMA 2002.29.132.1–7

The large compote and six miniature "satellites" make up the *Ritz* almond set. The stepped foot was echoed inversely in the conical bowl of each, a treatment that produced a tiered, "telescoping" effect. The *Ritz* holloware group included low candleholders, a compote, various bowls and servers, and a three-piece coffee service with tray.

Reference: "June . . . Weddings . . . And Silver . . . Now and Forever," *House Beautiful* 64 (June 1929): 92.

254. *Ritz* coffee service, 1929*

Harold E. Nock (attributed to)
American (b. England), 1876–1952

Patent 75,585 (for a compote or analogous article) filed Apr. 1, 1929, granted May 21, 1929. Silver, plastic. Coffeepot 8 × 7 × 3⅞ in. (20.3 × 17.8 × 9.8 cm); Creamer 4¹⁄₁₆ × 4½ × 2¾ in. (10.3 × 11.4 × 7.0 cm); sugar bowl and lid 3½ × 5⅜ × 4¼ in. (8.9 × 13.7 × 10.8 cm); tray 1¼ × 11¾ in. (3.2 × 29.8 cm). Coffeepot marked: *By Towle* [in script]/[lion in script *T*]/*STERLING*/55290/*PATENTED MAY 21, 1929*/*5 HALF PINTS*/5. Creamer: *Towle*/[lion in script *T*]/*STERLING*/55290/*PATENTED*/*MAY 21, 1929*. Sugar bowl: *By Towle* [in script]/[lion in script *T*]/*STERLING*/55290/*PATENTED*/*MAY 21, 1929*/4. Tray: [lion in script *T*]/*STERLING*/55290/*PATENT*/*APPLIED FOR*. Engraved (each): *CTF*
Dallas Museum of Art, The Jewel Stern American Silver Collection, gift of Jewel Stern in honor of her children Lori Schainuck and James Schainuck, DMA 2002.29.1.1–4

Unsigned blueprints for the *Ritz* coffee service are all dated January 14, 1929.[1] The service was probably designed by Nock, who filed for the patent on the *Ritz* compote. Only the telescoping bases of the vessels and the rim of the circular matching tray of this coffee service bear any resemblance to other pieces in the *Ritz* holloware group (see, for example, the *Ritz* almond set, above).[2] Many nuances of *art moderne*

were combined to create this exuberant 1929 design, including the odd feet that refer to Erik Magnussen's *Modern American* production-line holloware for Gorham designed the previous year (see chapter 3). Happily, the owner selected an appropriate modern engraved monogram for the service. Only two other *Ritz* coffee services are known, a three-piece service at the Newark Museum (accession number 89.21); and a monogrammed three-piece service in a private collection.[3] This *Ritz* service is the only one with the matching tray.

1. Jane Sullivan, Towle Silversmiths, letter to Jewel Stern, July 18, 1990.
2. "June . . . Weddings . . . And Silver . . . Now and Forever," *House Beautiful* 64 (June 1929): 92.
3. See Alastair Duncan, *American Art Deco* (New York: Abrams, 1986), 84, for the Ritz service in a private collection.

255. Bowl, c. 1937

Silver. 4¾ × 5½ in. (12.1 × 14 cm). Marked: *TOWLE*/*STERLING*/38
Dallas Museum of Art, The Jewel Stern American Silver Collection, acquired through the Patsy Lacy Griffith Collection, gift of Patsy Lacy Griffith by exchange, DMA 2002.29.158

This bowl was featured in *House and Garden, Interior Decorator,* and *Art News* in 1937, the year in which it was exhibited in *Silver: An Exhibition of Contemporary American Design by Manufacturers, Designers and Craftsmen* at the Metropolitan Museum of Art (see chapter 8). It was called the "Nordic" bowl by one author, who admired the simplicity of its form and modest decoration. In a sense it was a harbinger of Scandinavia's international ascendance in design after World War II.[1] The bowl was made in at least three sizes, this being the medium size.[2]

1. Elizabeth Brown, "Contemporary Table Decoration," *Interior Decorator* 97 (Aug. 1937): 41.
2. "Gifts," *House and Garden* (Dec. 1937): 67.

256. *Contour* flatware (knife*), 1950

Robert J. King
American, b. 1917
and
John Van Koert
American, 1912–1998

Patent 161,720 (for a fork or similar article), filed Aug. 30, 1950, granted Jan. 23, 1951. Silver, stainless steel knife blade. Place knife ½ × ¾ × 8⅞ in. (1.3 × 1.9 × 22.5 cm); place fork ¾ × 7⅞ × ¹⁵⁄₁₆ in. (1.9 × 20.0 × 2.4 cm); salad fork ⅝ × 6¹¹⁄₁₆ × 1 in. (1.6 × 17.0 × 2.5 cm); teaspoon ½ × 6⅜ × 1¼ in. (1.3 × 16.2 × 3.2 cm). Knife marked: *TOWLE*/*STERLING HANDLE*/*STAINLESS BLADE*. Fork/salad fork/spoon (on back of handle): [lion in script *T*] *CONTOUR*/*TOWLE STERLING*
Dallas Museum of Art, 20th-Century Design Fund, DMA 1995.109. 1–4

Contour, the first sterling pattern to manifest post–World War II organic modernist design, was the only production-line American flatware included in the Museum of Modern Art's *Good Design* exhibitions of the 1950s. A six-piece place setting (knife, fork, salad fork, butter spreader, teaspoon, and cocktail fork), together with a serving spoon, a cream ladle, a tablespoon, and a carving set, were selected by Edgar Kaufmann Jr., William Friedman, Philip C. Johnson, Hugh Lawson, and Eero Saarinen to be exhibited in *Good Design 1951*. Although the pattern was developed by Van Koert, Towle's design director, and King, who was a staff designer, it was Van Koert who assumed credit (see chapter 10). Ross Pollard, a former employee in Towle's product development department, said that he "saw Bob King make *Contour*" and that John Van Koert "did not" design *Contour* (either the flatware or the holloware).[1]

1. Ross Pollard, telephone conversation with Jewel Stern, June 9, 2000.
Reference: "Knife Fork and Spoon; exhibition by the Walker Art Center and the Towle Silversmiths," *Interiors* 110 (Mar. 1951): 94.

257. *Contour* beverage set, 1953 (designed 1951–1952)*

Robert J. King
American, b. 1917
and
John Van Koert
American, 1912–1998

Silver, polystyrene. Coffeepot 10 × 7⅜ × 3⅞ in. (25.4 × 18.7 × 9.8 cm); creamer 4½ × 3⅜ × 2 in. (11.4 × 8.6 × 5.1 cm); sugar bowl 3½ × 3 × 2¾ in. (8.9 × 7.6 × 7 cm). Coffeepot marked: *TOWLE*/*STERLING*/162/[lion in script *T*]/350; (coffeepot lid): *162*. Creamer: *TOWLE*/*STERLING*/[lion in script *T*]/350; (creamer lid): *16*. Sugar bowl: *TOWLE*/*STERLING*/16/[lion in script *T*]/350
Dallas Museum of Art, The Jewel Stern American Silver Collection, Decorative Arts Fund, DMA 2002.29.18.1–3

Contour holloware was designed after the flatware was launched (see chapter 10). The beverage set was advertised in 1953 as a "contemporary buffet ensemble" and priced by the piece at $200 for the beverage server, $75 for the sugar bowl, and $50 for the creamer.[1] This beverage server has the original lid that could be removed and the vessel used as a coffeepot, cocktail mixer, or water pitcher. Because of damage caused when the separate lid accidentally slipped off, Towle redesigned it and attached it permanently to the pot with a discreet hinge. Other holloware in *Contour* are candleholders, salt and pepper shakers (no. 380), and small accessory dishes (no. 347).

1. "A truly distinguished gift . . . *new* Sterling Holloware CONTOUR by Towle," Towle advertisement, *House Beautiful* 95 (Dec. 1953): 107.
References: Martin Eidelberg, ed., *Design 1935–1965: What Modern Was* (Montreal: Musée des Arts Décoratif de Montréal; New York: Abrams, 1991), 200–201; "Silver and Tableware," in Rathbone Holme and Kathleen Frost, eds., *1954–55 Studio Year Book of Furnishing & Decoration* (London and New York: Studio Publications, 1955), 73; "Last minute shoppers' guide to the right gift," *House and Garden* 104 (Dec. 1953): 125.

258. *Contour* candleholders (pair), 1953

Robert J. King
American, b. 1917
and
John Van Koert
American, 1912–1998

Patent 175,658 (for a candle holder or the like) filed May 12, 1953, granted Sept. 20, 1955. Silver. 2 × 3½ × 3⅜ in. (5.1 × 8.9 × 8.6 cm). Marked (each): *TOWLE / STERLING / [lion in script T] / 330*
Dallas Museum of Art, The Jewel Stern American Silver Collection, Decorative Arts Fund, DMA 2002.29.79.1–2

Although the patent holder was Towle's design director, John Van Koert, it was Robert King, a staff designer, who made the model for the sculptural *Contour* candleholders to coordinate with the *Contour* beverage set (see chapter 10).[1] These gently contoured, mound-shaped candleholders are not weighted. When they were introduced in 1953 the price was $35 for a pair.[2]

1. Robert J. King, telephone conversation with Jewel Stern, Feb. 11, 2002.
2. "A truly distinguished gift . . . *new* Sterling Holloware in CONTOUR by Towle," Towle Silversmiths advertisement, *House Beautiful* 95 (Dec. 1953): 107.
Reference: "Silver and Tableware," in Rathbone Holme and Kathleen Frost, eds., *1954–5 Studio Year Book of Furnishings & Decoration* (London and New York: Studio Publications, 1955), 73.

259. Trivet, 1954

Marion Anderson Noyes
American, 1907–2002

Silver, plastic. ¼ × 10 in. (0.6 × 25.4 cm). Marked (on rim): *TOWLE STERLING 81.* Paper label: *TOWLE / THE PROUDEST NAME IN / STERLING*
Dallas Museum of Art, The Jewel Stern American Silver Collection, Decorative Arts Fund, DMA 2002.29.198

Eight scrolling and pointed loops in relief form the radial motif that decorates this trivet. In the spaces between the connected loops a rhythmic pattern of raised dots alternates in single and double units. This ten-inch-diameter trivet was the largest of three produced in the design (see chapter 10).

References: "Every good casserole deserves a silver dish," *House and Garden* 107 (May 1955): 118; "15 silver presents under $15," *House and Garden* 106 (Nov. 1954): 106; "I Do," Towle Silversmiths advertisement, *New Yorker* 35 (May 30, 1959): 50.

260. Tazza, c. 1955*

Enameled silverplate. 2 × 7⅞ in. (5.1 × 20.0 cm). Marked: *TOWLE• SILVERSMITHS•* [in circular form surrounding mark] / [lion in script T] / *EP 5004*
Dallas Museum of Art, The Jewel Stern American Silver Collection, Decorative Arts Fund, DMA 2002.29.220.1

In the mid-1950s, Towle experimented with decorative contemporary designs in genuine enamel on silverplate and on sterling. These designs were primarily applied to low coupe-shaped dishes on pedestals, which are designated in this catalogue as "tazzas." A group comprising four related designs has been identified. Each has a black border surrounding a field stamped with an abstract design. The bright blue enamel field of this tazza is filled with asterisk-shaped motifs to suggest stars.

261. Tazza, c. 1955*

Enameled silverplate. 2 × 7⅞ in. (5.1 × 20.0 cm). Marked: *TOWLE•SILVERSMITHS•* [in circular form surrounding mark] / [lion in script T] / *EP 5005*
Dallas Museum of Art, The Jewel Stern American Silver Collection, Decorative Arts Fund, DMA 2002.29.220.2

A looping, linear design flows energetically in all directions across the rose-copper enamel field of this black enamel–bordered tazza.

262. Tazza, c. 1955

Enameled silverplate. 2 × 7⅞ in. (5.1 × 20.0 cm). Marked: *TOWLE•SILVERSMITHS•* [in circular form surrounding mark] / [lion in script T] / *EP 5007*
Dallas Museum of Art, The Jewel Stern American Silver Collection, Decorative Arts Fund, DMA 2002.29.220.3

The gold-colored enamel field of this tazza is covered with identical linear seed shapes that radiate in alternate rows from the center outward to the black enamel border at the rim.

263. Tazza, c. 1955

Enameled silverplate. 1½ × 7⅝ in. (3.8 × 19.4 cm). Marked: *TOWLE•SILVERSMITHS•* [in circular form surrounding mark] / [lion in script T] / *EP 5006.* Paper label: *Towle Silversmiths* [in script] / *PRECIOUS ENAMEL / AND SILVER PLATE*
Dallas Museum of Art, The Jewel Stern American Silver Collection, Decorative Arts Fund, DMA 2002.29.231

The oxblood-red enamel field of this tazza has a single spiraling-pinwheel motif.

264. Tazza, c. 1955*

Earl Pardon (attributed to)
American, 1926–1991

Enameled silverplate. 1¾ × 7½ in. (4.4 × 19.1 cm). Marked: *TOWLE• SILVERSMITHS•* [in circular form surrounding mark] / [lion in script T]
Dallas Museum of Art, The Jewel Stern American Silver Collection, Decorative Arts Fund, DMA 2002.29.10

In addition to the group of four related enameled tazzas from c. 1955, another tazza was produced with a very narrow black enamel border and a single, centered motif, a linear, abstract construction that, in this tazza, is stamped in a field of turquoise enamel (see chapter 13). The design is attributed to Earl Pardon, who was a consultant at Towle in 1954–1955. The same motif was applied to sterling tazzas in chartreuse enamel with a black border. These were produced in two sizes, the larger, no. 1902, the smaller, no. 1901.

265. Bowl, c. 1955

Enameled silver. 3½ × 5¾ in. (8.9 × 14.6 cm). Marked: [scratched] *S2139 / TOWLE / STERLING / 47*
Dallas Museum of Art, The Jewel Stern American Silver Collection, gift of Jewel Stern, DMA 2004.13.13

This bowl has an unusual decorative enamel interior. For a very small number of conservatively shaped sterling bowls, Towle experimented by scattering confetti-like bits of color randomly into the enamel interior. The design of each bowl is therefore unique, unlike the uniform stamped designs of the silverplated tazzas. This example is one of the few known surviving examples of this brief experiment.

266. Butter dish, c. 1955*

Silver, plastic, ceramic. 2½ × 3⅝ × 8 in. (6.4 × 9.2 × 20.3 cm). Marked (on cover): *TOWLE / STERLING / 54*
Dallas Museum of Art, The Jewel Stern American Silver Collection, Decorative Arts Fund, DMA 2002.29.189.A–B

In the mid-1950s Towle produced several items in which sterling and black ceramic components were combined. This dish of black ceramic has a sterling cover with a black plastic handle. Other examples included a black ceramic jam jar with a sterling cover, spoon, and tray, a black ceramic casserole with a sterling cover and heating stand, and a tray with a divided black ceramic insert.

References: "Good Things in Towle Sterling Come in All Shapes and Prices," Towle advertisement, *House Beautiful* 97 (Nov. 1955): 15; "Gourmet Goes Shopping," *Gourmet* 15 (Dec. 1955): 24.

267. Butter dish, c. 1955

Silver, enamel, ceramic. 2¾ × 6½ × 3¾ in. (7.0 × 16.5 × 9.5 cm).
Marked (on tray): *TOWLE / STERLING*. Marked (on cover): *TOWLE / STERLING / 53*
Dallas Museum of Art, The Jewel Stern American Silver Collection, Decorative Arts Fund, DMA 2004.13.12.A–C

The handle of this butter dish has two green enamel studs akin to the jade green enamel tips on Towle's *Contempra House* flatware, which was designed by the enamelist and jeweler Earl Pardon. The enamel studs on this butter dish are also similar to the finials of a sugar bowl and covered pot produced by Towle and Lenox at around the time when Pardon was a consultant at Towle, 1954–1955. The price of the butter dish when embellished with enamel was $25.[1] The butter dish was also produced without enamel touches.

1. "Last-Minute Gift Guide for Armchair Shoppers," *House and Garden* 108 (Dec. 1955): 101.

268. Creamer and sugar bowl, c. 1955*

Porcelain, silver, enamel. Creamer 3½ × 4¼ in. (8.9 × 10.8 cm); sugar bowl 5 × 4¼ in. (12.7 × 10.8 cm). Creamer marked: *TOWLE / STERLING 465*. Sugar bowl: (on bottom) *L* [in a laurel wreath; gold] / *LENOX / MADE IN USA*; (on rim) *TOWLE STERLING / 466*
Dallas Museum of Art, 20th-Century Design Fund, DMA 1994.225.1–2

This set was produced by Towle in collaboration with Lenox China. The jade green enamel accented lids on the sugar bowl and on a related covered pot suggest the influence of Earl Pardon, a consultant at Towle from 1954–1955.

269. Covered pot, c. 1955*

Porcelain, silver, enamel. 7 × 3½ in. (17.8 × 8.9 cm). Pot marked: *L* [in a laurel wreath; green] / *LENOX / MADE IN USA*. Lid: *TOWLE STERLING / 464*
Dallas Museum of Art, The Jewel Stern American Silver Collection, Decorative Arts Fund, DMA 2002.29.206.A–B

The function of this pear-shaped covered pot, which has a jade green enamel-tipped finial that matches the creamer and sugar bowl in the previous entry is unclear, but it may have been a container for artificial sweeteners. Its form is an attenuated version of the covered sugar bowl.

270. Candlesticks (pair), c. 1957*

Marion Anderson Noyes
American, 1907–2002

Silver, plastic. 9 × 11 × 5½ in. (22.9 × 27.9 × 14.0 cm) and 6⅛ × 10 × 4¾ in. (15.6 × 25.4 × 12.1 cm). Marked (each) [in a circular shape]: *TOWLE STERLING / [lion in script T] / 11 / WEIGHTED & REINFORCED*
Dallas Museum of Art, The Jewel Stern American Silver Collection, Decorative Arts Fund, DMA 2002.29.20.1–2

These serpentine, asymmetrical candlesticks are organically dynamic and can be arranged in intriguing configurations. In 1957, the pair retailed for $30.[1] The candlesticks appeared in the exhibition *Vital Forms: American Art and Design in the Atomic Age, 1940–1960* held in 2001 at the Brooklyn Museum of Art, the repository of the Marion Anderson Noyes Archive.

1. "Towle Gifts—for this season of gift occasions," Towle advertisement, *New Yorker* 33 (May 11, 1957): 123.
Reference: "Be An Angel . . . Give Towle Sterling!" Towle advertisement, *House Beautiful* 99 (Dec. 1957): 81.

271. *Contessina* flatware (fork*), 1965

Silver, stainless steel knife blade. Place knife ¾ × 8¹⁵⁄₁₆ in. (1.9 × 22.7 cm); dinner fork ¹⁵⁄₁₆ × 7⅞ in. (2.4 × 20.0 cm); salad fork 1¹⁄₁₆ × 6⅝ in. (2.7 × 16.8 cm); teaspoon 1¼ × 6¹⁄₁₆ in. (3.2 × 15.4 cm). Knife marked: *NEW FRENCH BLADE TOWLE / STERLING HDL / STAINLESS BLD*. Fork / salad fork / spoon: *TOWLE STERLING 1965 C CONTESSINA*
Dallas Museum of Art, gift of Beverly Hart Bremer, DMA 1998.174.1–4

For *Contessina* flatware, see chapter 14. This pattern was not patented.

272. Candlesticks (three), c. 1969*

Silverplate, brass. 16 × 4 in. (40.6 × 10.2 cm); 12½ × 4 in. (31.8 × 10.2 cm); 9¼ × 4 in. (23.5 × 10.2 cm). Paper label (on each): *TOWLE / T* [in shield] *THE PROUDEST NAME IN / SILVERPLATE*. Paper label (on two tallest): *T* [in shield] / *TOWLE E.P.-GERMANY / 4144*
Dallas Museum of Art, The Jewel Stern American Silver Collection, Decorative Arts Fund, DMA 2002.29.93.1–3

The slender rods of these candlesticks may be unscrewed at the brass spheres and their height adjusted. This trio is staggered in units of two, three, and four rods and use one, two, and three spheres, respectively. The candle cups are in the form of a stylized tulip, a shape popular in the 1950s and 1960s. Towle outsourced the production of these candlesticks in Germany (see chapter 13). They were featured in *House and Garden* several times from 1969 to 1972 as dramatic accessories for table settings.

References: "Decorating Zest: Blondes and Silvers," *House and Garden* 137 (Feb. 1970): 84; "Rooms Ready For Celebrating," *House and Garden* 140 (Dec. 1971): 59; "The whole house works for a party," *House and Garden* 135 (Jan. 1969): 71.

273. Wine cooler, c. 1969

Silverplate, teak. 8½ × 8 × 6½ in. (21.6 × 20.3 × 16.5 cm). Paper label: *TOWLE SILVERSMITHS*. Marked (on handle): *T* [in shield] / *TOWLE / GERMANY / EP 4142*
Dallas Museum of Art, The Jewel Stern American Silver Collection, Decorative Arts Fund, DMA 2002.29.268

The burgeoning appreciation of wine by Americans provided the impetus for this insulated wine cooler outsourced in Germany but designed by Towle. Primarily of teak, this contemporary object has a smooth silverplated collar rim and projecting disk-shaped handles.

CONTEMPRA HOUSE
NEWBURYPORT, MASSACHUSETTS
ACTIVE C. 1954–1960

DIVISION OF TOWLE SILVERSMITHS

274. *Contempra House* spoon, 1956 (designed 1955)

Earl Pardon
American, 1926–1991

Patent 180,748 (for a fork or similar article) filed Oct. 11, 1955, granted Aug. 6, 1957. Silver, stainless steel, enamel. ⁹⁄₁₆ × 1 × 8 in. (1.4 × 2.5 × 20.3 cm). Marked (on handle): [raised letters within an impressed rectangle] *contempra house / STERLING HANDLE*. Marked (on neck of bowl): *STAINLESS*
Dallas Museum of Art, The Jewel Stern American Silver Collection, gift of Jewel Stern, DMA 2003.34.6

Contempra House flatware was made in four variants. This spoon is an example of the variant that has a handle with vertical incised lines on the front and a jade green enamel inset at the squared tip. In an article in *Modern Bride* in 1957, this variant was described as: "Jade (Lined) a new pattern with sterling handles, stainless blades, tines, bowl, by Contempra House."[1] At $16 a place setting, it was half the price of the least expensive sterling pattern featured (see chapter 11).

1. Unidentified clipping, *Modern Bride* (spring 1957) (Tiffany Archives).
Reference: "Annual Design Review," *Industrial Design* 3 (Dec. 1956): 104.

275. *Contempra House* spoon, 1956 (designed 1955)

Earl Pardon
American, 1926–1991

Silver, stainless steel. ¼ × 1 × 8⅜ in. (0.6 × 2.5 × 21.3 cm). Marked (on handle): [raised letters within an impressed rectangle] *contempra house / STERLING HANDLE*. Marked (on neck of bowl): *STAINLESS*
Dallas Museum of Art, The Jewel Stern American Silver Collection, gift of Jewel Stern, DMA 2003.34.14

There is no patent for this version of *Contempra House* flatware in which the handle is incised with vertical lines on the front side only and comes to a point without an inset of enamel at the tip. The handle in this shape was also made completely plain, without lines and without an enamel tip.

276. *Contempra House* spoon, 1956 (designed 1955)

Earl Pardon
American, 1926–1991

Patent 180,749 (for a fork or similar article) filed Oct. 11, 1955, granted Aug. 6, 1957. Silver, stainless steel, enamel. 15/16 × 15/16 × 67/16 in. (2.4 × 2.4 × 16.4 cm). Marked (on handle): [raised letters within an impressed rectangle] *contempra house* / *STERLING HANDLE.* Marked (on neck of bowl): *STAINLESS*
Dallas Museum of Art, The Jewel Stern American Silver Collection, gift of Jewel Stern, DMA 2003.34.15

Contempra House flatware was made in two versions with enamel insets at their tips. In one version, the handle was incised with vertical lines on the front side. In the other version, of which this teaspoon is an example, the entire shaft of the handle is plain.

277. *Contempra House* salad serving set, 1956 (designed 1955)*

Earl Pardon
American, 1926–1991

Patent 180,748 (for a fork or similar article) filed Oct. 11, 1955, granted Aug. 6, 1957. Silver, enamel, plastic. Fork 1 × 2¼ × 127/16 in. (2.5 × 5.7 × 31.6 cm); spoon 1 × 2⅜ × 127/16 in. (2.5 × 6.0 × 31.6 cm). Marked (on each): [raised letters within an impressed rectangle] *contempra house* / *STERLING HANDLE*
Dallas Museum of Art, The Jewel Stern American Silver Collection, gift of Jewel Stern, DMA 2003.34.16.1–2

This set of *Contempra House* salad servers came in a specially designed box covered with a decorative diamond pattern. The serving ends of the fork and spoon are of black plastic. The handles are in the "Jade Lined" version of *Contempra House* and have vertical incised lines on the front sides and insets of jade green enamel at the ends of the squared tips.

TUTTLE SILVERSMITHS
BOSTON, MASSACHUSETTS
ACTIVE 1890–1955

278. Candlesticks (pair), introduced 1929–1933*

Silver. Each 5 × 41/16 in. (12.7 × 10.3 cm). Marked (on each): *STERLING* / *801S* / [female bust in oval] *HH* [in a crescent] / *I* / *THE WEBB C. BALL CO.*
Dallas Museum of Art, The Jewel Stern American Silver Collection, acquired through the Patsy Lacy Griffith Collection, gift of Patsy Lacy Griffith by exchange, DMA 2002.29.134.1–2

The ubiquitous stepped and staggered form of the late 1920s was employed for the round bases of these candlesticks that rise like a pyramid in five narrow tiers to smooth columnar stems that hold the removable candle cups. The candle cups flare inversely in telescoping fashion to contrast with the bases, to function as bobeches, and to provide aesthetic interest. The candlesticks bear the name of the retailer, the Webb C. Ball Company. The initials "HH" within the crescent in the Tuttle mark indicates that the candlesticks were made during the presidency of Herbert Hoover, March 4, 1929–March 3, 1933. The Roman numeral "I" below the crescent indicates that the candlesticks were produced during his first term in office. Hoover was not reelected to a second term, thus these candlesticks will have been made between March 4, 1929, and the inauguration of the next president, Franklin Delano Roosevelt, on March 4, 1933. This date mark system, begun during the presidency of Calvin Coolidge, is unique to Tuttle.

UNKNOWN MAKER

279. Cocktail shaker, c. 1928

Silverplate. 10½ × 4 in. (26.7 × 10.2 cm). Unmarked
Dallas Museum of Art, The Jewel Stern American Silver Collection, acquired through the Patsy Lacy Griffith Collection, gift of Patsy Lacy Griffith by exchange, DMA 2002.29.138.A–C

See chapter 7 for this telescoping shaker.

A. L. WAGNER MANUFACTURING COMPANY, INC.
NEW YORK, NEW YORK
ACTIVE 1927–1931

280. Tea and coffee service, 1928*

Silver, ebony. Coffeepot and lid 6¼ × 7½ × 4½ in. (15.9 × 19.1 × 11.4 cm); teapot and lid 5¼ × 8¼ × 5½ in. (13.3 × 21.0 × 14.0 cm); creamer 3¾ × 5¼ × 3 in. (9.5 × 13.3 × 7.6 cm); sugar bowl and lid 3½ × 6½ × 4 in. (8.9 × 16.5 × 10.2 cm); waste bowl 1¾ × 3¾ in. (4.4 × 9.5 cm); tray 1¼ × 19½ × 11 in. (3.2 × 49.5 × 27.9 cm). Coffeepot marked: *CSC* [in shield] / *STERLING* / *1352* / *1¾ PINTS* / *WM. WISE & SON, INC.*; (coffeepot lid): *STERLING.* Teapot: *CSC* [in shield] / *STERLING* / *1352* / *1½ PINTS* / *WM. WISE & SON, INC.*; (teapot lid): *STERLING.* Creamer: *CSC* [in shield] / *STERLING* / *1352* / *WM. WISE & SON, INC.*; (creamer lid): *STERLING.* Sugar bowl: *CSC* [in shield] / *STERLING* / *1352* / *WM. WISE & SON, INC.*; (sugar bowl lid): *STERLING.* Waste bowl: *CSC* [in shield] / *STERLING* / *1352* / *WM. WISE & SON, INC.*; (waste bowl lid): *STERLING.* Tray: *CSC* [in shield] / *STERLING* / *411* / *WM. WISE & SON, INC.*
Dallas Museum of Art, The Jewel Stern American Silver Collection, acquired through the Patsy Lacy Griffith Collection, gift of Patsy Lacy Griffith by exchange, DMA 2002.29.38.1–6

The six-piece tea and coffee service, including matching tray, inspired by the newly fashionable *art moderne,* was advertised by the Marshall Field & Company department store of Chicago in 1928 and priced at $575. "By contrasting ebony and silver, a simple carved line and a hand-fluted surface, a modern designer has achieved this exceptionally lovely tea or coffee service."[1] On this service A. L. Wagner kept the hallmark of its predecessor earlier in the century, the Central Sterling Company of Brooklyn, New York. The service also bears the imprint of the retailer, William Wise & Son of Brooklyn (see chapter 3).

1. Marshall Field & Company, *Fashions of the Hour,* Christmas number, 1928, 5.

R. WALLACE & SONS MANUFACTURING COMPANY
WALLINGFORD, CONNECTICUT
1871–1956

WALLACE SILVERSMITHS
1956–1984
AND
WALLACE BROTHERS SILVER COMPANY
FOUNDED 1875

281. Cocktail shaker and cups, c. 1928*

Silverplate, glass. Cocktail shaker 14½ × 91/16 × 415/16 in. (36.8 × 22.9 × 12.5 cm); cups (each, with glass insert) 4 × 4½ × 2¾ in. (10.2 × 11.4 × 7.0 cm). Cocktail shaker marked: *TRADE* [in scroll] *WB* [in shield surmounted by lion] *MARK* [in scroll] *3880.* Cups (each): *3882* / *TRADE* [in scroll] *WB* [in shield surmounted by lion] *MARK* [in scroll] / *3880*
Dallas Museum of Art, the Patsy Lacy Griffith Collection, bequest of Patsy Lacy Griffith, DMA 2001.135.1–5

The whimsical rooster design of this beverage set forms a clever visual pun denoting its intended purpose as a *cocktail* service. Unlike Napier's penguin-shaped cocktail shaker of the 1930s, which wittily evokes urbane gentlemen in tuxedos, the hammered finish and choice of a farm animal as the motif for this shaker suggests a sophisticated indulgence in rural themes that is sympathetic to colonial revival styles and other celebrations of Americana during the 1920s. The Wallace Brothers Silver Company was formed in 1875 for the manufacture of silverplated wares and was acquired by R. Wallace & Sons in 1879.

282. Sandwich tray, c. 1928

Silver. 1½ × 10 in. (3.8 × 25.4 cm). Marked: *RW* [stag head] *& S* / *STERLING* / *3696_3* / *WALLACE*
Dallas Museum of Art, The Jewel Stern American Silver Collection, acquired through the Patsy Lacy Griffith Collection, gift of Patsy Lacy Griffith by exchange, DMA 2002.29.129

This modern tray has a distinctive border of equally spaced and pierced small stepped motifs that subtly suggest 1920s skyscrapers. In 1931 the price was $25.[1] A bowl was also made in this design.

1. R. Wallace and Sons Manufacturing Company, *Sterling Hollow Ware* (1931), 62.

283. *Rhythm* tea and coffee service, 1929*

Percy B. Ball
American (b. England), 1879–1957

Silver, plastic. Coffeepot 10½ × 9½ × 3¼ in. (26.7 × 24.1 × 8.3 cm); teapot 8 × 10½ × 3¼ in. (20.3 × 26.7 × 8.3 cm); creamer 5¼ × 5 × 2¼ in. (13.3 × 12.7 × 5.7 cm); sugar bowl and lid 3½ × 6¼ × 3 in. (8.9 × 15.9 × 7.6 cm); waste bowl 3½ × 6 × 3 in. (8.9 × 15.2 × 7.6 cm); tray 1½ × 26½ × 11 in. (3.8 × 67.3 × 27.9 cm). Coffeepot marked: *RW* [stag head] *&S / STERLING 3900/3 PTS WALLACE / 6*. Teapot: *RW* [stag head] *&S / STERLING 3900/18/ RHYTHM/ 2½ PTS / WALLACE*. Creamer: *RW* [stag head] *&S / STERLING 3900/ ¾ PT. / WALLACE*. Sugar bowl: *RW* [stag head] *&S / STERLING 3900/ RHYTHM/ WALLACE*. Waste bowl: *RW* [stag head] *&S / STERLING 3900/ RHYTHM/ WALLACE*. Tray: *RW* [stag head] *& S / STERLING 3900/ RHYTHM/ WALLACE*
Dallas Museum of Art, The Jewel Stern American Silver Collection, gift of Jewel Stern in honor of Charles L. Venable, DMA 2002.29.36.1–6

The *Rhythm* tea and coffee service with waiter was part of the holloware line designed to coordinate with Wallace's 1929 *Rhythm* sterling flatware pattern. Wallace assured the trade that *Rhythm* was "far removed from the old order of things," yet "stands out in the maze of modernism."[1] In 1929, the five-piece *Rhythm* service and the waiter was priced $765, a formidable sum for the time. The provenance of this complete *Rhythm* service indicates that it originally belonged to the Horwitz family, owners of the Chateau Crillon Apartment House on Rittenhouse Square in Philadelphia, which had been designed by the architect Horace Trumbauer in the Art Deco style and built in 1928.

A full line of *Rhythm* holloware was produced: almond dish, bonbon dish, bowl, bread and butter plate, bread tray, candlesticks in two heights, two centerpieces with mesh, a centerpiece with mesh and under tray, entrée dish, goblet, gravy boat and tray, luncheon tray, meat dish in two sizes, salt and pepper set, sandwich tray, service plate, vegetable dish, goblet, water pitcher, dessert set, and compote. The only items embellished with white Catalin to suggest ivory were the pieces of the tea and coffee service (see chapter 3). The Depression quashed production of *Rhythm* holloware and consequently surviving examples are rare. This is the only known complete tea and coffee service with waiter.

1. "'Rhythm' modern enough to win the admiration of your most discriminating customers," Wallace advertisement, *Keystone* 98 (May 1929): 114.
Reference: A. Frederick Saunders, "Modernism in American Silverware," *Jewelers' Circular* 100 (Feb. 27, 1930): 105.

284. *Rhythm* compote, 1929

Percy B. Ball
American (b. England), 1879–1957

Silver. 5½ × 6½ in. (14.0 × 16.5 cm). Marked: *RW* [stag head] *& S / STERLING 3909/ RHYTHM/ WALLACE*
Dallas Museum of Art, The Jewel Stern American Silver Collection, acquired through the Patsy Lacy Griffith Collection, gift of Patsy Lacy Griffith by exchange, DMA 2002.29.131

Percy Ball worked at various times for Gorham, Frank M. Whiting, Wallace, and Watson (for whom he designed *Dorian* flatware and holloware in 1935; see chapter 6). Like William Warren (1887–1965), Wallace's head designer, Ball was born in England, but unlike Warren, who had a long affiliation with Wallace (1909–1959), Ball had a peripatetic career as a silver designer. Although Warren applied for the patent on the *Rhythm* flatware pattern, former Wallace employees consider that it was Ball who designed the holloware.[1] *Rhythm* holloware was designed and produced in two variants (see chapter 3). This compote is in one variant, the tea and coffee service is in the other.

1. James Luca, conversation with Jewel Stern, Wallingford, Conn., May 31, 1991; William Toth, telephone conversation with Jewel Stern, June 17, 1991; and William Regan, telephone conversation with Jewel Stern, May 4, 2001.

285. Mayonnaise dish, c. 1929*

Silver, Catalin. 3½ × 4½ in. (8.9 × 11.4 cm). Marked: *RW* [stag head] *& S / STERLING 3733/ WALLACE*
Dallas Museum of Art, The Jewel Stern American Silver Collection, acquired through the Patsy Lacy Griffith Collection, gift of Patsy Lacy Griffith by exchange, DMA 2002.29.124

The base of the segmented and notched bowl consists of a black Catalin disk surmounted by a fluted, brownish Catalin pedestal in a smaller diameter, imparting a classical note to the piece (see chapter 3). Produced for only a short time, this mayonnaise dish did not appear in the 1931 Wallace catalogue. The design was also produced in a large bowl (no. 3767).

286. Tea strainer and drip, c. 1929*

Silver, Catalin. 2¼ × 5 × 3¼ in. (5.7 × 12.7 × 8.3 cm). Drip marked: *RW* [stag head] *&S/ STERLING 3708/ WALLACE*. Strainer: *RW* [stag head] *& S STERLING 3708*
Dallas Museum of Art, The Jewel Stern American Silver Collection, acquired through the Patsy Lacy Griffith Collection, gift of Patsy Lacy Griffith by exchange, DMA 2002.29.34.A–B

This is one of three modernist Catalin-trimmed tea strainers with matching drips produced by Wallace. The round faceted base of the drip and the strainer handle are Catalin in green, marbled with a mustard color. The rim of the silver strainer bowl is also faceted and the Catalin handle is stepped and layered in a skyscraper motif. The tea strainers and drips were briefly in production and, like the mayonnaise dish were no longer offered in Wallace's catalogue for 1931.

287. Tea strainer and drip, c. 1929

Silver, Catalin. 2¼ × 6½ × 3¼ in. (5.7 × 16.5 × 8.3 cm). Drip marked: *RW* [stag head] *& S/ STERLING 3707/ WALLACE*. Strainer: *RW* [stag head] *& S STERLING 3707*
Dallas Museum of Art, The Jewel Stern American Silver Collection, acquired through the Patsy Lacy Griffith Collection, gift of Patsy Lacy Griffith by exchange, DMA 2002.29.35.A–B

This is one of the three Catalin-trimmed, modernist tea strainers and drips produced by Wallace. Of black and red Catalin, the handle of the strainer telescopes from a scalloped rim with incised radiating lines. For the drip base a black disk was superimposed on a larger one in red.

288. Tea strainer and drip, c. 1929*

Silver, Catalin. 2¼ × 6 × 3 in. (5.7 × 15.2 × 7.6 cm). Drip marked: *RW* [stag head] *& S/ STERLING 3725/ WALLACE*. Strainer: *RW* [stag head] *& S STERLING 3725*
Dallas Museum of Art, The Jewel Stern American Silver Collection, acquired through the Patsy Lacy Griffith Collection, gift of Patsy Lacy Griffith by exchange, DMA 2002.29.128.A–B

In contrast to the other two modernist tea strainers and drips made by Wallace with Catalin trim, the square is the predominant motif here. The base of the drip is made of a ring of black Catalin that rests above a square of green Catalin with mustard color marbling. A simple rectangular rod of matching green Catalin with black tips serves as the strainer handle. A radiating design of eight stepped squares perforates the circular strainer and emphasizes the geometry of the design. Rimless, the strainer rests on the drip by means of its extended handle, which fits into two V-shaped notches in the drip.

289. Salt and pepper shakers, c. 1929*

Silver, Catalin. Each 4 × 1³⁄₁₆ in. (10.2 × 3.0 cm). Marked (each): *RW* [stag head] *& S STERLING 3749*
Dallas Museum of Art, The Jewel Stern American Silver Collection, acquired through the Patsy Lacy Griffith Collection, gift of Patsy Lacy Griffith by exchange, DMA 2002.29.32.1–2

Wallace produced two modernist salts and peppers with Catalin bases. Red disks above black squares form the bases of these shakers. They were still offered in the 1931 Wallace catalogue, the price, $10.[1]

1. R. Wallace & Sons Mfg. Co, *Sterling Hollow-Ware* catalogue S-31, 1931, 75.

290. Salt and pepper shakers, c. 1929

Silver, Catalin. Salt shaker 4 × 2⅝ in. (10.2 × 6.7 cm); pepper shaker 4 × 2⅝ in. (10.2 × 6.7 cm). Marked: *RW* [stag head] *& S STERLING 3731/ 3781*
Dallas Museum of Art, The Jewel Stern American Silver Collection, acquired through the Patsy Lacy Griffith Collection, gift of Patsy Lacy Griffith by exchange, DMA 2002.29.125.1–2

The gear-shaped bases of these shakers are of green Catalin with mustard color marbling and are layered with smaller black Catalin disks. One of two modernist salt and peppers with Catalin elements that were made by Wallace, this design, like the other, was in production at least until 1931 and cost $10.[1]

1. R. Wallace & Sons Mfg. Co, *Sterling Hollow-Ware* catalogue S-31, 1931, 75.

291. Tea bell, c. 1929*

Silver, Catalin. 2½ × 1½ in. (6.4 × 3.8 cm). Marked: *RW* [stag head] *& S 3742–2 WALLACE STERLING*
Dallas Museum of Art, The Jewel Stern American Silver Collection, acquired through the Patsy Lacy Griffith Collection, gift of Patsy Lacy Griffith by exchange, DMA 2002.29.33

One of four tea bells made by Wallace and incorporating Catalin elements, this model is packed with modernist imagery. The handle is stepped inversely, and "hand engraved" triangles[1] circle the skirt and shoulders of the bell to approximate cubist planes. A black Catalin collar sets off the green marbled Catalin handle. In the 1931 catalogue the price was $5.50.[2]

1. R. Wallace & Sons Mfg. Co. "Sterling Silver Tea Bells," salesman's catalogue, pl. 428-S, April 1929.
2. Idem, *Sterling Hollow-Ware* catalogue S-31, 1931, 66.

292. Tea bell, c. 1929

Silver, Catalin. 3 × 1½ in. (7.62 × 3.81 cm), Marked: *RW* [stag head] *& S 3741 WALLACE STERLING*
Dallas Museum of Art, The Jewel Stern American Silver Collection, acquired through the Patsy Lacy Griffith Collection, gift of Patsy Lacy Griffith by exchange, DMA 2002.29.126

This, the smallest of Wallace's four modernist tea bells, has a bright red telescoping and flared Catalin handle accented with a black Catalin disk. A series of four "turned lines"[1] decorates the bell. In 1931 the price of the bell was $5.[2]

1. R. Wallace & Sons Mfg. Co, *Sterling Hollow-Ware* catalogue S-31, 1931, 66.
2. Ibid.

293. Tea bell, c. 1929

Silver, Catalin. 3¾ × 2¼ in. (9.5 × 5.7 cm). Marked: *RW* [stag head] *& S 3743 WALLACE STERLING*
Dallas Museum of Art, The Jewel Stern American Silver Collection, acquired through the Patsy Lacy Griffith Collection, gift of Patsy Lacy Griffith by exchange, DMA 2002.29.127

The largest of Wallace's four tea bells with Catalin elements, this is flared and "hand engraved" with vertical radiating lines.[1] The stepped shoulder rises to hold a black and red inversely flared Catalin handle. The most expensive of the four bells, it cost $7.50 in 1931.[2]

1. R. Wallace & Sons Mfg. Co, "Sterling Silver Tea Bells," salesman's catalogue, pl. 428-S, April 1929.
2. Idem, *Sterling Hollow-Ware* catalogue S-31, 1931, 66.

294. *Vogue* pie server, 1935*

William S. Warren
American (b. England), 1887–1965

Patent 94,931 (for a spoon or similar article) filed Jan. 19, 1935, granted Mar. 19, 1935. Silverplate. 1⁷⁄₁₆ × 2⁵⁄₁₆ × 9¼ in. (3.7 × 5.9 × 23.5 cm), Marked: *LUXOR PLATE–WALLACE*
Dallas Museum of Art, The Jewel Stern American Silver Collection, gift of Jewel Stern, DMA 2003.34.11

The Ionic order of Greek architecture was the inspiration for *Vogue*, one of several modern classical flatware patterns of the mid-1930s (see chapter 8).

295. *Classic Modern* pitcher, c. 1935

Silverplate. 10 × 5 in. (25.4 × 12.7 cm). Marked: *WALLACE / E.P.N.S. / SUPERFINE / N6700*
Dallas Museum of Art, The Jewel Stern American Silver Collection, acquired through the Patsy Lacy Griffith Collection, gift of Patsy Lacy Griffith by exchange, DMA 2002.29.169

The pitcher was part of Wallace's *Classic Modern* full holloware service (no. N6700) (see chapter 6).

296. 1939 New York World's Fair spoon, 1939

Enameled silver. ⅞ × 6 × 1¼ in. (2.2 × 15.2 × 3.2 cm). Inscribed: *NEW YORK WORLD'S FAIR WORLD OF TOMORROW 1939*. Marked: *WALLACE AI + N.Y.W.F. LIC. 1113*
Dallas Museum of Art, The Jewel Stern American Silver Collection, gift of Jewel Stern, DMA 17.2004.10

For 1939 New York World's Fair souvenir spoons, see chapter 8.

297. *Discovery* flatware (knife*), introduced 1957

Raymond Loewy
American, 1893–1986

Patent 181,692 (for a spoon or similar article) filed Sept. 26, 1957, granted Dec. 10, 1957. Silver, stainless steel knife blade. Dinner knife ¼ × ¾ × 9½ in. (0.6 × 1.9 × 24.1 cm); place fork 1 × 7½ × 1 in. (2.5 × 19.1 × 2.5 cm); teaspoon 1 × 6¼ × 1 in. (2.5 × 15.9 × 2.5 cm). Knife marked: *WALLACE / STAINLESS / STERLING HANDLE*. Fork / teaspoon: *WALLACE / STERLING*
Dallas Museum of Art, The Jewel Stern American Silver Collection, gift of Jewel Stern, DMA 2004.13.15.1–3

Although *Discovery* was advertised by Wallace as the creation of Raymond Loewy,[1] the patent was applied for by Ernest Frederich Thomson and Frederick Allen Burke—two men who are likely to have been designers in Loewy's firm. The slender seed-shaped gashes scattered on the handles of this unusual pattern bring to mind the slashed canvases of the Italian artist Lucio Fontana.

1. "Discovery," Wallace advertisement, *New Yorker* 33 (Apr. 20, 1957): inside front cover.

298. *Soliloquy* flatware, 1963*

Clark L. Lofgren
American, b. 1936

Silver, stainless steel knife blade. Place fork ¾ × 1 × 7⅝ in. (1.9 × 2.5 × 19.4 cm); salad fork ¾ × 1⅛ × 7 in. (1.9 × 2.9 × 17.8 cm); teaspoon ½ × ¾ × 9⅜ in. (1.3 × 1.9 × 23.8 cm); place knife ¾ × 1¼ × 6⅝ in. (1.9 × 3.2 × 16.8 cm). Fork / salad fork / spoon marked: © *WALLACE W* [formed by two overlapping V's] / *STERLING*. Knife: *WALLACE / STERLING HANDLE / STAINLESS BLADE*
Dallas Museum of Art, gift of Beverly Hart Bremer, DMA 2000.404. 1–4

Lofgren, who graduated from the University of Illinois with a degree in industrial design in 1959, worked for Wallace from 1961 until 1963 and has worked for Reed & Barton since 1969. He is currently the design director there (see chapter 15). In 1963, early in his career, Lofgren created the Wallace sterling flatware pattern *Soliloquy*, for which he made the first prototype and samples (see chapter 14). *Soliloquy* was produced in several iterations in 1963. With the Firenze textured finish added to one panel, it became *Evening Mist*; with a delicate leaf motif it became *Still Mood*; and with the Firenze texture added to *Still Mood*, the pattern became *Dawn Mist*.[1] Lofgren designed Wallace's *Cosmopolitan* four-piece tea and coffee service with matching tray in silverplate (1963–1964) to accompany the *Soliloquy* sterling pattern.[2] The *Cosmopolitan* vessels have sculptural finials modeled in the shape of the flatware handles. Technically competent, Lofgren made the initial samples of all of this silverware.

1. "Soliloquy and Still Mood. New contemporary patterns in sterling from Wallace," Wallace advertisement, *Brides' Magazine* 29 (summer 1963): 22–23; and "500 years later: Firenze Sterling Silver by Wallace," Wallace advertisement *Town and Country* 118 (June 1964): 39.
2. "Only Wallace does it this way," Wallace advertisement, *New Yorker* 43 (Apr. 29, 1967): 92.

299. Bowl, c. 1963*

Silverplate with applied color. 2¼ × 4¼ × 12¼ in. (5.7 × 10.8 × 31.1 cm). Marked: [mark with five connected loops] / *W* [formed by two overlapping V's] / *WALLACE / 9022*
Dallas Museum of Art, The Jewel Stern American Silver Collection, Decorative Arts Fund, DMA 2002.29.13

To compete with Reed & Barton's groundbreaking *Color-Glaze* line introduced in 1961, Wallace countered with *Color-Clad*, an applied color surface that also emulated genuine enamel (see chapter 13). This canoe-shaped bowl tapers to spout-like ends and rests on four ball feet. One of the most popular items in the *Color-Clad* line, it has a green interior and functioned as a small centerpiece or candy dish. Bowls in this shape were also offered in red, blue, and copper *Color-Clad*.

300. *Royal Satin* flatware (fork*), 1965

David B. Hoover
American, 1928–2002

Patent 202,926 (for a fork or the like) filed March 4, 1965, granted Nov. 16, 1965. Silver, stainless steel knife blade. Place knife ¼ × 9 × ¾ in. (0.6 × 22.9 × 1.9 cm); place fork ½ × 7¾ × 1 in. (1.3 × 19.7 × 2.5 cm); salad fork ½ × 6¾ × 1 in. (1.3 × 17.1 × 2.5 cm); spoon ¾ × 6½ × 1¹³⁄₁₆ in. (1.9 × 16.5 × 4.6 cm). Marked (each): *WALLACE / W* [formed by two overlapping V's] / *STERLING / Royal Satin* [in script]
Dallas Museum of Art, gift of Beverly Hart Bremer, DMA 2004.39.1–4

For *Royal Satin* flatware designed for Wallace by the staff designer David B. Hoover, see chapter 14.

301. *Golden Aegean Weave* flatware (fork*), 1970 (designed 1969–1970)

Charlotte Schwarz (Hallet)
American, b. 1943

Gilded silver, stainless steel knife blade. Knife ½ × 9½ ×¾ in. (1.3 × 24.1 × 1.9 cm); fork ¾ × 8 × ¹⁵⁄₁₆ in. (1.9 × 20.3 × 2.4 cm); salad fork: ¾ × 6¾ × 1⅛ in. (1.9 × 17.1 × 2.9 cm); spoon ¾ × 6⅝ × 1⅜ in. (1.9 × 16.8 × 3.5 cm). Knife marked: *WALLACE STERLING / 925*. Spoon / salad fork / fork marked: © *WALLACE W* [formed by two overlapping V's] *STERLING*
Dallas Museum of Art, gift of Beverly Hart Bremer, DMA 2004.40.1–4

In 1968, Charlotte Schwarz Hallet graduated summa cum laude from the University of Bridgeport, Connecticut with a degree in medieval history. As an apprentice to her stepfather, a specialist in the restoration of decorative arts, she had acquired a strong background in ornamental design. On her own initiative she contacted Wallace Silversmiths in 1969 and was hired as a staff designer. An analytic thinker, she described the sources of her inspiration for *Aegean Weave*.

At the time (in 1970) she had developed a theory about the size of flatware, having observed that, when people were shorter, flatware was shorter. Now that Americans were growing taller, flatware should be made longer. Pondering contemporary life styles, Hallet also took into account the feminist movement and what she referred to as the "awakening for women." She wanted her silver pattern to reflect this in a "bold" manner and with "grace." She viewed "weaving" and "fabric" as an integral "part of feminine life" and gave expression to this in *Aegean Weave*. At the time she was also studying Native American forms and the use of natural materials such as tree branches. Her interest in these was transformed abstractly into the innovative, pencilslim handles of *Aegean Weave*.

Hallet made the model of the dinner fork by hand in Plastilene, after which it was cast in sterling silver for evaluation. The prototype was subsequently included in a market research survey involving a competition, which she won, thus ensuring its production.[1] In less than a year after the pattern was introduced, it was offered with gold highlights (an idea from someone else at Wallace) as *Golden Aegean Weave*, and that version precipitated a new trend in American flatware (see chapter 15).[2]

1. Charlotte Schwarz Hallet, telephone conversation with Jewel Stern, Nov. 24, 2004.
2. "A new generation should create its own traditions: Introducing Aegean Weave," Wallace advertisement, *New Yorker* 46 (Feb. 13, 1971): 58; and "A new generation should create its own traditions: Introducing Golden Aegean Weave," Wallace advertisement, *House and Garden* 140 (Oct. 1971): 3.

WATSON COMPANY
ATTLEBORO, MASSACHUSETTS
ACTIVE 1919–1955

302. *Dorian* coffeepot, 1935*

Percy B. Ball
American, 1879–1957

Silver, ebony, plastic. 9¾ × 9¾ × 5½ in. (24.8 × 24.8 × 14.0 cm). Marked: [crown in circle] *W* [in shield] [lion in circle] / *STERLING SILVER 11 / B513 / 2¼ PINTS*. Engraved: *MCB* [in shield]
Dallas Museum of Art, The Jewel Stern American Silver Collection, acquired through the Patsy Lacy Griffith Collection, gift of Patsy Lacy Griffith by exchange, DMA 2002.29.160.1

A complete holloware service was produced by Watson to match the *Dorian* flatware pattern patented by Percy B. Ball in 1935. As the name implied, the theme of the pattern was the austere Doric order of Greek architecture, which was expressed in the holloware primarily through vertical fluting. A less radical interpretation of modern classicism than others of the mid-1930s (see chapters 6, 8), *Dorian* was, when introduced, lauded for its "classic dignity."[1] The *Dorian* coffeepot has a traditional spout and looped handle with a thumb rest. The subtle layering of the dome-shaped lid and finial added a modern touch. The coffeepot was advertised as part of a coffee set, but Watson also made a *Dorian* teapot.

1. "Sterling," *American Home* 14 (June 1935): 25.
References: "Original Designs in Silver," *Arts and Decoration* 42 (Apr. 1935): 29; "Sterling Plate," *Creative Design* 1 (spring 1935): 14.

303. *Dorian* bowl, 1935

Percy B. Ball
American, 1879–1957

Silver. 10 × 2½ in. (25.4 × 6.4 cm). Marked: *J.E. CALDWELL & CO.* / [crown in circle] *W* [in shield] [lion] / *STERLING SILVER / B513 / 9½*
Dallas Museum of Art, The Jewel Stern American Silver Collection, acquired through the Patsy Lacy Griffith Collection, gift of Patsy Lacy Griffith by exchange, DMA 2002.29.154

Four panels of five flutes rise from the interior and extend over the flared rim of the *Dorian* bowl. This bowl was exhibited with the *Dorian* tea and coffee service in the Metropolitan Museum of Art's exhibition *Silver: An Exhibition of Contemporary American Design by Manufacturers, Designers and Craftsmen* in 1937 (see chapter 8). Helen Bishop commended the bowl for its "unfretful proportions," which made it "particularly appropriate for the modern home."[1]

1. Helen Bishop, "Silver—The Hostess' Great Heritage," *Arts and Decoration* 48 (Aug. 1938): 22.
Reference: "Fascinating Dorian," Watson advertisement, *Vogue* 85 (Mar. 1935): 14.

WEIDLICH BROTHERS MANUFACTURING COMPANY
BRIDGEPORT, CONNECTICUT
ACTIVE 1901–1950

304. Dessert set ("Sunray"), c. 1928*

Gilded silverplate. Creamer 3⅛ × 5 × 2¹⁄₁₆ in. (7.9 × 12.7 × 5.2 cm); sugar bowl 2¹¹⁄₁₆ × 5 × 2¹⁄₁₆ in. (6.8 × 12.7 × 5.2 cm); tray ½ × 14½ × 6 in. (1.3 × 36.8 × 15.2 cm). Creamer and sugar bowl marked: *B.M. MTS. / MADE IN U.S.A. / E.P.* [shield with *W. B. / MFG. CO.*] *N.S. / 3831*. Tray: *B.M. MTS. / MADE IN U.S.A. / E.P.* [shield with *W. B. / MFG. CO.*] *N.S. / 3815*
Dallas Museum of Art, The Jewel Stern American Silver Collection, acquired through the Patsy Lacy Griffith Collection, gift of Patsy Lacy Griffith by exchange, DMA 2002.29.45.1–3

Because of the similarity of the patterning on this Weidlich holloware line with an *art moderne* decorative motif popular at the 1925 Paris exposition, the Weidlich line was later dubbed "Sunray." However, no contemporaneous reference to the nickname has been found.

The hexagonal form of the creamer and sugar bowl of this dessert set with matching tray, and the angularity of the spout and handles, add to the prismatic effect while the glowing gold-washed interiors suggest sunlight. The creamer is a smaller version of the pitcher (model no. 3806). The complexity of the stamped ray pattern on these shapes visually fractures the planes, the designer's reprisal of cubist imagery (see chapter 3).

305. Tray ("Sunray"), c. 1928

Silverplate. 2½ × 14 × 10¼ in. (6.4 × 35.6 × 26 cm). Marked: *B.M. MTS. / MADE IN U.S.A. / E.P.* [shield with *W. B. / MFG. CO.*] *N.S. / 3800 / 8To* [scratched]
Dallas Museum of Art, The Jewel Stern American Silver Collection, gift of Jewel Stern, DMA 2005.25.13

The stylized, stamped sunray motif with its dynamic shifting of planes that convey movement radiates exuberantly from the center of this octagonal tray with angular handles (see chapter 3).

306. Salt and pepper shakers, 1929*

Alfred J. Flauder
American, active 1901–1950

Patent 78,388 (for a combined salt and pepper shaker) filed Mar. 2, 1929, granted Apr. 30, 1929. Silverplate. Each 5 × 1⅞ in. (12.7 × 4.8 cm). Marked (each): *W.B. / MFG. CO.* [in shield] / [six-pointed star] / *PAT APRIL 30 '29 / U.S.A. / B-75*
Dallas Museum of Art, gift of Martin K. Webb and Charles L. Venable in honor of Jewel Stern, DMA 2001.298.1–2

These shakers are a pastiche of French *art moderne*, the source from which the designer took his cues (see chapter 13).

<h1>SELECTED BIBLIOGRAPHY</h1>

ARCHIVAL SOURCES

Brooklyn Museum of Art, Brooklyn, N.Y.

Cranbrook Archives, Cranbrook Educational Community, Bloomfield Hills, Mich.

Gorham Archives, John Hay Library, Brown University, Providence, R.I.

Gorham Company Archives, Smithfield, R.I.

International Silver Company Archives, Meriden Historical Society, Meriden, Conn.

Lunt Silversmiths, Greenfield, Mass.

Marshall Field & Co., Chicago, Il.

Metropolitan Museum of Art, New York, N.Y.

Museum School, Museum of Fine Arts, Boston, Mass.

Newark Museum, Newark, N.J.

Reed & Barton, Taunton, Mass.

Syracuse University Library, Syracuse, N.Y.

Tiffany & Company, Parsippany, N.J.

University Archives, Carnegie Mellon University, Pittsburg, Penn.

University Art Museum, University of California, Santa Barbara, Calif.

Wolfsonian–Florida International University, Miami Beach, Fla.

BOOKS

Bonneville, Françoise de. *Jean Puiforcat.* Paris: Editions du Regard, 1986.

Carpenter, Charles H., Jr. *Gorham Silver, 1831–1981.* New York: Dodd, Mead, 1982.

———, with Mary Grace Carpenter. *Tiffany Silver.* New York: Dodd, Mead, 1978.

Cheney, Sheldon, and Martha Candler Cheney. *Art and the Machine.* New York: Whittlesey House, 1936.

Darling, Sharon S. *Chicago Metalsmiths.* Chicago: Chicago Historical Society, 1977.

Duncan, Alastair. *American Art Deco.* New York: Abrams, 1986.

Frankl, Paul T. *Form and Re-Form: A Practical Handbook of Modern Interiors.* New York: Harper & Brothers, 1930.

Garrelick, Renee. *Sterling Seasons: The Reed & Barton Story.* Taunton, Mass.: Reed & Barton, 1998.

Gibb, George S. *The Whitesmiths of Taunton: A History of Reed & Barton, 1824–1943.* Cambridge, Mass.: Harvard University Press, 1943.

Hogan, Edmund P. *An American Heritage: A Book About the International Silver Company.* Dallas, Tex.: Taylor Publishing, 1977.

Kirkham, Pat, ed. *Women Designers in the USA, 1900–2000.* New Haven: Yale University Press, 2000.

Krekel-Aalberse, Annelies. *Art Nouveau and Art Deco Silver.* London: Thames and Hudson, 1989.

May, Earl Chapin. *A Century of Silver, 1847–1947: Connecticut Yankees and a Noble Metal.* New York: Robert M. McBride, 1947.

Meikle, Jeffrey L. *Twentieth Century Limited: Industrial Design in America, 1925–1939.* Philadelphia: Temple University Press, 1979.

———. *American Plastic: A Cultural History.* New Brunswick, N.J.: Rutgers University Press, 1995.

Neumann, Martha Cross, ed. *Kingswood: Study in Design.* Bloomfield Hills, Mich.: Kingswood School Cranbrook, 1982.

Rainwater, Dorothy T., and Colette Fuller. *Encyclopedia of American Silver Manufacturers.* 5th rev. ed. West Chester, Pa.: Schiffer, 2004.

Stern, Robert A. M., Gregory Gilmartin, and Thomas Mellins. *New York 1930: Architecture and Urbanism Between the Two World Wars.* New York: Rizzoli, 1987.

Visakay, Stephen. *Vintage Bar Ware: Identification and Value Guide.* Paducah, Ky.: Collector Books, 1997.

ARTICLES

Boykin, Elizabeth MacRae. "Modern Silver Put on Display; Metropolitan Museum Has Contemporary Showing." *New York Sun,* Apr. 10, 1937.

Braznell, W. Scott. "The Advent of Modern American Silver." *The Magazine Antiques* 125 (Jan. 1984): 236–41.

———. "A 'New Way of Life': A Candelabrum from Reed & Barton's 'Contemporary Group.'" *Yale University Art Gallery Bulletin* (1997–98): 76–83.

Davidson, Gail S. "Perfection: Jean E. Puiforcat's Designs for Silver." *The Magazine Antiques* 163 (Jan. 2003): 174–83.

"Exhibition Silver at the Metropolitan Museum." *House and Garden* 72 (July 1937): 58.

Fagan, Dudley T. "Modernism: Its Possibilities in America." *National Jeweler* 25 (Jan. 1929): 23.

Gold, Annalee. "Reed & Barton Goes Crafty." *Jewelers' Circular-Keystone* 147 (July 1977): 318–19.

Hood, William P., Jr., "Modern Flatware Design: The Viande/Grille/Vogue Style." *The Magazine Antiques* 158 (Feb. 2003): 78–85.

"June . . . Weddings . . . And Silver . . . Now and Forever." *Harper's Bazaar* 64 (June 1929): 92.

Keyes, Helen Johnson. "Contemporary American Silver." *Christian Science Monitor,* Boston, May 1, 1937, sec. 10, p. 6.

———. "Contemporary American Silverware," *Christian Science Monitor,* Boston, Nov. 27, 1937, 13.

Kogan, Belle. "Modern Trend in Silverware Design." *Jewelers' Circular-Keystone* 107 (Jan. 1937): 74.

Lounsbery, Elizabeth. "Modernistic Influence on Sterling Silver: The Lights and Shadows of a Skyscraper Are Reflected in this New Table Silver." *Arts and Decoration* 28 (Apr. 1928): 52.

McCann, Lee. "Sterling Goes Modernist." *Country Life* 54 (May 1928): 93.

———. "Sterling Silver, 1929," part 2, *Country Life* 56 (June 1929): 94.

McDevitt, Jan. "The Craftsman in Production." *Craft Horizons* 24 (Mar./Apr. 1964): 22–29.

"Modern Designs in Silver." *House and Garden* 54 (Sept. 1928): 85–87.

Muschamp, Herbert. "Silver's Shiny Journey from Craft to Art." *New York Times,* Oct. 24, 2003, 31.

Myers, Ella Burns. "Trends in Decoration." *Good Furniture Magazine* 31 (Dec. 1928): 127–30.

"Original Designs in Silver." *Arts and Decoration* 42 (Apr. 1935): 28–29.

Patterson, Augusta Owen. "The Decorative Arts." *Town and Country* 83 (Apr. 15, 1928): 70.

Prip, John. "John Prip and Reed & Barton ' . . . it's been a good relationship . . . .'" *Craft Horizons* 24 (Mar./Apr. 1964): 52.

Rainwater, Dorothy T. "Alphonse La Paglia, Silversmith and Designer." *Silver* 28 (May/June 1995): 8–11.

———. "Kurt Eric Christoffersen, Designer and Silversmith." *Silver* 28 (July/Aug. 1995): 10–12.

Read, Helen Appleton. "New Architecture at the International Exposition of Decorative Arts in Paris Illustrating the Use of Reinforced Concrete; Strange Geometric Shapes." *Brooklyn Daily Eagle,* Aug. 16, 1925. Archives of American Art, Helen Appleton Read Papers (hereafter as AAA, Read papers), reel N736, frame 112).

———. "International Exposition of Decorative Arts in Paris Has Practical Background for Display of the Bizarre and Exotic Atmosphere of Luxury." *Brooklyn Daily Eagle,* Aug. 23, 1925. AAA, Read papers, reel N736, frame 113.

———. "Selections from French Exposition Come to Metropolitan Museum." *Brooklyn Daily Eagle,* Feb. 21, 1926. AAA, Read papers, reel N736, frame 138.

———. "Swedish Decorative Art Display at the Metropolitan Museum." *Brooklyn Daily Eagle,* Jan. 16, 1927. AAA, Read papers, reel N736, frame 166.

———. "Department Stores Rival Museum in the Formation of Taste in Industrial Art." *Brooklyn Daily Eagle,* Dec. 25, 1927. AAA, Read papers, reel N736, frame 198.

———. "Twentieth-Century Decoration: The Modern Theme Finds a Distinctive Medium in American Silver." *Vogue* 72 (July 1, 1928): 58.

Saunders, A. Frederic. "From L'Art Nouveau to L'Art Moderne." *Jewelers' Circular* 98 (Feb. 1929): 105–108.

———. "Modernism in Silverware." *Jewelers' Circular* 100 (Feb. 27, 1930), 103.

Shean, Charles M. "The New Art: A Personal and Creative Art." *The Craftsman* 8, no. 5 (August 1905).

Singer, Patricia F. "Alfred G. Kintz, an American Designer." *Silver* 19 (Sept.–Oct. 1986): 14–19.

"Sterling Plate." *Creative Design* 1 (spring 1935): 14–15.

Stickley, Gustav. "Thoughts Occasioned by an Anniversary: A Plea for a Democratic Art." *The Craftsman* 3, no. 1 (October 1904).

Exhibition Catalogues and Brochures

Adams, Henry. *Viktor Schreckengost and 20th-Century Design,* exh. cat. Cleveland: Cleveland Museum of Art, 2000.

The Architect and the Industrial Arts: An Exhibition of Contemporary American Design. New York: Metropolitan Museum of Art, 1929.

Benton, Charlotte, Tim Benton, and Ghislaine Wood, eds. *Art Deco: 1910–1939.* Victoria and Albert Museum, London. Boston: Bulfinch Press, 2003.

Braznell, W. Scott. "Metalsmithing and Jewelrymaking, 1900–1920." In *The Ideal Home, 1900–1920: The History of Twentieth-Century American Craft,* edited by Janet Kardon. New York: Abrams, in association with the American Craft Museum, 1993.

Callahan, Ashley. *Enchanting Modern: Ilonka Karasz.* Athens, Ga.: Museum of Art, University of Georgia, 2003.

Clark, Robert Judson, et al. *Design in America: The Cranbrook Vision, 1925–1950.* New York: Abrams, in association with the Detroit Institute of Arts and the Metropolitan Museum of Art, 1983.

Contemporary American Industrial Art. Thirteenth exhibition, November 5, 1934–January 6, 1935. Metropolitan Museum of Art, New York.

Contemporary American Industrial Art. Fifteenth exhibition, April 29–September 15, 1940. Metropolitan Museum of Art, New York.

Contemporary Industrial and Handwrought Silver. New York: Brooklyn Museum, 1937.

Davies, Karen. *At Home in Manhattan: Modern Decorative Arts, 1925 to the Depression.* New Haven, Conn.: Yale University Art Gallery, 1983.

Decorative Metalwork and Cotton Textiles: Third International Exhibition of Contemporary Industrial Art. American Federation of Arts, New York, 1930–1931.

Design in Scandinavia: An Exhibition of Objects for the Home. Oslo: Kirstes boktr., 1954.

Duncan, Alastair. *Modernism: Modernist Design 1880–1940; The Norwest Collection.* Woodbridge, Suffolk, Antique Collectors' Club, 1998.

Eidelberg, Martin, ed. *Design 1935–1965: What Modern Was: Selections from the Liliane and David M. Stewart Collection.* Montreal Museum of Fine Art. New York: Abrams, 1991.

Friedman, William, ed. *20th Century Design: U.S.A.* Buffalo, N.Y.: Albright Art Gallery, Buffalo Fine Arts Academy, 1959.

Gebhard, David. *Kem Weber: The Moderne in Southern California: 1920 through 1941.* Santa Barbara, Calif.: Art Galleries, University of California, 1969.

Jackson, Lesley. *The New Look: Design in the Fifties.* London: Thames and Hudson, 1991.

Johnson, Bruce E. *Handwrought Silver and Architecture: The Artistry of William Waldo Dodge.* Asheville, N.C.: Asheville Art Museum, 2005.

Kardon, Janet, ed. *Craft in the Machine Age, 1920–1945: The History of Twentieth-Century American Craft.* New York: Harry N. Abrams in association with the American Craft Museum, 1995.

Knife, Fork, and Spoon. Minneapolis: Walker Art Center and Towle Silversmiths, 1951.

Krekel-Aalberse, A., J. R. ter Molen, and R. J. Willink, eds. *Silver of a New Era: International Highlights of Precious Metalware from 1880 to 1940.* Museum Boymans van-Beuningen, Rotterdam, and Museum voor Sierkunst, Ghent. Seattle: University of Washington Press, 1992.

Living Today: An Exhibition of Contemporary Architecture, Furniture, Interior Decoration. Washington, D.C.: Corcoran Gallery of Art, 1958.

McFadden, David Revere, and Mark A. Clark. *Treasures for the Table: Silver from the Chrysler Museum.* New York: Hudson Hills Press; Washington, D.C.: American Federation of Arts, 1989.

Michie, Thomas S., and Christopher P. Monkhouse, eds. *John Prip: Master Metalsmith.* Providence, R.I.: Museum of Art, Rhode Island School of Design; New York: American Craft Museum, 1987.

Official Catalog: Department of Fine Arts Division of Decorative Arts, Golden Gate International Exposition, San Francisco, 1939. San Francisco: H. S. Crocker Co. and Schwabacher-Frey Co., 1939.

Renwick Gallery. *Georg Jensen Silversmithy: 77 Artists, 75 Years.* Washington, D.C.: Smithsonian Institution Press, 1980.

Rust, Robert, et al. "Alchemy in East Aurora: Roycroft Metal Arts." In *Head, Heart and Hand: Elbert Hubbard and the Roycrofters,* edited by Marie Via and Marjorie B. Searl. Rochester, N.Y.: University of Rochester Press, 1994.

Silver: An Exhibition of Contemporary American Design by Manufacturers, Designers and Craftsmen. New York: Metropolitan Museum of Art, 1937.

Streamlining America. Dearborn, Mich.: Henry Ford Museum and Greenfield Village, 1986.

Venable, Charles L. *Silver in America, 1840–1940: A Century of Splendor.* Dallas, Tex.: Dallas Museum of Art, 1994.

———. *China and Glass in America 1880–1980: From Tabletop to TV Tray.* Dallas, Tex.: Dallas Museum of Art, 2000.

Warren, David B., Katherine S. Howe, and Michael K. Brown. *Marks of Achievement: Four Centuries of American Presentation Silver.* Museum of Fine Arts, Houston. New York: Harry N. Abrams, 1987.

Wilk, Christopher. "Looking at the Past Through Modernist Eyes." In *Viennese Silver: Modern Design, 1780–1918,* edited by Michael Huey. Ostfildern-Ruit: Hatje Cantz Verlag, 2003.

Wilson, Richard Guy, Dianne H. Pilgrim, and Dickran Tashjian. *The Machine Age in America, 1918–1941.* New York: Abrams, in association with the Brooklyn Museum, 1986.

INDEX

All photography, unless otherwise noted below, is by Brad Flowers, © 2005 Dallas Museum of Art

Figure for Charles Venable
Fig. 2: Dallas Museum of Art, from the Stephen Vaughan Collection and the Charles R. Masling and John E. Furen Collection, photograph: Tom Jenkins

Figures for Jewel Stern
Fig. 1.1: *L'Architecture Officielle et les Pavillons* (Paris: Charles Moreau, 1925), 7; fig. 1.2: Patent No. 75,655, June 28, 1928; fig. 1.5: *Good Furniture Magazine*, May 1926, p. 291; fig. 1.9: Museum of Art, Rhode Island School of Design, Providence. The Gorham Collection, gift of Textron, Inc., photograph: Cathy Carver; figs. 1.10, 1.11: Brown University Library, photograph courtesy of the Jewel Stern American Silver Collection Archives; fig. 1.12: Courtesy of *Jewelers' Circular-Keystone*; figs. 1.13, 1.15, 1.16, 1.18, 1.20: Brown University Library; fig. 1.22: Art and Architecture Collection, Miriam and Ira D. Wallach Division of Art, Prints, and Photographs, The New York Public Library, Astor, Lenox and Tilden Foundations and courtesy of *Jewelers' Circular-Keystone*; fig. 1.23: Courtesy of Syratech Corporation; fig. 1.24: Courtesy of The Wolfsonian–Florida International University, Miami Beach, Florida, the Mitchell Wolfson Jr. Collection; fig. 1.25: Photograph: Jacques Boulay; fig. 1.27: Courtesy of Reed & Barton

Fig. 2.1: Courtesy of *Business and Professional Women/US*; fig. 2.2: *Good Furniture Magazine*, July 1928, p. 15; fig. 2.5: Photograph courtesy of the Jewel Stern American Silver Collection Archives; fig. 2.12: Courtesy of Lord & Taylor, photograph courtesy of the Science, Industry, and Business Library, The New York Public Library, Astor Lenox and Tilden Foundations

Fig. 3.1: Photography by Mark Darley. Photograph © 1989 The Metropolitan Museum of Art. Reproduced by permission of The Metropolitan Museum of Art. All rights reserved; fig. 3.4: Courtesy of The Wolfsonian–Florida International University, Miami Beach, Florida, the Mitchell Wolfson Jr. Collection, photograph: Silvia Ros; fig. 3.11: Courtesy of Reed & Barton; fig. 3.12: Photograph: Henri Delage; fig. 3.15: Brown University Library, photograph courtesy of the Jewel Stern American Silver Collection Archives; fig. 3.16: Courtesy of the Jewel Stern American Silver Collection Archives; fig. 3.18: Photograph: Jacques Boulay; figs. 3.19, 3.29, 3.30: Photograph: Clive Russ, courtesy of John P. Axelrod, Boston, Mass.; fig. 3.20: Courtesy of Mr. and Mrs. Roger D. Redden; figs. 3.27, 3.49: Brown University Library; fig. 3.28: Courtesy *Jewelers' Circular-Keystone*; fig. 3.36: Courtesy of Ilonka Sigmund, photograph: Ashley Brown; fig. 3.37: Herbert Photos Inc., New York City; fig. 3.38: Collection of Solveig Cox, photograph: Michael McKelvey, courtesy of the Georgia Museum of Art, University of Georgia; fig. 3.39: Courtesy of the Kem Weber Archives, Architecture and Design Collection, University Art Museum, University of California at Santa Barbara; fig. 3.40: Photograph, all rights reserved, The Metropolitan Museum of Art

Fig. 4.1: The Metropolitan Museum of Art; fig. 4.2: Courtesy of John C. Waddell, photograph: John P. Goodbody; fig. 4.3: Courtesy of Ronald S. Swanson and Robert S. Swanson; fig. 4.6: Courtesy of the Jewel Stern American Silver Collection Archives; fig. 4.7: Cleveland Museum of Art Archives. Records of the Registrar. Gallery Views. "Danish Silver, A.F.A. Dec. Metalwork and Cotton Textiles," 1930–31. Box 22, folder 48

Fig. 5.2: The Metropolitan Museum of Art; fig. 5.3: International Silver Company, Wilcox Plate Division, Meriden, Connecticut (Manufacturer) Tea Urn and Tray, 1934 or earlier. Silverplate Collec-

tion of Cranbrook Art Museum, Bloomfield Hills, Michigan. Gift of George Gough Booth and Ellen Scripps Booth through the Cranbrook Foundation (CAM 1935.8), photograph: Dirk Bakker, courtesy of the Cranbrook Art Academy and the Detroit Institute of Arts; fig. 5.4: Courtesy of MAK– Austrian Museum of Applied Arts/Contemporary Art, Vienna, © Asenbaum Photo Archive; fig. 5.5: The Metropolitan Museum of Art; fig. 5.7: Photograph: Jacques Boulay; figs. 5.8: *Country Life*, January 1935, p. 66; fig. 5.9: Courtesy of the Carnegie Mellon University Archives; fig. 5.10: Metropolitan Museum of Art; fig. 5.11: Courtesy of the Science, Industry, and Business Library, The New York Public Library, Astor, Lenox and Tilden Foundations

Figs. 6.3, 6.6: Courtesy of the General Research Division, The New York Public Library, Astor, Lenox and Tilden Foundations; fig. 6.4: Courtesy of Lunt Silversmiths; fig. 6.7: *Vogue*, April 15, 1935, p. 120; fig. 6.9: Courtesy of The Wolfsonian– Florida International University, Miami Beach, Florida, the Mitchell Wolfson Jr. Collection, photograph: Silvia Ros; fig. 6.14: Photograph: Bachrach, courtesy of Bernard Banet, Ann Arbor, Michigan; fig. 6.21: Photograph: Underwood and Underwood; courtesy of the *Chicago Tribune*; fig. 6.23: *Fortune*, July 1934; fig. 6.26: Courtesy of the Mitchell J. Wolfson Jr. Private Collection; fig. 6.30: Art and design © 1998 Fox Lorber Video. All rights reserved; fig. 6.31: Courtesy of the Meriden Historical Society, Inc., Meriden, Conn.

Fig. 7.3: *House Beautiful*, May 1934, p. 117; figs. 7.7, 7.14: Courtesy of Reed & Barton; fig. 7.9: Courtesy of Nicholas Roerich Museum; fig. 7.15: Courtesy of American Airlines

Fig. 8.1: The Metropolitan Museum of Art; fig. 8.4: Photograph courtesy of the Museum of Fine Arts, Boston, and John P. Axelrod, Boston, Mass.; fig. 8.6: Courtesy of The Wolfsonian–Florida International University, Miami Beach, Florida, the Mitchell Wolfson Jr. Collection, photograph: Silvia Ros; fig. 8.10: Courtesy of Tiffany & Co. © Tiffany & Co. Archives 2004; figs. 8.11, 8.12: © Tiffany & Co. Archives 2004; fig. 8.13: Courtesy of Tiffany & Co., © Christie's Images Inc. 2002; figs. 8.23, 8.25, 8.26: The Metropolitan Museum of Art

Fig. 9.1: Courtesy of Oneida Ltd. © Oneida Ltd. All rights reserved; fig. 9.2: Courtesy of Reed & Barton

Fig. 10.1: © 2004 Artists Rights Society (ARS), New York/ADAGP, Paris. Photograph: Willy Maywald; fig. 10.3: Digital image © The Museum of Modern Art/Licensed by SCALA/Art Resource, N.Y. © 2004 Artists Rights Society (ARS), New York/VG Bild-Kunst, Bonn; fig. 10.4: Photograph: Richard P. Goodbody; fig. 10.6: Digital image © The Museum of Modern Art/Licensed by SCALA/ Art Resource, N.Y. © Artists Rights Society (ARS), New York; fig. 10.7: © Austrian Frederick and Lillian Kiesler Private Foundation, photograph: Berenice Abbott, Archive of the Kiesler Foundation; fig. 10.8: Photograph: Ezra Stoller © Esto. All rights reserved; fig. 10.9: © Christie's Images Inc. 2005, photograph: Herbert Gehr; fig. 10.10: Art and Architecture Collection, Miriam and Ira D. Wallach Division of Art, Prints and Photographs, The New York Public Library, Astor, Lenox and Tilden Foundation and courtesy of *Industrial Design*; fig. 10.13: Courtesy of Robert J. King; fig. 10.15: Brooklyn Museum Archives, Records of the Department of Decorative Arts, Exhibitions: Contemporary Industrial and Hand Wrought Silver, 1937; fig. 10.18: Sterling Silversmiths Guild of America; figs. 10.20, 10.25: Courtesy of Reed & Barton; fig. 10.21: Courtesy of Michael Malling, photograph by Ole Woldbye; fig. 10.24: Courtesy of Robert H. Ramp; fig. 10.29: Courtesy of the

Jewel Stern American Silver Collection Archives; fig. 10.33: Courtesy of the Meriden Historical Society, Inc., Meriden, Conn.; figs. 10.37, 10.38: Courtesy of Syratech Corporation; fig. 10.39: Courtesy of Oneida Ltd. © Oneida Ltd. All rights reserved; fig. 10.40: Herbert Gehr/Getty Images; figs. 10.47, 10.48, 10.50, 10.52, 10.56: Brown University Library

Fig. 11.1: *House Beautiful*, November 1954, p. 1

Fig. 12.1: Courtesy of Syratech Corporation; figs. 12.2, 12.3, 12.4, 12.6, 12.11: Courtesy of Reed & Barton

Fig. 13.4: Courtesy of *House and Garden*, Condé Nast Publications, Inc.; fig. 13.12: Photograph courtesy of Richard Huggins; fig. 13.13: Courtesy of Syratech Corporation, photograph courtesy of the Meriden Historical Society, Inc., Meriden, Conn.; figs. 13.14, 13.23: Courtesy of Syratech Corporation; fig. 13.17: Courtesy of Robert J. King; fig. 13.24: Courtesy of Reed & Barton; fig. 13.29: Courtesy of Oneida Ltd., © Oneida Ltd. All rights reserved, photograph courtesy of the Jewel Stern American Silver Collection Archives

Fig. 14.1: Cleveland Museum of Art Archives, Records of the Registrar. Gallery Views. Gallery 27, "20th Century Design, U.S.A.," 1959. Box 37, folder 49; fig. 14.3: Photograph courtesy of Gerald Gulotta; fig. 14.4: Courtesy of American Craft Council Archives; fig. 14.5: *House Beautiful*, April 1962, pp. 14–15

Fig. 15.1: *New Yorker*, December 9, 1967, p. 189; fig. 15.2: *House Beautiful*, October 1955, p. 35; fig. 15.3: Courtesy of Oneida Ltd., © Oneida Ltd. All rights reserved; fig. 15.5: Courtesy of Syratech Corporation and the Jewel Stern American Silver Archives; figs. 15.6, 15.9: Courtesy of Reed & Barton; fig. 15.7: Courtesy of Syratech Corporation; fig. 15.13: *House and Garden*, May 1987, p. 107; fig. 15.14: *New Yorker*, October 17, 1983, p. 165

Fig. 16.1: Courtesy of Lella Vignelli and the Jewel Stern American Silver Collection Archives, photograph: Denis Piel, courtesy of Denis Piel and the Arnell Group; fig. 16.4: Photograph: Hiro, © Tiffany & Co.; fig. 16.6: © Tiffany & Co. Archives 2004; fig. 16.10: Photograph: Dan Howell; fig. 16.11: Photograph: Denis Piel; fig. 16.13: Courtesy of Bergdorf Goodman, photograph: Roxanne Lowit; fig. 16.18: Designed by Michael Graves for Swid Powell/Reed & Barton, 1990, photograph: Franz Walderdorff, courtesy of Michael Graves and Associates; fig. 16.23: © Stanley Tigerman, courtesy of Tigerman McCurry Architects, photograph © Swid Powell; fig. 16.24: Courtesy of R. A. M. Stern Architects

The extract from the song "South American Way," words by Al Dubin, music by Jimmy McHugh © 1939 (renewed 1967) Cotton Club Publishing and Warner Bros. Inc. All rights for Cotton Club Publishing controlled and administered by EMI April Music Inc. All rights reserved. International copyright secured, used by permission; for the extract from the song "Fly Me to the Moon," words and music by Bart Howard, TRO—copyright 1952 (renewed), Hampshire House Publishing Corporation, New York, N.Y.; for the extract from the song "If You Are Going to San Francisco," words and music by John Philips, courtesy of Universal Music Group

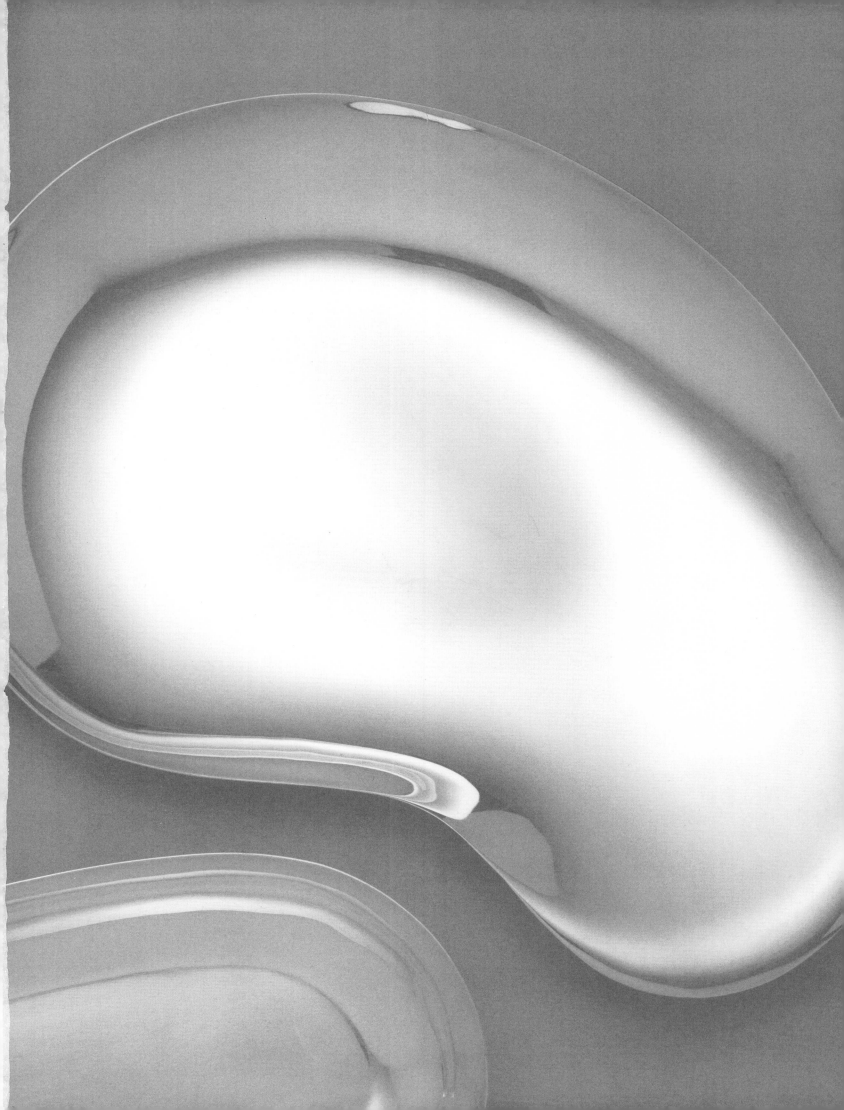